ECONOMIC GEOGRAPHY

ECONOMIC

SECOND EDITION

Prentice-Hall, Inc., Englewood Cliffs, New Jersey 07632

GEOGRAPHY

John W. Alexander
Formerly, Professor of Geography
University of Wisconsin
Madison

Lay James Gibson
Professor of Geography
University of Arizona
Tucson

Library of Congress Cataloging in Publication Data

ALEXANDER, JOHN WESLEY (date)
  Economic geography.

  Includes bibliographies and index.
  1. Geography, Economic. I. Gibson, Lay James,
joint author. II. Title.
HF1025.A53-1979   330.9   78-15735
ISBN 0-13-225151-5

Economic Geography, Second Edition
John W. Alexander and Lay James Gibson

© 1979 by Prentice-Hall, Inc.
Englewood Cliffs, New Jersey 07632

Printed in the United States of America

10 9 8 7 6 5 4 3 2 1

PRENTICE-HALL INTERNATIONAL, INC., *London*
PRENTICE-HALL OF AUSTRALIA PTY. LIMITED, *Sydney*
PRENTICE-HALL OF CANADA, LTD., *Toronto*
PRENTICE-HALL OF INDIA PRIVATE LIMITED, *New Delhi*
PRENTICE-HALL OF JAPAN, INC., *Tokyo*
PRENTICE-HALL OF SOUTHEAST ASIA PTE. LTD., *Singapore*
WHITEHALL BOOKS LIMITED, *Wellington, New Zealand*

Dedicated to
Clarence F. Jones and the late Vernor C. Finch

Economic geographers and friends
to whom the authors are deeply indebted

CONTENTS

PREFACE TO THE SECOND EDITION

The field of economic geography has grown a great deal since *Economic Geography* appeared in 1963. The first edition was written to span the gap between the traditional and "new approaches" to geography. The use of statistical methods of analysis is no longer new to professional geographers but it is still often foreign territory to the beginning student. The second edition of *Economic Geography*, therefore, is still a "bridge" textbook—one that will take the student through the broad range of material that is covered by the field of economic geography and then introduce him or her to a number of different methods used to describe and analyze the spatial patterns that have been identified.

In terms of organization, the second edition is similar to the first. Those familiar with the original edition will notice that the two chapters that focus on manufacturing regions outside of Anglo-America have been dropped. Some of the more important points and information from these chapters have been added to the topical discussions found in earlier chapters. In most other respects the second edition follows the first.

Wherever appropriate new material has been added, tables have been updated, and generalizations have been restated to reflect contemporary patterns. Perhaps one of the strongest features of the first edition was the wide use of maps to illustrate the patterns analyzed in the text. This feature has been retained. There are over 225 line drawings, a large share of which have been revised and redrafted.

A number of people have contributed to the making of the second edition but three who can be credited with exceptional effort are Steven Meyer, who took on the awesome task of map making, and Joan McLellan and Clair Shenk, who took time from their graduate studies to comment on the manuscript, help with the selection of illustrations, and generally keep the revision on track. Similarily, support on the home front was an essential ingredient in the revision process and for this, thanks go to Janet, Stephen, and Jim.

Finally, we would like to reiterate a request. We desire the suggestions of any reader for improving this book—suggestions for clarifying ideas, organization, and presentation, suggestions for giving illustrations a stronger role, We would also appreciate having any errors of fact brought to our attention.

John W. Alexander
Lay James Gibson

PREFACE TO THE FIRST EDITION

In writing this text, I have adopted a deliberate strategy. Geography, like most disciplines, is going through a transition period in which increasing attention is being given to quantification and the use of statistical methods of analysis. The reaction of geographers has been varied. Consequently, it seemed to me that there was a need for a "bridge" textbook, one to span the gap between the traditional and new approaches to geography. Accordingly, the early portion—in fact, most—of this text conforms to traditional geographic methods. The chapters have been deliberately structured around three basic geographic questions that apply to all economic activities, the questions of location, characteristics, and relationships. After this method is introduced, attention is directed to individual types of endeavor, moving through the sequence of primary, secondary, and tertiary economic activities. The later chapters weave in, very gradually at first, some of the "new geography," until finally, in Part Nine, statistical methodology is the main subject matter. By being introduced slowly and gradually to statistical concepts, even the student with little mathematical background may find it easy to glide into an understanding of these ideas. In a phrase, I have adopted the strategy of the soft sell. I trust that my educational engineering is sound, and that this bridge proves to be useful and sturdy.

Many scholars and friends have had a role, either direct or indirect, in the making of this book. First, I owe a general debt to teachers who have stimulated my interest and understanding of the field: to Harland James, high school teacher in Urbana, Illinois; to W. O. Blanchard, my undergraduate mentor at the University of Illinois; and to Vernor C. Finch, Glenn Trewartha, and Richard Hartshorne, under whom I took graduate work at the University of Wisconsin. I must acknowledge, too, Clarence F. Jones, of Northwestern University, whose concept of economic geography has strongly influenced my thinking.

Second, my thanks to colleagues. Any strong points in this textbook are attributable, at least in part, to my fellow geographers at the University of Wisconsin. I am grateful to: Arthur Robinson, for interesting me in statistical techniques; Andrew Clark, for showing me the value of historical geography (See Chapter 15); Henry Sterling, for information (and a photograph) on primitive cultivation; Kirk Stone, for information (and photographs) on Scandinavia; Clarence Olmstead, for reading a portion of the manuscript and teaching me a lot on the geography of agriculture; John Hidore, for permission to use two maps in Chapter 31; and Edwin Hammond, Fred Simoons, Robert Finley, and Karl Butzer, for stimulating my thinking in many ways. I shall happily share with them credit for any strengths in this textbook; but, needless to say, the reverse does not hold—I cannot share with them blame for any flaws.

I owe a great debt to Randall Sale who designed and directed the production of most of the maps, which were drawn in the University of Wisconsin Cartographic Laboratory, principally by Miss Mei-Ling Hsu, Rodney Helgeland, and George McCleary. Special thanks, too, to Robert Taaffe of Indiana University, who made numerous constructive comments on the Soviet Union section of Chapter 25.

There is insufficient space here to express appreciation individually to fellow economic geographers at other institutions upon whose ideas, maps, and photographs I have drawn in the pages to follow. Due credit is given them with quotations and illustrations. Several of my graduate students have helped by constructing maps, contributing ideas, and commenting on the manuscript, particularly Tom McKnight, William Wallace, George Stevens, Kenneth Martin, Roy Officer, Richard Hough, James Lindberg, and George McCleary. The United States Census authorities graciously made available numerous maps. Most of the burden of typing the manuscript and the mass of correspondence pertaining to this book has been cheerfully and neatly executed by Mary Jane Johnson and Judy Christenson. My wife, Betty, has graciously and patiently endured those exigencies of life associated with a husband's ups and downs in trying to haul a book over the long road from preliminary planning to final publication. And I gratefully acknowledge the patience, criticism, and suggestions of my editor, Ronald Nelson.

Finally, a request: I desire the suggestions of any reader for improving this book—suggestions for clarifying ideas, organization, and presentation, suggestions for giving maps, photographs, and other illustrations a stronger role. I would appreciate, too, having my attention called to any errors of fact alert readers might detect.

John W. Alexander

ECONOMIC GEOGRAPHY

PART

ONE

INTRODUCTION

Economic geography: What is it? Many people have at least a vague idea of the meaning of the term *economic*. They know that it pertains to farming and fishing, incomes and expenses, transportation and taxes, and a good deal else that is somehow related to money. And most people likewise have some notion of what geography means. But here opinions vary sharply. Some think it merely involves the memorization of place names, whereas others regard it as a twin sister of geology. Clearly, then, because of this prevalent vagueness and confusion, before we can pin down the concept of *economic geography* we should find out what each of the component words means.

This will be precisely our first task in Chapter 1. Then, after fixing our definitions, we can go on to a consideration of the distinctive method of economic geography. As we shall see, it involves three basic questions, which deal with the locations, characteristics, and relationships of economic activities.

We shall first apply this geographic method of analysis in Chapter 2 to population—for people are the fundamental subject matter of the economic geographer. Then we shall use the method to approach the principal economic activities in which the people of the world are engaged.

We shall give attention first to subsistence economic activities (Part Two) and then to commercial activities (Parts Three to Eight), treating the latter in the following sequence: commercial gathering, commercial agriculture (or bioculture), mining, manufacturing, transportation, and services (or tertiary activity). Finally, in Part Nine (Chapters 29 to 31) we shall take up measurements and geographic theory as applied to economic endeavors.

Early chapters are structured explicitly around the three basic questions in order that the reader may become familiar with the method of geographic analysis as well as with content material. In these early chapters, geographical relationships are usually approached in terms of the pairs of physical and cultural phenomena or of intraregional and extraregional phenomena, the reason being that information now available in the geographic literature makes these approaches more feasible for these topics.

Later chapters will be different in that usage of the three basic questions will be more implicit than explicit (for by this time they will have become second nature to the reader). Another difference is that later chapters will weave in certain aspects of correlation analysis. This topic is reserved for later stages of the book because it is more difficult to grasp, and has been used mostly by researchers in producing information which deals with topics covered in Parts Six, Seven, and Eight.

The names of many nations and of other places will be mentioned in the chapters to follow. Therefore, every reader should own an atlas, an indispensable tool for mastering the material of geography as well as for comprehending world affairs. Among the best atlases for economic geography are *The Oxford Economic Atlas of the World; The Oxford Regional Economic Atlas, The United States and Canada; The Oxford Regional Economic Atlas, Western Europe; Man's Domain, A Thematic Atlas of the World; The National Atlas of The United States of America;* and *Goode's World Atlas.* In addition, it would often be helpful to procure blank maps at a bookstore to make notations about places and areas discussed in the text.

CHAPTER

economic geography: meaning and method

Primary production. The Morenci open-pit mine in Arizona, the second-largest copper pit in the United States, has its ore removed by rail. The mine is the most significant employer in the remote east central part of the state. (*Courtesy Phelps Dodge Corporation.*)

THE MEANING OF ECONOMIC

The word *economic* pertains to all the activities that men engage in the world over in the production, exchange, and consumption of items of value. Anything man will pay money for, or will barter, or will work to produce is an economic item.

Production

In the *production* of economic items, men busy themselves in a wide range of pursuits that can be classified primary, secondary, and tertiary (see Table 1-1). *Primary production* includes the age-old activities involved in withdrawing objects of value from nature's storehouse and in collaborating with nature to increase the generation and proliferation of items that are available in their "wild" state. For example, in agriculture, man harvests crops from the soil; in mining, he harvests ores from the earth's crust; in fishing, he harvests animals from the rivers, lakes, and oceans; in forestry, he harvests trees from the wooded areas of the earth.

In *secondary production* man increases the value (that is, the utility) of an already existing item by changing its *form*. Such activity is called manufacturing. The miller, for instance, changes grains of wheat into a more usable product, flour. Steelmakers turn iron ore into a more durable metal in blast furnaces and steel mills.

In *tertiary production* man does not harvest substances from nature, nor does he upgrade their worth by changing their form. Rather, he renders services that are of value to his fellows. Repairmen hammer the dents out of automobile fenders. Teachers impart knowledge and try to stimulate thought. Government employees enforce laws, collect taxes, and maintain highways. Other services are rendered by musicians, lawyers, doctors, real estate people, bankers, and housekeepers. It would, of course, be possible to use more terms to categorize production activities than we have employed here. Terms such as "quaternary sector" and "quinary sector" are sometimes used—usually to refer to specific activities which we have included in the tertiary sector. Unfortunately, however, these terms are used in different ways by different people, so for the sake of clarity we will

Table 1-1

Classification of Economic Activities

A. Production

1. Primary
   Harvesting commodities from nature (agriculture, forestry, fishing, mining)
2. Secondary
   Increasing the value of commodities by changing their form (manufacturing)
3. Tertiary
   Performing services (repair, banking, teaching, entertainment, etc.)

B. Exchange

1. Location
   a. Increasing the value of commodities by changing their location (freight transportation)
   b. Satisfying the needs of people by changing their location (passenger transportation)
2. Ownership
   Increasing the value of commodities by changing their ownership (wholesale and retail trade)

C. Consumption

Use of commodities and services by human beings to satisfy their desires.

adhere to the terms and definitions that are given in Table 1-1.

Exchange

The *exchange* of items of value (whether the result of primary, secondary, or tertiary production) may be accomplished through *freight transportation*, which increases the value of commodities by changing their *location*. Iron ore, for example, is worth more in Chicago than in Hibbing; wheat is more valuable in Buffalo than in Saskatchewan. Changing the location of people

Secondary production. The mile-long Volkswagen plant in Wolfsburg, Germany. This single factory produces 4850 passenger cars each working day. (*Courtesy German Information Center.*)

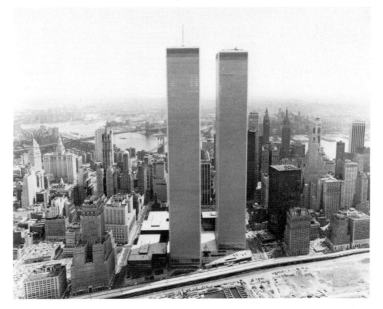

Tertiary production. In the heart of such metropolitan areas as New York, retail and wholesale trade, banking, government administration, and many other tertiary services become concentrated. The two 1350 foot buildings of the World Trade Center in lower Manhattan represent a tremendous concentration of tertiary activity, accommodating exporters, importers, customs brokers, freight forwarders, manufacturers, international banks, government agencies, and a wide range of additional services essential to international trade. This section of the city also contains Wall Street, the stock brokerage center of the U.S. (*Courtesy The Port Authority of New York and New Jersey.*)

themselves, through *passenger transportation*, is another activity which man rates highly. Still another way to increase the value of a commodity is by change of *ownership*. This is the purpose of wholesale trade and retail trade. A radio is worth more to a distributor than to its manufacturer, and its value continues to increase as it passes from distributor to retailer and from retailer to ultimate consumer.

Consumption

The final stage in the *economic* sequence is the *consumption* of goods and services. Until recently, the geography of consumption has been largely ignored by geographers. Today there is a relatively small but growing literature which deals with both the patterns of consumption and the spatial aspects of consumer behavior.

The term *consumption* refers to the final or direct use of goods and services to satisfy the wants and needs of human beings. Some forms of consumption destroy goods quickly—eating food or burning coal, for instance. Other forms use up a commodity slowly, bringing about its gradual depreciation—wearing a suit of clothes or driving a car. Still other forms of consumption do not destroy the commodity at all—gazing at the Alps or skiing down the snowy slopes. Occasionally, indeed, consumption may actually increase the worth of an object, as in enjoying an antique table or a Rembrandt painting.

Now, all these economic activities are studied by economists, historians, and several other social scientists, as well as by geographers. Just how does geography differ from these other disciplines in the study of economic activity? A partial answer can be found in the meaning of *geography* itself.

THE MEANING OF GEOGRAPHY

First of all, there are three widely held false notions of geography that should be dispensed with in order to clear the air for a definition of what geography really is.

A good many people seem to think that geography is simply a matter of *place names*: to them, a geographer is a person who knows the location of county seats, state capitals, rivers, and seas. When a contestant on a quiz program announces that he is an "expert" on geography, he is invariably asked a series of questions that involve nothing but place names.

Other people have the idea that geography is the study of the *natural environment*. To them, the geography of Illinois would deal only with climate, topography, drainage, natural vegetation, soil, and minerals. In this view geography is nothing more than a medley of excerpts from geology, meteorology, and biology. Indeed, some people may think that geography and geology are inseparable. They cannot understand why a geographer should be interested primarily in such things as the manufacture of flour or the circulation of newspapers. The trouble with this concept is that it omits man and all his doings. A geographer who sets about to interview factory managers in a city-wide study is likely to encounter surprise. If he were an economist or a historian, they would not be astonished, for they expect economists and historians to study manufacturing. But when he identifies himself as a geographer, they ask, "What is the connection between geography and manufacturing?"

Still a third group believes that geography is the study of the *influence of the natural environment on man's activities*. *Environmentalism* is the term applied to this still widely held concept. At one time, indeed, it was the prevailing notion among many American geographers themselves. But many of them have now concluded that it covers only *part* of geography and that by itself it may lead to false conclusions. Admittedly, natural environments set certain limits on what man can do; but, as we shall learn, two regions with similar environments may have dissimilar economies because their cultures are different.

These three concepts of geography are deeply

ingrained in the minds of many people. Perhaps the reader will have to make an effort to shake off these old and unacceptable notions in favor of the new and expanded concept of geography about to be presented.

The word geography comes from two Greek roots, *geo*, which means earth, and *graphos*, which means description. The meaning would seem to be simple and clear. But many scholarly disciplines "describe the earth," for instance, geology, pedology, botany, zoology—and meteorology. Surely geography cannot claim to be the sum total of all earth sciences. In fact, the hallmark of geography is not so much *what* it studies as *how* it studies. Geography is unique because of the perspective from which its practitioners study the earth.

Analogy with History

In many respects, geography is similar to history. There would be no history if human events were invariable from day to day; it is because of variation through time that the discipline of history is possible. Because of *temporal* variations, the historian can identify *periods*, such as the Elizabethan Period, the Middle Ages, the Atomic Era. A scholar primarily interested in military developments can break down the record into successive ages of armed conflict and strategy. If his main concern is with the manner in which people express themselves, he can identify various cultural periods, such as the Renaissance or the Victorian. Regardless of the historian's predilection, then, the fundamental fact that phenomena differ from one time to another enables him to distinguish chronological periods.

But this is only the beginning. The historian's main objective is to understand *relationships* between events. He wants to know how an incident in 1914 is related to other events that took place in that year, in subsequent years, and in earlier years.

The geographer is primarily concerned with variation *from place to place*, rather than from time to time. And he is bent on understanding relationships among places. There would be no geography if physical and human phenomena were distributed uniformly over the face of the earth. But rainfall, elevation, temperature, population, farming, mining, and manufacturing do vary markedly from one location to another. Any phenomena that differ from place to place are termed *spatial variables* and qualify as the *elements of geography*.

Definition of Geography

It is at present impossible to formulate a definition of geography that is both complete and simple—and that all geographers will accept. Nevertheless, beginning students are entitled to some declaration of position on the field. To that end, the following definition is proposed: *Geography is the study of spatial variation on the earth's surface*. "Earth's surface" is construed rather broadly here to refer to the milieu in which human life exists—the lower portion of the *atmosphere*, which man breathes, the outer part of the *lithosphere*, upon which he walks and from which he extracts minerals, and the *hydrosphere*, through which he sails and from which he withdraws fish and other aquatic substances.

Spatial variation, like temporal variation, has profound significance for human life and underlies many of the problems facing nations, states, cities, farms, factories, families, and individuals. The historian, we saw, deals in temporal variables, discerns distinct periods, and seeks to discover temporal relationships. In like manner, the geographer deals in spatial variables, identifies regions or areas, and searches for relationships among variables of location, or place. Thus, a more complete definition of geography would be: the discipline that *analyzes spatial variation in terms of areas (regions) and relationships among spatial variables*. Other definitions embodying the same concept are: *the study of places*, and *the analysis of areal (regional) variation*.

Unfortunately, the word geography itself does not connote accurately any of these concepts. Perhaps a better name for the discipline just described might be *spatial science* or *areal science*. Still, despite its limitations, geography remains the common term, so we shall retain it here.

THE METHOD OF ECONOMIC GEOGRAPHY

Now, we are in a position to answer our original question: What is economic geography? By blending our definitions of the two constituent terms we can derive this statement: *Economic geography is the study of areal variation on the earth's surface in man's activities related to producing, exchanging, and consuming wealth*.

In pursuit of that goal the economic geographer asks three basic questions. As we present these questions in the following paragraphs, consider how they compare with the basic questions asked by economists, historians, and other scholars.

Question 1:

Where Is the Economic Activity Located?

The fundamental geographic fact is *location*. If someone wants to investigate corn farming, he begins by asking: Where is corn being farmed? The best way to find out is to inspect a map, because maps provide the clearest and quickest answers to the question "where?" Perhaps an agricultural economist or a corn specialist has already produced a "corn map," such as Figure 1-1, which shows the location of corn production in the United States. If no such map exists, the geographer will have to construct one for himself. In any case, maps are his basic tools and are essential to his ultimate understanding of areal relationships.

The idea of *pattern*, or *distribution*, may facilitate our grasp of the concept of location. A pattern for us is the

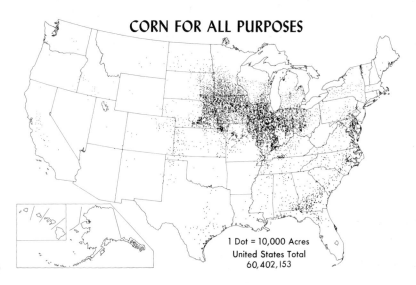

CORN FOR ALL PURPOSES

1 Dot = 10,000 Acres
United States Total
60,402,153

Figure 1-1 (*After U.S. Bureau of the Census.*)

arrangement of an element over the face of the earth. The general pattern of world population (shown on the front endpaper), for example, reveals some densely populated areas in Asia and Europe, some spots of less extreme density in these regions, and some sparsely settled stretches in Oceania, Africa, and South America. (Since we shall use "distribution" as a synonym for "pattern," we could also say that the population map shows the distribution of people over the earth.) In a way, maps are pictures of locational patterns that enable a geographer to begin delimiting areas of interest.

And this brings us to another term whose definition we need to settle. *An area is any portion of the earth's surface that is homogeneous in terms of any selected geographic element or group of elements.* An area, in short, is a distinctive portion of the earth's surface. In this book, we shall also employ the terms *region, belt, zone, land,* and *realm* to identify such portions of the earth.

Question 2:

What Are the Characteristics of the Economic Activity?

After the geographer has pinpointed all the places where corn is grown, he will want to investigate other matters. What are the characteristics of corn farming that distinguish the regions devoted to it? How many acres do the farms occupy? What kinds of buildings are on them? What kinds of animals? How much corn is grown? What other crops are grown? In what respects are these regions different from dairy belts, from wheat-raising regions, from cotton-growing areas? Careful observation of the various aspects of corn farming will enable him to distinguish the American Corn Belt both from regions of contrasting activities (such as cotton belts and lumbering regions) and from other regions of corn production (for example, the corn areas in Iowa are similar in many respects to those in Argentina, but in some ways they are different). Clearly, the geographer must first decide what the significant characteristics of corn-farming regions are. Then, in terms of these characteristics, he finally decides where on his map to draw the boundaries of those distinctive regions.

Thus, question number two deals with *description* and number one with *location.* But these two questions are not enough. A person can know the location of every place on earth without knowing much geography. And he can go on to familiarize himself with the characteristics of all these places and still not understand areal variation. He must go beyond these matters and search out the significance of the location and characteristics of the regions under study. Only then does he raise the question of analysis, which is the mark of mature scholarship. To this end, then, the economic geographer asks a third basic question.

Question 3:

To What Other Phenomena Is the Economic Activity Related?

There are four ways to investigate relationships: (1) One useful approach is through an analysis of *cause* and *effect.* (2) Some geographic studies, however, concentrate fruitfully on relationships with *physical* and *cultural* phenomena. (3) An alternative approach is to consider relationships *within* a region and those *between* regions. (4) Finally, some geographers prefer to study relationships in terms of *correlations.* Let us look at each of these four analytical approaches more closely.

Cause and Effect. An understanding of *causal relationships* enables us to answer such questions as these: Why is the Corn Belt located where it is? And why has the Corn Belt developed its distinguishing characteristics?

An understanding of *consequential relationships* enables us to answer such questions as these: What has been the impact of corn farming upon soil erosion? What roles does corn farming play in the economic life of Iowa and of other Corn Belt states?

There are some geographers who believe these questions to be the most important parts of analysis. Accordingly, they contend that there should be four basic questions in economic geography. With the Corn

Belt as an example, these would be: (1) Where is the Corn Belt? (2) What is it like? (3) Why is it there? (4) What are the consequences of its being where it is and as it is?

Physical and Cultural Relationships. Physical phenomena constitute the *natural environment*—the stage on which man plays out his drama. That environment is the sum total of the physical elements (moisture, heat, soil, terrain, and so on) that exist in a region apart from man and his works. In a sense, the physical environment consists of everything that was present before man appeared on the scene. Thus, analyzing the geography of corn production, we should understand the relationship between the rate of plant growth on the one hand and the inches of summer rainfall and the number of consecutive frost-free days on the other.

But a word of caution is not amiss here. The physical environment *does not determine* what man will produce or consume in a given region of the world, though, to be sure, it does have an enormous effect. For one thing, it may *prevent* man from carrying on certain economic activities. Coal cannot be mined in regions that lack coal deposits. Sometimes, too, the physical environment *promotes* certain endeavors. Although oranges can be grown anywhere on earth if men want to go to the expense of constructing adequate buildings, transporting soil, and providing moisture, heat, and light in handicapped regions, certain areas of the world naturally have a physical environment that is particularly well suited to orange cultivation. Thus, the environment may prevent some endeavors and promote others, but it never *determines* that man will support himself in a particular manner in a particular place. Still, an economic geographer must always recognize that a significant relationship may exist between a region's economic activities and its physical environment.

To the economic geographer, *culture* means the sum total of human achievements: knowledge, attitudes, arts, tools, social institutions, political organizations, religious convictions, systems for controlling capital investments, patterns of marketing, and habits of consumption. Cultural attributes differ from place to place as surely as do physical ones, and economic activity is strongly related to both.

Here is an example that illustrates the importance of culture in the economic life of a region. Most of northern Africa has a physical environment so dry that there is insufficient moisture for abundant vegetation. Yet there is some plant life, enough to support sheep and goats. The prevailing economy is nomadic herding, which yields scarcely any surplus of wool, skins, or meat to ship from this region to the huge nearby European market. Now, ten thousand miles to the southeast, in Australia, there is a physical environment highly similar to that of northern Africa. Little rain falls and vegetation is scanty. Yet in this region the prevailing economy

is commercial grazing—quite different from the nomadic herding of North Africa—which yields a surplus of wool, skins, and meat. The reason for the contrast between the economic activities of these two arid regions lies mainly in the differences between African and Australian cultures, a factor which will be discussed more fully in Chapters 3 and 7.

There are some geographers who believe it unrealistic to distinguish between physical and cultural features. They contend that cultivated soil, for example, is a cultural, not a physical phenomenon because it bears man's imprint. Similarly, the climate over cities is a cultural phenomenon because so much of its dust, gas, and heat content has come from the city. They argue that many of the features we term "physical" actually have been produced by nature and man together. "Both nature and man are intrinsic to the particular character of the areas, and indeed in such intimate union that they cannot be separated from each other."[1] This school of thought contends that if we are going to study relationships with physical features and those with cultural features, it would be just as logical to analyze relationships with animate and inanimate phenomena, with visible and invisible features, or with the material and nonmaterial.

However, some topics lend themselves to analysis in terms of relationships with physical and cultural features. Accordingly, some chapters in this book are built along this approach. Other topics however, are suited better to analysis from one of the other viewpoints, as will be seen in subsequent chapters.

Internal and External Relationships. Another fruitful way to analyze relationships between spatial variables is to consider those that involve features *within* a region and those that link the region *to other* regions. For example, to understand the geography of the American Corn Belt we must know how corn farming is related to such local phenomena as length of the frost-free season, temperature of summer nights, degree of mechanization, and transportation costs within the corn-growing area. Such associations within a region are termed *internal relationships*.

But to understand the geography of Corn Belt farming as it occurs in Iowa and Illinois we also need to know that there are millions of people in Indiana, Michigan, Ohio, Pennsylvania, and New York who do not live on farms and who therefore depend on others for the food they eat. Moreover, these people have developed dietary habits in which meat plays a large role. Not only do they want meat, but they can also afford to buy it, for they have great purchasing power. Much of their meat comes from animals fattened in the Corn Belt. In short, demand for meat in one region is related to specialized agriculture in another. Such

[1] Richard Hartshorne, *Perspective on the Nature of Geography*, Association of American Geographers Monograph, Rand McNally, (Chicago: 1959), p. 51. This quotation is from Alfred Hettner's "Das Wesen und die Methoden der Geographie," *Geographische Zeitschrift*, (1905), p. 554.

associations between different regions are termed *external relationships.*

To illustrate the power of such relationships, we can turn again to the two arid regions specializing in animal production, northern Africa and Australia. Neither contains many customers for animal products. But western Europe has millions of people who want animal products and can afford to pay for them. We might suppose that dry Africa, thousands of miles closer to Europe than dry Australia, would dominate the European market. Yet the trade between Africa and Europe is far less developed than that between Australia and Europe. The external relationships of these two dry regions with the European market are markedly different. Consequently, thousands of tons of wool, skins, and meat move annually from Australia along the longest sea lanes on earth, past the very doors of Africa, to European customers.

Analysis of Correlation. These first three approaches to the question of relationship have been used for some time and are rather well known. More recent is a fourth approach, *analysis of correlation.*

Correlation analysis employs statistical techniques to measure the variance or covariance of geographic elements. If two variables reach their peak value in region A and their lowest value in region Z, and if they become progressively lower from regions B and C down through regions X and Y, they covary to a high degree. That is, they have a *high positive correlation* in their geographic distribution, or a *high geographic correlation.* To illustrate, let's examine the correlations in Table 1-2 between six variables (in the columns) as they vary spatially through the four states of Ohio, Indiana, Iowa, and North Dakota. There seems to be a correlation between number of people, population density per square mile, employment, and median personal income. Since each of these elements attains its highest value in the same place (Ohio) and its lowest value in the same place (North Dakota) and has similar intermediate values in Indiana and Iowa, we can say that they covary *positively* through this quartet of states. Conversely, there is a *negative* (or *inverse*) correlation between these four variables and a fifth: farm population as a percentage of

all population. That is, as population, density, employment, and income go *up* (in the states under consideration), the farm population percentage goes *down*. The correlation with a sixth variable, median age, is weakly positive with the first four variables.

The need for scholarly investigation along the lines of this fourth approach has been expressed as follows:

> It seems clear that geographic investigation is concerned with discovering and describing areal variations in the occurrence of phenomena on the earth's surface, and also with the search for other areally associated factors that may help to explain the observed distributions. In all such cases, questions are bound to arise as to the degree of association that exists between two (or more) phenomena. Areal association is indicated when a variation from place to place in the occurrence of one variable is accompanied by a similar place-to-place variation in the occurrence of another.
>
> In geographic research, areal associations in the occurrence of related phenomena (such as wheat yields and rainfall) have often been discovered by comparing maps of the distributions of those phenomena; and the resulting generalizations have usually taken a form such as, "In this region, there is a tendency for wheat yields to decrease as rainfall decreases." Vague generalizations such as these leave much to be desired, but they have been extremely useful in teaching and explaining areal variations in land-use patterns. Many associations, however, are not so clearly discernible as the wheat-rainfall association to which we have just referred. In those situations in which associations are less clearly defined, it has often been difficult to secure agreement even among competent professional geographers as to the degree, or even the existence, of such associations. Under these circumstances, it is impossible to escape the conclusion that these types of generalizations would have more value if they could be quantified. If some objective, quantified measure of association could be applied that would make such expressions as "slight tendency" or "strong tendency" more precise, it appears that the advancement of geographic analysis would be expedited materially.[2]

[2]Harold H. McCarty, John C. Hook, and Duane S. Knos, *The Measurement of Association in Industrial Geography* (Iowa City: State University of Iowa, 1956), p. 20.

Table 1-2

Selected Spatial Variables for Selected States

State	Number of People in Thousands	Population per Square Mile	Number Employed in Thousands	Median Family Income	Farm Population as a Percentage of All Population	Median Age
Ohio	10,652	260	4,064	$10,309	3	27.9
Indiana	5,194	144	2,016	$9,966	7	27.3
Iowa	2,824	51	1,088	$9,016	18	29.1
North Dakota	618	9	205	$7,836	25	26.4

Within the ranks of professional geographers a school of thought has emerged which holds (a) that correlation analysis should constitute the heart of the geographic method, (b) that the term *relationship* should be reserved only for covariation (in this connection, no two variables can be said to be *positively* related unless both are high in the same regions; conversely, a negative relationship exists when one variable is high in regions where the other variable is low), and (c) that the term *association* should be used only for geographic elements that vary similarly from place to place.

At this point a statement is in order concerning *correlation* and *cause and effect:* High correlation between two variables does not prove cause and effect. Indeed it is possible for the two variables to have absolutely no functional relationship; both might be unrelated results of a third variable as yet unobserved. The authors recognize that the whole notion of *cause and effect*, except in a highly restricted and technical sense, has been so thoroughly attacked by philosophers that some people think it a useless concept. The authors frankly declare, however, that they belong to a different school of thought, which holds that railway lines, for example, are where they are and their traffic is as it is *because* of definite forces which have influenced their location and the characteristics of their traffic. Although complete scientific proof cannot be given that markets influence the location of roads or that topography influences the position of railways, it seems reasonable to believe that a *probabilistic* relationship exists in both cases. Where it appears *probable* that railways have been influenced by factor *X*, we would use the term *causal relationship* on the assumption that *X* has had at least some effect in causing railways to be *where* they are and *as* they are. Conversely, where it appears *probable* that railways have exerted an influence on variable *Z*, we would use the term *effect relationship*, assuming that railways have played some part in the location and character of *Z*. In brief, the term *cause*, as used in this book, applies to factors which *probably* have had an *influence on* the topic being studied;

the term *effect* applies herein to elements which *probably* have been *influenced by* the topic analyzed.

Of the four approaches to Question 3 (on relationships) in this book we proceed from the premise that the relationships derived by the fourth approach (covariation) are *corelationships*, or *correlations*, whereas those appropriate to the first three approaches (cause-effect, physical-cultural, internal-external) are *functional* relationships. Synonyms for *functional relationships* are *connections* and *linkages*. For example, Minnesota and Pennsylvania are functionally related, or connected, or linked together, by the flow of iron ore from northern Minnesota mines to Pittsburgh steel mills. Again, there is functional relationship, or connection, or linkage, between Israel, southern Africa, and the United States by means of diamond traffic. Rough diamonds are mined in Africa, shipped to Israel for cutting and polishing, and then sent to customers in the United States.

The Value of Geographic Analysis

The geographic method of analysis enables us to understand more fully the world in which we live. In satisfying the innate curiosity of the human intellect, geography contributes knowledge in a distinctive dimension. Beyond that, there are practical applications: Federal officials can deal better with the governments of other nations if they are informed about geography; state government officials will have a sounder base for making decisions regarding state policies if they understand the geography of their state; city officials and city planners can plan more wisely for future developments if they are familiar with geographic principles; industrialists, wholesalers, retailers, and other businessmen can find geographic analysis helpful in making decisions regarding location of factories, warehouses, stores, and advertising efforts. Every person, whether businessman, housewife, or student, will find that the ability to apply the geographic method of analysis to the events of everyday life will add a new dimension of interest and satisfaction to his intellectual experiences.

SUGGESTED READINGS

ACKERMAN, EDWARD A., *Geography as a Fundamental Research Discipline*, Chicago, 1958, 37 pp.

AMEDEO, DOUGLAS, and GOLLEDGE, REGINALD G., *An Introduction to Scientific Reasoning in Geography*, New York, 1975, 431 pp.

BERRY, BRIAN J. L., "Further Comments Concerning 'Geographic' and 'Economic' Economic Geography," *The Professional Geographer*, January, 1959, pp. 11–13.

BLAUT, J. M., "The Language of Maps," *The Professional Geographer*, January, 1954, pp. 9–12.

BROWNING, CLYDE E., "The Question, 'But is it Geography?' Revisited or Are There Criteria for Establishing the Geographic Content of Topics?" *The Professional Geographer*, 1974, pp. 137–139.

GIBSON, LAY JAMES, "Climate and Other Amenities as Factors in the Growth of Arid-Area Population," *Urbanization in the Arid Lands*, Carle O. Hodge and Carl N. Hodges, eds., Lubbock, 1974.

GINSBURG, NORTON, "Natural Resources and Economic Development," *Annals of the Association of American Geographers*, 1957, pp. 196–212.

HARTSHORNE, RICHARD, "What Is Meant By Geography as the Study of Areal Differentiation?" *Perspective on the Nature of Geography*, Chicago, 1959, pp. 12–21.

HUNKER, HENRY L., ed., *Erich W. Zimmermann's Introduction to World Resources*, New York, 1964, 220 pp.

ISARD, WALTER, *Introduction to Regional Science*, Englewood Cliffs, N.J., 1975, 506 pp.

———, et al., *Methods of Regional Science: An Introduction to Regional Science*, New York, 1960, 784 pp.

JAMES, PRESTON E., "The Hard Core of

Geography," *New Viewpoints in Geography*, Preston E. James, ed., 29th Yearbook of the National Council for the Social Studies, Washington, 1959.

——, "The Region as a Concept," *Geographical Review*, 1962, pp. 127–129.

McCarty, H. H., "An Approach to a Theory of Economic Geography," *Economic Geography*, 1954, pp. 95–101.

——, "Toward a More General Economic Geography," *Economic Geography*, 1959, pp. 283–289.

——, and Lindberg, James B., *A Preface to Economic Geography*, Englewood Cliffs, 1966, 261 pp.

McNee, Robert B., "The Changing Relationships of Economics and Economic Geography," *Economic Geography*, 1959, pp. 189–198.

——, *A Primer on Economic Geography*, New York, 1971, 208 pp.

Morrill, Richard L., "The Future of Geography," *The Professional Geographer*, 1975, p. 1.

Pattison, William D., "The Four Traditions of Geography," *The Journal of Geography*, 1964, pp. 211–216.

Robinson, J. Lewis, "A New Look at the Four Traditions of Geography," *The Journal of Geography*, 1976, pp. 520–530.

Sauer, Carl O., "The Education of a Geographer," *Annals of the Association of American Geographers*, 1956, pp. 287–299.

Schaefer, Fred K., "Exceptionalism in Geography: A Methodological Examination," *Annals of the Association of American Geographers*, 1953, pp. 226–249.

Schnore, Leo F., "Geography and Human Ecology," *Economic Geography*, 1961, pp. 207–217.

United Nations, Food and Agriculture Organization, *Production Yearbook*, Rome (annual).

United Nations, Food and Agriculture Organization, *Trade Yearbook*, Rome (annual).

White, Gilbert F., "Geography and Public Policy," *The Professional Geographer*, 1972, pp. 101–104.

CHAPTER

people — the producers and consumers

A major business street in Frankfurt, Germany. Increased urbanization of the world's population has been accompanied by increased specialization in the production of goods and services. (*Courtesy German Information Center.*)

To the economic geographer the most important single topic is *people*—the producers, the exchangers, and the consumers of every item and service of economic value. Therefore, we must first have a clear picture of the distribution of the world's population before we can develop an understanding of the geography of agriculture, forestry, manufacturing, railroading, or any other economic activity.

How many people are involved in the world's economic life? Most of us have only a foggy notion of the number of human beings who are living today. If you were to stand on a street corner and put this question to passersby, only about one in ten could give you an answer that was even approximately correct. Are there a hundred million people, a billion, ten billion, a hundred billion? Try this question on your friends and notice the range of answers.

At present, the total population of the earth is approximately four billion. But what does a figure of this magnitude really mean? Take the number of years that have elapsed since Christ was born (approximately 1980 years), and multiply it by the number of days per year. The product—722,700—is not even close to the number of world inhabitants today. Now multiply that figure by 24 to get the number of hours in 1980 years, 17,344,800. But this is merely the approximate present population of New York State. Now multiply this by 60 to give the number of minutes, 1,040,688,000. But this is less than the number of people in the two nations of China and India. We would still have to multiply the number of *minutes* since Christ was born by four to equal the number of human beings on earth today.

THE DISTRIBUTION OF POPULATION

As geographers we want to know how these four billion are distributed around the globe. So the first thing we must do is consult a map (see the front endpaper or use an atlas). Three-fourths of the earth's surface is covered by water where naturally few people live. Thus, the four billion people live on the quarter of the earth composed of land and its adjacent water fringes.

As we analyze Table 2-1 or a map of population, we discover several important facts. First, most of the people are packed into a tiny part of the earth's land area. Asia and Europe, for example, have over two-thirds of the world's people but less than one-quarter of its land area. Clearly, population is very unequally distributed over the face of the earth.

The map (or Table 2-1) further reveals that this unequally distributed population is concentrated in four major regions—eastern Asia, southern Asia, western Europe, and eastern Anglo-America (that is, southeastern Canada and the eastern United States). The map also reveals several large regions of population void, and several transitional areas that lie between the two extremes of population centers and sparsely inhabited wildernesses.

The Four Major Regions of Population Masses

The most heavily populated major region of the world lies in eastern Asia, embracing China, Japan, Korea, the Philippines, and Vietnam. Probably 30 per cent of all the people in the world live in this area. China alone has a population of over 800,000,000—almost one of every five pepole living in the world today. Japan has 106,000,000. In eastern China along the coast there is an area that extends from north to south for nearly 1000 miles; people are crammed into it as densely as in the most heavily populated portion of the United States. A similar belt runs from east to west through China along the Yangtze (Ch'ang) Valley. The Yangtze Valley and the North China Plain (which includes the delta of the Huang Ho or Yellow River) are two of the largest areas of extremely dense settlement on the face of the earth. To appreciate the magnitude of congestion, imagine an area as thickly settled as northeastern Illinois that extends all the way from Canada to the Gulf of Mexico and spreads from the Mississippi River to the Atlantic Ocean.

The second region, southern Asia, consists essentially of India (563,000,000 inhabitants), Sri Lanka (13,000,000), portions of Pakistan (65,000,000), and Thailand (36,000,000). We might also include Indonesia (120,000,000), parts of Burma (29,000,000), and Cambodia (Khmer Republic) (6,000,000). India contains the Ganges Valley, the most intensely congested long valley in the world. If transposed to the United States, this Ganges belt would extend from New York City almost to Salt Lake City. In southeastern Asia, population clusters occur at the deltas of the Irrawaddy, Menam, and Mekong rivers. The number of people in these countries is astonishing compared with the 209,000,000 in the United States. In total, this

Many vast portions of the earth are still largely uninhabited, such as this area in southeastern Colorado. Like most of the other regions primarily void of population, human activity is still present, in this case, primarily ranching. (*Courtesy Clair A. Shenk.*)

second region has well over 800,000,000 people, over 20 per cent of the world's inhabitants.

Thus, over half the earth's people are jammed into the comparatively small space of eastern and southern Asia. This is one of the most significant facts in economic geography; its importance cannot be overemphasized, for it is fundamental to an understanding of many of the economic, social, and political problems that confront mankind in the twentieth century.

The third major region of habitation is Europe. Approximately one-fifth of the world's population is located within a wedge-shaped zone that is broad to the west along the Atlantic Coast (from Gibraltar to Scotland) and tapers as it runs eastward more than 3000 miles into central Russia. Over 700,000,000 people live in this area, which contains most of the Soviet Union (248,000,000), West Germany (62,000,000), the United Kingdom (56,000,000), Italy (54,000,000), France (52,000,000), Spain (34,000,000), Poland (33,000,000), and Romania and Yugoslavia (21,000,000 each). For comparison, remember that Canada has 22,000,000 people, and New York State 18,000,000. Visualize this third region transposed to the United States: It would reach from the Atlantic seaboard clear across the continent and into the Pacific Ocean.

Compared with these three gigantic areas, the fourth seems small in population and limited in extent. Roughly 3 per cent of the world's people are situated in eastern Anglo-America, along the southern border of

Table 2-1

Population and Area for Selected Nations

	Population in Millions	Land Area in Millions of Square Kilometers*	Persons per Square Kilometer*	Arable Hectares per Person*
WORLD	3,788	135.9	28	0.38
Asia	2,154	27.6	78	0.21
Afghanistan	18	0.6	28	0.44
China	801	9.6	83	0.14
Hong Kong	4	0.001	3,942	0.003
India	563	3.3	172	0.29
Indonesia	120	1.5	81	0.15
Iran	31	1.6	19	0.54
Israel	3	0.02	149	0.14
Japan	106	0.4	287	0.05
Korea	47	0.2	214	0.09
Pakistan	65	0.8	70	0.29
Philippines	39	0.3	130	0.28
Saudi Arabia	8	2.1	4	0.10
Thailand	36	0.5	71	0.32
Turkey	37	0.8	47	0.74
Europe	469	4.9	95	0.31
Austria	7	0.08	89	0.24
Belgium	10	0.03	318	0.08
Czechoslovakia	14	0.1	113	0.38
Denmark	5	0.04	116	0.53
Finland	5	0.3	14	0.54
France	52	0.5	95	0.37
Germany (E)	17	0.1	157	0.28
Germany (W)	62	0.2	248	0.13
Hungary	10	0.09	112	0.56
Italy	54	0.3	180	0.23
Netherlands	13	0.04	326	0.06
Norway	4	0.3	12	0.20
Poland	33	0.3	106	0.46
Romania	21	0.2	87	0.50
Spain	34	0.5	68	0.61
Sweden	8	0.4	18	0.38
Switzerland	6	0.04	156	0.06
United Kingdom	56	0.2	229	0.13
Yugoslavia	21	0.3	81	0.39

Canada and in the northeastern quadrant of the United States, from the Mississippi River to the Atlantic Coast.

The Eignt Major Voids

At the other extreme from these thickly peopled zones are vast stretches of land where hardly anyone lives. By far the most extensive is the African-Asian void, which runs almost 10,000 miles from the Atlantic shores of northern Africa eastward through the Sahara Desert, Arabia, and Afghanistan, deep into the heart of Asia. Mongolia marks its eastern extremity. Interrupted by only a few populous ribbons (such as the Nile Valley) and scattered oases (such as in Turkestan and western Sinkiang), this tremendous void extends over 20 per cent of the earth's land. And only a narrow, but con-

spicuous, band of settlement across southern Siberia separates it from another void that stretches 6000 miles across northern Eurasia from the Atlantic cliffs of Norway to the Pacific coast of Kamchatka.

Then there is northern North America, most of which is very sparsely settled, which, in fact, is virtually empty (except for military outposts) of permanent occupants all the way across northern Alaska, Canada, and Greenland. A southward prong extends, with only a few small anomalies, through the western United States deep into Mexico.

About equal in size to the North American void is Antarctica's 5,000,000 square miles (for comparison, the

Table 2-1 (Cont.)

	Population in Millions	Land Area in Millions of Square Kilometers*	Persons per Square Kilometer*	Arable Hectares per Person*
Africa	364	30.3	12	0.59
Algeria	15	2.4	6	0.45
Egypt	35	1.0	35	0.08
Ethiopia	26	1.2	21	0.51
Kenya	12	0.6	21	0.14
Nigeria	58	0.9	63	0.37
Rhodesia	6	0.4	15	0.31
Sudan	16	2.5	7	0.44
Tanzania	14	0.9	15	1.16
Uganda	10	0.2	44	0.49
South Africa	23	1.2	19	0.52
Zaire	23	2.3	10	0.31
North America	332	24.2	14	0.82
Canada	22	10.0	2	1.99
Cuba	9	0.1	76	0.39
Mexico	53	2.0	27	0.45
United States	209	9.4	22	0.92
South America	201	17.8	11	0.42
Argentina	24	2.8	9	1.08
Brazil	99	8.5	12	0.30
Chile	9	0.8	12	0.51
Colombia	22	1.1	20	0.23
Peru	14	1.3	11	0.21
Venezuela	11	0.9	12	0.47
U.S.S.R.	248	22.4	11	0.94
Oceania	20	8.5	2	2.35
Australia	13	7.7	2	3.43
New Zealand	3	0.3	11	0.28
Papua New Guinea	3	0.5	6	0.14

Sources: United Nations *Demographic Yearbook* (1973), Tables 1 and 2, and *Food and Agricultural Organization Production Yearbook* (1973), Table 1.
*A kilometer is 3,281 feet (approximately 5/8 of a mile). A square kilometer covers 39% of a square mile. The world population density of 28 people per kilometer can also be expressed as 72 per square mile. One hectare equals 2.471 acres; one acre equals 0.4047 hectares.

land area figure for the United States is 3,000,000). A fifth population void (about the same size as the United States) shows up in the Amazon Basin, which makes up a major segment of South America. A comparable expanse is that part of Oceania which comprises Australia and New Guinea. Other areas where few people have chosen to live are southwestern Africa and the southern tip of South America.

Altogether, these eight sparsely settled sections constitute about 75 per cent of the earth's land area.

Transitional Regions

Between the two extremes are several transitional areas, some of which are beginning to stand out as conspicuous, if minor, clusters of people—for example, the Nile Valley and the Near East (particularly Israel, Lebanon, Turkey, and the northern portions of Iraq and Iran). In addition, there are the oases of Russian Turkestan and Sinkiang, which have already been mentioned. And deep in the heart of Africa is a surprising population cluster—in Rwanda and Burundi. Nigeria and the southeastern coast of South Africa are also noteworthy. A counterpart to these areas appears at Africa's other margin, along the coasts of Morocco, Algeria, and Tunisia.

South America's population pattern resembles beads on a string. The continent is encircled with appreciable concentrations on the coasts of Brazil and Argentina and on the peripheries of Venezuela, Colombia, and Chile. In Middle America, we find a concentration in southern Mexico, along with a few small aggregates elsewhere.

Man/Land Ratios

Another way of approaching the question of where mankind is located is to strike off ratios between numbers of people and amounts of land. The most familiar ratio, of course, is population per square mile or square kilometer. Such a statement expresses a relationship known as "density of population" or as "the man/land ratio." The distribution shown in Figure 2-1 is based on this relationship.

Table 2-1 presents information on density of population by means of two measurements: number of persons per square kilometer, and number of arable hectares per person. Both measurements vary markedly from nation to nation. When we use the persons-per-square-kilometer ratio, we discover a sharp contrast between Australia and the Netherlands. In between these two extremes, there are many shadings. But notice that the average *for the world as a whole* is 28 persons per square kilometer (72 per square mile). (These ratios are based on *land* areas; they do not include the surface areas of oceans or inland seas.) The average for the United States is below the world average. It is scarcely surprising, though, to find that the average number of

Figure 2-1   (*After U.S. Bureau of the Census.*)

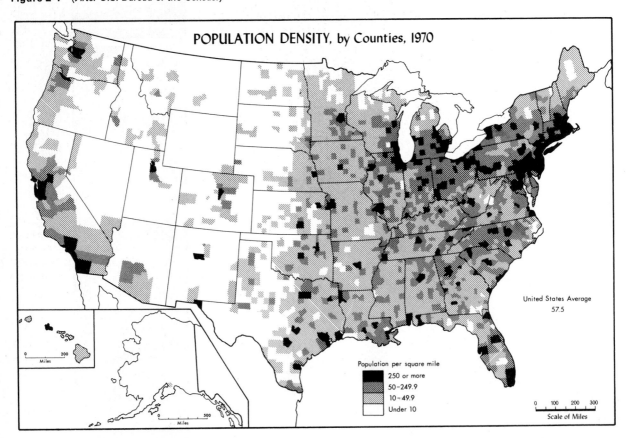

persons per square kilometer in the other three dense regions is markedly higher than in the United States and in the sparsely settled areas.

But what do these bald figures really tell us? Are the citizens of Australia scattered evenly all over the landscape? For so large and varied a country as the United States, how meaningful is it to say that there are 22 persons per square kilometer? The point, of course, is that land is not all of equal value. Some lands produce an abundance of the items that man cherishes. Others are unproductive—at least of what twentieth-century man desires and of what his present knowledge enables him to produce. So a more meaningful way of stating land-per-person ratios is to specify the number of *arable* acres or hectares per person, arable land being land that can be cultivated to produce useful crops. When we modify our ratios in this way, we discover substantial changes. As Table 2-1 shows, although Saudi Arabia has a vast amount of open land, very little of it is arable; in fact, there is 0.1 hectare of arable land per person. At the other extreme is Australia, where there are over 3.4 hectares per inhabitant. For the world as a whole, the figure is 0.38, and the average for the United States is about two and one-half times the world average. Notice how little arable land there is per person in such countries as Japan, Belgium, the Netherlands, China, the United Kingdom, and West Germany.

Although these ratios appear in the table simply as statistics, they tell a vivid story about the economic problems of nations. For impersonal statistics often stand for empty stomachs and low standards of living. Study these data carefully, compare them, and keep them in mind as we come to the economic activities by which the people in the nations of the world are trying to support themselves. (Anyone interested in population problems can find considerable information in the United Nations' *Demographic Yearbook*. The United Nations has published several other studies of population that you may find in your college library. For the first time in history, we have in these sources something resembling world census materials.)

The observations we have made on the basis of the ratios listed in Table 2-1 lead to some provocative questions. Why are so many people located in the densely settled regions? Why are so few people located in the sparsely settled regions? Can the sparsely populated regions be used to support more people? These are major questions challenging mankind today, questions on which there is wide difference of opinion. Topics presented in this book will shed at least some light on them.

This picture of the present-day population of the world becomes more meaningful when we compare it with scenes in years gone by. For in geography, as in many other disciplines, it is impossible to understand the present without some knowledge of the past. So let us familiarize ourselves with the principal changes that have taken place in the total number of people and in their location.

THE PAST

Changes in Number of People

Only recently has the earth teemed with nearly four billion people; for centuries only a few million people lived at any one time. We do not know for sure how many people there were at any given moment in the past, but the most reasonable estimate is that during the centuries before Christ there were never more than 200 or 300 million people. In fact, when Christ was born the population of the whole world was probably about 250 million, considerably less than the present-day population of India alone. A thousand years later the world figure was still less than 500 million; by the year 1650, it had apparently passed the half-billion mark. By 1800, it stood at one billion, and by 1900 it had reached about 1.5 billion. Then, in the few decades since 1900, the population of the world seems suddenly to have exploded. In just five decades the number of people shot up by over 1.5 billion.

How can we account for this rapid growth in just a few decades when for so many centuries the number of inhabitants changed so little? Here is one general explanation—not completely satisfactory, but nevertheless suggestive. Theoretically an increase in the number of people can result from either an increase in the number of births (while the death rate holds steady), from a decrease in the number of deaths (while the birth rate holds steady), or from both. Regardless of how high the birth rate is, if the death rate is equally high the population will not increase. Again, no matter how low the death rate is, if the birth rate is similarly low the total population will not increase. Now, birth rates have scarcely changed over the centuries. The population explosion of recent times, then, seems to have resulted directly from a sharp reduction in death rates.

Before about 1650, the total population remained low because the death rate was kept high by starvation, disease, and war. Then man learned some new lessons. He discovered ways of improving his agriculture and increasing his food supply; he learned to irrigate arid lands, drain wet lands, and develop hardier strains of seeds. Man also discovered better methods of transportation. Surfaced roads, railroads, power-driven vehicles, larger ships: These and other inventions made it possible to distribute the new supplies of food to deficient areas. So starvation became less menacing and death rates began to fall.

Man also learned to combat diseases. He discovered germs and the manner in which they live and reproduce. He devised new methods for destroying their habitats, remedial measures that we call sanitation. By pushing forward the science of medicine, he learned how to prevent disease and to cure people who had been infected.

Figure 2-2

All these advances in science served to reduce the high death toll that had been levied by starvation and disease since the dawn of history. Although birth rates remained about the same, fewer newborn babies died, and those who lived began to live longer. All these discoveries have sharply reduced the death rate and so have enabled the population of the world to multiply at a dramatic pace. Unquestionably science has added years to our lives. (A relevant issue is whether science has added "life to our years.")

Changes in Location of People

The regions that are most densely settled today have not always been in the top positions. At one time the most populous area was located in southwestern Asia, in the valley of the Tigris and Euphrates rivers. A few centuries later, three new spots had appeared on the map: southeastern Asia (especially India and China), northern Africa, and southern Europe. By 1700 west-central Europe had become a conspicuous region, but North and South America were still very sparsely settled. Only recently have people streamed across the oceans from regions of high densities to occupy the American voids.

The front endpaper in the book, then, is simply a single picture in a long series. If we were to run through the series chronologically, we would have a picture of the continuous changes in the population regions of the world, a complex pattern of population shifts from place to place and from time to time.

PROSPECTS FOR THE FUTURE

What about the future? How many people will the earth have to support? Will the number of people continue to multiply at the present rate, with the curve shown in Figure 2-2 shooting steadily upward?

If so, a host of troublesome new questions will arise. Will there be enough food? What is the maximum number of people the earth can feed? Will enough fuel be available for heat and power and enough fiber for clothing? Or will the rate of growth slow down so that the curve, though continuing upward, will rise more gradually? Is there any evidence that the graph will level off, with the population stabilized at one figure? Is there any likelihood that the curve will reverse itself

some time in the future to indicate a shrinkage of the world's population? If so, at how many billions and in what period might that occur?

Since even well-informed authorities disagree on the answers to these questions, the reader need not hesitate to make a start at forming his own opinion. And there are a number of other questions to ponder as well. What about the school of thought that regards the spread of population over the face of the earth as analogous to the spread of cancer in the human body? In cancerous growth, the normal body cells begin to multiply at an excessive rate, and, for some reason that we still do not understand, accumulate in abnormal concentrations. According to this analogy, although the rapid increase in population may not be undesirable in itself, the danger is that billions of people swarming over the globe may eventually exhaust and vitiate the host on which they live, the earth itself. There is just so much energy available to man for use in producing the food, fuel, colthing, shelter, and tools he needs, and all that is at his disposal either arrives from the sun moment by moment or is already stored up in the substances of the earth—in the form of coal, petroleum, or nuclear fuel. How many billions of people—and at what standard of living—can be supported by the energy resources of the earth? Can the resources of other celestial bodies be tapped? Clearly, these questions are crucial to anybody who is interested in the future economic activities of the earth's people.

Trends in location are also worth pondering. Where will the populous regions be two centuries from now? Will man infiltrate today's vacant stretches as he makes further discoveries in science and further changes in his economic and social organization? Or have human beings reached a climax at which we have finally worked out the locational pattern that most perfectly fits our needs—the pattern that makes it possible for us to be supported at the highest possible level by the earth's resources? Or will the locational pattern of resources continue to interact with changes in culture to produce some new regional pattern of population?

At the present level of economic and cultural development, certain regions are better equipped than others to support people. Throughout most of man's history, people have had to live rather close to their food supply. And even today most food does not have to be transported very far to get it from the place it is produced to the place it is consumed. But the relatively recent revolutions in transportation and economic productivity may one day make it possible for great numbers of men to live in regions far removed from their food-producing regions.

We have already seen evidence of this tendency in the shift of population in the United States. A great wave of people has moved to the West Coast, where life is easier, where winters are less severe, where many of the amenities of life are ready at hand. And yet the West Coast connot provide all the varieties of food, in the quantities demanded, for this new population. The region does provide the means, however, by which people can produce items and services of value to exchange with food-producers in other regions. Inhabitants of the Pacific Coast now generate a surplus of airplanes, motion pictures, timber, fruit, and vegetables. But this blossoming of a new population region never could have occurred had it not been for the efficient transportation system that enables the surplus of the West to be exchanged for food from other regions. As transportation becomes more and more efficient, people everywhere can, if they wish, settle in regions ever farther and farther removed from the areas in which their food is grown.

For the present, at least, most of our food still comes from the soil. The plants we eat subsist on soil nutrients, moisture, sunshine, and the atmosphere. The animals we consume also subsist on the same botanical base. The fundamental truth is that, at our present level of knowledge, some regions are distinctly handicapped in their ability to produce the kind of food we can and want to eat. Some regions are too cold, some are too hot, or too

dry, or too wet, or too rough, and some have very poor soil. And the location of these physical factors is not very likely to change.

Consequently, if the regions of population shift, the change will come about through the cultural efforts of man—in devising new techniques that will make it possible to irrigate deserts and drain swamps. Man has had some success in terracing hilly regions and in transforming rough lands into productive areas. Can he devise techniques for improving soils that are now too poor to produce crops? If so, the sparsely settled regions that now appear on the world population map may, in the future, rank among the chief population centers on earth.

An even more striking shift in the location of people would probably occur if we could devise some means of producing food from sources other than soil. If, for example, we could produce an adequate supply of nutrients from the oceans or in chemical laboratories, the people of the world would suddenly be freed from their attachment to the soil. The criteria by which human beings evaluate places for living would change, and with improving means of transportation they could—and many perhaps would—eventually move into areas that are now completely devoid of human life.

The reader should think about these problems for himself. Nobody has a ready-made set of answers that can be set forth in a neat list, so he should try to look into the future and predict the regional patterns that the world's population is likely to follow.

SUGGESTED READINGS

EHRLICH, PAUL R., and EHRLICH, ANNE H., *Population, Resources, Environment*, San Francisco, 1972, 509 pp.

GRAF, WILLIAM L., "Resources, the Environment, and the American Experience," *The Journal of Geography*, 1976, pp. 28–40.

GREENWOOD, NED H., and EDWARDS, J. M. B., *Human Environments and Natural Systems*, North Scituate, 1973, 429 pp.

HECOCK, RICHARD D., and ROONEY, JOHN F., JR., "Towards a Geography of Consumption," *The Professional Geographer*, 1968, pp. 392–395.

JEANS, D. N., "Changing Formulations of the Man-Environment Relationship in Anglo-American Geography," *The Journal of Geography*, March 1974, pp. 36–40.

LOUNSBURY, JOHN F., "Recent Demographic and Economic Changes and World Crises," *The Journal of Geography*, 1975, pp. 411–418.

LOWENTHAL, DAVID, and COMITAS, LAMBROS, "Emigration and Depopulation: Some Neglected Aspects of Population Geography," *Geographical Review*, 1962, pp. 195–210.

Rockefeller Foundation, Progress Report, *Toward the Conquest of Hunger*, 1965–1966.

STERNSTEIN, LARRY, "Migration and Development in Thailand," *Geographical Review*, 1976, pp. 401–419.

TAYLOR, CARL E., and TAYLOR, DANIEL C., "Population Planning in India and Nepal," *Growth and Change*, April, 1976, pp. 9–13.

TREWARTHA, GLENN T., *A Geography of Population: World Patterns*, New York, 1969, 186 pp.

United Nations, *Demographic Yearbook*, New York (annual).

United States Department of Agriculture, *The World Food Situation and Prospects to 1985*, Washington, D.C., 1975, 90 pp.

VERMEER, DONALD E., "Population Pressure and Crop Rotational Changes Among the Tiv of Nigeria," *Annals of the Association of American Geographers*, 1970, pp. 299–314.

WAGLEY, CHARLES, ed., *Man in the Amazon*, Gainesville, 1974, 330 pp.

ZELINSKY, WILBUR, *A Prologue to Population Geography*, Englewood Cliffs, N.J., 1966, 150 pp.

PART

TWO

SUBSISTENCE ECONOMIC ACTIVITIES

All the world's four billion people are supported by economic activity of one sort or another. Given such a bewildering amount of activity, how can we detect the patterns by which it is organized from place to place? In a sense, doing so is precisely the task of economic geography.

In this book we shall apply the geographic method of analysis to, and organize our discussion around, *production* rather than *consumption*. We do so for two reasons. First, spatial variation is more pronounced for the former than the latter. Coffee-drinkers are more ubiquitous than coffee-growers; paper is consumed in almost every inhabited area of the world, but paper is manufactured in only a few spots; and although the consumption of cotton is well-nigh universal, cotton growing and cotton-textile production are carried on only in certain specific regions that can be clearly delimited. Second, there is much less information, scientifically analyzed, about consumption compared to the information dealing with production.

For our purposes, we can divide production efforts into two great categories—

subsistence and *commercial*. In *subsistence* endeavors, each producer lives directly on what he produces. He bends all his efforts to meeting the immediate needs of himself and family and so has little left over for bartering or selling. He and the members of his family must provide the food they eat, the clothes they wear, the fuel that warms them, the dwelling that shelters them, the implements they use, and any items of culture they enjoy.

In *commercial* economies, by contrast, each producer generates a surplus of something that he can exchange for surpluses of other things others produce. Little of his effort goes into directly providing the food, clothing, fuel, and shelter his family needs.

The basic distinction between subsistence and commercial economies lies, then, in the source of satisfaction of economic needs. Obviously, there are variations in the degrees of either subsistence or commercial economies. Businessmen who live in city apartment houses are entirely dependent on other producers for every one of their economic needs. Primitive tropical tribesmen who avoid contact with outsiders provide themselves with everything they consume. But in between these two extremes are countless shadings—areas in which the economy is partly subsistence and partly commercial.

We shall confine our discussion to regions that are clearly either subsistence or commercial—or at least we shall confine our chapter headings to such activities. For now, in Part Two, we shall deal primarily with subsistence economies. Chapter 3 treats of primitive subsistence economies, while Chapter 4 deals with a more advanced activity—intensive subsistence cultivation.

CHAPTER

primitive subsistence activities

Several herdsmen with a herd of goats and a few cattle in the drought-stricken village of Bume, Ethiopia. The drought of the mid-1970's, which affected much of northern Africa, took the lives of about 85 per cent of the cattle in southern Ethiopia. Goats generally fare better in dry weather than do cattle. (*Courtesy United Nations/Jerry Frank.*)

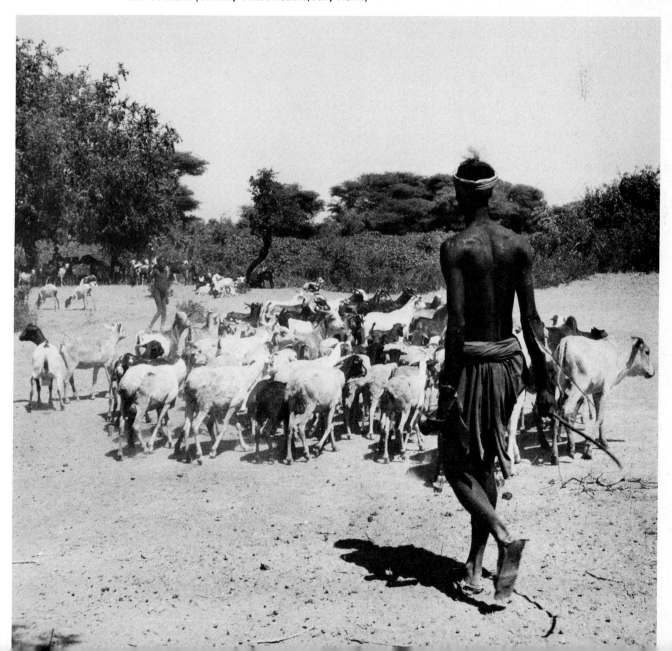

On the subsistence level, man's economic efforts fall into two main categories: primitive and intensive (or advanced). Chapter 3 deals with endeavors in the first category: primitive gathering, primitive herding, and primitive cultivation. We shall investigate each according to our method of identifying locations, characteristics, and relationships.

PRIMITIVE GATHERING

Primitive gathering, the lowest order of economic activity, is fading rapidly from the face of the earth, and is currently practiced by only a few thousand people. Nevertheless, it still warrants a brief treatment in any survey of economic endeavors.

Where Is Primitive Gathering Located?

Primitive gathering persists in isolated pockets within two major realms: the very high and the very low latitudes (Figure 3-1). The high-latitude zone includes portions of northern Canada, northern Eurasia, and southern Chile. The low-latitude area consists of the territories of some Indian tribes dispersed through the Amazon Basin (Brazil, Peru, Ecuador, and Venezuela) along with a few stretches within tropical Africa, the northern fringe of Australia, the interior of New Guinea and Borneo, and even the interior of southeastern Asia (Burma, Thailand, and China).

What Are the Characteristics of Primitive Gathering?

Primitive gathering is the oldest economy known, for it was by collecting items from nature's bounty that early man supported himself. Even today, in regions of primitive gathering, man collects fruits, nuts, and wood from trees, and gathers berries, roots, leaves, and fibers from shrubs and smaller plants. He hunts wild animals, preys upon wild birds, and snares fish. From all kinds of wild life, plant and animal, on land, in the air, and in the waters, he extracts enough to satisfy his needs for nourishment, shelter, warmth, clothing, and tools. He plants few seeds and spends little time cultivating the soil. He exerts no effort to breed, feed, or protect animals, nor does he try to control or improve their habitat. Of all economic endeavors, gathering requires the least amount of capital investment. Yields per acre and yields per man are so low that surpluses are virtually nonexistent.

Primitive gathering in the high latitudes is based almost entirely on animal life, especially caribou and musk ox from the land, seal, walrus, and salmon from the seas, birds from the air, and eggs snatched from nests. Typical of the peoples of this realm are the North American Eskimos, who have developed hunting into a fine art: They have become skillful in fashioning kayaks from skins and harpoons from bones and they display remarkable ingenuity in adapting animal products to satisfy all their physical needs. Farther south, in a few parts of Canada, occasional Indian tribes remain essen-

Figure 3-1

SUBSISTENCE GATHERING

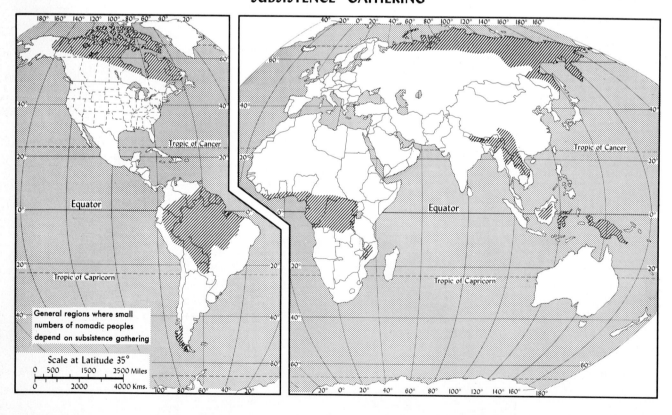

General regions where small numbers of nomadic peoples depend on subsistence gathering

Scale at Latitude 35°
0   500   1500   2500 Miles
0   2000   4000 Kms.

A fisherman on the Volta Lake in Ghana. He is one of 25,000 fishermen around the lake, which was created by the construction of a hydroelectric dam to power industry in the nation's urban areas. (*FAO Photo by Peyton Johnson.*)

tially at the gathering stage. These Indians are landsmen, whose main targets are deer; they themselves are sometimes called "people of the deer." The Yukaghirs of Siberia and the Yahgans of southern Chile are other high-latitude peoples who still subsist mainly on harvests of wild animals.

Primitive gatherers in the tropics utilize plant life as well as animal life; they collect fruits, roots, leaves, and wood. Fish also constitute an important part of their diet, specially on tropical islands of the Pacific. Typical primitive gatherers in the tropics are the Auca Indians of Ecuador, the bushmen of northern Australia, and the pygmies of the Congo region. A fascinating description of one such group appears in the passage entitled "The Aucas" in Elizabeth Elliott's *Through Gates of Splendor*.[1]

To What Other Phenomena
Is Primitive Gathering Related?

For this economic type we shall consider the third question of the geographic method in terms of physical and cultural relationships.

Physical Phenomena. The physical environments in which primitive gatherers are located seem forbidding in many ways. In the *tropics*, the atmosphere is hot and humid, and vegetation grows profusely. This is the land of the *rainforest* where great trees tower into the sky, often with crowns spreading out 60 or 70 feet. The dense canopy shuts out the sunlight and cloaks the ground in semidarkness. Since there is little in the way of browse, or ground-covering plants, this is a rather poor habitat for wildlife. Only on the fringes of the rainforest, where trees are shorter, smaller, and farther apart, and in the adjacent savannas (regions of tall, coarse grass) is there abundant animal life. The heavy

[1](New York, 1957), pp. 96–120.

precipitation of the rainforest, however, creates numerous rivers that are endowed with nutrients—a good habitat for fish.

In some other low-latitude regions of subsistence gathering the environment is exceedingly dry. For example, in central Australia the Bindibu tribe has lived for 10,000 years in a desert, surviving on drought-resistant plants and on animals dependent on the same type of vegetation.

In the *high latitudes*, primitive gathering is carried on in a physical environment of low average temperatures and short growing seasons. The barren land supports a meager growth termed *tundra* (mosses, lichens, and shrubs), which makes poor food for humans. But tundra provides an adequate diet for caribou, musk ox, and deer, and these animals in turn furnish food to the human beings who range over these uninviting expanses in search of animal prey.

Cultural Phenomena. Subsistence-economy cultures are backward. The people still live in the Stone Age, much like their ancestors of a hundred centuries ago. Indeed, some of them are not even that far advanced; the Charante and Camayura tribes in the wilds of Mato Grosso, western Brazil, do not yet have stone points for their arrows, according to Edward M. Weyer, formerly of the Museum of Anthropology at the University of California in Berkeley. Primitive gatherers lack written languages. Their health is generally poor; life expectancy is short. The Eskimos are probably the most advanced of all the gatherers, yet even they never domesticated a herd until they were taught to do so by Laplanders from Scandinavia.

Clearly, by our standards, their way of life has little to recommend it. Yet primitive gatherers can be credited with maintaining a fine balance between the supply and the harvest of animal resources, in sharp contrast to the performance of some members of more "advanced" economies who have seriously damaged such resources and have actually extinguished certain types of animals. Of course, we might argue that the poor health of these primitive peoples prevented them from becoming numerous enough to threaten their food supply. But when we realize that these peoples waste scarcely any part of the animals they capture—using skins for shelter, tendons for cord, bones for tools—we must recognize their conservation of natural resources. Primitive gatherers seem never to have destroyed their economic base by overharvesting the food supply except where techniques or tools—such as firearms—were introduced from other cultures.

Gathering economies are associated with tribal societies in which individuals or single families rarely function as independent units, for the jobs of tracking down wild animals with primitive weapons and protecting the families against enemies are conducted more efficiently in groups.

The man-to-land ratio is extremely low in regions of subsistence gathering—in fact, the number is often less than two persons per square mile. But this figure in itself is almost meaningless, for a traveler can pass for miles through these regions without meeting a single person. Then he comes upon a small cluster or tribe before traveling on across more empty miles. Plainly that portion of the earth's surface on which primitive gathering appears supports a very small fraction of the earth's four billion inhabitants. (This raises an interesting question about the best way of indicating population on a map: Would it be more realistic to portray these regions, not by working out over-all averages of the total number of people divided by the total area, but rather by identifying areas that are altogether unpopulated and those that have some population?)

With no surplus production, there is little need for transportation or trading centers. Cities are absent in primitive-gathering regions, except as enclaves of other economic activities such as mining. Economic relationships with other regions are virtually nonexistent.

The Future

Occasionally, explorers discover a new tribe of primitive gatherers unknown to civilization. In 1956, Brazilian surveyors stumbled on to just such a tribe, the Xetas, in the rugged, jungle-tangled, almost inaccessible Serra dos Dourados mountains in the western part of Paraná, one of Brazil's southern states. How many more such tribes await discovery is open to speculation. In any case, the extent of gathering as an activity is decreasing as more and more tribes, in contact with outside cultures, begin to upgrade their means of livelihood.

Thus, primitive gathering, which once was widespread, once the prevailing economy of the inhabitants of Europe, Asia, Africa, North America, South America, and Australia, has steadily retreated in the face of advanced economies and now holds out only in isolated pockets.

It is indeed puzzling why these ancient peoples—the Eskimo, the Auca, the Xeta, and others of their type—have taken no step "upward" on the ladder of economic production, whereas other cultures of much later vintage have scurried up that ladder. The term "upward" is used advisedly, though, for some observers think that the Aucas and Eskimos will continue to inhabit the earth long after "civilized" man and his "higher" economies have disappeared, and that the economic activity of subsistence gathering will, at some future date, blanket all the populated portions of the earth as it once did, at the dawn of history.

PRIMITIVE HERDING

Primitive herding is a step above primitive gathering in that men who live by it make at least some investment to enhance natural production. The product is animal, and the investment is labor—not just the labor required to extract from the natural supply, but the labor necessary to *increase* that supply.

The domestication of animals marks the step upward from animal gathering to primitive herding. Once this step has been taken, man begins to play a significant role in producing his commodities—that is, in bringing them to maturity—as well as in harvesting them. No longer is he merely a parasite living off the earth's bounty, for now he is making an investment of his own.

Location

By the mid-twentieth century, man had occupied the earth in such a way that one vast area of primitive herding (see Figure 3-2) extended across northern Africa, all the way from the Atlantic shores eastward through the Arabian Peninsula, then deep into the heart of Asia, almost to the Pacific—a longitudinal extent of over 8000 miles. This is one-third the circumference of the earth! Latitudinally, the region extends from 5° south latitude (on the east coast of Africa) to 50° north latitude (in inner Asia)—a range of over 3500 miles. This is the largest single economic region on earth.

A lesser region of primitive herding runs across northern Eurasia, reaching over into Alaska. In the Southern Hemisphere, too, there are small areas in Southwest Africa and Madagascar. Primitive herding is absent from Australia, South America, and most of North America.

A word of caution: The existence of the foregoing pattern does not mean that there are *no other types* of economic activity in the regions identified as primitive (or nomadic) herding, rather that primitive herding is the *predominant* form of employment activity there.

Characteristics

The economic needs of the primitive herders are met by animals that feed on wild plants rather than on cultivated crops. The animals supply food (milk, cheese, and meat), materials for clothing (fibers and skins), shelter (skins),

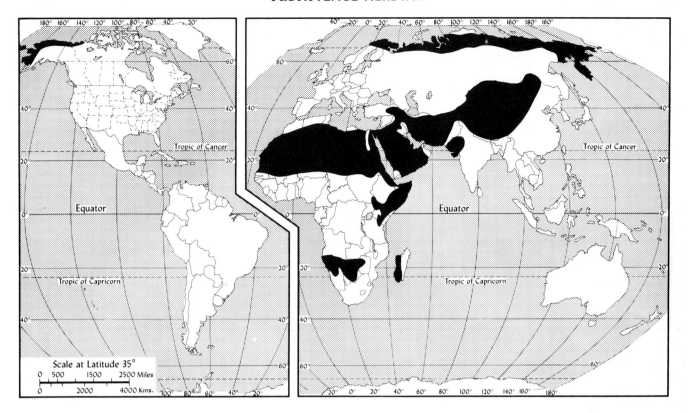

Figure 3-2

fuel (refuse), and tools (bones). The animals that have proved most satisfactory in these roles are sheep, goats, cattle, camels, yak, and deer. Horses are used in some areas, but they perform the special function of transporting the herdsmen as they tend their herds.

Primitive herding is a migratory undertaking, and these people are typically nomads. (Indeed, some scholars prefer *nomadic herding* over *primitive herding* as a label for this endeavor.) Their migrations are both horizontal (often hundreds of miles) and vertical (often thousands of feet.)

Internal Relationships

We shall consider primitive herding in relation to several other phenomena, first, those *within* its regions and then those in *other* regions.

Regions of primitive herding invariably have rigorous physical environments, in terms of aridity and vegetation, and rather backward cultures; each of these topics merits comment in some detail.

Aridity. Most of these lands have a dry climate. In a dry climate annual precipitation is *less than* the annual evaporation, no matter how many inches of rain (or snow) fall. A place that gets 8 inches of rain has a *humid* climate if its annual evaporation is only 7 inches; a place with 16 inches of precipitation has a *dry* climate if its annual evaporation exceeds 16 inches. Thirst—and the search for water—are critical facts of life in these regions.

Vegetation. Plant life reflects the amount of available moisture. In general, the earth's wetter lands tend to have forests, the drier lands grass. This generalization applies, of course, to *natural* vegetation undisturbed by human activity. The relationship between vegetation and amount of available moisture is suggested by Figure 3-3, in which the solid line represents variation in amount of moisture available and the sketches represent types of natural vegetation.

Most primitive herding occurs in the regions of shrubs, bunch grass, and short grass. Goats, which can endure considerable aridity, constitute the herds in the driest regions; sheep and camels predominate in regions with somewhat heavier rainfall. The moister fringes of these vast dry realms can support herds of cattle.

Not only the type but also the amount of natural vegetation is conditioned by the precipitation. The vegetative cover in these areas is extremely sparse, which means that the amount of food available for fodder is severely restricted. So the search for forage is never-ending. The herdsmen leave their animals in one place as long as possible until forage gives out; then they move on to some other place where a meager supply of water and grass suffices briefly—until the next move.

The unending migration of subsistence herdsmen and animals is, as was mentioned, both lateral and vertical. They must move hundreds of miles across the earth both because supplies at any given time in any one place are limited and because the rains come at different times in different areas. And since highlands tend to be wetter than lowlands, the nomadic herdsmen often move *up* to higher altitudes to find grass for their herds. Again,

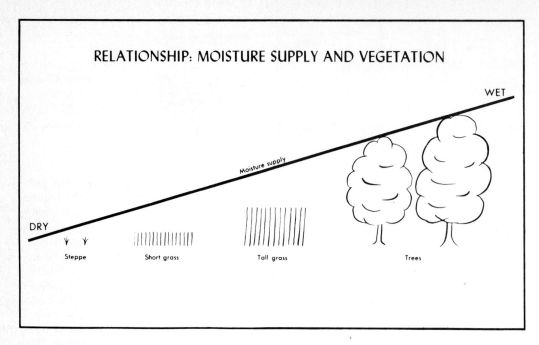

RELATIONSHIP: MOISTURE SUPPLY AND VEGETATION

WET

Moisture supply

DRY

Steppe   Short grass   Tall grass   Trees

Figure 3-3

there are seasonal variations in the forage supply, the determining factor usually being temperature rather than precipitation. Herdsmen tend to winter in the lowlands and migrate upward to mountain pastures during the summer. As autumn approaches and the frosts begin, they drive their herds back to the lowlands.

Here is a vivid description of the arid setting and nomadic herding as carried on in Saudi Arabia.

> On either side the land rolled away tan and light gold beneath the burning sun of May, with little more than thistles and stubbly grass rising seared above the sand. Over the land herds of camels wandered, sometimes in long single lines, with their awkward necks thrust ungainly forward and their bodies almost the color of the sand. Always the landscape was the same, beneath a sky milky with haze at the horizon, ranging to deeper blue at the zenith, and white puffballs of cloud drifting high. Once, far to the east, a range of sandy hills, carved in the most delicate pastel shades all based on brown, rose out of the sand. Flocks of black goats moved over the tan of the earth, and here and there a Bedouin's black goat hair tent was staked out upon a slope. This was nomad country, and the Bedouins filed past on their way to a new location.[2]

One might wonder why nomadic herdsmen do not set their sights on green pastures in humid regions, head straight for them, and stay there. Would not this move unshackle them forever from the need to roam? It would. But there seems to be a geographic law at work that subsistence herding quickly fades as a way of life in humid regions. Newly arrived nomads soon settle down, and economic metamorphosis sets in. Usually the change is from subsistence herding to subsistence cropping, or to commercial livestocking. Underlying this metamorphosis are various cultural forces, which will be considered in later chapters.

[2]Harry B. Ellis, in "Desert Road to Arabia," *The Christian Science Monitor*, August 13, 1955.

The physical environment is different in the primitive herding region of northern Eurasia. Precipitation is low but evaporation is lower resulting in humid climates. However, temperatures drop so low that cold climates prevail and the natural vegetation is tundra; there are no trees, just a few shrubs, and only a little grass. Forage is scanty, like steppe and desert, but here the major handicap is cold, not aridity. Plants that withstand the climate of the tundra are no more palatable to man than are the shrubs of the deserts or the grass of the steppes. But certain animals—in this case, caribou and deer—can exist even on this meager vegetation, and in some parts of the tundra (for example, the Lapland area of Europe) man has learned the art of domesticating them. Where he has not, the economy persists at the level of primitive gathering.

Because of limited forage, the herds migrate—toward the pole in summer when the tundra plants germinate and mature, toward the equator in winter when the intense cold drives the plants into dormancy.

But the physical environment is only part of the story. There are other areas of the world that have an environment as meager in forage as that of North Africa and Central Asia, yet have little subsistence herding. Australia, southern South America, and western North America are conspicuous examples. If the natural environment were the determining factor on the economic activities of men, these places would also be regions of subsistence herding. Clearly, we cannot understand the geography of herding without investigating the *cultural* phenomena with which it is associated.

Antiquity of Cultures. Without exception, subsistence herding occurs in areas of surviving ancient cultures. At some time in the distant past, an alert gatherer first conceived the idea of protecting wild animals (from predators) and helping them in their search for food and water. This introduction of domestication, one of the major cultural developments in man's history—a significant economic step forward—occurred long ago in southwestern Asia and northeastern Africa.

By contrast, dry regions that have been settled by peoples with more recently developed cultures are not areas of subsistence herding. Australia, South America, and North Amercia were settled by peoples of European culture, which is of much more recent vintage than that of the nomadic herders. And, as far as we know, the first European immigrants did not find nomadic herdsmen when they arrived in Australia and the Americas. They found gatherers. The conclusion seems to be that during the long period when man subsisted in the gathering stage he migrated from the starting point in southwestern Asia to each of several continents. Later, at that same starting point, he developed the idea of domesticating animals. Here we encounter an interesting question, whose answer is still obscure: Why did not this new idea of domesticating animals radiate outward to all the continents? Apparently it penetrated only into Asia, Africa, and Europe.

Low Man/Land Ratio. The relationship of numbers of people to land area is marked by a low ratio in regions of subsistence herding. Some of the great voids on the population map coincide with these areas. But this correlation is not reversible, for there are many population voids that do *not* have nomadic herding.

It is a basic principle that subsistence herding simply cannot sustain great numbers of people. This generalization leads to another which will unfold fully later: The earth can support fewer people by means of animal food that it can by means of plant food. Acre for acre, a larger number of vegetarians than meat-eaters live on the land. This recalls one of the questions raised in Chapter 2: How many people can the earth feed? If man were content with a vegetarian diet and did not insist on eating meat, one answer might be "a great many more."

Tribal Settlements. There are no isolated herdsmen. The people cluster in clans or tribes, and their settlements are temporary in location. The flexibility demanded by a migratory economy of this sort has led to the development of a peculiar type of dwelling —usually the tent—which is easy to fold up and carry along. Some nomads live in huts that can be disassembled and loaded on the backs of camels, or else stored in tree tops when the dry season keeps the herders on the move day after day.

To be sure, the herding regions on the map do contain a few cities and towns, but these rest on some other economic base, such as mining, or else they are centers on trade routes that cut across the herding regions.

Tribal Spirit. Another cultural phenomenon is an intense *esprit de corps*—the fierce loyalty to the tribe. Some of these people are friendly to outsiders, but many of them are hostile—tough people, lean people,

always hungry, always on the move, always searching for water and forage—as were their forefathers, who lived for millennia on these same barren plains and slopes. Success in their unceasing search for water and grass and their mutual protection depend on membership in a loyal, tightly knit group.

Political Boundaries. In recent years, the political boundaries that thread through these vast regions have involved the nomadic herders in some troublesome problems; even though, in some instances, the very existence of such man-defined boundaries was unknown to the herdsmen. In inner Asia, for example, tribes wander back and forth across the frontiers of Siberia, China, Afghanistan, and Iran, without thinking about leaving one "country" and entering another. The movement of Laplanders between Russia and Finland caused disputes between these governments. To which of these two nations do the nomads owe citizenship? Or are they men without a country?

External Relationships

Normally, there is little contact between the people in regions of primitive herding and those in other places. Since the herdsmen have no surplus to export, outsiders have no incentive to ship commodities to them. Moreover, some of the nomads feel a genuine aversion toward the rest of the world. Proud of their ancient traditions and imbued with a fiery tribal spirit, they disdain other cultures. Nevertheless, they have experienced some contacts with the outside world. In some instances the herdsmen moved outward, and in other instances the outsiders penetrated nomadic herding regions.

Outward Movements of Subsistence Herders. Occasionally, during periods of starvation induced by unusually severe droughts, herdsmen have struck fiercely into neighboring areas. From the African Sahara they have raided southward into zones of primitive subsistence farming, and northward into more advanced agricultural regions. As far back as 1000 B.C., farmers along the Mediterranean coast of Asia were being attacked by nomadic tribes from the east. One such assault was described as follows:

> And so it was, when Israel had sown, that the Midianites came up, and the Amalekites came up, and the children of the east, even they came up and encamped against them and destroyed the crops in their fields as far as Gaza. They came up with their animals and their tents . . . and lay along the valley like grasshoppers for multitude, for they and their camels were without number, as the sand by the seaside for multitude. (*Judges* 6:2 and 7:12)

Similar outbursts marked the history of the European frontier. In the 5th century A.D., the Huns (nomads from eastern Asia) swept westward across Europe almost to the Atlantic. In 1242, Mongol nomads poured into the West again, annihilating every army that dared stand against them. And in 1529, the Turks, nomads from southwestern Asia, besieged the walls of Vienna. Often these invaders settled down in the regions they had penetrated, losing their identity in the indigenous population. The Huns, for example, never returned to Asia; they simply "disappeared" in the melting pot of Europe.

But not all out-movements of nomadic herdsmen are belligerent. Take, for example, the following relationship of Laplanders and Eskimo. For ages, the economy of the Eskimo in northwestern Alaska was based on *subsistence* hunting and fishing. Then, in the 1880's, the federal government of the United States arranged for the shipment into Alaska of a small herd of caribou from Lapland (the nomadic herding region of northern Europe). A few Lapps were persuaded to visit Alaska to teach the art of their husbandry to the Eskimo. The successful transplanting of this economic activity transformed the northwestern edge of North America from a primitive gathering area into a region of nomadic herding.

And on the margins of other nomadic herding areas there frequently occurs a process which might be termed "cultural osmosis" whereby some nomads quietly shed their herding habits, settle down at the edge of advanced agricultural areas (to be discussed in later chapters), and adopt agricultural techniques from their more progressive neighbors. Such migration is occurring in western Asia and in northern Africa, especially along the margins of the Nile Valley.

Inward Movements of Outsiders and Their Cultures. External relationships are discernible also in terms of movements of people and ideas from other regions into the herding realm. Since antiquity, trade routes have cut across the realms of nomadic herding from China to Europe, from India to Europe, from Central Africa to Northern Africa. The merchants traveling over these routes were simply passing *through* these regions; they had no interest in going *to* them, since the herdsmen had little to sell and little with which to buy. Countless times the nomads ambushed the traders, whom they regarded as interlopers at best and as competitors for precious water at worst, because the typical trade route was strung out from oasis to oasis across the desert.

Now not only transient traders but also settlers are moving into many of the nomadic herding regions from territories with higher economies. And they bring with them modern scientific methods: irrigation, drought-resistant strains of crops, healthier animals, and improved methods of handling them. In Africa, advanced agriculture is pushing its way south from the Mediterranean into Morocco, Algeria, and Libya. In Central Asia the

In a temporary settlement in Nigeria, a small boy builds a fire under a tree to kill it. In this slash-and-burn economy the land is not completely cleared, as evidenced by the tree stumps throughout the clearing. (*Courtesy Robert Netting.*)

Chinese peasants have been pushing ever northward and westward, staking out farms on the shrinking margins of nomad country. Perhaps one of the most dramatic invasions in recent years has been on the north slope in Alaska where the discovery of oil has brought in literally thousands of "outsiders."

Settling the Nomads. Many nations containing nomad country have decided that the wanderers must be settled. The most vigorous programs are being undertaken by the Soviet Union, China, and Iran. The Iranian government, for example, launched a program in the 1930's to induce Iran's 500 nomadic tribes (2,000,000 tribesmen) to stay put in permanent settlements. At first, these proud, independent people resisted stubbornly—almost violently. But the government helped them dig wells and construct irrigation systems and, in lean years, it augmented their food supply. The nomads' children are being educated in government schools, so the new generation may be willing to concede that permanent occupancy of the land is more desirable than following the flocks. Some Iranians even think that nomadism will vanish from their country within the next one or two generations.[3]

The Future

On maps of the world's economic regions, the areas of nomadic herding will probably shrink as nomads are

[3]Two interesting case studies of this phenomenon are Mohamed Awad's "The Assimilation of Nomads in Egypt," *Geographical Review* (1954), pp. 240–252, and Anthony D. Marshall's "Somalia: A United Nations Experiment," *Focus* (April 1956), pp. 1–6. Both are excellent analyses of the developments, problems, and prospects of improving the economic life of primitive herdsmen. These articles go into such matters as the stratagems employed by the governments of Egypt and the United Nations in Somalia to induce the migrants to settle down, the relative successes of these stratagems, the consequences of outside influence on the nomads, and the resulting impact on the rest of the nation in which they live.

assimilated along the margins. And even within their domain, some herdsmen are beginning to settle down themselves, often assisted or even coerced by national governments. In such places, an economic and social revolution is currently underway.

PRIMITIVE CULTIVATION

From primitive gathering, some peoples have taken a step "upward" on the economic ladder by learning the art of domesticating plants, and their economy has moved into primitive cultivation. This activity encompasses large portions of the earth's surface and brings us for the first time to an economic endeavor that involves large numbers of people.

Location

There are three broad regions of primitive cultivation (termed *rudimental cultivation* by some scholars) portrayed on Figure 3-4. The largest is in Central Africa; it straddles the Equator and abuts on the realm of nomadic herding. On the west, it fronts the Atlantic Ocean almost continuously for nearly 3000 miles. Eastward it reaches the Indian Ocean, though the frontage is less than on the Atlantic coast. A portion of Madagascar lies in this zone.

A second major region appears in the Western Hemisphere, embracing most of the Amazon Basin, all the way from the Atlantic coast to the Andes Mountains and from Bolivia to Venezuela. It leaps the Andes in Ecuador and Colombia to reach the Pacific coast and

runs northward through Central America to southern Mexico. A good part of the West Indies is included.

The third major region lies in southeastern Asia and the adjacent off-shore islands, from Sumatra eastward through Borneo, New Guinea, New Hebrides, and numerous tropical islands of the Pacific. On the mainland of Asia, primitive cultivation tends to be absent along the coast and to be confined to the interior of Burma, Thailand, Cambodia, and adjacent portions of India and China.

Once again, of course, all other economic activities are not necessarily absent from the regions of primitive cultivation, for here and there are pockets of less advanced primitive gathering or of more advanced commercial gathering, mining, and so on. Nevertheless, the *prevailing* endeavor is primitive cultivation.

Characteristics

This is a crop-based economy, the leading crops being corn (maize), millet, rice, manioc (the source of tapioca), yams, and sugar. The diet is heavy in carbohydrates, although some protein is provided by peanuts and beans. Tomatoes, cucumbers, and bananas are common adjuncts. There is some regional variation in the leading grain: maize in the Western Hemisphere, millet in Africa, and rice in the Far East.

For these farmers, fire plays a unique role in the clearing of land. Most of the trees and underbrush they

Figure 3-4

PRIMITIVE SUBSISTENCE FARMING

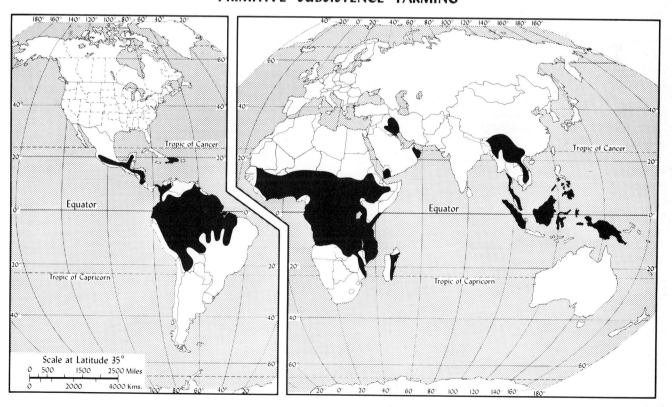

hack out by means of primitive knives and then burn the cuttings, though sometimes they dispense with the cutting and let fire alone do the job of clearing. Accordingly, this primitive technique is often called *slash-and-burn* farming. Methods of preparing the soil for planting are equally primitive. These people simply scratch the surface of the soil with sticks or crude hoes. Plows are almost unknown.

The farmers have scarcely any knowledge of soil science, and they return few nutrients to the soil by means of fertilizers. Erosion is severe, particularly on the slopes, since they usually leave crops untended until harvest time, and the harvest consists of plants that have managed to compete successfully with the weeds. Animals play only a minor role in these economies—all food produced is required to feed the people—but there are a few poultry and swine, which subsist on waste or what they can scavenge. Farm units are small and consist of a few tiny fields, often isolated from one another by patches of forest or brush. The aggregate of all these clearings makes up only a small proportion of the total area—mere droplets of cultivation sprinkled lightly on a sea of wild vegetation.

Three general subtypes of primitive cultivation are distinguishable in terms of permanence of settlement: shifting, semi-shifting, and sedentary. In *shifting* cultivation, which is the most common type, the farmers abandon both their fields and their dwelling sites every three or four years and move on to fresh territories. In the *semi-shifting* type, the farm dwellings remain fixed but the farmers change their fields throughout the environs, actually abandoning the fields, turning them back to wild vegetation after a few years of cropping. So at any given moment most of the area encompassing a settlement is in the wild—either having been cast away or waiting its turn for clearance. The most advanced variety is the *sedentary* type in which the farmers shift neither their fields nor their dwellings but maintain the same dwellings and the same fields year after year. These farmers evidence a rudimentary soil science; they clear the soil, plant their seeds carefully, and husband and harvest the crops with some diligence so they need not move.

But in all three types, agricultural methods are primitive at best. No other form of cultivation has such low yields per acre and man.

Relationships within the Regions

Temperature. Primitive cultivation generally occurs in areas that lack a cold season. Only in very high altitudes and on the poleward margins of the tropics is there threat of frost. On a map of climate (in any atlas) notice that there is a moderately strong correlation between the tropics and primitive cultivation.

Precipitation. These regions are wet. No zone of primitive subsistence farming receives less than 20 inches of rainfall a year, most areas have over 60 inches, and some parts (the Amazon Basin, Indonesia, and a part of Central Africa) are drenched with 80 or more inches. A warm, moist environment explains, in part, why animals play such a small role in this economy. Meat spoils rapidly and must be eaten within a few hours of slaughter. Hence, small animals such as poultry are the most numerous.

Vegetation. The regions of this endeavor tend to have one of the following types of flora—*tropical rainforest, lighter tropical forests, scrub and thorn forests,* or *savannas*—which reflect variation in precipitation from the wetter to the drier areas respectively (as a map of vegetation in any atlas demonstrates). Thus the first problem that confronts a primitive farmer is how to clear land that is either forested or overgrown with savanna. Handicapped by his primitive tools, he often finds it easier to fell a few large trees from a forested acre than to clear the same amount of savanna land of thousands of grass stalks, some of which are ten feet tall and exceedingly coarse. Ages ago, the people in these regions discovered that fire was a useful ally in clearing land of wild vegetation, and for years fire has supplemented hand-cutting operations. But the use of fire boomerangs by damaging the soil, as we shall now see.

Soil. Most forest soils are deficient in plant nutrients. At least two factors are responsible for this condition: slow accumulation of *organic matter* and *leaching.* Organic matter (which consists of the remains of dead plants and animals—such as roots and earthworms) is an important source of nutrients to living plants. But trees do not return much organic matter to the soil. And although savannas tend to have somewhat better soils than rainforests, even they are less fertile than mid-latitude grasslands. Man compounds the problem by his use of fire, for organic matter is combustible and burns like peat. Thus, the fire that clears the surface simultaneously destroys a part of the soil's precious organic matter.

Leaching is the process by which ground water filtering downward robs the soil of nutrients. In order to be assimilated by plant roots, soil nutrients must be soluble—the very attribute that makes them so vulnerable to leaching. Steadily percolating downward, water robs the nutrients from the soil and carries them beneath the reach of the roots of crop plants. Rapid depletion of nutrients in naturally infertile soil is the basic reason why primitive farmers shift their cultivation. In many places they can grow satisfactory crops for only three or four consecutive years. Then they abandon the fields and wild vegetation quickly takes over. If the need for land is great enough, they may clear the plots again for the next cycle of cultivation in a few decades. Usually, though, 40 or 50 years must elapse before the soil has recovered.

Landforms. Topography is related to several different aspects of primitive cultivation. For content of

A large number of workers planting in a field in Nigeria. They have cleared by slash-and-burn methods. Some large trees, while killed, are left standing. (*Courtesy Robert Netting.*)

organic matter the best tropical soils are in the valleys, having been deposited there by surface run-off from adjacent slopes. But lowland farming frequently has two enormous handicaps: poor drainage and disease.

Lowlands in the humid tropics tend to be very wet. Swamps are numerous. Crops are in danger of drowning. Therefore, the farmers often choose hillside plots. But the hills have a severe disadvantage too, since exposing the raw soil of a rainforest slope to the heavy rainfall of the tropics results in erosion.

Lowlands are warmer than highlands, and in the tropics they furnish an ideal breeding ground for insects and other pests that not only are bothersome in themselves but also carry disease. Malaria, for instance, is prevalent throughout tropical lowlands. Sometimes a lowland village becomes so infested with insects and rats that it must be abandoned and burned to the ground.

Man/Land Ratio. Primitive cultivation supports more people than primitive gathering or primitive herding. Even so, the density scarcely exceeds two persons per square mile in South America, Borneo, and New Guinea, and 25 per square mile in Africa. But the ratio does vary considerably within each area, being most obviously correlated with altitude and type of cultivation. Thus, low population density tends to occur in lowlands, high density in highlands: note the contrast, for example, between the vast population void of the Amazon Lowland and the greater settlement of the Andes. In Equatorial Africa ratios exceeding 100 people per square mile coincide with the highlands of Rwanda and Burundi, Uganda, Ethiopia, and western Kenya. That most of South America's zone of primitive cultivation is lowland while most of Africa's is upland helps to explain, partially, why the population of equatorial Africa exceeds that of equatorial America (see back endpaper).

Man/land ratios also vary with type of cultivation. Where methods have been devised for better treatment of the soil and better techniques of cultivation, yields have increased to sustain a higher man/land ratio. The sedentary variety supports higher densities than does the semi-shifting type, which in turn supports more people per square mile than does the shifting kind. (This is not to say that all dense populations in the tropics correlate with sedentary primitive cultivation. As we shall see later, plantations, mines, and other complex economic activities support large numbers of people in the tropics.)

An Old Culture. Long ago primitive cultivators took a single step upward from primitive gathering and have remained at that level ever since. The farming techniques they use today have prevailed for thousands of years. Their living standards are low, and, for all the "time" they have had, most of them have not developed a written language. Again we encounter the puzzle of why these peoples have remained at this level. Why, after graduating from primitive gathering to primitive cultivation, did they not continue to advance up the economic ladder?

Relationships to Other Areas

Primitive cultivators, in contrast to primitive herders, initiate few contacts with peoples of other areas. More numerous are the contacts initiated by representatives of other regions: nomads, traders, plantation operators, immigrants, and political authorities.

Nomads. For centuries, primitive farms on the drier margins of the tropics were subjected to sporadic depredations of hungry nomadic herdsmen, goaded by excessive droughts into adjoining areas where food was being produced by primitive cultivators.

Trade. Although subsistence farmers rarely have a surplus crop of their own cultivation, they can gather small amounts of nuts, gums, wax, spices, ivory, dyes, cinchona (for quinine), and rubber. If the farmers are located in villages that are accessible to the outside world (along navigable rivers), they can bolster their economy by selling these gathered items to traders. Where this occurs, the farmers need not keep shifting around because their economy no longer depends entirely on what is produced by cultivated patches of land. For this reason, the sedentary type of primitive farming frequently occurs along rivers while the *shifting* type occupies the interfluves (land between streams).

Plantations. In certain equatorial areas (to be studied in Chapter 12) promoters from Europe and Anglo-America have developed plantations, with large labor forces of native workers, that specialize in sugar cane, pineapples, rubber, or other plants native to the tropics. When prices are high for a plantation's crop, the demand usually exceeds the supply, and the primitive cultivators in the immediate vicinity often respond by growing a little of the crop. But the quality is inferior to that from plantations and is never in demand during periods of low prices and low demand. Since these primitive farmers adopt some of the superior plantation-type methods of tending crops, primitive cultivation near plantations is often *sedentary*.

Immigration. For several decades there has been a gradually increasing rate of migration from regions of intense population pressure in the mid-latitudes to the sparsely populated tropics. Thousands of Japanese are now in Brazil. There are a million Indians in tropical Africa. Thousands of Europeans have immigrated into Kenya, Ghana, and other present and former European colonies in Africa. But these immigrants were not lured by prospects for primitive cultivation, but by rich opportunities in plantations, commercial livestocking, mining, and trading.

Political Control. These immigrants made capital investments in docks, roads, warehouses, marketing facilities, and agricultural equipment. And since these investments had to be protected, the outsiders took steps to insure political stability. Before long, nations in distant regions, especially Europe, had established control over most of the primitive-cultivation realm.

Spanish, Portuguese, French, Dutch, Italian, German, and British colonies soon covered the tropics from the Americas through Africa and the Far East. The U.S. controlled the Philippines.

This political penetration, following in the wake of the original economic penetration, has had severe repercussions. The markets of the outside world have benefited economically, of course, from the relationship. And the regions of primitive cultivation have derived such benefits as hospitals, schools, and roads. But the indigenous peoples bristle under outside political control, as was illustrated in the trouble the British settlers of Kenya had with the Mau Mau movement among the Kikuyu tribe, who are primitive cultivators.

After World War II, many of the foreign powers began to ease the political reins and to return control to the nationals, but some have been forcibly ejected through revolution. In 1946 the United States granted independence to the Philippines; French Indo-China has been replaced by Vietnam, Cambodia, and Laos. Malaya and Indonesia have been granted independence from Britain and the Netherlands. On the African scene, a remarkable number of nations have become independent, such as Angola, Ghana, Ivory Coast, Guinea, Nigeria, Cameroon, Gabon, Congo, and Zaire.

The realm of primitive cultivation appears destined to shrink in the future, both as the indigenous peoples abandon it for more complex activities and as immigrants bring more advanced techniques into the tropics.

SUGGESTED READINGS

AKINBODE, ADE., "Population Explosion in Africa and Its Implications for Economic Development," *The Journal of Geography*, 1977, pp. 28–36.

CLARKE, JOHN, "Studies of Semi-Nomadism in North Africa," *Economic Geography*, 1959, pp. 95–108.

HARRIS, DAVID R., "The Ecology of Swidden Agriculture in the Upper Orinoco Rain Forest, Venezuela," *Geographical Review*, 1971, pp. 475–495.

PELZER, KARL J., "The Shifting Cultivator," *Pioneer Settlement in the Asiatic Tropics*, New York, 1945, pp. 16–34.

PLATT, ROBERT S., "Six Farms in the Central Andes," *Geographical Review*, 1932, pp. 245–259.

RUDDLE, KENNETH, *The Yukpa Cultivation System: A Study of Shifting Cultivation in Colombia and Venezuela*, Berkeley, 1975, 207 pp.

SEAVOY, RONALD E., "The Shading Cycle in Shifting Cultivation," *Annals of the Association of American Geographers*, 1973, pp. 522–528.

SONNENFELD, JOSEPH, "An Arctic Reindeer Industry: Growth and Decline," *Geographical Review*, 1959, pp. 76–94.

———, "Changes in an Eskimo Hunting Technology, an Introduction to Implement Geography," *Annals of the Association of American Geographers*, 1960, pp. 172–186.

SPENCER, J. E., *Shifting Cultivation in Southeastern Asia*, Berkeley, 1966, 247 pp.

STEWART, NORMAN R., BELOTE, JIM, and BELOTE, LINDA, "Transhumance in the Central Andes," *Annals of the Association of American Geographers*, 1976, pp. 377–397.

WHITTLESEY, DERWENT, "Fixation of Shifting Cultivation," *Economic Geography*, 1937, pp. 139–154.

———, "Shifting Cultivation," *Economic Geography*, 1937, pp. 35–52.

CHAPTER

4

intensive subsistence farming

Thrashing rice by hand in Rajasthan, India. Foreign experts assisted here in establishing irrigation projects and carrying out soil surveys. (*FAO photo by T. Loftas.*)

For decades geographers have used the term *intensive subsistence farming* to describe a general type of agriculture characterized by high output per unit of land and relatively low output per worker. These characteristics and others that will be discussed later in this chapter still apply to most of the Far East's agriculture. But this term, like any general term, has its shortcomings. For example, it is used to cover agriculture in a number of different geographic and culture areas. The degree to which the specific agricultural practices of a particular place fit the specifications of the general model for intensive subsistence agriculture are highly variable. Perhaps the most obvious problem is with the use of the term *subsistence*, since some areas of *intensive subsistence farming* have for centuries produced at least a small surplus, which was used to pay rent on the land or to secure trade goods. Since the late 1940's and early 1950's additional problems in usage have come with the land reform programs in such countries as China, India, and Vietnam and, with the shift toward commercial agriculture, in such places as Japan. Since the Second World War, many of the Far East's traditional systems have undergone massive change in terms of the use of machinery, land tenure practices, the use of fertilizers, and even in the types and varieties of crops planted.

Despite these changes *intensive subsistence agriculture* is still used today to describe those agricultural systems which are clearly more sophisticated than the primitive activities which we discussed in Chapter 3 but which do not have the attributes that we normally ascribe to the commercial systems discussed in Chapters 7 to 13.

In the introduction to Part Two we noted that there are countless shadings between the two extremes of subsistence and commercial activities. With this caution in mind, we will continue to use the term *intensive subsistence farming*, rather than coining our own term.

Of the world's four billion people, perhaps one-third support themselves by intensive subsistence farming. From the standpoint of sheer numbers of people directly involved, this is the most important economic activity on earth.

THE GENERAL PATTERN

Location

The principal region of intensive subsistence farming is the Far East, the bulk of it in China and India; Japan and Korea mark the eastern frontier of the realm. From Manchuria in the north, it stretches southward to blanket all of eastern China. At the widest point, it spreads from the East China Sea to the frontier of Tibet. Further south it thins rapidly to a narrow band that runs along the coast of Vietnam. Westward it covers most of Cambodia and Thailand, much of Burma, alomst all of India, eastern Pakistan, and a good part of western Pakistan. Adjacent island territories that are included in this region are Taiwan, the northern parts of the Philippines, part of Sumatra, and Java. What we have then is a broad zone that covers 40 degrees of latitude and 80 degrees of longitude. It covers about twice as much land as the United States. Notice that this vast expanse of

Figure 4-1

INTENSIVE SUBSISTENCE FARMING

The village of Khoranaq, northeast of Yazd, Iran, has a population of about 350. The terraced fields are used to grow wheat in the winter and vegetables in the summer. (*Courtesy Michael Bonine.*)

intensive subsistence farming is nearly cleft in two by a wedge of primitive subsistence farming that runs 1500 miles from inland Burma through Laos almost to the Vietnam coast.

Outside of the Far East the only intensive subsistence farming of any consequence shows up in the valleys of the Tigris and Euphrates rivers and of the Nile. It is absent from Europe, North America, South America, nearly all of Africa, western Asia, northern Asia, and Australia.

Characteristics

Intensive subsistence farming can be distinguished from other economic activities on several counts: crops grown, cropping methods, farm layout, the role of animals, and the role of fishing. In recent years, changing attitudes and new technology have had their impact in regions of intensive subsistence farming. Nevertheless, the traditional systems discussed in this chapter are still fairly characteristic throughout much of the Far East.

Heavy Emphasis on Crops. Crops are substantially more important than animals in this farming economy. Of the various crops grown, grains are by far the most numerous. Of the grains, rice is the most widespread. Rice predominates in most of Japan, Korea, southern China, the coastal fringes of Vietnam and Burma, eastern India, and a narrow belt along the western coast of India. The deltas of the Mekong, Menam, Irrawaddy, and Ganges rivers are particularly productive rice-growing lands. There are least two reasons for the widespread popularity of rice. First, it produces more food per acre than any other grain except corn. For example, the world average yield per acre is 2038 pounds for rice, 2369 pounds for corn, and 1418 pounds for wheat. Second, because of its tightly fitting husk, the rice kernel keeps well in humid climates.

There are two kinds of rice—wet and dry. The more important by far is the *wet* (or *lowland* or *paddy*) type. It requires tremendous amounts of moisture, which is often provided through the careful irrigation of rice fields (known as *paddies.*). Yields of wet rice are high, sometimes soaring to 3000 pounds per acre or more annually. *Dry* (or *upland*) rice will thrive on less water and can be grown in highland plots that would be difficult to irrigate. But upland rice yields considerably less per acre than does paddy rice.

Other grains predominate in areas unfit for rice culture. Wheat, barley, sorghum, and millet carry the dietary burden in northern China, Hokkaido, western India (except the coast), Pakistan, the Tigris and Euphrates valleys, and the Nile Valley. But rice and other grains are not the only food crops. Most farmers augment their cereal supply with beans, peas, corn, peanuts, yams, sugar cane, melons, and a wide variety of vegetables and fruit. In addition to food crops, considerable cotton is grown, since cotton garments comprise most of the clothing of Asia's millions.

Cropping Methods. Whatever the crop, the yields reflect a tremendous investment of human effort. Draft animals are used in some places, but traditionally farm machines have been virtually unknown. Agricultural implements in fact are often rather crude, for this is another realm of hoe culture. Nevertheless, the use of tractors and other farm machinery has increased considerably in Japan and to a lesser degree in China. In 1970 China had only 300,000 tractors, whereas the United States had 4,619,000 (5,424,000 including garden tractors). Although China's figure is small when compared with figures for the United States or other advanced nations, it is five times greater than her 1959 figure.

Although their tools are often primitive, these farmers display a remarkable understanding of the soil. Ages ago these Oriental farmers had devised ingenious schemes for conserving this precious resource. By terracing rough land, transporting baskets of eroded soil back to its starting place, draining swampy areas, irrigating subhumid land, and fertilizing every patch of ground that might conceivably be coaxed into productivity, these peasants transformed their treatment of the soil into a fine art. This is an endeavor that requires vast expenditures of muscle and sweat, and these are probably the hardest-working farmers on earth. Still, cropping methods differ considerably within this realm, being most intensive in Japan, moderately so in China, and only slightly so in India.

Two unusual methods are *interculture* and *multiple-cropping*. Interculture is the practice whereby two different crops grow together in the same field. Their plantings are timed so that as one crop matures the other is getting started. Multiple cropping is the technique of growing two successive crops on the same land per year; the first is harvested before the second is sown. Sometimes, if climate permits, rice is followed by rice; otherwise rice is grown in the summer and another grain in the winter. Where the environment is unusually favorable, three crops of rice can be harvested annually from one plot of ground.

With so many millions of farmers applying such intensive methods, rice is the world's second leading cereal (see Table 4-1). Although rice is cultivated to some extent in many parts of the earth, the Far East generates some nine-tenths of the total and stands unrivaled as the rice bowl of the world.

Table 4-1

World Production of Leading Grains

Grain	Total Metric Tons	Average Yield in Pounds per Acre
Wheat	339,954,000	1418
Rice	304,413,333	2038
Corn	289,438,667	2369
Barley	147,745,000	1628
Millets, sorghums	92,739,667	761
Oats	54,861,000	1542
Rye	29,195,000	1432

Source: Food and Agricultural Organization of the United Nations, *Production Yearbook.*

Nevertheless, in spite of such intensive cropping methods, the result is not an abundant surplus. The yield *per farmer* is usually low, just enough to meet his family's needs without much of a remainder for sale. Where yields *per acre* are high (as in Japan) the farms are usually small; where somewhat larger farms exist (as in India) the yields *per acre* are usually low. In either case, this intensive farming is frequently a *subsistence* economic activity. As previously noted, this generalization does not hold throughout all of the Far East. Although Japan's farmers do not produce enough to feed that nation's urban masses, farm surpluses are fairly typical.

Similarly, surplus rice from southeastern Asia has long been exported to Japan and other countries with an agricultural deficit. Unfortunately, however, the generalization does hold true for India and China, two countries which have undergone major land reforms since 1950. For example, collectivization of China's agriculture was accomplished by 1960, and since that time there have been many technological advances. Productivity has been increased, but the population has also increased. As a result, agricultural production per capita has not increased substantially, nor has there been a significant increase in the amount of agricultural surplus.

Farm Layout.   Farms are small. In a few places they cover little more than an acre. In the lowlands of Japan farms are often only 3 or 4 acres, China's farms (before collectivization) were somewhat larger, and a few in India are more than 10 acres. In general, however, the individually held rice farms of the Far East are the smallest farms on earth.

Still, although the individual farms are often small, in the aggregate they cover an enormously high percentage of the usable land. In few other regions has the terrain been so completely modified by man's agricultural activities as in the Orient. Indeed, the natural flora was stripped away hundreds of years ago by the unceasing efforts of these vigorous farmers. Yet not all the land in these countries is blanketed by farms. In fact, only 17 per cent of Japan's land is in agriculture, only 30 per cent of China's, and 55 per cent of India's. The point here is that where the environment *is* favorable, man has pressed into cultivation every square inch of land that he could.

Tiny as these farms are, they are (or were) usually chopped up into several smaller plots separated from one another by intervening plots belonging to other farms. Figure 4-2 shows the traditional pattern of land holdings around a Chinese farm village. The land ownership pattern shown in this figure is typical of China before the 1949 revolution and is similar to that in much of the Far East today. Notice in Figure 4-2 that the property of farmer C is made up of 13 plots in 7 different locations, separated from one another by distances of from 1000 to 2000 feet, and that farmer E has 19 plots clustered in 8 separate groups. Such a land pattern adds immeasurably to the already staggering burden of these farmers, for they must trudge many miles each year just to reach their fields. A major reason behind such fragmentation is the inheritance system by which a man's land is subdivided among his children, who marry and acquire other land that may be widely separated from the first parcels.

India became independent of the British in 1947, and the People's Republic of China was established in 1949. In an effort to increase efficiency of farmers and to raise agricultural production, consolidation of small and fragmented holdings was made a top priority issue by both of the new governments. It took China only 10 years to (a) break up large landholdings and distribute this land to the previously landless peasants, (b) to

Figure 4-2 [*After Clarence F. Jones and Gordon Darkenwald* (*from John L. Buck*), Economic Geography, *p. 223, Macmillan, 1954.*]

organize the peasant landholders into collectives, and (c) to group the collectives into communes. A collective might include all the farmers in a fairly large village or, where villages are small, several villages together might make up the collective. A collective is a producing unit but the commune, which is made up of several collectives, is both an economic and administrative unit. Thus, in an extremely short period China's landscape and her institutions underwent considerable change. India has made significant progress in the area of land reform, but her story is much less dramatic than China's.

Role of Animals. Animals have a subordinate role in this economy because less human food can be produced per acre if crops are fed to livestock than if the food is consumed directly by people. Plots of ground that are totally unfit for cropping may be left in pasture, but rarely is arable land devoted to the support of animals. Still, certain domestic animals are maintained. Draft animals, particularly cattle, are fairly common. In hot and humid zones the water buffalo performs most of the heavy work. And in the hillier and cooler places, a few mules or asses are kept to help with the daily round of farming. Fortunately, draft animals can subsist on the by-products of food crops: straw, bran, and bean meal.

Certain other animals (swine, poultry, and goats) play an entirely different role. These are all small creatures that occupy little space and do not compete with crops for use of the land, for they do not require feeding but thrive as scavengers. The goat is an especially avid scavenger although chickens and swine produce a greater amount of human food from the waste and garbage they consume. Indeed, the hog has been dubbed by J. Russell Smith the world's best "animated, productive, and edible grabage can."

The function of these animals is twofold: to provide fertilizer for the soil and to provide what little meat and milk these people consume. Swine produce most of the fertilizer, although the excrement of poultry, goats, and cattle is also carefully collected. Understandably, meat is only a negligible component of the diet of these farmers, but they occasionally vary their fare by goat milk or by meat dishes of poultry, pork, or goat.

In China, Japan, or India nearly every farm has chickens and, in the lowlands, ducks and geese. Farms too small to afford cattle or an ox usually have at least some poultry and one hog. China alone has 220,000,000 hogs, one-third of the world total! (This seems to be a tremendous pork supply, but remember that China has 800,000,000 people.) India and Pakistan have 82,000,000 goats—21 per cent of the world total.

Role of Fishing. Since the land does not provide enough food for its millions of people, and since the crops it does yield are heavy with carbohydrates, many of these peoples resort to fishing both to augment the quantity of food and to increase the protein supply. Two practices are followed: *fish farming* and *fish gathering*.

Fish farming is characteristic in humid places with cool winters but warm summers; the paddies are planted to rice in one season and stocked with carp in the other. Like pigs in a pen, these carp are fed exclusively on garbage; they even rival pigs in their ability to convert waste into human food. Carp also perform the function of fertilizing paddy soil. In addition to these seasonal fish farms, swamps and ponds unfit for cropping are diked off to serve as permanent pens for carp. In inland China carp has for generations been the leading fish.

In the early 1950's the Thailand Ministry of Agriculture, in conjunction with the United States Mutual Security Agency and the United Nation's Food and Agriculture Organization, launched an experiment with *tilapia*, a fish that is native to Africa. The tilapia multiplies with incredible rapidity. In just one year, a single pair will produce progeny numbering 10,000. And it takes only four months for a fingerling to attain a weight of eight ounces, which makes a good meal. Moreover, at that age tilapia begin to reproduce and they continue to hatch 500 young fish every three months. These remarkably productive fish are no trouble to keep and they live well in either brackish water or fresh water, in tanks, ditches, canals, swamps, or rice paddies. They thrive on garbage and whatever small aquatic plants and animals they can find. The Thai government launched a campaign in 1953 to describe the merits of fish to its people. Illustrated pamphlets were distributed showing how to cultivate the fish; specimens were taken on tour; radio talks advertised the venture. King Phumiphot Aduldet stocked the fish in palace pools, and the Minister of Agriculture set up a big tank teeming with tilapia for free distribution to anyone willing to raise them. Tens of thousands of householders now have "pens" of tilapia, which are adding, at almost no cost, valuable protein to the Thai diet.

Fish gathering is practiced elsewhere, along rivers and the seacoast, where people augment their diet by gathering fish from the natural habitat. Some persons, in fact, have abandoned farming and gone into full-time fishing. Along the coasts of China and Japan the population pressure has become so intense that many people have literally been forced off the land and now reside on their boats. When these subsistence fishermen do come in to shore, they tie up their boats in tightly packed masses like cars in a New York City parking lot.

In order to understand why intensive subsistence farming occurs where it does, we must inquire into its geographic relationships. Let us begin with the *internal* ones.

Internal Relationships

Temperature. If this realm straddled the Equator, temperature would be rather uniform throughout it. But it does not straddle the Equator—it runs from 10° north latitude to 50° north latitude. This means that the southern areas of intensive subsistence agriculture are located in the tropics, where temperatures are always high—even in the coldest month the average temperature here is nearly 70°, frosts are unknown in the lowlands, and the growing season is uninterrupted from one end of the year to the other.

But the northern areas of this zone experience appreciably lower temperatures. In parts of Hokkaido, for example, the average temperature of the *warmest* month is only 63°, and during three months of the year the average is below freezing: February averages 22°. Hokkaido's temperatures are rather mild, being ameliorated by the encircling sea. On the mainland of Asia, though, the range is more extreme; Mukden, for example, in Manchuria averages a high of 77° in July

but is exposed to five months of subfreezing temperatures: January's average is only 8° above zero.

Clearly, then, there is little homogeneity of temperature in the realm of intensive subsistence farming. And this pronounced spatial variation in temperature helps explain some of the agricultural characteristics that we have just observed. For instance, anywhere from four to six months are required to plant, cultivate, and harvest a single rice crop, and during this growing period an average temperature of about 70° must prevail. Therefore, rice cannot be grown successfully in the northern parts of this region. The line that separates the territory which is warm enough for rice from that which is too cold for rice runs between Hokkaido and Honshu, bisects Korea, and splits China just north of the Yangtze Valley.

Because of regional variation in temperature, it is possible to distinguish three cropping zones. (1) A warm zone in the tropics permits rice to grow in both summer and winter so that at least two crops of rice can be grown every year on a parcel of land. The first is set out in the spring and harvested in July; after that harvest, the second, which is started beforehand in seedbeds, is transplanted to the main plots and is harvested in November. A few particularly favorable tropical sites can even generate *three* crops of rice every year from each field. (2) In somewhat cooler zones rice grows well only in the summer; however, winters are still mild enough to permit multiple cropping. Fields that grow rice in the summer are subsequently sown with wheat, millet, barley, beans, or some other hardy plant. Multiple cropping in both these zones helps explain why small farms can support entire families in the Far East. (3) The coolest areas prohibit rice even in summer and the hardier crops even in winter. As new varieties of rice and other crops are introduced, the locational patterns of cultivation do change. Nevertheless, the general patterns which we have described are fairly stable.

Moisture Supply. Precipitation varies greatly within the area of intensive subsistence farming. Extremely heavy annual rainfall (over 80 inches) distinguishes southwestern India, the lower Ganges and Brahmaputra valleys, southern Burma, northern Luzon, and a portion of southern China. Yet some parts of this realm are very dry: The extreme northern areas of China receive less than 20 inches of rain, and the Huang Ho Basin and western India less than 40.

These spatial variations in precipitation have great significance for the locational pattern of cropping practices, just as temperature variations do. Three zones can be observed on this basis, too. (1) The wettest zone, which gets over 80 inches, is devoted to *wet* rice. High yields of wet rice are maintained by intensive conservation of water, the farmers keeping their fields inundated for two or three months. Paddies are enclosed by dikes so that during the period of maturation the rice plants can be engulfed with half a foot of water. To prevent stagnation, the water is kept moving slowly. (2) A drier zone, which receives between 50 and 80 inches, contains the lands given over to dry rice. Dry rice does not need to be inundated and can be sown like wheat. But it needs more rainfall than wheat. Since its yields per acre are lower than those of wet rice, it occupies a minority of the land. Indeed, in most countries of the Far East, wet rice occupies at least ten times as much acreage as does dry rice. (3) The driest zone of intensive subsistence farming receives less than 50 inches of annual rain, a figure of significance on two counts. For it is the traditional *bottom* limit for rice culture and the *top* limit for wheat culture. Excessive moisture causes the wheat plant to produce straw instead of grain, and what grain there is shrivels before harvest and molds quickly thereafter. Moreover, in a humid climate the wheat plant is highly vulnerable to *wheat rust* and other fungus diseases. In this dry zone, barley and millet supplement wheat as the predominant grains.

Seasonal Precipitation. In the Far East, regardless of the annual amount of moisture in any one place, the striking fact is that most of it falls in the *summer* months. This is of particular significance for northern India and China for it means that the wettest season *coincides with* the hottest season, a coincidence that favors seed germination and plant growth; conversely, the dry season in northern India and China comes in winter, when the temperatures are too low for good plant growth. Indeed, winters in northern China are too cold for any crops even if moisture were available In Table 4-2 we see an indication of the pronounced seasonal variation of rainfall at selected Far Eastern places. Compare these with the much more uniform rainfall distributions in selected American stations.

The explanation for the dry winters and wet summers of the Far East lies in the *monsoon* wind system. It tends to work this way: In winter the interior of Asia becomes very cold; high air pressures develop over the land, much higher than those over the warmer Pacific Ocean to the east and Indian Ocean to the south. Accordingly, winter winds blow *out* from the land mass. They contain very little moisture since they travel over no expanses of water before they reach the zone of intensive subsistence farming. But in summer the pressures and winds are reversed. Then the interior of Asia heats up, so that a vast area of low pressure develops,

much lower than the pressures over the oceans. Therefore, summer winds blow *in* toward central Asia and are laden with moisture sucked up in their long glide over thousands of miles of ocean.

From year to year, the precipitation is comparatively reliable, with relatively slight variations from year to year. Occasionally, however, the summer monsoon fails to bring the usual heavy rains, and then the results are catastrophic. In some districts famine has devastated a third of the population in a single year.

Landforms. Intensive subsistence farmers prefer lowlands, but where population densities are high the lowlands simply cannot support the human load. Then the farms creep up the hillsides, in some places to as high as 2000 feet above sea level. There are certain identifiable relationships between landforms on the one hand and the types of crops grown and cropping methods employed on the other.

Since wet rice must be inundated during a good part of the growing season, it must be cultivated on *flat land*. Valley bottoms provide the ideal topography for this crop, especially in areas where temperature and rainfall are high. Wet rice predominates even in valleys where the precipitation is too low, so long as irrigation is feasible. A common method is to impound water from the surrounding hills and to lead it down gradually under the influence of gravity to the rice paddies on the valley floor. When even this supply is inadequate, additional water can be pumped up from valley streams to the nearby paddies.

But the amount of flat land in this part of the world is quite limited. In fact, the only extensive areas of flat land are the deltas of the Ganges-Brahmaputra, Irrawaddy, Mekong, Yangtze, and Huang rivers. The only flat plain that does not front on the sea is a small area 500 miles up the Yangtze Valley, though a few other areas, not quite as flat as the deltas, occur inland along several major rivers. Unfortunately, most of the land that is warm enough and wet enough for rice growing is in hill country. So the industrious farmers of those hilly regions have revised the topography by constructing

Table 4-2

Average Inches of Monthly Precipitation

Place	J	F	M	A	M	J	J	A	S	O	N	D	Yearly Total
Calcutta, India	0.4	1.1	1.4	2.0	5.0	11.2	12.1	11.5	9.0	4.3	0.5	0.2	58.8
Rangoon, Burma	0.2	0.2	0.3	1.4	12.1	18.4	21.5	19.7	15.4	7.3	2.8	0.3	99.6
Wuhan, China	2.1	1.1	2.8	4.8	5.0	7.0	8.6	4.6	2.2	3.9	1.1	0.6	43.8
Mukden, Manchuria	0.2	0.3	0.8	1.1	2.2	3.4	6.3	6.1	3.3	1.6	1.0	0.2	26.5
Boston, Mass.	3.7	3.5	4.1	3.8	3.7	3.1	3.5	4.2	3.4	3.7	4.2	3.8	44.6
Chicago, Illinois	2.1	2.1	2.6	2.9	3.6	3.3	3.4	3.0	3.1	2.6	2.4	2.1	33.2
Mobile, Alabama	4.7	5.2	6.4	4.9	4.4	5.4	7.0	7.1	5.3	3.5	3.7	4.9	62.5

terraces—steps of flat paddies that march up and down the hillsides. Where the natural slopes are gentle only low dikes are needed to create broad paddy flats. But steeper slopes require higher dikes. In some places—northern Luzon, for example—the farmers have terraced slopes with nearly a 30 per cent incline (that is, 30 feet of vertical drop with every 100 feet of horizontal distance). There, the hillsides are tiered like bleacher seats and the height of the dikes measures a third of the width of the paddies themselves.

A prodigious amount of labor is required to remodel such natural landforms. First, the farmer must clear the land of all natural vegetation, then construct the dike and level off the paddy. At many points he has to tap streams that flow down the hillsides to lead off water to each tier of paddies. The dikes must be strong enough to withstand the gentle underground seeping of this water. Think of the catastrophe that would result if the higher dikes were to give way during a heavy downpour. The suddenly released mass of water would cascade down the hillside with accelerating momentum, completely demolishing the lower terraces. But the farmer's job is not done when he has completed the construction of

This woman is harvesting rice in the Solo River Basin of Indonesia by hand, cutting each stalk separately. (*FAO Photo by J. Dornbierer.*)

his carefully engineered terraces, for the maintenance of the dikes requires constant attention.

Land that is too rough to terrace is devoted to dry rice if temperature and precipitation are favorable. Otherwise the rough land may be in wheat, millet, vegetables or other crops. Where land is too rough to crop it is left in pasture or woodland.

Soils. The soils of the Far East are moderately well endowed in soluble plant nutrients. They are richer than the leached soils of the tropics, but poorer than the grassland soils of the mid-latitudes. Erosion of hill slopes invariably carries off soluble materials and small particles of soil. Hard as these farmers try, it is impossible for them to prevent erosion completely. The materials picked up by the moving water are carried along to the lowlands, where as the velocity of the water slackens, they are deposited on the valley floor as alluvium.

Rice plants will tolerate a variety of soils, but they prefer about two or three feet of alluvium deposited on a clay subsoil. This combination is propitious because alluvium usually is friable and permits the rootlets to penetrate and spread, while the impervious clay checks the downward movement of water. If the underlying soil were indefinitely pervious, of course, it would be almost impossible to keep the paddies flooded during the growing season. Such soil conditions help to explain the limited role of draft animals in this economy, for only the water buffalo can work belly-deep in the muddy alluvium of a rice paddy under a hot and humid sky.

Yet many parts of the world have an environment comparable to that just sketched out for the Far East, but they are not regions of intensive subsistence farming. We can understand the presence of this economic activity only as we look also at the cultural phenomena with which it is associated. Within the region of intensive subsistence farming the cultural environment is marked by a staggering man/land ratio, by cultural antiquity, by a distinctive understanding of soil, an unusual religious concept, a village pattern of settlement, and limited transportation.

Man/Land Ratios. In no other rural region on earth is the population density as great as here. On the alluvial soils of the lower Ganges Valley, for example, the density ranges between 1,000 and 2,500 per square mile, or from two to four people *per acre*! The pressure of such population is a major reason for the heavy emphasis on rice growing and the intensive cropping of the soil. But population density varies from place to place within the Far East. For India as a whole there is 0.72 acre of arable land per person, for China the figure is 0.35 acre, and for Japan 0.12. The yields of rice per acre correlate inversely with these ratios: 5200 pounds in Japan, 2900 in China, and 1500 in India.

With population so delicately balanced against food production, it is no wonder that famines have been so severe in this region—indeed, among the worst in the world. In India, for instance, the total quantity of food available allows only 2000 calories per person per day. This figure is 800 calories less than is recommended for good health for a 30-year-old male of average size in the United States. In a sense, India is caught up in a perpetual famine. Were the population burden less severe, the lower yields resulting from an unusually dry year, an unusually cool summer, or a season of violent floods would be less catastrophic. But the trouble is that the number of people is so large that even the best harvests cannot feed everybody. Consequently, millions of these people never go to bed with a full stomach—even in good years. And the margin of production is so narrow, the line between life and death so thin, that in poor years millions starve to death.

Thus, for all their tremendous investment of labor, the people of this realm have insufficient food to nourish themselves. With little surplus production of any kind, a subsistence economy is all they can manage. If they had some other economic base from which to operate— mining, for example, or manufacturing, or even a surpuls of forest products or fish—they could barter some of their output in exchange for more food, thereby reducing the pressure on their own land. Precisely such an attempt to broaden the economic base is behind the strategy of all political powers in these regions today, especially in Japan, India and China. Industrialization has already come (principally to Japan, and to a degree to China and India); nevertheless, the latter two still have a tremendous reliance on agriculture as their major economic activity.

The problem would be serious enough if the population figures remained constant. But they do not. The greatest *increments* in the world's population are occurring in the very regions that already bear the heaviest population burden. Since 1940 China's population has increased by an astonishing 300,000,000. And the increase is continuing; China now has an active birth control program, but there is still some question as to exactly *how much* this program is slowing growth. India is now adding 150,000,000 to her population every decade (she too has a birth control or family planning program). Even though the population is rising, the *rate* of increase in India still does not seem particularly high in itself—only 2.6 per cent a year. But with such tremendous numbers involved, even small percentage gains produce a dramatic increase in the demand for food supplies.

Cultural Antiquity. Regions of intensive subsistence farming are among the oldest inhabited areas on earth. This type of agriculture has prevailed here for at least 4000 years, and over the centuries the peoples have developed advanced cultures. They had developed written languages and formal literatures when Europe and the Americas were still in a state of semibarbarism, and philosophers in China and India were searching for the principles of religious and intellectual wisdom before Greece had stepped forth as a major power. It seems paradoxical, then, that such an ancient culture—so advanced in many respects and with such an "early start" on the rest of humanity—has not produced a more "advanced" economy as well. There are now certainly some bright spots. Japan has become one of the world's industrial giants, and China, since midcentury, has made dramatic advances. But China is, by European or Anglo-American standards, still a backward country, and most of the remainder of the Far East is even less well developed. After so long a time, why have farmers throughout much of the Far East failed to devise a "better" system? Is it that they have been too lacking in natural resources to produce metal hoes instead of sticks, metal blades instead of crude wooden plows? Is it that education has been traditionally reserved for the few? Until fairly recently, 80 per cent of the people in India and China were illiterate. In any case, social science has yet to answer completely *why* the cultures of the Far East have often remained at their economic levels.

Soil Science. On one front, at least, these farmers, especially in Japan and China, have made noticeable advancements. Early in history they developed a remarkable understanding of soil science, an awareness of the simple fact that plants rob the soil of its nutrients and that man can help restore those nutrients to the soil. And so they recognized what is now known as *the manure cycle*, in which waste products from plants, animals, and human beings are ultimately returned to the soil.

The waste products are fed back in the form of *green manure* (plant tissues), *animal manure* (urine contains greater amounts of soluble potash, phosphorus, and nitrogen, and is preferred to feces, which contain largely insoluble matter), and *night soil* (human excreta).

> The manure of draft animals is commonly reserved for the rice seed-bed. . . . Japanese farmers have discovered that the presence of fish in flooded rice paddies acts as a fertilizer and increases rice yields as much as 10 to 20 per cent. The use of night soil in China, Japan, and Korea has been so emphasized that the importance of animal manure has been overshadowed. Shen, for instance, estimates that night soil represents only one-fifth of the manure produced in China. Trewartha indicates that night soil comprises only one-third of the manure used in Japan. Throughout China large numbers of swine are kept as scavengers and manure-producers. . . . Farm manure provides only one-fourth of the fertilizer required on Japanese farms, and much of the so-called manure is actually compost, green manure crops, seaweed, ashes, and other farm refuse; fertilizers are in such short supply that even silkworm excrement is used.[1]

The art of fertilizing is more highly developed in Japan than in China, where in turn it is more advanced than in India. This is true for green manure, animal manure, and chemical fertilizers. Japan both produces

[1]Eugene Mather and John Fraser Hart, "The Geography of Manure," *Land Economics* (February 1956), page 35.

and consumes huge amounts of chemical fertilizers—Japan has one of the world's highest rates of chemical fertilizer use in terms of pounds consumed per unit of land. Use levels are also high in Taiwan. In recent years China has become a big producer of chemical fertilizers and she is a major importer. But in terms of consumption per unit of land, China's level is low by world standards.

Theology. Religious concepts have economic significance in explaining the role of animals in specific areas of intensive subsistence farming. In Japan and China, where relatively few people practice religions that forbid the consumption of meat, the meat of scavengers is a welcome addition to the diet, even though the land shortage is too acute to permit livestocking. In India, however, the leading religions forbid the consumption of some or all meat. Approximately 85 per cent of India's people are Hindus. Although adherents of some of the numerous branches of that faith can eat no meat whatsoever, nearly all Hindus are permitted to eat fish and goat; only a fourth of them, however, may

partake of beef, and then only provided it meets certain rituals of slaughter. Moreover, since many Hindus consider animals to be the embodiment of former human souls, they are reluctant to kill animals or even to disturb them when they molest the crops. Hence, this amazing paradox in India: 225,000,000 cattle and millions of hungry people. A tremendous meat supply goes untouched—left to die of old age. India and Pakistan also have millions of Moslems to whom pork is forbidden though goat is permitted. It is not surprising that these two countries have a fifth of the world's goats.

Village Pattern of Settlement. Intensive subsistence farming is associated with a system of *farm villages* whereby the rural millions occupy the land by grouping themselves in agglomerations of residences rather than dispersing in individual farm dwellings over the countryside. Some of these clusters contain only 250 people, but others contain 10,000. These farm villages are *not* primarily commercial centers; they are dormitory settlements from which the land workers commute every morning to their respective fields.

If we could fly over these settled areas, we would be impressed with a multitude of small villages dotting the landscape, surprisingly close to one another. Picture an

Figure 4-3

SETTLEMENT PATTERN ON NORTH CHINA PLAIN

■	Walled City	—— River or Stream	
▪	Town or Village	�咖啡 Levee	
•	Settlement	▨ Rice fields	+ Intersections of Meridians and Parallels

Scale of Miles
0   5   10   15

intensively cultivated plain on which the average farm consists of two acres. Assume that the average family has five members, and that everyone lives in villages of no more than 1000 inhabitants. How far apart would the villages be? Let's work it out this way: With an average of two acres per farm, there would be 320 farms on *one* square mile. If each farm supported five people, one square mile would support 1600 people! And if all these people were clustered in villages of 1000 each, these settlements would be sprinkled over the plain at intervals of *less than* one linear mile!

This pattern of settlement is a cultural phenomenon generally unknown today in the United States. Figure 4-3 shows a portion of the North China Plain, 45 miles by 60 miles, as it appeared before collectivization of agriculture. In this area (which is similar to other areas in the Far East today) there were nearly 400 farm villages and settlements. Contrast this with the pattern prevailing in agricultural regions of the United States, where the individual farmstead (that is, the buildings occupied by one farmer and his immediate family) is the distinctive form of land occupancy, where, in fact, farm villages are virtually nonexistent.

The Oriental farm-village system is fostered by two conditions—one economic and one sociological. The *economic factor* is the ever-present threat of hunger which helps weld each family into a cohesive production unit. In a subsistence economy where each family's daily ration must be wrested directly from the land the family works, mutual dependence among family members is bound to develop in order to get all the work accomplished.

The *sociological factor* is family loyalty. The philosophy of life of these peoples puts strong emphasis on reverence for deceased family members and on responsibility for the living. When children marry, the bride becomes a member of the groom's family and often moves into that family's abode. As son after son marries, the population of a household expands to the point where more houses are needed. Such a process, in time, transforms what was originally a one-family residence into a one-family village.

One of the most startling sociological revolutions in all human history has been accomplished by the Chinese Communists. Their aim is to destroy the family loyalty of the peasants, and replace it with loyalty to the state. They have retained the village pattern, but each village is no longer a family of workers who choose to abide there but a collection of laborers who have been assigned to it.

Transportation. Intensive subsistence farming is generally associated with poorly developed transportation. This realm, for all its millions of people, has comparatively few railroads and surfaced roads. Footpaths and dirt roads predominate. The rivers serve as important thoroughfares, and the open sea is a "main street" over which much of the traffic moves. It may seem surprising that a region which supports such a mass of humanity should have so few transportation facilities. We might expect some sort of positive correlation between population density and transportation media. But this correlation does not always exist, as we shall see in subsequent chapters on transportation. In the region that we are exploring here, the basic reason for the lack of a highly developed system of transportation is that the economy is still in the subsistence stage. Little surplus for outbound shipments means little buying power for inbound purchases. Furthermore, since these farmers have little money with which to pay for commercial transportation, they travel by foot, by animal, or by boat. Even so, they take trips only rarely, for they can spare little time from their constant round of farming activities. Millions of them are born, grow up, marry, raise a family, and die without ever leaving their villages and fields. In short, since there is very little movement of freight, and even less movement of passengers, there has been no pressing need to develop elaborate transportation systems.

There are several notable exceptions to this generalization. The southeastern Asiatic peninsula (consisting of Burma, Thailand, Cambodia, and Laos) *does* generate a surplus of rice. Japan, India, and to some extent even China have deficiencies of rice. (One explanation for the contrast between these rice-surplus and rice-deficient countries lies in the following ratios of number of arable acres per person: Japan 0.12, China 0.35, India 0.72, Burma 1.53, Thailand 0.80, and Cambodia 0.57. Transportation has been set up to link these rice-surplus and rice-deficit areas.

A second exception is Japan, and to a lesser extent India, where railway transportation is highly developed. Japan is laced with a network of trackage over which electric trains run at high speeds and short intervals with probably the world's best record for punctuality. The explanation for the transport development is not to be found in the type of agricultural development in the rural countryside but in the high development of manufacturing and commerce in Japan's cities. Both freight and passenger traffic is heavy, but passenger traffic seems to dominate (see Chapter 24). India has a substantial railroad system that is part of their legacy from the British. China, on the other hand, is a large country with a relatively sparse railway network. Nevertheless, what railroads there are, carry huge volumes of freight.

External Relationships

We can consider the relationships between the region of intensive subsistence farming and other geographic areas under three headings: international trade, political maneuvering, and migrations.

International Trade. The international trade of the Far East is, for the most part, small. China, with a fifth of the world's people, exports commodities worth less than those exported by Norway, a nation with only 4,000,000 people. India contributes little more than *half* as much export traffic as Austria. Here is one of the most significant aspects of the world's economic geography in the final quarter of the twentieth century: The world's two most populous countries generate only a small volume of international trade, in part, at least, because they are essentially subsistence-farming regions.

Japan is an exception in this region, however, for she carries on a large amount of trade, the largest in Asia. For countless generations the Japanese subsisted on a rice-based economy similar to that of other parts of Asia. Then, a century ago, they launched into new activities that eventually brought them into the mainstream of world trade. Although they had no surplus of food to sell, they did produce a surplus of tea and silk. And with these commodities as a starter, they purchased modern machinery abroad and began to manufacture textiles, mainly from raw cotton imported from other areas. In one century they have advanced to the stage at which their subsistence agricultural economy has been overlaid by an industrial and commercial economy. Whereas 66 per cent of China's population is active in agriculture and 68 per cent of India's, Japan's proportion is down to 21 per cent. (Compare these figures with highly industrialized western nations: West Germany 9 per cent; United States 4 per cent; United Kingdom 3 per cent.) Present governments in China and India are endeavoring to duplicate Japan's achievement.

Political Maneuvering. At the moment, the most significant relationship between this realm and the rest of the world lies, perhaps, in the area of political ideologies. Since almost half of the world's inhabitants live here, many of the more advanced countries of the world are vitally concerned with the attitudes and ideas (political, religious, and economic) that these people will embrace as they move away from subsistence farming. We cannot escape the conclusion that the choices these people make will have a profound effect on every other part of the world. Consequently, the Western powers and the Soviet Union have engaged in a bitter struggle in their attempts to win over the minds of these Far Eastern peoples. No scholar of international relations and political ideologies can ignore the dependence of most of the people of China and India and many other Far Eastern countries on intensive subsistence farming or the hunger that dogs them year after year in spite of their best efforts.

Population Migrations. One of the five major migrations of human beings in world history[2] has flowed

[2]The other four major migrations in world history were (1) the 15,000,000 Negroes who were hauled from Africa to slave markets in the Americas; (2) a smaller number of Europeans who traveled southeastward to Africa, Australia and New Zealand; (3) approximately 18,000,000 Europeans who went to Latin America; and (4) 25,000,000 Europeans who migrated to the United States and Canada.

out from China and India. Millions of Chinese and Indians have migrated from these hunger-ridden lands; they and their progeny now reside in many other parts of the world. Most of the migrants have headed toward the less densely settled countries of southeast Asia. Several hundred thousand others moved to Africa's eastern and southern territories and to the Americas.

INDIA: A CASE STUDY

We shall conclude this chapter with a closer look at India, a nation whose problems are intimately related to intensive subsistence farming, a country that is typical of the economic realm we have been discussing.

India's population is approaching 600,000,000—greater than the population of the United States and the Soviet Union combined. Her population density is six times the world average. With an annual birth rate of 43 per 1,000 against a death rate of 17 per 1,000, her population is increasing at a rate of 2.6 per cent a year. Better medical facilities and the use of modern drugs have reduced the threat of epidemics and have effectively lowered the death rate. The population, meanwhile, is rising. India now is adding 15,000,000 a year to her population total. Were this an industrial nation, such an increment might be absorbed by manufacturing, commerce, and other urban economic activities. But India is still an agrarian country, and this astonishing population increase has simply brought additional people onto the arable land which already was overcrowded. Although 68 per cent of India's people are farmers, only one-half of her land is suited for even marginal farming, and most of this would support less than 50 persons per square mile. Today, as we have seen, there is only 0.7 acre of cultivated land per person; 65 years ago there were 1.5 such acres. These two ratios provide dramatic evidence of the problem that is now facing this nation. In 1901 the area that is now known as India had a population of 235,000,000 of whom over three-fifths (146,000,000) were farmers. The proportion has only increased to about two-thirds. But today, India has almost 600,000,000 people, over 380,000,000 of whom are living directly off the land! In short, here is a country where the pressure on the land, intense enough to begin with, has steadily mounted as the number of farmers has increased, not only absolutely (by an astounding 235,000,000) but also proportionately to the national total.

Since this dramatic rise in population has not been accompanied by any substantial increase in the total amount of cultivated land, the food shortage has grown more acute every year even though crop yields have increased substantially. The quantity of food produced per capita each year slumped from 600 pounds in 1901 to 450 pounds in 1951. Since 1951, thanks to national planning efforts and the *Green Revolution*, productivity has actually been increasing. Still, the threat of famine hovers constantly over large portions of the land, and most Indians struggle along on starvation rations. As we saw, the average diet provides only 2,000 calories per day per person—a figure which is below the *minimum* health requirement for much of India's population. And this is substandard in quality as well as in quantity, for as we have seen, there is a dearth of meat and protein.

Although food is in short supply in much of Asia, the fact that there has been progress in increasing supplies should not be overlooked. Professor A. K. Chakravarti[3] summarizes recent innovations in Indian agriculture as follows:

Recent Innovations

Before independence was achieved in 1947, agriculture was decaying under a predominantly feudal system. Small farmers had very little opportunity and incentive to raise production. Crop failures and famines were frequent. World War II and the partition of the nation further compounded the problem of food supply. Immediately after independence, therefore, the Government launched a program to develop agriculture and particularly to raise the foodgrain production. A series of Five Year Plans were initiated beginning in 1950–51. By the end of 1972, three Five Year Plans and two Annual Plans had been completed, and the fourth Five Year Plan is in progress.

During the planned period the nation has achieved significant progress despite the tremendous increase in population, a large inflow of refugees, and costly border conflicts with the People's Republic of China and Pakistan. Since 1950–51, the agricultural growth rate has increased by 3 per cent per year from an almost stagnant condition. Between 1951 and 1970, as many as 500 major- and medium-sized irrigation projects were launched and 345 have been completed. During the same period the total irrigated area jumped from 51 million acres to 94 million acres. Various soil conservation and land reclamation programs have helped to increase the net cultivated area from 297 million acres in 1950–51 to 407 million acres by 1970, and the double-cropped or triple-cropped area from 32 million acres to 58 million acres.

Efforts have been made to implement the new land-reform measures. The old landlord system (zamindari) has been abolished and the land is being distributed to the cultivators. Because of the scarcity of land, ceilings on landholdings have been fixed. Also Multipurpose Community Development Programs have been launched; they are self-help programs planned and carried out by the villagers themselves, with technical guidance and financial assistance from the Government. Eventually the whole of rural India will be part of a block, each of which will generally comprise 100 villages and a population of 60,000 to 70,000. Agriculture receives the highest priority but the program also includes the improvement of communications, health, sanitation, housing, education, and welfare, and the development of cottage industries.

The mechanization of farming has increased, but only slightly because only rich landowners can afford the equipment needed, and in any case, there is a large supply of unemployed and underemployed farm laborers, most farm holdings are small and scattered and hence unsuited to mechanical operations, repair facilities are scarce, and maintenance and fuel are expensive. Most of the farm machines are imported, but local production is rising rapidly. For example, tractor production

rose from 880 in 1961–62 to about 30,000 in 1970. Further, the Agro-Industries Corporations, which have been set up in all but three states (Himachal Pradesh, Meghalaya, and Nagaland), are enabling more and more farmers to acquire mechanized agricultural implements on a hire or hire-purchase basis.

Great progress has also been made in such areas as the use of chemical fertilizers and pesticides and the extension of electrical power to farming communities. The consumption of chemical fertilizers in India increased from 64,000 tons in 1950 to 2.4 million tons in 1971. The manufacture and use of chemicals used as pesticides is being promoted and the area benefited by plant-protection measures has increased from 41 million acres in 1955–56 to 130 million acres in 1970–71. In the past electricity was used mainly in the cities and for industries. Now it is spreading to rural areas and about one out of six villages has electricity; more than a million wells have been fitted with power-driven pump sets.

As a result of these efforts, in the mid-1960's India appeared to have solved its food problem. But then the monsoon rains failed over large areas and the 1966–67 crop production declined seriously. Famine conditions were recorded over extensive areas and millions of people were close to starvation. The drop in foodgrain production dramatically illustrated the scale of achievements and the desperate need for more extensive and intensive measures to reach and help farmers in every part of the country.

There are several reasons for India's slow progress in agricultural development. Increases in production are offset by large increases in the population: about 13 million persons are added every year to an already vast population of about 547 million people. The completion of a large number of expensive irrigation projects has certainly raised foodgrain production, but they have benefited only the farmers in the area concerned, and mainly the rich. Large areas and a large proportion of the rural population still depend on the mercy of erratic monsoons. Small farmers may get adequate food when the rains are adequate; they may starve when the rains fail and crops fail. There may be a surplus of foodgrains produced in one part of the country, but many subsistence farmers in a drought area may not have savings or cash to purchase the needed food. The fundamental requirement is to raise the purchasing power of the small farmers and stabilize agricultural production in every part of the country—in fact, every farm—if periodic starvation or famines are to be avoided.

The Green Revolution

In recent years, agriculture in India has experienced a most important technological breakthrough with the introduction of new high-yielding varieties of seeds. These include varieties of hybrid rice, Mexican wheat, maize, jowar, and bajra. The new varieties are capable of giving two to four times the yield of indigenous seeds. The benefits of planting the fields with new seeds have been demonstrated and those farmers who can afford to are rapidly changing over to the high-yielding programs. By the end of the 1969–70 cropping season, the land planted with high-yielding varieties of wheat, rice, maize, jower, and bajra amounted to 28.5 million acres, or about 7 per cent of the total cultivated area. The new varieties

[3]A. K. Chakravarti, "India's Agriculture," *Focus*, American Geographical Society, January, 1973, pp. 5–8.

require adequate use of fertilizers, pesticides, and irrigation, however. Therefore, only those farmers can participate who have enough money. In other words, many small farmers who cannot afford canal-or tube-well irrigation or fertilizers and pesticides are not in a position to participate in this new program. Thus they are left far behind and the gap between the rich and small farmers will widen further. The Government recognizes this problem, however, and has launched schemes such as Small Farmers' Development Agencies. These agencies are to be set up in selected districts throughout the nation during the fourth Five Year Plan. They will identify the problems of small farmers and ensure the availability of services, inputs, and low-interest loans.

Only a few years ago farming in India was considered a menial job and practiced mostly by uneducated and poor villagers under a rich *zamindar* (landlord). Now the high foodgrain prices, tax-free agricultural income,

price-support policies, low-interest agricultural loans, and the new high-yielding varieties of seeds have attracted many educated and wealthy people into farming. In a recent field-study trip to India, the author was greatly impressed to observe the rapid strides that agriculture has made during the last ten years. Through samplings and case studies in ten states, it was found that most villagers are better dressed, and have better housing, health, and educational facilities. A significant point noticed was that most farmers in India are aware of the advantages of the new techniques of farming and are eager to adopt them. It appears that the awareness and willingness might contribute a great deal toward the success of the Green Revolution and the elimination of famines in India.

This has been a long chapter. But in it we have been exploring economic activity that supports *almost half of the people of the world.* For most of the world's people are still farmers, and most of those farmers are still operating at or near the intensive subsistence level.

SUGGESTED READINGS

BHALLA, G. S., *Changing Agrarian Structure in India*, Meerut, Delhi, 1974, 127 pp.

CHAKRAVARTI, A. K., "Foodgrain Sufficiency Patterns in India," *Geographical Review*, 1970, pp. 208–228.

———, "Green Revolution in India," *Annals of the Association of American Geographers*, 1973, pp. 319–330.

———, "The Impact of the High-Yielding Varieties Program on Foodgrain Production in India," *The Canadian Geographer*, 1976, pp. 199–223.

———, "India's Land Reform," *Focus*, May, 1973, pp. 1–8.

———, "Population Growth Types in India, 1961–71," *The Journal of Geography*, 1976, pp. 343–350.

DUTT, ASHOK, and AHMED, DR. NAWAJESH, "Population Pressures in Bangladesh," *Focus*, November-December, 1974, pp. 1–10.

FARMER, B. H., *Agricultural Colonization in India Since Independence*, London, 1974, 372 pp.

KARABENICK, EDWARD, "Morocco, A

Microcosm of Evolving Agriculture in the Arab World," *The Journal of Geography*, 1976, pp. 531–540.

KEEN, E. A., "Maps, Models, and East Asian Intensive Subsistence Agriculture," *The Journal of Geography*, January, 1973, pp. 31–39.

LENTNEK, BARRY, "Economic Transition from Traditional to Commercial Agriculture: The Case of El Llano Mexico," *Annals of the Association of American Geographers*, 1969, pp. 65–84.

MA, LAWRENCE, J. C., "China's Agriculture: Institutional and Technological Changes," *Focus*, May-June, 1975, pp. 1–11.

MACNAB, J. W., "Cultivation and Field Form on Three Japanese Islands," *Geographical Review*, 1970, pp. 176–191.

NATH, V., "The Growth of Indian Agriculture: A Regional Analysis," *Geographical Review*, 1969, pp. 348–372.

PROSTERMAN, ROY L., "Land Reform in Vietnam," *Focus*, January, 1972, pp. 1–8.

RUTHERFORD, JOHN, "Double Cropping of Wet Padi in Penang, Malaya," *Geographical Review*, 1966, pp. 239–255.

SEAVOY, RONALD E., "The Transition to Continuous Rice Cultivation in Kalimantan," *Annals of the Association of American Geographers*, 1973, pp. 218–225.

SIDDIQI, AKHTAR HUSAIN, "Cropping Patterns in West Pakistan," *The Journal of Geography*, 1972, pp. 96–108.

SORKIN, ALAN L., "In Punjab: The Green Revolution," *Growth and Change*, July, 1971, pp. 36–41.

SPENCER, J. E., and STEWART, NORMAN R., "The Nature of Agriculture Systems," *Annals of the Association of American Geographers*, 1973, pp. 529–544.

TAYLOR, CARL E., and TAYLOR, DANIEL C., "Population Planning in India and Nepal," *Growth and Change*, April, 1976, pp. 9–13.

TIRTHA, RANJIT, "Population Problems in India: A Battle With Hydra," *Focus*, May, 1974, pp. 1–8.

THREE

COMMERCIAL GATHERING OF ANIMALS AND PLANTS

There are several distinguishing characteristics by which we can recognize a region of commercial economic activity: surpluses, specialization, transportation and trade, and services.

Where commercial economy prevails each individual produces a *surplus* of something above the needs of himself and of his dependents. In a subsistence economy, where each family performs the roles of farmer, fisherman, hunter, miner, and manufacturer, there is likely to be no surplus—or a very small one at best. But when a family's breadwinner concentrates on one of these roles and becomes a full-time farmer or fisherman or miner or manufacturer, the usual result is an immediate surplus—more of some commodity than the family can consume.

A region of commercial economy is also characterized by a division of labor whereby everyone *specializes* in turning out goods for which he is best suited. As the economy of a region tends more and more toward commercialism, producers intensify their specialization and produce larger quantities of fewer items. Thus, there is specialization in *agriculture* when farmers stop trying to grow a little bit each of several crops in favor of concentrating on the most salable items, becoming wheat farmers, vegetable farmers, fruit growers, and dairymen. Frequently there is comparable specialization in the other forms of primary production: *fishing, forestry*, and *mining*. Specialization appears also in secondary production, or *manufacturing*, as some manufacturers narrow their lines: Tool makers, say, concentrate on hand tools or on power tools, or on metal-working machines. The result is greatly increased surpluses.

But the existence of a surplus in a region usually means that there is a dificiency in that region of something else, because energies are being directed toward the surplus commodities. The inevitable result is an exchange of commodities: The surpluses go out and the goods that are in short supply come in. This exchange requires and gives rise to *transportation and trade*.

With a still further intensification of commercialism, an entirely new type of production arises—commercial *services*. Now we find specialists who concentrate not on producing or handling goods but on meeting personal needs. Physicians, teachers, entertainers, clergymen, government officials, stenographers, lawyers, repairmen, household help: All exemplify the service type.

In light of the foregoing ideas, we can make the following generalizations about the stages through which any region's economy will progress. As yet, we have insufficient evidence to prove these generalizations—they are still only hypotheses —but they provide matter for stimulating speculation.

1. The lower the level of commercial development in a region, the higher the proportion of its people who are engaged in *agriculture, fishing*, and *forestry*.
2. As the degree of commercialism in a region begins to increase, the proportion of people engaged in those three activities tends to shrink, the proportion engaged in *trade and transportation* to rise.
3. As a region continues to advance up the ladder of commercialism, it reaches a third stage, at which *manufacturing* is the most rapidly expanding endeavor. Indeed, manufacturing may eventually claim more workers than any other activity.
4. With further commercial development, the most rapid rate of growth obtains in *services*, which ultimately take over as the leading endeavor in the region's economy.

As you read through the following chapters, and as you become more alert to the economic life of the world, you will find considerable evidence in support of these hypotheses.

From now on, our attention will be focused on regions where the economy is geared to commercial endeavors. First, we shall turn to the harvesting of biotic and mineral resources: In Part Three we shall deal with commercial gathering of plants and animals, in Part Four with commercial agriculture, and in Part Five with mining. Then, Part Six is devoted to activities in which the form of products is altered (manufacturing), Part Seven to activities in which the location and ownership of economic items are changed (transportation and trade), and Part Eight to *services*. The accompanying diagram on page 51 suggests the framework in which we shall be considering these topics.

Gathering, in our usage, refers to the harvesting of natural, uncultivated resources whether for subsistence or commercial objectives. From wild plants, from wild animals, or from the earth's crust, man extracts the commodities he needs. Nature produces the entire supply; man's only role is to collect it.

Commercial gathering is the term used if the primary objective of collecting is sale. In certain regions the product is animal life, as we shall see in Chapter 5, in others, it is plant life, as we shall see in Chapter 6.

MAJOR CATEGORIES OF ECONOMIC ACTIVITIES

commercial gathering of wild animals

A bed trawling net is being emptied on the deck of a German fishing vessel. (*Courtesy German Information Center.*)

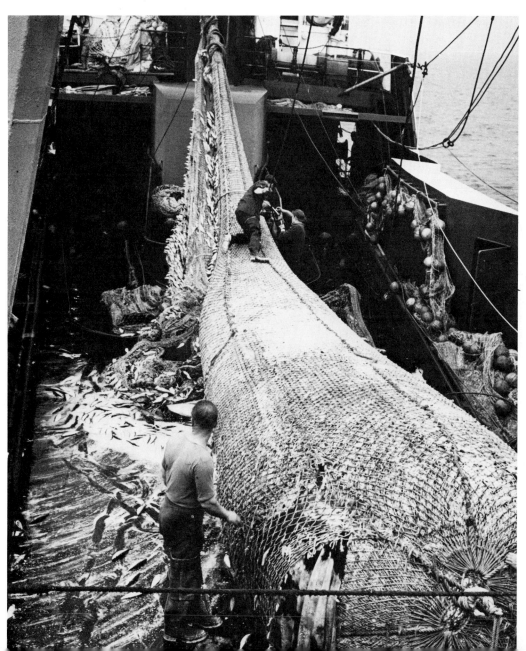

Men gather substantial surpluses of animal products from both land and water by hunting and fishing. The latter is by far the more important, so the bulk of this chapter will be devoted to it.

COMMERCIAL HUNTING

Commercial hunting is rapidly fading away, generally giving way to ranching and animal farming. A good illustration of this change is what happened in the Great Plains of North America over the last few centuries. Until the arrival of white men, the Indians carried on a subsistence economy based on the hunting of buffalo, which supplied them with meat, skins, and bones for tools. Then, with the white man's demand for buffalo robes and the introduction of firearms, hunters went swarming over the Plains, ruthlessly slaughtering the great herds, and subsistence hunting gave way to commercial hunting. Today only a few buffalo are left—in reservations, parks, and zoos. The Great Plains still support millions of animals—but now they are sheep, cattle, and horses raised on commercial ranches and farms.

The smaller animals of North America, such as the fox, and raccoon, were at first hunted on the subsistence level. This activity too has been replaced by commercial hunting. Even so, comparatively few men earn their living by commercial gathering of these animals.

Historically, commercial hunting played an important role in launching the economic development of many regions, for instance, the interior of North America. Two centuries before the signing of the Declaration of Independence, French, British, and Spanish fur trappers were working through the St. Lawrence Valley, the Mississippi Valley, and the Great Lakes area. Because furs were extremely valuable and relatively small in bulk, they could be profitably transported even from sparsely settled hunting grounds far from populous centers. By establishing isolated fur-trading posts, these trappers and hunters took the first step toward developing a commercial economy. Many such posts later became sizeable cities (for example, Detroit and Green Bay). Even today, fur-trading posts persist in northern Canada and Alaska, where trapping remains as the sole economic base of many small communities. Trapping lines radiate from these communities much as fishing fleets radiate from coastal villages. Elsewhere in Anglo-America, the only notable remaining hunting region is the lower Mississippi Valley, where muskrat harvests bring in an appreciable amount of money to trappers.

The progress of commercial economy has been similar in the far reaches of the Soviet Union, where fur trappers have led the way for settlers from the Urals to the Pacific. Even today, fur-trading posts are scattered throughout eastern Siberia, northern Manchuria, and Mongolia; the U.S.S.R. is now the world's leading source of wild fur.

Commercial hunting probably will remain a prominent endeavor in many areas unsuitable for agriculture. But as soon as land is cleared of trees for farms, or as soon as grasslands are occupied by ranches, commercial hunting quickly fades in importance.

COMMERCIAL FISHING

Location

Now that we have swung over to commercial economies, we have access to more complete data than that available for subsistence economies. So we can now construct meaningful maps: Figure 5-1, for instance, shows which countries front on waters that abound in large-scale fish activity. (For convenience we shall apply the term "fishing" to the harvest of all water creatures, whether fish, mollusks, or mammals.) And we can compile meaningful tables. Table 5-1 shows which countries lead in fishing activity. Japan, the U.S.S.R., and China are conspicuously in the forefront, ranking far ahead of Norway and the United States. Notice that many of the leading nations are situated in the middle latitudes of the Northern Hemisphere. We shall see why in the following paragraphs.

Table 5-1

Fish Catches by Leading Nations, in Thousand Metric Tons

Country	Amount	Percent of World Total
WORLD	65,700	100%
Japan	10,701	16%
U.S.S.R.	8,618	13%
China	7,574	12%
Norway	2,974	5%
United States	2,669	4%
Peru	2,299	3%
India	1,958	3%
Thailand	1,692	3%
South Korea	1,654	3%
Spain	1,570	2%
Denmark	1,464	2%
South Africa	1,331	2%
Indonesia	1,300	2%
Philippines	1,248	2%
Canada	1,151	2%
United Kingdom	1,144	2%

Source: United Nations, Food and Agricultural Organization, *Yearbook of Fishery Statistics*, (1974).

Fishermen from these nations range near and far in search of fish. Eighty-five per cent of their catch comes from the ocean, 15 per cent from rivers and inland seas.

Ocean Fishing. Ocean fishing is most prominent in four regions. (1) The foremost area is in the northwestern Pacific, extending from Kamchatka to southern China, enveloping Japan, and following the China coast. (2) Also important is the northeastern Atlantic Ocean

COMMERCIAL FISHING

Figure 5-1

and adjacent waters of the Arctic Ocean. An arm reaches northward around Norway to the Barents Sea and the shores of the Soviet Union. Southward, it envelops the British Isles and touches Spain. Westward it encircles Iceland. (3) Considerably less important is a fishing zone in the northwestern Atlantic running from the west coast of Greenland, down along the coast of Nova Scotia and the United States, to about Virginia. (4) Another region, in the west central Pacific, runs from southern China to Australia, then from Sumatra to the middle of the Pacific. These four areas account for two-thirds of the fish harvested from the world's oceans. The northwestern Pacific alone yields 29 per cent of the world total, and the northeastern Atlantic fishery yields another 20 per cent.

For the United States, the principal fishing areas and the leading states are given in Table 5-2. Our leading fish, by weight, is menhaden—responsible for 40 per cent of all fishing tonnage. But by value, shrimp, tuna, and salmon are the principal products (Table 5-3).

Inland Fishing. Commercial fishing is also carried on in inland waters throughout the world, particularly in the Great Lakes and Mississippi River, and in the inland seas of southeastern Europe (especially the Black and the Caspian) and their tributary rivers (the Danube, Don, Dnieper, Dniester and Volga).

Characteristics of the Fishing Industry

Although a few million people make their living at it, fishing does not rank high in world economy, though it

Table 5-2

Unites States Fisheries

Place	Value of Catch in Millions of Dollars	Quantity of Catch in Millions of Pounds
United States Total	907	4,732
Leading Areas, 1973		
New England States	118	524
Middle Atlantic States	42	256
Chesapeake Bay States	60	698
South Atlantic States	57	241
Gulf States	268	1,547
Pacific Coast States	340	1,330
Great Lakes States	9	69
Mississippi River States	8	54
Hawaii	5	13
Leading States, 1973		
Alaska	162	456
California	103	669
Louisiana	98	1,036
Texas	91	98
Florida	64	174
Massachusetts	57	269
Washington	47	117
Maine	43	143
Virginia	39	631
Oregon	28	88

Source: U.S. National Oceanic and Atmospheric Administration, *Fishery Statistics of the United States* (1975).

Table 5-3

Leading Species of Fish in the United States

Species	Value, 1973, Millions of Dollars	Quantity, 1973, Millions of Pounds
Shrimp	219	372
Pacific salmon	125	213
Tuna	90	342
Crabs	88	292
Menhaden	73	1,890
Lobsters	42	29
Clams	35	106
Oysters	35	49
Flounder	31	163
Pacific halibut	13	24
Atlantic cod	9	50
Sea herring	5	100

Source: U.S. National Oceanic and Atmospheric Administration, *Fishery Statistics of the United States* and *Fisheries of the United States* (1975).

Tuna boat stationed in San Diego, California. This modern fishing vessel is equipped with both an observation tower and radar for locating the schools of tuna. The small craft on the rear deck drags the net away from the boat and then encircles the fish. The catch is then hauled on board and stored in large holds. (*Courtesy Clair A. Shenk.*)

contributes a good deal to the economy in a few countries. Japan and the U.S.S.R. are the largest fishing nations—together they account for almost one-third of the tonnage which is harvested annually. But it is the smaller countries such as Iceland that are most dependent upon fishing as a source of national income. For example, fish accounts for 65 per cent of the value of all exports from Iceland and 10 per cent of Panama's exports. Nor is the *quantity* of fish caught so very large. The world's total of 66,000,000 tons is about the same as the tonnage of milk produced on North America's farms, and by *value*, the world's imports and exports of fish are about equal to the value of whole milk sold in the United States. Yet in Iceland and parts of Japan, China, and Indonesia, fish is a major component in the diet.

Since fish migrate through their extensive feeding areas and, in the course of a year, may traverse thousands of miles, commercial fishing is mainly a seasonal endeavor. Where market prices are high enough, fishermen may find it profitable to pursue their prey over these vast distances. Otherwise, though, they wait until the schools return to waters closer to home. Depending on local condition and circumstance, some crews put out from port each morning and return in the evening of the same day, while others spend weeks or months at sea.

Equipment. Most commercial fishing these days is a corporate affair; the lone commercial fisherman is rare. Fishing fleets are highly modernized. They even employ electronic sounding devices (adapted from naval sounding equipment used to track submarines in World War II) that reveal the direction, distance, rate of movement, and size of great schools of fish. Occasionally experts can even identify types of fish from electronic

reports. The fleets also are streamlined in numerous other ways.

Commercial fishermen use craft that vary all the way from primitive boats run by manpower and sail to modern machine-driven vessels. Steam was first used in fishing vessels during the 1880's, and gasoline and diesel internal combustion engines appeared 50 years later. Today, steam and diesel ships make up most of the world's commercial fishing fleets, although sailing vessels persist in all regions. In the United States, there are 85,000 commercial fishing craft, including 70,000 smaller motor boats and 14,000 large vessels which are 5 tons or more. The European fleets are also highly modernized, although not to so high a degree. The Japanese and Russian fleets still have many sailing vessels, even though mechanical power is rapidly coming into use.

Over the years a variety of ingenious nets have been devised for different depths, types of ocean bottom, and types of fish. Bulk catches are snared in *purse nets*, which are looped around whole schools of fish and then drawn in, like a cowboy's lasso around a steer. Another technique is to float a *trawl line*, several hundred feet long, from which hang hundreds of vertical lines carrying hooks. Trawl nets, or *drags*, are cone-shaped nets towed behind powered vessels called *trawlers*. Some fish, however, such as tuna, are still caught by rod, line, and hook. This once common means of taking tuna has largely been replaced by net fishing. But the use of nets has led to over-fishing and as a result, there is a movement to make nets illegal. Should this happen, a return to the rod and hook method of tuna fishing is likely. Other sea creatures, such as lobsters, are trapped in crates.

Some modern fishing boats are fitted with refrigeration equipment to preserve the catch until it is brought in to port. Among the most complex of these are the Japanese *floating canneries* and the European whaling ships. Some years ago, Japanese fishermen began to roam so far to the east in search of salmon (almost to the shores of North America) that the cost of transporting and preserving their catch over the 5000-mile voyage home proved excessive. Moreover, the time required for the return trip was wasted. To combat both problems, the Japanese designed special ships fitted out with canning equipment so that the fishermen could spend the return trip in preparing the fish for market.

Modern whaling ships are also equipped to serve as floating factories. The largest fishing vessels ever built (some of them weigh 20,000 tons), they are specially designed so that whales can be towed aboard across the stern and then cut up on deck. The ship itself is a combination slaughter house, packing plant, and refrigerator. Every bit of the whale is put to some use, and no scrap is thrown overboard.

Species. Of the thousands of species of animals that dwell in the waters of the world, only a few are significant to man—few overall, and very few in any one region. Consider this breakdown. Off northwest Europe lie the world's best cod-fishing grounds; the catch there is augmented by masses of herring and haddock. In the Mediterranean, valuable economic items are sardine, eel, and sprat. Off Greece, the commercial fishermen concentrate mainly on sponges, in the Black Sea, Caspian Sea, and tributary rivers, on sturgeon. Off eastern Asia, the main commercial creatures are cod, herring, salmon, and crab. From the northwest Atlantic the catches are haddock, rosefish, flounder, and cod. Menhaden and shrimp constitute the major catches in the Gulf of Mexico, except for sponges in the waters right off Florida. In the northeast Pacific, we find leading salmon and halibut grounds. And from California to the Equator, the waters are rich in tuna. No more than four types are important in any one region, and there is a great deal of duplication among regions.

The distribution of sea creatures in the main fishing regions follows a latitudinal pattern. In the northern waters, for example, we find abundant supplies of cod, herring, mackerel, haddock, sole, and pilchards, all of which are scarce or absent in the waters to the south. And in the lower latitudes we find menhaden and

Part of the fleet at Fisherman's Wharf in San Francisco. The families which operate these boats are often of sourthern European ancestry, though they have been operating out of San Francisco for a number of years. (*Courtesy Clair A. Shenk.*)

sponges, which are relatively thinly represented in the higher latitudes. Originally, whales swam in all the seas, but some species have been virtually exterminated. Today, the Antarctic Ocean and adjacent waters of the Pacific and Atlantic form the most important single whaling area in the world.

Transplantings. Occasionally man has succeeded in transplanting sea life from one region to another. For one notable instance, a successful oyster industry in Puget Sound and the mouth of the Columbia River in the northwestern United States was built up with oysters introduced from Japan.

Physical Relationships

In nature, all these regions are typified by shallow, cool, mixed waters, by nearness to continental runoff, indented shorelines, and forests, and by periodic exposure to storms, fog, and icebergs.

Shallow Waters. The profile of the ocean bottom consists of three recognizable sections: (1) The part that drops gently away from dry land is known as the *continental shelf*. The width of shelf varies considerably. Off the western United States, for instance, the shelf is very narrow, rarely reaching out as far as 20 miles. Off our Atlantic Coast, however, it is much wider, extending as far as 150 miles from shore. (2) The shelf ends in a precipitous stretch called the *continental slope;* the average depth at which the one gives way to the other is 450 feet, although off some coasts it occurs as deep as 1200 feet. (3) The slope plunges sharply to an average depth of 12,000 feet before leveling off in the third section, the *abyss.* Scarcely any commercial fishing is carried on in the waters of the abyss or the continental slopes, for reasons to be seen in a moment. Instead, the fishermen draw most of their catch from the relatively shallow waters of the continental shelves.

Sealife is concentrated over the continental shelves because that is where the most abundant food supply is. This is so because of the *biotic pyramid* which prevails in the ocean just as it does on land. Since animals cannot manufacture their own food, they must consume either plants or other animals that subsist on plants. Thus, plants provide the foundation of the biotic pyramid. In the ocean, tiny plants, such as the *diatoms*, drift through the surface waters like fine dust; indeed, a cupful of water may contain millions of these minute organisms. These sea vegetables extract nutrients in the form of dissolved minerals and organic matter from the sea water and, in the presence of sunlight, convert them into substances that can be assimilated by animals. Those that feed directly off the diatoms and other unicellular flora are minute animals such as protozoa, crustacea (for example, small crabs and barnacles) sea worms, and tiny fish. In turn, larger carnivores feast off the grazers.

Neither the microscopic plants nor the microscopic animals can propel themselves through the water. Since they move only when they are borne along by currents and other water movements, they are known collectively as *plankton*, derived from a Greek word meaning "wandering." *Phytoplankton* are the plants, *zooplankton* the animals.

Plankton supply the complete diet of many fish, such as herring, menhaden, and mackerel. Carnivores—like bluefish, tuna, shark and some of the large jellyfish—in turn prey on the plankton-eaters. Not all the large sea animals live off smaller fish, however; certain whales, for example, live entirely on plankton.

Each type of fish tends to concentrate in the waters where its favorite food is most abundant. That is why we find some species in warm waters, others in cold; some in clear waters, others in turbid; some in waters rich in phosphates, others in waters rich in silicates.

There is one condition, however, that seems to be essential to almost every kind of fish, and that is *shallow water*. One reason is that the penetration of sunlight, which is required by all plants for photosynthesis, diminishes as the depth of the water increases. In fact, below 600 feet so little sunlight penetrates that few plants can live. In most waters, the limit is 200 feet. But sunlight alone is not enough to insure abundant plant and animal life. After all, the surface water in the middle of the oceans receives as much sunlight as does the water over the continental shelves, and yet the mid-ocean waters are normally poorer in plankton. Apparently, something more than sunlight is needed.

A second reason is access to plant nutrients (such as the remains of dead sea life) which tend to drift downward and accumulate on the ocean floor. In the abyss such nutrients are beyond the reach of sunlight. But on the shelf they collect in shallows where plants can utilize them in photosynthesis.

Thus, the most propitious environment for sea vegetables is in shallow waters, and these prevail either just offshore or else farther from the continents above elevated portions of the shelves known as *banks*.

Most offshore (or coastal) shallows are in the Northern Hemisphere. (Off the coast of Africa in the Southern Hemisphere there is virtually no continental shelf, and the ledges around South America and Australia are very narrow.) The shallows encircling Iceland, the Faeroe Islands, the Lofoten Islands, and other margins of northwestern Europe provide that region with 300,000 square miles of excellent fishing grounds. Off the coasts of eastern Asia we find approximately 100,000 square miles of shallow water. There is about an equal extent off the coast along the northwestern Atlantic.

As for the banks, some are enormous. The Dogger Bank in the North Sea (Figure 5-2), for instance, covers nearly 20,000 square miles, and over this whole extent

NORTH SEA AREA

Figure 5-2

the depth of the water ranges from only 40 to 100 feet.[1] In the western Atlantic several banks are dispersed along a zone 1100 miles long and from 50 to 250 miles wide that runs from Newfoundland to Massachusetts (Figure 5-3). In this part of the world the largest bank is Grand Bank, which covers 37,000 square miles, much of it lying less than 300 feet beneath the surface. Georges Bank, which covers 8500 square miles, is at no point more than 100 feet below the surface, and in a few places it lies under only 20 feet of water.

Continental Run-Off. Much of the dissolved minerals and organic matter (nutrients for the one-celled plants) in the ocean is brought in by river waters. Through erosion the land loses such resources to the rivers, but those losses provide nourishment for the plants and creatures of the sea. Obviously these dissolved nutrients are most abundant in water that is adjacent to the land from which the dissolved substances have been carried.

Mixed Waters. Food for sea plants at the base of the biotic pyramid is most abundant in *mixed* waters. The reason is that mineral and organic matter in the sea —which consists of material eroded from the continents, and the shells, skeletons, and other remains of sea organisms—drifts slowly toward the bottom. But, since most of the plant and animal life that needs these nutrients is restricted, by the plants' need for sunlight, to water near the surface, they could better survive if this organic and mineral matter were somehow churned upward once

[1]Apparently this great bank once protruded as an Island. North Sea fishermen trawling over the Dogger Bank have dragged up pieces of trees, animal bones, and flint heads used by hunters in tracking game. It appears that the Dogger Bank once supported an economy in which man preyed on land animals as he now preys there on the fish of the sea.

again. This mixing action takes place in the following three ways.

1. Convectional mixing: In the higher latitudes the winter is severe enough to lower the temperature of surface water almost to the freezing point. As water becomes cooler, its density *increases* (reaching its greatest density at 39° Fahrenheit) and it "sinks," thereby churning up water from the depths. But this process does not go on indefinitely, for when water is cooled below that critical temperature (39°F. for fresh water, somewhat lower for salt water, depending on salinity) its density *decreases*. As the water approaches the freezing point and gets lighter, it floats upward to the surface. With the approach of springtime, the temperature of surface water rises; if the winter temperatures have been below the critical point, the warming water sinks once more, again churning up water from below. This vertical movement of water under the influence of temperature changes is known as convectional mixing.

2. Conflict of currents: Where a cold-water current encounters a warm-water one, the warm usually glides over the cool, driving it downward to churn up the mineral-laden water at the lower depths. Fortunately for commercial fishermen, the areas in which cool and warm currents meet are located along the coastlines in latitudes from 40° to 70°; it so happens that these are the very areas in which convectional mixing is also most effective. The most significant interactions are those between the Labrador Current and the Gulf Stream in the northwest Atlantic and between the Kamchatka Current and the Japanese Current in the northwest Pacific.

3. Upwelling: Another phenomenon that helps replenish the surface layers with nutrients from the ocean basement is known as *upwelling*. This action develops when surface currents swing away from the land masses, leaving a "vacuum" which is filled by water rushing in from the depths. The most vigorous upwellings are caused by the California Current, the Humboldt Current, and the Benguela Current, which benefit the coastal fisheries of, respectively, California, Peru and Chile, and South Africa.

Cool Waters. Average sea temperatures vary from a high of 96° in the Persian Gulf to 28° in polar waters. Sea creatures are much more abundant in polar seas than the Persian Gulf. As a rule, cool waters yield far more commercial fish than do warm waters. Why is this so? In the first place, fish from warm-water habitats have a high oil content which makes them unpalatable to most people. In the second place, warm waters contain less plant food because of the presence of water-borne denitrifying bacteria that destroy organic material.

A characteristic of cool-water fish which makes them susceptible to large-scale fishing is that they tend to cluster together and move about in *schools*. Why the fish of the mid-latitudes exhibit this tendency more than the fish of the tropics is a question that awaits an answer from ichthyologists. The significance of this *schooling* tendency for us is that fishermen can specialize in one kind of fish—cod, for example. The point is, their production costs are lower than when they have to handle different types of equipment for different kinds of fish, and they also save on marketing costs by selling boat loads of one fish rather than small amounts of several species.

Figure 5-3 (*After Clarence F. Jones and Gordon Darkenwald,* Economic Geography, *Macmillan, 1954.*)

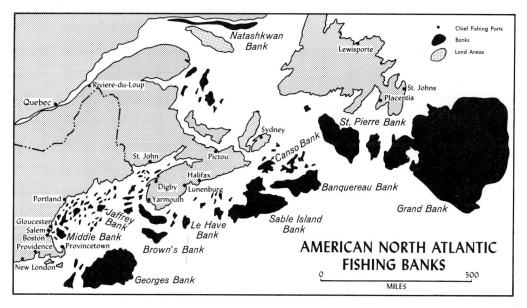

Indented Shorelines. An area characterized by the foregoing physical characteristics, *plus* an irregular, indented shoreline, would provide an ideal natural setting for commercial fishing. The reason is simple: The abundance of good harbors along an indented shoreline makes it easy to develop the port facilities that are essential for commercial fishing.

Forests. By coincidence, some of the best ocean fishing grounds adjoin land that is to a large extent well forested. The forests, of course, historically facilitated the construction of ships. Even with the advent of steel for ship construction, though, wood is still needed for dories and other small boats, for fuel to smoke fish, and for the making of barrels, boxes, and crates for marketing the catch.

Physical Disadvantages. All the physical conditions we have considered so far expedite commercial harvests of fish. But the environment in fishing regions is not completely favorable to this business. There are three definite physical handicaps: storms, fogs, and icebergs.

According to meteorologists, cyclonic storm tracks that cross North America converge over the Atlantic where cool and warm air masses converge. Thus, the fishing regions of the northwest Atlantic (off New England and Newfoundland) are plagued by rough seas and stormy weather associated with cyclonic storms. The same conditions exist in the northwest Pacific fishing grounds, where the storms converge in their movement from eastern Asia.

Over oceans, cyclonic storms usually suck in warm moist air from their sides toward the equator; and when a mass of warm moist sea air glides over a cool ocean current, condensation occurs, and countless droplets of water fill the atmosphere. Consequently, the foggiest seas coincide with the major fishing regions.

In the northwest Atlantic the southward-moving Labrador Current often carries great masses of ice that have broken away from the glacier fronts of Greenland. Spring thaws unlock these monsters and send tremendous blocks of ice slipping into the sea to drift southward across the shipping lanes and into the fishing grounds. The worst months for icebergs are April through July.

Market Factors

The commercial harvesting of fish is closely related to several aspects of cultural environment, especially market factors, international relations, and problems resulting from man's activities.

The demand for fish depends on such factors as population density, dietary habits, the inability of agriculture to provide adequate diets, market price of fish, and use of fish by-products in industry. Meeting the demand involves some unusual marketing procedures.

Population Density. If you compare the front endpaper (map of world population) and Figure 5-1, you will see that the four principal regions of commercial fishing are located near dense populations. Of the world's four most heavily populated areas, only India is not adjacent to a major commercial fishing realm.

Dietary Habits. In some areas strong cultural forces foster the consumption of fish. One of these forces derives from religious practices. In southern Europe, for example, the population is predominantly Catholic. Traditionally, the people here ate no meat on Fridays and on many other holy days. Even though the Church now permits meat to be eaten on Fridays, many Catholics have elected to stay with the fish-on-Friday tradition. And there are enough of them to constitute an enormous market for fish not only from the Mediterranean and mid-Atlantic, but also from the North Sea and the Norwegian coastal waters. Similarly, in the Far East, most adherents of Hinduism and Islam are prohibited from eating the meat of at least some, if not all, land animals; but most of them can eat fish. Fish is a big item in the diet of millions of Indians, Pakistani, and Burmese.

Catamaran being launched at Mutham, India. The rather crude vessel was recently mechanized with overseas and government counterpart funds, which were aimed at improving these commercial fishing ventures. (*FAO photo by D. Mason.*)

Limited Agriculture. A scarcity of arable land is a strong factor in driving people to the sea in search of a livelihood. Notice the low proportion of arable acres per person in the following countries, all of which have large relative numbers of fishermen: Norway 0.49, Iceland 0.01, the United Kingdom 0.32, and Japan 0.12. It is scarcely surprising, then, that the Japanese and Scandinavians look to fish as a major source of protein in their diets. Alaska, British Columbia, Maine, Nova Scotia, Newfoundland, and Scotland are other areas where fishermen have been encouraged by an environment which is rather inhospitable to agriculture.

In some places, people work one season as farmers and another season as fishermen. Norway, for instance, has fishermen who go to sea in February for the cod runs, return to their farms in the summer, and then go to sea for herring runs in October and November. Similarly, in Iceland, virtually all fishermen are biooccupational, working part time in the fishing fleets and part time in filet-freezing plants and at other occupations.

Meat Prices. Until recently, one basic reason behind the demand for fish has been cheapness. Fish cost less than many other kinds of meat, not only in port cities, but also in cities far from the sea. This situation is changing, however; since the 1960's fish prices in the United States have risen faster than most meat prices.

Illustrative of such differences as do exist are these recent average retail prices in the United States. Examples of fish prices per pound: perch $1.08, tuna $1.60, haddock $1.51, shrimp $2.25. Some examples of meat prices per pound: ground beef $0.81, pork loin roast $1.20, chuck roast $0.91, rump roast $1.70, standing rib $1.56, ham, $1.10, pork chops center cut $1.61, round steak $1.71, Swiss steak $0.99, sirloin steak $1.73.

Other Uses for Fish. Although the main use for fish has always been as human food, increasing quantities are going into the manufacture of soil fertilizers and animal feed. Today, in fact, the most important species in United States fishing, by quantity, is the oily, unpalatable menhaden (Table 5-3). The carcasses of all these fish are ground up for use as oil, animal feed, and fertilizer.

Manufacturing and Marketing. Fishing regions and market regions are linked by highly organized processing and transportation systems. Historically, most of the fish shipped to consumers were salted or dried, though ice-packed fish in barrels were sent inland from New England as far as central Pennsylvania in the nineteenth and early twentieth centuries. Then, with the development of canning processes in the late nineteenth century, salting and drying began to give way to canning. Next came refrigeration, and now freezing. All these techniques permit fish to be sold and eaten thousands of miles from port.

Fishing Ports. The processing and marketing functions have long been concentrated in fishing ports. Countless small villages in which fishing is the principal economic activity dot the coasts of Norway, Iceland, Newfoundland, Nova Scotia, Maine, British Columbia, Alaska, eastern U.S.S.R., and Japan. Frequently such settlements are extremely small—only a few people whose life centers around a cannery and its fishing fleet. On the rugged Pacific coasts of North America, completely isolated out in the wilderness, sit several canneries that are built on the flat land near the mouth of a salmon stream. Surrounded by steep forested slopes, their only avenue of transportation with the outside world is the sea. Some of these Pacific Coast settlements are merely semipermanent villages inhabited by migrants who come in only for the fishing and canning season. Those that are permanent experience a sizable influx of workers during fishing season. For example, the salmon canners in Alaska annually import hundreds of seasonal laborers from other states and Canada.

Where fishing villages are somewhat larger they function not only as home bases for fishing boats, for personnel, and for canning, but also as manufacturing centers of boats and equipment, and even as headquarters for fishing companies.

With increasing mechanization of techniques and complexity of manufacturing and marketing, the small fishing villages are beginning to disappear. More and more their functions are becoming concentrated in cities, notably Gloucester, Boston, Baltimore, and Los Angeles. Although fishing is a small component in the economy of such cities (this industry only employs about 225,000 in the entire United States), these places now dominate the fishing industry. Particularly noteworthy fishing settlements in other countries are Grimsby and Hull in England and Bergen and Stavanger in Norway (Figure 5-2).

Commercial Fishing and International Relations

International Trade. The world's leading fishing nations (Japan, the U.S.S.R., China, Norway, and the United States) consume much of what they catch. Nevertheless, three of these nations—Japan, Norway, and to a lesser extent, the United States, are also major exporters of fish (Table 5-4).

Fish products constitute a considerable portion of sales abroad for a few countries, notably Iceland, whose economy is based to an astonishing degree on this one type of commodity. By percentage of value of fish in all exports for each nation, the important fish-exporting countries are Iceland 65 per cent, Norway 8, Panama 10, Denmark 5.

International Agreements. Fishermen from England, France, the Netherlands, Germany, Denmark,

Table 5-4

International Trade in Fish, Millions of U.S. Dollars

Country	Leading Importers	Country	Leading Exporters
(Fish—Fresh and Simply Preserved)			
World	2,255	World	1,869
United States	744	Canada	227
Japan	382	Norway	181
France	154	Denmark	135
Italy	154	Japan	115
(Fish—Tinned and Prepared)			
World	692	World	603
United States	133	Japan	224
United Kingdom	113	Canada	45
France	63	Norway	39
West Germany	39	United States	36

Source: United Nations, *Yearbook of International Trade Statistics* (1974).

and Norway have mingled for centuries on the waters of the North Sea. And for over 400 years European fishermen have pushed across the Atlantic to the Grand Bank and the other fishing grounds off North America. Japanese craft range 5000 miles across the Pacific, and tuna boats from California strike west to Hawaii and along the cool California Current southward to Panama.

Inevitably, these wide-ranging activities have led to negotiations among the governments concerned. On the one hand, some treaties have been designed to conserve the valuable resources of the sea. In 1930, for example, the United States and Canada signed a treaty to limit the size of halibut catches. And back in 1911 the United States, Canada, Russia, and Japan agreed to control the killing of seals in the Pribilof Island area. From a population of 10,000,000, the herd had been reduced to 12,000. In response to the virtual extermination of whales from the oceans of the world except in the southernmost Pacific and the Antarctic, in 1935 an international agreement was worked out prohibiting the catching of calves and females with calves; subsequently a limit was set on the number of adult whales that can be caught. In the North Sea Conventions of 1936, 1943, and 1946, several European nations collaborated in establishing net regulations and size limitations for fish.

On the other hand, the purpose of certain government actions seems to have been to limit the freedom of fishermen from other nations. Nowhere has this been more apparent than in the Pacific. Before World War II, Japanese fishermen cruised at will over the whole Pacific. Then in 1952 Korea established the "Rhee Line" barring Japanese vessels from the western Sea of Japan, an area

rich in sardines, mackerel, and flatfish. And just to the southwest, the Chinese Communists ruled that the Japanese could not approach closer than 100 miles to the China coast, thus blocking them from the best trawling grounds in the East China Sea. Next, the United States established a 420,000-square-mile nuclear testing area in the tuna and bonito grounds of the mid-Pacific.

The plight of Japanese fishermen was further intensified in 1953 when the United States and Canada signed an agreement barring them from the northeast Pacific where they had previously fished for salmon and halibut. Finally, in 1956, immediately after the Japanese broke off treaty talks with the U.S.S.R., the Russians retaliated by closing the Sea of Okhotsk, the western Bering Sea, and part of the northwest Pacific to Japanese fishermen. For decades, the Japanese had been coming to this area to harvest the tremendous runs of salmon. On March 1, 1977, the United States extended her territorial limits to 200 miles; this has had significant impact on the Japanese, Russians, and others who have grown accustomed to fishing off our shores, and the political implications for U.S. foreign relations are substantial.

The question of how far a nation's territorial limits extend has caused a number of international incidents; from time to time in recent years the newspapers have carried accounts of the seizure of American fishing boats by Ecuador or some other Latin American country because the boat was fishing in waters claimed by that nation. Perhaps the best known controversy is the British-Icelandic Cod War. In September, 1972, Iceland extended its fishery jurisdiction from 12 to 50 miles, which, as might be expected, had severe repercussions. At one point, an Icelandic military vessel actually shelled a British fishing boat.[2]

Problems Facing Commercial Fishing

Aside from international restrictions and bad weather, the successful harvesting of fish is adversely affected by ocean shipping, overfishing, pollution, and the encouragement of predators.

Ocean Shipping Lanes. Unfortunately, some of the world's most-traveled shipping routes cut across fishing grounds. The most direct route between New York and the ports of western Europe, for example, passes through Georges Bank and the Grand Bank. In daytime during clear weather, there is no particular problem, but at night and on foggy days (remember that this is one of the world's foggiest zones), there is a constant danger of collision between freighters and fishing boats. Less dangerous but more frequent is damage to nets and trawl lines. The same perils exist on the busy lanes of the North Sea.

[2]A fascinating analysis of the Cod War is provided in Bruce Mitchell, "Politics, Fish, and International Resource Management: The British-Icelandic Cod War," *The Geographical Review*, Vol. 66, April, 1976, pp. 127–138.

Overfishing. Not very many years ago, men regarded the supply of sea animals as inexhaustible, and they pulled in all kinds in unlimited amounts. But then something happened: Fishermen began to bring smaller and smaller catches back to port. It now appears that some species of sea life do not multiply indefinitely regardless of how favorable the habitat. We now realize that some animals were snatched up faster than they reproduced themselves. The examples of halibut, salmon, and seal illustrate this problem.

The *halibut* lies lazily on its side on the floor of the continental shelf, feeding on the nutrients that drift down from the surface and on the organisms that live on the floor. Thousands of halibut congregate in relatively immobile schools. Back in the late 1800's, fishermen hauled in tremendous catches of halibut from fishing grounds off the American shores. But when they returned to the same grounds, they had very poor luck. Concluding that the school had moved on, the fishermen moved along to a new spot and once again they came up with huge catches. Once more, however, on their return, they found that the fish had vanished. Almost too late, around 1920, the fishermen realized that the schools of halibut were not moving from place to place at all; instead, one school after another was being exterminated. The fishing fleets were simply scraping the bottom clean. As a result, today catches of halibut in American waters are controlled by American (United States-Canada) agreements.

Salmon are intensely mobile, migrating hundreds of miles. Yet they have a peculiar homing instinct which man has capitalized on. After being spawned upstream in fresh water, the salmon go out to the open sea where they spend most of their lives. Then, usually five years later, they come back to do their own spawning in the very stream from which they came. (It is said that one loyal salmon came home to the University of Washington Fisheries School up a pipe!) These regular, predictable runs make it easy for fishermen to draw in tremendous catches in a few days' time. But the effects of the severe overfishing of a stream in any one year do not show up generally until five years later—when the inbound spawners would be markedly fewer than normal. As a result of excessive catches in spawning rivers, salmon are nearly extinct in New England where they were once numerous. The salmon runs have also declined sharply in the rivers of northern California, Oregon, and Washington. At the turn of the century the Sacramento River supplied salmon meat for hundreds of thousands of cases; since 1920 it has supplied none. By tonnage, the United States harvest of salmon is now about a quarter of what it was in our record year—1936 (see Table 5-2).

Fur seals of the northern Pacific were also once seriously decimated. They are especially vulnerable because once a year they are impelled to go "home" to the Pribilof Islands west of Alaska, where they are, in effect, sitting ducks. From an original population of 10,000,000 the herd was nearly exterminated by 1911. As we have seen, though, through international agreement the herds have been protected and enabled to expand. Still, the fur seal harvest in the north Pacific is only 35,000 to 45,000 animals annually.

Over and over again, hampered by inadequate knowledge of the living habits of sea animals but armed with powerful ships and modern equipment, men have proceeded to devastate some of the world's best resources of sea life. The pattern has become painfully familiar: tremendous harvests followed by declining supplies and by the subsequent shifts of the fishermen to more distant seas. As yet, the commercial fisherman has failed to maintain the conserving balance between supply and demand that the subsistence fisherman achieved ages ago. A belated awareness of the problem has developed, though, and stringent laws have been passed to protect some species—for instance, controlling the type of nets and other devices used in catching salmon, controlling the quantity of halibut and salmon that will be accepted at commercial ports, and controlling the number of seals that can be slain.

Overfishing is a menace, and yet it is evidently not the only problem. When a single mackerel or sole spawns from 100,000 to 1,000,000 eggs a year, and a cod or haddock produces 5,000,000 eggs, it would seem that enough would mature to replenish the adult population if fishermen were the only enemy. Clearly, other factors are in the equation. One of these is pollution.

Pollution. In countless fresh water streams and in the ocean margins at the mouths of many rivers, the habitat of sea life has been damaged by excessive mud from eroded land, and by slime and poisonous chemicals from agricultural, industrial, and city wastes (Table 5-5). Such noxious substances destroy fish eggs and increase the death rate of small fry. Pollution has severely damaged mackerel, cod, sole, and haddock grounds fringing large urban areas; it has virtually ruined the waters off

Table 5-5

Pollution-Caused Fish Kills in the United States, 1973

Source of Pollution	Fish Reported Killed in Thousands
Agricultural operations	2,464
Industrial operations	1,794
Municipal operations	10,385
Transportation operations	565
Unknown	22,256
Other	350
Total	37,814
Type of Water	
Fresh	5,447
Salt	61
Estuary	32,306

Source: U.S. Environmental Protection Agency, *Pollution-Caused Fish Kills* (1975).

our northern Atlantic coast where shad fishing has nearly disappeared and oyster harvests have plummeted.

Predators Further, man has ruined some fisheries by unwittingly unleashing predators that destroy commercial fish. As far as we know, this disruption is more serious in inland waters than in oceans. What has happened to commercial fishing in Lake Michigan will serve as a good example of the problem. Table 5-6

Table 5-6

Quantity and Value of Catch from Lake Michigan

Year	Catch in Millions of Pounds	Value in Millions of Dollars
1950	27	4
1955	30	3
1960	24	2
1965	27	2
1970	53	4
1972	44	4

Source: U.S. National Oceanic and Atmospheric Administration, *Fishery Statistics of the United States* (1975).

presents the story. Notice that although the tonnage of the yield from Lake Michigan is steadily *increasing*, the value of the catch has been relatively *constant*—and this in a period of inflation! What is the explanation? First of all, the two fish—trout and whitefish—that for years brought the highest prices and provided Lake Michigan fishermen with their greatest revenue are now in short supply. By the mid-1950's trout were extinct and whitefish were rapidly becoming so. These valuable fish were victims, not of overfishing, but of the ravages of a predator, the sea lamprey. The lamprey is a water worm that measures up to 2 feet in length, and looks somewhat like a garden hose with a suction cup at one end. The lamprey fastens this mouth, which is lined with dozens of needle-sharp teeth, to the side of a fish and then lives as a parasite by sucking the lifeblood from its host. Eventually the host dies and the lamprey moves on to another fish. The average lamprey destroys 20 pounds of fish during its four years of mature existence.

Apparently there has always been a population of lampreys in the St. Lawrence River and Lake Ontario, but Niagara Falls formerly barred them from entering the other Great Lakes. Then, in 1829, the Welland Canal was constructed to make it possible for ships to bypass Niagara. The new canal also provided a convenient bypass for the lampreys into Lake Erie. For reasons that are still obscure, the lampreys have never been much of a problem in the shallow water of Lake Erie; apparently they reserved their attack for the fish of the deeper waters of Lakes Huron, Michigan, and Superior.

In the 1930's, trout catches in Huron dwindled sharply and fishermen noticed that, of the fish they were drawing in, an increasing number bore circular scars on their sides. In 1948, Lake Huron's trout industry collapsed.

The first lamprey was discovered in Lake Michigan in 1936. From that time on, the number of scarred fish steadily increased, and the trout harvest began to slip. From a peak year in 1944 the catch rapidly declined until 1952 when it amounted to less than 1000 pounds, and by 1955 there was no catch at all—Lake Michigan's trout were extinct.

Now that the best fish of the Great Lakes had been destroyed, the fishermen turned to the next best—the whitefish. But so did the lampreys. In 1947, the peak year for whitefish, the catch amounted to 1,806,000 pounds. Then the lampreys, deprived of their trout diet, closed in. Nine years later the whitefish catch was only 18,295 pounds, even though the fishermen had constantly been improving their techniques and equipment.

But this it not the end of the story. As a result of these shifts in the natural life of the lakes, a small species of lake chub, unmarketable except as animal feed, has increased in number by 300 per cent, and is particularly abundant in Lake Michigan. Formerly, this small chub provided the lake trout with their main source of food. But now that the trout have been exterminated by the lampreys, the chub population has increased spectacularly. Unfortunately, these fish are a nuisance to the fisherman, for their gills become ensnared in the nets and they have to be removed by hand—a time-consuming task. And when they are marketed as animal feed they bring only a few cents per pound.

There is a larger species of chub, however, which in smoked form has proved palatable. So commercial fishermen have now turned to this chub and to perch as their major sources of revenue. But once again they are bedeviled by the lampreys, which, now that the whitefish are disappearing, are feasting not on the small species of chub but the large ones! So the harassed fishermen of Lake Michigan are now shifting to lake smelt, a fish that ranks even lower on the income ladder.

For several years, researchers have been searching for means to combat the lamprey nuisance. One method which held some promise was that of establishing electrical weirs at the mouths of spawning streams—the idea being to generate a mild electric shock to the lamprey, discouraging it from entering the stream to spawn. Thousands of lampreys have been killed at the weirs since their inception in 1955. But this method is slow and very expensive, and probably could never eliminate the lamprey population. Recently a chemical has been discovered which kills lamprey larvae but causes no injury whatsoever to other forms of life in the stream or to animals which drink its water. Results have been astonishingly successful—100 per cent kill in streams where the method has been tried.

One encouraging indicator of the success of these measures is the definite signs of recovery in the whitefish harvest by fishermen from Lake Michigan. The take had skidded steadily downward to a nadir in 1958, but since then there has been a conspicuous reversal. It looks as if the battle tide against the lamprey is turning. Indeed, authorities are so encouraged that they have initiated a program to restock Lake Michigan with trout from fish hatcheries.

The Future

At present men annually pull in 66,000,000 tons of fish and other animals from the oceans. This may seem an appreciable amount, yet one square mile of plankton-rich sea water produces 4000 tons of vegetable matter—about six times the yield from a comparable area of good Kansas wheat land. The question is whether plankton can ever be used as food for man, and if so, whether it can be extracted economically. If scientists ever produce affirmative answers to these questions the day may come when *aquaculture* supersedes commercial fishing in the water world as surely as agriculture superseded commercial hunting on the continents.

SUGGESTED READINGS

ALFORD, JOHN J., "The Chesapeake Oyster Fishery," *Annals of the Association of American Geographers*, 1975, pp. 229–239.

CHAPMAN, J. D., "Natural Resource Developments in Canada, 1970–75," *The Canadian Geographer*, 1976, pp. 15–40.

CRAIG, ALAN K., "The Grouper Fishery of Cay Glory, British Honduras," *Annals of the Association of American Geographers*, 1969, pp. 252–263.

DICKINSON, JOSHUA C., III, "Fisheries of Lake Izabal, Guatemala," *Geographical Review*, 1974, pp. 385–409.

HELIN, RONALD A., "Soviet Fishing in the Barents Sea and the North Atlantic," *Geographical Review*, 1964, pp. 386–408.

MARTS, M. E., and SEWELL, W. R. D., "The Conflicts Between Fish and Power Resources in the Pacific," *Annals of the Association of American Geographers*, 1960, pp. 42–50.

MITCHELL, BRUCE, "Politics, Fish, and International Resource Management: The British-Icelandic Cod War," *Geographical Review*, 1976, pp. 127–138.

PADGETT, HERBERT R., "The Sea Fisheries of the Southern United States," *Geographical Review*, 1963, pp. 22–39.

United Nations, Food and Agriculture Organization, *Yearbook of Fishery Statistics* (annual).

United States Department of Commerce, *Marine Fisheries Review* (monthly). Contains reports on fishing developments in the United States and in numerous foreign countries.

CHAPTER

commercial forest gathering

Seedlings grow in an old clearcut. An example of regeneration at Glacier Peak National Forest, Washington. (*Courtesy Weyerhaeuser Company.*)

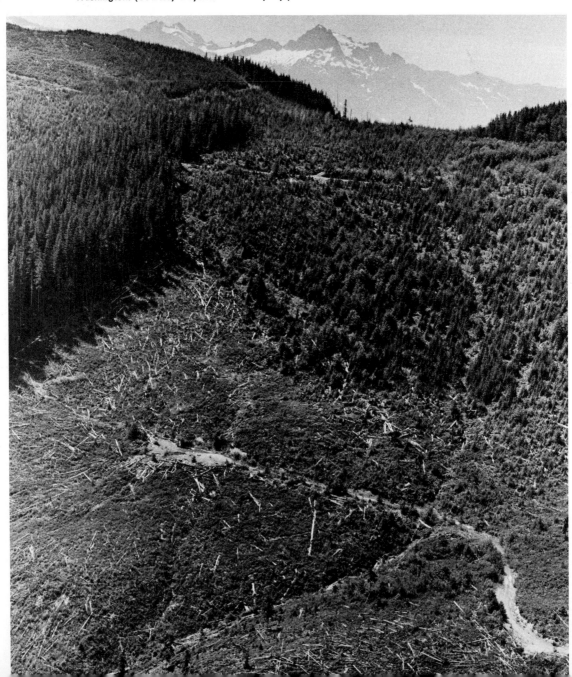

Chapter 3 included some comments about the gathering of forest products for subsistence purposes. The present chapter deals with economic activities in which man gathers trees and tree products for commercial exchange.

Location

Men gather surplus products from natural stands of trees chiefly in two huge belts, as shown on Figure 6-1. The first virtually encircles the globe in the mid-latitudes of the Northern Hemisphere, southern Alaska, Canada, and contiguous parts of the United States, picks up again in a swath through central Europe, and stretches across Scandinavia and the northern Soviet Union and covers most of Japan. This region is one of the most extensive and comprehensive in all economic geography.

The second forest-gathering realm is found around the tropics, widely through South and Central America, in a long strip in western and central Africa, and again in Southeast Asia.

Apart from these two general regions commercial forest gathering is of significance only in small zones in southern Chile, in southeastern Australia, in New Zealand, and in some of the countries flanking the Mediterranean Sea.

Characteristics

Forest gathering consists of two general types of activity: *lumbering*, in which the trees themselves are harvested, and *collecting*, in which only tree products (that is, nuts, leaves, sap, fruits, and so on) are taken, leaving the trees intact. When we compare the mid-latitude region with the tropical region, we find contrasts in the relative extents of collecting and lumbering and in the particular commodities gathered.

Gathering in the Tropics. Forest gathering generates much less wealth in the tropics than in the mid-latitudes. In the tropics, collecting—principally of sap, nuts, leaves, and bark—is often for more important than is lumbering.

The sap of many different types of trees is collected to be used in manufacturing a diversity of products— from rubber and chewing gum to wiring insulation and golf balls.

Nuts are collected for a variety of purposes. The oil used in the manufacture of soap, margarine, candles, and glycerine is extracted from various tropical nuts. The coconut is the biggest prize because copra (white meat) is over half oil. Commercial copra comes from forest gatherers in the Philippines, Indonesia, and Malaysia. Another oil-yielding nut comes from the oil plam tree, which is common in Nigeria, Malaysia, and Indonesia. But oil is not the only use for nuts. Nuts from *cacao* trees and *castanheiro* trees are food items. *Ivory nuts*, which are white and very hard, are useful in making buttons and knife handles. Silky fibers from seeds of the *kapok* tree are made into mattress filler and life-jackets. *Coir*, the fiber from coconut husks, is used in cordage and door mats.

Forest gatherers also pick a wide array of leaves for a variety of purposes. For instance, fibers from the leaves of a tree native to the Philippines are peculiarly resistant

Figure 6-1

COMMERCIAL FOREST GATHERING

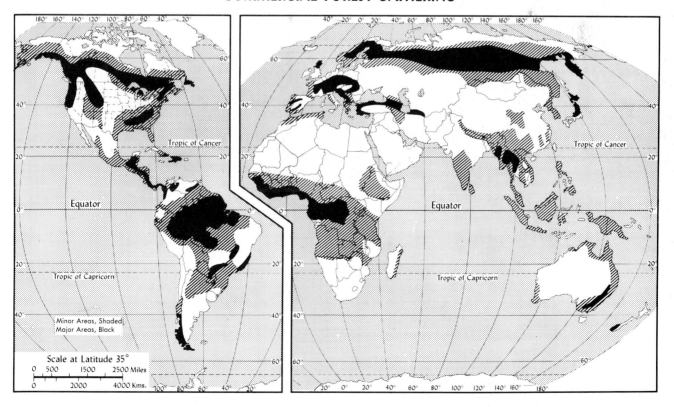

to salt water; known as *abaca* (or *Manila hemp*, because most of it is marketed through Manila), the fiber is indispensable in the making of ropes, twine, and cordage. Leaves of the *coca* bush contain the drug cocaine.

As for bark, quinine is manufactured from the covering of the *cinchona* tree, and the aromatic bark of the cinnamon tree, which grows in Sri Lanka and Malaysia, is used as a spice.

Thus, forest gathering in the tropics yields a great diversity of commodities from a wide assortment of plants. Some of these commodities, such as bananas, have become so highly valued that today they are produced primarily on carefully managed *tree farms* rather than in wild forests.

Tropical *lumbering* is less varied than collecting, but it yields an important group of commercial products. The most valuable are certain timbers, tanning chemicals, and drugs.

A principal timber is mahogany, which comes primarily from tropical America, including Haiti and the Dominican Republic, though some comes from the Guinea coast of Africa. Other important woods are cedar, teak, and ebony. Cedar, a soft, fragrant wood, is shipped mainly from Mexico, Central America, and Brazil. Teak is a strong, hard wood that contains an unusually high amount of oil which acts as a natural preservative in both fresh and salt water. The wood also resists both rot and white ants, and does not burn easily. Accordingly, teak is highly valued in the construction of wooden boats and as pilings for wharves and piers. Teak trees are rarely found outside Burma, Thailand, Laos, Cambodia, Vietnam, and Java. One of the earliest woods to be gathered commercially in the tropics was ebony, a hard, jet-black, fine-grained wood from Central Africa, Madagascar, and southeast Asia. Ebony has for a long time been used in making chests, figurines, and handles.

Until the late nineteenth century, most commercial tannin (for tanning leather) was extracted from the oak, chestnut, and hemlock trees of the mid-latitudes. Then it was discovered that the quebracho tree of South America was rich in tannin, and it soon became the single most important natural source of tannin. Northern Argentina yields the greatest supplies, although the output of southern Brazil is also important.

Gathering in the Mid-Latitudes. In the mid-latitudes, collecting is much less important than lumbering. At one time large quantities of commercial tannin were extracted from the bark of chestnut, oak, and hemlock trees in the United States and Europe, but as we just saw, the quebracho tree proved a better source. Certain wood products are still economically valuable, however, notably cork and naval stores. Cork comes primarily from oak trees in Portugal (half the world total) and along the northwestern fringe of Africa. Turpentine, tar, and pitch (collectively termed naval stores because of their wide use in caulking wooden

ships) are derived from the sap of yellow pine trees. When this resinous fluid is heated, the turpentine is driven off and collected for use in paints and varnishes; the distillate, called rosin, is employed in the manufacture of soap and a wide array of chemicals. Most of the world's commercial supply of naval stores comes from the southeastern United States (South Carolina, Georgia, Florida, and Alabama) and from southwestern France.

Lumbering in the mid-latitude region provides roughly 80 per cent of the world's industrial wood (Table 6-1); Figure 6-1, which shows the world pattern of forest gathering, provides an illustration of the regional concentration. Within the United States the leading states by volume in sawtimber removals are Oregon and Washington; by general area, the Pacific Coast states now account for 40 per cent of the sawtimber cut from the nation's forests.

Table 6-1

World Harvest of Wood by Leading Countries
(Millions of Cubic Meters)

	Total Roundwood	Industrial Roundwood	Fuelwood and Charcoal
WORLD	2,453	1,313	1,140
Africa	307	41	266
Ethiopia	24	1	23
Nigeria	59	3	56
Tanzania	32	1	31
North America	518	468	50
Canada	119	116	3
United States	355	342	13
South America	237	43	194
Brazil	163	23	140
Colombia	26	4	22
Asia	657	179	478
China	178	44	134
India	116	10	106
Indonesia	120	16	104
Japan	46	44	2
Philippines	33	13	20
Europe	320	262	58
Finland	42	35	7
France	33	28	5
Sweden	57	54	3
U.S.S.R.	383	298	85

Source: United Nations, Food and Agriculture Organization, *Yearbook of Forest Products* (1974).

For the world as a whole, almost as much wood is cut for fuel as for boards, pulp, veneer, and other industrial purposes. But the proportion between fuelwood and industrial wood varies sharply from place to place. Within the tropics the chief use is as fuelwood—86 per cent in Brazil, 87 per cent in Indonesia, 91 per cent in

India, nearly 100 per cent in Ethiopia, Tanzania, and other tropical nations. Throughout the continent of South America, 82 per cent of the wood cut is for fuel; in Africa that figure is 87 per cent. By contrast the harvest in mid-latitude forests is mainly for industrial use, in France 85 per cent, Sweden 95, Japan 96, and Canada 97.

The woods of the mid-latitudes serve such a wide array of uses that it is impossible to associate any one item with a few distinctive purposes. In general, these woods have great strength and are very easy to work. Consequently, they can be adapted to such widely diversified uses as building materials, shingles, implements, wagons, railroad ties, mine props, and furniture. The softwoods (especially poplar and pine) are well suited for conversion into paper pulp; fir and pine are best for structural timbers, studs, and joists; and the hardwoods are most suitable for furniture, wagons, sleds, and tools.

Physical Relationships

Of the several aspects of the natural environment that have an influence on forest gathering, we shall first consider the forest resource itself and then look at other physical elements such as climate, soils, and drainage.

The Forest Resource. Originally, one-fourth of the earth's land was blanketed with trees, but man has removed nearly half of the tree cover. Today, only about 15 per cent of the land is forested. (The world regions of this forest resource, by types of trees, are shown in almost any atlas.)

The forest resource of the tropics is considerably different from that of the mid-latitudes. In the heart of the tropics lies the *rainforest*, the most luxuriant and variegated community of plants on the face of the earth. The features of the rainforest that are most directly related to forest gathering are profusion of species, "confusion of stands," size of trees, and hardness of woods.

The remarkable profusion of species means a profusion of products. The reasons for the abundance of plant types are not entirely clear, but it appears that the warm humid tropical environment permits rapid maturation and frequent mutations resulting in numerous different species.

The "confusion of stands" in the rainforest means that any given acre of timber land is usually heterogeneous, frequently containing from 15 to 30 different species! Why the stands of timber are mixed rather than uniform is obscure, but the economic consequence is clear: Confusion of stands increases the cost of gathering the forest products. (The cost of logging mahogany, for example, would be lower if pure stands of mahogany existed.)

The large size of tropical trees is an advantage that, to some extent, counteracts the lack of pure unmixed stands. Many soar 150 to 180 feet into the air. As a consequence, the *volume* of timber that can be harvested from an acre is great. The large size of its trees is one reason why Brazil ranks so high among the nations in quantity of wood logged.

Most tropical woods are hard and very heavy—indeed, some are too heavy to float. In fact, since almost all these woods are too hard to work easily, many tropical countries with a surplus of *trees* have to import *lumber* from the mid-latitudes for building materials and other purposes. One exception is balsa, a tropical wood that is very light; many natives of the tropics have been using balsa logs for centuries in the construction of rafts.

In addition to the rainforest itself, there are in the tropics zones of *light tropical forest*, which consists of shorter trees with thinner trunks. Here the trees grow farther apart and stand over a dense undergrowth of shrubs and grass. All told, the tropical forests constitute nearly half of the world's woodland.

By contrast, the forest resource of the *mid-latitudes* is characterized by fewer species, purer stands, and a mixture of softwoods and hardwoods. The original settlers of the New World often established their villages near pure stands of timber, and today the countryside is still dotted with communities bearing such names as Maplewood, Oak Ridge, Elm Grove, and Pine Village. The purity of stand has important economic consequences, for when foresters work a given stand of timber in the mid-latitudes they can concentrate on gathering one kind of wood. Being able to harvest whole groves rather than isolated trees means, in effect, that they can employ mass-production techniques, with all the resulting savings of time and expense.

The forest resource of the mid-latitudes is distributed according to the regional patterns of hardwoods and softwoods. The hardwood belt is located along the side toward the Equator of the mid-latitude forest region. This belt is typified by oak, chestnut, hickory, maple, birch, and beech. We find only a few softwoods in this region. Originally, hardwoods were distributed over the eastern United States and over Europe from the Baltic to the Mediterranean, with the belt narrowing into western Siberia. Most of China and Korea, too, were once forested with hardwoods; parts of Japan and Manchuria still are. In the Southern Hemisphere this northern hardwood belt has only limited counterparts: the narrow coastal fringes of Chile, southern and eastern Australia, New Zealand, and the tip of Africa.

The softwood belt is much vaster and occupies the poleward flanks of the mid-latitude forests. In Eurasia it forms the world's single largest forest zone, stretching 7000 miles from Scandinavia to eastern Siberia, where it fans out broadly to nearly 2000 miles. It stretches on across North America from Alaska to Labrador; on the west it reaches southward along the Pacific Coast, extending even into Mexico. On the east there is a detached segment in the southeastern United States. The most common trees in this softwood belt are pine, spruce, fir, and larch.

Mixed forests, consisting of both hardwoods and softwoods, are typical of a transition strip that runs along between the hardwood and softwood belts.

The trees in the mid-latitudes are generally smaller than those in the tropics. Yet there is one notable excep-

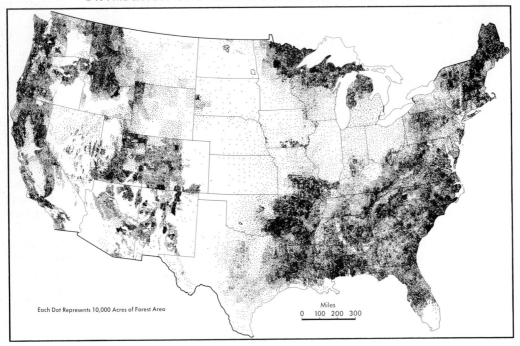

Each Dot Represents 10,000 Acres of Forest Area

Miles
0 100 200 300

Figure 6-2   (From U.S. Department of Agriculture.)

tion to this general rule: The earth's tallest trees grow in the fir and pine forest of northern California, where giant redwood *sequoias* attain heights of 300 feet and diameters of 20 feet. Douglas fir trees in this region grow 250 feet tall and have trunks that measure 6 feet across.

Although accurate data are not available for the volume of timber now standing in the world's forests, such measurements have been compiled for the United States by the Forest Service. These indicate that four states dominate our volume of sawtimber: Oregon, Washington, California, and Alaska, which contain respectively 19 per cent, 13 per cent, 11 per cent, and 7 per cent of the nation's total resource—50 per cent altogether.

Climate.   There is a close correlation between moisture supply and forests. Except where average temperatures are too low or drainage too poor, most of the wet regions of the world were tree-covered. It is difficult to generalize on the number of inches of precipitation required for satisfactory tree growth. Forests in the tropics are associated with 60 or more inches of rain a year, while in Canada and Siberia, forests exist in areas that receive only 10 inches. In part this discrepancy can be explained by this condition: In regions of high average temperatures, the rate of evaporation is also high, consequently more precipitation is required to support trees. In any case, trees require more water than grass and shrubs, because trees have larger transpiring surfaces than other plants have.

Trees also require temperatures favorable to the

annual formation of new shoots that need time to mature sufficiently to survive the dormant season. The average temperature during the warmest month must be at least 50°. Since summers become progressively cooler and shorter toward the poles (or upward in highlands) the forests consist of fewer and shorter and smaller trees along the poleward margins of the great softwood belt across Eurasia and North America as well as along the lofty highlands to the south. At high latitudes as well as high altitudes trees cannot survive at all and give way to *tundra*—a stunted growth of shrubs and lichens.

Thus, a warm, moist climate tends to favor maximum forest growth. This explains why in the United States the greatest volume of new sawtimber growth is not in the Northwest but in the South where the forests are *adding* a net volume of about five billion board feet of lumber each year.

That the most luxuriant forests develop in warm, humid regions serves, as we have seen, as both a blessing and a curse to the gatherers in the tropical rainforests. On the one hand the volume of tree growth is large, but on the other hand there is a profusion of species in confused stands. Furthermore, since physical activity is burdensome in a hot, humid climate, a forester in the tropics is likely to produce less than a forester in the mid-latitudes. To complicate matters, the muddy ground in many tropical areas makes it difficult to transport products after they have been gathered. And the *lianas* and other climbing plants—giant vines which thread their way like huge cables running from tree to tree—fostered by such climates are no help. For vines impede the movement of the lumbermen through the forest, and after a tree trunk has been severed, the tree itself sometimes remains standing, held upright by these vines.

Soils.   But warm weather and plenty of rain are not enough, for water that evaporates or runs off the surface is of no use to plants. The soil around the tree roots must be able to retain enough of the precipitation to remain moist throughout the year, since trees are *perennials*, not annuals. Therefore, to overcome short periods of drought, roots of trees drive much deeper than do those of the grasses, which are *annual* plants. This is why green trees may be surrounded by parched grass in an area suffering from a short dry spell. If the dry season lasts too long, however, the trees will die. Thus, not only must the annual supply of moisture be adequate in itself, but the subsoils of the region must also be able to retain it throughout the year.

Apparent exceptions to this rule are the pine forests in the southern United States (from Virginia to Texas) and in southern France. In these places the soils are sandy and the rain sinks rapidly into the ground. But pine trees are able to thrive on sandy soils by driving their roots extremely deep into the subsoil supply of water.

Streams and Rivers.   Water courses are essential to forest gathering. In both the tropics and the mid-latitudes, they provide the main arteries of transportation for the products that are lumbered or collected from the forests. In the higher mid-latitudes, where the streams are frozen during the winter months, forest harvesting follows a regular seasonal pattern. In the colder stretches of North America and Eurasia, the foresters spend the long winters transporting logs by

Rafting on the Coos Bay River, Oregon. (*Courtesy Weyerhaeuser Company.*)

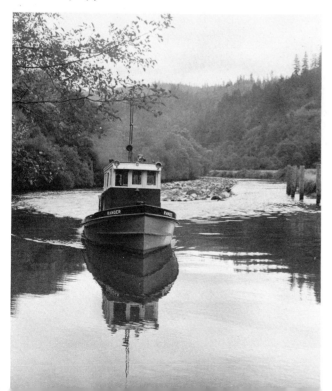

sled over the snow-covered countryside to the banks of the frozen streams. By early springtime, the river banks are lined with great piles of logs—the fruits of the winter harvest. When the return of warm weather breaks up the river ice, the streams once again become thoroughfares down which the logs are floated to sawmills and river ports.

The orientation of rivers in a forest region is critical. Where the streams flow in the general direction of the final market, as in Sweden, Finland, and southern Canada, production and marketing costs are relatively low. But where they flow in the opposite direction, as in northern Russia and on the West Coast of the United States, the trip to market must be roundabout and correspondingly more expensive. Where the rivers flow into the sea, however, the cheapest form of transport on earth (ocean transport) becomes available for the remainder of the journey.

Where the general trend of flow is poleward, seasonal flooding imposes a severe handicap on foresters. The rivers of the northern U.S.S.R., for example—the Dvina, Vashka, and Pechora in European Russia, and the Ob, Yenisey, and Lena in Siberia—all flow toward the north. During the winter, all these rivers are frozen over. Then, with approaching springtime, the southern portions naturally begin to thaw first, while the downstream portions to the north are still ice-blocked. The thaw water rushes downstream and floods out over the river banks of the still frozen stretches. Orderly log drives become extremely difficult to conduct, and even the logs piled up along the banks are sometimes floated away by the flooding water.

Topography.   Irregular terrain favors the growth of forests by discouraging competing types of land use. This was true "in nature" as well as after man's appearance on the scene. In drier climates like that of southern California, for example, the warmer lowlands produced a natural growth of grass and shrubs, while the cooler, moister mountains developed a coverage of trees. The same relationship has persisted in forested regions where man has cleared the low, level lands for farms, leaving the rougher land in trees.

Thus, we can say that if moisture, temperature, and subsoil conditions are satisfactory, forests tend to be associated with high lands in regions of irregular topography. In North America, the three southerly prongs of the mid-latitude softwood belt correspond to three mountain ranges—the Appalachian, the Rocky, and the Cascade-Sierra Nevada.

Unfortunately, however, rough terrain handicaps workmen. The steep slopes impede the transportation of equipment into the forest, the actual harvesting of timber and other products, and the transportation of products out of the forest. It so happens that some of the best forests in the mid-latitudes—in parts of Scandinavia and western Canada and the United States—are associated with just this sort of topography. Precipitous waterfalls and treacherous rapids make log drives difficult and, on some rivers, quite impossible. The locational pattern of forests in Europe (Figure 6-3) gives evidence of many of the relationships cited so far with topography, climate and soils.

Role of Animals. The fauna within forest regions both help and, more often, hinder forest gathering. In Burma and Thailand, for example, elephants are indispensable in moving teak logs to river banks where they can be floated downstream. But in the African forest the tsetse fly, a small, blood-sucking, disease-carrying fly that attacks cattle and horses, prohibits the use of animal power. Here large numbers of human beings are obliged to tug the felled trees out of the forests to the river banks. In Venezuela and adjacent parts of the Amazon Basin, a carnivorous fish known as the *piranha* poses a moderate threat to logging operations. Frequenting shallow waters at the river's edge, they often attack any unfortunate animal or human being that happens to fall in.

In the softwood forests of the mid-latitudes deer, hare and other browsing animals destroy tremendous numbers of seedlings and young trees. Yet the foresters encounter a firm obstacle in a sentimental public that favors laws designed to protect the deer herds from hunters.

Cultural Relationships

The activity of forest gathering depends on several human factors, especially demand, international trade, transportation, forest settlements, manufacturing, agriculture, government policies, and problems of forest gathering.

Demand. The largest single use of wood is for fuel. Worldwide, by percentages, consumption lines up as follows: fuel 46 per cent and industrial roundwood (for lumber, paper, railroad ties, and mine props) 54 per cent. In the United States the percentage breakdown is quite different: fuel 4 per cent and industrial roundwood 96 per cent (lumber 50, pulpwood 30, plywood 12, and other uses 4).

The main markets for industrial roundwood products are in the middle latitudes of the Northern Hemisphere—notably in the U.S.S.R., Europe, and Anglo-America (see Table 6-1). Nearness to these three market regions is one factor helping to explain why lumbering is more extensive and more lucrative in midlatitude forests than in tropical forests.

Notice how the relationship to markets influences forest gathering in the tropics. There is little demand

Figure 6-3 *(By B. F. Dietrich, courtesy* Economic Geography.*)*

DISTRIBUTION OF THE FORESTS OF EUROPE

A Sikorsky Skycrane helicopter delivers logs to an off-highway landing site in northern California from which they will be delivered by truck to a mill in Happy Camp, California. While being a rather expensive operation, this method has made many rugged and remote areas easier to log. (*Courtesy Southwest Forest Industries.*)

for industrial roundwood within this region either because there are few people (as in Amazonia, much of tropical Africa, and New Guinea) or because the economy is not very industrialized. Moreover, tropical forests are remote from customers. To be sure, this distance can be overcome, but transport costs are excessive in proportion to the price wood will bring. Still, lightweight products collected from tropical forests such as rubber and copra can be transported easily and they fetch a price that compensates for transport costs. Thus, the market handicap compounds the physical difficulties already noted. The combination explains why the world's most luxuriant and most rapidly regenerating forests are not the principal areas of forest gathering.

One particular source of demand—house construction— shows an interesting relationship with forest gathering. Within forested regions houses are, naturally enough, likely to be built of logs or boards. In Brazil and Colombia, for instance, many houses are of solid mahogany! Frame houses typify central Europe, eastern Anglo-America, the American Pacific coast, and Japan. But in southern Europe and China—where the forests have long since been cut—houses are of stone or brick or a mixture of earth substances plastered onto a framework of wood. Reeds from marshes or river banks often serve as base for the plaster. But since even in these generally denuded regions the *mountains* are usually forested, wood houses are common in highlands, such as the Swiss Alps, the southern Urals, and the Himalayas. Latitude has a comparable effect in Russia where log cabins and frame houses distinguish the north, sod houses characterize the grassland middle zone (though they are being replaced by wooden structures as the economy improves), and stone houses typify the steppe-desert region in the far south.

In other words, when wood is readily available and offered at a reasonable price it is a commonly used material. When scarcity or production costs drive the price up, people start substituting other building materials for wood. In the United States, for example, per capita consumption of lumber is falling and consumption of plywood is growing. Nevertheless, the per capita consumption of lumber and plywood together has dropped about 20 per cent since 1950. During this same period, however, the wholesale price of these building materials has increased substantially. Lumber is up more than 100 per cent.

One final observation on the location of demand and location of forests: The world's four chief clusters of population (see Chapter 2) are all in regions that were naturally forested. What accounts for this relationship between large populations and forest lands? Can it be that trees provided for more of man's needs (fuel, clothing, tools, housing) than did grasses and therefore attracted man in the early stages of his economic development? Then, as he developed into an agriculturalist, did he find it easier to farm forest land than grass land? This may seem inconceivable at first, but in the early days of farming—until very recently, in fact—only wooden plows were available, and they simply could not break up the matted sod of grasslands. Clearing land of trees took lots of work, but once cleared, such soil could be easily worked.

International Trade. The geographic separation of regions of demand and supply gives rise to a lively international trade in forest products. Most of the trade is southward—from Canada to the United States and from Sweden and Finland to Britain and Germany (Table 6-2). We can account for the high rank of some nations in both exports and imports by the fact that a country can grow a surplus of one type of wood yet be short of another.

Six nations stand out in relative terms as wood exporters (Table 6-3). Lumber and other shaped wood products and pulp are an important source of export income in Finland, Sweden, and Canada. Rough (unmilled) wood is a major export item from the tropical forests of the Philippines and Indonesia. Cork, lumber, other shaped wood, and especially pulp all contribute to Portugal's total exports.

Table 6-2

International Trade in Wood
(in Millions of United States Dollars)

Commodity	Major Exporters		Major Importers	
Fuel, wood,	(World	37)	(World	68)
and charcoal	France	6	Italy	16
	Yugoslavia	4	Finland	9
	West Germany	3	West Germany	8
Rough wood	(World	1,361)	(World	2,449)
	United States	301	Japan	1,327
	Philippines	215	West Germany	149
	Indonesia	157	Italy	127
Shaped wood	(World	2,365)	(World	3,072)
	Canada	832	United States	746
	Sweden	394	United Kingdom	562
	Finland	237	West Germany	293
Raw and	(World	36)	(World	33)
waste cork	Portugal	22	Italy	4
	Spain	7	Japan	3
	Morocco	3	France	3
Pulp and	(World	2,332)	(World	2,387)
waste paper	Canada	797	United States	491
	Sweden	548	United Kingdom	393
	United States	386	West Germany	280

Source: United Nations, *Yearbook of International Trade Statistics* (1974).

Table 6-3

Wood, Cork, and Pulp Exports as a Percentage
of Total Exports

Nation	Percentage
Finland	20
Philippines	19
Indonesia	13
Sweden	13
Canada	10
Portugal	9
Yugoslavia	4
Morocco	2
United States	2
France	1
Spain	1
Italy	less than 1
Japan	less than 1
United Kingdom	less than 1
West Germany	less than 1

Source: United Nations, *Yearbook of International Trade Statistics* (1974).

Transportation. For moving wood from forest to mill, men have threaded railroads and roads into forest regions to augment streams. But since truck and rail transportation are more expensive than the waterways, they have generally been constructed in only the accessible fringes of forest regions. In Scandinavia, flumes have been constructed (sometimes parallel to roads) for floating logs down to sawmills.

Vast stretches of mature trees in remote locations (for instance, central Canada, Alaska, Siberia, and also in the tropics) remain untouched except where river or ocean transport is possible. Thus, regions of forests and forest gathering are not coextensive.

Where railroads are used, often narrow-gauge tracks are laid down in the woods. As cutting moves from one location to another, the tracks are relocated. Such use of the railroad has usually been restricted to regions where waterways are inadequate for log drives. Railways are being superseded by trucks in this function, however, especially in the United States and Canada. Some of these trucks have detachable wheel mounts that are affixed to the rear ends of logs too large to load on a truck—occasionally, a loaded truck is 50 feet long. Since such trucking is usually developed in forested regions with rough topography (where rivers are tortuous) the routes are necessarily circuitous with many tight curves. A frequent sight on forest highways is a queue of autos trailing after a log truck snaking its way down the hillside.

For moving lumber from mill to market, man again augments waterways with railroad and truck transportation. In Eurasia, forest products are frequent commodities in the freight traffic of the Trans-Siberian railway and the railroads crossing the Arctic Circle to Vorkuta (just west of Ural Hills), to Arkhangelsk, and also to Murmansk. The same is true for the northernmost railroads in North America, those serving Fairbanks (Alaska), Churchill (Manitoba), and the several ports in Newfoundland. Within the United States the Great Northern and the Southern Pacific are among the railroads that connect western lumber regions with eastern markets. About 8 per cent of all railroad freight revenues come from the transport of lumber and wood products and another 6 per cent from pulp and paper products.

Nevertheless, tremendous tonnages still move to market by waterway from northern to central Europe, from Canada to the United States, and from northern Russia and Siberia to central Russia. For instance, huge rafts of logs and ships loaded with lumber move by sea along the Arctic coast of Siberia, through the Barents Sea, and along the Atlantic Shores of Norway. Other water "highways" for lumber are the gulfs of Bothnia and Finland, the Baltic and North seas in Europe, the Great Lakes in Anglo-America, the Pacific shores of Alaska, Canada and the United States, and the Pacific shores of U.S.S.R. and Japan. Considerable interoceanic traffic in lumber moves from Washington, Oregon, and California via the Panama Canal to New York and other eastern ports.

Logging truck being loaded at Clemons Tree Farm near Raymond, Washington. This particular area is being clearcut. (*Courtesy Weyerhaeuser Company.*)

Forest Settlements. Transportation routes converge on forest settlements, which thus serve as ganglia in the forest economy. Upon these points the logs and collected items come together from the forest; from these points they move on to markets. Countless such settlements are sprinkled throughout the world's forests. And there are numerous types of them. At one extreme are the temporary *lumber camps*, semipermanent settlements that serve the simplest functions: residence for workers and assembly point of outbound freight. Little sorting and no processing take place. Such settlements may be on banks of rivers where log drives begin, or at the junctions of minor roads or small railroads. Somewhat larger forest settlements may support the additional functions of sawmilling or manufacturing veneer or pulp. Still larger forest settlements may contain businesses supplying saws, ropes, and other equipment used in forest gathering. The largest ones contain headquarters of forestry firms and the financial institutions serving them.

At this point we should have a world map of forest settlements. But so far as the authors know, no such map exists. Before one can be made, somebody must devise a system for classifying *forest settlements*. Is it possible to distinguish *forest hamlets, forest villages, forest towns, forest cities*? If so, by what criteria? If not, what categories *can* be delimited? And when this is done, where does each type occur? Such a study would be a real contribution to economic geography.

Manufacturing. Lumbering invariably leads to manufacturing. Forest settlements, except for the very smallest, usually have at least a saw mill. Some places have a group of factories such as veneer mills, planing mills, or sash and door factories. In Finland and Sweden, many a stream flowing into the Gulf of Bothnia has one or more of these factories at its mouth.

In Europe, too, wood carving is a distinctive industry that occupies many farmers during the winters; their wooden carvings, dolls, and toys are exported in large numbers to America.

But the future will see wood used less and less as lumber or fuel and more and more as a raw material

from which scientists will manufacture paper, rayon, and alcohol, among other things. Necessity has already proved what can be done with wood. For instance, during World War II the Germans manufactured cattle feed from pulp, lubricating oil from stumps, and synthetic rubber tires from cellulose. Wood has so many useful by-products that it is a universal raw material. More and more the forester will play the role of provider of raw materials for factories. The remarkable aspect of this function is that forests, if properly treated, are a *renewable* resource in contrast to minerals which, once mined, do not replenish themselves.

Agriculture. In Norway we have found farmer-fishermen; we find farmer-forestrymen in Sweden, Finland, the northern U.S.S.R., and a few in Canada (and at an early date, in the United States)—men who till crops in the summer and cut down trees in the winter. This practice is restricted essentially to regions where the winters are too cold for agriculture.

Agricultural principles are being increasingly applied to trees themselves as the years go by. Cleared land planted in trees (in particular, rubber, cacao, banana, orange, apple, peach, pine, fir, and spruce) which are then protected and harvested is a farm as truly as if it were planted in corn. *Tree farming* is a type of agriculture regardless of whether the tree crop takes a century to mature (for instance, fir, pine) or just a few years (apples, rubber).

Governmental Policies. Forest gathering is influenced by govermental policies in many ways, three of which are reforestation, government ownership of forest land, and the taxing of private forests.

China, India, and Japan illustrate contrasts in governmental attitude toward reforestation. Each exhausted its virgin timber long ago. The Chinese and Indian governments did little about it. So today they are forest-poor lands starved for firewood (the people must burn manure in many places) and lumber (they have little wood for implements and even coffins). The

Japanese government, on the other hand, was one of the first to urge its people to plant trees on a large scale. Today growth exceeds cut. Indeed, 60 per cent of the land is now forested—an astonishing percentage for a nation so densely populated. In no country outside the tropics (except Finland) is so high a proportion of the land in trees.

Some nations believe that trees are a resource that should be owned by the public for both best usage and conservation. Canada's forests, which were not exposed to commercial exploitation until comparatively recently, are still largely (90 per cent) owned by the government. Where public domain was sold to private holders, some governments have repurchased land to re-establish forests. The United States federal government now owns 21 per cent of our forest land; state and local governments own an additional 6 per cent.

Government taxing policies influence forest practices on private land. Where such land is taxed at the same rate as crop land, the owners are discouraged from conserving trees. After all, it can take from 75 to 100 years to produce a tree crop in the mid-latitudes. Few men would spend $1000 in replanting trees on a piece of land knowing that neither they nor their son, perhaps even grandson, would realize any direct return on it—all the while paying regular taxes on it. Taxation policy is of significance in this instance not to good crop land but to *marginal* land—territory that might or might not yield an agricultural crop within a year. If regular taxes prevail, the owner will be tempted to plant an annual crop (say, wheat) that will yield an imminent return. But if lower taxes are assessed on wood land, he may decide to leave marginal land in trees or even reforest it.

Problems of Forest Gathering

Numerous problems stem from carelessness in forest gathering. The most important are cut-over, erosion, and floods. After describing them, we shall consider remedial measures.

Cut-over. This term applies to places where virgin forests have been removed without replenishing themselves. Two agents have usually been responsible. One is the farmer who wants land for tillage and considers trees as nuisances—something to be destroyed. This attitude motivated much of the land-clearing in the central United States. The other agent is the lumberman to whom trees are items of value. Together they have nearly deforested the populous areas of the world. China has suffered the most. Endowed ages ago with extensive and excellent forests, China now has trees on less than 10 per cent of its area, mostly in the remote and very hilly west and south. The forests of central Europe, particularly Germany, France, and Britain, suffered the same fate. The woods of New England, the southeastern United States, and the Great Lakes states were devastated as if by an invading army. Rarely in the history of man has a resource been so ravaged as were mid-latitude forests. As yet, the rainforest bears few such scars.

Erosion. Tree roots and the litter of leaves anchor soil in place. On flat or gently sloping land, trees can be removed and soil cultivated without danger of severe erosion. But moderate slopes must be protected at least with grass (such as pasture) which has roots deep enough to hold soil in place. But even grass roots are unable to bind soil to steep slopes. These must be left in trees, else through erosion the soil is speedily carried away. Conservationists estimate that a fourth of the original soil in the Mississippi Basin has been swept into the Gulf of Mexico. A good deal of this soil was originally firmly anchored by trees.

Floods. The litter of leaves and the tree roots also act like a sponge to retard the rate of run-off, whether of water from heavy rain or melting snow. When forests are removed the water rushes unchecked into the rivers. By carelessly removing trees, man has cursed himself with floods. To be sure, floods occurred in primeval forests occasionally, but man's modification of the landscape has increased both the frequency and severity of floods.

Remedial Measures. Man is learning his lesson and is beginning to practice conservation of forest resources. Conservation is a broad term that means, not preservation, but *wise use*. Two broad practices apply: reforestation and sustained-yield forestry.

These conservation measures are being practiced to an increasing degree by owners of forest land whether they are farmers on small woodlots, industrial companies (such as lumber and pulp manufacturers), or governments (national, state, county, or municipal). The conservation movement originated in regions of dense population and advanced technologies where the forest resource quickly gave out and where the exposed land was poor for farming. These conditions were met best in Germany, Sweden, and Japan, and they are where the movement started.

Reforestation is necessary in cut-over lands, which are handicapped for more productive uses, that is, if the terrain is too rough, the climate too severe, or the soil too poor for agriculture. Thousands of sandy acres in midwestern and in southeastern states are being reforested by high school conservation classes, by sporting clubs, by paper companies, and by government agencies. One of the first such ventures in reclaiming sandy soil occurred in "The Landes," a sandy region of southwestern France where an army of sand dunes was advancing eastward from the Atlantic, swallowing farms and villages. Shortly after 1800 the French launched a successful experiment to anchor these dunes with pine trees. Today the pine forest of southern France protects farms and settlements, and also supports a respectable business in naval stores.

The notion and practices of reforestation are spreading rapidly in the northern United States and northern Europe where land, once cleared for farming, is now being replanted in trees. Agriculture turned out to be a poor venture here for two reasons: Winters are too severe for most cropping, and soils that develop under softwood trees are poor for most crops. Much of the soil here is *podzol*. Now, some farmers are selling their farms to lumber companies, the government, or other agencies who then bear the costs of transforming the land from farm back to forest.

Even on acreage that is technically forested, tree-planting programs are often urged by forest specialists for the simple reason that natural regeneration of under-stocked land is just too slow. The federal government distributes over 500,000,000 seedling forest trees each year as part of their tree planting program; over 1,500,000 acres of forest land are planted annually. Although our sawtimber removals exceed net annual growth, we have finally reached the point where our net annual growth of growing stock (which includes both sawtimber and seedlings and other trees too small to be called sawtimber) is greater than annual removals.

Sustained-yield forestry involves three ideas.

1. The rate of cut must not exceed the rate of growth. This balance has already been achieved in Japan, Germany, and Sweden. The United States has achieved this objective—not in every part of the nation yet, but for the country as a whole. Our annual increment in volume of standing timber (growing stock) is 18.6 billion cubic feet; the annual cut is 14.0 billion. But in the West—where our best-quality wood occurs—cutting greatly exceeds growth. The reverse is true in the South and especially the Northeast where growth is now twice the rate of cut. This net gain in the East, however, is mostly from seedling and pulpwood trees while the net loss in the West is of sawtimber.

2. Cuttings must be small enough in extent so that surrounding trees may easily reseed the cut-over segment.

3. Trees must be protected from three major enemies: insects, diseases, and fire. Diseases such as heart rot, leaf mold, blister rust, oak wilt, and root diseases wreak more havoc than all other offenders combined. Regionally, disease is more devastating in the Northeast and the West than in the South. Fire not only destroys growth but also makes surviving trees vulnerable to disease and insects. Fire does more damage in the West and South than in the Northeast where more progress has been made in fire protection. Each year over 100,000 fires strike our forests; 90 per cent of them are started by man, some deliberately. Insects such as bark beetles, borers, weevils, moths, spittlebugs, and aphids do most of their damage in the West and the least in the North.

The key to the successful application of conservation policies rests in the hands of farmers and other owners of private forests who, together, hold the deeds to about 75 per cent of our nation's commercial forest acreage. The problem at this point is that the interests of most of these owners is *not primarily* in growing timber.

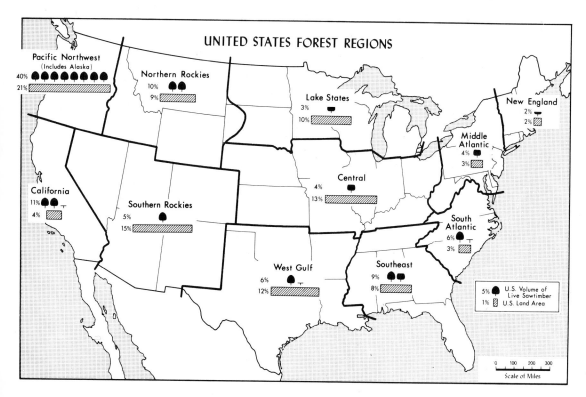

Figure 6-4

77

SUGGESTED READINGS

CHAPMAN, J. D., "Natural Resource Developments in Canada, 1970–75," *The Canadian Geographer*, 1976, pp. 15–40.

Clawson, Marion, *Forests for Whom and for What?* Baltimore, 1975, 175 pp.

DINSDALE, EVELYN M., "Spatial Patterns of Technological Change: The Lumber Industry of Northern New York," *Economic Geography*, 1965, pp. 252–274.

HAYTER, ROGER, "Corporate Strategies and Industrial Change in the Canadian Forest Product Industries," *Geographical Review*, 1976, pp. 209–228.

STOKES, EVELYN, "Kauri and White Pine: A Comparison of New Zealand and American Lumbering," *Annals of the Association of American Geographers*, 1966, pp. 440–450.

United Nations, Food and Agriculture Organization, *Yearbook of Forest Product Statistics* (annual).

FOUR

COMMERCIAL BIOCULTURE

Besides merely extracting (or gathering) commodities from nature, man also manipulates the natural creation of plants and animals he values. These activities will be the subject matter of Part Four. We shall use the term *bioculture* in this book to apply to all such collaborations between man and nature. Thus, bioculture includes all endeavors traditionally known as agriculture and animal husbandry plus others, such as fish farming and fur farming, in which plants or animals are raised for sale.

Activities whereby income is derived mainly from the sales of tended animals or their products will be considered first, in Chapters 7, 8, and 9. Chapter 7 deals with livestock ranching (or commercial grazing), in which domesticated animals are supported largely by natural forage and raised primarily for the sale of meat, wool, and hides. Chapter 8 covers dairying, in which domesticated animals are supported mainly by cultivated crops and raised primarily for milk production. Chapter 9 takes up "mixed" farming, where the emphasis is on production of both animals and crops.

The next two chapters are devoted to types of bioculture in which farmers specialize primarily in the production of commercial crops. Chapter 10 is on the "Mediterranean" type, which is distinguished by a wide variety of crops, while Chapter 11 deals with one of the most highly specialized of all agricultural endeavors: grain farming.

The last two chapters of Part Four will deal with a diversity of biocultural endeavors—Chapter 12 with miscellaneous cropping ventures and Chapter 13 with miscellaneous types specializing in producing animals. The end of Chapter 13 provides a summary of general facts and patterns about bioculture as a whole.

Throughout the chapters on bioculture it will help to refer frequently to five source materials:

1. The most important is the United States *Census of Agriculture*. For decades the United States government has published a periodic agricultural census that contains a wealth of data. For no other economic activity does the federal government compile and make available to the public so vast a body of information.
2. The government has also published the *National Atlas of the United States,* which contains numerous maps and generous analytical comments.
3. The United Nations' Food and Agricultural Organization *Yearbook* contains a wealth of data on biocultural endeavor in member countries of the UN.
4. *The Oxford Economic Atlas of the World* provides excellent colored maps of production and excellent data on international trade of biocultural products, as do the *Oxford Regional Economic Atlas of Western Europe* and the *Oxford Regional Economic Atlas of the United States and Canada.*

CHAPTER
7

livestock ranching

An infrequently used barn and corral on a ranchstead in western Wyoming, below the Tetons. This is a center of activity during roundups of cattle which graze the adjacent range much of the year. (*USDA Photo by Jonathan Write.*)

Location

The characteristic economy in several parts of the world is the tending of animals for sale (see Figure 7-1). In North America, the region extends from Canada to central Mexico and blankets a third of the United States. South America has two zones. The larger runs 4000 miles northward from Tierra del Fuego through Argentina and Brazil to the Atlantic; with only three interruptions it covers the southeastern third of the continent and actually penetrates through Chile to the Pacific Coast. A smaller counterpart occupies the coast and interior lowland of Venezuela. Livestock ranching is found all over that portion of Africa which is south of central Angola and Rhodesia except for most of the coastal areas. It prevails over a great portion of Australia and New Zealand—no other land masses have so high a percentage of space devoted to this economy. As in southern Africa, long stretches of the Australian coast are taken by other biocultural types. Livestock ranching is absent in Eurasia save for an area northeast of the Caspian Sea where this activity has recently replaced nomadic herding.

Characteristics

The bioculture of these ranching regions is strong on animal husbandry, with comparatively little crop cultivation. Although almost any animal could be grazed commercially, only certain ones are deemed really worthwhile, namely sheep, cattle, and goats. This is not to say that most of the world's number of these animals is in these regions but rather that these animals typify the bioculture here (for the distribution of sheep, see Figure 7-2).

The items of revenue are mainly wool and hides. Some meat is sold, but there is an increasing tendency to sell live meat animals to farmers in other regions that are better endowed to fatten them.

Scientific methods are applied in the care of both animals and their habitats. With the animals, for instance, breeding practices are scrupulous in order to upgrade strains. Herds are carefully protected not only from marauders but from parasites and diseases; on the most advanced ranches the animals are run through chemical baths and sometimes are inoculated against disease. Natural supplies of water are augmented by wells, which are often powered by windmills and pumps. Although the feed supply is largely natural forage, it is often augmented by alfalfa, grains, or other crops.

The habitat is tended in order to realize its "carrying capacity" to the full. Carrying capacity refers to the number of animals a given amount of land can support with its natural vegetation. The variation is great. Over the desert area of the southwestern United States 100 acres or more may be required to supply forage necessary for just one steer. In the steppes and mountain meadows the carrying capacity generally varies from 25 to 75 acres per steer. On the eastern margins of the Great Plains the capacity improves to 10 to 25 acres per steer. These figures can also be phrased in terms of "animal units" whereby, for measuring carrying capacity, one steer is equated with one horse or five sheep. If an area has a

Figure 7-1

LIVESTOCK RANCHING

Scale at Latitude 35°

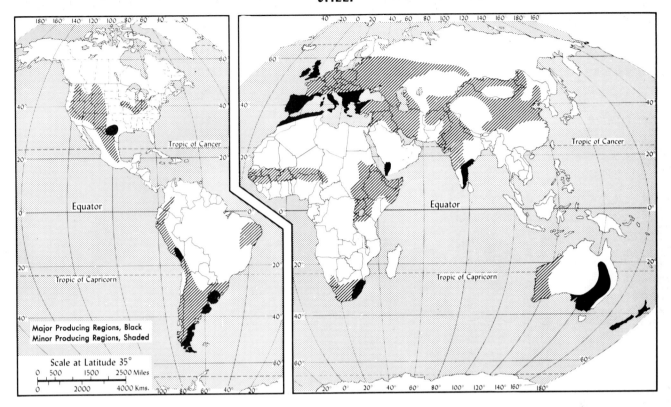

Figure 7-2 Distribution of sheep does not coincide with pattern on Figure 7-1 because sheep are raised as a sideline in many areas where livestock ranching is not the predominant activity.

carrying capacity of 10, a rancher could count on successfully raising 10 steer or 10 horses or 50 sheep or any combination thereof so long as the 10-unit figure was not exceeded.

A key role in controlling carrying capacity is played by the fence, a simple structure with a profound agricultural impact.[1] Essentially a fence protects a piece of range land by preventing interlopers from bringing the number of grazers above carrying capacity and so exhausting the forage. Further, the fence prevents the herd from wandering and interbreeding with poorer strains of animals; it also protects against marauders.

In contrast to nomadic herding, livestock ranching restricts the animals to parcels of land owned or leased by herdsmen or ranching organizations. The "operating units" consist not only of the natural pasture land but also the ranch house and often acreage given over to supplementary feed crops. Livestock ranching has the largest operating units of any type of bioculture. In the United States they frequently exceed 1000 acres. Ranches in Wyoming, Nevada, Arizona, New Mexico, and Texas are often over 2500 acres in size. One ranch in southern Texas encompasses 865,000 acres—over 1000 square miles. But the world's largest ranches are found in Australia where several spread over 5000 square miles; one Australian ranch even covers an astonishing 12,000 square miles!

[1]An interesting analysis of the significance of the fence to agricultural economy is "The American Fence" by Fraser Hart and Eugene Mather in *Landscape*, Vol. 6, No. 3, 1957, pages 4–9.

Physical Relationships

In many respects, livestock ranching is involved with the same kinds of forces as is nomadic herding, particularly the physical environment; on the other hand, some relationships are quite different, notably those with cultural phenomena, which we shall consider a little later.

Precipitation. Most commercial grazing occurs in dry lands. Dry climates prevail in five of the largest ranching areas—those of North America, southern South America, South Africa, Australia, and the U.S.S.R. Anomalies are New Zealand and portions of South America where climates are humid. Rainfall varies from less than 10 inches in the five dry regions to as high as 60 inches in the wet ones. Precipitation is significant in its effect both on natural vegetation (as we shall see in a moment) and on alternate possibilities of bioculture. Generally it is held that 20 inches of annual rainfall marks the limit for unirrigated farming in the mid-latitudes. Beyond that line, the drier regions are too risky for cropping and generally are devoted to animal culture. Most of the plants that can survive in dry lands are not valuable enough to cultivate. But animals can live off such scattered vegetation. This is the basic reason why animal husbandry rather than cropping is the prevailing form of bioculture on dry land which is not irrigated.

Natural Vegetation. For the above reason, livestock ranching occurs in regions of grasslands and

Cattle in Hill County, Montana, being driven to a summer range in the Beaver Creek Watershed. The animals are generally kept in protected pastures and corrals in the winter. (*Courtesy USDA, Soil Conservation Service.*)

desert shrub. But the correlation between ranching and these vegetation types is not complete since nomadic herders also occupy vast stretches of such environments. Conversely, there is some livestock ranching in forest zones—in coniferous forest in portions of North America and in "light" tropical forests in parts of South America and southern Africa. But in these anomalous regions, individual trees are far enough apart so a grass cover can develop.

The type of grass varies regionally. In the low latitudes are the tropical grasslands, generally termed savannas—such as the *llanos* of Venezuela, the *campos* of Brazil, and the *Gran Chaco* of Argentina-Paraguay-Bolivia. Generally, these tropical grasses are tall, coarse, and fibrous, so not very edible, and their carrying capacity is low. Yet some tropical grasses, which are softer and more palatable, can support animals fairly well and would provide rather good range land if their spreading could be encouraged. In a few places, strains of lusher African grasses have been sown in forest clearings in the tropics and, in some instances, seem to be taking hold satisfactorily enough to provide pasturage.

The mid-latitudes have the best grasslands: prairies and steppes. Prairies, however, rarely sustain a ranching economy for very long. Why? Because the rainfall in these regions, though inadequate for trees, does support tall lush grass, and tall grasses are particularly edible and lucrative crops—such grasses as wheat, corn, and oats, for instance, once grew wild but today are domesticated and often hybridized. Consequently, prairies have yielded to the plow and the cultivator, and the rancher has been replaced by the farmer. Not so in the steppes. With decreasing rainfall the carrying capacity decreases —but so do the opportunities for cultivation. Thus, in the mid-latitudes the principal domain of livestock ranching is the steppe. Marginal grasslands are also used, such as

the desert fringes adjoining steppes and grassland patches on the edges of forests that adjoin steppes.

Landforms and Elevations. Sheep and cattle are only slightly deterred by rough land, and goats are famous for their ability to scale steep slopes. There is little direct correlation, then, between ranching regions and landforms: Ranching occurs on plains, hills, plateaus, and mountains, in lowlands and in highlands. If mountains are high enough, they pass the *tree line*, above which grasses are unrivaled. If the country at these altitudes is not too rough, excellent mountain pastures prevail.

Temperature. In the mid-latitudes, variations in temperature are associated with a distinctive practice, called *transhumance*, in which herdsmen move their herds to different altitudes at different seasons. This system prevails in regions where the climate has one severe season, say, a very cold winter. The usual practice is to graze the herd on lowland forage in the winter when the mountain pastures are inaccessible and then in summer to move the herd to the slopes. This permits the lowland grasses to be replenished. Transhumance is not customary in mild climates where the highland meadows can feed a herd year around. In such places the lowlands can be given over to more remunerative forms of bioculture, and ranching is largely confined to the highlands. This is the case in southern California.

In the tropics, the combination of heat and humidity handicaps commercial grazing (particularly in Venezuela, Brazil, Paraguay, Bolivia, and northern Argentina); furthermore, animal diseases flourish in that climate, as do flies, ticks and other pests. Native animals that have developed a resistance to these environmental handicaps do not, unfortunately, produce the kind of wool, hide, and meat that man esteems. The best fleeces and skins are those of animals in the mid-latitudes.

Cultural Relationships

Population Density. Livestock ranching, not surprisingly in view of its physical requirements, is associated with low population density. The regions of commercial grazing generally have densities of less than 25 people per square mile and often less than 2 per square mile. To be sure there are enclaves of denser settlement, but these are based on some other type of economic activity.

Settlements. Livestock ranching regions contain two types of settlement: *dispersed* and *agglomerated*. The dispersed settlements consist of *ranchsteads* (the dwellings of ranching families plus associated buildings), each of which is located on its own ranch. This arrangement contrasts with the settlement patterns in the other economic regions we have studied—those of subsistence farming, of commercial fishing, and of commercial foresting (and also, as we shall see, of commercial mining) —where homes tend to be clustered together.

Agglomerated settlements in ranching areas are mainly service centers (see Chapter 27). A service center is a dual-purpose settlement found only in regions of commercial economies. One function is to assemble the surplus production from its environs (in this case, wool, hides, and so on from the ranches) for forwarding to major markets. The other function is to supply the producers in its surroundings (in this case the ranchers) with everything they do not provide for themselves. Such services are *tertiary* endeavors (see Chapter 1). In ranch country, there may be a little manufacturing, but typically these settlements are service centers rather than manufacturing centers.

What kind of work do people do in these ranching towns? *Employment structure*, which provides a breakdown by percentages of the employment in each economic activity for any given political unit, will be useful to apply here. Unfortunately, nobody has ever made a study of the employment structures of ranching settlements to discover what a "typical" ranching center is like. But Table 7-1 does give data for one ranching center which may be fairly representative. St. Johns is the county seat for Apache County, Arizona; its population has for years been about 1,300, and its main reason for staying in existence has been to provide goods and services for its own population and the people living on ranches in the surrounding area. Perhaps someday somebody will investigate the employment structures of all ranching settlements to discover what the group as a whole is like and how they vary among themselves, not only for St. Johns and other towns in the United States but also for ranching centers abroad, such as Torreón (Mexico), Ciudad Bolívar (Venezuela), Correntina (Brazil), San Jose (Bolivia), Puerto Casado (Paraguay), Kuruman (South Africa), and Cloncurry (Australia).

Table 7-1

Employment Structure of a Selected Livestock Ranching Center, St. Johns, Arizona

Activity	Percentage of Total Employment in Each Economic Activity
Manufacturing	7.4
Restaurants, bars, and service stations	8.2
Hotels and motels	0.3
Other services	3.0
General retail trade	14.8
Wholesale trade	5.7
Finance, insurance, and real estate	5.4
Transportation, utilities, and communication	0.9
Government and schools	54.3

The size of a ranching center depends on the amount of service demanded by its hinterland. Obviously, the small centers greatly outnumber the larger ones. Depending on the general density of ranches (which in turn depends on the carrying capacity of the land and the standard of living of the ranchers), the small centers may be from 20 to 50 miles apart. Any traveler in the American West, for example, knows how few and far between the towns are. Larger settlements are even farther apart. In the Great Plains of the Dakotas, Nebraska, Wyoming, and Montana, it is often 100 miles between settlements that have even 2500 people. In Nevada the distance reaches 300 miles.

The combined population in larger settlements makes up a rather low percentage of the region's total inhabitants, the proportion of rural to urban populace being high. According to the United States Census (in which a settlement must have 2500 inhabitants to be considered "urban"), the urban population in dozens of counties in the livestock ranching region is zero.

In brief, the settlements of commercial ranching regions are small in size, few in number, far apart, and account for only a small proportion of the region's total population.

Age—A New Economy. Livestock ranching is a newcomer on the world map. Whereas nomadic herding has been practiced for millennia, commercial grazing is little more than 200 years old. Not until the period 1750–1800 did world markets generate enough demand for wool, hides, and meat to support a commercial animal economy based on natural vegetation in the dry lands.

Western Culture. The physical environment of nomadic herding is essentially the same as that of livestock ranching. But the cultures are dissimilar. At one time nomadic herding was common to most dry lands with scanty vegetation.

But immigrants to the present regions of livestock ranching were mainly European farmers accustomed to tilling the soil. They found that the dry lands in the new continents would not permit satisfactory farming. Consequently they resorted to raising animals. Although they adopted the nomadic herders' means of existence, they shunned the nomads' way of living, retaining instead their European traditions such as fixed houses and private ownership of the grazing lands. Furthermore—and most importantly—Europeans had different notions of how animals should be tended in a dry habitat. Only they developed the ideas for advanced scientific animal culture mentioned earlier. Europeans also developed breeds of animals that produce particularly prized kinds of fleece (such as Merino sheep) or of hides and of flesh (such as Angus and Hereford cattle).

More recently, scientists have tried to cross certain breeds to develop a strain endowed with the resistance of tropical animals to disease and insects yet with the qualities of meat and hides attributed to mid-latitude animals. They have made some progress. Such strains as the Brahmin cattle, probably the most successful of this type, may herald a new day for commercial grazing in tropical grasslands. As more scientific methods are adopted to overcome environmental handicaps in Venezuela, Brazil, Paraguay, and other tropical grazing regions, it seems likely that their inherent environmental advantages can be capitalized on, thereby increasing their role in livestock production.

Markets. Ranchers do not use up much of their own product. In few other economic activities are producing regions so remote from customers. Livestock ranchers in the major world regions depend for their livelihood on two markets: western Europe and Anglo-America. In the early days of commercial grazing the demand was for hides, wool, tallow, and only slightly meat—and even that in dried form. Before the days of refrigeration, fresh meat simply could not stand the long trip from the western United States to the Atlantic Seaboard, from Buenos Aires to Berlin, from Capetown to London, from Freemantle to Liverpool. The population explosion and the increased purchasing power attributable to the Industrial Revolution of these two market areas triggered the development of commercial animal economies. Before these two world markets experienced the Industrial Revolution, their own economies were largely on the same subsistence level as the distant regions that subsequently yielded up surplus animal products.

Source of Personnel and Capital. It takes both money and people with ideas to build a commercial venture. Livestock ranching requires capital investments for fences, herds, lands, and hired hands. Europe and eastern Anglo-America served not only as the destination for products of ranching regions but also as the point of origin for much of the investment capital and personnel that established grazing enterprises in South America, western North America, South Africa, and Australia. Until rather recently, ranching areas themselves could not raise enough capital to finance ranching ventures.

Transportation. Commercial grazing areas are so far from their markets that cheap transportation is essential to their existence. Fortunately for the most distant ones (Australia, southern Africa, and South America), cheap ocean transportation is possible. Railroads converge from the grazing country on a few port cities such as Buenos Aires, Montevideo, Salvador (Brazil), Lobito (Angola), Capetown (South Africa), and Freemantle (Australia). In the early days of commercial grazing in the United States, southern Californians shipped hides and tallow clear around Cape Horn to New York and the East Coast. Galveston and New Orleans dockworkers still load ships with wool and hides, but by and large the American grazing region is dependent on truck movements rather than rail and waterways. Notice that on the world map of railways (in almost any economic atlas) railway networks spread over the regions of commercial grazing; however, the density of railroads is not as high as in more heavily populated and highly developed areas. It is ironic that the livestock ranchers, who historically were a major force in the expansion of railroads in the United States, now depend mainly on trucks. Some livestock products are still shipped by rail, but virtually no cattle are moved by rail in the United States today.

International Trade. Most surplus wool, skins, and meat must be transported across international boundaries to reach their markets. In some countries they attain rather high percentages of total exports:

Uruguay	81%
New Zealand	52%
Australia	37%
Argentina	33%
Paraguay	26%
South Africa	11%

The six countries all have mid-latitude grasslands except for Paraguay. Of the three items—wool, skins, and meat—meat provides over one-half of the export income in four of these countries. In Australia and South Africa wool provides over one-half of the total export income from these commodities.

There is a paradox involving regions of nomadic herding and those of livestock ranching. Since the foremost market for wool and hides is western Europe, it would seem that the nearest dry regions of steppe vegetation would serve that market. Northern Africa and the Middle East satisfy these environmental requirements and lie from 500 to 3000 miles from Europe. Moreover, the Mediterranean Sea links them to Europe. But environmental factors are not enough. Here is a vivid instance of the effect of cultural forces—Australians have bridged the 10,000 miles from their continent to England with wool and hide shipments while in northern Africa, though it is much nearer to England, the people have plodded along with nomadic herding.

Manufacturing. Valuable as wool, hides, and tallow are, their values are increased when their form is changed. Essentially the sequence of movement is from ranch to settlement to port—all on the way to the factory. In the days before commercial grazing, leather and textiles were largely manufactured by consumers at home or by local specialists. But with the dawn of livestock ranching woolen mills, leather factories, and meat packing factories mushroomed. (The development of these industries will be analyzed in later chapters on manufacturing.)

Farming. In two quite different ways, livestock ranchers find themselves involved with farmers. In some areas they ship their cattle to farmers in humid regions for fattening before final sale. This relationship holds particularly in North America where the ranchers of various western states collaborate with Corn Belt farmers.

On the other hand, as population has increased, the demand for food has risen, and new farms have been staked out, often on the humid margins of range country; the tillers of the soil have steadily invaded grazing land. Friction between farmer and rancher has flamed out many times in open feuds.

Now, it is a basic principle of bioculture that any given amount of land can sustain more human beings if it is used for grains and vegetables eaten directly rather than for raising animals for meat. The diet may be better and more enjoyable in the latter instance, but fewer individuals can be supported. Is it not likely, then, that as population mounts, farmers will continue to make inroads on ranching land, even resorting to irrigation, if necessary?

Without irrigation, indeed, cultivating these dry lands is extremely risky. Once the sod is broken by the plow, the soil is no longer anchored by grass roots, and upon drying out, the soil particles become vulnerable to wind erosion. *Dust bowls* (areas where wind erosion strews dust around like sand dunes) are the inevitable result unless there is enough rainfall to enable a grass cover to take root immediately. But annual rainfall in the borderlands between humid climates and dry climates is a rather unreliable affair. The critical boundary sweeps back and forth across a climatic no-man's land several hundred miles wide. For example, during one five-year period on the United States Great Plains the boundary between the *dry* and the *humid* climates oscillated from western Iowa to central Montana (see Figure 7-3). Tilling the soil is clearly a risky business in this transitional area. In United States economic history repeated waves of farmers have invaded this zone—their hopes aroused by a series of a few unusually wet years—only to be driven to bankruptcy during subsequent drought years. Left behind have been two monuments to man's ignorance of nature's ground rules: abandoned farmsteads and ruined land.

An interesting example of how both the characteristics and the relationships of a ranching region can change with the passage of time is illustrated by what has happened in the United States.

LIVESTOCK RANCHING IN THE UNITED STATES

As Figure 7-1 shows, livestock ranching is the predominant economic activity in over a third of the United States, a greater area than that of any other type of bioculture. It extends from Canada to Mexico and from an eastern border which runs through the Dakotas and western Texas almost to the Pacific Ocean. Twelve states are either totally or partially included in this region.

Clarence F. Jones, applying historical geography to commercial grazing, points out that 1880 separates two distinct periods: the *open-range* period and the *organized-ranch* period.

During the *open-range* period, which prevailed from

The Friona Feedyard in the Texas Panhandle. Cattle are brought in from the range and collected in feedlots like this to be fattened prior to shipment to markets. Feed and equipment are stored in the buildings in the background. (*Courtesy USDA, Soil Conservation Service.*)

BOUNDARY OF HUMID CLIMATES

Figure 7-3 (*After Henry Kendall, in Glenn T. Trewartha's* An Introduction to Climate, *McGraw-Hill, 1954.*)

the mid-1700's, commercial grazing characterized the western half of the country. Hides, wool, and tallow were far more important commodities than meat, which was either marketed in dried form or left to rot on the carcass after the hide was removed. The animals on which this economy was based were introduced from abroad. Many

of the cattle had been brought in by the Spaniards by way of Mexico. There were no operating units such as those that now exist. Animals were semiwild and were left to graze on the open range, little of which was owned by the men who owned the animals. At that time the federal government still held most of it in the public domain. Harvest season was round-up time, and the herdsmen and their cowboys roamed hundreds of miles corralling the wandering animals. Branding was an essential practice in these days for only by the brand symbol burned into the hide of an animal could a grazer claim possession of it.

During the open-range period, transportation was slow. Railroads had made only a few penetrations of range country (Figure 7-4), so most of the animals were driven long distances to the nearest railway station. In the earliest days they were driven all the way from Texas, Oklahoma, Colorado, and other grazing states to the northeastern market states.

These were the days of unbridled independence, of rudimentary law enforcement. Each cowman and sheepman was a law unto himself. Western novels, movies and television shows still embody the spirit of that age, or at least a reasonable facsimile thereof. These were also the days when there were no limits to the number of herdsmen, or to the number of animals, or to the extent of their wanderings. Such uncontrolled grazing exceeded the carrying capacity of the land. It overloaded the pastures and ruined thousands of acres of western dry lands, exposing them to wind erosion. It is doubtful that anywhere else on earth so much semiarid country has ever been destroyed in so short a time by wind erosion as the American steppes. They were laid bare both by overgrazing and by the cultivating of land that never should have felt the plowman's blade.

The *organized-ranch* period began around 1880. Well-planned commercial grazing now emerged. Several characteristics differentiate this phase from the preceding one. Meat was now the main cash item, wool and hides secondary. Since the emphasis turned to beef, cattle became the most numerous animals, especially the white-

RAILWAY MAP OF THE UNITED STATES: 1870

FIGURE 7-4 (*From the Association of American Railroads.*)

CATTLE AND CALVES

1 Dot = 10,000 Head

United States Total
106,380,541

Figure 7-5 *(From U.S. Bureau of the Census.)*

Figure 7-6 *(From U.S. Bureau of the Census.)*

SHEEP AND LAMBS SOLD

1 Dot = 5,000 Head

United States Total
18,308,083

faced; reddish-brown Herefords and the black Augus (Figure 7-5), followed by sheep (Figure 7-6), and goats. Cattle received priority in the less dry regions, sheep and goats got what was left. The main sheep region today is in west central Texas although numerous smaller zones are conspicuous in Colorado, Utah, Wyoming, and other ranching states.

The chief new feature was the organized ranch. Tremendous pieces of land were purchased by private operators who fenced them in and built ranchsteads. They put in windmills, which became conspicuous features of the landscape, to power pumps in the wells drilled to augment the natural water supply. Similarly they supplemented the natural forage supply by growing crops which tided the animals through the winter in regions where natural grasses were dormant.

The railway network expanded, threading its strands into the grazing regions (Figure 7-7). Irrigation was developed (often from government irrigation projects) to expedite the growth of supplementary feed. The government restricted grazing on public lands—forests as well as grasslands—renting out the privilege each year to ranchers in accordance with the capacity of the range. In 1934 the government's policy was formalized in the Taylor Grazing Act, which divided the public domain into numerous *grazing districts* in which privileges could be leased, established rules and regulations for grazing, and provided for the hiring of personnel to supervise these rules. Over 150,000,000 acres are now in these grazing districts.

Another development in the organized-ranch period was a closer collaboration between ranchers in the West and farmers in the Midwest and East. It came about this way. Animals lose weight in transit from range to market. Moreover, the short grass of ranch country is insufficient for producing cattle as fat as can be produced in the Corn Belt. In the days when the main cash product was hides, this was no handicap. But when meat became the premium product, the animals either had to be shipped to a humid region for fattening, or fattening feeds had to be imported to the dry lands—or grown locally under irrigation. Since the final markets were mostly in the East it made sense to ship the lean steers eastward, first for fattening and then for slaughtering. At the turn of the century farmers as far east as New York

Figure 7-7 *(From the Association of American Railroads.)*

RAILWAY MAP OF THE UNITED STATES: 1890

Part of a ranch near Eads in southeastern Colorado. The windmill is used to pump groundwater to the surface for the livestock. In only a few parts of this region is groundwater economically usable for the irrigation of crops. (*Courtesy Clair A. Shenk.*)

were getting animals through the Buffalo stockyards for fattening on their farms. Today this is a thriving business throughout the humid Midwest along the routes from ranch to market.

With the swing to meat, ranching became more sensitive to economic booms and depressions of the general economy, since there is a close relationship between beef consumption and general prosperity. Only the most prosperous peoples consume much beef, and their demand plunges sharply with depressions.

As late as 1900 the United States was the world's leading exporter of fresh beef and a major exporter of wool. Europe was the principal customer. Europe is still an important customer but the United States has reversed position to become an importer of wool, hides, skins, and meat. This reversal resulted from several forces: The American market has expanded so much that there is no longer a surplus for export; other forms of agriculture invaded ranch territory; and vigorous competition from more recently developed ranches in the Southern Hemisphere captured the European market.

SUGGESTED READINGS

CARLYLE, W. J., "Livestock Markets in Scotland," *Annals of the Association of American Geographers*, 1975, pp. 449–460.

CROWLEY, JOHN M., "Ranching in the Mountain Parks of Colorado," *Geographical Review*, 1975, pp. 445–460.

DORAN, MICHAEL F., "Antebellum Cattle Herding in the Indian Territory," *Geographical Review*, 1976, pp. 48–58.

KOLLMORGEN, WALTER M., and SIMONETT, DAVID S., "Grazing Operations in the Flint Hills-Bluestem Pastures of Chase County, Kansas," *Annals of the Association of American Geographers*, 1965, pp. 260–290.

MEALOR, W. THEODORE, JR., and PRUNTY, MERLE C., "Open-Range Ranching in Southern Florida," *Annals of the Association of American Geographers*, 1976, pp. 360–376.

SPRAGUE, HOWARD B., editor, *Grasslands*, Washington, 1959, 406 pp.

commercial dairy farming

Dairy cattle grazing in Trout Lake, Washington. In this case the Meadow Foxtail in the pasture is being browsed in a rotation grazing program. (*Courtesy USDA, Soil Conservation Service.*)

For hundreds of years men in certain parts of the world have consumed animal milk, principally from cows although the milk of goat, sheep, buffalo and reindeer is used in some places. On the other hand, some peoples —as in portions of Africa—consider animal milk to be excrement and so refuse to partake of it. But among people whose cultural traditions are favorable, milk has long been a staple food. Through most of human history, milk has been produced on a subsistence level. What little was sold commercially came from general farmers. Only within the past 100 years has there been much specialization by farmers in milk production. Today, however, there are thousands of farmers who gear their enterprise to production of this salable fluid. From many dairy farms, though, milk is not the only commodity sold; income is augmented by sale of eggs, poultry and other items.

Location

There are three main regions where commercial farms derive a major portion of their income from the sale of milk (Figure 8-1). The largest is in western Europe, a belt extending 2,000 miles from the Atlantic Coast almost to Moscow. A continuation of this belt runs east of Moscow. The second dairy region, that of Anglo-America, is likewise a belt, this one beginning at the Atlantic Coast and running 2,000 miles inland to the Prairie Provinces of Canada. Dairying is the prevailing

type of bioculture in eastern Pennsylvania, New York, every New England state, the St. Lawrence Valley of Canada, the Ontario peninsula, and the states of Michigan and Wisconsin. For all its fame for wheat, Minnesota is largely a dairy state. The third region, again a belt, is halfway around the world—in Australia, Tasmania, and New Zealand.

Two other types of dairy areas appear by the hundreds as small pockets, but they are too widely dispersed and too small to show up on a world map. In one type, dairy farms hover around cities outside the main dairy belts in Europe and Anglo-America, and around cities in Latin America and South Africa; each zone radiates outward from a city for only a few miles, displacing the prevailing type of bioculture, whatever it might be, in the general region. In the second type, minute areas are tucked away in valleys (some irrigated) of the western United States; they dot the Pacific coast from San Diego, California, to Vancouver, British Columbia (the general distribution is shown by dots in Figure 8-1).

From the standpoint of world milk production, the leading countries are listed in Table 8-1. The U.S.S.R., United States, France, and West Germany are the leaders, in that order. However, when weight of milk per milking cow is the criterion, then the noteworthy countries are the United States, the Netherlands, Japan, and Denmark (Table 8-1).

Figure 8-1

DAIRY FARMING

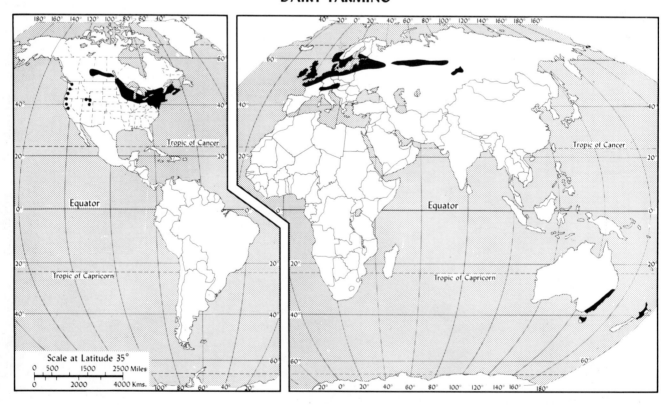

Table 8-1

Ch. 8 / Commercial Dairy Farming

Milk Production for Selected Countries

Area	Annual Production 1,000 Metric Tons	Kilograms of Milk per Milking Cow
WORLD	374,823	1,856
Africa	10,180	485
South Africa	2,850	2,591
Sudan	1,400	549
North America	68,472	3,406
United States	54,557	4,659
Canada	8,041	3,216
South America	19,883	988
Brazil	8,100	821
Argentina	5,000	1,976
Asia	28,682	629
India	8,100	476
Japan	4,939	4,396
Europe	151,529	3,114
France	29,177	3,445
West Germany	21,318	3,909
Poland	15,150	2,500
United Kingdom	14,200	4,057
Italy	9,180	2,900
Netherlands	8,860	4,520
East Germany	7,250	3,356
Czechoslovakia	4,900	2,619
Denmark	4,500	4,049
Spain	4,400	2,362
Ireland	3,750	2,500
Oceania	13,477	2,559
Australia	7,130	2,460
New Zealand	6,289	2,700
U.S.S.R.	82,600	2,004

Source: United Nations, *Production Yearbook* (1973).

Characteristics of The United States Dairy Belt

Although the principal type of bioculture in all these regions is milk production, there are regional differences that warrant separate consideration. We shall look at the United States dairy belt first.

Number and Size of Farms. In the United States there are approximately 260,000 dairy farms, roughly one out of every seven commercial farms in the nation. The average size is around 250 acres; however, the range in size is considerable, since many are less than 100 acres and many exceed 300. Generally, the shorter the distance to a major city and the better the land, the smaller the dairy farm tends to be. Altogether, the dairy farms of the nation occupy almost 65,000,000 acres of land.

Cows. The number of milk cows per farm varies. A one-man farm may have only 10 or 12; a farm with hired labor may have 100; the average is around 37. Breeds have been developed through the years to produce particular types of milk. The Holstein, a large cow, yields the most milk, but the yield is low in butterfat. The Jersey, a small animal, yields the least amount but the richest in butterfat. Between these extreme types are the Guernsey, Brown Swiss, Ayrshire, and other breeds. A dairy cow does not begin to give milk until two years of age; on the average the milking lifetime lasts about three or four years. The lives of dairy cows contrast with those of beef cattle, which mature quickly and make the trip to market at the age of two.

All the best breeds of dairy cattle, whether in the Netherlands, Denmark, or England, whether in Maine, Wisconsin, or Oregon, whether in Australia or New Zealand were developed in Europe—Guernseys and Jerseys from the Channel Islands, Ayrshires from Scotland, Holstein-Frisian from the coastal lowlands of Netherlands and Germany, the Brown Swiss from Switzerland.

Milk Sales. Unquestionably, by revenue the main commodity on these farms is derived from milk cows; other supplementary income is received from the sale of calves, eggs, poultry, and swine. But more than three-fourths of the income of most dairy farmers derives from the sale of dairy products. Milk is sold either as fluid *market milk* or as *manufactured milk*, the latter being purchased by creameries, dairies, and other factories that turn it into cheese, butter, powdered milk, condensed milk, or ice cream mix. All told, the nation's milk cows annually produce dairy products valued at approximately $5.5 billion.

On Figure 8-2, which shows the distribution of milk cows in the United States, it is clear that the main dairy belt is split into an eastern portion (especially New York

Figure 8-2 *(From U.S. Bureau of the Census.)*

MILK COWS

1 Dot = 1,000 Head

United States Total
11,174,521

ALFALFA CUT FOR HAY

1 Dot = 5,000 Acres

United States Total
22,139,038

Figure 8-3 (*From U.S. Bureau of the Census.*)

State and eastern Pennsylvania) and a western one (mainly Wisconsin, Minnesota, and fringes of Illinois and Iowa). The western valleys, particularly the Puget Sound, Snake, San Joaquin, and those in the Los Angeles area all stand out conspicuously too.

Wisconsin is unquestionably the leading milk-producing state. Its dairymen sell $783,000,000 worth of dairy products annually, which is 14 per cent of the national total. Other leaders are New York with $530,000,000, California with $401,000,000, and Pennsylvania with $385,000,000.

Other Animals. Milk revenues are augmented by the sale of calves, old dairy cows, poultry, eggs, and swine. There is always a surplus of calves because the breeding of the cows, to keep the milk flowing, automatically means more calves than are required to maintain the size of the herd. Veal thus originates largely in the dairy belt. There is some sale, too, of old beef, though it never brings a high price because the beef market is met primarily by Hereford, Angus and other cattle bred specifically for that purpose in other regions (see Chapter 7). Poultry and eggs bring supplementary income; the fowl are fed largely on skim milk, a by-product from the sale of cream, or whey, a by-product from the manufacture of cheese. Swine likewise enable the dairy farmer to convert otherwise waste material (whey or skim milk) into a salable product. (Of course some grains and other solid foods must be grown to supplement the diet of the poultry and swine.)

Land Use. The average American dairy farmer allocates his 250 acres as follows: He has 162 acres in cropland and harvests 107 of these acres (33 in corn, 23 in hay, 14 in oats, 5 in wheat, 4 in soybeans, and the remainder in a variety of minor crops). Unharvested cropland includes that which is used only for pasture, that planted in unused cover crops, that on which all crops failed, and idle land. About 53 acres are in noncropland pasture and range, which supports the cattle in spring, summer, and fall. Approximately 13 acres are devoted to farmstead and feed lot (for poultry, swine, and calves), vegetable gardens, roads, and other such uses. A surprising amount of acreage (22) is in woodland which is not pastured.

Crops. The main purpose of growing crops is to feed the animals during the winter when pastures are dormant. The three most common crops are hay, corn, and oats, as we saw in the acreage allocation above. Yet many dairy areas are deficient in hay (for the distribution of alfalfa see Figure 8-3) and must bring it in from adjoining regions. For example, the Los Angeles area still produces a great deal of milk, but the dry land there grows little natural forage. Some hay is irrigated, but most is trucked in from the San Joaquin Valley and other nearby areas of production; copra feed comes from the Philippines. Dairymen in Wisconsin and Michigan have to buy corn, oats, and hay from farmers of richer croplands to the south. When occasional droughts hit the dairy region, hay is trucked into Wisconsin from as far south as Tennessee. Corn grown on dairy farms is usually cut green, chopped, and stored in silos for winter feeding. Even more conspicuous in their purchases of feed are the drylot dairies that are frequently found near large urban centers. Because land is valuable they are usually fairly small in size; in many cases literally all of the feed that they use must be trucked in from outlying areas.

Research over a four-year period at a United States Agricultural Experiment Station at Marshfield, Wisconsin, indicates a correlation between yield of milk and type of crops fed to cows. When land is devoted to pasture, and cows are sustained by grazing it, the average yield is 4436 pounds of milk per acre. When the land is devoted to hay and grain—which are then harvested and fed to the cows in feedlots—the average yield is 5796 pounds of milk per acre. The advantages of the latter system (keeping cows in a feedlot and feeding them from the silo and hay mow all year long) is that the farmer can let his hay and grain mature completely in the field and then harvest them at the best stage of growth. Not all farmers, of course, face this option since much dairy land is not physically suited to growing grain (as we shall see later).

This family-run dairy farm is located near Lake Geneva, Wisconsin. Farms like this produce milk for shipment to large dairies, which handle processing. (*Courtesy Clair A. Shenk.*)

This is only part of a large dairy complex in southern Wisconsin. Here, dairy cattle are raised primarily on local pasture and grains. Milk and milk products are being produced in complexes like this for shipment to both regional and national markets. (*Courtesy Clair A. Shenk.*)

But the research just cited suggests that on those farms where more grain and hay can be produced than are now being grown, it might be possible to increase milk output by revising cropping and feeding methods.

Large Amounts of Capital Invested. In few types of bioculture is so much money invested per farm. Large amounts of capital are required for buildings, machinery, and stock, although the land itself is not as expensive as in some other regions. The average dairy cow is worth around $700, so an average-size herd is worth the price of a college education.

A small fleet of machinery—tractor, plow, drill, cultivator, mowing machine, harvester, silo-filler—is required for the crops. Then there are milking machines and milk-handling equipment, which must comply with sanitary regulations imposed by the government. Finally, a truck is usually essential.

But the largest investment is in buildings. A large barn is needed to house the herd during the daily milking routine and to store the winter supply of hay. In addition a silo is required to preserve *ensilage*—crops which are cut green and kept green for winter feeding (such as corn and sometimes alfalfa). Most states require still another building for handling milk—the *milk house*—to comply with sanitary regulations. The aggregate costs of herd, land, machinery, and buildings call for tremendous volumes in capital, often $100,000 and frequently more.

Labor Demands. No other type of bioculture requires the day-after-day, week-after-week, year-after-year, unrelentingly faithful attention of dairy farming. The dairy cow is a valuable possession and must be treated almost as thoughtfully and carefully as a human being. Carelessness can ruin a herd in a matter of days—a herd that has taken years of meticulous attention to build up. It takes scrupulous planning also to maintain an even flow of milk from the herd. Since it takes nine months for a cow to freshen (that is, to calve, and so to begin produc-

ing milk again), a farmer must arrange the breeding and freshening periods so that he is always milking essentially the same number of cows. In the average herd, only 80 per cent of the cows yield milk at any given time. The others either are too young or are between freshening periods.

The milking itself is a twice-daily routine. This is the requirement that ties the dairyman as close to his farm as a Chinese peasant. But caring for the cows is not the only work. A farmer with, say, 37 milk cows is likely also to have hogs and chickens to feed. In the summer there is corn to be cultivated, oats to be sprayed for weeds, and hay to be cut. Anyone who knows a dairy farmer personally can appreciate the tremendous number of things to be done—and the significance of what they call "bent-back work."

It all adds up to the heaviest year-around work load of any kind of bioculture outside the Far East. Many dairy farmers never take a vacation. Some Wisconsin dairymen have never been outside the state. The authors know of one dairy farmer in New York who, in 22 years, has been away from his herd only *one* day—to attend a county fair. He even spent his honeymoon on his farm!

Little Tenancy. Such a stringent demand for work discourages owners from renting their farms because the supply of dependable tenants for this type of farm is very small. For the United States as a whole, 13 per cent of all farms are tenant-operated, but in the dairy states (see Figure 8-4), the figures are all lower, as the following selections reveal:

Percentages of Farms Operated by Tenants

Minnesota	12
Connecticut	8
Wisconsin	7
Massachusetts	5
Michigan	5
New York	5
Maine	4
New Hampshire	3

Figure 8-4 (*From U.S. Bureau of the Census.*)

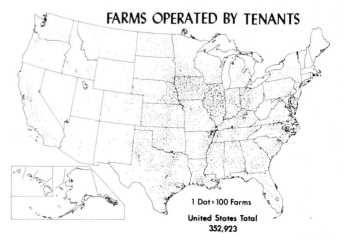

FARMS OPERATED BY TENANTS

1 Dot = 100 Farms

United States Total
352,923

Changing Characteristics. Currently the trend is toward more mechanization, larger herds, and larger farms. In recent years the total number of dairy farms and milk cows has decreased but the average number of cows per dairy-type farm and the value of products sold have both increased. Since 1964 the number of dairy farms has dropped by more than 25 per cent, but the average milk cow herd has grown more than 20 per cent and the value of dairy products sold per farm has risen over 40 per cent. An increasing share of the output of milk and other dairy products is coming from very large farms, but family-sized farms are also being expanded thanks to new equipment and other technological advances which allow for increased output per worker.

Foreign Dairy Regions

Essentially the same characteristics apply to dairying in other countries; however, a few exceptions deserve comment.

Canada. Canada is essentially a manufactural milk region. Although Montreal, Toronto, Quebec, Hamilton, and other cities form a market for fluid milk, many of the farmers of the Ontario Peninsula and Maritime Provinces send butter, cheese, and condensed milk to Britain. Comparatively little goes to the United States because of import restrictions designed to protect the United States dairymen. Typical Canadian dairy farms have more acreage in hay, less in corn and oats than do the warmer farms to the south.

Europe. Dairying is more intense in western Europe than in America because the man/land ratio is higher. Farms therefore are smaller, around 40 acres. Obviously such small farms are not based on natural forage; the farm is not a producer of feed for cows but serves only as a place of residence. The farmers import feed, usually as a more concentrated food than hay. Corn from Argentina and cotton seed meal from the United States are common. Farmers who do grow feed devote little land to pasture, most to crops. In the Netherlands, considerable salt hay is grown, it being one of the few crops that thrive on the polder lands—former sea bottom reclaimed from the ocean. Root crops such as potatoes, beets, turnips and rutabagas are the leading feed items because the very cool European summers discourage corn and oats. Considerable crop land is heavily fertilized.

Expanding urbanization is extending the fluid milk zones contiguous to cities outward into former cheese and butter districts. Thus, the city markets of France, Belgium, Germany, and southeastern Britain absorb most of the milk produced locally. Outside sources are being turned to. Thus, milk is now being brought from eastern Ireland to London. Manufactural milk for much of England now comes from western Ireland, Scotland, Scandinavia, Finland, Denmark, Switzerland, and the hills of central France.

In the mountainous sections of Switzerland and Scandinavia, transhumance is a distinctive practice; in summer the animals graze mountain pastures (termed *alps*). Dairymen migrate with the herds and manufacture cheese on the spot. But in the winter the dairymen, bringing the cheese made in summer, the herd, and even some surplus hay, move down to the valleys where summer-grown root crops can carry the herd through the winter.

Most of these manufactural milk areas are renowned for certain products. The Danes specialize in butter, for which they are world-famous. The Dutch specialize in cheese. Many cheeses bear the name of the area in which they originated: Edam is a town north of Amsterdam; Gouda is north of Rotterdam; Muenster and Limburger are cheeses of the German area. Every village in these localities has a cheese factory. Italians, too, are great cheese eaters, and the Po Valley is their leading dairy area. Because of Italy's dry, warm, sunny climate many meadows are diked and irrigated. Denmark is, relatively, the continent's leading dairy exporter in that 6 per cent of her sales are dairy products.

Within the European dairy realm, there is spatial variation in the style of dairy barns. Near the seacoasts, winters are mild and there is comparatively little need for sturdy winter shelter for the herd; but inland the barns are larger and sounder in order to provide more protection for the herd against the cold.

In the U.S.S.R., dairying has become the leading activity in a major region developed in the late 1920's in two former Baltic states (that is, Estonia and Latvia). On stony and rough pastures this dairy zone has spread eastward to Leningrad and Moscow and beyond.

New Zealand and Southeastern Australia. The lands Down Under are ideal for dairying. Grass grows in profusion nearly all year round. So there is little need for growing supplementary feed or for protective storage buildings. The Taranaki area on the North Island of New Zealand has one of the densest concentrations of dairy cows in the world. Dairymen there have developed highly efficient methods of pasture management, which have attracted study by visiting American and British agriculturalists. New Zealand dairymen are probably the most efficient producers of milk in the world, and can, even with the 10,000 miles of ocean to cross, put cheese and butter on the European market. Were it not for import restrictions in the United States, New Zealanders would probably compete successfully on that market too. Dairy products account for about 23 per cent of New Zealand's exports (by value)—the highest ratio in the world.

Cultural Relationships

Western Culture. Dairying is closely related to the western world. In many other cultures milk is either taboo or too expensive. Many Africans, as was mentioned earlier, consider milk to be animal excrement. In most of Asia the obstacle is insufficient cash. The people like milk well enough (Middle Easterners, for instance, typify the perfect land as one flowing with milk and honey), but just a little is produced, mostly on a subsistence level. Only in Europe and Anglo-America are there large numbers of milk-drinkers with the ability to pay for this food which is rather expensive (compared to rice, for example). Much of the expense is attributable to storage and preservation since fresh milk sours quickly.

Urbanism. Within the western world there is a close relationship between dairying and urbanism. The concentration of cities in eastern Anglo-America and western Europe is the basic reason for their having the world's two main dairy regions. But wherever there is an Occidental city—whether in Middle America, or South America, or South Africa, or Australia—there is likely to be at least a small ring of dairy farming around it. The city may be so small that the surrounding farmers produce milk only as a sideline, but settlements of 2500 inhabitants or more are likely to have a few full-time dairy farmers close by.

From this point on in this discussion of relationships, we will deal principally with the North American dairy belt, simply because of expediency.

The specific type of dairy farming in a dairy region depends to a large degree on the distance to urban markets. Invariably the farms nearest the city sell *fluid milk* to the urban dairies. Today, such milk must meet rigid sanitary standards and is termed *Grade A* milk. Other grades of milk (Grades B and C) come from farms that do not measure up to certain sanitation codes, and this milk is sold only for manufactural purposes. Grade A milk commands the highest price, so most farmers prefer to sell milk this way. But fresh milk is costly to transport, since it is both bulky (not worth much relative to weight) and perishable. Thus, there is a critical distance from every city beyond which it is uneconomical to transport fresh milk. Obviously, the absolute mileage of this distance depends on the size of the city, the rate of milk consumption, the price of milk in that city, the transport costs to the city, and the production costs to the farmer. Large urban centers may draw milk from as far as 300 miles away.

Milk Sheds. A *milk shed* is the area from which a city receives its market, or fluid, milk and is a tangible expression of the relationship between city and farm. Where many large cities are near together as on the Atlantic seaboard, the areas coalesce into one tremendous milk shed.

Every day without fail tank trucks, often bearing the name of city dairies, but sometimes operated by milk marketing associations, wear a steady path up and down the rural roads of milk sheds collecting fresh milk. Before the automobile era, the marketing associations were poorly developed and the milk was either hauled in by the farmers themselves or shipped in on milk trains. Today the milk trains have faded from the picture except for a few long hauls to very large cities. Even Chicago gets almost all its milk by truck.

Manufactural Milk Areas. But urban centers consume milk in other forms, such as cheese, butter, powdered milk, condensed milk, and ice cream. Only in smaller cities are these products manufactured locally. For large cities it is cheaper to pay transport charges on dairy products made in the manufactural milk areas. The reason is that fresh milk is bulky and perishable, whereas the derivatives are both less bulky and less perishable. Thus, these zones within dairy regions: Milk sheds are adjacent to cities, while the manufactural milk areas are farther out.

Within manufactural milk regions there is a further tendency toward regional specialization in cheese and butter. Cheese regions have traditionally been closer to markets than butter areas. The leading cheese states with their percentages of the national total are Wisconsin (31), Missouri (11), and Minnesota (10). But the leading butter states are, by percentage shares of total national value, Minnesota (34), Wisconsin (16), and Iowa (6). Two basic forces seem to be at work in determining the two somewhat different regional patterns: transportation and the cultural background of producers.

Transportation. It takes about 10 pounds of milk to make a pound of cheese, but a pound of butter requires about 20 pounds of milk. Thus, butter is the more economical form. This is one reason butter makers could, historically, survive farther from markets. The law at work is that if a raw material is turned into a product higher in value per unit of weight, it will bear greater transport costs to market. Thus, the overall pattern within a dairy region bears this out: The greater the distance between production and consumption, the more concentrated the dairy product in value per weight. Prices reflect this principle, too. Butter is more expensive than cheese, and cheese than milk. In the United States, for example, the average retail prices of these items by the pound have been roughly: butter 95 cents, cheese 74 cents, and homogenized milk 20 cents (in half-gallon cartons). Other manufactured dairy products likewise lend themselves to long hauls because they are not as bulky or perishable as fresh milk.

The transportation networks in dairy regions (particularly the fluid milk sheds) comprise the best systems of rural roads in the world—they are well kept because milk must be delivered quickly. Therefore, rural roads must be closely spaced, well surfaced, and open all year round.

Cultural Background of Producers. But the areal concentration of cheese and butter regions is more complex than transportation alone suggests. Otherwise rather sharp concentric boundaries would separate cheese and butter regions. Cultural background has historically been equally important, particularly in influencing the location of cheese-making areas.

When milk is curdled it separates into a liquid *whey* and a solid *curd*. The whey is waste but the curd can be pressed to form cheese. A wide variety of cheeses can be made, the particular type depending on two things: how the curd is treated, and what *molds* (or bacteria) are cultivated in the curd. The complex techniques involved in cheese-making constitute quite a study in themselves. But the significant fact here is that different groups have developed different traditions and aptitudes for cheese-making. The art is handed down from fathers to sons. In time, areas build up a reputation for a particular type of cheese—which in itself has value for advertising. This is a major factor explaining the regional concentration of cheese-making in such areas as "the heart of Swissconsin," and other cheese regions in New York, Pennsylvania, Michigan, Utah, and Oregon and, of course, in Europe.

Changing Patterns. Fluid milk sheds have flooded out into regions of manufactural milk. This expansion is related to the rapid growth of urban population. Once-famous cheese districts in central, northern, and western New York, for instance, have been engulfed by the great milk sheds of the Atlantic Seaboard. Former cheese areas in southeastern Wisconsin have disappeared with the advancing front of the Chicago and Milwaukee milk sheds.

Another development has been the appearance of condenseries and powdering plants. Techniques have been devised for concentrating and preserving the attributes of fluid milk in liquid and in powdered form. But these factories require fresh milk, a great deal of equipment, and, to operate efficiently, they must process large quantities of milk (in contrast to creameries and cheese factories that can be very small operations). Therefore, condenseries and powdering plants tend to locate where large amounts of milk are yielded in a small area.

The trend has been toward multiple-purpose plants, often operated by cooperative organizations, that are equipped to manufacture everything from cheese and butter to ice cream mix depending on demand.

Physical Conditions

The dairylands around cities are not perfectly circular, of course. A principle seems to be at work that dairymen use the poorer land while more remunerative forms of farming get the better land. This generalization needs qualification, however. Let us examine the individual components of the physical environment.

Precipitation. Dairying is associated with humid regions. Beef cattle and animals grown for hides and fleece may wander for miles in search of forage in dry lands, but good milk is not produced that way. The better pastures for dairying require 30 or more inches of annual rainfall, the critical amount increasing with temperature. Dairying in drier regions must depend on irrigated pastures (as in the valleys in Wyoming, Idaho, Utah, and California) or on forage imported from grass-producing areas.

Temperatures. A critical average daily temperature of 43°F. delimits the *growing season* for most forage grasses. This is an important factor. Regions that have an almost year-long pasture season offer a tremendous advantage, for a farmer can save on the costs of producing supplementary feed crops, on expenditures for machinery to handle those crops, and on investments for buildings to protect not only the supplemental feed but also the herd. Severe winters are the curse of many American dairy farmers and are responsible for much of his bent-back work.

Dairying is associated with cool summers, too. For one thing, the best dairy cows so far developed are cool-summer animals. They simply do not yield much good milk in hot weather. What is even more important, in the regions with warm summers farmers can grow crops such as corn, which is more remunerative than raising cows, at least in the American Corn Belt.

Soils. Forage grasses such as alfalfa, timothy, and clover tolerate poorer soils than corn and wheat do. The original natural vegetation in the world's great dairy regions was forest. The soils that through eons of time developed under those forests are grayish-brown in color and rather low in organic material. Termed *podzolic soils*, they are less fertile than those developed under prairies and steppe grasses. When men cleared off the trees in what are now the main dairy regions they soon discovered that the most prized crops—wheat and corn—fared poorly. But hay did well. Theoretically, perhaps, they could have switched to a hay diet, but they chose not to—an important geographic factor often ignored because it is so obvious. But dairy cattle convert that hay into a substance men do like—at least in Europe and America. Dairy farming is therefore an efficient use of rather poor soils. This explains in part the strange configuration of the American Dairy Belt in the portion which lies south and west of Lake Michigan. The belt's southern boundary swings northward to be displaced by the Corn Belt (which offers a more remunerative type of farming) in the good prairie soils of Chicago's Illinois hinterland.

In most of the American and European dairy belts, the soils are rendered even harder to work by boulders, stones, and gravel from glacial deposits. Though handicaps to plowing and cultivation, these substances scarcely inhibit the growth of pasture grasses. And the stones can be used to make good fences.

Topography. Dairying is closely associated with rough topography. Farm machinery can negotiate flat land devoted to crops, but rough land is better traversed by animals. Furthermore, pasture grasses do better on slopes than do corn and other tilled crops. If the land is very rough, woodlots replace pastures on dairy farms. Again the glaciers played a part, by dumping their sand, gravel, and boulders in irregular moraines which blanket much of the dairy belt with ridges and swamps, swells and swales.

Summarizing these several influences on the location of dairying, we may say that the main American and European dairy belts are essentially coextensive with the main belt of urban settlement. But within those great urban realms the dairy region is bounded on the *north* by severe winters (hence, too short a growing season for grasses) and soils too poor for pastures; on the *south* by high summer temperatures (warm enough for corn and other crops) and by better soils (good enough for more remunerative crops); and on the *west* (in America) by aridity (land too dry for the lush grasses required by dairy cattle).

The Pacific Northwest and The Southeast United States

A fortunate combination of precipitation and temperature spells out peculiar advantages for dairymen in opposite corners of the United States—the Northwest, which already has pockets of dairying in dozens of valleys, and the Southeast, where dairying has only recently been established on a large scale. In both these regions winters are mild; average January temperatures are 39° in Nashville, Tennessee, and 36° in Seattle, Washington. Both regions are humid: The Pacific Northwest highlands receive over 60 inches of rain a year; the lowlands get only 25 to 40 inches; but so much of it is drizzle and so many days are rainy (150 or more a year) that evaporation is low and pastures are lush. The Southeastern United States receives over 40 inches a year.

For all their advantages, though, neither region has many large urban markets. The dairymen of the Pacific Northwest, however, have developed cheese, butter, and condensing industries that sell to distant markets.

The American Southeast, for all its cities, has few large ones and has never generated a great demand for milk. Nor did its farmers choose to concentrate on manufactural milk as did those in the Pacific Northwest. Still, the economic revolution is now underway in the South (see later chapters on manufacturing) and is bringing with it an expansion of dairying. Perhaps in a few years the South too may be a major dairy region.

SUGGESTED READINGS

FIELDING, GORDON J., "Dairying in Cities Designed to Keep People Out," *The Professional Geographer*, January, 1962, pp. 12–17.

———, "The Los Angeles Milkshed: A Study of the Political Factor in Agriculture," *Geographical Review*, 1964, pp. 1–12.

GREGOR, HOWARD F., "Industrialized Drylot Dairying: An Overview," *Economic Geography*, 1963, pp. 299–318.

HALE, GERRY A., and GIBSON, LAY JAMES, "A City Designed to Keep People In," *Yearbook of the Association of Pacific Coast Geographers*, Vol. 33, 1971, pp. 161–171.

KYSER, DEWAYNE, "Change in the Rural Landscape of Southern Britain," *The Journal of Geography*, 1975, pp. 37–54.

LEWTHWAITE, GORDON R., "Cows in the Corn: The Emergence of the Tri-State Butter Region," *Proceedings of the Association of American Geographers*, 1975, pp. 113–117.

———, "Wisconsin and the Waikato: A Comparison of Dairy Farming in the United States and New Zealand," *Annals of the Association of American Geographers*, 1964, pp. 59–87.

———, "Wisconsin Cheese and Farm Type: A Locational Hypothesis," *Economic Geography*, 1964, pp. 95–112.

PATTEN, GEORGE P., "Dairying in Nicaragua," *Annals of the Association of American Geographers*, 1971, pp. 303–315.

WIKKRAMATILEKE, RUDOLPH, and SINGH, KARPAL, "Tradition and Change in an Indian Dairying Community in Singapore," *Annals of the Association of American Geographers*, 1970, pp. 717–742.

CHAPTER

mixed farming

Breeding sow near Bad Godesberg, Germany. (*Courtesy German Information Center.*)

MIXED FARMING

Figure 9-1

In commercial mixed farming, a farmer combines the cultivation of crops and the husbanding of animals *and* gets income from both. Mixed farming can, therefore, conveniently serve as a transition between the animal-raising economies just studied (ranching and dairying) and the crop-raising ones to be taken up in subsequent chapters.

Location

The two most extensive regions of mixed farming are in Eurasia and the United States (see Figure 9-1). This activity takes up more land than any other type of bioculture in Europe and is prevalent eastward in an ever narrowing belt that stretches from the Atlantic to the Pacific, with only one interruption in eastern Siberia. At its thickest point, between the Ukraine and central Finland, it is over 800 miles wide.

Mixed farming is the second most extensive type of agriculture in the United States, after ranching, and covers a large part of the eastern half of the country. It is the prevailing form of farming through Ohio, Indiana, Illinois, Iowa, and Nebraska on the north, and Virginia, Tennessee, Georgia, Oklahoma, and much of Texas on the south. Small areas of this type in the Pacific Northwest are intermixed with dariy farming.

Outside these two principal regions, the distribution is spotty: central Mexico, southern South America, southern Africa. Elsewhere there are occasional patches of mixed farming in the vicinity of Occidental cities; but, as is true for dairy farming, they cover areas too small to constitute important world regions.

Characteristics

Both Crops and Animals. On each mixed farm, crops are grown for sale and as feed for animals which are also sold. Only two other types of bioculture have significant places for both crops and animals: the Mediterranean type, in which some farms specialize in crops while other farms raise animals (see Chapter 10), and dairy farming, in which an animal product rather than the animals themselves is sold (see diagram, Figure 13.6, p. 154).

Role of Crops. Crops, then, play a triple role, being grown for animal feed, for cash sale, and for use by the farm family. The relative importance of each role varies from place to place within the mixed-farming regions. In some places, particularly Iowa and northwestern Illinois, almost all the crops are grown for animal feed. But in northeastern Illinois, in Indiana, and in Ohio, a considerable portion of the crops is sold. In many of the mixed farms of Mexico and eastern Europe a large share of the crops is consumed by the farm family.

1. Feed Crops: The most prevalent feed crop in the United States is corn. Compare the pattern of mixed farming in Figure 9-1 with that of corn, Figure 9-2. *The Corn Belt* is 900 miles long, running from central Ohio westward through Indiana, Illinois, and Iowa, where it fans out into Minnesota, South Dakota, and Nebraska. In the nation as a whole, corn occupies 22

CORN FOR ALL PURPOSES

1 Dot = 10,000 Acres

United States Total
60,402,153

Figure 9-2   (*From U.S. Bureau of the Census.*)

per cent of all harvested cropland, but in the Corn Belt states the percentages are much higher: 35 in Ohio, 47 in Indiana, 50 in Illinois, 52 in Iowa, and 34 in Nebraska. In the Southeast, the figures are also high (Georgia 45, Kentucky 31, Delaware 43). There, though, the yields per acre are low.

Wherever possible, farmers prefer to grow corn because of both its effectiveness in fattening animals and its large yields per acre. In the United States, for example, the average number of harvested bushels per acre is as follows: corn 85, sorghum 53, wheat 29, and soybeans 27. Moreover, virtually the whole of the corn plant makes edible ensilage.

Secondary feed crops in the United States are hay and oats. Notice how the region of mixed farming correlates rather closely with the location of oats and hay on Figures 9-3 and 9-4.

In Europe, corn is a major feed crop only in the Danube Basin. Over most of Europe hay takes the place of corn; potatoes, turnips, sugar beets and oats are also important as animal feed.

2. Cash Crops: Wheat is a main cash crop in mixed-

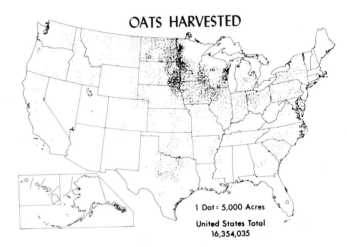

OATS HARVESTED

1 Dot = 5,000 Acres

United States Total
16,354,035

Figure 9-3   (*From U.S. Bureau of the Census.*)

Figure 9-4   (*From U.S. Bureau of the Census.*)

On this Amish farm near Lancaster, Pennsylvania, tobacco and corn are being grown while other fields are left to pasture. Grain silos and livestock pens are visible, as well as multi-purpose barns which are used to house animals during much of the winter. There are a number of houses on this one farm, testifying to the fact that Amish frequently live in extended family groups. (*Courtesy Clair A. Shenk.*)

LAND FROM WHICH HAY WAS CUT*

1 Dot = 5,000 Acres

United States Total
53,203,606

* Excluding sorghum hay.

A soybean crop and driers near Charleston, Missouri. Soybeans are becoming a major crop in the mixed farming portions of the Mississippi Valley, as well as in the Corn Belt. (*Courtesy Clair A. Shenk.*)

farming regions of both the United States and Europe (see Figure 11-2). In the United States, corn and oats are secondary. In recent years soybeans have come into prominence in the central United States (Figure 9-5).

3. Subsistence Crops: These include wheat and a wide array of field crops such as potatoes, cabbage, beans, peas, turnips, beets.

Crop Rotation. One of the most distinctive characteristics of mixed farming is the practice of crop rotation whereby each field is devoted to a succession of different uses. There is a dual purpose here: restoring soil nutrients and combating erosion. Since each plant removes different nutrients in different proportions, soil must be rich indeed to support the same crop year after year. Crops differ too in protecting soil against erosion. On both counts, corn is hard on soil.

Rotation often follows a four-part sequence: (1) A cultivated crop—often corn, although in central Europe it may be potatoes, turnips, or sugar beets—that is the main feed for animals. (2) Hay, particularly alfalfa, timothy, and clover (clover is a legume that is particularly desirable because its roots put nitrogen back *into* the soil); in recent years an Oriental grass, Lespedeza, has been successfully introduced into southern

United States as hay. (3) Pasture. (4) A small grain (most often wheat) that is usually grown for cash sale; in Europe, rye replaces wheat where soils are poor and winters cold. Notice that three of the four components in the rotation system are animal feeds. Crop rotation is used in other types of bioculture also, but it is most widely practiced in mixed farming.

Percentage of Land in Crops. The emphasis on crops means that only a small portion of animal feed is natural vegetation. Indeed, a very high percentage of each farm's acreage is cropped: Illinois 83, Iowa 83, and Indiana 77 (Figure 9-6). The national average is 43 per cent.

Role of Animals. The sale of animals brings in most of the revenue of mixed farms. On many farms, in fact, all the income is realized from marketed animals; but on some farms crops are more lucrative.

Hogs, beef cattle, sheep, and poultry are raised in the greatest numbers on mixed farms. Although skins, hides, wool, and eggs are useful by-products, the main product is meat. Many animals could be raised for this purpose, but in mixed-farming regions, the customers prefer beef, bacon, and ham. Notice on the world maps of swine and cattle (Figures 9-7 and 9-8) the concentrations in the mixed-farming regions. These two maps, however, include animals on subsistence as well as commercial farms. Closer parallels would be observable between a map of mixed farming and maps of hogs *sold* and cattle *sold*. Such maps are presently possible to construct for the United States but not for the world.

1. Hogs sold: There is a very close correlation between the locational pattern of hogs sold (Figure 9-9) and the mixed-farming region from eastern Nebraska to Ohio. Few other areas in the United States have many swine at all. The hog population numbers 55,000,000, almost 80 per cent of which are in the

Figure 9-5 (*From U.S. Bureau of the Census.*)

SOYBEANS HARVESTED FOR BEANS

1 Dot= 10,000 Acres
United States Total
38,549,663 Acres

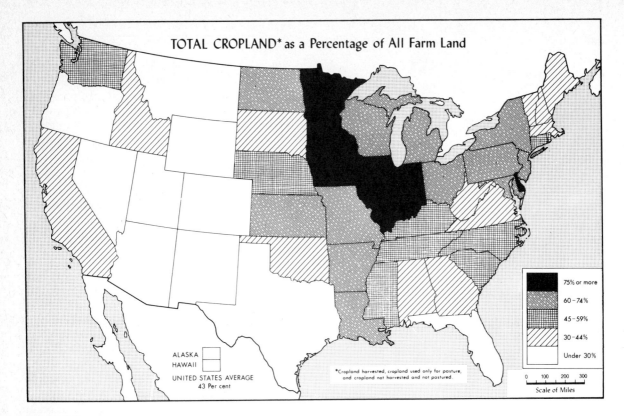

Figure 9-6

Figure 9-7

SWINE

CATTLE

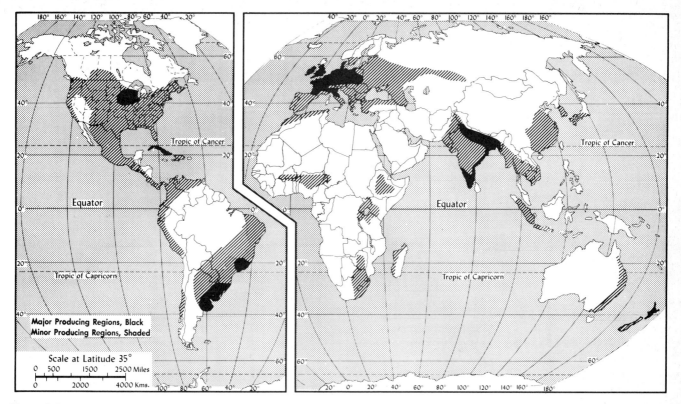

Figure 9-8

Figure 9-9 *(From U.S. Bureau of the Census.)*

HOGS AND PIGS SOLD

1 Dot = 10,000

United States Total
89,313,449

conspicuously on the second, livestock ranching regions would dominate the third, and the first would be dominated by the dairy belt.

The cattle in the United States number 106,000,000, of which 11,000,000 are milk cows, most of them in the dairy regions. The remaining 95,000,000 cattle are being raised primarily for meat. Forty-three per cent of the nation's cattle and calves are located in the North Central region. Leading states within the region are Iowa and Nebraska with a total of 13 per cent of the nation's cattle between them. The average farm in the heart of the mixed-farming region of the United States has 62 head of beef cattle in addition to its 135 hogs.

Mixed farms in Europe tend to have fewer cattle and fewer hogs than do American farms mainly because farms are smaller there. There are more farmers per square mile of land.

Size of Farm. To shelter all these animals and grow their feed requires an average of about 250 acres per farm in the United States. The size range is typically from 200 to 300 acres. Note that these operating units are about the same size as dairy farms but markedly smaller than livestock ranches. The farms in Europe are about half the size of those in the United States, those in South America and South Africa almost as large.

In the United States Corn Belt each farm has a farmstead, covering perhaps ten acres, which consists of the farm dwelling, a barn for sheltering animals and storing grain for winter feeding, a silo for storing corn cut green, a corn bin for storing ripened corn, a shed or

twelve north-central states. Each farm in the mixed-farming region has an average of 135 hogs.

2. Cattle sold: A different pattern appears on the map of cattle sold (Figure 9-10). Regions are more widely spread and less conspicuous because farms selling cattle are virtually ubiquitous in the United States. We could define the picture more carefully if three other maps were available: (a) old milk cows sold to slaughter houses, (b) mature beef cattle sold to slaughter houses, and (c) young beef cattle sold to farms for additional fattening. Were such maps available, the mixed-farming regions would stand out

CATTLE AND CALVES SOLD

1 Dot = 10,000 Head

United States Total
74,616,155

Figure 9-10   (*From U.S. Bureau of the Census.*)

two for machinery, and a feed lot for swine, cattle, and chickens. It is the feed lot in which most of the fattening is done—on crops harvested from the field—although sometimes the fields are "hogged off" or "cattled down" by letting the animals roam the fields to forage for themselves.

Farming Methods.   In Europe mixed farming is less mechanized than in the New World where farmers use a wide assortment of machines to plow, disc, harrow, and cultivate the soil as well as to plant and harvest the crops. It would be instructive to have a world map of agriculture plotted by degrees of mechanization. None is available. But for the United States, at least, a

map has been prepared by the Census Bureau that does show by percentages how many farms have tractors (Figure 9-11). Throughout most of the Corn Belt (which is the heart of the mixed-farming region) over 80 per cent of the farms have these machines. As Figure 9-11 indicates, though, in addition to the Corn Belt, farms in other areas, such as the dairy belt and the ranching region, are also highly mechanized.

Use of Manure.   No other type of commercial farmer makes such intensive use of manure over as broad a region as do the men in mixed farming (Figure 9-12). (Dairymen use almost as much manure but cover a smaller portion of the earth. Intensive farmers

Figure 9-11

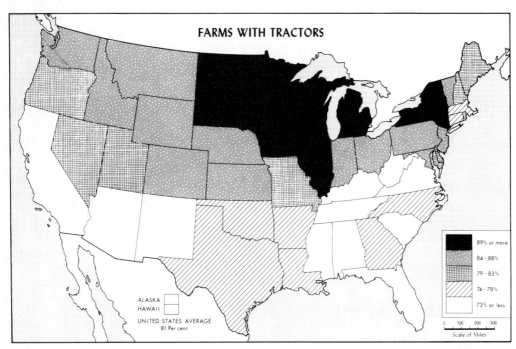

FARMS WITH TRACTORS

ALASKA
HAWAII

UNITED STATES AVERAGE
81 Per cent

89% or more
84 – 88%
79 – 83%
74 – 78%
73% or less

0   100   200   300
Scale of Miles

of the Orient use tremendous quantities of manure also, but they are not engaged in commercial ventures primarily.) The purpose in using manure is to return nutrients to the soil. In Europe, in fact, many cash-crop farmers maintain a few livestock primarily to ensure a steady supply of barnyard manure.

In a fascinating analysis of the role of manure in bioculture, Eugene Mather and John Fraser Hart write:

> The European attitude is best summarized by the statement that "farmyard manure . . . has formed the basis of arable farming throughout the ages. In spite of the great development of fertilizers during the last ninety years, farmyard manure is still the standby of arable farmers; it has been supplemented—not supplanted—by chemical fertilizers." (H. V. Garner, *Manures and Fertilizers*, Great Britain: Ministry of Agriculture and Fisheries Bulletin No. 36, London, 1952, p. 1). Conversely in newer societies, manure is not given the esteem accorded it in older and more stable agricultural communities. The hazards of continuous cropping with little manure are now beginning to be recognized in newly settled lands, however, and Americans can no longer continue to ignore the importance of manure in the agricultural economy. . . . .
>
> Manure is obtained from a greater variety of animals, and in greater quantities, in the Corn Belt than in any other part of the western hemisphere. Cattle, hogs, poultry, and sheep all produce significant amounts of manure here, but the most distinctive manurial aspect of the Corn Belt is associated with the feed lot. Most feed lots exist for the fattening of cattle and hogs. The rich

grain and protein supplements fed to the cattle produce rich manure. Grain which passes through the cattle undigested is greedily sought by hogs which consume considerable quantities of feces as they root after the grain. Two to four shoats commonly follow each steer.[1]

Degree of Commercialism. The degree of commercialism varies considerably. In west-central Europe, the northern United States, and Argentina, mixed farming is highly commercialized, each farmer and his family consuming only a small fraction of their output. At the other extreme are farmers in the American Appalachian highlands, in eastern Europe (particularly Poland, eastern Austria, Hungary, Yugoslavia, Romania, and Bulgaria), and in the Soviet Union who have only a comparatively small surplus for sale. Yet change is rapid now behind the Iron Curtain as mixed farmers are advancing from the subsistence stage (where they had been for generations) and are now in the commercial stage, prodded upward by the planned economy of the Soviet system. Just as they converted lands from subsistence herding to commercial grazing, the Soviets have upgraded mixed farming. Southern Brazil and eastern Paraguay are the only other major areas where mixed farmers are still on the subsistence level.

[1]Eugene Mather and John Fraser Hart, "The Geography of Manure," *Land Economics*, February, 1956, pp. 25–38.

Figure 9-12 (*Courtesy Eugene Mather and John Fraser Hart, and Land Economics.*)

MANURE MAP OF THE WORLD

Value of Sales. Revenues from cash sales also vary considerably. Very low in the subsistence areas, they rise to respectable heights in the highly commercialized zones. Indeed, farmers there can be among the most prosperous of all farmers. In Figure 9-13, which shows the average value of farm products sold per farm in the United States, the Corn Belt stands out conspicuously. For the nation as a whole, the average is $17,000, but throughout much of the Corn Belt average sales are between $20,000 and $30,000.

Capital Invested per Acre. Finally, the value of operating units is low in the subsistence portions and high in the commercial areas. Figure 9-14 shows that some of the most valuable farms in the nation (in terms of value of land and buildings *per acre*) are in the mixed-farming region. Notice particularly the Corn Belt—the largest single region of highly valued farms (per acre) in the country. The phrase *per acre* is emphasized because some of the huge ranches and wheat farms in the West are, farm for farm, as valuable as those in the Corn Belt, but some of them are ten times as large.

Physical Phenomena

Where mixed farming predominates, the environment is propitious for the raising of animals for meat. The advantages lie in soil, precipitation, growing season, and topography.

Soils. The soils in mixed-farming regions are intermediate in quality; they are not so rich in plant nutrients as the grassland soils, but they are richer than

Figure 9-13

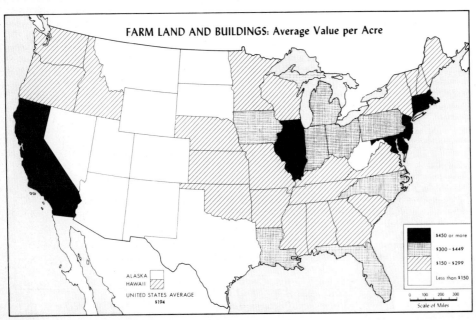

Figure 9-14

the leached soils of the forested tropics. Mixed farming is associated with two kinds of soil. Western Europe and the eastern United States have *podzolic* soils, which developed mostly in broadleaf forests. Such soils tend to be more fertile and less acidic than those associated with needle-leaf forests. The west-central United States and eastern Europe have *chernozem* soils, which developed under grasses and are superior to podzolic soils. If fertility of soil were the controlling factor in the location of mixed farming, the less remunerative, subsistence zones would coincide with the poorer soils of eastern United States and western Europe, while the more prosperous commercialized zones would be on the better soils of the western United States (say, Iowa) and eastern Europe (Hungary, Romania, and Russia). Although this correlation tends to hold in the United States, the opposite is true in Eurasia. One reason for this somewhat strange situation involves available moisture supply, for eastern Europe is drier than western Europe.

Available Moisture. Good soil alone is not enough for prosperous farming since plants need water as well as nutrients. Moreover, the nutrients are actually unavailable if there is insufficient moisture in the soil to dissolve them. Annual rainfall in mixed-farming regions varies from 20 to 60 inches. Most of it falls during the warmer months when growing plants need it, and it falls in *convectional* showers (a considerable volume of rain that falls from a minimum amount of cloud cover). No other type of weather favors growing plants with so much sunshine *and* so much moisture throughout the growing season.

Temperature. There is a rather close locational correlation between mixed farming and intermediate temperatures.

On the basis of *winter* temperatures, climatologists recognize two climatic types: mesothermal and microthermal. Where the average temperature of the coldest month stays above freezing, the climate is called *mesothermal*, the winters *cool*. If the average is below freezing, the climate is *microthermal* and the winters are *cold*.

On the basis of *summer* temperatures, climatologists recognize three types of climate. If the average temperature of the warmest month exceeds 72°, the climate is described as *warm summer*, if the average is between 50° and 72°, *cool summer*, if under 50°, *subarctic*.

Thus, the largest regions of mixed farming occur where the climates are either (a) *cool winter—cool summer* as in most of western Europe and in the Pacific Northwest, or (b) *cool winter—warm summer* as in the southeastern United States (this type of climate occurs in only a small part of southeastern Europe), or (c) *cold winter—warm summer* as in the east-central United States (this climate in Europe is restricted to the lower Danube Valley), or (d) *cold winter—cool summer* as in the Soviet Union. Smaller regions of mixed farming in the Southern Hemisphere all have one of the above climates.

The growing season varies from 120 days on the poleward and interior margins of the Soviet mixed-farming region to 220 days on the southern margin of the United States region. Any period within this range permits the growth of crops which make good animal feed. Even so, corn, the best grain for fattening animals, requires not only a long growing season (140 days) but also warm summers. It thrives best where summer nights as well as summer days are warm. This condition prevails in the mixed-farming region of Anglo-America but not in Europe. Here, then, is a basic reason why livestock are fattened on corn in the United States but on potatoes, sugar beets, and turnips in France, Germany and Poland.

Topography. Beef cattle on livestock ranches can roam hills and mountains in search of food. But in mixed-farming areas feed is brought to them, and that feed is best produced on relatively flat land. This holds whether the farmer works largely by hand or by machinery. The regions of mixed farming occur largely in plains—eastern Nebraska, Iowa, and Illinois in Anglo-America and France, Germany, Poland, and vast stretches of European Russia. Only small pockets occur in the hills of the eastern United States, central France, and southwestern Germany.

Cultural Features

A physical environment with the attributes just discussed does not inevitably lead to mixed farming. North China has somewhat the same general association of temperatures, precipitation, topography, and soil as do the mixed-farming regions of Europe and Anglo-America. But the millions of farmers in North China busy themselves with subsistence cropgrowing. Then, too, for thousands of years the physical features of Europe and Anglo-America were virtually what they are today, but only recently have the inhabitants practiced mixed farming. Obviously it depends on certain cultural phenomena as well as certain physical factors.

Dense Populations. Nearly all the mixed-farming regions on Figure 9-1 are associated with dense populations, notably in western Europe. Through Germany and southern Poland, the man/land ratio often exceeds 250 per square mile. A slightly lower density prevails over most of the remaining European mixed-farming territory, continuing eastward as far as Moscow, beyond which the population gradually thins out. A somewhat different situation obtains in the Western Hemisphere and in southern Africa where mixed farming frequently coincides with densities of 20 to 50 per square mile; nevertheless, even here, mixed farming is associated with the areas of each continent where the population is relatively dense.

But dense population is not the only cultural force

that applies, else China and India would be strong in mixed farming. Is there something relevant in the way the people are distributed?

Urbanization. Mixed-farming regions also turn out to have a heavy concentration of people in *cities*. Of the nearly 150 cities with one million or more people, perhaps 60 are located either within mixed-farming zones or on their poleward margins where they merge with dairy areas. Yet on this basis, the Far East, again, should have a mixed-farming economy because it can boast 35 cities with a million or more inhabitants. We must look at still other phenomena.

Diet. Here is an important factor that we must not overlook just because it seems so obvious: Mixed farming is associated with meat diets. Millions of the earth's peoples—many in the Far East—are vegetarians, many for religious convictions; if their cultures took over in western Europe and Anglo-America, the realm of mixed farming would be drastically reduced.

Purchasing Power. The large numbers of meat-eating urbanites have a large purchasing power. And it is purchasing power, as we have already seen, that stimulated the development of livestock ranching and commercial dairying. Notice the data in Table 9-1 dealing with diet components (note especially animal protein supply) for several selected countries. These figures relate closely not only to such productive activities as mixed farming, ranching, and dairying, but also to customers' eating habits and buying power.

Transportation. No other type of farming (except dairying) has stimulated the spread of as wide a network of good transport facilities as mixed farming has (see Figure 24-1 and the world map of railroads and roads in any economic atlas). Being highly productive, mixed farming generated much of the tax money with which good roads were built, and the roads in turn facilitated the shipments of farm products to markets.

Prices and Transportation Costs. A bushel of corn commands a lower price on the market than does a bushel of wheat, mainly because the customers of the mixed-farming regions prefer wheat bread and wheat cereal to corn bread and corn cereal for their own diets. Even though wheat will bring a higher price than corn, transport charges by the carload are usually about the same on the two grains. Obviously, the ratio of transport costs to value of product is *higher* for corn and *lower* for wheat—a strong factor discouraging trade in corn and encouraging trade in wheat.

Table 9-1

Food Supply per Capita for Selected Countries

Area	Total Calories per Day	Total Protein in Grams per Day	Animal Protein in Grams per Day
Europe			
Austria	3230	86	51
Denmark	3250	88	58
Finland	2940	90	59
France	3270	103	64
West Germany	3180	83	54
Greece	2900	99	43
Hungary	3190	98	43
Iceland	2900	99	73
Ireland	3510	96	63
Italy	3020	88	38
Netherlands	3200	85	53
Norway	2940	82	51
Spain	2770	80	35
Sweden	2850	80	55
United Kingdom	3170	87	53
U.S.S.R.	3180	92	36
North America			
Canada	3200	96	64
United States	3300	99	71
Latin America			
Argentina	3160	105	62
Brazil	2820	67	21
Chile	2560	66	28
Colombia	2140	50	25
Ecuador	1970	45	15
Panama	2370	59	26
Paraguay	2540	65	29
Venezuela	2430	60	26
Near East			
Israel	2990	91	44
Lebanon	2360	70	20
Sudan	2090	59	19
Far East			
China	2050	57	8
India	1990	49	6
Indonesia	1920	43	5
Japan	2470	77	32
Pakistan	2410	55	10
Taiwan	2620	68	21
Africa			
Egypt	2770	80	10
Kenya	2200	68	16
South Africa	2730	77	28
Tanzania	1700	42	15
Zaire	2040	33	9
Oceania			
Australia	3160	91	61
New Zealand	3380	108	74

Source: United Nations, Food and Agricultural Organization, *Production Yearbook* (1972).

But the farmer has the option of converting corn (or potatoes, hay, or whatever) into meat, which *will* bring him a high price. To be sure, freight rates are higher for meat than for corn, but the value of meat is so much higher than that of corn that the ratio of transport costs to value of the product is lower. Moreover, the farmer has fewer tons of product on which to pay transport costs if he feeds his corn to animals. Six pounds of corn make 1 pound of pork. Beef is an even more concentrated product—it takes 8 or 9 pounds of corn plus 2 or 3 pounds of hay to make a pound of beef—and beef often gets a still higher price.

Because of these variations in prices and transport costs, the farmers in mixed-farming regions enjoy a certain flexibility of production. When prices on meat are low, they can devote their fields to growing crops for sale; when meat prices are high they can concentrate on livestock sales.

Contract Farming. Some farmers within the United States mixed-farming region have turned to *contract farming.* Under this system the individual farmer surrenders his independence as a producer for the general market in favor of signing a contract with a commercial meat-packing company. He accepts the company's decisions on exactly how much of what kinds of meat he will produce; the firm in turn covenants to pay him within the limits of a certain price range. Frequently, the packers also have contracts with distributors and chain stores that sell the meat products. If contract farming succeeds, mixed farmers in the United States will be spared some of the uncertainty of planning each year's activity. Instead of guessing what the market will be, they will have a firm commitment around which to budget their time, effort, and investment.

Settlements. Trade and service centers are spaced about 12 miles apart in the American mixed-farming region. They are closer in Europe where farms are smaller, rural roads poorer, and transportation less mechanized.

The employment structure in such a settlement is geared to service the needs of surrounding farmers (see, for example, Bloomfield, Iowa, in Table 9-2). Yet, since some of the larger settlements have food-processing plants, in those places manufacturing accounts for a larger number of jobs (for instance, Waterloo, Iowa, in Table 9-2).

Table 9-2

Employment Structures of Two Settlements in a Mixed-Farming Region

	Bloomfield, Iowa		Waterloo, Iowa (urbanized area)	
Population	2,847		113,100	
Total employment	1,101		43,513	
Percentage of Employment:				
Construction	4		4	
Manufacturing	10		30	
Nondurable goods		4		9
Transportation	3		2	
Communications and utilities	4		3	
Trade	25		23	
Finance, insurance, business, and repair services	8		6	
Professional and related services	28		28	
Educational services		10		11
Public administration	6		3	
Other industries	12		1	

Source: U.S. Bureau of the Census, *Census of Population 1970*, Vol. I, Part 17 (1971).

Source Regions for Feeder Animals. A certain distinctive regional specialization has become important to mixed farmers in the United States. Western ranchers breed cattle and sheep, raising them to semimaturity (approximately one year of age) and then ship them for final fattening to the more humid regions where lusher grasses and grains grow (see Chapter 7). Many of the beef cattle in Iowa, Nebraska, Illinois, Indiana, and Ohio were born in Montana, Wyoming, and other western range states.

Men in the feeder business deal mostly with cattle. Hogs are bred and raised (as well as fattened) more satisfactorily right where the crops are. If Americans had as strong a taste for lamb and mutton as for beef, there might be a greater feeder business in sheep.

Meat-Packing Areas. In recent years a great many meat-packing factories have left New York, Cincinnati, and Chicago for new locations in smaller

The exceptional soils and intensive cropping methods characteristic of many mixed farming regions allow for a very dense pattern of farms. This farm is near Lancaster, in southeastern Pennsylvania, the size and condition of the farm building attesting to the success of intensive mixed farming in this region. (*Courtesy Clair A. Shenk.*)

cities, such as Omaha, within the mixed-farming regions. The reasons for this shift are rather complex, as we shall see in the chapters on manufacturing; but whatever they are, a movement is clearly underway.

International Trade. Although Europe and Anglo-America have the most highly developed regions of mixed farming, the demand for meat still exceeds the domestic supply. Meat therefore is imported from areas of mixed farming (as well as livestock ranching areas) on other continents. The leading importers of fresh and frozen meats are West Germany, the United Kingdom, and Italy. The leading exporters are Australia, the Netherlands, New Zealand, Argentina, and the United States. For some countries, the value of meat exports makes up a large share of total sales abroad: Australia 11 per cent, Denmark 17, New Zealand 30, and Argentina 36.

SUGGESTED READINGS

GIBSON, LYLE E., "Characteristics of a Regional Margin of the Corn and Dairy Belts," *Annals of the Association of American Geographers*, 1948, pp. 244–270.

KIEFER, WAYNE E., "An Agricultural Settlement Complex in Indiana," *Annals of the Association of American Geographers*, 1972, pp. 487–506.

REITSMA, HENDRIK J., "Crop and Livestock Production in the Vicinity of the United States-Canada Border," *The Professional Geographer*, 1971, pp. 216–223.

WEAVER, J. C., HOAG, L. P., and FENTON, B. L., "Livestock Units and Combination Regions in the Middle West," *Economic Geography*, 1956, pp. 237–259.

CHAPTER

10

mediterranean agriculture

Grapes are laid out to dry into raisins in a California field. (*Courtesy USDA.*)

Figure 10-1

The term *Mediterranean agriculture* applies to a particular mixture of diverse biocultural activities (both animal husbandry and crop farming) that has developed in five major world regions. The largest of these nearly encircles the Mediterranean Sea—and it is from there that the type derives its name, not only because it is the most extensive of the five but also because it was the first. Of the economic activities discussed in this book this is the only one for which the name derives from a *type area*, rather than from characteristics of the economy itself.

Location

The Mediterranean Basin, where this agriculture prevails, is situated amid three continents (see Figure 10-1). The type zone includes a narrow coastal belt 1,000 miles long across North Africa, from Tunisia to the Atlantic coast, stretches across southern Europe, and bends around southwestern Asia (from Turkey a prong extends eastward through the valleys of Georgia and Azerbaydzhan in the U.S.S.R. to northern Iran). Between Israel and Tunisia, however, nomadic herding predominates, except for intensive cultivation in the Nile Valley and the Barqah section of Libya.

Elsewhere, this biocultural type prevails in almost half of California, particularly the Great Valley and the coast south of San Francisco; in central Chile; and at the southwestern tip of Africa.

Thus, Mediterranean agriculture occurs in both the Northern and Southern Hemispheres, and in the midlatitudes, roughly between 30 and 45 degrees.

In applying the geographic method of analysis, at this point we would normally turn to the characteristics of the economic activity under study. But, for the sake of variety, and also for a better understanding of the characteristics to be mentioned later, let us instead take up relationships with the physical environment first.

Physical Relationships

The natural setting that lends itself to Mediterranean agriculture is distinguished by erratic rainfall, mild temperatures, irregular topography, and nearness to large bodies of water.

Amounts of Precipitation. The climate in these regions is subhumid, which means that there is just enough rainfall to keep the climate from being classed as dry. The formula for deciding whether a climate is dry or humid is rather complex, but for our purposes, we only need to know that Mediterranean-type rainfall varies from 10 inches to 40 inches annually. Annual average precipitation in inches at representative cities are: Los Angeles 15, Rome 33, Jerusalem 25, and Capetown, South Africa 25.

Unpredictable Precipitation. These averages do not tell us much about any one year, though, for precipitation is fickle. Some years are very dry, others are quite humid. It is an axiom of physical geography that the lower the annual precipitation the greater its annual variation. Table 10-1 illustrates this principle with data for three cities. Notice that the *higher* the rainfall average, the *lower* the percentage range between exceptionally dry and wet years. Sharp fluctuations can occur between consecutive years. In Los Angeles, for instance, 33 inches fell in 1941 but only 11 inches came in 1942; a scant 8 inches came in 1951, but they were followed by 26 inches in 1952.

Monthly Distribution of Precipitation. In most climatic regions that have pronounced wet and dry seasons the former is in summer, the latter in winter. The reasons for these conditions are complex, involving some of the basic principles of physical geography, but the chief factor is that cold air holds less water vapor than warm air does. In a phrase, summer air in most regions is a richer mixture for forming rain.

Not so in Mediterranean regions. Winters there are markedly wetter than summers which are often exceedingly dry. Climatologists and geographers recognize a specific *Mediterranean Climate* (sometimes termed *Humid Sub-Tropical Dry Summer*), the most distinguishing feature of which is the dry summer-wet winter sequence. Compare the monthly precipitation figures at the weather stations listed in Table 10-2.

Mediterranean climates are invariably bounded on the *equatorial* side by steppes and deserts; the air masses that hover over these dry realms most of the year drift toward the *poles* in the summer. As a result, actual desert

conditions prevail in some Mediterranean areas in the summer. For the whole six-month period from May through October, Los Angeles receives less than one inch.

Natural Vegetation. The flora of Mediterranean regions is a mixture of trees, shrubs, and grass. The trees, comparatively short and rather widely spaced, form a distinctive type known as *Mediterranean Scrub Forest*. Some of them are deciduous and drop their leaves in summer; they stand dormant in the hot season, thus preventing the loss of too much water in transpiration through leaf surfaces. Other trees are evergreen and endure summer aridity through such adaptations as thick oily leaves and husky bark which reduce evaporation. Examples of Mediterranean trees are the cork oak, the olive, and the fig.

More numerous than the trees are the shrubs and bushes that make up the brush known as *chaparral*. Finally, there are vast areas of grass, lush in winter and dormant in summer. The relative location of trees, shrubs, and grasses within Mediterranean areas is a highly complex association (treated by physical geographers), determined by the landforms, by the variation in precipitation between lowlands and highlands, and by soil types.

Table 10-1

Annual Precipitation Data for Selected Cities

City	Annual Average in Inches	Inches in Wet Year	Inches in Dry Year	Range in Inches	Range as a Percentage of Annual Average
Los Angeles	15″	38″ (1884)	5″ (1899)	33	220%
Chicago	32″	46″ (1954)	22″ (1956)	24	75%
New York City	42″	59″ (1889)	33″ (1935)	26	60%

Source: Personal communications from United States Weather Bureau offices.

Table 10-2

Monthly Precipitation at Selected Weather Stations

Place	J	F	M	A	M	J	J	A	S	O	N	D
Mediterranean Regions												
Jerusalem, Israel	6.2	4.6	3.5	1.5	0.3	*	*	*	*	0.4	2.5	5.7
Rome, Italy	3.2	2.7	2.9	2.6	2.2	1.6	0.7	1.0	2.5	5.0	4.4	3.9
Los Angeles, California	3.1	3.0	2.6	1.0	0.3	*	*	*	0.1	0.5	1.1	2.7
Other Regions												
Chicago, Illinois	2.1	2.1	2.6	2.9	3.6	3.3	3.4	3.0	3.1	2.6	2.4	2.1
Berlin, Germany	1.7	1.4	1.6	1.5	1.9	2.3	3.0	2.3	1.7	1.7	1.7	1.9
Fuchou, China	3.1	2.5	4.8	5.3	4.6	6.0	4.3	8.7	3.0	1.3	0.8	1.3

*Less than 0.1

Temperature. Temperatures are mild for most of the year. Summers are warm, with averages for the warmest month ranging from 71° in Los Angeles up to 80° in Athens, Greece, and down to 67° in Santiago, Chile. More significant, though, are the mild winters. Representative averages for the coldest months are 54° in Los Angeles, 48° in Athens, and 46° in Santiago. The growing season in these regions is almost continuous, so most farming is geared to that expectation. Summer and winter therefore are matters of dryness and wetness rather than of heat and cold. This generalization applies to the lowlands. Frosts do occur there occasionally, but they are frequent and severe in the highlands.

Thus, heat and maximum precipitation come at different seasons, which is a handicap to many plants.

Relation to Water Bodies. Mediterranean regions are rarely very far inland. Usually they front on the sea itself, although a few zones extend inland quite a way from the Mediterranean, Black, and Caspian seas. Nearness to large bodies of water is one reason why Mediterranean winters are comparatively mild, especially where the prevailing winds come from the sea. (The oceans remain warmer than the land masses do in winter.)

Landforms. Nearly all Mediterranean regions are mixtures of lowlands and highlands, of flat lands and rough lands, both hilly and mountainous. Mountains often mark the poleward border of Mediterranean regions, and therefore provide effective barriers against invasions of cold air. Such air moving southward in Europe encounters the Pyrenees, Alps, and Dinaric Alps. In California and Chile the mountains lie to the east, protecting the Mediterranean regions from colder air blowing westward in winter from the continental interiors. These mountains, by the way, are one reason why California's lowlands, although farther north than Florida's, never have such severe winter temperatures. Florida's lowlands have no mountain bulwarks against outbursts of cold continental air.

Relation to Prevailing Winds. In the midlatitudes on the western portions of continents the prevailing winds are westerly. This fact, coupled with the nature of landforms, the nature of cyclonic storm tracks, and the tendency of land masses to heat and to cool at different rates from those of oceans, explains why the Mediterranean region of California has no counterpart in the same latitude on the east coast of the United States, and why the Mediterranean realm of Europe-Asia-Africa is not repeated in China.

In the physical environment just described, a distinctive type of agriculture becomes possible. Mediterranean agriculture is distinguished by an unusual combination of crops and livestock, an association which has prevailed for centuries in the land surrounding the Mediterranean Sea and which has tended to be recurrent in the other four realms of Mediterranean bioculture. The combination involves particular sets of winter crops, of summer crops, and of animals.

Winter Grains. Winter crops, whether grains or vegetables, are sown or planted in the fall and nourished by winter rainfall; they ripen in the spring and are harvested in early summer.

The grains usually grown are wheat and barley, the two cereals that survive best on limited amounts of moisture through cool growing seasons. Corn and oats, for instance, require more rainfall and warmer periods of maturation. Moreover, wheat and barley do not require land as flat as does corn, which must be cultivated—a technique that combats weeds but simultaneously lays bare the soil, making sloping land subject to increased erosion. Accordingly, wheat and barley often occupy the sloping land on the fringes of valleys in Mediterranean regions. Wheat is the preferred cereal and bread grain; Italians eat a lot of it as spaghetti. Barley is the poor man's cereal.

Because of the limited moisture, grain yields per acre in Mediterranean regions are low. It takes several acres to produce the cereal crop for even one family, and each worker tends a considerable amount of land.

Dry farming is a grain-growing technique that is frequently resorted to in the drier portions of all Mediterranean regions, wherever the rainfall of a single year is inadequate for a grain crop although the total precipitation in consecutive years is sufficient. The objective in dry farming is to tend the soil in such a manner that it absorbs and retains the greatest amount of water possible. Fields are cropped only once every two years (occasionally once every three years during unusually dry periods) and they lie fallow the other year in order to store up moisture. The soil is tended as carefully during the fallow year as during the cropped year, but the treatment is different. In the former, fields are plowed and harrowed at intervals of approximately three months. During the autumn they are cultivated in order to open the ground for the autumn rainfall. But since rainfall hardens bare soil, increasing the run-off and reducing the intake, the land is plowed and harrowed again in winter. Once more in spring it is cultivated to promote absorption of rainwater. The last plowing and harrowing in the fallow year come in summer, the aim being to break up the soil capillaries through which moisture moves toward the surface where it evaporates. Obviously, in a dry season the rate of upward capillary action exceeds that of downward seepage, so there is a net loss of moisture during these months; however, enough is retained to be useful the following year. Dry farming is practiced on the highlands and upper slopes of valleys where it is too costly to irrigate.

Winter Vegetables. The winter crop in valleys is usually vegetables. The alluvial soils of the valleys are usually better than those of the slopes and so are devoted to crops that yield more food per acre than do wheat and barley. Nearly every vegetable will grow: beans, peas, carrots, onions, radishes, tomatoes, lettuce, cabbage. Planted in the fall, some of these mature so rapidly that two or even three crops can be harvested before the summer drought. Yields per acre of vegetables are high; therefore, valley farms are likely to be smaller in size than those on the slopes. Surplus vegetables can be dried during the summer.

Summer Crops. Summer crops mature during the summer and are harvested in the autumn. They must be hardy plants capable of enduring a long dry period. Several plants can endure this ordeal, however, by having (a) long tap roots that penetrate soil moisture far below the surface, (b) extensive root systems that reach far out horizontally, and (c) little foliage, which reduces evaporation. Certain trees and vines meet these speci-

fications although most grasses and vegetables do not. Typical summer crops are olives, figs, and grapes. For centuries they have been basic to the Mediterranean diet.

Ninety per cent of all olive acreage is in the Mediterranean Basin (Figure 10-2). Olive trees are planted 30 feet apart. Closer spacing would be all right in winter but would overtax the soil's supply of moisture in the summer. *Interculture* enables the farmers to reap a dividend from this open space between olive trees during the winter; then, they plant vegetables or winter grains between the trees.

In contrast to the olive tree, the *fig* tree yields two crops of figs a year, one in early summer and one in autumn. Again the trees must be far enough apart so that the land in summer is not overtaxed. Winter interculture also prevails on fig plots.

Most of the world's *grapes* are grown in Mediterranean-type regions (Figure 10-3). Vineyards are rarely interplanted with winter crops, though, for grapes do not tolerate competition. Grapes can be processed into a diversity of foods, and some Mediterranean areas are famous for their grape products: wine from Algeria and Portugal, fruit grapes from the Malaga district in southern Spain, raisins from Greece.

Figure 10-2

OLIVES

Major Producing Regions, Black
Minor Producing Regions, Shaded

Scale at Latitude 35°
0   500   1500   2500 Miles
0   2000   4000 Kms.

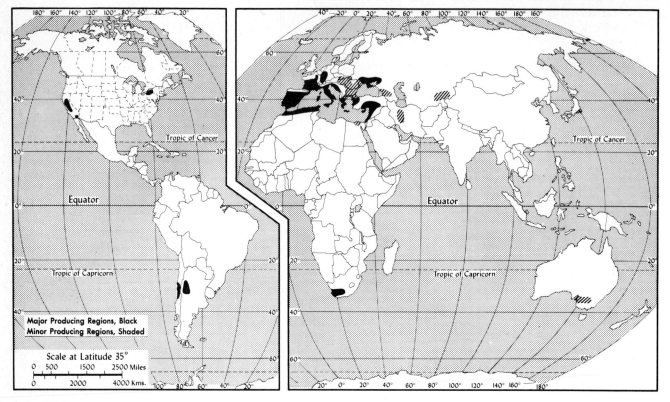

Figure 10-3

All told, winter crops and summer crops together use up less than one-fifth of the land in regions of Mediterranean agriculture. What cropland there is tends to be on the valley bottoms and lower slopes. Most of the land, though, is either too dry or too rough for growing anything. There is some tendency toward zonation: Valley bottoms often are devoted to vegetables and intercultured olive and fig groves; the lower slopes have cereals; the steeper slopes, if cropped at all, are in vineyards, or olive or fig groves. Interculture is avoided, however, because of the risk of erosion.

Livestock Agriculture. The role of livestock tending in Mediterranean bioculture varies from farm to farm. At one extreme are farms where the emphasis is almost entirely on crops, and the function of the few animals, if any, is to meet the needs of farm operator and family. At the other extreme are operating units where animals constitute a major source of revenue—but never the only source, else they would be classified as commercial grazing or dairying.

There are two types of livestock husbandry in Mediterranean regions: livestock "grazing" and livestock "farming."

Livestock grazing is based on natural vegetation. Goats and sheep make up most of the herds because they can subsist on the meagre vegetation of these subhumid lands where the carrying capacity varies from 15 acres

to 80 acres per animal. As Figure 7-2 shows, considerable numbers of sheep are in areas of Mediterranean agriculture. The main handicap is the dry summer. But since there is usually a little more rainfall in the highlands than in the lowlands as well as less evaporation because of lower temperatures, mountain ranges can often be grazed all year long. Where the economy is mainly on the subsistence level, the people get milk, meat, wool, and skins from the herds. Where commercialism prevails, the main product is wool. Turkey, for example, is famous for Angora wool.

Most grazers do some farming, too, of course, otherwise these grazing areas should be included in the nomadic herding regions (to which they are adjacent in Africa and the Middle East) or to the livestock ranching areas (to which they are adjacent in the United States).

Livestock farming is based on tended vegetation such as alfalfa, clover, pastures of sown grasses, or other forage crops. Swine, beef cattle, and dairy cattle are the main animals on livestock farms, which are located in valleys, often near large cities. Sometimes the crops for these animals are irrigated. Swine, though, succeed particularly well in certain parts of the Mediterranean Basin where they graze on acorns in oak forests.

Other Characteristics. *The degree of commercialism* varies markedly within and among Mediterranean regions. In parts of the Mediterranean Basin (notably southern Italy, central Spain, and the interiors of Greece, Turkey, and Syria) the economy is still largely subsistence —as it has been for thousands of years. But in northern Italy, southern France, coastal Spain, and coastal Algeria there is a good deal of surplus production. In the three other Mediterranean regions, the farming is on the whole rather highly commercialized.

There is no typical *size* of operating unit in Mediterranean agriculture. The largest number of valley vegetable farms is small, sometimes as small as 10 acres. Those depending on grapes, olives, figs, or grains are larger. And those located far from the valley bottoms take up hundreds of acres, most of which are range land.

The characteristics so far mentioned have prevailed for a long time. In the last few decades some new attributes have developed in response to the influence of certain cultural phenomena.

Cultural Relationships

Age of Culture and Agricultural Methods. The cultures in the Mediterranean Basin are ancient; in the other regions newer cultures prevail. Areas with recent cultures practice the commercial phase of Mediterranean agriculture while many areas of the old cultures are still in the subsistence stage.

In many of the older areas, methods are crude. Farmers still sow wheat and harvest it by hand in many parts of Spain, Italy, Greece, and Algeria. They use wooden hoes, wooden harvesting equipment, and primitive carts for transporting produce from the fields. But in South Africa, Chile, and California, more modern equipment and considerable machinery are employed.

Man/Land Ratio. A moderately high population density is sustained by this economic activity. Rarely is the density less than 25 per square mile, and in many places (Italy, and the coastal zones of Spain, Greece, Turkey, Syria, Lebanon, and Israel) it exceeds 200 per square mile.

Settlements. Settlements vary widely. In the Mediterranean Basin most farmers reside in farm villages in buildings made of stone. Timber is scarce in these lands. But in areas of newer cultures most farmers reside on their own land in farmsteads made of wood, some of which is brought in from afar. Few settlements function as trade centers where the subsistence phase prevails. But in California and Chile most settlements are service centers, where exactly the same functions are performed as in their counterparts in regions of other commercial activities.

Contacts with Other Regions. Although Mediterranean farming is associated with a very old culture, it did not develop many contacts with distant market regions until recently. In response to these contacts, Mediterranean agriculture has gone through several changes. Let us look at them chronologically. It will be convenient to delimit three time periods with the years 1300 and 1880 as our pegs. Admittedly, no one year clearly marks the boundary between two stages, but it can serve as a rough identification of the point of transition.

1. The period before 1300: Throughout most of history, Mediterranean agriculture has been a subsistence activity. It was, though, one of the first phases of bioculture to emerge from subsistence gathering. Then for centuries the world's major biocultural regions were given over to either subsistence herding, subsistence farming, or to Mediterranean agriculture, which was a blend of both. During this period Mediterranean agriculture was confined to the Mediterranean Basin and its practitioners made comparatively few sales to customers in other regions.

   There was some surplus production in this period, but it went to citizens in Athens, Rome, Alexandria, Carthage and other cities within the Mediterranean Basin rather than to other regions. But people from other regions approached the Mediterranean farmers —particularly the nomadic herdsmen who made annual attacks on the fields and settlements of Mediterranean fringes.

2. The period between 1300 and 1880: The cultural revolution in the western world that ended the Middle Ages and brought the Italian Renaissance, also saw the flowering of commercialism. Agricultural surpluses that for centuries had gone only a few miles from farms to nearby cities now began to move hundreds and thousands of miles to other realms. The contributions of Mediterranean agriculture to this trade were surpluses of her three main commodity groups: (1) easily preserved summer crops (olives, olive oil, figs, wine, raisins), (2) animal products (wool, hides, skins),[1] and (3) winter crops—mostly grains (more wheat than barley because wheat makes better bread and finer cereal), but also some dried winter vegetables. In every instance, the exported products were relatively imperishable and valuable in proportion to weight so that they were worth the cost of transport. The principal market in this period was western Europe although eastern Anglo-America was beginning to come into prominence.

3. The period after 1880: Most regions of Mediterranean agriculture went through a mild revolution near the end of the nineteenth century in response to four major developments incipient in other regions: (1) the Industrial Revolution in northwestern Europe and America where purchasing power skyrocketed, (2)

---

[1]Richard Dana's *Two Years Before the Mast* is a fascinating description of life on a ship which operated in the movement of hides from a region of Mediterranean agriculture in southern California clear around South America's Cape Horn to the markets of New England.

grain regions (Chapter 11) were beginning to specialize and to capture the wheat markets.

rapidly increasing population (in Europe and America) which multiplied the number of consumers of Mediterranean products, (3) the transportation revolution, whereby railroads, steamships, and later trucks sharply reduced the time required to move commodities between regions, and (4) the invention of refrigeration.

As a result of these developments, several changes occurred in the geography of Mediterranean agriculture in several categories: location, amount of exports, types of exports, addition of new crops, labor supply, size of farms, and regional specialization.

New Locations. Settlers from western Europe developed new regions of Mediterranean agriculture. They recognized the Mediterranean climate and Mediterranean vegetation when they encountered them in California, Chile, and South Africa, and they were also sensitive to the demand in Europe for the products of Mediterranean agriculture.

A Modest Increase in Traditional Items. Summer crops have become items of commerce in increasing amounts. Today 90 per cent of all olive oil comes from the Mediterranean Basin (mainly Italy, Spain, Greece, and Turkey). Wine is a money-maker, and more dried fruits (such as figs and raisins) are also shipped out than before. About one-half of the world's raisin exports come from Greece and Turkey alone.

Some of the new regions began exporting these items, too. California exports wine, and Australia now rivals Turkey in exporting raisins. Exports of wool did not keep pace with the increased shipments of crops, however, for livestock ranchers captured the wool market. Wheat shipments also declined because commercial

Tremendous Increase in New Exports. For centuries, the Mediterranean farmer grew winter vegetables, but he had little incentive to produce a surplus of something that would spoil en route to market. But the transport revolution and the development of refrigeration enabled him to deliver these perishables in good condition to distant regions. The status of winter vegetables changed immediately: They became major items of export.

In response to this development, summer cropping practices also quickly changed. For centuries, the main drawback of summer was lack of water, a handicap that could be remedied only by irrigation. But irrigation was costly and there was little incentive to incur this expense in the early days. But with a boom in the vegetable market, prices rose high enough to warrant the investment of labor and capital in constructing dams and conduits for irrigation systems. If winter rainfall and snowfall in the high mountains are impounded, gravity will bring water to the valley bottoms. Such water is reasonably inexpensive. By this method, the irrigated valleys of California receive water from the Coast Ranges and the Sierra Nevada Mountains; in addition, Los Angeles and the Imperial Valley of California are supplied by water from the Colorado River.

Introduction of Fruits from Elsewhere. The Mediterranean regions had always been warm enough for many tropical plants. Now, with irrigation, their soils could be made wet enough. Moreover, most Mediterranean farmers were considerably closer than their tropical competitors to the main markets. Several tropical fruits were transplanted successfully to irrigated fields in Mediterranean realms, but the most striking success was with citrus fruits. Oranges and lemons have

Orange grove near Riverside, California. Erosion control is being practiced by growing winter and summer annual grasses, which are controlled by mowing. The grove is irrigated by sprinklers. (*Courtesy USDA, Soil Conservation Service.*)

Figure 10-4

joined vegetables as the most distinctive exports of the Mediterranean Basin today (see Figure 10-4).

Irrigation likewise permitted the successful introduction to Mediterranean cropping systems of peaches, walnuts, almonds, apricots, and other humid-area fruits from the mid-latitudes.

This revolution emphasizing fruits and vegetables in the commercial regions of Mediterranean agriculture is reflected in the export structure of these areas. The value of fruit and vegetable exports as a percentage of total exports is Turkey 26, Greece 21, Israel 17, Spain 16, Lebanon 13, and Italy 5.

Relationships to Labor Supply. Raising fruits and vegetables requires tremendous amounts of hand labor. Some of the work can be mechanized (preparing soil, for instance, or harvesting such crops as onions), but a vast amount of hand labor is still needed to set out plants, extract weeds, and harvest fruit. The Mediterranean Basin has always been one of the world's more densely settled areas. So the abundant labor supply there has been rather cheap. As yet, commercial Mediterranean agriculture elsewhere has not been able to pay very high farm wages either. This has been a problem in California and Arizona where the demand for labor has been met by immigrants from foreign countries, particularly Mexico. But some of the Mexican labor does not immigrate; retaining their Mexican citizenship they cross the border seasonally to work on United States farms.

Farm Size. Many small farms were one result of all these developments. The high cost of irrigation meant that an irrigated acre might better be devoted to fruit and vegetables than to grains, for they would bring a higher return on investments. Not only did they command higher prices; but two or three crops of vegetables could be harvested in a single year. As a result, the individual farmer in Mediterranean valleys began applying more intensive methods of farming to smaller parcels of land. But in some instances, rather large farms (sometimes called "ranches") have been organized with a sizable force of hired hands and machinery operating scores of acres.

Regional Specialization. There is an increasing tendency for neighboring farmers in the United States portion of this realm to specialize in the same crops. By doing so, they benefit as a group from certain aspects of large-scale operation. Instead of small shipments of lettuce, full truck loads or full carloads can be assembled. Transport agencies generally quote lower rates on carload shipments than on smaller ones. Where the shipments are large enough, entire trainloads of vegetables and fruit can be sped along to market.

Emperor grapes ready for harvest near Fresno, California. (*USDA, Soil Conservation Service.*)

Concomitant with such regional specialization has been the growth in *marketing associations* by which fruit growers and vegetable growers pool their resources to expedite the collecting, grading, sorting, and selling of their produce. These associations operate efficiently in shrinking the interval between the times of harvest and of delivery. The Salinas Valley of California is one of the many areas that have specialized in a single crop for the foregoing reasons. The crop is lettuce, and the valley claims to be "The Salad Bowl of the Nation."

But such specialization is not typical for the Mediterranean Basin, where most of the farmers engaged in this type of bioculture reside. Their endeavors continue to be a mixed type of farming, with both crops and animals present on each farm, and a diversity of crops (winter and summer, grains and vegetables and fruit) being grown.

In its truest form, Mediterranean bioculture is the most "mixed" of all types of farming—mixed in two respects. First of all, most farms as individual operating units are a mixture of productive efforts. Secondly, when farms do specialize (in citrus, or grapes, or avocados, or any other crop) a diverse mixture of such specialized operating units occurs in Mediterranean realms.

SUGGESTED READINGS

ACKERMAN, EDWARD A., "The Influences of Climate on the Cultivation of Citrus Fruits," *Geographical Review*, 1938, pp. 289–302.

GREGOR, HOWARD F., "The Plantation in California," *The Professional Geographer*, March 1962, pp. 1–4.

STANISLAWSKI, DAN, "Dionysus Westward: Early Religion and the Economic Geography of Wine," *The Geographical Review*, 1975, pp. 427–444.

———, *The Individuality of Portugal; A Study in Historical-Political Geography*, Austin, 1959, 248 pp.

———, *Landscapes of Bacchus: The Vine in Portugal*, Austin, 1970, 210 pp.

———, *Portugal's Other Kingdom, the Algarve*, Austin, 1963, 273 pp.

CHAPTER
11

commercial grain farming

Grain elevators at Hutchinson, Kansas. The largest one is almost one-half mile long and contains 1000 bins, each with a capacity of from 9000 to 18,000 bushels. These elevators, as well as the smaller ones in each of the service communities throughout the Wheat Belt, are served by railroads. The crop is preserved by keeping it dry until it is needed by the food industry or for international trade. (*Courtesy USDA.*)

Figure 11-1

Human beings need starch, gluten, and oils for proper physical health; and many kinds of grasses store up these nutrients in their seeds. It is biologically possible for man to eat the seeds of a wide array of plants, but in the dietary tastes he has developed, he gives first preference to rice, wheat, and corn, with barley, millet, oats, and rye as second choices. These crops can be grown rather widely over the earth; however, in only a comparatively small number of regions do men specialize in producing surpluses of these grains for sale. Commercial grain farmers concentrate primarily on wheat for reasons that will be explained later.

Location

The major world regions of commercial grain farming are shown on Figure 11-1. The largest one, in Eurasia, stretches for 2000 miles from Kiev in southern Russia to Omsk in western Siberia; at its widest it extends 700 miles, from the Caucasus to Saratov on the Volga River. A few hundred miles to the east is a second region including much of the Uzbek Republic.

In North America there are several grain areas, the largest running from Alberta, through Saskatchewan and Manitoba, to the Dakotas. Another area centers on Kansas and spills over into neighboring states. Smaller regions appear in eastern Washington and Oregon, eastern Illinois and northern Iowa.

South America has commercial grain farming in Argentina. Australia has two areas, one in the southwest and one in the southeast.

Commercial grain farming is a mid-latitude activity —it is all between 30° and 55° latitude in both the Northern and Southern Hemispheres. None of the regions devoted to it is very large compared to other agricultural regions. Altogether, they take up only a small fraction—less than 5 per cent—of the earth's surface.

In this chapter, we shall start with Anglo-America and then take a look at other countries to see how they differ.

Table 11-1

World Production of Leading Crops

Crop	Production in Millions of Metric Tons	Area Harvested in Millions of Hectares*	Yield in Kilograms per Hectare
Wheat	347.6	213.4	1,628
Maize	301.3	108.2	2,785
Rice, paddy	295.3	131.2	2,251
Potatoes	279.8	22.0	12,666
Barley	152.2	84.9	1,793
Sweet potatoes	124.9	14.9	8,355
Oats	51.2	31.2	1,640
Sorghum	46.7	39.9	1,170
Millet	42.9	65.0	660
Rye	28.1	17.0	1,654

Source: United Nations, *Production Yearbook* (1973).

*United Nations data are published in terms of the metric system, in which the basic unit of area is a square meter. A *hectare* is 10,000 square meters, the equivalent of 2.471 acres. Similarly, a kilogram is 1,000 grams, the equivalent of 2.2046 pounds; 1 metric ton equals 2204.6 pounds.

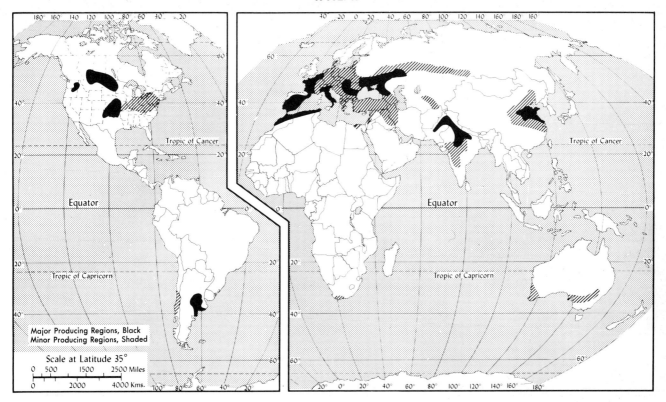

Figure 11-2

Characteristics: Anglo-America

Specialization in One Single Cash Crop. Commercial grain farmers are highly specialized. They concentrate on crops instead of animals, and each usually selects one single grain as the main source of income. In most commercial grain regions that crop is wheat.

Wheat. There are two kinds of wheat—*soft* wheat and *hard* wheat—and they are grown in distinctively different regions. Soft wheat has a low gluten content; therefore, its flour does not rise well with yeast, and it spoils fast. Soft wheat is better for spaghetti, crackers, and pastry.

Hard wheat has a high gluten content; flour made of it rises well and makes good bread. Further, it stands transportation without spoiling readily. For these reasons hard wheat is the type used in international trade and is the more widely grown variety.

The locational pattern of wheat in the United States is shown in Figure 11-3. Wheat occupies 17 per cent of all cropland, but in the commercial grain regions, sometimes over half the farm land is given over to it. Many people are surprised to see states outside the Great Plains on a map such as shown in Figure 11-3. Thinking only of Kansas, North Dakota, and other well-known wheat states, they fail to realize that the farmers of northern Missouri, southern Illinois, Indiana, Ohio, and Michigan place heavy emphasis on wheat.

The value of the United States' wheat crop comes to around $2 billion in most years—less than half the value of dairy products. The leading wheat-growing states are Kansas, North Dakota, Oklahoma, Montana, and Washington.

Other Crops. There are two important grain regions in the United States where the farmers specialize in producing corn for sale: east-central Illinois and north-central Iowa. Frequently these are termed *cash-corn* areas because corn is the main crop grown—but grown for sale rather than for feeding animals on the corn-growing farm as is done through most of the corn belt. The reason for this apparent anomaly will be considered later under the topic of relationships. For the

Figure 11-3 (*From U.S. Bureau of the Census.*)

WHEAT HARVESTED

1 Dot = 10,000 Acres

United States Total
45,372,868

nation as a whole, corn sold is valued at well over $5 billion. Occasionally, some other grain may be the major cash product. Farmers in southern Louisiana and the Sacramento Valley of California, for instance, specialize in rice. All other crops play secondary roles. A farmer may put in barley, oats, and rye in small amounts for consumption by his family, for feeding a few farm animals, or for supplementary income.

Area Cropped. The proportion of land devoted to crops attains unusually high percentages in commercial grain regions. Cropland accounts for 80 per cent of the total in the Red River Valley of North Dakota and in parts of western Kansas. Over large stretches of the grain regions the figure surpasses 60 per cent (see Figure 9-6).

Role of Animals. Animals—some chickens, perhaps a dairy cow, and a few swine—are raised to meet the subsistence needs of the farm family though many wheat farmers raise no animals at all. There are, however, small anomalous areas where cash animals are important, but these usually surround large cities. At one time horses were essential on every grain farm for pulling wagons and machinery, but their number declined as farms became mechanized. Draft horses are absent from most grain farms today.

Mechanization. No other type of agriculture is as highly mechanized as is commercial grain farming. Indeed, the very birth of commercial grain farming is attributable largely to the invention of two pieces of equipment—the steel plow and the harvester—that enabled man to unlock the resources of handicapped land. Today the typical grain farm has a fleet of machines: tractors, plows, disks, harrows, drills, reapers, combines, wagons, and trucks. There is scarcely a job to be done for which a machine has not been designed. The distribution of farm machinery in the United States can be typified by a map of farms with tractors (see Figure 9-11). Over 80 per cent of commercial grain farms have tractors.

Number and Size of Farms. There are approximately 370,000 cash-grain farms in the United States; roughly 20 per cent of all farms are of this type. Cash-grain farms cover an aggregate of 186,000,000 acres, about 20 per cent of all land in farms.

Commercial grain farms are the largest on earth. (Livestock raising takes up more acres, but it is based on natural vegetation rather than crops, so the holdings are more properly called ranches rather than farms.) Commercial grain farms average 924 acres in North Dakota, 1,506 acres in Washington, and 2,013 acres in

Montana. Farther south they are smaller—694 acres in Kansas and 593 in Oklahoma. The United States average is 500 acres.

Labor Force. The labor force on any farm is small, consisting of the farmer, members of his family, and perhaps two hired hands except for the brief period of harvest when large numbers of laborers are hired. In the entire United States there are only 68,000 "permanent" hired workers, those working more than 149 days a year. Were it not for mechanization, a farmer could never handle the tremendous acreage of commercial grain farms.

Wheat farming has one peak period for work: harvest time. Thousands of extra laborers had to be hired before the invention of *combine* machines (which cut and thresh wheat in one operation) and cornpicking machines (which pick and husk ears of corn). Today extra hands are still needed to man the fleet of combines that sweep northward, beginning in May with winter wheat harvest in Texas and finishing in September with spring wheat harvest in Alberta.

Farmsteads. Structures on grain farms are small and unpretentious compared to farmsteads in regions of dairy farming or of mixed-farming. With so few animals there is little need for large barns and silos to store feed, or for barns and sheds to shelter animals, or for large feedlots. In addition to the family residence, the only building needed is a garage for the machinery. At harvest time the grain is sped to market so that the farmstead needs no structure to store or process the crop.

Value of Farms. Commercial grain farms are far above the average in total value for both farm land and farm buildings—around $130,000 per farm. As Figure 11-4 shows, commercial grain regions stand out favorably compared with the national average of $104,000 per farm. The average farm value in North Dakota is $87,000 and in Kansas $91,000. But these farms are large, and their value per acre is relatively low—land values in commercial grain regions are perhaps one-fourth as much as Corn Belt land values (see Figure 9-14).

Physical Relationships

Precipitation. Commercial grain farming occurs usually where the annual rainfall is between 10 and 20 inches. But the effectiveness of precipitation depends not only on number of inches but also on rate of evaporation; where evaporation exceeds precipitation, a *dry*, or *arid*, climate results. Regions of commercial grain farming usually are associated with subhumid climates, that is, the drier margins of humid climates.

More critical than annual amount of precipitation and evaporation rate, though, is the seasonal distribution. Since wheat is a grass, it begins to grow by sending up a tuft of green blades. Then stalks of straw shoot up that

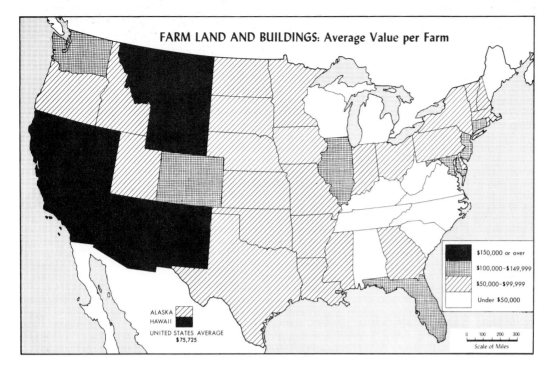

FARM LAND AND BUILDINGS: Average Value per Farm

$150,000 or over
$100,000–$149,999
$50,000–$99,999
Under $50,000

ALASKA
HAWAII
UNITED STATES AVERAGE
$75,725

0   100   200   300
Scale of Miles

Figure 11-4

carry the seeds. In this formative period, moist weather is essential if numerous large heads of grain are to develop. At the next stage, however, the weather should be sunny and dry if the grain is to mature properly. Excess rainfall at that time causes the plant to grow straw instead of seeds, makes it vulnerable to fungus and wilt, and induces molding of the grain after harvest. Humid summer weather may be excellent for corn but it is undesirable for wheat.

Hard wheat does well in subhumid lands. *Soft* wheat, though, can tolerate more moisture; it is the prevailing type east of the Mississippi River. But in humid lands, soft wheat must compete with corn, which is better than wheat for fattening animals. Moreover, wheat produces a lower yield per acre than do corn, oats, rye, and barley (Table 11-1). Humid regions in the mid-latitudes do grow wheat (Figures 11-2 and 11-3), but only secondarily to some other specialty crop.

The cash-grain areas of Illinois and Iowa are exceptions to these generalizations about precipitation and specialization. Illinois and Iowa are humid enough for corn and farmers there specialize in growing that crop for sale. They do so because of relationships with other factors to be considered later.

Combines in the Palouse Hills of Washington, cutting and threshing wheat in one operation. In the quest for more land on which to grow food, farmers have begun to grow grains on rather steep hillsides. (*USDA Photo by Doug Wilson.*)

Droughts. Since the variability of precipitation generally *increases* as the annual amount *decreases*, the threat of drought is serious in commercial wheat lands. In the chapter on livestock ranching, we observed that the grazing regions of the United States have often been invaded by farmers who thrived during humid years and went bankrupt during dry years. Most of these farmers were commercial wheat producers.

In drier country, *dry farming* (see p. 116) is commonly practiced. In the nation as a whole, about 5 per cent of all land in farms is in cultivated summer fallow. But in the leading wheat-producing states the nation's highest percentages of land in summer fallow are reached: North Dakota 22, Washington 17, Kansas 15, and Montana 10.

Temperatures. Wheat is widespread throughout the mid-latitudes (see Figure 11-2), being cultivated as far north as Finland and as far south as Argentina. Hardy strains of wheat need growing seasons of only 90 days. On the other hand wheat cannot stand excess heat, particularly in the formative period when the straw stalks are shooting upward and the cereal grains are developing. Therefore, little wheat is grown in areas where the average summer temperatures are over 68°. When both rainful and temperature are considered, the best wheat climate is one with a cool, moist season for early growth followed by a warm, sunny, dry period for maturation.

By temperature, there are two general types of wheat region: winter wheat areas and spring wheat areas.

Winter wheat grows where winters are mild. Seed is sown in the autumn, begins to sprout before the growing season ends, lies dormant through the mild winter, and matures in early summer. Winter wheat predominates throughout the United States except in the Dakotas and Minnesota.

Spring wheat grows where winters are too severe for wheat seedlings. Seed is sown in early spring and is harvested in the autumn. The spring wheat belt of Anglo-America starts in Minnesota and South Dakota, extends northwestward into Montana and the Prairie Provinces of Canada (Manitoba, Saskatchewan, and Alberta), and finally penetrates to the Peace River valley of Alberta, almost 60° north of the Equator.

Spring wheat is usually hard wheat. Winter wheat grown in dry areas is ordinarily hard, while that grown in humid areas is generally soft. Winter wheat yields are typically about 10 per cent higher than spring wheat yields.

The average wheat yield in the United States is about 31 bushels per acre. The states with high average wheat yields by bushel per acre are frequently states where winter wheat dominates: Arizona 68, California 51, and Idaho 45. The astonishing thing about the states with the highest yields per acre is that none of them is in either of the two main commercial grain-farming regions! The highest average yield per acre within the heart of the two major regions is found in Kansas (33). North Dakota averages 26 bushels per acre, Montana 25, Oklahoma 25, and South Dakota 24. Obviously, farmers in a region do not specialize in wheat just because its yields per acre surpass those of competitive regions but because, among their alternatives, wheat is the most remunerative.

Flora. Nearly every present commercial grain region originally had a natural cover of grass. The only exception is the area in the Soviet Uzbek Republic where commercial grain farming extends into a region of desert shrub. The contemporary significance of the original vegetation lies in both fertility of soil and ease of cultivation.

Fertility of Soil. Mid-latitude grasslands have developed some of the world's most fertile soils. Known as *chernozem*, these soils are extremely rich in plant nutrients for two reasons. First, a very high content of organic matter has been imparted by the grasses, so much so that their color is black. Second, leaching is limited because the rainfall in the grasslands is limited.

Chernozemic soils are so rich they can stand repeated cropping of the same grain year after year. Many fields have been in wheat for 20 consecutive years with no decline in yield. Wheat farmers accordingly practice very little crop rotation. Nor do they spend much money for fertilizer. Taking all cropland in the United States the average expenditure is about $4.75 per acre for commercial fertilizer. As Figure 11-5 shows, commercial grain areas require relatively low expenditures. The national average application is 0.17 tons of commercial fertilizer per acre; the figure for Kansas is 0.09 and for North Dakota 0.04. Low expenditures in Nebraska or Iowa would be understandable in the light of large supplies of manure produced on the farms themselves. But commercial grain farmers have no such supply; their low investment in phosphates, nitrates, and potash can be understood only in light of the inherent, matchless fertility of chernozemic soil.

Ease of Cultivation. The original cover of mid-latitude grass has also influenced the amount of effort required to cultivate soil. In the days of the wooden plow the grasses were a curse; wooden plows simply could not cut through the sod mat of grass roots. It was easier for pioneers to clear forest lands. But things quickly changed when the steel plow was designed. Grasslands that were formerly avoided were now eagerly sought. Now, in fact, they could be cultivated more easily than tree lands! They had no stumps. Thus did a single cultural factor—the invention of the steel plow—completely reverse the relative merits of two environments.

Landforms. Wheat will grow in rather rough land, but the major commercial wheat regions occupy plains because mechanized methods, absolutely essential to successful commercial grain cropping, work best on flat land. The Columbia Plateau is no exception; although it is high land, its surface is that of a rolling plain.

It is landforms that seem to explain the presence of the two anomalous cash-corn areas in the midst of the American Corn Belt mentioned earlier. East-central Illinois and north-central Iowa are unusually flat areas endowed with fertile soils. On most farms in that region corn is the principal crop, and most of them are on rolling plains. Therefore there is a good deal of land with at least a gentle slope—enough to foster erosion when the land is devoted to corn, a crop that lays bare the soil for a considerable length of time. To combat erosion, Corn Belt farmers put the slopes in alfalfa, clover, or permanent pasture, the flats usually in corn. A Corn Belt farm with such a diversity of landform is likely to be a stock farm—the animals being sustained by crops from that farm. But if a Corn Belt farmer is blessed with a large farm that is entirely flat, he is likely to realize more profit from it by devoting it all to corn—and then selling the grain as a cash crop.

In summation, the hypothesis . . . is that in the Corn Belt, and certain peripheral areas, even where permanent pasture is negligible, cash-grain farming will be found concentrated in those portions least subject to erosion, and livestock farming will prevail in the more rolling areas. Flat land will not dictate cash-grain farming, but it is the crucial factor which will permit cash-grain farming as a reasonable choice over long periods. On lands subject to erosion, good soil management suggests a crop rotation including alfalfa or clover. Cash-grain farming in such areas may not be impossible, but it certainly is not a wise choice.[1]

Cultural Relationships

Commercial grain farming occurs in areas typified by low population density, recent development, "frontier economies," a particular type of trade-center, milling industries, and intricate transportation networks. And some areas have odd freight-rate structures.

Population Density. Population densities are low in areas specializing in commercial grain, ranging from 2 to 25 people per square mile. Densities are higher, though—up to 125 people per square mile—in the few areas specializing in corn. If the population continues to shoot upwards from its present four billion it will be interesting to see what happens to the man/land ratios in these grain regions, especially the wheat lands. Will the ratios increase, and if so, will wheat growing persist as the leading activity or will it yield to other types of farming that today are associated with higher man/land ratios?

[1] Leverett P. Hoag, "Location Determinants for Cash-Grain Farming in the Corn Belt," *The Professional Geographer*, May 1962, pp. 6–7.

Figure 11-5

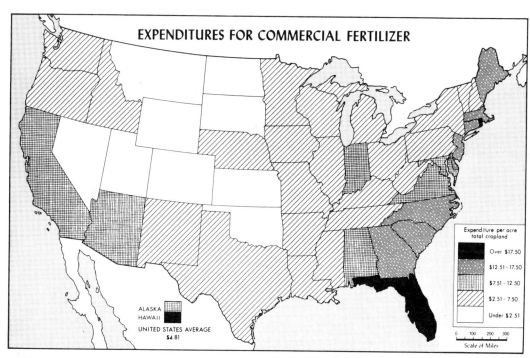

EXPENDITURES FOR COMMERCIAL FERTILIZER

Expenditure per acre total cropland

Over $17.50
$12.51 - 17.50
$7.51 - 12.50
$2.51 - 7.50
Under $2.51

ALASKA
HAWAII

UNITED STATES AVERAGE
$4.81

Recent Development. Commercial grain farming is a comparatively new economic activity, occurring in regions that have been settled, in general, within the last 150 years. One reason for this is the recent development of a large wheat market in Europe and America. A second reason is the recency of the mechanical revolution, which provided steel plows, harvesting machines, and other equipment for grain farming. To appreciate the significance of these inventions, we must recall the limited rainfall in commercial grain regions. In their natural state, these subhumid lands may be exploited successfully by livestock grazing, but they can not be cropped commercially with hand labor. Unless they are irrigated, dry lands have low yields per acre; therefore, each farmer must work a great deal of land in order to earn a living. This requires machinery, that is, *extensive* farming methods in which the ratio of number of acres to number of workers is high.

Frontier Stage of Development. Commercial wheat farming is particularly adapted to frontier areas. As waves of Europeans moved into the sparsely settled mid-latitudes of North America, South America, Australia, and Africa they invariably started raising wheat. With the following waves of settlers, wheat farming was displaced by other kinds of agriculture; but it took root again on the more distant frontier. At one time the leading wheat state in the United States was New York, then Ohio, then Illinois; now it is Kansas. Wheat is an ideal crop for frontier areas because it is worth more per weight and volume than many other grains and therefore bears transport costs better over long hauls; it keeps well and can be easily stored; and the market is relatively stable (that is, wheat-eaters consume about as much wheat in depressions as in times of prosperity). Since 1850 most of the world frontiers have been settled by Europeans familiar with wheat, and European financiers investing in these frontiers were interested in developing new sources of the grain most wanted in Europe.

"Sidewalk Farmers" and "Suitcase Farmers". Farms are linked to settlements by an increasing percentage of people who operate commercial grain farms but reside elsewhere than on the farms they run. Sully County, South Dakota, for instance, was selected as a sample area for studying this phenomenon; it had a total of 516 farms in 1950; 418 (81 per cent) of these were operated by farmers who lived on the farm; but 44 (8.5 per cent) of them were operated by *sidewalk farmers* —those who lived in a nearby settlement; 54 (10.5 per cent) were operated by *suitcase farmers*, operators, that is, who live 30 miles or more from the nearest border of the county containing their farm. These last are not to be confused with absentee owners who reside elsewhere and rent their farms to tenants. Most suitcase farmers in fact own their farms as well as operate them. As late as 1948 there had been only 12 suitcase farmers in Sully County; by 1952 their number had jumped to 78. Their homes were dispersed through twelve states; Texas was home for 20, Oklahoma for 17, Kansas 16, South Dakota 6, Minnesota 5, Colorado 5, Nebraska 3. Two others lived in Canada. By 1952 suitcase farmers were operating one-third of Sully County's wheat land.

On the other hand there was little change in number of sidewalk farmers between 1948 and 1952.

The amenities of life in a large, even if more distant, city are apparently a stronger draw than those of the isolated farmstead or the nearby town. Automobiles and airplanes enable the farmers to commute. Wheat is peculiarly adapted to *suitcase* farming because the farmer need not be on hand all the time.[2] Many of the "snow-birds" who live much of the year in Arizona, Florida, and other states with warm winters are wheat farmers from the Plains States or Prairie provinces of Canada.

Settlements and Their Employment Structures. Most towns and cities in commercial grain regions are fundamentally service centers whose existence depends on surplus grain. On the one hand they serve as transportation centers, where carloads of grain are assembled for shipment to larger centers; on the other hand, they serve as distribution points to supply farmers with lumber, coal, repair services for machinery, financial and other services.

There is an inverse correlation between the spacing of these settlements and general population density. In the commercial grain area of North Dakota the settlements are 40 miles apart; in that of Kansas they are 20 miles apart while in the Illinois cash-grain area the average is 7 miles apart.

Most of the jobs in small cities in commercial grain regions are in trade and services. Look at the employment structure of two sample settlements in Kansas (Table 11-2). Some settlements are also railroad division points and trucking centers.

The larger settlements have factories that transform a large portion of the grain output. Throughout the winter wheat region there are numerous flour mills, particularly in Kansas City, Topeka, Wichita, and Oklahoma City. In the spring wheat zone, Minneapolis and Winnipeg are the chief milling cities. Northeastern Illinois has several corn mills where starch and oil are made. Decatur, Illinois, is the seat of one of the nation's biggest processors of soybeans—one of the secondary cash crops in commercial grain regions (as well as in mixed-farming areas). We shall have more to say about the milling industry in Chapter 17.

[2]A fascinating analysis of this development has been written by Walter M. Kollmorgen and George F. Jenks, "Suitcase Farming in Sully County, South Dakota," *Annals of the Association of American Geographers*, 1958, pp. 27–40.

Table 11-2

Ch. 11 / Commercial Grain Farming

Selected Employment Structures in the Commercial
Grain Region of Kansas

Type of Employment	Norton	Dodge City
Population	3,602	14,127
Total employed	1,478	5,895
Percentage employed		
Total	100	100
Construction	12	7
Manufacturing	4	12
Transportation	5	4
Communication, utilities and sanitary services	3	6
Wholesale and retail trade	26	27
Finance, insurance, business, and repair services	7	6
Professional and related services	27	28
Educational services	8	8
Public administration	5	5
Other industries	11	5

The largest settlements contain grain exchanges—places where buyers of grain contact sellers. The largest exchange is the Chicago Board of Trade.

Truck and Railroad Transportation. The wheat moves to market (flour mills primarily) by a series of transportation links. Usually the grain is trucked directly from the harvesting machinery to a grain elevator which serves not only as a huge storage facility but also as a place of testing and grading the grain. Elevators are also equipped to clean and dry the kernels. Elevator owners generally buy the wheat and provide the farmers with marketing information. From farms within a few miles' radius, grain is trucked in directly to flour mills, but most of the grain is first assembled at country elevators. Elevators are located alongside railways, and railway box cars serve as the carriers which transport the grain from country elevators to flourmills, brewers, exporting points, or other terminals. In the flat, treeless plains of commercial grain country, such clusters of buildings are visible for miles. Indeed, the most conspicuous features of the landscape as one travels through the countryside of southern Saskatchewan, North Dakota, central Kansas, eastern Washington, or northeastern Illinois are the tall white elevators that mark each town and many a village.

At harvest season in wheat belts these settlements face a unique type of traffic congestion. The maturing of wheat crops cannot be scheduled evenly over a long time as can harvests of milk or vegetables. In any one area, all the wheat ripens simultaneously and must be harvested at once. All wagons and trucks in the area are pressed into service, some on 24-hour-a-day schedules, to move the wheat from farm to transportation center.

There the wheat is dumped into the country elevators and then into railroad cars for shipment to the main milling centers. American railroads begin shifting boxcars into the wheat regions several days in advance of harvest dates. The subsequent trainloads of wheat invariably clog the railroad yards in Winnipeg, Kansas City, Topeka, and other centers where huge elevators await filling. In no other economic region do the cities have, relatively, such large rail yards for storing freight.

In all this movement the railroad plays a major role —indeed, commercial grain regions did not develop until railways were constructed to and through them. The surge of railroad building west of the Mississippi River between 1870 and 1890 contained several companies (termed "*The Granger Roads*"), which wove a tight net through the leading commercial grain states, Kansas, Nebraska, Iowa, Minnesota, and the Dakotas (see Figure 7-7), and were financed for purposes of developing these granger states.

Today, grain is still an important source of revenue for railroads in the United States. Grain accounts for about 6 per cent of all cars of revenue freight loaded on Class I railroads (railroads with more than $1,000,000 gross annual operating revenue), and grain mill products account for another 4 per cent.

Water Transportation. Waterways play an important role in moving wheat from regions of surplus to deficit areas. Port Arthur, Fort William, Duluth, Chicago, and other Great Lake ports, as well as New Orleans and Houston—all have impressive dockside grain elevators for storing grain which is being transshipped from rail to boat. Generally speaking, hauling grain by truck is more expensive than hauling by rail, and rail is more expensive than boat. This explains why shippers, when given a choice, will often use water transportation to reach an important flour-milling center such as Buffalo.

Grains and cereal preparations account for about 10 per cent of the total value of all exports from the United States and are a major source of traffic in some ports. For example, grains and cereal preparations account for 33 per cent of the value of all commodities shipped from the New Orleans customs region, 27 per cent from the Houston region, and 15 per cent from the San Francisco region.

Market Regions. Most of the world's wheat is consumed as human food in Europe and Anglo-America. Most of the world's commercial grain regions are vitally linked with these two zones, which provide not only human consumers of wheat but also animal consumers of corn and oats. In 1800 these areas had a population of less than 200,000,000. Now their population is five times that figure. This population boom and

Wheat plunges from a railroad car tipped on its side through a huge funnel into a ship's hold. This device at Newport News, Virginia, which was originally designed for handling coal, can empty a carload of grain in approximately three minutes. (*USDA Photo by Jack Schneider.*)

the associated industrial revolution generated a tremendous purchasing power, a powerful stimulant to the development of commercial grain regions (as well as livestock ranching, dairy farming, and mixed farming) in distant regions of the world. Another linkage between commercial grain regions with Europe and with eastern Anglo-America involved the flow of capital funds that developed grain farms and serviced them with railroads. Moreover, Europe and eastern Anglo-America were the source regions of the settlers who opened up the world's commercial grain regions.

Most of the world's commercial corn is consumed as animal feed in the dairy belts, mixed-farming regions, and on poultry farms.

Government Price Support. For years, United States grain farmers produced more grain than the domestic and foreign markets were able to purchase. Normally this situation would produce such low prices that many a wheat or corn farmer would be confronted with bankruptcy. To avoid such a development the federal government guaranteed the farmers a minimum price which the Secretary of Agriculture established each year. The net effect of this arrangement was that the government would buy up surplus wheat and corn and store it in huge cylindrical steel bins which are still common sights in many settlements within the commercial wheat and commercial corn areas. But since the early 1970's the price of wheat grains has been so high that price supports have become meaningless. Grain prices have been kept high by increased domestic and foreign demand, including large wheat deals made with the U.S.S.R. by wheat exporters in the United States. Major factors explaining increases in demand are increased affluence in many of the world's nations, decreases in production caused by crop failures in some nations, and general population increases.

International Trade. Table 11-3 indicates the volume of international trade in four major grains. The

United States and Canada are the major wheat exporters. Even though most of their wheat is spring wheat (which, as we saw, gives low yields per acre) Canadians export tremendous tonnages for several reasons. Their own population is small, about that of California;

Table 11-3

World Trade in Cereal Grains, Leading Nations in Millions of U.S. Dollars

Country	Exports	Country	Imports
Wheat–Unmilled			
World	2,806	World	2,787
United States	1,004	Japan	342
Canada	824	United Kingdom	336
Australia	489	West Germany	194
France	304	India	155
Rice			
World	919	World	872
United States	257	South Korea	150
Thailand	139	Hong Kong	52
Japan	134	Cuba	35
Burma	65	India	31
Barley–Unmilled			
World	620	World	691
France	210	West Germany	151
Canada	193	Belgium-Lux.	86
Australia	69	Italy	84
United States	65	United Kingdom	71
Maize–Unmilled			
World	1,878	World	2,058
United States	746	Japan	363
France	357	Italy	319
Argentina	348	West Germany	251
Thailand	105	Netherlands	220

Source: United Nations, *Yearbook of International Trade Statistics* (1974).

Canadian wheat is high-quality hard wheat; and the Great Lakes and St. Lawrence Seaway provide a waterway across almost half of the continent.

Commercial Grain Farming in Other Regions

Commercial grain regions on other continents are essentially similar to those in Anglo-America, but there are some differences that are worth noting.

U.S.S.R. The Soviet Union, with the largest grain belt, is now one of the world's foremost wheat producers. The western part of this belt is in the Ukraine, the most humid and productive wheat region of Russia. Winter wheat predominates there but in the rest of this expansive grain belt spring wheat does. All of it is hard wheat. Notice (Figure 11-2) that the region tapers off in Siberia, impinged on by low temperatures on the north and by low precipitation on the south. The Uzbek region, however, receives adequate rainfall for wheat, due to the influence of the Pamirs and Tien Shan mountains. The Soviet wheat regions are distinguished by the Soviet system of collectivized farms on which thousands of acres are farmed by large labor forces, organized and managed by the government.

Argentina. The *pampas* of Argentina are vast flat grasslands west of Buenos Aires. The physical environment meets all the specifications for grain farming; it shows up clearly on a world map of wheat and of corn. In the east is the corn area, in the drier western portion is *the wheat crescent* (so-called because it bends around the populous area to the east). Because the region is near the sea, temperatures are so mild that farm buildings are few and small; instead of using elevators, distributors in some transport centers simply stack sacks of grain in huge piles. A railnet that is threaded through the pampas converges on the ports of Buenos Aires and Rosario. The propitious environment and good seaports have put Argentina in a competitive position for exporting grains. She is a noteworthy exporter of corn (Table 11-3).

Australia. Farmers in Australia's main commercial grain zone specialize in wheat. This zone extends 1000 miles inland from Adelaide in the general vicinity of the Murray and Darling river basins. A second zone is in the southwestern extremity of the continent. Australia's grain regions resemble Argentina's in both environment and nearness to the sea.

SUGGESTED READINGS

CHAKRAVARTI, A. K., "The Impact of the High-Yielding Varieties Program on Foodgrain Production in India," *The Canadian Geographer*, 1976, pp. 199–223.

DANDO, WILLIAM A., "Wheat in Romania," *Annals of the Association of American Geographers*, 1974, pp. 241–257.

FIELDING, GORDON, J., "The Role of Government in New Zealand Wheat Growing," *Annals of the Association of American Geographers*, 1965, pp. 87–97.

HOAG, LEVERETT P., "Location Determinants for Cash-Grain Farming in the Corn Belt," *The Professional Geographer*, May, 1962, pp. 1–6.

JOHNSON, HILDEGARD BINDER, "King Wheat in Southeastern Minnesota: A Case Study of Pioneer Agriculture," *Annals of the Association of American Geographers*, 1957, pp. 350–362.

KOLLMORGEN, WALTER M., and JENKS, GEORGE F., "Sidewalk Farming in Toole County, Montana, and Traill County, North Dakota," *Annals of the Association of American Geographers*, 1958, pp. 209–231.

———, and ———, "Suitcase Farming in Sully County, South Dakota," *Annals of the Association of American Geographers*, 1958, pp. 27–40.

MEINIG, DONALD W., *On the Margins of the Good Earth*, Chicago, 1962, 234 pp.

SAARINEN, THOMAS F., *Perception of the Drought Hazard on the Great Plains*, Chicago, Department of Geography Research Paper No. 106, 1966, 183 pp.

SIMS, JOHN, and SAARINEN, THOMAS FREDERICK, "Coping with Environmental Threat: Great Plains Farmers and the Sudden Storm," *Annals of the Association of American Geographers*, 1969, pp. 677–686.

CHAPTER

miscellaneous crops

Yellow sweet Spanish onions windrowed by mechanical harvester. The onions are planted in double rows, 1300 feet long, and the yield is about 42 tons per acre. (*Courtesy USDA, Soil Conservation Service.*)

The world has thousands of commercial crop farms that fit none of the agricultural types discussed so far. Many low-latitude farmers specialize in coffee, bananas, rubber, cacao, or other tropical crops. Their mid-latitude counterparts concentrate on cotton, tobacco, vegetables, or fruit. Some grow only flowers or bulbs. There is an increasing number of farmers in the higher latitudes who specialize in growing trees for wood. Clearly, there is quite a diversity. This chapter, however, will take up all these miscellaneous types of crop farms together, distinguishing only between farms in the tropics and farms in the mid-latitudes.

TROPICAL COMMERCIAL CROP FARMING

Location

Commercial crop farming, as Figure 12-1 shows, is widely dispersed throughout the tropics, those areas in which the average temperature for the coldest month is above 64°F. Three general tropical zones can be recognized: the American (extending through North America, South America, and the Caribbean Islands), the African (including Madagascar), and the Australasian (from India through Malaysia and Indonesia to northeastern Australia).

All told, tropical commercial crop farming occupies only a small percentage of the earth's surface in both the Northern and Southern Hemispheres. It occurs in numerous small areas rather than in broad regions.

Characteristics

Specialization in One Crop. Most farmers in these areas concentrate on growing a single crop for sale, such as bananas, cacao, pineapples, coffee, sisal, or rubber. A farmer may grow several other crops (often beans, yams, rice, corn, or manioc) for subsistence, but he selects one main source of revenue in an attempt to achieve the efficiencies of large-scale production.

There is regional specialization in each of the cash crops. For instance, over half of the world's coffee is produced in the Western Hemisphere (see maps of world distribution of these crops in almost any economic atlas), but most of the tea comes from the Far East. A large share of the cacao and palm oil comes from Central Africa, whereas copra comes mostly from Southeast Asia. From tropical farms come three valuable fibers for making twine and rope: in the Far East abaca, in Africa sisal, and in North America henequen. Almost all natual rubber comes from Southeast Asia.

Two plants grow widely in the tropics: bananas and sugar. But in most sections these are grown either for subsistence or for local sale. Commercial operations are conspicuously confined to the Americas.

Figure 12-1

MISCELLANEOUS COMMERCIAL CROP FARMING

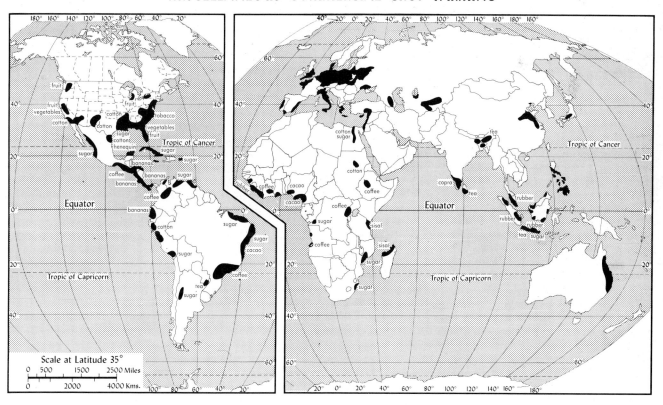

Hand Labor. A large amount of hand labor is required to plant, tend, harvest, and process the cash crop. Occasionally, machinery is used to clear the land, but other operations are most often done by hand. The hoe and the machete are typical tools.

Operating Units. The distinctive operating unit is the *plantation*, which is typified by large acreage, a small community of workers and families, a headquarters containing the central offices, and a processing plant in which the cash crop is prepared for shipment. The labor force often numbers several hundred people. This is *intensive* agriculture on a large scale.

But even taken all together plantations cover only a small part of the tropics. Extensive areas of natural vegetation usually surround each individual plantation; they constitute standby land that can be turned into fields as the soil in the old ones is depleted. In this respect, plantations resemble tropical subsistence farms; the subsistence farmers, however, shift their fields much more frequently.

Most plantation land is owned by foreign interests— a fact which, at times, has given rise to intense friction between indigenous people and the outsiders.

Not all commercial farms in the tropics are plantations, of course. Some small operations are run by individual farmers. These, though, are usually in the vicinity of large plantations, and they specialize in the same crops as do the plantations, and market their surplus during years of high prices through the same agencies as the plantations. They represent a transitional type between plantations and the small-scale primitive subsistence farms that cover most of the tropics (see Chapter 3).

Physical Relationships

Climate and Soil. Tropical plantations occur in regions where temperatures are relatively high and precipitation abundant throughout the year. With an uninterrupted growing season and plenty of moisture, the tropics are a natural greenhouse where crops can be harvested year around. But because of rainforest vegetation and rapid soil leaching, tropical soils usually contain little organic matter. To cope with the problem, some plantations even employ soil scientists whose main duty is to supervise the tending and fertilizing of the soil.

Diseases and Pests. Fungi, insects, and other forms of life thrive in this warm, humid environment. Plantations are sometimes shifted from one location to another not only to take advantage of fresh soil but also to escape infested areas. For instance, until 1930 the banana industry was centered on the *eastern* coast of

Panama, Costa Rica, and Nicaragua. But about 1890 a wilt disease, known as *Panama Disease*, had begun to attack the root systems of banana trees. The banana companies, unable to check the spread of this blight, set about abandoning the infested plantations and clearing land for new fields. But within three or four years the new fields too began to display symptoms of the disease. Finally, around 1930, the banana-growers conceded defeat, abandoned the humid eastern coast of Central America, and shifted their operations to the western coast. Here, there was a regular annual dry season that, though it made irrigation necessary, did check the disease.

Another plant disease, *Sigatoka*, attacks the banana leaves and limits the crop to small bunches of poor fruit. This blight can be controlled, but only at great expense. The trees must be sprayed every three weeks; the harvested fruit must first be dipped in sodium acid sulfate to remove the spray and then in water to rinse off the sulfate. These spraying and washing operations can account for one-fourth of the labor costs of a banana plantation in the affected areas. And the capital invested in pipes, pumps, and other spraying equipment almost equals the initial cost of preparing the land and planting the banana trees.

Winds and Landforms. Strong winds are also a serious menace, particularly to the larger fruits. Mature bunches of bananas, for example, fall in even a 25-mile-per-hour wind. The frequent hurricanes on the East Coast of Central America were a consideration, along with Panama Disease, in the relocation of the banana industry to the West Coast.

Most tropical plantations are situated on the lowland plains. There the alluvial soils are richer than the soils of the highlands, the land is easier to clear, the crops are easier to tend, and transportation is less costly.

Tropical plantations also tend to cluster along coasts or along navigable rivers, for water shipment is the main means of transportation in the tropics.

Cultural Relationships

Labor Supply. Since almost all the work on tropical plantations is performed by hand, commercial cropping in these regions is invariably associated with high population densities. For example, the Amazon Basin has an excellent physical environment for rubber growing but has few workers. By contrast, the coasts of Southeast Asia have both a satisfactory environment and many people. Consequently, most natural rubber comes from Malaysia and Indonesia.

Transportation. Plantations that are not on natural waterways must be near to railroads that lead to ports, for virtually all the cash crops in the tropics are shipped to distant regions.

Regions of Demand. The commercial farming regions of the tropics are intimately related to the populous northern mid-latitudes, specifically Europe and Anglo-America—the same regions that gave rise to livestock ranching, dairy farming, mixed farming, grain farming, in fact, almost every major commercial activity. Before 1300 A.D., very few tropical products were consumed in the mid-latitudes. Europe still had comparatively few people and eastern Asia, though it supported large masses, produced little purchasing power. Then with the cultural revolution that swept Europe in the fourteenth and fifteenth centuries, purchasing power increased and European traders scattered around the world. Tropical commodities now began to trickle back to Europe, but without exception they were the fruits of gathering rather than of agriculture. As the European market expanded, European settlers, in cooperation with native populations, launched agricultural enterprises to augment commercial gathering and increase the production of indigenous plants. Some plants were transplanted to other tropical regions, either to take advantage of a better labor supply, as in the case of rubber, or to be nearer the market regions, as in the case of bananas. (The details of these shifts will be explained below.) In the nineteenth century Anglo-America became the second major market for tropical crops.

Europe and the United States also supply the tropical farms with investment capital (most plantations are foreign-owned), machinery for clearing and cultivating the land, personnel for managing the enterprises, soil scientists to tend the soil, fertilizers with which to replenish soil, chemicals for combating diseases and pests, railway facilities for hauling the crops to ports, and ships for transporting the cargoes overseas.

Tropical crops usually undergo the final stages of manufacturing in the market regions; thus, rubber refineries, sugar refineries, and copra oil factories are seldom in plantation country. The main reason for this situation is simply that it is cheaper to ship the raw materials than the finished products.

Political Factors. The heavy influx of plantation managers, settlers, and investment capital from Europe and the United States in the late 1800's and early 1900's led to their political control over many tropical lands. This type of development has already been discussed in the treatment of primitive agriculture (see Chapter 3).

The political factor has also been operative in government attempts to control the price of the tropical commodity. The clearest example of how this has influenced the regional location of an industry is the rubber industry. In the early 1900's, for example, Brazil had almost a monopoly on rubber; and the Brazilian government kept rubber prices higher than those charged by British companies in the Far East—thereby unwittingly aiding the development of the Malayan industry. In the 1930's the British producers similarly attempted to keep prices up, only to discover that the plantations in the Dutch East Indies could make severe inroads into the market by producing rubber at a lower price.

Characteristics and Relationships of Specific Crops

The general pattern of tropical commercial agriculture can be seen more clearly, perhaps, as it applies to individual crops.

Sugar Cane. Sugar cane requires a total of 50 to 65 inches of rainfall a year, with a dry period to allow for final ripening; continuous rainfall encourages stalk growth but discourages the formation of sucrose. Growth usually ceases when the temperature falls below 65° and is best above 80°. Sugar cane is a perennial. The first crop, which is called *plant cane*, requires 15 to 24 months to ripen; thereafter, the harvests are annual. Succeeding crops are termed *ratoon crops*; they decline in yield as the years go by. The sugar yield of the first two ratoon crops is satisfactory, but then it falls off. So, many planters set out entirely new canes after the second ratoon crop. The variety of sugar most widely grown today was indigenous to Melanesia, perhaps New Guinea. Until the fifteenth century it was almost unknown in Europe (honey was the main source of sweetening) and was regarded as a luxury until the nineteenth century. The Spaniards and Portuguese introduced sugar culture to the Caribbean area in the early years of western colonization. Today, though India produces more sugar cane than any other one nation, the Americas provide about one-half of the sugar in world trade. The leading exporters and importers of cane sugar are indicated in Table 12-1.

Cacao. These trees begin to bear at the age of five years and continue to do so for two decades. The plant demands a continuously warm and humid climate. Sensitive to temperatures under 60°, cacao trees do best in the warm lowlands. They are also sensitive to strong winds, which increase transpiration and cause the fruit pods to drop prematurely. Indigenous to remote areas of the Upper Amazon and Upper Orinoco valleys, cacao now comes mainly from tropical Africa where the first seedlings were planted around 1880. Ghana, the world's leading producer, has over 3,700,000 acres in cacao farms. In Nigeria, which produces only two-thirds as much cacao as Ghana, there are both small native farms (2 or 3 acres) and plantations (exceeding 30 acres). The major exporters and importers of cacao are listed in Table 12-1.

Table 12-1

International Trade in Selected Tropical Crops—
Percentage of World Total by Weight

Leading Exporters		Leading Importers	
Sugar			
Cuba	20	United States	21
Brazil	12	U.S.S.R.	11
Australia	9	Japan	10
France	7	United Kingdom	9
Philippines	6		
Cacao (Cocoa Beans)			
Ghana	35	United States	21
Nigeria	20	West Germany	13
Ivory Coast	14	Netherlands	10
Brazil	9	U.S.S.R.	10
Bananas			
Ecuador	21	United States	31
Costa Rica	16	Japan	15
Honduras	15	West Germany	11
Panama	8	France	8
Natural Rubber			
West Malaysia	46	United States	20
Indonesia	26	Japan	12
Thailand	11	China	9
Sri Lanka	5	U.S.S.R.	8
		West Germany	7
Coffee			
Brazil	29	United States	36
Colombia	11	West Germany	9
Uganda	6	France	7
Angola	6	Italy	5
Copra			
Philippines	70	West Germany	26
Papua New Guinea	9	United States	19
Mozambique	5	Japan	13
Indonesia	4	Netherlands	10

Source: United Nations, *Trade Yearbook* (1974).

Bananas. Native to southern Asia, bananas were brought to the Western Hemisphere in the early 1500's where they now serve as a subsistence food. Bananas had already become an important commercial crop in the lowlands, encircling the Caribbean Sea by the late 1800's. Since the fruit spoils rapidly, however, only with the advent of air-conditioned ships (which are cool in summer, warm in winter) has it been possible to ship bananas from the tropics to Europe and Anglo-America all year round. Since such transportation is costly, the regions nearest the major markets have won an advantage.

The banana tree, which matures in one year, demands from 75 to 100 inches of annual rainfall with no dry season (it responds well to irrigation when the rain is inadequate), uniformly high temperatures, and well-drained soils to keep the roots from becoming waterlogged. It depletes soil nutrients so rapidly that it is called a soil killer.

Rubber. This plant thrives best in a hot, humid environment where rainfall is at least 70 inches (preferably 100 inches) and average temperatures are above 75°. Temperatures above 95°, however, unless accompanied by high humidities, cause the plant to dry out and discourage the flow of *latex*, the sap from which rubber is made. The soil must be well drained, for rubber trees will not grow with wet feet. Rubber trees are lowland plants that become vulnerable to viruses and other diseases at elevations above 1000 feet. In virgin rainforests there is an average of one rubber tree per acre; plantations, though, average 100 rubber trees per acre.

The rubber tree is indigenous to Brazil. The Brazilian government, in an effort to preserve Brazil's monopoly over the rubber industry, banned the export of rubber seeds and rubber shoots. But in 1878 an Englishman, Henry Wickham, smuggled out several thousand rubber seeds. Planting them in Ceylon, he successfully launched the rubber industry in the Far East. In 1905, the year the first shipment of rubber left Malayan shores, Brazil was producing 99 per cent of the world supply; today she produces less than 1 per cent. Malaya, with a larger and more efficient labor supply, easy access to ocean shipping, and satisfactory environment, quickly gained a competitive superiority to Brazil in rubber production.

Although the synthetic rubber factories of the United States could produce most of the nation's domestic rubber needs, the United States deliberately encourages imports of natural rubber from the Far East. Natural rubber is better than synthetic rubber for most purposes. Moreover, if the nations of this area were deprived of their export trade, their economies would be severely jolted and, then (many Western statesmen believe), the national people would become more receptive to communist appeals.

Coffee. Coffee is an evergreen tree that originated in the highland forests of Ethiopia. The most widely grown variety (which demands uniform but moderate temperatures of from 60° to 80°) is a tropical highland crop that does best at altitudes between 3000 and 6000 feet. It requires from 50 to 90 inches of rainfall well distributed throughout the year, but with the least during the flowering period. Like other forest plants, it prefers shade; in fact, shade trees are planted to protect it in sunny regions where adequate protection is lacking.

Sugar cane being harvested on the Warren Harang farm in Thibodaux, Louisiana. The cane, which yields 30 tons per acre or more, is often burned in the field, a process which rids the crop of insects and foliage. (*Courtesy USDA, Soil Conservation Service.*)

Copra. Copra is the white lining of the nut of the coconut palm tree. Rich in both oil and protein, copra is mainly used for margarine, soap, and animal feed. The coconut palm requires a mean annual temperature between 72° and 88°, a daily temperature that never falls below 50°, and annual rainfall of at least 50 inches. It prefers a coastal lowland but it will grow inland at surprising altitudes—up to 5000 feet in the Philippine Islands, which are the world's foremost source of surplus copra (Table 12-1).

MID-LATITUDE COMMERCIAL CROP FARMING

The *mid-latitudes* (areas which are not always warm—in contrast to the tropics—or always cold—as are polar zones) are generally defined by these limits: an average temperature below 64°F for the coldest month and an average above 50° for the warmest month. Many crops will grow successfully under such conditions and several are produced commercially. Commercial grain farming, an outstanding example, has already been discussed in detail in Chapter 11.

Location and Characteristics

The commercial production of crops (other than grains) in the mid-latitudes is restricted to small areas dispersed through broader regions that are typified by other forms of commercial bioculture, such as mixed farming, and livestock ranching. Most of these small areas occur in Anglo-America and Europe, though there are some in

Asia and a few in other continents. The only really large example of this type is in the eastern United States along the Atlantic and Gulf coasts.

Some farmers concentrate on a single cash crop such as cotton, tea, or tobacco; others specialize in groups of vegetables or fruit; a large number sell a diversity of crops. In any case, the income derives mainly from crops.

Major World Crops. The staple crops in mid-latitude commercial farms vary from region to region. Most of the *cotton*, for example, is grown in the southern United States, southern Soviet Union, northeastern China, western India, Pakistan, and the Nile Valley (Figure 12-2). *Tobacco* conforms to somewhat the same pattern, although it is grown in Europe but not in Egypt. *Tea* is essentially a Far Eastern product although one type of tea (called *yerba mate*) is produced commercially in South America. No single map is available of all fruit- or vegetable-growing, but for *apples* Europe and Anglo-America are the most productive areas, and Europe and the Soviet Union dominate the world *potato* map (Figure 12-3). Europe and Anglo-America are the main areas of horticulture—flowers, flower bulbs, flower and vegetable seeds, potted plants, vines, shrubs, and nursery trees. (World maps of these and numerous other

Cotton harvesters work their way through a field in Louisiana. While mechanization comes rather slowly to cotton harvesting, these machines can now pick as much in an hour as a man could pick in 72 hours. (*USDA Photo by Larry Rana.*)

COTTON LINT

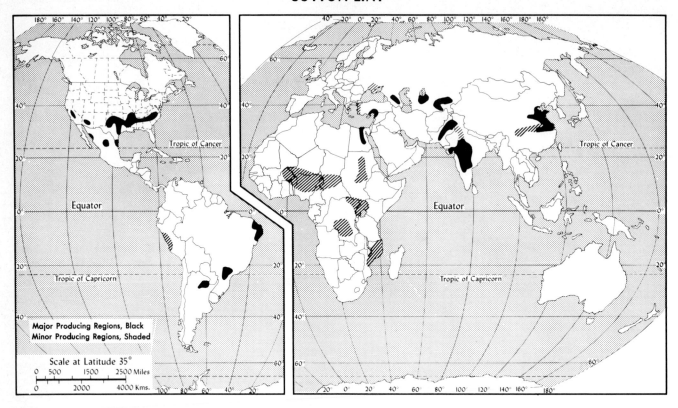

Figure 12-2

Major Producing Regions, Black
Minor Producing Regions, Shaded

Scale at Latitude 35°

0   500   1500   2500 Miles

0   2000   4000 Kms.

Figure 12-3

POTATOES

Major Producing Regions, Black
Minor Producing Regions, Shaded

Scale at Latitude 35°

0   500   1500   2500 Miles

0   2000   4000 Kms.

mid-latitude crops are available in the economic atlases recommended earlier.)

Major Crops Within the United States. The Graphic Summary volume of the *Census of Agriculture* breaks the regions of commercial crops within this country down into great detail. The chief categories (other than grains) are cotton, fruits, tobacco, vegetables, and horticultural specialties including nursery and greenhouse products.

1. Cotton: There are four important regions of cotton farming in the United States (Figure 12-4). The first is in the middle portion of the Mississippi Valley, beginning at its confluence with the Ohio River and spreading south. A second region swings eastward from Alabama through Georgia and the Carolinas. A third region, which consists of fewer farms yet produces as much cotton as the first two, is located in Texas and Oklahoma. Finally, cotton is harvested in California and Arizona. Texas accounts, by weight, for one-fourth of the national total, about twice as much as does California, the second-ranking state. The total value of the cotton crop is less than one-half that of wheat.
2. Fruits and nuts: The regional pattern of commercial fruit and nut farming is very spotty (Figure 12-5). The West Coast states clearly predominate, but central Florida also produces a great deal, as do the Northeastern states. Small pockets of this activity are scattered elsewhere.
3. Tobacco: The major tobacco region (Figure 12-6) spreads over the eastern Carolinas and southern Virginia; it includes most of Kentucky, southern Georgia, and northern Florida. Shares of the nation's tobacco crop by value are as follows: North Carolina 41 per cent, Kentucky 22 per cent, and South Carolina 8 per cent.
4. Vegetables: Vegetables harvested for sale (Figure 12-7) occupy many small areas widely dispersed throughout the nation, particularly in the North-

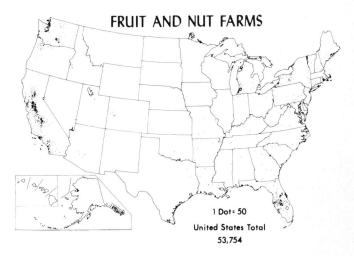

FRUIT AND NUT FARMS

1 Dot = 50

United States Total
53,754

Figure 12-5 *(From U.S. Bureau of the Census.)*

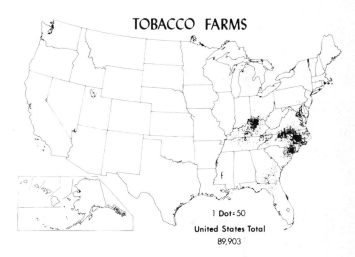

TOBACCO FARMS

1 Dot = 50

United States Total
89,903

Figure 12-6 *(From U.S. Bureau of the Census.)*

Figure 12-4 *(From U.S. Bureau of the Census.)*

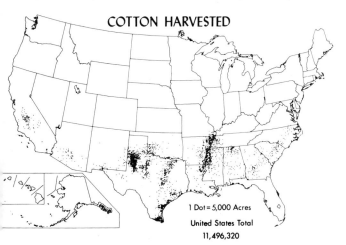

COTTON HARVESTED

1 Dot = 5,000 Acres

United States Total
11,496,320

Figure 12-7 *(From U.S. Bureau of the Census.)*

VEGETABLES HARVESTED FOR SALE

1 Dot = 1,000 Acres

United States Total
3,352,383

east, from Minnesota to New Jersey. Several sections appear throughout the southern states. But most commercial vegetable production is in the far west; California alone accounts for 36 per cent of all vegetables sold from the nation's vegetable farms.

5. Nursery and greenhouse products: The pattern of farms specializing in flowers, mushrooms, and similar products is also rather spotty (Figure 12-8). California is the leading state with 20 per cent of national sales, and Florida is second with 10 per cent. But the Northeast is the leading area and contains the other ranking states.

6. Trees: Tree farming is a new activity that is difficult to classify. Does it belong with forestry or with bioculture? Indeed, some people would contend that these two paragraphs belong in Chapter 6 on forest gathering. We are assigning tree farming to agriculture because, as in banana plantations and apple orchards, particular plots of land are set aside for a particular tree crop, seedlings are deliberately planted, the growing trees are tended and protected, and the harvest is carefully gathered. The main differences between tree farming and traditional types of agriculture are that the trees are grown not for fruit (like coconuts) or for leaves (like tea) but for wood, and that the crops require several decades rather than a few months to mature.

Tree farms now cover millions of acres of the United States. Much of this acreage is in the southern states from North Carolina to Texas. But the largest tree farms, planted mostly in Douglas fir, are in the Pacific Northwest, where the first large mass planting took place in 1941. The first large harvest will probably

Tobacco is a crop which requires a large amount of hand labor, as well as specially designed barns for drying. This crop, being grown near Lancaster, Pennsylvania, is destined for processing into cigars, while cigarette tobacco is generally grown farther south in Virginia and North Carolina. (*Courtesy Clair A. Shenk.*)

Carrots piled on a truck in Holtville, California. The Imperial Valley of California provides the nation with many types of fruits and vegetables. Thanks to mild winters and extensive irrigation facilities, these crops often can be harvested during seasons when fresh fruit and vegetables are not locally available in most of the rest of the nation. (*Courtesy Clair A. Shenk.*)

Figure 12-8

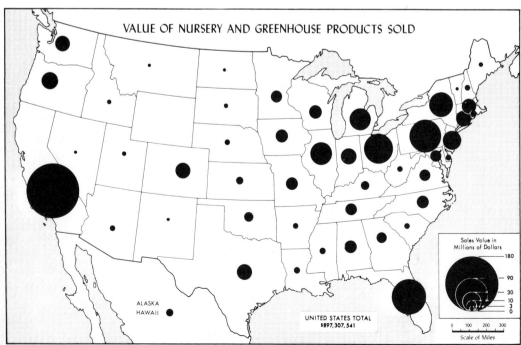

VALUE OF NURSERY AND GREENHOUSE PRODUCTS SOLD

ALASKA
HAWAII

UNITED STATES TOTAL
$897,307,541

Sales Value in
Millions of Dollars

180
90
30
10
3
0

0   100   200   300
Scale of Miles

not be ready before the year 2020. Here is one reason why tree farming has not been conducted on a large scale in the past: The long time lag between the date of investment and the date of harvest has discouraged risk capital.

Operating Units. All of these diverse commercial crops are grown on operating units that range from vegetable farms of only a few acres to tree farms of thousands of acres. But some generalizations can be made from the figures given in Table 12-2. First, cotton,

Table 12-2

Characteristics of Selected Farm Types

Type of Farm	Number of Farms of in Thousands	Average Value of Farm Products Sold per Farm in Thousands	Average Size of Farms in Acres
Cotton	41	$19.9	463
Tobacco	90	10.5	122
Vegetable	20	58.7	250
Fruit and nut	54	31.1	148
Total—Farms of all types	1,734	$25.7	529

Source: U.S. Bureau of the Census, *U.S. Census of Agriculture* (1973).

tobacco, vegetables, and fruit and nut farms are only a small portion of the total number of farms in the United States. Second, these types of farms tend to be relatively small. This is especially true of tobacco and fruit and nut farms, but even vegetable farms are only about one-half the size of the average United States farm, and this figure is inflated by a few large vegetable farms located mostly in California, Arizona, Texas, and Florida. Finally, the fact that there are many small and economically marginal tobacco and cotton farms shows up in the low figures on average value of farm products per farm. Vegetable farms, and to a lesser extent fruit and vegetable farms, produce a high-value product, which helps account for the high average value figures for these farms.

Fertilization. Animals play a minor role on commercial crop farms; consequently, there is a dearth of manure, and plant food must be purchased. Most of the expenditure is for *commercial fertilizers* manufactured from phosphate rock, nitrate rock, potash rock, and limestone. In the United States, the average expenditure *per acre* on fertilized cropland for commercial fertilizer is over $13 a year, but on vegetable, flower, fruit, tobacco, and cotton farms the figure sometimes exceeds $20. Figure 12-9 shows several conspicuous areas in which a good deal of money is spent for fertilizers; notice that these areas are generally either in the Corn Belt or

EXPENDITURES FOR COMMERCIAL FERTILIZER

1 Dot = $250,000
United States Total
2,209,185,456

Figure 12-9 (*From U.S. Bureau of the Census.*)

in those regions where cotton, tobacco, vegetables, and fruits are grown. See also Figure 11-5, page 129.

Plantations and Neoplantations. The predominance of the plantation system in the American Cotton Belt before the Civil War is well known. There seems to be a widespread impression, however, that after the War this plantation system disintegrated with the abolition of slavery. To be sure, the nature of the plantation *labor force* did change radically, but the *landholdings* remained generally intact and have persisted to the present time. Indeed, the term *plantation* is still common coin in the South to apply to agricultural enterprises that meet the following criteria: (1) A landholding considerably larger (averaging between 700 and 800 acres) than "family farms" (those operated by a single family). (2) A division of labor and management duties. (3) Specialization in commercial production. Rarely, however, is the specialization in just one single item; rather, *groups* of two or three specialties are the norm today, principally some combination chosen from cotton, rice, sugar, soybeans, pecans, cattle, and hogs. (4) Location somewhere in the South where the plantation tradition is part of the cultural heritage: namely, the Mississippi Valley and a broad belt from the Brazos River in Texas to the James River in Virginia. (5) Centralized location of dwellings (in a "plantation village") and of farm operations. (6) A large input of cultivation power per acre.

The term *neoplantation* applies to a type of plantation operation that has evolved since World War II. What mainly distinguishes the type from regular plantations is a high degree of mechanization. This has been associated with migration of rural labor to cities in the North and the South in response to the lure of higher wages in industrial plants and an increase in labor costs and other production costs relative to market prices. To resolve these two problems, farm operators have mechanized. Such a solution has been expedited by the mass production of tractors selling at reasonably low prices. On one plantation, for example, three tractors replaced fourteen teams of mules and the labor force has decreased from sixteen to seven.

Merle Prunty has this to say about neoplantation development in the South:

> Such evidence as exists suggests that mechanization has not displaced large numbers of laborers on plantations; on the contrary, landowners have been compelled to mechanize because of voluntary labor migrations. . . .
>
> However, acquisition of tractors and cultivating implements alone customarily does not signify the inception of neoplantation occupance. . . . . Neoplantation occupance is established when *harvesting* implements are added in sufficient numbers to justify large fields for their efficient use.
>
> The functional focus of the neoplantation is the tractor station, which also shelters harvesting, cultivating and accessory machinery, spare parts, repair tools and fuel. Neoplantation occupance eliminates most share-paid labor. Cash-wage labor, which works machines under central direction, and which is applied as a unit to the whole acreage of the holding in a manner approximating the employment of gangs of slaves on large fields under ante-bellum occupance, predominates on these holdings today. The tractor station is always located close to the manager's or owner's residence, a locational factor suggesting the intimate interrelationship of centralized management and cultivating power. Thus its location approximates, closely, that of the mule barn under ante-bellum occupance.
>
> The neoplantation differs from the ante-bellum unit in a few significant spatial aspects. The proportion of woodland is less, generally, than on the ante-bellum form . . . and beginnings of sensible legume-livestock rotations are implied by the crops now grown. There are fewer houses than on the ante-bellum unit of the same acreage, and their arrangement customarily is more linear (along roads) than rectangular or compact.[1]

Physical Relationships

The several crops dealt with in this chapter—cotton, tobacco, tea, vegetables, and fruits—are diverse enough in their environmental requirements to warrant separate mention. But in their cultural aspects, they are similar enough to be considered as a group.

Cotton requires a growing season of about 200 frost-free days. Usually the longer the growing season, the longer the staple length (that is, the length of fiber). There must also be five months of high temperatures, preferably above 70°. Cloudy weather, though, prevents the cotton boll from ripening. Unless irrigated, at least 20 inches of rainfall are needed annually, with eight of

[1]Merle Prunty, Jr., "The Renaissance of the Southern Plantation," *Geographical Review*, 1955, pp. 459–491.

them distributed through the growing season. Excess moisture in the growing season, however, promotes attacks by funguses and bollworms. Cotton grows on a large variety of soils; it does particularly well on less rich ones that limit excess vegetative growth at the expense of boll growth.

Tobacco is one of the most tolerant crops in terms of temperature requirements. Some varieties prefer warm humid conditions as in the Carolinas, while others thrive in more rigorous climates such as Wisconsin and Connecticut. High humidity produces thin leaves with low nicotine content—"mild" tobaccos.

Tea is an evergreen plant that grows best where temperatures stay above 55° and below 90°. Few plants require as much moisture as tea, which demands over 100 inches well distributed through the year. Humidity must be high to assure abundant leaf formation, consequently heavy dews and fogs are welcome.

Vegetables need only rather short growing seasons but they demand considerable moisture during the season. In California, Arizona, Texas and Florida the climate is warm enough to permit two and three crops a year of several vegetables.

The trees and vines that flourish in mid-latitude can endure severe winters; but their *fruits* are sensitive to frosts. The best locations, therefore, are those where the springs are cool enough to discourage blossoming until the threat of severe frost is past and the autumns are mild enough so that late summer growth can be completed before the winter cold sets in. These conditions frequently prevail on the *leeward* side of large bodies of water, where the water warms up more slowly than the land in spring and cools off more slowly in autumn. Notice how the leeward shores of Lake Michigan, Lake Erie, Lake Ontario, and central Florida stand out on Figure 12-5. This helps explain the contrast on this map between the West Coast states, on the leeward side of the Pacific Ocean, and the East Coast states, on the windward side of the Atlantic Ocean. (Remember that *prevailing* winds in the United States blow from the West).

Unfortunately, many regions with good environments for cotton, tobacco, tea, vegetables, and fruits are far from urban markets. As a result, low production costs are partially offset by the high transport charges due to both long hauls and refrigeration. To overcome these disadvantages, producers in distant areas concentrate on large crops of a few commodities so that they can ship each in carload and trainload lots.

Regions of Mediterranean climate have particularly favorable environments for many of the crops discussed in this chapter. Consequently, the agriculture in such areas is now a mixture of traditional Mediterranean farming and commercial growing of vegetables, fruits, vines, and even cotton.

Cultural Phenomena

Market. Nearness to market saves both time and money in transportation, an advantage that is critically important in the case of perishables such as vegetables and fruits. Many large cities are surrounded with vegetable farms intermixed with dairy farms.

But commercial crop farming on the outskirts of cities suffers certain disadvantages as well: The land is expensive, the growing seasons around many mid-latitude cities are short, the soils may be poor, and the terrain may be rough. Therefore, market gardeners must employ very intensive methods in order to squeeze out the maximum yield per acre. Usually they grow a multiplicity of crops, scheduling their plantings to ensure a harvest of both early crops (such as radishes and lettuce) and later crops (such as carrots, tomatoes, and cabbages). They cram the greatest number of harvests they can into the growing season, which lasts for 189 days on the farms around New York City, about 177 days around Detroit, and 162 days around Chicago. Increasingly large amounts of these perishable crops are being produced locally in the artificial environment of a greenhouse or are imported by air from Mexico and other places with mild climates.

Farm Management. Even regions that enjoy easy access to markets and favorable environments do not automatically develop commercial crop farming, however. This activity develops only where the farmers recognize and exploit natural advantages. The role of this factor as well as market and the physical environment is analyzed by Clarence W. Olmstead as follows:

Three conditions were necessary for the development of orchard and vineyard regions: (1) a market demand for the produce, (2) a permissive, if not favorable, natural environment, and (3) recognition of the opportunity afforded by these conditions and the desire and ability to profit therefrom. In the early days of small, widespread kitchen and farm orchards, the market was correspondingly small and widespread; environmental conditions were not carefully evaluated. Then came the change

which has stimulated the revolution in agriculture in America and the world—the multiplication and alteration of market demand.

Urbanization separated most householders from their kitchen orchards, as from their milk cows and vegetable gardens. Increase of population, especially in cities, multiplied demand for the product of farm orchards. As farm orchards were expanded to meet the demand for quantity, they became subject to new demands—for quality. Only those growers who took advantage of the new developments in plant improvement, pest control, pruning, thinning, tillage, fertilization, harvesting, and selling, could survive the competition that ensued.

Specialization resulted. The farmer with three or four acres of orchard and the remainder of his 80 acres devoted to field crops and livestock does not postpone corn-planting in order to spray apples, or interrupt haying so as to thin peaches. Unsprayed apples and un-thinned peaches lost out in the increasingly quality-conscious market. Thus, the general farmer faced the alternatives of expanding and intensifying his farm orchard enterprise, or of abandoning it. Most were abandoned. Where the first alternative, specialization, was chosen, orchard regions began to emerge. The evolution occurred where one or a combination of three sets of conditions existed: (1) advantageous location with respect to market, (2) advantage with respect to natural growing conditions, especially climate, and (3) a particular desire to specialize in orchard or vineyard enterprise.

Successful development and maintenance of a regional orchard and vineyard specialty requires the expert attention of many people, not only farmers but also processors, packers, brokers, shippers, researchers, inspectors, laborers, labor recruiters, bankers, and handlers of equipment and supplies. A small farm orchard, or even a few large modern orchard establishments, may operate successfully on the basis of a limited local market. But such an individual operator is handicapped in meeting the keen competition offered in large, distant markets by

Harvesting cabbage on the Krunmueller farm near San Juan, Texas. Workers cut the mature cabbage heads and drop them onto a conveyor belt, which carries them to a wagon. Immature heads may never be picked because it won't pay to g o over the field again. (*USDA Photo by Cornelius Keys.*)

established orchard and vineyard regions which have developed the organization and services not only for efficient production, but also for low-cost grading, packing, processing, advertising, shipping, and selling.[2]

The appraisals farmers have made of the potentialities of various areas, of the costs of farming particular crops there, and of the profits available by marketing those crops in urban regions have led to pronounced specialization in many places: citrus fruit in Florida, southern Texas, and southern California; peaches in Georgia (for early marketing), in Arkansas, southern Illinois, and Colorado (for August marketing), and in western Michigan (for autumn marketing); tung trees (for vegetable oil) in southern Mississippi and Alabama; apples in the Yakima and Wenatchee valleys of Washington and in numerous Appalachian valleys of the eastern United States; cherries in western Michigan and Wisconsin's Door Peninsula; and strawberries in the Delmarva Peninsula (the land mass between Chesapeake Bay and the Delaware River). And as for California—nearly every mid-latitude fruit and vegetable thrives in at least one of its valleys.

Labor Supply. The tending of most mid-latitude crops requires large numbers of laborers, particularly during the harvest season. Every year, with the coming of summer, thousands of migrant laborers (largely Mexican and Puerto Rican) travel north from the harvest fields of the southern United States as farm jobs open up in the higher latitudes. On most vegetable plantations, the migrant labor force is nearly 8 times the permanent force. For example, a 2000-acre "ranch" in Arizona has a permanent labor force of 25 (tractor drivers and irrigators) plus 200 seasonal migratory workers (mostly Mexican nationals) who weed and harvest the crop.

International Trade. The leading exporters and importers of several of the crops discussed in this chapter appear in Table 12-3. Since so many mid-latitude vegetables and fruits (carrots, lettuce, onions, cabbage, potatoes, apples, pears, peaches) are grown in the general vicinity of their main markets, there is comparatively little international trade in these commodities. Most of what limited trade there is is within Europe or

Table 12-3

International Trade in Selected Mid-Latitude Crops—
Percentage of World Total by Weight

Leading Exporters		Leading Importers	
Apples			
France	24	West Germany	24
Hungary	15	United Kingdom	14
Italy	14	U.S.S.R.	14
South Africa	7	Brazil	5
Cotton			
United States	27	Japan	19
U.S.S.R.	16	China	12
Turkey	7	West Germany	6
Brazil	6	France	6
		Italy	6
		Hong Kong	4
Tea			
Sri Lanka	27	United Kingdom	28
India	25	United States	10
China	7	Pakistan	5
Kenya	7	U.S.S.R.	5
		Australia	4
Tobacco			
United States	23	United States	12
Turkey	9	United Kingdom	12
India	7	West Germany	11
Bulgaria	6	U.S.S.R.	7
Brazil	5	Netherlands	5
Greece	4	Japan	5
		Spain	5
Potatoes			
Netherlands	31	West Germany	23
Poland	10	Italy	12
France	7	Czechoslovakia	7
United Kingdom	6	France	6
		United Kingdom	6

Source: United Nations, *Trade Yearbook* (1974).

[2]Clarence W. Olmstead, "American Orchard and Vineyard Regions," *Economic Geography*, 1956, pp. 189–236.

Table 12-4

International Trade as a Percentage of Production
of Selected Crops

	World Totals: Thousands of Metric Tons		
Crops	Production	Export Trade	Export Trade as a Percentage of Production
Tropical			
Sugar	626,599	22,973	4
Bananas	35,520	6,637	19
Coffee	4,102	3,651	89
Copra	3,741	1,052	28
Cocoa beans	1,354	1,161	86
Mid-latitude			
Cotton	13,396	4,614	34
Potatoes	315,732	3,922	1
Apples	22,373	2,440	11
Tobacco	4,959	1,188	24
Tea	1,571	768	49

Source: United Nations, *Production Yearbook* (1975) and *Trade Yearbook* (1974).

across the North Atlantic. Whereas only 1 per cent of the world's potatoes cross international boundaries, 34 per cent of the cotton, 49 per cent of the tea, and 24 per cent of the tobacco (Table 12-4) cross such borders.

Some countries appear in both the exporter and importer column for the same crop in Table 12-3. Thus, the United States exports over 20 per cent of all tobacco yet imports 12 per cent. Such apparent incongruity is often explained by the fact that a country has a surplus of one specific *type* of a crop but is deficient in another type. In this case, considerable tobacco comes from Turkey for blending with domestic leaves.

SUGGESTED READINGS

AUTY, RICHARD M., "Caribbean Sugar Factory Size and Survival," *Annals of the Association of American Geographers*, 1976, pp. 76–88.

CARLSON, ALVAR W., "Specialty Agriculture and Migrant Laborers in Northwestern Ohio," *The Journal of Geography*, 1976, pp. 292–310.

JOHANNESSEN, CARL L., "The Dispersal of Musa in Central America: The Domestication Process in Action," *Annals of the Association of American Geographers*, 1970, pp. 689–699.

JUMPER, SIDNEY R., "Wholesale Marketing of Fresh Vegetables," *Annals of the Association of American Geographers*, 1974, pp. 387–396.

MANSHARD, WALTHER, *Tropical Agriculture: A Geographical Introduction and Appraisal*, translated by Dorothea A. M. Naylon, New York and London, 1974, 226 pp.

Plantation Systems of the World, Social Science Monographs, Pan American Union, Washington, D.C., 1959, 212 pp.

PRUNTY, MERLE C., and AIKEN, CHARLES S., "The Demise of the Piedmont Cotton Region," *Annals of the Association of American Geographers*, 1972, pp. 283–306.

RAITZ, KARL B., and MATHER, COTTON, "Norwegians and Tobacco in Western Wisconsin," *Annals of the Association of American Geographers*, 1971, pp. 684–696.

SCHUL, NORMAN W., "A Philippine Sugar Cane Plantation: Land Tenure and Sugar Cane Production," *Economic Geography*, 1967, pp. 157–169.

SMITH, DEREK L., "Market Gardening at Adelaide's Urban Fringe," *Economic Geography*, 1966, pp. 19–36.

SOUTH, ROBERT B., "Coca in Bolivia," *Geographical Review*, 1977, pp. 22–33.

CHAPTER 13

miscellaneous animals; review of bioculture

The Hildinger Hodge catfish farm at Bonham, Texas. Raising catfish for commercial sale is a rapidly growing industry in the southern states. (*USDA-SCS photo by John Doak.*)

Our purpose in this final chapter on bioculture is twofold: (1) to consider several branches of animal raising not taken up in previous chapters, and (2) to generalize about bioculture as a whole, now that we have examined individual types. The United States will serve as the case-study area, essentially because of availability of statistical measurement.

MISCELLANEOUS ANIMAL FARMING

Location and Characteristics

There is no satisfactory world map available showing the regions of commercial animal farming other than livestock ranching, dairying, and mixed farming. The reason for this deficiency is that the specialization of farms in producing other animals and products is a rather recent development, is still comparatively limited, and has not been widely studied by regional analysts. Nevertheless, from what information is available, it seems clear that commercial farms that specialize in the production of animals (other than cattle, sheep, and swine) are generally located in Anglo-America and western Europe.

Products Sold. Eggs and poultry, fur animals, and fish are all produced for sale on specialized farms. We have seen that some of these products, notably eggs and poultry, are minor sources of income on farms that specialize in other items, but in recent years a substantial number of farms have come to depend for their income *primarily* on the sale of these products. Let us take them up separately.

1. Poultry: Chickens are probably the most widespread farm animal. Almost every farm, regardless of type, whether subsistence or commercial, in tropical climates or in severe climates, has a few laying hens. And a sizable amount of commercial poultry is indeed sold from farms with other specialties. But we are concerned here with farmers who raise poultry for sale. Some specialize in poultry to such a degree that poultry sales account for at least half their revenue.

Flock of turkeys on the Karl Herkamp farm in Clackamas County, Oregon. (*Courtesy USDA, Soil Conservation Service.*)

Actually, the United States has over 55,000 such farms. Although they make up less than 4 per cent of all farms in the country, they constitute unusually high percentages in certain states: Delaware 39 per cent, Georgia 20, Connecticut 19, Maine 19, Alabama 19, and Arkansas 17. In Delaware, in fact, poultry farms outnumber any other type of farm. As revealed in Figure 13-1, which shows the locational pattern of poultry farms, the major area is in the South Atlantic and South Central states, especially Georgia, Alabama, and Arkansas. Poultry farms are thinly sprinkled throughout the Corn Belt and New England. There are very few poultry farms in the western half of the country, with the conspicuous exception of southern and central California.

The value of poultry products sold by United States poultry farms, augmented by the value of poultry sold by dairy farms, mixed farms, and other establishments, reaches the astonishing sum of $6 billion annually.

Figure 13-2, based on the value of all poultry and their products, shows somewhat the same pattern as Figure 13-1. But notice that two different types of region are discernible: (1) the major producing region

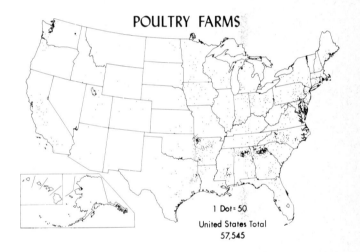

POULTRY FARMS

1 Dot = 50

United States Total
57,545

Figure 13-1 (*From U.S. Bureau of the Census.*)

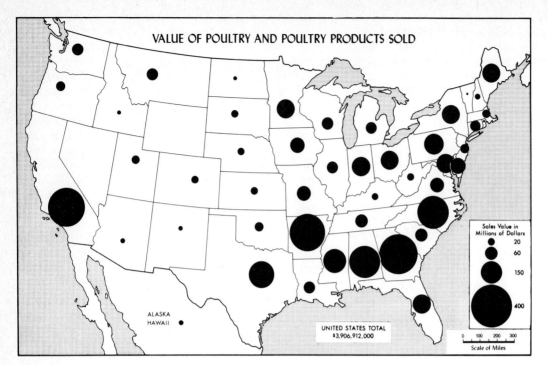

VALUE OF POULTRY AND POULTRY PRODUCTS SOLD

Sales Value in Millions of Dollars
20
60
150
400

UNITED STATES TOTAL
$3,906,912,000

ALASKA
HAWAII

0 100 200 300
Scale of Miles

Figure 13-2

which runs from New York, south to Florida, and then west to Arkansas and Texas, and (2) a secondary region which runs from Ohio to Iowa and north to include Wisconsin and Minnesota. The major region includes five states which each produce more than $200 million in poultry products and together account for almost 40 per cent of the total U.S. value of poultry and their products: Georgia $396,000,000, Arkansas $356,000,000, North Carolina $278,000,000, Alabama $267,000,000, and Texas, $209,000,000. States in the second region generally produce $50,000,000 to $120,000,000 annually.

Chickens and chicken eggs are, of course, the leading poultry products (Figures 13-3 and 13-4 and Table 13-1). The map of chickens sold (Figure 13-4) reveals a highly unusual regional pattern. Notice that the map is extremely spotty with numerous centers of intense activity surrounded by areas where scarcely any chickens are sold. (The influence of a cultural factor, contract farming, is a major explanation of this pattern and will be explained in the following paragraphs.) Imagine a line drawn diagonally from central Maine to Oklahoma City and then straight south to Mexico. Southeast of this line lies the main chicken-selling region of the nation. Nearly 2 dozen concentrations stand out there of which the most extensive are in northern Georgia, the Delmarva Peninsula, northwestern Arkansas, central Mississippi, and northern Alabama. A few equally sharp concentrations appear elsewhere, e.g., California and Maine. By states, Georgia is the unquestioned leader; farmers there raise 11 per cent of the chickens sold in the United States.

Visual inspection of Figures 13-3 and 13-4 suggests that chickens of all types are much more widely

CHICKENS 3 MONTHS OLD OR OLDER

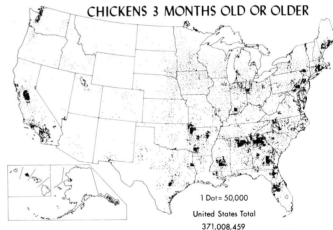

1 Dot = 50,000

United States Total
371,008,459

Figure 13-3 *(From U.S. Bureau of the Census.)*

Figure 13-4 *(From U.S. Bureau of the Census.)*

**MEAT-TYPE CHICKENS
LESS THAN 3 MONTHS OLD SOLD**

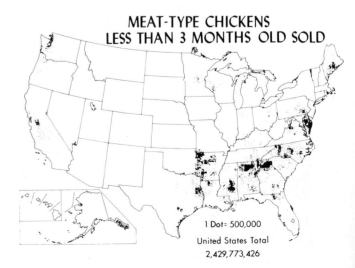

1 Dot = 500,000

United States Total
2,429,773,426

distributed than meat-type chickens. A substantial portion of the nation's eggs are produced in the Northeast, especially in New York, New Jersey, and southeastern Pennsylvania. In the West, California is an extremely important egg producer. Although the Corn Belt has relatively few poultry farms, chickens are frequently kept on the mixed farms in this region, and income from egg sales is often a small but important source of farm income.

2. Fur: Fur farming is a new type of bioculture less than 50 years old. The main emphasis is on silver foxes and mink, although rabbits, muskrats, racoons, and martens are also raised. A large share of the world's mink fur and all the silver fox fur now come from commercial farms. Where land is cheap, the animals are allowed to roam freely in a natural habitat enclosed by fences. But where land is expensive, the animals are kept in small pens or dens. In both cases, the animals are bred, protected, fed, and handled like ordinary domestic livestock.

The major areas of fur farming in North America are Prince Edward Island (where this type of bioculture originated), the Adirondack hill country of northern New York, Manitoulin Island in Lake Huron, the upper peninsula of Michigan, northern Wisconsin, and southeastern Wisconsin. In Europe, fur animals are farmed in Russia and Scandinavia.

In the future, there will probably be a sharp increase in the relative importance of farming over hunting in satisfying the world's fur markets. At one time man procured all his furs from wild animals—just as he once gathered all his rubber from wild rubber trees. But farmed rubber now exceeds wild rubber, and the same thing is likely to develop in the fur business.

3. Fish: As yet there is very little commercial farming of fish—subsistence farming of fish in the Far East has already been cited in Chapter 3—for the natural supply of wild fish is still adundant enough to meet man's needs. In only a few places are fish farmed—that is, penned, fed, and protected—as if they were cattle or swine. Commercial fish farming is carried on in the U.S.S.R., Poland, Germany, Hungary, the

Netherlands, Denmark, Italy, and Israel. The principal fish raised are carp, goldfish, catfish, and game fish fingerlings; in addition, oysters and pearls are cultivated in a few places.

The main species farmed commercially is the *carp*, which multiplies almost as rapidly as the tropical tilapia, and produces more pounds of meat per acre than any other edible fresh-water fish of the mid-latitudes. European immigrants to the United States brought along live carp for transplanting to streams and lakes. A few carp farms are now operated in Wisconsin, Illinois, and Iowa.

Many farms raise *game fish fingerlings* (especially trout, muskellunge, and pike) which are transplanted to lakes, rivers, and streams, to augment the natural supply. Most of these farms are operated by state governments; Wisconsin, for example, maintains a dozen trout farms and two muskellunge farms, which supply millions of fish a year to the state's rivers and lakes. Many *oysters* are now quasi-farm products. In Chesapeake Bay, for example, "fields" are staked out in shallow coastal waters and "prepared" by dumping in cement blocks, tile, and shells to provide surfaces to which the oysters can attach themselves, oysters being sedentary creatures that sift their food out of the water. *Pearls* are now produced artificially in oyster beds. The oysters are extracted from the water and small fragments of foreign matter are inserted inside their shells. The oysters are then placed in small cages or baskets which are replaced in the water. Japan leads the rest of the world in this type of pearl production.

Size of Farms. Poultry farms, fur farms, and fish farms are usually small in size, often less than ten acres. Fur farms in northern Wisconsin, upper Michigan, and Canada are larger because few people live there, so land is less expensive, and because forests rather than grasslands serve as "pastures"—the point is that generally acre for acre trees produce less animal food than grass or bushes.

Supplementary Feed. Most of these farms produce at least some of the feed consumed by their animals. But an increasing number produce *none* of it (see Figure 13-5) serving only as a place of residence for the animals. In this respect, these farms are unique, and the question comes to mind whether such animal culture is "agriculture" or "manufacturing." For example, some poultry farms in Delmarva produce 10,000 chickens on no more than two acres of land. Crowded together in one long building, these birds spend their entire life on sawdust litter, never getting out from under the roof. (This way they are less vulnerable to disease than when they roam around on dirt.) To be sure, the "machine" that converts corn, soybean-meal, menhaden-meal, food concentrates, and water into eggs and broilers is animate, while the machine that changes tin plate into tin cans is inanimate.

A poultry house in Frederick County, Maryland. The house contains its own feed bin, which can deliver feed to approximately 10,000 chickens at the press of a button. (*Courtesy USDA.*)

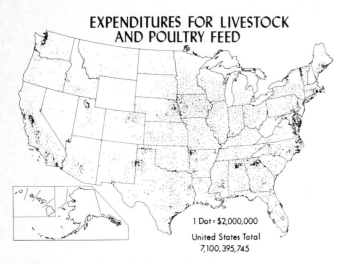

EXPENDITURES FOR LIVESTOCK AND POULTRY FEED

1 Dot = $2,000,000

United States Total
7,100,395,745

Figure 13-5 *(From U.S. Bureau of the Census.)*

But otherwise the operation of the two enterprises is rather similar.

Five Phases of Animal Culture. On the basis of source of feed and degree of animal husbandry in a region, we are able to identify five different phases of animal-producing economies.

1. Hunting: Animals subsist entirely on wild fauna and wild flora, with no supervision by man of the habitat or the animals.
2. Herding: Animals subsist entirely in the wild state, but man tends the animals and gathers them in for his purposes.
3. Ranching, or grazing: Animals subsist mostly on wildlife, but man tends them and also provides supplementary feed.
4. Animal farming: Animals subsist largely on feed grown on the farms where they reside.
5. Animal "manufacturing": The operating units simply provide a place of residence for animals that subsist entirely on feed, which, like raw materials arriving at a factory, comes from other places.

Here is an interesting hypothesis awaiting verification: As population density and the standard of living increase in a region, the production of meat (and perishable animal products) tends to move progressively from phase 1 toward phase 5. To prove this contention, we would have to draw evidence that would support it and to consider carefully any that would refute it. The reader may wish to ponder the problem for himself.

Physical Relationships

The regional pattern of these animal-raising activities reveals very little association with any physical features. There seems to be no critical growing season.

Chickens thrive in the tropics and the mid-latitudes— almost everywhere that man lives. The best fox and mink fur do come from colder climates, but good muskrat fur is produced as far south as the Mississippi River delta.

These animal farms tend to be located in humid regions, but there is no evidence to suggest that they would be less successful in dry regions; indeed, southern California, one of the major poultry areas in the nation, has a climate that is subhumid at best and often dry.

The association between soil and poultry farming was once thought to be a critical factor in the success of Delmarva's poultry industry, for the sandy soil of this peninsula was said to discourage the spread of chicken diseases. Perhaps the most that can be said about the soil relationship is that enterprises that do not grow their own feed crops need not compete with commercial grain farms, dairy farms, and mixed farms for better soils.

No particular type of landform is associated with these farms. They thrive on the plains of Delmarva and on the hills of Arkansas, Georgia, and northern New York. All other environmental features being equal, these farmers seem to take the cheaper, rougher land, leaving the flatter, more expensive land to crop farmers.

All in all, there appears to be no other type of bioculture in which the regional pattern is so unrelated to the physical environment as is the commercial farming of these animals.

Table 13-1

United States: Poultry Products Sold, 1974, in Millions

State	Eggs Produced	Broilers Produced
Total	66,045	2,993
Alabama	2,945	398
Arkansas	3,601	482
California	8,485	90
Georgia	5,827	427
Mississippi	1,908	227
North Carolina	3,037	287
Pennsylvania	3,492	63

Source: U.S. Department of Agriculture, *Agricultural Statistics* (1975).

Cultural Phenomena

Specialized farming of poultry, fur animals, and fish is a very recent activity. It is associated with an agricultural revolution marked by (a) increased output and (b) intensified specialization, phenomena that are associated with the development of urban markets. This agricultural revolution was triggered by the amazing expansion of urban settlements in recent years. Millions and millions of city people are now totally dependent on commercial bioculturalists for food and fibers.

Distance to Market. Urban markets are powerful influences on the location of commercial animal farms. The line of great metropolises stretching from

Boston through New York, Trenton, Philadelphia, Baltimore, and Washington, D.C., is edged by poultry farms (as well as by vegetable farms and dairy farms). Notice on Figures 13-1, 13-2, 13-3, and 13-4 that many other cities also have a near-by concentration of poultry farming: for instance, Louisville, South Bend, Fort Worth, Austin, Los Angeles, and San Francisco.

This urban association seems to be particularly important in egg production. Scarcely any large city is far from an egg area. Accordingly, the northeastern quadrant of the United States has a significant share of the nation's people and produces most of its eggs.

There is less correlation between cities and chickens grown for sale than between cities and eggs. To be sure, several large urban areas are associated with major producers of meat-type chickens. However, several large cities lack nearby chicken farms, among them Chicago, Detroit, Pittsburgh, St. Louis, Milwaukee, Minneapolis, and Buffalo. Moreover, many areas full of chicken farms are remote from large cities: the Shenandoah Valley of western Virginia, the Blue Ridge Mountains of northern Georgia, the Tennessee River Valley of northern Alabama, and northwestern Arkansas. Obviously, the farmers in areas adjoining certain cities have chosen not to specialize in raising poultry, since vegetable farming, dairying, and other agricultural activities are more rewarding. Yet farmers in remote rural areas have chosen this specialty. Much of the explanation of this pattern lies on *contract farming*.

Contract Farming. Sometimes known as *integrated farming*, contract farming is a relatively new type of bioculture conceived by the managers of commercial feed corporations. In the 1930's these men, sensing the increasing demand for broiler chickens, began to line up farmers who would agree to buy the corporation's feed, to concentrate on raising broiler chickens, and to market all their birds through distributors with whom the feed corporations also had contracts. The term *integrated* describes the series of contracts between the feed manufacturer on the one hand, and the farmer, slaughterer, wholesaler, and retailer on the other. In a sense, then, the contract-broiler farmer is no longer an independent producer whose profit depends on the difference between expenses for feed (and other production costs) and income from an unpredictable market. Rather, he is like an employee in a factory, a hired technician who is paid a stipulated fee, regardless of whether prices rise or fall, by a company to whom he guarantees a certain output.

To save transportation and distribution costs and to expedite the shipment of birds to market, the commercial feed manufacturers contracted with many farmers in a few areas rather than with a few farmers in many areas. Poultry feed is shipped in carload lots to the farmers in these specialty areas; the largest farms even have their own railroad sidings, and several smaller farms are often serviced by one siding. In selecting the areas that would respond most readily to broiler specialization, the commercial feed manufacturers tended to choose regions of "problem farms."

Understandably enough, prosperous farmers in the Corn Belt and Dairy Belt were not very enthusiastic about the idea of contract poultry farming. Most of the farmers who did respond to the scheme were located in areas characterized by rather backward farm methods, small acreage, rough terrain, or poor soil. This new scheme seemed an ideal solution to these farmers: Equipment would be provided and methods specified under the terms of the contract, small acreages would suffice, rough land would serve well enough for broiler houses, and the quality of the soil would be immaterial. Almost any part of the South, except the more lucrative cotton, tobacco, vegetable, and fruit areas, was perfectly suitable. Even an area located rather far from a sizable urban market was satisfactory, for the higher transport costs were offset by lower production costs.

For the nation as a whole, 90 per cent of the poultry is now produced by only 23,000 farms, a few of which are huge and many of which operate under integration contracts held by commercial feed corporations. Much California poultry production now comes from contract farms, which are known locally as *poultry ranches*.

The success of contract farming in the poultry business has led agriculturalists to scrutinize its possibilities for other types of production. Some mixed farms are already engaging in integrated farming. What the advantages and the disadvantages might be of applying this concept to dairy farming, to livestock ranching, to wheat farming, to cotton farming are open to speculation.

Feed-Producing Regions. Most poultry feed comes from crops grown in the Corn Belt, and much of the feed for fur farms and fish farms comes from meat-packing plants in the same region. This is one reason for the dispersed pattern of poultry farming in the Corn Belt, where almost every farm has a few chickens, but where farmers have chosen to specialize in dairying, cattle fattening, swine raising, or cash-grain cropping rather than poultry.

Feed is expensive. In many of the chicken-producing areas the expenditure for feed exceeds 50 per cent of the value of animal products sold (Figure 13-5). (Notice the similarities between Figures 13-4 and 13-5.)

GENERALIZATIONS ABOUT BIOCULTURE

The several types of bioculture that have been discussed in Chapters 3, 4, and 7 through 13 may be diagrammed as in Figure 13-6, page 154. By synthesizing these various activities, we can make certain generalizations about the geography of bioculture as a whole.

Location

Less than half the land on earth is devoted to bioculture (in even the broadest use of the term), and a large portion of even this land is used for nomadic herding. Land under

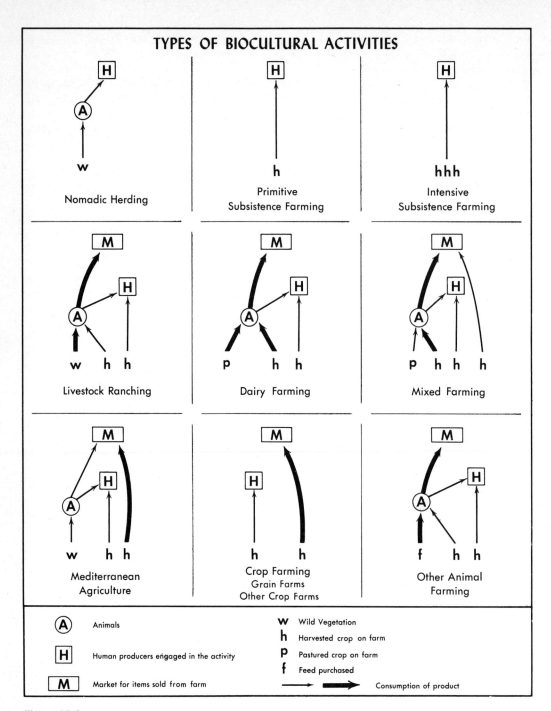

TYPES OF BIOCULTURAL ACTIVITIES

Nomadic Herding

Primitive Subsistence Farming

Intensive Subsistence Farming

Livestock Ranching

Dairy Farming

Mixed Farming

Mediterranean Agriculture

Crop Farming
Grain Farms
Other Crop Farms

Other Animal Farming

Ⓐ Animals

🄷 Human producers engaged in the activity

🄼 Market for items sold from farm

w Wild Vegetation
h Harvested crop on farm
p Pastured crop on farm
f Feed purchased

⟶ ⟹ Consumption of product

Figure 13-6

cultivation accounts for a considerably smaller proportion, perhaps 20 per cent of the total. The pattern of cultivated land (Figure 13-7, page 155) shows a marked concentration in humid portions of the mid-latitudes. Four major regions loom up: western Eurasia, eastern Anglo-America, eastern Asia, and south-central Asia. Remember that these are also the four major regions of population.

A detailed map of the location of farm land is available for the United States (Figure 13-8, page 155). Notice the blanket of closely spaced dots sweeping northward from Texas to the Dakotas. An eastward prong

projects through Iowa, Missouri, Illinois, Indiana, and Ohio. East of the Mississippi River and south of the Ohio River the amount of farm land is high but the pattern is irregular.

Characteristics

Unfortunately, we do not have enough accurate worldwide information to show the differences in the characteristics of bioculture from place to place. But enough data for this purpose are available for the United States, thanks to the federal Bureau of the Census and the

Department of Agriculture, which has published detailed reports on such characteristics as types of farms, sales of all farm products, and changes in agriculture.

Types of Farms in the United States. *What is a farm?* The definition of places to be counted as farms for United States Census purposes has changed several times since 1850. The essential characteristics have however been constant: (1) The land is under the control of a single management, and (2) the land is used for or connected with agricultural operations. Places of less than 10 acres are counted as farms if their annual sales of agricultural products amount to at least $250 or normally would be expected to amount to that value or more. Places of 10 acres or more are counted as farms if

the sales of agricultural products amounts to at least $50 or normally would be expected to amount to that value or more.

A number of different systems are used to classify farms:

Economic Class This system is based upon dollar value of farm product sales. The economic classes used are as follows:

CLASS 1 $40,000 or more of farm product sales
     Class 1a $100,000 or more
     Class 1b $40,000 to $99,999

Figure 13-7 (*From Office of Foreign Agricultural Relations.*)

Figure 13-8 (*From U.S. Bureau of the Census.*)

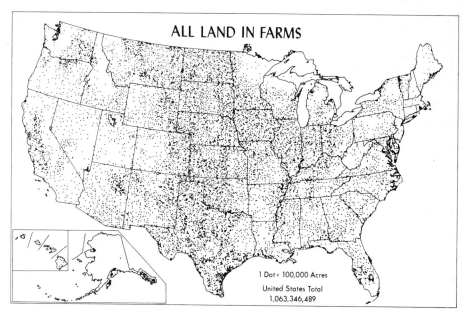

ALL LAND IN FARMS

1 Dot = 100,000 Acres
United States Total
1,063,346,489

CLASS 2 $20,000 to $39,999 of farm product sales

CLASS 3 $10,000 to $19,999 of farm product sales

CLASS 4 $5,000 to $9,999 of farm product sales

CLASS 5 $2,500 to $4,999 of farm product sales or a value of products sold of less than $2,500 provided the farm has the acreage or livestock operations which would normally yield sales in excess of $2,500. These would include new farm operations, farms with crop failures, and farms with large inventories and small census year sales.

CLASS 6 $50 to $2,499 of farm product sales and a farm operator who is under 65 years of age and did not work off the farm 100 days or more in the census year.

PART-TIME $50 to $2,499 of farm product sales and a farm operator who is under 65 years of age and who worked off the farm 100 days or more in the census year.

PART-RETIREMENT $50 to $2,499 of farm product sales and a farm operator who is 65 years of age or over.

ABNORMAL   Includes institutional farms, experimental and research farms, and Indian reservations.

In general, commercial farms are those assigned to Classes 1 to 5 (Figure 13-9). Subsistence farms and farms operated as a hobby make up a large share of the farms shown in Figure 13-10.

Size   All farms are classified by size according to the total land area established for each farm. The size categories used vary depending upon what is being described but, for example, data on number of farms by acres harvested are presented using the following breakdown:

1 to 49 acres
50 to 99 acres
100 to 199 acres
200 to 499 acres

Figure 13-9   *(From U.S. Bureau of the Census.)*

COMMERCIAL FARMS

1 Dot = 250
United States Total
1,733,683

PART TIME AND
PART RETIREMENT FARMS

1 Dot = 250
United States Total
994,456

Figure 13-10   *(From U.S. Bureau of the Census.)*

Figure 13-11   *(From U.S. Bureau of the Census.)*

FARMS OPERATED BY FULL OWNERS

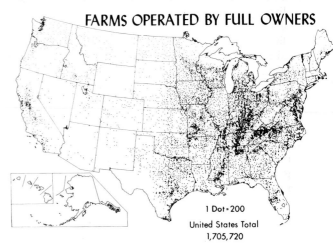

1 Dot = 200
United States Total
1,705,720

500 to 999 acres
1000 to 1,999 acres
2,000 acres and over

Tenure of Operator   The classifications of tenure used in the census are

a. Full owners who operate only land they own (Figure 13-11),

b. Part owners who operate land they own and also land they rent from others,

c. Tenants who operate only land they rent from others or that they work on shares for others (Figure 8-4).

Type of Organization   Patterns of ownership are covered by this system.

a. Individual or family farms,

b. Partnership,

c. Corporation, including family-owned,

d. Other, including estates, trusts, cooperatives.

Farms by Type This classification system is based on the type of product produced. To be classified as a particular type, a farm must have sales of a particular product or group of products amounting to 50 per cent or more of the total value of all farm products sold during the year. The following types of farms are recognized:

a. cash-grain;
b. cotton;
c. tobacco;
d. other field crop (peanuts, sugar beets, etc.);
e. vegetable;
f. fruit and nut;
g. poultry;
h. dairy;
i. livestock other than dairy and poultry (except for farms in the 17 western states, plus Louisiana, Florida, Hawaii and Alaska, that qualified as livestock ranches. Included are farms producing cattle, calves, hogs, sheep, goats, wool, and mohair);
j. livestock ranches (farms in the 17 western states, plus Louisiana, Florida, Hawaii, and Alaska, are classified as livestock ranches if the sales of livestock, wool, and mohair represent 50 per cent or more of the total value of farm products sold and if pasture land or grazing land amounts to 100 acres or more and is 10 times or more the acreage of cropland harvested);
k. general (field seed crops, hay, grass, and silage). A farm is also classified as general if it has cash income from three or more sources and does not meet the criteria for any other type;
l. miscellaneous (nursery and greenhouse products, forest products, mules, horses, colts, ponies, fur-bearing animals, bees, honey, goat's milk, and farms with no value of farm products sold).

The number of commercial (Class 1 to 5) farms by type, expressed as a percentage of all United States farms, is shown in Table 13-2.

Table 13-2

Percentage of All United States Farms by Types

Type	Percentage
Cash-grain	14
Cotton	1
Tobacco	3
Other field crop	1
Vegetable	1
Fruit and nut	2
Poultry	2
Dairy	10
Livestock other than poultry and dairy	21
Livestock ranches	3
General	5
Miscellaneous	1
All commercial farms	64

Sales of All Agricultural Products from United States Farms. American farmers sell over $90 billion worth of products annually. For decades the value of crops sold exceeded the value of animal products sold from farms. By the early 1950's the two were approximately equal. In 1960 the value of animal products was clearly greater than that of crops and the gap continued to widen through 1973. Data for 1974 (Table 13-3) show that at least temporarily the trend has been reversed. Thanks largely to a substantial jump in the value of food grains and oil-bearing and feed crops, the total value of crops sold was greater than the value of livestock and livestock products in that year. It will be interesting to review these figures again in the 1980's to see if 1974 was an unusual year or one that marked a return to the pre-1950's situation.

Table 13-3

United States: Farm Income—Cash Receipts from Farm Marketings in Millions of Dollars

Type of Product	1960	1974
TOTAL	34,248	93,521
All Crops	15,259	52,097
Cotton (lint and seed)	2,362	2,975
Tobacco	1,154	2,146
Food grains	2,450	9,276
Oil-bearing crops	1,362	9,604
Feed crops	2,986	13,882
Vegetables	1,980	5,358
Fruits and nuts	1,529	3,476
Other	1,436	5,380
All Livestock and Products	18,989	41,424
Hogs	2,869	7,002
Cattle and calves	7,380	17,889
Sheep and lambs	325	366
Wool	108	79
Dairy products	4,760	9,399
Eggs	1,738	2,878
Broilers and farm chickens	1,122	2,604
Turkeys and other poultry	433	803
Other	254	404

Source: United States Department of Agriculture, *Farm Income Statistics* (1975).

The relative importance of each product is shown in Table 13-3; the locational pattern of the nation's total agricultural output is shown in Figure 13-12, page 158. Perhaps someday such data will be available for the rest of the world; then it will be possible to construct maps showing regional patterns of *value* of farm products for the world as a whole, as Figure 13-12 now does for the United States. In studying this map, it will be helpful to recall the characteristics given in preceding chapters for

VALUE OF ALL FARM PRODUCTS SOLD

1 Dot= $5,000,000

United States Total
45,609,090,417

Figure 13-12 (*From U.S. Bureau of the Census.*)

each "white" area and each area where dots are close together.

Changes in United States Agriculture. The number of farms in this country is steadily decreasing. The figure plummeted from an all-time high of 6,800,000 in 1935 to 2,800,000 in 1975, an amazing decline of 59 per cent in just 40 years. Much of this change is attributable to the amalgamation of many small farms into fewer larger ones, which, with improved machinery, can be operated by fewer persons. Consequently, thousands of farmers have left agriculture for other employment.

But acreage in farms, farm population, and employment in agriculture is also declining. The peak for acreage was reached in the early 1950's when our farm land totaled 1,206 million acres. By 1975 the total was 1,086 million acres, a decrease of 10 per cent. The drop in farm population has been even more dramatic. In 1950 the farm population was about 23 million. By 1974 the figure had fallen to under 10 million—a drop of over 50 per cent. Similarly, the number employed in agriculture has dropped; in the 10 years between 1960 and 1970, employment fell from 4,000,000 to 2,300,000. This trend seems truly astonishing when we recall that United States population increased from 150,000,000 to about 210,000,000 between 1950 and 1975. Obviously, through improved agricultural methods fewer people can operate more acres (reducing the number of farms), and fewer acres can produce larger yields.

Change in acreage by states during the 1960's presents an interesting pattern (Figure 13-13). The farm acreage in almost every state declined. There were a few exceptions. North Dakota, Texas, and Nevada all showed a tiny increase, and Illinois, South Dakota, and Oklahoma showed no change. But all other states show a decline in farm acreage. The greatest relative drop in total acreage is in the New England states, but other northern and southeastern states also had often substantial declines. The most severe reductions were in Rhode Island (down 34 per cent) and in Maine and New Hampshire (each down 32 per cent). Decline in farm acreage in these eastern states is attributable to (a) the transformation of marginal farm land (that is, handicapped land yielding small profits from farming) into forest or recreational areas, (b) the invasion of rural land by cities, and (c) the obliteration of farm acreage by new or widened highways.

Figure 13-13

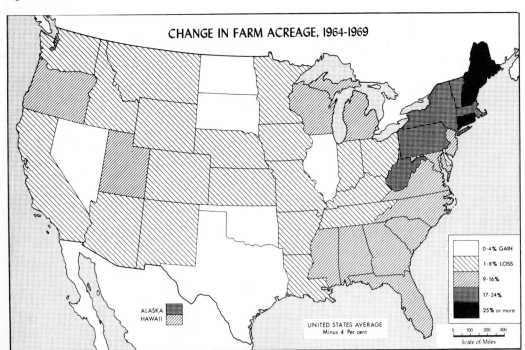

CHANGE IN FARM ACREAGE, 1964-1969

ALASKA
HAWAII

UNITED STATES AVERAGE
Minus 4 Per cent

0-4% GAIN
1-8% LOSS
9-16%
17-24%
25% or more

0   100   200   300
Scale of Miles

Deserted farmstead near Beatrice, Nebraska. Consolidation of farms and the increasing popularity of suitcase farming has led to the abandonment of many Great Plains farmsteads in recent years. (*Courtesy Clair A. Shenk.*)

Relationships

Relationship of Biocultural Employment to Total Employment. For the world as a whole, approximately one-half of all breadwinners are in bioculture. Although precise data are not available on total biocultural employment, the United Nations publishes data on agricultural employment. Table 13-4 is based on these figures and indicates that the proportion of the labor force in agriculture varies sharply from one part of the world to another, from a minimum of 3 per cent in the United Kingdom to 92 per cent in Nepal. An inspection of Table 13-4 makes one wonder whether there is any correlation between the variation in this ratio and the age of a country or a political unit, location, standard of living, or to some other variable.

Between 1935 and 1959 every state in the East except Florida showed a decline in farm acreage, but every western state experienced a gain. The most rapid expansion was in Nevada and Arizona where farm acreage increased 200 per cent and 190 per cent, respectively. Extension of farm land in the West was associated with (a) the expanding population and purchasing power within the western states, which created a larger demand for farm products, and (b) the appearance of new farm land in dry areas as a result of expanded irrigation facilities. Judging from the picture provided by Figure 13-13, it appears that the period of rapid growth of western farm acreage has ended.

Relationship of Land Area in Farms to Total Land Area. A somewhat different regional view of bioculture emerges when we compare the amount of agricultural land with the total area of a country. For the world as a whole, the percentage is 33, but the variation is considerable—from 3 per cent in Egypt and Norway to 84 per cent in South Africa (see Table 13-5).

In the United States, 47 per cent of all land is in farms, but this percentage varies sharply from region to region, as in Figure 13-14, page 159. Note how high the percentages are in the Plains and Corn Belt states and how low they are in New England and most western states.

Figure 13-14

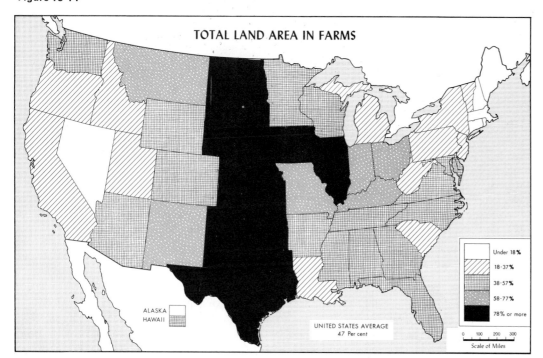

TOTAL LAND AREA IN FARMS

ALASKA
HAWAII

UNITED STATES AVERAGE
47 Per cent

Under 18%
18-37%
38-57%
58-77%
78% or more

0   100   200   300
Scale of Miles

Table 13-4

Per cent of Economically Active Population in Agriculture in Selected Countries

Continent	Countries—under 33%		Countries—33% to 66%		Countries—over 66%	
Europe	U.S.S.R.	32	Yugoslavia	53		
	Ireland	27	Romania	52		
	Hungary	25	Greece	46		
	Finland	25	Bulgaria	42		
	Italy	21	Poland	38		
	Iceland	17	Portugal	37		
	Austria	16	Spain	34		
	Czechoslovakia	15				
	France	14				
	Norway	14				
	East Germany	12				
	Denmark	12				
	West Germany	10				
	Sweden	9				
	Switzerland	7				
	Netherlands	6				
	Belgium	5				
	United Kingdom	3				
North America	Puerto Rico	14	Guatemala	63	Haiti	77
	Canada	8	Nicaragua	56	Honduras	67
	United States	4	Mexico	47		
			Costa Rica	45		
			Panama	43		
			Cuba	33		
South America	Guyana	32	Bolivia	58		
	Venezuela	26	Ecuador	54		
	Chile	25	Paraguay	53		
	Argentina	15	Colombia	45		
			Brazil	44		
Asia	Japan	21	China	66	Nepal	92
	Israel	10	South Korea	58	Thailand	76
			Malaysia	56	Pakistan	70
					Philippines	69
					Turkey	69
					India	68
Africa	South Africa	30	Rhodesia	63	Tanzania	86
			Morocco	61	Guinea	83
			Algeria	56	Zaire	78
			Egypt	55	Mozambique	72
			Ghana	55	Nigeria	67
			Tunisia	46		
			Congo	45		
Oceania	New Zealand	12				
	Australia	8				

Source: United Nations, *Production Yearbook* (1973).

Physical Phenomena That Deter Bioculture.
The blank areas on Figures 13-7 and 13-8 seem to be
associated with regions that are cold, or dry, or have
poor soils, or have rough topography. But these statements oversimplify the relationships, because they ignore
the fact that land is cultivated not only in accordance
with its physical attributes but also in response to human
needs for crops and animals.

Human Needs for Biocultural Products.
Man's need for crops and animal products varies spatially
as surely as do climates, landforms, and soils. Furthermore, it changes more swiftly than do the physical
attributes of land. Two hundred years ago, Figure 13-7
would have shown most of Anglo-America as a blank
area, not because it was too cold, too dry, too wet, or too
rough, but because there was no active need to cultivate

it. Since then the physical environment has remained essentially unchanged but the need for farms and ranches, generated by widespread settlement, has changed markedly. It is interesting to speculate what a map based on the same criteria as Figure 13-7 will look like 200 years hence.

The intensity of human need for biocultural products varies with three major elements: the number of people in the area, their standard of living, and their cultural attitudes. The first two are obvious enough, but the third merits comment, since both the quantity of commodities demanded and the type of commodity consumed are closely related to such cultural factors as

religion and dietary habits. Take attitude toward diet in the United States, for example. Changing tastes and changes in the prices charged for food products have had an interesting effect on the patterns of consumption in America. In 1940 Americans consumed 19.4 pounds of butter and margarine per capita and most of it was butter; now they eat only 16 pounds, most of it margarine. Per capita intake of fruit has dropped from 158 pounds to 100 pounds per year. Before World War II each United States citizen ate an average of 155 pounds

Table 13-5

Total Area and Agricultural Area: Selected Countries in 1,000 Hectares

Location	Total Area	Total Agricultural Area	Percentage of Total Area in Agriculture
Europe	493,000	236,000	48
Austria	8,385	3,894	46
Belgium	3,051	1,586	52
Bulgaria	11,091	6,009	54
Czechoslovakia	12,787	7,077	55
Denmark	4,307	2,951	69
East Germany	10,576	6,275	59
Finland	33,701	2,782	8
France	54,703	33,035	60
Greece	13,194	8,870	67
Hungary	9,303	6,855	74
Iceland	10,300	2,280	22
Ireland	7,028	4,794	68
Italy	30,123	17,649	59
Netherlands	3,671	2,128	58
Norway	32,422	931	3
Poland	31,268	19,508	62
Portugal	8,894	4,900	55
Romania	23,750	14,935	63
Spain	50,478	34,560	68
Sweden	44,975	3,758	8
Switzerland	4,129	2,176	53
United Kingdom	24,401	18,831	77
West Germany	24,288	13,500	56
Yugoslavia	25,580	14,520	57
U.S.S.R.	2,240,000	607,000	27
North America	2,242,000	633,000	28
Canada	997,614	68,663	7
Costa Rica	5,070	2,362	47
Cuba	11,452	5,980	52
Guatemala	10,889	2,499	23
Haiti	2,775	870	31
Honduras	11,209	4,236	38
Mexico	197,255	102,909	52
Nicaragua	13,000	1,793	14
Panama	7,565	1,622	21
Puerto Rico	890	562	63
United States	936,335	436,595	47
South America	1,783,000	447,000	25
Argentina	277,689	170,975	62

Table 13-5 (Continued)

Location	Total Area	Total Agricultural Area	Percentage of Total Area in Agriculture
Bolivia	109,858	14,414	13
Brazil	851,197	137,034	16
Chile	75,695	15,814	21
Colombia	113,891	22,138	19
Ecuador	28,356	6,015	21
Guyana	21,497	3,261	15
Paraguay	40,675	10,947	27
Venezuela	91,205	19,061	21
Asia	2,753,000	974,000	35
China	959,696	288,200	30
India	326,809	178,490	55
Israel	2,070	1,235	60
Japan	37,208	6,396	17
Nepal	14,080	3,878	28
Pakistan	80,388	24,235	30
Philippines	30,000	11,631	39
South Korea	9,848	2,329	24
Thailand	51,400	13,415	26
Turkey	78,058	53,513	69
Africa	3,031,000	1,036,000	34
Algeria	238,174	44,208	19
Congo	34,200	14,930	44
Egypt	100,145	2,852	3
Ghana	23,854	14,072	59
Guinea	24,586	4,500	18
Morocco	44,505	15,550	35
Mozambique	78,303	46,700	60
Nigeria	92,377	47,595	52
Rhodesia	39,058	6,693	17
South Africa	122,104	102,448	84
Tanzania	94,509	56,453	60
Tunisia	16,415	7,760	47
Zaire	234,541	72,700	31
Oceania	851,000	510,000	60
Australia	768,681	494,688	64
New Zealand	26,867	13,514	50
World Total	13,393,000	4,443,000	33

Source: United Nations, *Production Yearbook* (1973).

GENERALIZED SOIL EROSION

SLIGHT OR NONE

MODERATE
(25 TO 75 PERCENT OF TOPSOIL LOST, MAY HAVE SOME GULLIES)

SEVERE
(MORE THAN 75 PERCENT OF TOPSOIL LOST, MAY HAVE NUMEROUS
OR DEEP GULLIES. INCLUDES SEVERE GEOLOGICAL EROSION IN
PARTS OF LOW RAINFALL AREAS.)

(MANY SMALL AREAS COULD NOT BE SHOWN AT THIS SCALE.)

BASED ON DATA FROM 1934 RECONNAISSANCE EROSION SURVEY OF THE UNITED STATES
AND OTHER SOIL CONSERVATION SURVEYS BY THE SOIL CONSERVATION SERVICE

Figure 13-15

of wheat flour a year; now he eats only 110. On the other hand he is eating more chickens, turkeys, and vegetables. Further, the annual per capita consumption of beef rose from 55 pounds in 1940 to 116 in 1974, but veal dropped from 7 pounds to 2 pounds; consumption of pork remained about the same.

Impact of Bioculture Upon Soil. One of the consequences of man's use of land for growing crops is destruction of the soil—*if* the soil is not properly tended. Figure 13-15 is a dramatic expression of how farmers in the Southeast, the Midwest, and the Far West have laid bare the topsoil, over three-quarters of which has been carried away. If the rainfall in the eastern United States were of the gentle, drizzly type characteristic of western Europe, erosion would not have been nearly so severe. But the climate in America's most populous areas has a high incidence of thunder showers which dash torrents of water against the earth within a few minutes. The combination of tilled soil, thunder showers, and sloping land creates the worst possible conditions for maintaining topsoil.

SUGGESTED READINGS

BLAUT, J. M., "Microgeographic Sampling: A Quantitive Approach to Regional Agricultural Geography," *Economic Geography*, 1959, pp. 79–88.

BOWLER, I. R., "Regional Agricultural Policies: Experience in the United Kingdom," *Economic Geography*, 1976, pp. 267–280.

CARLSON, ALVAR W., "Seasonal Farm Labor in the San Luis Valley," *Annals of the Association of American Geographers*, 1973, pp. 97–108.

CLARK, ANDREW H., "The Sheep/Swine Ratio as a Guide to a Century's Change in the Livestock Geography of Nova Scotia," *Economic Geography*, 1962, pp. 38–55.

DILLMAN, C. DANIEL, "Land and Labor Patterns in Latin American Agriculture: A Review of the 1960s," *The Journal of Geography*, 1975, pp. 223–242.

GREGOR, HOWARD F., "The Changing Plantation," *Annals of the Association of American Geographers*, 1965, pp. 221–238.

———, *Geography of Agriculture: Themes in Research*, Englewood Cliffs, N. J., 1970, 181 pp.

———, "The Plantation in California," *The Professional Geographer*, February, 1962, pp. 1–4.

GRIGG, DAVID, "The Agricultural Regions of the World: Review and Reflections," *Economic Geography*, 1969, pp. 95–132.

MERCHANT, JAMES W., JR., and MAROTZ, GLEN A., "Agricultural Water Pollution: Some Problems Associated With Its Control," *The Journal of Geography*, 1975, pp. 419–429.

SAUER, CARL O., *Agricultural Origins and Dispersals*, New York, 1952, 110 pp.

STOUSE, PIERRE A. D., JR., "Instability of Tropical Agriculture: The Atlantic Lowlands of Costa Rica," *Economic Geography*, 1970, pp. 78–97.

WOOD, HAROLD A., "Spontaneous Agricultural Colonization in Ecuador," *Annals of the Association of American Geographers*, 1972, pp. 599–617.

COMMERCIAL MINING

The plant and animal kingdoms are not man's only sources of economic commodities. He also extracts goods from what we loosely call the mineral kingdom. Among geographers, the term *mining* applies to all endeavors by which minerals or other resources, whether solid or liquid, are extracted from the earth regardless of method, whether through shafts, open pits, quarries, or any other technique.

Several difficulties beset a geographer when he comes to the study of mining. In some respects, indeed, the geography of mining is more formidable than the geography of any other economic activity. One reason is that regions of mining are so hard to visualize. Forests, which cover extensive areas of the earth's surface, can be readily seen, as can dairy regions, wheat belts, and rice areas. Farms, like forests, take up appreciable stretches of land; so agriculture areas too can be apprehended rather easily. But mines are mere pinpoints on the earth's surface, for most of them are small holes in the ground through which men descend to the harvest realms below. Since mines are often dispersed through regions of farms or forests, an aerial photograph in mining country would show some other land use prevailing. Plainly, delimiting the regions of mining is an exacting task.

Moreover, the heterogeneous distribution of minerals makes it difficult to delimit types of regions. In some places coal alone occurs; elsewhere there is only iron ore; other localities have only petroleum. But there seem to be no combinations of minerals that distinguish kinds of mining regions, "typical associations" of minerals comparable to the "typical associations" of crops in intensive subsistence agriculture or to those of trees in mid-latitude softwood forests.

Nor is there any readily discernible regional association of mining techniques. Methods simply differ from place to place: Coal mining in Pennsylvania is highly mechanized, in Britain it is less so. But the regional associations of methods are missing that would permit us to delimit broad regions for mining as we can for, say, primitive subsistence farming.

Finally, there are at present few discernible correlations between areas of mining and the location of other phenomena. Mining is carried on in the high latitudes north of the Arctic Circle, in the mid-latitudes, and in the tropics; in mountains and in plains; in hot countries and in cold; in dry land and in wet; in densely populated areas and in sparsely settled ones; in regions of advanced cultures and in regions of culture which the advanced people consider backward.

For all these reasons it is difficult to regionalize mining activity very effectively. Consequently, we shall discuss the subject in terms of individual minerals. In Chapters 14 and 15 we shall deal with a few of the more important minerals; then, in Chapter 16 we shall endeavor to summarize the general geography of mining.

CHAPTER 14

selected minerals

The Sierrita Copper Mine, located south of Tucson, Arizona. Mining is accomplished by establishing a series of levels or benches, each being approximately 50 feet high. The first step in the mining cycle is the blasting of the various benches. To blast, rotary drills bore holes 59 feet in depth; the holes are then loaded with explosives. A typical blast involving 40 holes breaks loose 200,000 tons of rock—enough material to keep one power shovel in production for approximately four days. (*Courtesy Duval Corporation.*)

Through the ages man has discovered in and on the earth's crust a wide variety of valuable minerals that meet his needs for fuels, lubricants, building materials, gems, coins, fertilizers, tools, weapons, synthetic fabrics, and medicines. Obviously we cannot go into the whole vast array of materials man has found in the earth. So we shall choose for discussion a few of the economically more important ones: coal, iron ore, ferro-alloys, copper, bauxite, diamonds, nuclear fuels, fertilizers, asbestos, building materials, and water.

Man places economic value on many additional minerals, of course. Some of these are located in relatively few places, they lend considerable geographic distinctiveness to their localities. Here are a few examples: the lead and zinc mines of Upper Silesia; the tin mines of Malaysia, the U.S.S.R., and Bolivia which together account for over one-half of the world total; the Broken Hill district of Australia which can boast of the richest lead and zinc ores on earth; the silver-mining belt that runs from Mexico to British Columbia; the famous Witwatersrand of South Africa which produces much of the world's gold, notably in the vicinity of Johannesburg; and the Rustenberg district (also in South Africa) where a substantial share of the earth's platinum is extracted. But the minerals we are concentrating on are the most valuable.

Since we shall be dealing with these substances one by one—and for the sake of variety—the three basic questions of the geographic method will be implicit rather than explicit in our discussion.

The three main kinds of coal are anthracite, bituminous coal, and lignite. Anthracite is the hardest variety and is almost smokeless. Lignite is the softest, has the most impurities, and is the dirtiest. Bituminous coal is the all-purpose type that is most widely used.

Coals vary considerably in quality. Two regions may produce the same quantity of coal, but if one has high-grade bituminous coal and the other only lignite, the significance of the two areas will be quite dissimilar. Coals differ in three components: moisture, carbon, and volatile gases. As these vary, so do three potentials: heat energy, coking ability, and available by-products.

The world's miners annually extract from the earth's crust more than three billion tons of coal of which over 850,000,000 tons are lignite. The regional patterns of the types of coal are distinctive. Bituminous coal is the most widespread, occurring in nearly every coal region. Lignite is mined chiefly in Europe and European Russia (Germany alone accounts for almost one-half of the world's lignite—more in East Germany than in West Germany—and the U.S.S.R. accounts for one-fifth of the total, mostly from the Tula field south of Moscow). And three areas produce about 70 per cent of all of the world's anthracite, the Soviet Union, China, and North Korea.

COAL MINING

Producing Regions

The world's principal coal belt runs through the middle latitudes of the Northern Hemisphere (see Figure 14-1). Four major regions stand out: Europe, the Soviet Union, China, and Anglo-America, a quartet that accounts for about 90 per cent of the world's coal harvest (see Table 14-1).

Figure 14-1

COAL MINING: Percentage of World Total

Table 14-1

World Production of Coal and Iron Ore

Region	Coal			Iron Ore	
	In Millions of Tons	As Percentage of World Total		In Millions of Tons	As Percentage of World Total
WORLD	3,264 (862*)	100		744	100
Western Europe	484 (130*)	15		126	17
West Germany	240 (117*)	7		6	1
United Kingdom	159	5		11	2
France	44 (3*)	1		55	7
Belgium	13	—		—	—
Luxembourg	—	—		5	1
Sweden	—	—		32	4
Spain	15 (3*)	—		7	1
Eastern Europe	726 (525*)	22		15	2
East Germany	288 (287*)	9		—	—
Poland	190 (36*)	6		2	—
Czechoslovakia	120 (90*)	4		2	—
U.S.S.R.	683 (161*)	21		191	26
North America	600 (9*)	18		132	18
Canada	16 (3*)	—		42	6
United States	582 (6*)	18		86	12
West Virginia	118	4	Minnesota	54	7
Pennsylvania	82	3	Michigan	12	2
Kentucky	119	4	Alabama	—	—
Illinois	54	2	Utah	2	—
Ohio	51	2	New York and Pennsylvania	3	—
Virginia	31	1			
Indiana	21	1			
Alabama	18	1			
South America	8	—		78	10
Venezuela	—	—		20	3
Brazil	3	—		36	5
Peru	—	—		9	1
Asia (except U.S.S.R.)	614 (11*)	19		94	13
China	419	13		45	6
India	84 (4*)	3		31	4
Japan	43	1		2	—
Africa	67	2		56	7
South Africa	61	2		9	1
Liberia	—	—		23	3
Australia	79 (26*)	2		50	7

Source: United States Bureau of Mines, *Minerals Yearbook* (1973).
*Million tons of lignite included in total figure.

Western Europe. A distinct coal belt extends from the United Kingdom through northern France, Belgium, and northern Germany, to southern Poland (Figure 14-2). The United Kingdom, although now surpassed by West Germany, was for decades Europe's leading coal producer. Coal fields are widely dispersed throughout her territory, along the coast as well as inland. The chief mining areas are York, Derby-Nottingham, Northumberland-Durham, southern Wales, and the Scottish Lowland.[1] On the continent the richest areas are the Sambre-Meuse, which threads its way through

[1] An economic atlas should be consulted for the location of all fields mentioned in this chapter.

Lignite being mined southwest of the Ruhr in Germany. The lignite is scooped from a deposit having little overburden and taken by conveyor to the small train. (*Courtesy German Information Center.*)

the northernmost province of France into central Belgium; the Saar, which lies close by the French-German border; and the Westphalia (sometimes called the Ruhr), which is matched only by the United States' Appalachian field in volume of production. The quality of product in all these fields is high-grade bituminous coal. But beyond the Ruhr, the product changes character, for most of the coal in central and eastern Germany is lignite. Better coal appears again, though, in the Silesian field which straddles the Polish-Czechoslovakian border.

U.S.S.R.   The Soviet Union is rapidly approaching western Europe and has overtaken the United States in quantity of coal mined. Indeed, when the satellite nations of eastern Europe are included, the Soviet bloc leads the world.

Within the U.S.S.R., coal mines are clustered in several areas separated from 600 to 1000 miles apart (Figure 14-3). The Donbass coal field in the Ukraine is a major producer. Not surprisingly, it was a prime target in World War II for the German army that stormed

Figure 14-2

through the Ukraine to the Volga. Of less importance is the Tula lignite field near Moscow. The Ural field is a long linear area corresponding roughly in location with the Ural hills. One thousand miles to the southeast, the Karaganda area produces substantial amounts of a good product. Six hundred miles east of Karaganda is the Kuzbass field, which has been developed rapidly since 1930 to become one of the Soviet Union's ranking producers. Finally, almost 600 miles farther east is the Irkutsk coal field.

Anglo-America. A large portion of Anglo-America's coal is mined in the eastern half of the continent. The Appalachian field, which extends from north-

western Pennsylvania to Alabama, is one of the most productive coal-mining regions on earth; it accounts for over two-thirds of United States production. West Virginia and Kentucky are unquestionably the leading states (Table 14-2 and Figure 14-4, page 170). The East Central field, which produces about 15 per cent of our coal, underlies Illinois, fringes of Indiana, and western Kentucky. A small amount is produced in the West Central region, which stretches from Iowa to Oklahoma. Considerably more originates in the Rocky Mountain field, mostly in Utah, Wyoming, and Colorado. In

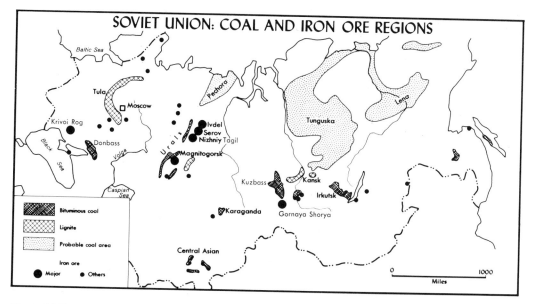

Figure 14-3

Table 14-2

United States Coal

| Production (Million Short Tons, 1969–71 Avg. | | Reserves (Billion Tons) Estimated Original Reserves | | | | |
State	All Coal	State	Bituminous	Sub-bituminous and Lignite	Anthracite	Total	Remaining Reserve (Jan. 1, 1970)
TOTAL	582	Total	724	877	24	1,625	1,557
West Virginia	134	North Dakota		351		351	351
Kentucky	118	Montana	2	220		222	222
Pennsylvania	87	Illinois	140			140	139
Illinois	63	Alaska	19	111		130	130
Ohio	52	Wyoming	13	108		122	121
Virginia	34	West Virginia	117			117	101
Indiana	21	Colorado	63	18		82	81
Alabama	19	Pennsylvania	75		23	98	69
Tennessee	8	Kentucky	72			72	65
Wyoming	7	New Mexico	11	51		62	61

Sources: U.S. Bureau of Mines; *Minerals Yearbook, 1971* (1973); *Minerals Yearbook, 1970* (1972); *Minerals Yearbook, 1969* (1971).

Canada, which produces about as much coal as Alabama, Nova Scotia and Alberta (at opposite sides of the country) are the leading coal-producing provinces.

Other Places. China has surged rapidly into world prominence in coal mining, and if her published data are correct, she is now mining about three-quarters as many tons of coal as the United States.

Elsewhere in the world only a few areas are conspicuous. Japan accounts for one per cent of the world's coal, mostly from the southern island of Kyushu and the northern island of Hokkaido. Most of India's coal is mined in the Northeast. Southeast Australia (Newcastle), southeastern Africa (Transvaal), and southern Brazil are the more prominent coal-producing areas in the Southern Hemisphere.

Reserves

The volume of the world's known recoverable coal reserves is tremendous—sufficient for another 200 years at the present rate of consumption. Geologists have established that certain kinds of rock never contain coal; on this basis vast areas of the earth have little likelihood of ever yielding that fuel. But in extensive regions that geologists have not yet penetrated, the rocks might contain coal. As far as known reserves are concerned, the following observations seem to hold true. Coal reserves are unequally distributed, and the nations most favored with reserves are generally the very ones that now domi-

nate coal mining. In order of coal assets, the leading areas are the United States, the Soviet Union, China, and western Europe (Table 14-3). China has in particular a tremendous reserve of high-quality coal in the provinces of Shenhsi and Shanhsi, probably the world's outstanding region of abundant good coal that is still only slightly tapped. The Soviet Union reports large reserves in the Tungas and Lena fields in northern Siberia.

Table 14-3

Recoverable Reserves of Coal in Megatons

Country	Anthracite, Bituminous and Sub-bituminous Coal	Lignite, Brown Coal	Total	Percentage of World Total
United States	158,725	23,056	181,781	30.7
U.S.S.R.	82,900	53,700	136,600	23.1
China	—	—	80,000	13.5
West Germany	30,000	9,571	39,571	6.7
United Kingdom	3,871	—	3,871	0.7
India	10,683	897	11,580	2.0
Japan	933	93	1,026	0.2
WORLD TOTAL	430,867	160,324	591,191	100.0

Source: U.S. National Committee of the World Energy Conference, *Survey of Energy Resources* (1974).

Within the United States the leading states in reserves are not the leading states in production. Most of the reserve tonnage is in the West with North Dakota and Montana heading the list (Table 14-2). It is perhaps

Figure 14-4

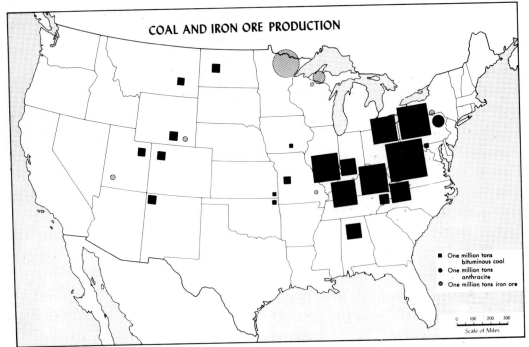

COAL AND IRON ORE PRODUCTION

- ■ One million tons bituminous coal
- ● One million tons anthracite
- ◉ One million tons iron ore

Scale of Miles

surprising that the principal producing state, West Virginia, is surpassed by five others in reserve tonnage; indeed, it has only a third as much coal as North Dakota. The Dakota and Montana stores, however, are mostly lignite. Illinois and West Virginia have the most abundant reserves of bituminous coal.

Relationship to Population

The main coal-mining regions tend to be comparatively densely populated. The correlation with population is not very high, however, since the reverse generalization definitely does not hold; that is, the world's most populous regions (China and India) are not necessarily the leading coal-producing countries.

Relationship to Manufacturing

Factories are the primary market for coal. To be sure, large quantities are used for other purposes, for instance, to heat buildings and to provide power for railroad engines, Since the early 1970's the use of coal for the generation of electricity has risen sharply in the United States. But to an increasing degree, coal is also being consumed by factories, not only to heat water in boilers and to smelt metallic ores in blast furnaces but also to be processed as a raw material. And since most of the world's manufacturing is situated in western Europe, Anglo-America, and the Soviet Union, the locational association between coal mining and manufacturing is immediately evident; it is, in fact, one of the most striking correlations in the economic geography of the world in the second half of the twentieth century. The correlations hold not only for the three great regions, but elsewhere as well. Japan, Manchuria, India, and southeast Australia—all are mining areas and manufacturing areas.

International Trade in Coal

Since coal is consumed for the most part in the general vicinity where it is mined, the international flow of this commodity is meager. The leading exporters today are the United States, West Germany, and Australia (Table 14-4). But for almost three centuries the United Kingdom alone served as the world's coal bin. She began shipping coal abroad in the early 1600's, and for nearly 250 years was the only country that produced a surplus. We cannot overestimate the role of coal in the reign of Britain during that period as the world's leading commercial and maritime power. But the United Kingdom has skimmed off the cream of her coal supply and is mining deeper and thinner seams, many of which dip at steep angles. These handicaps make it difficult to use the mechanized mining methods widely employed in the United States and Germany. Indeed, the United Kingdom is now actually importing small amounts of high-grade coal.

The world pattern of international trade in coal is unusual. It is not surprising to see the United States, West Germany, and Australia listed among leading exporters in Table 14-4. Nor is it surprising to find France, Canada, the Netherlands, and Japan among the leading importers. But why are France, West Germany, Canada, and the Netherlands on both lists? West Germany, France, and the Netherlands are explained partly by the encouragement the European Common Market (discussed in Chapter 25) gives to trade in coal by removing tariffs on shipments among the member nations. Thus, coal fields in a country that are near an industrial concentration in another country can serve the latter easily. Perhaps even more surprising is that the United States exports about one billion dollars worth of coal anuually. Approximately one-third goes to Japan and one-fourth to Canada, but substantial amounts also go to Europe, especially Italy, Spain, West Germany, the Netherlands, and Belgium-Luxembourg. The reasons for this anomaly are (a) much lower production costs in the United States due to mechanized mining methods, and (b) cheapness of ocean transportation.

In the foregoing discussion we have done little more than apply the first basic question of the geographic method to the topic of coal. The questions of characteristics and relationships, which normally should be considered at this point, will be postponed until Chapter 16; the same applies to the other substances taken up in this and the next chapter. We are doing so because many characteristics and relationships of coal mining are similar, in terms of geography, to those for iron ore mining, copper mining, and other mining activities. Consequently, it seems reasonable to treat all of these topics in one chapter that can generalize for all mining endeavors grouped as one major economic activity.

IRON ORE

Iron is ubiquitous, being one of the most abundant elements in the earth's crust, which averages 47 per cent oxygen, 28 per cent silicon, 8 per cent aluminum, and 5 per cent iron. The catch to this abundance is that it costs too much to extract that 5 per cent of iron from a mass of crustal rock. In several places, however, geological processes have concentrated iron in proportions far

Table 14-4

International Trade in Coal, in Thousands of U.S. Dollars

Leading Exporters		Leading Importers	
World Total:	5,606,015		
United States	950,757	Japan	1,011,396
West Germany	755,929	France	411,201
Australia	246,978	Belgium-Lux.	274,576
Netherlands	79,953	Italy	265,952
Canada	72,776	Canada	172,422
United Kingdom	54,332	West Germany	152,395
France	48,260	Netherlands	125,439

Source: United Nations, Yearbook of International Trade Statistics (1974).

above the average. Any mass of dirt or rock with a high enough concentration of a metal to pay for the cost of extraction is called an *ore*. Whether a material is ore depends, then, on *both* its chemical composition *and* the economics of the moment. The costs of extraction rise and fall as do the prices extracted metal will fetch, and what is iron ore today may be just so much dirt tomorrow, or vice versa. The principle tends to hold, then, that the *higher* the market price, the *lower* the percentage of metal content necessary to qualify a substance as *ore*.

The quality of iron ore depends not only on its percentage of iron but also on the absence of objectionable impurities. Thus, an ore may be half iron, but phosphorus or sulphur may make it unusable. In the early history of iron ore mining, some rocks rich in iron had to be bypassed because they contained considerable phosphorus; it was impossible by methods then known to separate the phosphorus from the iron. Not until 1878 did scientists discover that the two could be dissociated by the addition of calcium carbonate (in the form of limestone or dolomite) in smelting operation.

Producing Regions

Iron ore mining is concentrated in the same trio of regions that top the list for coal mining. Western Europe, Anglo-America, and the Soviet Union together account

for 60 per cent of the world's iron ore production (Table 14-1 and Figure 14-5).

Western Europe. Here, iron ore mining is located in the same general pattern as coal except for the absence of Silesia and the presence of northern Sweden. The United Kingdom has several iron mining areas in unusually close proximity to coal. The Midland field, about 60 miles north of London and only 15 miles from the interior coal field, provides much of Great Britain's total; the Lincoln field to the north (also very close to coal) is also important; most of the remainder comes from the Cleveland field (near Durham coal). No other nation has been favored with so much iron ore so close to so much good coal.

But Europe's largest quantities of iron ore are produced on the continent. The Lorraine field in northeastern France is less than 30 miles from Saar coal, 100 miles from the Sambre-Meuse field, and 150 miles from Westphalia. (The Lorraine ores were known but unused for decades because of their high phosphorus content. The largest known reserve of iron ore in Europe lay undeveloped in spite of its nearness to good coal fields. But shortly after the discovery mentioned above, the Lorraine became the foremost iron-mining region of Europe.) Lorraine ores are not unusually rich (they average 30 to 40 per cent iron), but in volume they constitute western Europe's most productive source and are a strong reason why France leads western Europe in iron mining, produc-

Figure 14-5

IRON ORE MINING: Percentage of World Total

Iron ore being stockpiled prior to shipment to a blast furnace. (*Courtesy American Iron and Steel Institute.*)

ing more than the next three nations—Sweden, West Germany, and the United Kingdom—combined.

Sweden's foremost field is in the vicinity of Kiruna (north of the Arctic Circle), where remarkably high-grade ores—up to 60 per cent metal—are unearthed. Germany's major mines are in the Siegerland (southeast of Köln) and Salzgitter (near Braunschweig). Many smaller iron-mining areas dot the rest of the map of Europe; nearly every nation in fact produces a little.

The United States and Canada. For several decades the world's most prolific iron mines have been those in the Lake Surperior district (see Figure 14-4), which consists of several iron ranges in Minnesota, Wisconsin, Michigan, and Ontario. This area yields over 80 per cent of Unites States ore (mostly from the Mesabi range in Minnesota, and the Marquette and Menominee ranges in Wisconsin and Michigan). In addition to their abundance, Lake Superior ores were traditionally uncommonly rich, as high as 60 per cent; today, most of the high grade ores have been mined out, so taconite and other low-grade ores are mined. Canada is represented here by Steep Rock and Michipicoten in Ontario. Elsewhere, the Alabama field, which produces less than 1 per cent of the nation's iron ore, is unusual in the United States in that beds of iron ore lie close to those of good coal. The Quebec-Labrador field is relatively new—the first ore was mined in 1954—but today large quantities of ore are coming annually from this area. The Adirondack field in northern New York and the Wabana field in Newfoundland also provide a little iron ore. In the entire western half of North America the only notable mines are near Cedar City in southwestern Utah, Eagle Mountain in southern California, and in the Atlantic City District in Wyoming.

The Soviet Union. Most of the iron ore in the U.S.S.R. comes from three areas, the foremost of which

is Krivoi Rog, approximately 250 miles west of the Donbass coal field. This general vicinity also yields iron ore in the Kerch penninsula. The Ural Hills boast extensive deposits and now rank second behind Krivoi Rog; "Magnet Mountain" near Magnitogorsk and Nizhniy Tagil are big producers. A thousand miles east lies Gornaya Shorya, another ranking source.

Other Places. South America's foremost nation in iron ore extraction is Brazil. Also important is Venezuela where, in the eastern forests, two mining districts, Cerro Bolivar and El Pao, have achieved world prominence. Asia's leaders are China (with approximately the same tonnage mined as Australia) and India.

Reserves

Unfortunately, we lack sufficient data for accurate mapping of world reserves of iron ore either by quantity or quality.

For the world as a whole, iron ore seems to have been deposited more widely than coal. Indeed, several countries that as yet mine comparatively little ore give promise of considerable endowments.

International Trade

A substantial share of the world's iron ore crosses international boundaries, some of it being transported over long distances. Leading exporters are Australia, Canada, Venezeula, Sweden, and Brazil. Leading customers are Japan, the United States, and West Germany (Table 14-5). This trade reflects the tendency of iron ore to move both to markets and to coal. The strongest reasons in support of this principle are these: (1) In the production of finished steel, more coal than iron ore is consumed, a fact with several ramifications, which are considered in Chapter 20 on steel manufacturing. (2) The buyers of steel are often fabricating factories that tend, themselves,

Table 14-5

World Trade in Iron Ore in Thousands of U.S. Dollars

Exports		Imports	
WORLD	2,337,172	WORLD	3,178,488
Australia	458,651	Japan	1,331,873
Canada	409,340	West Germany	482,697
Sweden	247,853	United States	450,644
Brazil	237,327	United Kingdom	262,830
Venezuela	166,294	Belgium-Lux.	195,629
Liberia	160,617	Italy	133,136
India	136,744	France	108,495

Source: Unted Nations, *Yearbook of International Trade Statistics* (1974).

to locate in areas which are nearer to coal than to iron ore (for reasons which will be analyzed in Chapters 20, 21, and 22, dealing with location of metal-processing industries). The general tendency is for iron ore to flow toward coal regions to join a raw material (coal) and to be near a market. Most of this flow is to Japan and western Europe (especially West Germany, Belgium, and Great Britain) and to the United States. Also a heavy trade moves from the U.S.S.R. to Poland, Czechoslovakia, and Hungary.

Heavy movements of iron ore in international trade relate directly to the trend of the world's main industrial regions to reach out into distant places to procure this mineral. Arctic Scandinavia, Quebec-Labrador, and eastern Venezuela are three such remote areas that function as ore suppliers for industrial regions in the middle latitudes of Anglo-America and western Europe.

The United States is importing large quantities of iron ore because our best ores have been used up, and it is cheaper to smelt high-quality foreign ores than low-grade domestic ones. We import around 35,000,000 to 45,000,000 tons of ore annually—40 to 50 per cent of the tonnage produced by domestic iron mines. Such dependence on foreign ore is a new development. As recently as 1950 the United States imported only 9,000,000 tons—in a year when domestic production was 100,000,000 tons.

United States links to other areas for iron ore are changing not only in quantity but also in location. As recently as 1953 the main foreign sources were Chile and Sweden; 1954 brought an abrupt change as the newly discovered fields in Venezuela (Cerro Bolivar and El Pao) and Canada (Quebec-Labrador) began producing. Now 90 per cent of United States imports of ore come from the Western Hemisphere, principally from Canada and Venezuela (see Table 14-6).

Case Study: Arctic Scandinavia

North of the Arctic Circle in Sweden and Norway is a nest of five iron ore fields. The three most productive are in Sweden on the eastern slopes of the Kjölen highlands. The leader is the world-famous Kiruna district, which boasts large quantities of extremely rich ore (much of it is 66 per cent iron) so close to the surface that mining can be carried on in open pits. An initial handicap was distance—Kiruna is over 500 miles from the principal population cluster of Sweden and 1000 miles from the blast-furnace centers of Europe. But ore so rich and so easily mined can bear high transport costs and still compete with those that are closer to the furnaces but leaner in content and harder to mine. Although located in the Arctic, these Scandinavian districts have mild enough winters so that year-round operations are feasible.

A railroad extends all the way from the Swedish port of Luleå, through the Malmberget, Gällivare, and Kiruna ore fields, to the Norwegian port of Narvik. One might think that all the ore would pass through Luleå— the gradient is downhill all the way, the port is in the same political state as the mine, and the town is 200 miles *south* of Narvik. But the Gulf of Bothnia freezes during the winter, while the ocean at Narvik remains ice-free. Thus, in order to benefit from the lower costs accruing from *year-round* operations (in both mining and shipping), Kiruna ore is shipped in freight trains up through the backbone of the Kjölen Mountains, across an international border, and northward in virtually the opposite direction from the German and British steel mills for which most of it is destined. As a result, Narvik is well equipped with docks and ore-handling facilities while Luleå, although closer to and downhill from Kiruna and within the same country, is less well set up.

The Malmberget and Gällivare minerals are less plentiful and poorer in quality than the Kiruna ore. And since the mines are farther than Kiruna from Narvik, little of their production can bear shipping costs through that port. So the ore goes to Luleå. There it is processed in a steel mill the government built shortly after World War II in an effort to bolster the economy of northern Sweden. This may appear, at first glance, to be dubious strategy since Luleå is so far from coal. But Scandinavia has a wealth of hydroelectric power—at Kiruna even the pit shovels are electrically powered—and Sweden tapped some of that energy for the Luleå mill, one of the largest electrified steel mills in the world.

Table 14-6

Breakdown of United States Imports of Iron Ore

Major Sources	Thousands of Tons	Percentage of Total
Canada	18,168	51
Venezuela	10,926	31
Liberia	2,761	8
Peru	1,318	4
Brazil	1,115	3
Australia	687	2
TOTAL	35,761	100

Source: U.S. Bureau of Mines, *Minerals Yearbook* (1974).

Thus, in the flow pattern of ore in Arctic Sweden, the greater tonnage and the richer ore move north to Narvik for foreign mills and the lesser tonnage and lower quality move south to Luleå for domestic mills. Through the latter port, in addition, a small amount of ore is forwarded to central Europe.

The Norwegian ore fields in the Arctic show a contrast between an older area ravaged by war and a newer area just coming into production. The Bjornevatn (or Kirkenes) field is in the far northeast corner of Norway, only two miles from the Russian border. Mining operations began here in 1906; ore was shipped out to England and Germany; a population of 7000 was supported by this economy. But in World War II the works were all but obliterated. The last shipments moved out in 1944 and the subsequent destruction was so complete that it took eight years to reconstruct the mines, railroad, and port facilities. Outbound flow of ore resumed in 1952.[2]

Dunderland is a newer ore field, 25 miles upstream from the fishing port of Moirana in a narrow valley only two miles from flanking mountain ice fields. The development here resembles that of Luleå in being a government project designed to bolster a national need for more job opportunities. The authorities have constructed a railroad through the valley, begun mining, and brought a hydroelectric plant into operation. Ore and power now converge in a new electric steel mill in Moirana, formerly a small fishing village.

Case Study: Quebec-Labrador Field

The Quebec-Labrador field illustrates how the geography of a region can be transformed by new dynamic ties with distant places. The vast triangular land mass of northern Quebec and Labrador is a cold, bleak, barren plain, almost devoid of population except for a few Indians and white villagers along the southern margin. For centuries, caribou and fish were the main subsistence supports, though a little commercial trapping, fishing, and lumbering were practiced.

Nature set an inhospitable stage for human occupancy. Winter temperatures reach 50° below zero. The ice-age glaciers scoured this land severely and left very little soil, so much of the surface is bare rock. The first white man here dubbed it "the land God gave to Cain." As early as 1892 a Montreal geologist discovered an extensive vein of rich iron ore straddling the Quebec-Labrador boundary. But the resource was in a wilderness, 200 miles from even the smallest human settlement, 250 miles from Ungava Bay to the north, 250 miles from the Atlantic, over 300 miles from the St. Lawrence. Here lay lots of ore, good ore, but it was inaccessible—inaccessible, that is, in terms of what man was willing to pay to get at it. Elsewhere on earth there were plenty of good ore fields, easier to work and easier to reach. But these other mines began to give out. So in 1936 the first of two companies was formed to explore Labrador's ores. It received a concession from the government of 20,000 square miles. But not until 1943 did a full-scale exploration begin. Every man, every piece of equipment, every bit of food had to be flown in—the greatest civilian airlift in history. Harvesting this resource required importing to this wilderness workmen and tools for modern production, facilities for a community in which the labor force could enjoy the amenities of civilization, and a railroad that could transport the ore to civilization and bring back the food, clothes, fuel, books—in short, every single item—needed by the miners. The local region had absolutely nothing with which these various needs could be met.

A total of 6900 men and $250,000,000 was required to get this economic organism into operation. On October 2, 1950, a small steamer tied up at Seven Islands, Quebec, with the first load of equipment. Dock facilities were built here for shipping at least 10,000,000 tons of ore a year; tremendous storage areas had to be built too because winter restricts the mining season to 165 days, although the St. Lawrence is ice-free for shipping 220 days a year. Railroad classification yards were built so that cars containing ores of different grades could be sorted, thereby facilitating the loading of ships with homogeneous cargoes. In 1950 Seven Islands numbered only 1000 people—a fishing village that exported pulpwood and served as a trading center for the fur-trapping Montagnais Indians.

A mainline railroad 357 miles long was built between Seven Islands and Schefferville, the heart of the mining country. Few railroads on earth encountered such difficulty: Swamps, lakes, and streams cover half the land. Elsewhere, bare rock made it difficult to anchor the rails and ties. Tunnels required blasting. In December, 1953, the construction gang averaged two miles of road per day for ten consecutive days in 30-below-zero weather.

The full extent of the Quebec-Labrador ores is not known. Only a fraction of this wilderness has been explored, but evidence at hand indicates 44 bodies of proved ore totaling 420,000,000 tons of ore averaging 50 per cent or higher iron content. This does not include much larger tonnages containing less than 50 per cent iron. Most of these iron-rich rocks are concentrated in a band 80 miles long and six miles wide that lies in an unproved area 225 miles long and 30 miles wide; but explorations indicate the presence of good ores not yet accurately estimated. The average overlay of rock or dirt covering the known beds is only 15 feet, so they can be readily strip-mined. Ore formation extends downward an average of 300 feet. The deepest hole drilled goes down 596 feet—and is still in ore!

Equally impressive, although on a somewhat smaller scale, is the more recent effort of a second company to unlock the iron ore resources of northern Quebec. In 1958 this organization began constructing three installations: Port Cartier (an iron-ore shipping port on the St. Lawrence River, 50 miles upstream from Seven Isles),

---

[2]A fascinating analysis of this area is Trevor Lloyd's "Iron Ore Production at Kirkenes, Norway" in *Economic Geography*, 1955, pp. 211–233.

a 193-mile railroad connecting Port Cartier with a newly discovered ore field near Lac Jeannine, and Gagnon (a new settlement hewn out in the wilderness at the focus of mining operations, 200 miles southwest of Schefferville). Iron ore was first shipped from this area in 1960. Since the ore is comparatively lean (averaging 31 per cent iron content for the company's entire holdings, with the richest ores around 45 per cent), a concentrating mill has been built just east of Gagnon.[3]

FERRO-ALLOYS

Ferro-alloys are metals that, in small amounts, are blended with iron to make steel. Each of these substances imparts a particular quality. Manganese provides tensile strength in rails and beams, and resistance to abrasives in rock-crushing machinery. Chromium renders iron resistant to corrosion from liquids. Nickel adds strength, ductility, and toughness to steels used in machinery. Tungsten is used in making high-speed cutting tools. The presence of molybdenum makes a steel that is useful in magnets and highly elastic steel. Steels containing cobalt resist rust and withstand high temperatures (as in jet engines). Springs, forgings, and high-speed tools require vanadium. To be sure, each of these metals is also used for many other purposes—but their main role in today's economy is as alloys with iron.

The world's combined annual ore yield of these seven metals is 28,000,000 tons, approximately 4 per cent of the figure for iron ore.

Most of the areas well endowed in coal and iron ore are *not* well endowed with ferro-alloys. For example, North America's major region of alloy minerals is in the western part of the continent, extending from Canada to Mexico, corresponding generally with the Rocky Mountains. This region leads the world in the mining of molybdenum and has at least modest reserves of every other major alloy mineral. Arizona and Colorado are predominant states. In eastern North America the ferro-alloys are neither as widespread, nor as numerous, nor as abundant as in the West. But one zone is notable for nickel: the Sudbury area of eastern Ontario.

Europe is poorly endowed with ferro-alloys. For only one of them—tungsten—does it produce even as much as 6 per cent of the world total and for that one its leading producer is Portugal. What ferro-alloys Europe does possess are located in either the South or the North. The southerly belt begins at the Atlantic coast and runs eastward through the Soviet Union; it includes not only European nations but a fringe of northern Africa (Mo-

rocco) and a fragment of Asia (Turkey). Not many ferro-alloys appear here, but the region does produce appreciable amounts of chromium and tungsten. In northern Europe, ferro-alloys are restricted pretty much to Scandinavia.

The Soviet Union has a long belt that runs the length of southern Russia clear to the Pacific with branches northward along the Urals. It is notable for its diversity (all ferro-alloys are available) and for the prominence of manganese—over one-third of the world total. The leading manganese mines are at Nikopol and Chiatura near the Black Sea.

In eastern Asia ferro-alloys are found in an arc running from Hokkaido in the northeast, around through southeast Asia to western Pakistan. All ferro-alloys are represented. China is the world's leading source of tungsten (25 per cent), notably in Chianghsi. The Philippines yield chromium. India accounts for 8 per cent of the world's manganese.

Africa, from Zaire to the Republic of South Africa, has a spectacular share in the mining of cobalt: The former alone mines 64 per cent of the world total. Southern Africa, particularly Rustenburg in South Africa and Selukwe in Rhodesia, is the world's foremost chromium-mining zone. Africa also produces 30 per cent of the world's manganese. Indeed, southern Africa does extensive mining of a wide array of ferro-alloy ores; the industry has developed rapidly since 1940.

South America, like Europe and Australia, has relatively few ferro-alloys. The ones mined there are scattered through the southern and western part.

Within the mining regions, ferro-alloy ores seem to be associated with igneous rocks and with hilly or mountainous terrain where the earth's crust has been subjected to folding and other forces associated with instability.

For the world as a whole, ferro-alloy ores are mined much more widely than coal and iron. Indeed, three outstanding areas for coal and iron (Europe, Anglo-America, and the U.S.S.R.) altogether account for only about 39 per cent of the manganese, 42 per cent of the chromium, 39 per cent of the tungsten, and 21 per cent of the cobalt. Only in nickel and molybdenum do the industrial leaders rank as high as in coal and iron ore.

The significance of this situation is that a lively foreign trade in ferro-alloys develops, virtually all in the direction of Europe and Anglo-America—the predominant miners and users of coal and iron. Some of the ores (or substances concentrated from them) travel long distances, indeed. Manganese moves 7000 miles from India to Europe, and over 3000 miles from Ghana to the United States. Chromium ore travels 8000 miles from the Philippines to the United States, and nearly 7000 miles from South Africa to Europe.

[3] Additional insights to the development of these two Canadian ventures can be gleaned in Graham Humphry's "Schefferville, Quebec: A New Pioneering Town," *Economic Geography*, 1958, pp. 151–166, and in a special report entitled "Precambrian Mining in Canada, Special Report," dated April, 1961, by the Quebec Cartier Mining Company.

COPPER

Western North America boasts one of the world's leading copper-mining regions. It extends from Canada to Mexico and accounts for almost a quarter of the world total. Arizona is the principal state, with important mines

A new 15-cubic-yard capacity electric shovel loading copper ore into an ore train in Morenci, Arizona. The locomotive engineer in the foreground is using remote control equipment to position the train for loading. (*Courtesy Phelps Dodge Corporation.*)

near Tucson, Morenci, and Globe-Miami. The largest single copper mine in North America though is at Bingham, Utah, where operations have been continuous since 1865. The Bingham ores are near the surface, permitting inexpensive open-pit mining. This is fortunate since more expensive operations might not be worthwhile. Ores taken from open-pit mines often average less than 0.5 per cent metallic content, that is, every 1000 tons of ore dug from the earth contain less than 5 tons of copper. Butte, Montana, is the northernmost important copper district. There, the mineral must be mined via shafts; ores from underground operations must be relatively rich to cover the high cost of operation. In eastern Canada, the Sudbury, Ontario, district yields copper as a by-product in refining nickel ores.

The interior of southern Africa, notably a zone straddling the Zambia-Zaire border, has in recent years become one of the world's main copper zones. Zaire's Katanga district is also important. Africa yields about one-fifth of the world's mine production of copper; Zambia with 10 per cent of the world total and Zaire with 7 are clearly Africa's leading countries.

The South American copper belt extends from northern Peru to central Chile. In most years, Chile mines more copper than any other single nation except the United States, and her Chuquicamata district may contain more ore reserves than any other deposit in the world.

The Soviet Union has ample copper in the Ural Hills, notably around Mednogorsk. But western Europe is almost barren of copper ore and has long been dependent on outside areas for its supply. Similarly, there appears to be relatively little in Asia.

The locational pattern of copper ore mining is closely associated with a significant volume of international trade. Much of Africa's production goes to Europe

as does a large share of Chile's copper. In spite of being the world's leading producer, the United States is a major importer. Sales of copper account for an astonishing 95 per cent of Zambia's exports by value.

BAUXITE

The Caribbean area (notably Jamaica, Surinam, and Guyana) has assumed world leadership in mining the aluminum ore, bauxite, and now accounts for over one-third of the world total. Bauxite shipments constitute 45 per cent of Guyana's sales abroad and 30 per cent of Surinam's.

Some bauxite is mined in Arkansas, the only portion of the United States that yields any significant quantity. Several European countries have bauxite, the most prominent being France (particularly the Var Valley), Greece, Yugoslavia, and Hungary. Hungary's bauxite, in fact, is an important reason for the tenacity with which the Soviet Union is holding on to that country, for along with Yugoslavia and Romania it produces more of that valuable mineral than the Soviet Union does in its own bauxite mines.

Whereas most nonferrous metals are associated with igneous rocks, bauxite tends to be associated with clay-limestone rocks which have been exposed to weathering in tropical climates. The presence of bauxite in Arkansas, France, Hungary, and other such areas suggests that at one time they must have had a tropical climate, which expedited the formation of bauxite. Rich bauxite ores have also been developed in tropical Africa (Guinea) and tropical Asia (Indonesia, India, and West Malaysia). Aluminum is one of the most abundant elements in the earth's crust (averaging 8 per cent) but current methods for extracting the element are too expensive for ores that contain less than about 20 per cent of the metal.

177

DIAMONDS

Of the several precious minerals—gold, silver, and platinum among them—we shall select the diamond for comment here because of its significance in the manufacture of machinery. Unlike the others mentioned, diamonds are not a metal but rather pure carbon in crystallized form.

By value, the gem trade takes most of the diamond harvest. But by weight the industrial trade predominates, since about three-fourths of the world's diamonds are built into cutting instruments, abrasives, and bearings in machinery. No other economically significant mineral is so geographically concentrated as the diamond. Over 75 per cent of all diamonds are mined in Africa. Zaire alone accounts for nearly one-third; Ghana, the Republic of South Africa, and Sierra Leone are also important. In most of these places diamonds are gathered by placer-mining methods, being washed out from alluvial gravels. Before the discovery of such gravels in 1867 (along the Orange River) diamonds had been mined by shaft methods in South Africa, especially around Kimberley. But alluvial diamonds are much cheaper to gather; consequently, many of the underground mines have been closed. The greatest alluvial deposits are in Zaire where the diamond-bearing gravels are scattered over an area 450 miles long and 300 miles wide along the courses of the Kasai and Sankuru rivers, which are southern tributaries of the Congo River.

Nearly all these African diamonds find their way to industrial Anglo-America and Europe; many of the gem-quality stones go to Israel and Belgium for cutting and polishing before moving on to the consumer markets. Diamonds make up 4 per cent of Belgium's export trade and 37 per cent of Israel's.

NUCLEAR FUELS

The most recent additions to the list of desirable items in the earth's crust resulted from the discovery that a pair of radioactive metals can be used to produce nuclear energy. Uranium is now the more important of these but thorium is a potential source. When one *ounce* of these nuclear fuels disintegrates, it yields energy equal to that produced in the burning of 100 *tons* of coal. When released rapidly, such energy explodes violently, as in a bomb. When slowly controlled and released, it can meet man's needs as does any other source of power.

Governments tend to keep secret the data on amount and location of uranium and thorium, but since uranium occurs mainly in veins associated with such metals as copper, silver, gold, vanadium, cobalt—and with some oil shales—it is possible to make estimates. Large known uranium deposits are near Lubumbashi in Zaire, and in the Western Hemisphere the richest apparent reserves are around Port Radium (next to Great Bear Lake) in

Canada's Northwest Territories. Most of the United State's uranium comes from New Mexico and Wyoming. Europe's sources seem to be largely in France. Supposedly the Soviet Union has considerable uranium deposits in the Turkestan district.

ASBESTOS

About 4,000,000 tons of asbestos are mined each year for use as fire-proof insulation. This mineral is unique. It occurs in the form of nonflammable fibers that can be spun and woven, these fibers making up 5 to 10 per cent of a rocky substance termed serpentine. In Canada, which is responsible for 40 per cent of the world's supply, a large portion of the product is taken from a narrow belt of serpentine rock that stretches for 150 miles near the Quebec-New York border. Some of the mining is open pit. Most of the output is exported to the United States and Europe. The Soviet Union mines one-third of the world's asbestos, mostly in the Ural Hills and mostly for domestic markets. South Africa, the only other notable producer, ships its product to the United Kingdom and other European customers.

FERTILIZER MINERALS

Soil supplies plant rootlets with plant foods, some of which are consumed in only small amounts and are restored by natural processes. But there are four nutrients that are returned too slowly to maintain crop yields in regions of intensive farming: phosphorus, potassium, nitrogen, and calcium. Man must add these to the soil if high yields are to continue.

Most farmers depend on manure to convey plant foods back to the soil. But regions with inadequate manure supplies must rely on commercial fertilizers that are manufactured largely from pulverized rocks. Three different types of rock (one high in phosphorus, another in potash, a third in nitrate) are crushed, treated by several chemical processes, dried, ground up into pellets or finer grains, and blended together in measured proportions. Since in very wet areas the soil is also poor in calcium, calcareous rocks must be ground into the mixture or applied directly to the soil.

The market for manufactured fertilizers is found in those humid regions where pressure on the land is intense and where farmers have enough capital to buy plant food for supplementing their manure supply. Specifically, the main consumers are Europe, eastern Anglo-America, central U.S.S.R., and China (Table 14-7). Acre for acre, Japan, the Netherlands, and Belgium are among the leading nations in the application of commercial fertilizer.

The source regions for most manufactured fertilizers are certain areas where ages ago there were deposited sediments from sea water containing high proportions of calcium, nitrogen, potassium, and phosphorus that are now suitable for mining.

Since *calcium* is available in the limestone that is

Table 14-7

Ch. 14 / Selected Minerals

Consumption of Manufactured
Fertilizers, Percentage of World Total*

Country	Amount
WORLD	100
Africa	3
North America	24
United States	21
South America	3
Asia	18
China	7
India	4
Japan	3
Europe	34
France	7
West Germany	4
Poland	4
Oceania	3
Australia	2
U.S.S.R	15

Source: United Nations, *Production
Yearbook* (1975).
*Metric tons of nitrogenous, phosphate,
and potash fertilizers.

widespread in many farming regions, local quarries can
provide the rock for pulverizing and spreading on the
fields. Because it is so widespread, limestone for fertilizer
is not shipped very far; hence, no specific areas achieve
renown for producing it.

At one time most of the *nitrogen* for fertilizer came
from a nitrate rock (known as *caliche*) of which the entire
known world supply was in the Atacama Desert of Chile.
Before World War I Chile monopolized world nitrate
production and price-setting. And for many years nitrates
constituted the major portion of Chile's sales abroad.
But Chile's industry is now in trouble due to competition
from chemical factories in other countries that are
manufacturing nitrogen from the air, which is 78 per
cent nitrogen, and from coal, which yields many volatile
gases, including ammonia—composed primarily of
nitrogen. Today only 1 per cent of Chile's exports are
nitrates and less than 1 per cent of the world demand is
met by Chilean mines.

Potash salts deposited from ancient seas are the prime
source of potassium. Although useful in tanning leather
and in making soap and a wide diversity of products, 90
per cent of the world's potash goes into fertilizer. For a
long time Germany and France were the principal
sources. In the vicinity of the Harz mountains (half-way
between Berlin and the Ruhr) lie potash beds from 10 to
100 feet thick, resting between 1,000 and 2,000 feet below
ground level. The Iron Curtain bisects this potash field.

So today 14 per cent of the world's potash comes from
West Germany, and 12 per cent from East Germany.
Shortly before World War I, the Alsace district of France
began producing potash from deep beds, but Germany
controlled Alsace at that time and restricted its output.
Since 1919, however, Alsace has been French, and the
French government has so stimulated the industry that
French companies now mine 9 per cent of the world
total. For years the United States was dependent on
these European sources, but after World War I a series of
potash deposits were discovered underlying thousands of
square miles east of Carlsbad, New Mexico. Commercial
mining began in the early 1930's; today the United
States mines 12 per cent of the world supply. The worst
handicap of the Carlsbad area is its location, far from the
eastern demand for fertilizer. The Soviet Union has
tremendous reserves in the vicinity of Solikamsk, just
west of the middle Urals, and is self-sufficient. The
U.S.S.R. is the world's largest producer with over one-
fourth of total production.

Fertilizer factories procure some *phosphorus* from
blast-furnace slag, but the bulk of their need is met by
phosphate rock. About 100,000,000 tons are mined a
year, that is, roughly one-tenth the tonnage of iron ore.
The United States is responsible for 40 per cent of that
total and is self-sufficient. Florida produces 85 per cent
of our supply from open-pit mines widely distributed in
a belt 100 miles long paralleling the western coast north
of Tampa. Heavy movements of phosphate rock account
for high percentages of the freight traffic on Florida's
railroads, for they start the rock on its way to numerous
fertilizer factories scattered widely and evenly over the
eastern United States, from the Gulf of Mexico to Minnesota, and from the Atlantic Coast to the Great Plains.
Ocean carriers, too, transport much of Florida's phosphate to New York and other Atlantic ports; barges take
it up the Mississippi. Although the Southeast is the
principal mining region, the nation's biggest *reserve* of
phosphate rock is in the West. Underlying Idaho,
Montana, Wyoming, and Utah are deposits of much
greater quantity and much higher quality than those in
Florida and Tennessee. Yet relatively little mining is
done. For one thing, the deposits are deep and must be
shaft-mined. Then once it is out of the ground, the rock
is far from customers, most of whom are hundreds of
miles to the east.

In Europe phosphate rocks are mined in numerous
places, but a century of digging has depleted the resource;
so it is now imported, mainly from Morocco and Tunisia,
which together produce 20 per cent of the world supply.
The Soviet Union, which accounts for 24 per cent of
world total, is self-sufficient; its mines are located in the
Kola Peninsula and in southern Russia west of the Volga
River.

Several Pacific islands (notably Nauru, Ocean, and
Makatea) produce strip-mined rock to go to Japan, New
Zealand, and Australia.

A unique source of phosphorus is guano from the arid Chincha Islands, a few miles off the coast of Peru. Guano is composed of the excrement and skeletal remains of milions of *guanay* birds and other ocean-birds which, for reasons still obscure, flock to these specific islands. When man discovered the islands, the guano deposits were several feet thick. Prized by the Incas, guano later became Peru's most valuable export, but the supply has been so depleted that the Peruvian government bans its sale abroad. Rich in nitrogen as well as phosphorus, guano today is consumed entirely by the sugar and cotton plantations of coastal Peru (see Figure 12-1).

Essential to the production of commercial phosphate fertilizer is another mineral—*sulfur*. Each year miners excavate about 26,000,000 tons of sulfur, the bulk of which goes into the manufacture of sulfuric acid. A large proportion of the acid is, in turn, used by the fertilizer industry in treating phosphate rock. Although pulverized phosphate rock can be effectively used without treatment, the phosphorus is more easily released to the soil if the rock is first treated with sulfuric acid. The result is termed "acid phosphate" or "super-phosphate." More than a ton of sulfuric acid is required in the treatment of each ton of phosphate rock.

Sulfur comes from mines in two forms: sulfide ores and "native" sulfur. Sulfide ores contain a metal (say, iron or copper) that is actually the principal object of mining; sulfur is merely a by-product. But over half of the earth's sulfur is mined in the "native" form, not combined with metals. Nearly 75 per cent of all native sulfur comes from the fringes of the Gulf of Mexico, 8 per cent from Mexico, and 67 per cent from the United States. Texas and Louisiana are the leading states. Here the sulfur deposits have been concentrated, by rather complex geological forces, as caprock atop salt domes. These salt domes are massive affairs, sometimes 3000 feet in diameter, that rise to within 1200 feet of the earth's surface and are capped with a layer of sulfur-bearing rock 100 to 200 feet thick.

The prominence of the Gulf Coast in sulfur production provides an excellent example of how several advantageous relationships can work together in the economic geography of a region. The region naturally has large amounts of sulfur-bearing mineral, which fortunately is of high quality (around 40 per cent sulfur); some rocks even have such a high content of that element that they can be used without further refining. Then, since the domes are located close to ocean ports, the mineral may be moved cheaply up the Mississippi River or to the Atlantic Seaboard, or to foreign ports. In addition, scientists were able to develop a peculiar mining technique that extracts the sulfur from the ground at a very low cost. Three concentric pipes are driven into the sulfur cap; hot water is forced down the outermost pipe and, escaping at the bottom, melts some of the sulfur. Compressed air is forced down the middle pipe and forces the water-sulfur mixture up the innermost pipe. At the surface this mixture is led to huge storage vats where the water evaporates, the sulfur hardens, and then is dug for transporting. Mining costs would be considerably higher if this area were not endowed with abundant water and abundant fuel (natural gas). Other sulfur mines, widely dispersed through the western states, can scarcely compete with inexpensively mined salt-dome sulfur.

Prior to discovery of the Gulf domes (around the turn of this century) Italy dominated the world mining of sulfur. The island of Sicily and the southern mainland have several deposits, averaging 26 per cent sulfur content, associated with old volcanoes.

BUILDING-MATERIALS MINERALS

In spite of the widespread occurrence of sand, gravel, and stone, few people appreciate their economic importance. For example, in the United States the value of sand and gravel mined is 115 per cent of the value of the iron ore mined; the value of crushed stone is almost that of copper.

A few places are endowed with distinctive stone resources. In this country, although limestone exists in every state, Indiana is blessed with masses of easily accessible stone that is solid yet easy to mine, is easy to cut in blocks, resists weathering, and hardens with exposure. Bedford is the center of this industry in Indiana which mines over half the nation's building limestone. But stone is a heavy commodity in proportion to its value, which means that after a few hundred miles transportation costs begin to equal the original cost of the stone when loaded at the quarry. Quarrymen in the Alpena district of northern Michigan—a world leader in the production of crushed limestone—ship stone via the Great Lakes to the industrial heart of Anglo-America.

WATER

Water is perhaps the most versatile—and surely the least expensive—of all the economic minerals. Water's versatility is demonstrated by its ability to meet man's need for nourishment, water power, navigation, recreation, irrigation, washing, air-conditioning, and in such industrial processes as forming solutions, cooling, and disposing of waste materials. In addition, sea water can serve as a raw material from which different chemicals are extracted. And steam is used to make electricity.

Clearly we cannot take the time to discuss the geographic aspects of each such individual use of water. Only two will be considered: water power and sea water as a raw material.

Water Power

Unlike coal, water has no capacity within itself for producing energy. But as a liquid which responds easily to the influence of gravity, water is mobile—and its *motion* does possess the ability to develop power. This ability varies with two major factors: (a) vertical distance of water fall, and (b) volume of water falling. Obviously, a large volume falling a great distance has the greatest power potential. Where one of these two factors is small, a small volume falling a great distance is to be preferred generally over a large volume falling a short distance—because of ease in harnessing the power. For it is easier to construct a narrow high dam than a broad low one. Accordingly, more power is produced by falling water of small rivers in the mountains than by the water of giant rivers in the plains.

The ideal physical environment for the production of water power has (a) a steep gradient in the river, (b) a uniformly large supply of water from month to month, and (c) a narrows somewhere in the river's course that can facilitate dam construction. Uniformity of supply of abundant water cascading over a dam is enhanced by the following conditions: a vast drainage basin over which a humid climate prevails and through which an extensive network of tributaries feeds the major river trunk. In such a situation, droughts in one portion of the drainage basin may be compensated for by wet periods in other portions so that water flow in the main artery is maintained. Uniform flow is also favored by the presence of numerous lakes and swamps which serve as reservoirs in the drainage system, impounding water during unusually wet seasons and regulating its passage through the river network.

The ideal cultural environment for production of water power has large consumers of power (for example, factories and cities) located rather close to the power site. In the early days of water power such consumers had to be within a few yards of the waterfall or dam. Many a grist mill and saw mill were actually alongside a water wheel, turned by the falling water. The number of factories at a single dam was increased in the early days by the construction of *millraces*. A millrace was a channel dug to divert water from a river at a point upstream from a dam and then to lead it in a downstream direction parallel to the river, though at a distance of at least 100 feet. The intervening land was an ideal site—a factory could take water in from the millrace, conduct it to a water wheel within or beside its building, and then let it flow out into the river which was several feet (depending on the dam height) lower than the millrace. Many a small city grew up around an industrial district consisting of several factories straddling millraces. It was possible also for power thus produced to feed factories on the opposite side of a millrace. Such factories, however, could not possess their own water wheels; rather, they were serviced by overhead rotating shafts which extended to the millrace site where, via leather belts, they were rotated by power generated at the water wheels. Such overhead shafts, often extending 100 feet or more—sometimes crossing streets—made millrace districts noisy parts of town.

In the early days of water power development two major world areas stood out, distinguished by a myriad of small water power installations: western Europe and eastern Anglo-America. These were the areas where the Industrial Revolution first flowered, and part of its power requirement was met by a host of small water power developments. Many a good power site (with an excellent physical environment) was totally undeveloped because of a poor cultural environment; whereas many a poor power site (with a limited physical endowment) was fully exploited because of a favorable cultural environment.

The discovery of electricity opened a new era for water power. Prior to this discovery, power generated by water-driven wheels could be transported only by mechanical means which spanned comparatively short distances measured, at most, in yards. But the discovery of electricity—a form of energy into which water power could be converted—unshackled factories and cities from the necessity of being located right by water power sites. Electricity is transportable and can be conducted scores of miles. But shipping electricity is not like shipping coal; a volume of coal does not decline with distance transported (a hopper car loaded with 50 tons of coal departing from Pittsburgh will contain 50 tons of coal when it arrives at Indianapolis). Electricity, on the other hand, dissipates with distance. But inventions have enabled it to be shipped economically as far as 400 miles or more. However, the actual distance which electricity is transported in any given area depends upon government subsidy and the costs of competing fuels; if coal, oil, or gas is cheap, a region is likely to manufacture more electricity from steam plants and to transport hydroelectricity only short distances.

Water power is thus a competitor with fuels. Wherever the cost of generating electricity at a water power site plus the cost of transporting it to a market is more than the cost of building and operating a thermal plant at the market, the choice is likely to be made in favor of fuel-consuming power plants near the customers.

Thus, the principle holds that hydroelectricity (electricity generated by water power) tends to be consumed in the general region of production. Even with inventions for transporting electricity, many excellent water power sites are still undeveloped while many poor power sites are totally developed!

Today, water power itself is relatively unimportant in the world's total power picture. Only as a generator of electricity is it significant in meeting the world's energy requirements. Even so, water power produces only 4 per cent of this country's total power demand. Even if every potential water power site in the nation were fully developed, only about 12 per cent of our power needs would be satisfied thereby.

Regions of Developed Water Power. Major areas measured in percentage of the world's annual generation of water power are western Europe 28 per cent, the United States 20, Canada 14, Japan 6, the Soviet Union 9. Asia, exclusive of the Soviet Union, accounts for 9 per cent, Latin America generates a little over 8 per cent, and Africa 2.

Figure 14-6 shows the general areal pattern of the world's developed water power. Southern Europe has numerous water power districts in the several nations through which the Alps and contiguous mountain ranges run. Indeed this part of Europe is distinguished by nations where water power development is so complete that the capacity (measured in horsepower) actually exceeds the potential power at ordinary minimum water flow. Examples of such nations are Italy and France (each accounting for over 3 per cent of the world total), Switzerland, and Austria. Recent developments in Norway and Sweden rank these nations ahead of Italy and France in capacity. Norway and Sweden together produce about 9 per cent of the world total.

Figure 14-6 also shows that eastern Anglo-America (from Canada to northern Alabama) is a major world region in the generation of hydroelectric power. The chief centers are the Shipshaw and Isle Maligne projects (in eastern Canada, harnessing the Saguenay River), Niagara Falls, and the series of dams in the Tennessee Valley. The St. Lawrence Seaway dams increase the power in eastern Anglo-America. The western part of the continent has several water power plants, from Kitimat (in British Columbia) to Hoover Dam. The state of Washington's Grand Coulee Project has a larger ultimate capacity than any other hydroelectric project in the world. The three Pacific Coast states, in fact, account for a large share of the nation's developed water power. Although developed power sites are more numerous and widespread in eastern states, the power produced is less than in the West.

The Soviet Union has both natural power sites (principally in the Caucasus Mountains and in the numerous mountain chains of eastern Siberia) and man-made sites, such as the Dnepropetrovsk dam on the Dnepr River in the rather flat Ukraine, and two installations at Kuybyshev and Stalingrad (now Volgograd) on the Volga. Japan, Korea, and Manchuria dominate hydroelectric power production in the Far East. Indeed, Japan's developed capacity almost equals her potential waterpower at ordinary low flow. Elsewhere, a few hydroelectric projects are of great significance to their immediate hinterlands in nations that, in the over-all view, otherwise have comparatively little power development. Examples are the Kariba Dam in Rhodesia, the Aswan High Dam in Egypt, and the Bhakra Dam in India. The periphery of South America and of southeast Australia and New Zealand should also be mentioned in this category. (A detailed hydroelectric power map in an economic atlas will serve to pinpoint the location of the foregoing districts.)

Prominent in the world's water power installations are some very impressive dams several of which exceed 500 feet in height—one in the U.S.S.R. reaches 1040 feet. However, the rivers flowing over these high dams are

Figure 14-6

DEVELOPED WATER POWER

Scale at Latitude 35°

0   500   1500   2500 Miles

0   2000   4000 Kms.

often relatively small compared with certain ones at other installations which have greater capacity. Western Europe has almost one-third of the world's hydroelectric capacity (Table 14-8), yet none of the world's 64 largest

Table 14-8

Installed Hydroelectric Capacity

Area or Nation	Installed Capacity (Mw)
Western Europe	97,822
United States	53,404
Canada	32,501
U.S.S.R.	31,500
Latin America	23,078
Japan	19,897
Other East Asia	14,521
South Asia	12,469
Africa	8,154
Eastern Europe	6,176
Australia	4,310
New Zealand	3,200
Other Oceania	99

Source: World Energy Conference, *Survey of Energy Resources* (1974).

Table 14-9

Hydroelectric Projects with Capacities of 1,000 Megawatts (Mw) or More

Hydroelectric Project, River Basin, and Country	Ultimate Capacity (Mw)
Grand Coulee, Columbia, U.S.	9,771
Guri, Orinoco, Venezuela	6,500
Sayansk, Yenisei, U.S.S.R.*	6,400
Krasnoyarsk, Yenisei, U.S.S.R.	6,096
Bratsk, Yenisei, U.S.S.R.	5,600
Sukhovo, U.S.S.R.*	5,225
Churchill Falls, Churchill, Canada*	5,225
Ust-Illinsk, Yenisei, U.S.S.R.*	4,300
Cabora Basa, Zambesi, Mozambique*	4,000
Ilha Solteira, Parana, Brazil*	3,200
Paulo Afonso, Sao Francisco, Brazil	2,939
John Day, Columbia, U.S.*	2,700
Nurek, Amu Darya, U.S.S.R.*	2,700
22nd Congress, Volga, U.S.S.R.	2,560
Mica, Columbia, Canada*	2,500
Sao Simao, Parana, Brazil*	2,500

Source: World Energy Conference, *Survey of Energy Resources* (1974).

*Under construction.

hydroelectric projects are located there. The United States, Canada, the U.S.S.R., and Latin America, however, are next in line in terms of installed capacity, and these regions hold 15 of the 16 largest hydroelectric projects (Table 14-9). The U.S.S.R. alone has 7 of these, Brazil 3, and the United States and Canada have 2 each.

Potential Water Power. The location of potential water power, however, is markedly different from the foregoing pattern. Asia, for instance, has 27 per cent of the world total. For other places the percentages are Africa 21, North America 15, U.S.S.R. 11, South America 17, and Europe 7. Notice that the world pattern of potential water power tends to correlate with areas having good physical environments but poor cultural environments for hydroelectric installations. Some of the world's greatest potential water power sites are the lower Congo River, the Parana River, the middle Yangtze, and some of the rivers in New Guinea—all of which are relatively far from customers demanding electric power. In contrast to the wet tropics of Africa, the Amazon basin has little potential water power. In spite of tremendous water volumes, the Amazon has a comparatively low water head, so it drops little in elevation along its course.

Water for Mineral Content

The earth's surface embraces almost 200,000,000 square miles. Continents occupy 56,000,000 square miles (roughly 28 per cent of the total surface) including the rivers, lakes, and inland seas. This leaves the staggering figure of 144,000,000 square miles as the area of the ocean surface. For every square mile of continent, there are almost three square miles of ocean. Most of the wet acreage is concentrated in the Pacific Ocean—approximately 65,000,000 square miles. If we could shift all the land masses in the world into the Pacific, we would still have 9,000,000 square miles of water left—the area of North America. The other oceans, in order of size, are: Atlantic 32,000,000 square miles, Indian 28,000,000, and Arctic 6,000,000. In addition there are numerous smaller bodies such as the Mediterranean, Caribbean, China, Red, Yellow, Okhotsk, Bering, Baltic, and Japan seas, as well as Hudson Bay and the Gulf of Mexico.

Oceans are deep as well as vast. The greatest known depth, 36,201 feet, is south of the Mariana Islands in the western Pacific.

The water world is indeed gigantic and so are its resources. One single cubic mile of sea water contains, on the average, 166,000,000 tons of dissolved minerals. If we multiply this by the number of cubic miles in the world's seas, we get the staggering product of 50,000,000,000,000,000,000 tons of minerals!

The sea averages 96.5 per cent water and 3.5 per cent dissolved minerals. The figures vary from region to region—in the rainy tropics, for instance, the percentage of minerals is slightly lower, the ocean being diluted by rainfall, and in the dry subtropics the percentage is higher because of reduced rainfall and increased evaporation.

The most abundant *elements* dissolved in sea water are sodium, chlorine, magnesium, calcium, potassium, and sulfur; the most prevalent *minerals* are:

Sodium chloride	78.0%
Magnesium chloride	11.0
Magnesium sulfate	5.0
Calcium sulfate	3.0
Potassium sulfate	2.5
All others	0.5
Total dissolved minerals	100.0%

Extracting minerals from sea water is an expensive business, with few exceptions. Chemists have identified some 50 elements in sea water, but technologists have succeeded in extracting only a few at costs that are competitive with the mining of these minerals from rocks. Sea water is evaporated in huge reservoirs in the open sunshine to produce residues of sodium chloride (common salt) on the shores of the Persian Gulf, China, Japan, and the Philippines. Bromine is now produced commercially by means of the same general technique. In 1941 scientists discovered methods for commercially extracting the strong light metal magnesium from sea water. During World War II much of the magnesium used in airplanes, star shells, incendiary bombs, boats, and even lightweight buildings was mined from the sea, a cubic mile of which contains 4,000,000 tons of the metal. A cubic mile of sea water also contains large amounts of gold and silver, but the labor and complex equipment required for extracting these precious metals would cost more than they are worth. As for the other elements known to exist in the ocean—lobsters absorb huge quantities of cobalt and their blood contains copper; mollusks contain nickel; it was not known that vanadium even existed in the sea until zoologists discovered it in the blood of sea cucumbers. Someday man may devise techniques for commercially extracting other minerals from ocean water. When that day comes, world regions of mining may go through a major transformation, as "mines" line the seacoasts near the world's major markets of mineral consumption.

SUGGESTED READINGS

BERMAN, MILDRED, "The Location of the Diamond-Cutting Industry," *Annals of the Association of American Geographers*, 1971, pp. 316–328.

BRENT, MILLARD D., and SANDIDGE, JOHN R., "Uranium Production in South-Central Texas," *The Professional Geographer*, 1969, pp. 15–17.

DEASY, GEORGE F., and GRIESS, PHYLLIS R., "Local and Regional Differences in Long Term Bituminous Coal Production Prospects in Eastern United States," *Annals of the Association of American Geographers*, 1967, pp. 519–533.

EARNEY, FILLMORE C., "New Ores for Old Furnaces: Pelletized Iron," *Annals of the Association of American Geographers*, 1969, pp. 512–534.

EYRE, JOHN D., "Development Trends in the Japanese Electric Power Industry 1963–68," *The Professional Geographer*, 1970, pp. 26–30.

GRIFFITHS, IEUAN L., "Zambian Coal: An Example of Strategic Resource Development," *Geographical Review*, 1968, pp. 538–551.

HEFFORD, R. K., and SMITH, DEREK L., "The Leigh Creek Coalfield, South Australia Resource Development in a Difficult Environment," *Annals of the Association of American Geographers*, 1967, pp. 503–518.

HIDORE, JOHN J., "Water, Water Resources, and Water Problems," *The Professional Geographer*, 1970, pp. 117–119.

HOLZ, ROBERT K., "The Aswan High Dam," *The Professional Geographer*, 1968, pp. 230–237.

HORDON, ROBERT M., "Selected Trends in Metropolitan Water Supply: A Case Study of the New York and New Jersey Metropolitan Area," *Proceedings of the Association of American Geographers*, 1975, pp. 96–100.

ISSERMAN, ANDREW M., "Some Policy Implications of Spatial Variations in Fuel Consumption by Manufacturing Activities," *Economic Geography*, 1977, pp. 45–54.

KINLOCH, ROBERT F., "The Growth of Electric Power Production in Malaya," *Annals of the Association of American Geographers*, 1966, pp. 220–235.

MASON, PETER F., "The Atlantic City Ore Mine, A Study in Economic Geography," *The Professional Geographer*, 1966, pp. 280–282.

———, "Some Changes in Domestic Iron Mining as a Result of Pelletization," *Annals of the Association of American Geographers*, 1969, pp. 535–551.

MIHALYI, LOUIS J., "Electricity and Electrification for Zambia," *Geographical Review*, 1977, pp. 63–70.

PALMEDO, PHILIP F., "Approaches to Regional Energy Analysis," *Growth and Change*, October 1976, pp. 25–32.

SWINDELL, KENNETH, "Iron Ore Mining in West Africa: Some Recent Developments in Guinea, Sierra Leone, and Liberia," *Economic Geography*, 1967, pp. 333–346.

UNITED STATES BUREAU OF MINES, *Minerals Yearbook* (published annually) and *Mineral Trade Notes* (published monthly).

YOUNG, B. S., "Jamaica's Bauxite and Alumina Industries," *Annals of the Association of American Geographers*, 1965, pp. 449–464.

ZOBLER, LEONARD; CAREY, GEORGE W.; GREENBERG, MICHAEL R.; and HORDON, ROBERT M. "A Geographical Systems Analysis of the Water Disposal Networks of the New York Metropolitan Regions," *Geographical Review*, 1976, pp. 32–47.

oil and gas: a study in historical geography

A drilling camp in Saudi Arabia. (*Courtesy EXXON Corporation.*)

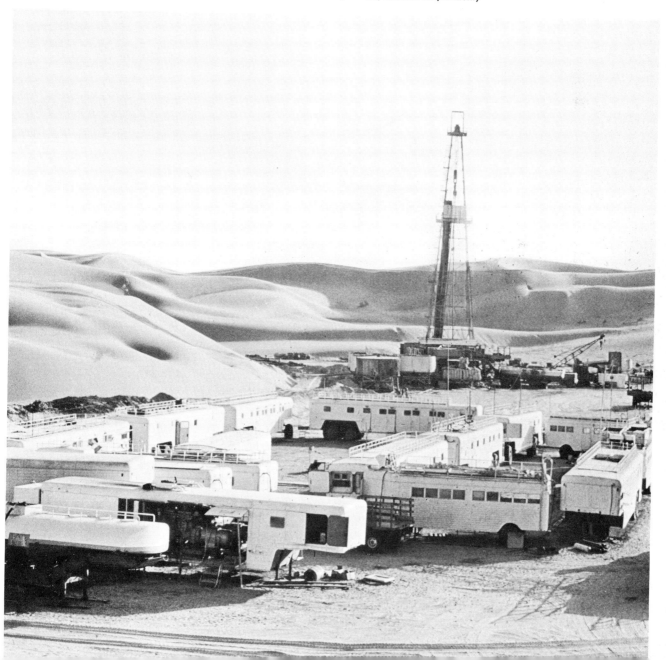

Petroleum is versatile in its uses: fuel; lubricant; source of illumination, wax, and tar; and raw material from which many chemicals can be extracted. Its high economic value automatically commends it to our attention. In addition, the mining of this liquid mineral is unusual in two respects that are of peculiar interest to the geographer. First, few other mining industries have experienced such abrupt locational changes in so few years as has that of petroleum. Second, of all mining, the petroleum industry provides the most complete collection of production records published year by year, country by country, and (in the United States) state by state.

For these reasons, petroleum mining is admirably suited to illustrate a particular type of geographic analysis which we have not touched on so far, but with which every student of geography should be familiar—historical geography.

Historical geography is not the history of geography nor the geography of history; rather, it is the geography of past periods. The historical geographer applies the basic questions of the geographic method to the past, age by age, in order to understand regions as they existed in whatever periods he wishes to study. Thus, historical geography adds a useful dimension of time to our understanding of world economic activity.

PETROLEUM

A complete portrayal of the location of oil mining in the world from one period of time to another would resemble a motion picture of a dynamic map showing the location of petroleum mining, a map that has been kept continually up to date ever since petroleum was first mined as a commercial venture. But such a movie, however informative, might run longer than "Gone with the Wind" so for our account we shall project individual frames from the total sequence of pictures. Each chosen frame will provide a view of the geography of petroleum mining at a particular time and will reveal some significant development. Occasionally, we may find we have to run our film forward and backward in order to bring a particular frame into meaningful focus.

1857

For thousands of years man had known about petroleum. In some places it bubbled to the surface in tar pits or small flows. From time immemorial people used the stuff to leakproof their boats, to make hot fires, or to burn for illumination. But not until 1857 was petroleum mined commercially. Although historical records unfortunately disagree about where and when the first commercial oil was produced, the authors accept the verdict of *World Oil* (a trade journal of the United States oil industry) that 1857 was the year and Romania the country. In that first year the wells, in the vicinity of Ploesti, 40 miles north of Bucharest, yielded 2000 barrels of petroleum—the entire world output—which was marketed in the surrounding hinterland. The rest of the world continued to use whale and other animal fats and vegetable oils for illumination, lubrication, and fuel.

1860

Three years later the world map showed two regions. Romania had increased her output to 9000 barrels, a respectable increase of 350 per cent. But her share of the world total had plummeted to 2 per cent! For another region, thousands of miles away, had burst upon the scene.

Since 1750 oil seepages had been observed in western New York and Pennsylvania. Several of these happened to be in the vicinity of salt wells. Several such wells near Tarentum, Pennsylvania, a few miles north of Pittsburgh, yielded not only salt but a nuisance product, oil. Many white people had adopted the Indian practice of using such oil for medicine, and since 1847 an astute druggist named Samuel Kier had been salvaging this discard and bottling it for sale under the following caption:[1]

> Kier's Petroleum or Rock Oil, celebrated for its wonderful curative powers . . . gets its ingredients from the beds of substances which it passes over in its secret channels. Its discovery is a new era in medicine.

Kier's advertisements carried a picture of a derrick, like those of the salt wells from which the oil had been taken, which caught the eye of a New York lawyer, George Bissell. Bissell got the idea that oil itsslf could be mined commercially. Under his leadership, the Seneca Oil Company was organized for the purpose of drilling for petroleum. The question of where to drill was decided in favor of Oil Creek (near Titusville in northwestern Pennsylvania) where seepage had been known for years not only to white settlers but earlier to the Indians. In late 1859 an experimental well struck oil here at a depth of 70 feet. In the very next year the wells of Pennsylvania yielded 500,000 barrels. Demand for this product came mainly from the illuminating-oil market in the northeastern United States, particularly the Atlantic Seaboard where most of the nation's populace resided.

1880

Twenty years later the total world production was up from 509,000 barrels to a surprising 30,000,000. The United States was the unrivaled leader (see Table 15-1, page 187). Within the United States, Pennsylvania still dominated; that state alone accounted for 80 per cent of the world's total. In addition, oil drillers began roaming, with success, into New York, Ohio, and West Virginia (Table 15-2, page 188).

In the rest of the world, Romania was still pumping oil, but several new areas had bobbed up on the map. Russia for one far surpassed Romania. The first oil in Russia was struck in 1863 at Maikop (Maykop) on the

[1] Wallace E. Pratt and Dorothy Good, *World Geography of Petroleum*, American Geographical Society, Special Publication No. 31, 1950, page 130.

Table 15-1

Crude-Oil Production by Leading Nations (for Selected Years) and Reserves (1974) (Thousands of Barrels)

Region	1860	1880	1900	1910	1920	1927	1940	1950	1960	1974	1974 Percentage	Reserves 1974
WORLD	509	30,019	149,137	327,763	688,884	1,262,582	2,149,821	3,802,995	7,663,184	20,338,290	100	556,177,194
Europe	9	355	4,346	23,480	13,751	33,038	61,494	65,293	205,683	284,073	1	22,096,450
Romania	9	115	1,629	9,724	7,435	26,368	43,168	32,000	85,169	107,964	†	1,300,000
Poland	—	229	2,347	12,673	5,607	5,342	3,891	1,205	1,442	2,847	†	42,500
Germany (East and West)	—	9	358	1,032	246	663	7,371	8,107	39,262	46,494	†	510,500
Austria	—	—	—	—	—	—	2,808	10,200	16,619	15,609	†	171,600
U.S.S.R.	—	3,001	75,780	70,337	25,430	77,018	218,600	266,200	1,080,400	3,314,200	16	48,550,000
North America	500	26,636	64,534	213,507	600,194	965,727	1,405,983	2,075,217	2,865,824	4,010,309	20	44,508,078
Canada	—	350	913	316	196	477	8,591	29,044	191,841	601,155	3	7,171,229
United States	500	26,286	63,621	209,557	442,929	901,129	1,353,214	1,973,574	2,574,933	3,199,328	16	34,249,956
Mexico	—	—	—	3,634	157,069	64,121	44,036	72,443	99,049	209,826	1	3,086,893
South America	—	—	274	1,421	7,068	102,822	268,764	644,056	1,265,333	1,551,405	8	21,766,291
Peru	—	—	274	1,258	2,817	10,127	12,126	15,012	19,255	28,230	†	830,000
Colombia	—	—	—	—	—	15,014	25,593	34,060	55,770	60,875	†	627,000
Venezuela	—	—	—	—	457	63,134	185,570	546,783	1,041,675	1,086,313	5	14,568,000
Trinidad	—	—	—	143	2,083	5,380	22,227	20,632	42,357	68,136	†	651,000
Africa	—	—	—	—	1,046	1,275	6,532	16,702	103,508	1,976,159	10	57,918,186
Egypt	—	—	—	—	1,046	1,267	6,505	16,373	22,559	53,715	†	2,761,000
Algeria	—	—	—	—	—	—	—	—	67,226	360,671	2	9,034,871
Middle East	—	—	—	—	12,230	40,026	102,691	640,862	1,929,789	7,947,713	39	325,959,301
Iran	—	—	—	—	12,230	39,688	66,317	242,475	390,754	2,197,877	11	68,050,000
Iraq	—	—	—	—	—	338	24,225	49,726	354,591	675,250	3	35,123,750
Saudi Arabia	—	—	—	—	—	—	5,075	199,547	456,453	2,996,543	15	103,480,000
Kuwait	—	—	—	—	—	—	—	125,722	594,278	830,580	4	70,890,000
Far East	—	26	4,203	18,998	29,145	42,663	85,740	94,657	212,643	1,254,431	6	35,378,888
Japan	—	26	871	1,829	2,221	1,789	2,639	2,048	3,730	4,526	†	76,178
Indonesia	—	—	2,253	11,031	17,529	27,459	62,011	48,400*	150,510	501,838	2	12,000,000
China	—	—	—	—	—	—	—	—	12,810	438,000	2	14,800,000

Source: World Oil, August 15, 1957, August, 1961, and August 15, 1975.
*In 1946 Indonesia's production had slumped to only 2,100 thousand barrels.
†Less than 1%.

northern flanks of the Caucasus, 60 miles east of the Black Sea; in 1871 another field was found near Baku on the Apsheronskiy Peninsula. Then a third field opened up in the vicinity of Grozny (Groznyy), midway between Maikop and Baku. Elsewhere, lesser flows were appearing in Poland, Germany, Japan, and Canada.

1900

Great changes are seen in our next frame, 1900 (Figure 15-1). Romania's yield had gone up steadily to 1,629,000 barrels. Much of her oil was now moving up the Danube River to the markets of western Europe, particularly the budding industrial power, Germany.

Yet her share of the world total was only one per cent. Poland, now ahead of Romania, led in Europe.

Many new regions were furnishing crude oil, especially Peru and the Dutch East Indies. Peru's production was small, but several islands in the Indies were, taken together, yielding a great deal. The story in the Indies began in 1885 when Dutch farmers, clearing tropical forests on the northeastern coast of Sumatra for plantation sites, noticed oil seepages. They drilled, struck oil, and began to produce commercial petroleum. The same story was repeated on Java in 1896 and on Borneo in 1897.

Things were different also in North America. Canada appeared with a small yield, but the chief

PETROLEUM PRODUCTION, 1900

Figure 15-1

Table 15-2

Crude Oil Production by Leading States for Selected Years and Reserves (Thousands of Barrels)

Region	1860	1880	1900	1910	1920	Production 1927	1940	1950	1960	1974	Proved Reserves as a Pecentage of U.S. Total	
U.S. TOTAL	500	26,286	63,621	209,557	442,929	901,129	1,353,214	1,973,574	2,574,933	3,199,328	35,299,839	100
Northeast												
Pennsylvania	500*	24,987*	13,258	8,795	7,438	9,626	17,353	11,859	6,213	3,924	39,613	†
New York	—	1,041	1,301	1,054	906	2,242	4,999	4,143	1,796	1,047	8,288	†
W. Virginia	—	179	16,196	11,753	8,249	6,023	3,444	2,808	2,306	2,597	32,126	†
Ohio	—	39	22,363*	9,916	7,400	7,593	3,159	3,383	4,886	9,383	124,911	†
Illinois	—	—	—	33,143	10,774	6,994	147,647	62,028	79,463	28,012	152,343	†
Mid-Continent												
Kansas	—	—	75	1,128	39,005	41,069	66,139	107,586	112,531	63,191	401,089	1
Oklahoma	—	—	6	52,029	106,206*	277,775*	156,164	164,599	191,553	176,724	1,270,964	4
Texas	—	—	836	8,899	96,868	217,389	493,209*	829,874*	932,321*	1,263,251*	11,756,613	33
Louisiana	—	—	—	6,841	35,714	22,818	103,584	208,965	392,712	743,248	4,576,826	13
New Mexico	—	—	—	—	—	1,226	39,129	47,367	108,383	96,923	642,994	2
Northwest												
Wyoming	—	—	6	115	16,831	21,307	25,711	61,631	134,441	142,651	916,763	3
Montana	—	—	—	—	340	5,058	6,728	8,109	30,135	34,516	219,343	1
N. Dakota	—	—	—	—	—	—	—	—	22,010	19,533	179,520	1
California	—	—	4,325	73,011*	103,377	231,196	223,881	327,607	304,535	322,236	3,488,100	10

Source: World Oil, Feb. 15, 1958, pages 127, 166–167, February 15, 1961, pages 81 and 100, and February 15, 1975, pages 98 and 114.

*Leading state for year indicated.

†Less than one per cent.

change was the dethroning of Pennsylvania as leader, a position she had held for a generation—from 1860 to 1895. Ohio now led the states (Table 15-2), and even West Virginia overtook Pennsylvania. But this was just a shift of focus within a single field—the Appalachian— that underlay all these states. More significant was the faint appearance of entirely new fields, one in the Southwest (Texas, Oklahoma, and Kansas), one in the Rockies (Wyoming), and one on the West Coast (California). All told, the United States flowed with 63,000,000 barrels of oil, Yet for all this volume, she could be credited with only 43 per cent of the world total—quite a comedown from her previous shares (98 per cent in 1860 and 88 per cent in 1880).

The most spectacular area on the 1900 map is southern Russia (Figure 15-1). The three Caucasian fields (Maikop, Grozny, and Baku) poured forth 75,000,000 barrels, an astonishing increase in 20 years that propelled Russia into first place among the nations. In fact, she was mining more crude oil—50 per cent— than the rest of the world combined. This period marks the apex of Russian oil mining in percentage of the world total. Never since has her share attained that figure.

The market for Caucasian oil was partly in the Moscow area (some oil moved by water across the Caspian and up the Volga), partly in the Ukraine (to which oil moved by pipe, rail, and river), but mostly in western Europe where industry was now using petroleum for lubrication and fuel. To get the oil to market, a pipeline was constructed from the Grozny field through the Maikop field to Tuapse, a Black Sea port, where it

then proceeded by barge and ship. Most of the Baku oil also moved to Europe by another pipeline along the south side of the Caucasus to Batum (Batumi). Thus, the pipelines, the ports of Batum and Tuapse, and the three mining areas all functioned together in moving oil from the Caucasian wells to the western European customers.

By 1900, petroleum mining was under way in other widely separated areas that were also becoming related to the market of western Europe—a region with a large population and tremendous industrial capacity that meant a voracious demand for petroleum. So capital flowed out of western Europe as payment for petroleum and as investment in property and mining equipment in the Dutch East Indies, Peru, and even Russia (where the Russian economy under the Czarist regime was incapable of providing much investment capital). Not only money but also personnel moved out from Europe (Britain and the Netherlands in particular) to most of the oil-producing regions of the world. In the geography of petroleum for 1900 even the United States was a supplier to Europe.

1910

The year 1910 shows a still different picture. Virtually all the areas on the 1900 map increased their output. Russia was the chief exception (Figure 15-2). During the ten-year interval her annual yield shrank to 70,000,000 barrels, and from the biggest cut of the pie her share

Figure 15-2

PETROLEUM PRODUCTION, 1910

shriveled to 21 per cent of the world total. Political and economic turmoil within Russia was beginning to affect oil mining.

Some of the older fields expanded substantially by 1910. Polish wells on the northern flanks of the Carpathian Mountains were enjoying a mild boom. But this proved to be their peak period, for the resources soon faded. Few oil fields on earth have been so fragmented by national boundaries as this Carpathian field which, in 1910, was at the juncture of southern Poland, eastern Czechoslovakia, and western Russia.

During this time an unusual advance occurred in the United States, which strode beyond the 200,000,000-barrel mark—more than half again the volume of the rest of the world combined. The sharp contrast in ten short years from 1900 (Russia 50 per cent and the United States 43 per cent of the total) to 1910 (Russia 21 per cent and the United States 64 per cent) is one of the most abrupt changes ever seen in historical economic geography.

A new regional pattern also appeared within the United States. Pennsylvania's oil yield had shrunk to a third of that in her best years. Ohio, the nation's leader just a decade earlier, was down to less than half her peak. Booms were underway farther west, in Illinois and Oklahoma. But the biggest boom of all was in California, which now ranked first in the nation and actually outproduced every foreign nation except Russia.

Two newcomers to the map were Mexico and Trinidad whose yields were still small.

1920

At the close of World War I North America dominated the world in petroleum production. Mexico in particular had made notable gains. Mexico and the United States together accounted for 86 per cent of the world's oil yield. In the decade since 1910 Mexico's production shot up from 3,000,000 to 157,000,000 barrels —about 22 per cent of the world total—the largest volume coming from the gulf fields in the vicinity of Tampico on the eastern coast. But this was the high mark in the history of Mexican oil. For in 1921 there was an event with far-reaching consequences—the Queretaro Convention. It had been long-standing Mexican policy that subsoil rights were vested in the landowners. Accordingly, oil prospectors (representatives of companies from California, Britain, and the Netherlands) purchased subsoil rights far and wide from the individual owners. The Queretaro Convention reversed this policy and transferred all petroleum rights to national ownership. Moreover, it made the action retroactive. The upshot was lengthy litigation between the government and the oil companies, which eventually reduced operations in Mexico.

The United States likewise had made rapid advances, boosting her output to 442,000,000 barrels. Within the United States the regional pattern was different from that of 1910. Oklahoma was now the leading state, California had slipped to second, and Texas, riding the crest of the most vigorous expansion in the industry so far experienced in the United States, was a close third. It was actually in 1901 that oilmen prospecting in Texas struck a gusher just north of Beaumont. This gusher, the most productive in the nation's history, was on a small hill called "Spindletop." From that date, there began a frenzy of prospecting and drilling in southwestern states. Thousands of dry wells disappointed their drillers, but hundreds came through successfully. So feverish was the activity that by 1920 the Gulf Coast field (along coastal Texas and Louisiana) and the Mid-Continent field (in northern Texas, Oklahoma, and Kansas) had far outstripped all other fields in the nation. Indeed, Kansas and Louisiana joined Oklahoma, California, and Texas as the five petroleum leaders. For the first time, the nation's crude-oil industry was clearly centered in south-central states. West Virginia, Pennsylvania, and Ohio had slumped; their wells were literally running dry.

Another development in the Western Hemisphere, though not prominent in 1920, had significant implications for the future: Venezuela appeared for the first time on the world oil map. Seepages in the northern part of the country had been reported centuries earlier by the conquistadores, but it was not until 1917 that geologists of the Royal Dutch Shell company drilled successfully and developed the Mene Grande field, the first large oil field in Venezuela. This development occurred in the northwestern part of the country on the eastern shores of Lake Maracaibo. An unusual geographical relationship arose between Venezuela and Curaçao, a Caribbean island 50 miles off the coast and a colonial possession of the Netherlands. There was little choice of where the mining should be located, but there was a choice of where the refineries should be built. Curaçao was selected as the site of the latter for several reasons: A refinery would provide job opportunities for the citizens of the colony; it would provide tax revenues for the Dutch government of the island; and capital invested in refining equipment would be protected by Dutch law-enforcement agencies. Thus, a flow pattern was established whereby a mining venture (combining a Venezuelan physical resource with a European cultural resource) shipped crude oil to Curaçao which in turn shipped refined products to Europe.

Another significant debut in the decade between 1910 and 1920 was that of the Middle East. It appeared with a larger volume than Venezuela and was destined to play a larger role. The first entry was Persia—now Iran. Shortly after the turn of the century the Persian government granted a concession to an Englishman named Willam D'Arcy who made the first successful oil strike in 1909 in the southern part of the country at Masjed-I-Sulaiman. But this was nomadic herding territory having no demand for petroleum within hundreds of miles. Even the populated heart of Persia 400 miles to the north and the populous Tigris-Euphrates valleys to the west had little purchasing power. The market was thousands of miles away in western Europe.

Figure 15-3

Ships could traverse that distance in a few weeks. But Masjed was 100 miles from the Persian Gulf—a distance that, for large oil movement, could *not* be conquered in a few weeks. Indeed, it required four years to overcome that 100-mile barrier—by constructing a pipeline to the port of Abadan. The year 1913 saw the initial shipment of Persian oil. That year she accounted for 1,000,000 barrels—not much in the world total (385,000,000 barrels), but a significant portent of things to come. Again, European capital and personnel interacted with the physical resource of Iran to give birth to an economic activity, most of which was administered by the Anglo-Iranian Oil Company.

Elsewhere, Indonesia, Trinidad, and Peru enjoyed increases. But yields in every European nation were down, reflecting depletion of the resource in some wells but, more importantly, the exigencies of war. The toll of conflict and disorganization was particularly severe in Russia, which was jolted by war and revolution. Volume was down to only 25,000,000 barrels, a mere 4 per cent of the world total—an astonishing decline in 20 years from the 75,000,000-barrel harvest which had exceeded that of all other nations combined. 1920 was the nadir of Russian oil mining. Not since 1889 had yields been that low; and they have never since been that low.

1927

Seven years later the United States and Mexico parted company in production trends. Mexico was in a nosedive not only in her share of world total (in seven years down to 5 per cent) but also in actual volume: from 157,000,000 down to 64,000,000. Some of her fields were giving out,

and some of the gulf fields were being infiltrated by salt water, but the most serious factor was political strife—legal tangles between oil companies and the Mexican government that were precipitated by the Queretaro Convention and discouraged oil extraction.

By contrast, prospecting and drilling in the United States enjoyed a healthy gain; over 900,000,000 barrels flowed from her wells in 1927—71 per cent of the world total. Not since 1860 had a single country so dominated the world. But this was the last year that a lone nation was responsible for such a percentage. Since this 1927 apex, the United States' share has slipped steadily downward even though the volume has moved steadily upward.

Within the country, three fields, Mid-Continent, Gulf Coast, and California, were leaping far ahead of all others. Among the leading states, Texas was gaining rapidly on Oklahoma and California.

Even more remarkable, though on a smaller scale, was the boom in Venezuela. In seven short years output rocketed from 457,000 barrels to 63,000,000. She quickly overtook all other nations except the United States and Russia. By this time a second mining company—an American one—had struck oil in the Lake Maracaibo district. And, like its Dutch predecessor, it chose to locate refineries just outside Venezuela in Aruba, another possession of the Netherlands. Nearly all of Venezuela's oil was exported, mostly to European consumers.

Russia had recovered dramatically from her earlier decline; since 1920 her yield had risen sharply to 77,000,000 barrels. In the Middle East, Iran was up to 39,000,000 barrels. Although this was a respectable increase over 1920, it still was a very small fraction of the world total. Worth noting also is Iraq's first appearance on the world map.

1940

Thirteen years later the world was going through a petroleum revolution. Consumption had reached the unprecedented figure of 2,000,000,000 barrels as the age of the internal combustion engine shifted into high gear. The world map of oil production in 1940 is substantially different from that of 1927.

For one thing, the United States was dropping—down to 63 per cent of the world total—despite a huge increase in production, now more than one billion barrels. Within the United States the most dramatic change was the emergence of Texas as national leader. Indeed, this single state now accounted for twice as much oil as any nation outside the United States. Hundreds of new wells were drilled in north, northwest, and coastal Texas, and in the Gulf itself. Derricks and wells were marched out to sea several miles from shore. At this point Texas and Louisiana found themselves enmeshed in an unusual and complex relationship with the United States government; many states contended that oil underlying the Gulf (that is, the "tidelands") was the property of the United States as a whole rather than the state off whose shores the wells were situated. California, now the second-ranking state, was also involved in this hassle because she too had wells reposing on stilts in the Pacific Ocean. The debate over tidelands oil raged for several years until, in 1953, the federal government enacted legislation recognizing state ownership of the tide-lands as far out as $10\frac{1}{2}$ miles from shore.

Southern Illinois had boomed into prominence with 147,000,000 barrels in 1940, only slightly behind third-ranking Oklahoma. But Illinois turned out to be a fast starter but slow in the stretch, for her wells dried up within a decade to yield less than half that volume.

For the United States as a whole, consumption was increasing more rapidly than production. Yet the country still had a surplus for sale abroad, primarily to three deficit areas: Europe, Japan, and Canada.

Russia, at the start of World War II, had climbed to second place in oil mining—with 10 per cent of the world total, nine-tenths of it still being mined in the Caucasus. But exploration in the '30's had uncovered another field west of the Urals, in the heart of the Volga drainage basin. The extent of this field was roughly 300 miles from east to west and 600 miles from north to south, approximately two-thirds as large as the state of Texas. In addition, just northeast of the Caspian Sea Russia had the Emba field, and far to the east there were wells on Sakhalin Island.

Venezuela also was enjoying successes in oil. Fortunately the government took an attitude that is fundamental to a successful mining economy. Broadly speaking, the Venezuelan government position was formally cast in the Petroleum Law of 1922, which charted a course followed assiduously by succeeding governments. The sturdiest planks in the Venezuelan platform are these: (1) Any person, national or foreigner, may freely explore

Figure 15-4

PETROLEUM PRODUCTION, 1940

An oil-drilling platform in the Persian Gulf off the coast of Saudi Arabia. (*Courtesy EXXON Corporation.*)

and carry on geological investigations in the national territory. (2) A specific governmental department (Inspectoria Tecnica de Hidrocarburos), supervises the oil industry and encourages all efforts to develop it. The effectiveness of this department has been demonstrated by its miraculous ability to maintain a continuity of action even during convulsive political changes and its ability to preserve cordial relations between the industry and the government. (3) The tax burden in oil is kept comparatively lenient, a policy that has helped to make Venezuelan oil the cheapest on earth.

Although the Venezuelan government both owned and controlled the production of all subsoil minerals in the nation, it realistically recognized that a strong mining economy requires both natural resources and the aptitudes needed to develop them. In the early days of her petroleum production, she had only the former, and western Eurcope had only the latter. So Venezuelan authorities permitted the two to interact. Without this enlightened policy, crude-oil mining in Venezuela would surely be considerably behind its present pace. And the Venezuelan economy, in turn, would be less developed.

The Venezuelan policy is clearly expressed as follows:

A nation in an initial stage of her development from a backward and disorganized agro-pastoral economy in which there suddenly appears, like an unnatural growth, the enormous creation of riches produced by the oil industry and which, in twenty years, changes from being the world's fifth or sixth exporter of coffee to its leading exporter of petroleum, finds herself faced with an upheaval so intense and so dangerous that out of it may come genuine and enduring greatness, or subjection to the fortunes of fuel and oil. This, expressed summarily and even brutally, is the way we should plan in what we may call Venezuela's fundamental economic problem: we must use petroleum to develop Venezuela instead of permitting her future and the course she follows to be diverted and unnaturally displaced by the violent torrents of wealth produced by that industry and by all the special conditions that its existence brings about day after day.[2]

Before 1920 Venezuela was not wealthy but was self-sufficient in food. The oil boom reversed this situation. The country gradually became more and more wealthy, attaining the highest per capita government budget in Latin America. Oil provided the government with over half its revenues, which were expended rapidly in an effort to give all Venezuelans a higher standard of living. But meanwhile, paradoxically, Venezuela was losing its ability to feed and clothe itself, and began to import rice, corn, wheat, flour, sugar, meat, textiles, and garments: commodities desired by a people with an increasing purchasing power, no longer satisfied with the modest diet accepted by their forebears.

The Venezuelan story stands in sharp contrast to that of Mexico where the government discouraged oil exploration by foreign technicians. The feud between Mexico's government on the one hand and the American and European oil concerns on the other depressed oil output through the 1920's and the 1930's (notice Table 15-1) until finally, in 1938, the Mexican government took the bold and unprecedented step of expropriating all property and equipment of foreign oil companies, whose activities were thereby abruptly terminated. The 1940 picture shows Mexico, which 20 years earlier had mined 157,000,000 barrels—23 per cent of the world's share—down to 44,000,000, a mere 2 per cent of the world total.

Almost as outstanding as Venezuela's expansion was that in the Middle East. Here, as in Venezuela, the mining economy was based on the blending of resources from two regions: the Middle East contributed the material and the Western world contributed the knowledge to exploit it. The very company names—Anglo-Iranian and Aramco (Arabian-American Company)—epitomize the forces at work. About 40 per cent of the crude oil was piped westward to ports on the Mediterranean Sea for shipping to Europe; a slight amount was moved by tanker from Persian Gulf ports to the same destination. But over half the oil was refined in large factories in new Gulf settlements and then moved by tanker—mostly through the Suez to Europe. Some of the refined product, though, was dispersed widely to markets in Africa and eastern Asia.

Indonesia was progressing, becoming one of the

---

[2]From Uslar Pietri as quoted by Guillermo Zuloaga in Wallace E. Pratt and Dorothy Good, *op. cit.*, pp. 74–75.

more prolific exporters. Since its market was almost entirely in the Far East, particularly China and India, where refineries were only scarcely developed, Indonesia processed all its oil before export.

Europe showed a few changes. Romania was still the leader, thanks to the Ploesti fields which in World War II were destined to be a goal for Nazi invasion and then a prime target for Allied aircraft. Germany's petroleum industry showed growth by 1940 in the Hanover district. This area (termed by oilmen as the North German Basin) is underlain by sedimentary rock somewhat like that of the American Gulf Coast field. Austria appeared for the first time; production in the vicinity of Vienna almost equalled home consumption.

The over-all world circulation of oil between nations in 1940 fell, in general, into the following pattern. Major exporters (with percentage of world exports) were:

Venezuela, Trinidad, and Colombia	37%
Unites States	35
Middle East	17
Indonesia	6
Others	5
	100%

From the three principal export areas, the destination of most of the product was western Europe; but as we noted above, Indonesia's oil went to the Far East.

1950

The economic geography of crude oil in 1950 showed some striking changes. There were no new nations on the scene but there were a variety of new relationships among established producers.

At mid-century the United States maintained its position of leadership, reaching the astonishing record of two billion barrels, but there were two significant developments. First, for all its boom, the United States was slipping in degree of world leadership; other regions were developing even more rapidly and closing the gap, so that for the first time in nearly half a century the United States could not claim appreciably greater production than the rest of the world combined. (The actual percentage in 1950 was 51 per cent—quite a drop from the 71 per cent peak of 23 years earlier.) The second development was that, for all its production, the United States was now an importer of petroleum. The consumption of gasoline, diesel oil, and other petroleum products had skyrocketed. The number of automobiles in the United States had jumped from 8,000,000 in 1920 to almost 35,000,000 in 1950; diesel engines had displaced steam engines on railroads; millions of homes had discarded coal furnaces and stoves for oil furnaces and heaters; World War II had brought with it an airplane

revolution, and the chemical industry now consumed millions of barrels of crude oil as raw material. Thus, the uses of oil for energy in driving engines, for heat, and as a raw material, all shot up so rapidly that they finally exceeded domestic production. Tankers began carrying oil in the opposite direction. From an exporter of oil, mostly to Europe, the United States turned into an importer, mostly from Venezuela.

The most conspicuous novelty on the 1950 map is the Middle East, which now surpassed Caribbean America (Venezuela, Colombia, and Trinidad). Not only did the older fields (Iran and Iraq) enjoy healthy gains, but Arabia's ten-year increase was fabulous (from 5,000,000 to 199,000,000 barrels). Most astonishing of all was the unparalleled debut of a little country whose name was practically unknown outside the Arab World: Kuwait, tucked in between Arabia and Iraq on the Persian Gulf. As late as 1945 Kuwait, a flat, sandy, treeless, hot stretch of desert about the size of Massachusetts, supported on a subsistence economy an unknown number of nomadic herdsmen and a few thousand settlers in villages along the coast. The main export business was pearl fishing. Then in 1946 British and American geologists struck oil. After four short years Kuwait was pumping more oil than any other country in the world except for the United States, Venezuela, the U.S.S.R., and its own neighbors, Iran and Saudi Arabia. Rarely in history has so small an area burst so dramatically upon the stage of the world's economy. Being of such recent vintage, the Kuwait oil industry had the advantage of modern methods and equipment so that the average oil well yielded 3700 barrels a day. The average for each well in Venezuela was 200, in the United States, 11. And the reserves awaiting future mining were enormous, estimated to be half those of the United States.

Another noteworthy development occurred in the Soviet Union, where the Volga-Ural field had experienced a soaring oil boom. This area, located about 450 miles east of Moscow, underlies a vast amount of land in the upper Volga River basin and extends upward into the western foothills of the Urals. Production is centered in the vicinity of Tatar, Bashir (Bashkir), and Kuibyshev (Kuybyshev), with lesser wells near Saratov and Stalingrad (Volgograd) to the south. Although a little petroleum had been drawn off here before 1940, it was not until 1950 that the field came into its own, accounting for 30 per cent of the Russian total. The opening up of this field was significant in that it occupies a strategic location in the heart of the Soviet Union between two great industrial regions, the Industrial Center and the Urals. Moreover, this new field is in an area served by Russia's main railway and waterway systems, and costs of distribution are low.

By 1950, Indonesia's oil mining was recovering from a severe experience. When World War II broke, crude oil was flowing from Indonesian wells at the rate of 60 million barrels a year. War strife cut her production down to 22 million as the Japanese moved in. But when the Japanese evacuated in 1945 they so thoroughly demolished the facilities that the 1946 yield trickled off to only 2 million barrels. Yet recovery was fast (Table 15-1).

Africa's only oil mining was in the far northeastern extremity of the continent, in the Sinai Peninsula. From the standpoint of landform configuration, these small oil fields are really outliers of the Middle East fields. But politically they lay within the boundaries of Egypt, and Egypt (at least for the keeping of statistics) is part of Africa. Yields were small, though, and provided Egypt with only a third of her own needs.

The 1950 pattern of world circulation showed only one minor and two major regions of surplus oil. The Caribbean area provided 50 per cent of the world surplus, the Middle East 45 per cent, and Indonesia a trace. The most profound change since 1940 in this aspect of the industry was the disappearance of the United States from the list of exporters.

1960

The world pattern for 1960 was basically the same as that for 1950. Old established areas continued to dominate, although some of the small areas were making unusual progress, notably Canada and western Europe. All told, the world's oil wells yielded over seven billion barrels—more than twice the 1950 output. Practically every producing nation showed an increase. Distinction depended not on growth, but on rate of growth.

The United States retained first rank and reported yields in two-thirds of the states. Texas alone produced almost one billion barrels. Other important oil states

were Louisiana, California, Oklahoma, and Wyoming in that order. But the mining of crude oil was expanding not only in terms of barrels from leading states but also in terms of numbers of states mining any oil at all. Thirty-two of the 48 contiguous states were producing some crude oil.

But United States production had begun to slip—both absolutely and relatively. A peak of 2,617,283,000 barrels had been attained in 1956, and 1960 marked the fourth consecutive year in which production had been less than that maximum. Moreover, the United States percentage of world total had steadily dropped—to 35 per cent. But this is not surprising. In an economic activity like petroleum mining, with reserves widespread among several countries, only the most naive would expect that any single nation could long maintain so disproportionate a share of world production as did Russia in 1900 or this country in 1927.

Canada was enjoying an oil boom in her prairie provinces—particularly Alberta. Unfortunately, since Canada's petroleum is considerably farther from her center of population than is the case in the United States, great transportation problems had to be overcome.

The most eye-catching advance was going on in the Middle East with Kuwait now the leader there. Only three other nations (United States, U.S.S.R., and Venezuela) produced as much oil as this amazing little nation.

Figure 15-5

PETROLEUM PRODUCTION, 1960

PETROLEUM PRODUCTION, 1974

Figure 15-6

Figure 15-7

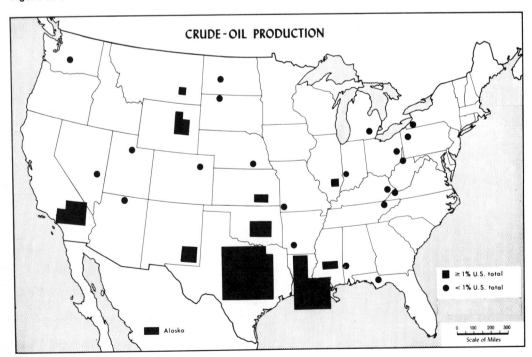

Within the Soviet Union the Volga-Ural field, which had overtaken the Caucasian field in the early 1950's, was rocketing upward and by 1960 was accounting for 67 per cent of Russian petroleum production. This astonishing performance ranks the Volga-Ural area as one of the world's foremost producers of crude oil and suggests that this will be Russia's main source of supply for many years to come. As recently as 1940 it appeared that 80 per cent of Russian oil reserves were in the Caucasus; but by 1955 the evidence provided by new discoveries showed that 80 per cent of Russian oil reserves were in the Volga-Ural area, which is closer to both Russian consumer and producer markets than is the Caucasus.

Since 1960 there have been some significant shifts in the world pattern of crude oil production. Europe's percentage of the world total has dropped slightly, and the percentages for the U.S.S.R. and the Far East have increased by a small amount. But elsewhere in the world changes have been much more dramatic. The big relative gains in production have been in Africa and the Middle East. In 1960 Africa had only 1 per cent of the world total and the Middle East had 25 per cent. In 1974 these percentages had jumped to 10 per cent and 39 per cent, respectively. The Western Hemisphere's share, however, declined. South America's share of production dropped from 16 per cent to 8 per cent, and North America went from 38 per cent to 20 per cent; the United States alone dropped from 35 to only 16 per cent.

It is interesting to note that although there were some significant *relative* shifts between 1960 and 1974, all important producers showed absolute gains during this period. The United States' share of world production may have declined, but she still produced 600,000,000 barrels more in 1974 than in 1960.

Interestingly, reserves have increased substantially since 1960 despite large increases in production. World reserves were estimated to be 266 billion barrels in 1960 and 556 in 1974! In the Middle East, which has the largest reserves, the figure jumped from 163 billion barrels to 326 billion. Even the United States has shown an increase, from 32 billion to 34 billion barrels.

Regions of Consumption

Much of the world's petroleum is consumed in Anglo-America; the United States and Canada together take 35 per cent of the world total. Non-Communist Europe takes 25 per cent, Japan takes 9 per cent, and the Communist countries 17 per cent. That leaves only 14 per cent for the rest of the world. Petroleum consumption plainly correlates with a high degree of industrialization. The bulk of the product is used up in regions that are rich in both producer goods (such as factory machines, railroads, trucks) and consumer goods (such as automobiles, oil furnaces, and so on). This relationship will be more apparent after we have studied the chapters dealing with manufacturing (Chapters 17 to 23).

International Trade

Because of the marked discrepancy between regions of production and regions of consumption, a tremendous volume of oil moves between regions. This transfer is one of the great movements in international trade in the twentieth century. The main supply and demand areas are tabulated in Table 15-3.

Only one region produces a great amount of surplus petroleum—the Middle East. Much less important but still conspicuous in this respect are the Caribbean and Africa. Most other regions are big importers. Non-Communist Europe leads the world in petroleum imports and accounts for one-half the world total. The other two major importers are the United States and Japan. It is interesting to note that the United States is the one region which is both a major producer and a major importer of petroleum. The flow pattern from surplus areas to deficit areas encompasses three chief arteries: from the Middle East to western Europe and Japan, and from the Caribbean to Anglo-America.

Consider particularly the setting in the Middle East. Large amounts of oil move out by tanker as a pro-

The drill ship *Discoverer 534* off the coast of Thailand. This type of drilling precedes the establishment of permanent platforms. (*Courtesy EXXON Corporation.*)

cessed product from Persian Gulf refining centers—including Abadan in Iran, the world's fifth largest refinery in terms of capacity; Ra's Tannūrah, Saudi Arabia, the world's third largest refinery; Bahrein in the Persian Gulf, 15 miles from Saudi Arabia; and Mina-Al-Ahmade in Kuwait.

The remainder moves in crude form westward via several pipelines. The older ones link the northern fields of Iraq (in the vicinity of Kirkuk) with Banias in Syria and Tripoli in Lebanon. Two other lines formerly connected Kirkuk with Haifa and Acre in Israel, but these are no longer in use. A newer line connects Persian Gulf fields with Sidon in Lebanon. These pipelines must go through one or more of the following nations: Jordan, Syria, and Lebanon, none of which produce much oil. However, the economies of these countries are bolstered by revenues from transit fees and income from transshipping services at the ports. Another consequence is that if the nations that lie between the oil and the market are so disposed, they can disrupt the flow of oil whether by tanker or by pipeline. Cessation of flow over the two older pipelines from Kirkuk to Haifa and Acre is attributable to strife between Israel and Arab nations; the Suez Canal was closed between June 1967 and January 1975 for the same reason.

For the United States, the pendulum continues to swing. Until after World War II (except for the brief period of 1920 to 1922), our exports always exceeded our imports. As recently as 1942 we shipped out three times as much oil and oil products as we imported. Then things changed; 1947 and 1948 saw the pendulum pass the point of balance. Since then our deficit has steadily increased. Today we produce only 64 per cent of our demand. Thirty-nine per cent of the inbound crude oil and refined products originate in Canada; in terms of imports of *crude* oil only, 23 per cent comes from Canada and 20 per cent from Venezuela. We also receive crude oil (20 per cent) from the Middle East. Foreign oil can be marketed in the United States more cheaply than much of the domestic product because of (a) lower labor costs, (b) newer more efficient wells abroad, (c) savings in production costs abroad, and (d) cheap ocean transport (the cost is so low it does not cancel out the savings attributable to the foregoing factors). These advantages, however, have been greatly diminished by actions of the OPEC (Organization of Petroleum Exporting Countries) nations which have greatly increased the cost of foreign petroleum.

The Future

In volume, the known world reserves of petroleum in 1974 totaled 556 billion barrels—enough to last 28 years at the 1974 rate of consumption (quite a contrast to the world coal situation).

In location, the world's petroleum *reserves* conform to a different pattern from that of production (see Table 15-1). An astounding 60 per cent of known reserves are

A remote drilling rig in Prudhoe Bay on Alaska's north slope. In 1969 proved crude oil reserves in the United States were 30 billion barrels, and Alaska's share was less than 2 per cent. In 1970 the United States figure was 39 billion barrels, and Alaska's share had jumped to 26 per cent. (*Courtesy EXXON Corporation.*)

in the Middle East! Saudi Arabia has nearly 19 per cent, more than any other country in the world and over three times as much as the entire United States. Kuwait ranks second. Iran has larger known reserves than the Soviet Union.

Iraq's reserves are greater than those of all South America. No other facts portray so telling a story of the future significance of the Middle East to the world's economy.

Within the United States a large share of the known petroleum reserves are located in the very regions that now mine it. Texas has almost one-third of our crude oil resources, but Alaska, which is now emerging as a major producer, has proved reserves comparable to those in Texas.

Prophets of doom cry that what remains in United States pools (some 35 billion to 40 billion barrels) will be used up in nine or ten years at the present rate of mining. This is indeed a gloomy prospect. But in 1924 our known reserves were only 7.5 billion barrels—in a year when we mined 713,000,000 barrels. Even then the wail might have been that we had only enough oil to last ten years! Had no new oil been discovered, the wells would have run dry in 1934. Fortunately, as oil miners increased their production, oil prospectors discovered more new oil than was mined. In 1930, the reserves at the start of the year were 13 billion barrels; one billion barrels were mined, and at the end of the year, reserves were almost 14 billion barrels. Twenty-five years later, reserves at the beginning and end of the year were approximately 30 billion barrels even though about 2.5 billion barrels had been mined. More recently, however, the pattern has changed. In 1973, proved reserves were 36 billion barrels at the start of the year and 35 billion at the end. Some 3.4 billion barrels were mined that year but that amount was partially offset by the discovery of 2.3 billion additional barrels. Nevertheless, these figures do represent a net loss of over 1 billion barrels. Discovery of new reserves, exploitation of oil shale and other such activities promise continued "growth" of our resources. Unfortunately, however, there is now strong evidence to suggest that we can exhaust our domestic supplies in the near term. Many authorities are convinced that we can no longer expand our supply of crude oil to meet the ever-growing demand. The question of how this resource should be allocated has certainly received a great deal of attention in recent years. The efficiency of pricing, direct government controls, and voluntary reduction of consumption of petroleum products have all been extensively debated topics.

NATURAL GAS

Crude oil generally occurs with natural gas. But the geography of mining natural gas is quite different from that of crude oil for the simple reason that whereas oil is easily trapped at the wells and lends itself to shipment via barrels, tank cars, trucks, barges, or ocean tankers, gas readily escapes at the wells, and what is trapped can be transported feasibly only by pipelines. Gas is an economic product only in those mining areas that are close enough to market to be connected by pipeline. Accordingly, most of the world's natural gas is "produced" in the United States, Russia, and Europe.

Within the United States, natural gas has experienced a dramatically growing role in the nation's total production of inanimate energy. In 1900, it accounted

Table 15-3

World Petroleum Demand and Supply Regions, 1974 (Thousands of Barrels per Day)

Region	Domestic Consumption	Supply	Excess Supply over Demand	Demand over Supply	Percentage of World Total Domestic Demand	Domestic Supply
United States	16,382	10,489		5,893	30.0	18.0
Caribbean	701	3,340	2,639		1.3	5.7
Canada and Mexico	2,462	2,597	135		4.5	4.5
Other Western Hemisphere	2,158	1,043		1,115	4.0	1.8
Non-Communist Europe	13,545	429		13,116	24.8	0.7
Africa	1,029	5,416	4,387		1.9	9.3
Middle East	1,221	21,835	20,614		2.2	37.6
Japan	5,057	15		5,042	9.2	
Other Eastern Hemisphere	2,734	2,231		503	5.0	3.8
Communist areas	9,340	10,749	1,409		17.1	18.6
WORLD TOTAL	54,629	58,144	29,184	25,669	100.0	100.0

Source: World Oil, August 15, 1975, p. 41.

Table 15-4

United States: Inanimate Energy Production

Source of Power	Trillions of BTU's 1900	1930	1960	1970	Percentages 1900	1930	1960	1970
Bituminous coal and lignite	5,563	12,249	10,886	14,820	71	55	26	24
Anthracite	1,457	1,762	478	247	18	8	1	<1
Crude petroleum	369	5,208	14,935	19,772	5	24	36	32
Natural gas	254	2,148	13,822	24,154	3	10	33	39
Water power	250	752	1,723	2,631	3	3	4	4
Nuclear power*	—	—	—	229	—	—	—	<1
TOTAL	7,893	22,119	41,844	61,853	100	100	100	100

Source: U.S. Bureau of Mines, *Minerals Yearbook* (1961 and 1973).
*39 trillion BTU's in 1965; insignificant amount in 1960.

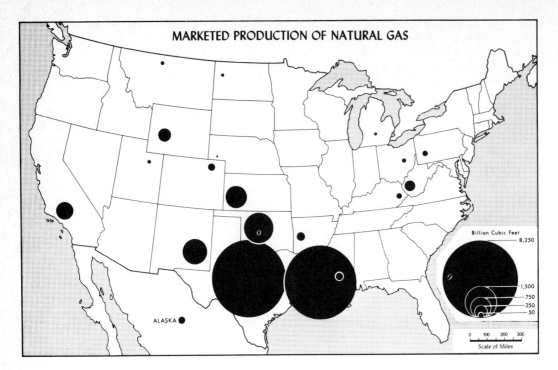

MARKETED PRODUCTION OF NATURAL GAS

Figure 15-8

for about the same volume of energy as water power—3 per cent of the national total. In those days coal was responsible for almost nine-tenths of such energy production. Subsequent years have seen a rapid shift in relative importance of energy sources. Table 15-4 reveals that by 1970 coal's share had dropped from 89 to 25 per cent, water power had remained steady at around 3 or 4 per cent, while petroleum and natural gas had soared from 8 to 71 per cent. Today, crude oil and gas produce approximately equal shares of the nation's total inanimate power output.

In view of the foregoing indication of the importance of natural gas, its treatment in these pages is disproportionately brief. Two reasons may be cited. First and foremost, very little research has, as yet, been done in analyzing the geography of natural gas. Secondly, although natural gas has overtaken coal as a source of energy in the United States, gas is still far behind coal and oil in meeting the world's energy demands.

Within the United States, 6 per cent of the natural gas "produced" (that is, removed from the ground) is either lost to the atmosphere, is burned for energy on the producing property, or returned to the underground reservoir for repressuring. Consequently, only 94 per cent of the production is available for commercial sale. Production of commercial gas occurs in 30 states, but the great bulk comes from wells in Texas and Louisiana, which, together, account for 73 per cent of the national total. See Figure 15-8 and Table 15-5.

In the United States, major users of gas are residential and commercial (37 per cent) and industrial customers (41 per cent). The number of gas house-heating customers has increased greatly since the early 1960's, so that today their number is well over 30 million.

Table 15-5

Quantity of Marketed Production of Natural Gas by Leading States

Area	Billions of Cubic Feet	Percentage
TOTAL	22,531.7	100
Texas	8,657.8	38
Louisiana	7,972.7	35
Oklahoma	1,806.9	8
New Mexico	1,216.1	5
Kansas	889.3	4
California	487.3	2
Wyoming	375.1	2

Source: U.S. Bureau of Mines, *Minerals Yearbook* (1974).

Furthermore, gas has now overtaken both coal and oil in providing heat to these customers. Indeed, in some states, gas outsells all other fuels combined in meeting this market, particularly in the states listed in Table 15-5. At the other extreme are New England, the Carolinas, and Florida, which neither produce gas nor are well served by gas pipelines (see Figure 24-12). These states, however, are well served by oil tankers and accordingly depend more upon petroleum derivatives for space-heating or (to a steadily decreasing degree) upon coal, which is more costly and less convenient than oil.

About 20 per cent of marketed gas is consumed by electric generating plants. Indeed, a significant share of all the electricity produced by public utilities in the Southwest is from generators driven by gas-fired boilers.

SUGGESTED READINGS

McNee, Robert B., "Centrifugal-Centripetal Forces in International Petroleum Company Regions," *Annals of the Association of American Geographers*, 1961, pp. 124–138.

Melamid, Alexander, "The Geography of the Nigerian Petroleum Industry," *Economic Geography*, 1968, pp. 37–56.

———, "Geography of the World Petroleum Price Structure," *Economic Geography*, 1962, pp. 283–298.

———, "Petroleum Product Distribution and the Evolution of Economic Regions in Iran," *Geographical Review*, 1975, pp. 510–525.

———, "Satellization in Iranian Crude-Oil Production," *Geographical Review*, 1973, pp. 27–43.

Osleeb, Jeffrey P., and Sheskin, Ira M., "Natural Gas: A Geographical Perspective," *Geographical Review*, 1977, pp. 71–85.

Peet, J. Richard, "Natural Gas Industries in Western Canada," *The Canadian Geographer*, 1963, pp. 23–32.

Rosing, Kenneth E., and Odell, Peter R., "A Predictive Simulation Model of Oil Province Development: The North Sea Example," *Proceedings of the Association of American Geographers*, 1975, pp. 189–195.

Thomas, Trevor M., "The North Sea and Its Environs: Future Reservoir of Fuel?" *Geographical Review*, 1966, pp. 12–39.

Weaver, Glen D., "A Decision Model for Oil Shale Development," *Proceedings of the Association of American Geographers*, 1975, pp. 268–272.

CHAPTER 16

mining:
general observations

Almost 5000 people live in San Manuel, Arizona, which was built by the Magma Copper Company to support its mine, smelter, and refinery.

In the two preceding chapters we considered the mining of selected minerals, giving major attention to location, making only occasional remarks about characteristics and relationships. The purposes of this chapter are to make some observations about location and characteristics of mining activities in general and then to give closer attention to the topic of relationships.

Location

Regions of the World. When we assemble all our jigsaw pieces of fact about the location of each individual mineral and fit them into a world-wide composite view of all mining, we can discern several regions of concentration. In the Western Hemisphere a wide zone spans the North American continent from the Atlantic to the Pacific and extends from southern Canada to central Mexico. A second region runs like a ribbon from Nicaragua to Chile; there are outlying clusters in northern Venezuela, Guyana and Surinam, and southeastern Brazil. In the Eastern Hemisphere a broad region that begins at the Atlantic coast of Europe runs eastward into southern U.S.S.R. and southward through the Balkan nations into Saudi Arabia and Iran. The Ural Hills stand out conspicuously as a north-south mining belt. A narrow band also runs east-west through the center of Asia. In southeastern Asia mining is found all the way from Japan and Manchuria on the east through southern China to India on the west. Burma, Malaysia, and Indonesia can be included in this region. Australia, like South America, is almost encircled with a peripheral pattern of mining. Africa has a long and wide zone that extends from South Africa to Ethiopia, with a secondary section along the Guinea Coast. Elsewhere there are scattered mining operations, though they are small in scale.

Thus, commercial mining appears on every continent, but mostly in the mid-latitudes, primarily in those of the Northern Hemisphere.

Regions in the United States. We can construct a more accurate map of mining for the United States than for the world because more information is available. Figure 16-1 shows the location of mining in terms of numbers of people employed. The most conspicuous region is the Appalachian belt which stretches 500 miles from western New York to northeastern Alabama. However, Texas has more employment in this sector than any other state with about one-sixth of the nation's total mining employment. Figure 16-1 is an example of the type of map that can be constructed when employment data are available for areal units as small as counties. It is based on data in *County Business Patterns*, one of the world's most detailed sources of published facts on the number of people engaged in specific economic activities in small areal units. The United States Government also publishes the *Census of Mineral Industries* and the *Minerals Yearbook*, which give figures on other measurements, such as value of product mined.

Characteristics

Two key characteristics for distinguishing mining regions are source of employment and value of mined product.

Employment in Specific Types of Mining. The combinations of minerals that support mining employees differ widely from place to place in the United States. Texas and West Virginia are the leading states in

Figure 16-1

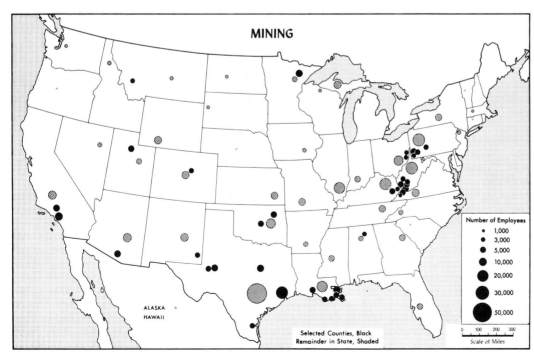

number of employees, but they are markedly unalike in the distribution of workers in mining industries: Texas miners are engaged largely in the petroleum and natural gas industries whereas West Virginia's are connected with coal. Oklahoma, Louisiana, and Texas report that employment in oil and gas accounts for over 90 per cent of their total mining labor force. Other high percentages appear in Arizona (92 per cent in copper), West Virginia (92 per cent in coal), Pennsylvania (74 per cent in coal), and Kentucky (83 per cent in coal). For the United States as a whole, employment in specific mining industries in shown in Table 16-1. Unfortunately, comparable data for the rest of the world are unavailable.

Value of Types of Products Mined. We have inadequate information for measuring the value of each mined product by individual nations; however, such figures are available for the United States. Statistics on value of shipments for the leading products are given in Table 16-1. By value, petroleum (with natural gas)

is three times as important as the nation's next-ranking mineral, coal, which is over three times as valuable as copper. Coal and oil also provide the most jobs. But, perhaps surprisingly, sand and gravel support the fourth largest payroll—almost as much as copper. And the mining of crushed limestone employs more people than does iron mining. Indeed, the mining of nonmetallic solids (sand, gravel, stone, sulfur, phosphate, clay) collectively provides employment to more people and yields almost as valuable shipments as does the mining of all the metallic ores.

During the last four decades, mining in the United States has shown contrasting trends. The number of employees has declined from an all-time peak of 1,084,000 in 1919 to 600,000 in the 1970's. But the number of mines increased in that time from 14,417 to 25,000, and the value of shipments shot up from $3,158,000,000 to $36,318,600,000.

Physical Relationships

Mining in any region is related with many physical factors, such as the resource pyramid, depth of mineral deposit, surface topography, subsurface conditions, natural waterways, and climate.

The Resource Pyramid. In the distribution of mineral resources, quantity and quality are inversely related. The pattern is like a three-tiered pyramid. The base of the pyramid consists of tremendous quantities of low-grade deposits widely distributed around the world. In the middle are moderate amounts of moderate-grade deposits which are less widely scattered. At the apex there are small amounts of high-grade deposits located in only a few areas. The rule holds that the higher the quality the less the reserve and the more restricted in location.

Herein lies a problem, for man is skimming the cream from the top of this resource pyramid. In the future he may face increased costs of exploiting the low-quality deposits in the mines now in operation, or else face high transport charges if he taps remote but rich sources. Still, there is always the hope that science will discover new techniques for cheaply processing the poor residue in mines from which the best has already been taken.

Depth of Mineral Deposits. Minerals at the earth's surface are obviously less costly to mine than those far underground. For the shallow deposits, *strip* or *open-pit* methods can be used whereby miners simply carry away the surface materials, digging downward and outward for as far as the mineral is rich enough and property rights can be acquired at a reasonable cost. Surface deposits are a large part of the explanation of the success of the Mesabi Range (where the mines are a series of tremendous open pits, some 300 feet deep and several hundred feet wide), of Bingham Canyon copper mines, and of the southern Ohio coal fields. These places have some of the most mechanized mining on earth;

Table 16-1

United States Mining

Product	Number of Establishments	Value of Shipments in Millions of Dollars	Thousands of Persons Engaged (All Employees)
U.S. TOTAL	25,269	36,318.6	595.1
Metallic ores			
Iron	111	1,065.0	19.7
Copper	181	1,588.6	36.4
Lead and zinc	101	251.3	7.7
Gold and silver	132	74.6	2.8
Ferro-alloys (except vanadium)	44	164.3	3.8
Fuels			
Bituminous coal and lignite	3,191	5,312.8	152.2
Anthracite	213	122.8	4.0
Crude oil and natural gas	7,609	15,688.1	116.6
Natural gas liquids	680	5,057.7	10.7
Nonmetals, Nonfuels			
Construction and industrial			
Sand and gravel	2,929	1,004.4	34.0
Crushed limestone	1,374	906.8	30.0
Chemical minerals			
Potash, soda, and borate	31	261.5	6.9
Phosphate	47	250.7	5.9
Sulfur	24	127.7	2.6
Fire clay	80	19.7	0.5
Dimension stone	198	31.4	2.0

Source: U.S. Department of Commerce, *Census Of Mineral Industries* (1975).

in some of them huge electric shovels scoop out 16 tons of ore per bite. In the United States, 2 out of every 5 tons of bituminous coal and lignite is mined in open pits, and in some states open pits yield more coal than do underground mines. For the leading states, here is the amount of coal in millions of tons mined by each type of mine annually:

Table 16-2

Coal Mined (Millions of Short Tons—1969 to 1971 Average)

Area	Underground	Strip
U.S. TOTAL	322	238
West Virginia	110	19
Kentucky	60	49
Pennsylvania	53	29
Illinois	30	32
Ohio	17	35
Virginia	27	5
Indiana	2	19
Alabama	8	10

Sources: U.S. Bureau of Mines, *Minerals Yearbook,* 1971 (1973); *Minerals Yearbook,* 1970 (1972); *Minerals Yearbook,* 1969 (1971).

Surface Topography. Flat topography expedites strip-mining, but a rough surface can also simplify operations by permitting *drifting*. In this method, horizontal tunnels are driven into the side of a hill in which mineral deposits occur in nearly horizontal strata (see Figure 16-2). The erosion of valleys performs the same function as the construction of mine shafts by providing access to mineral deposits too deep for strip-mining.

Subsurface Conditions. A combination of generally flat topography and unusual subsurface structure has given the East Central coal field of the United States a distinctive pattern of mining. Subsurface rock strata have been warped into the shape of a bowl. At this bowl's edges where the coal seams meet the earth's surface, strip-mines are numerous. But shaft-mines typify the interior of this area.

Shaft-mining is undertaken most easily where subsurface conditions meet the following specifications:

rock layers are horizontal, there has been little or no *faulting* (the movement of rock masses vertically along fractures), and minerals occur in thick layers. Horizontal layers facilitate the blasting, cutting, loading, and hauling of minerals in underground work rooms. Such operations are obviously awkward and hazardous in rock layers that dip at steep angles. But even where the seams are horizontal, faulting prevents continuous mining on the same floor and necessitates changes in level of operation. Thick seams are of course easier to work than thin, for in one, say, two feet thick, miners must either work flat on their stomachs or expend effort in digging out dross rock to make work room.

Subsurface water is a nuisance in most mines. Strip-mines can become temporary lakes after heavy rains, and shaft-mines can turn into drainage channels where underground water collects. So a big item of expense is pumping out water. In this matter drift-mines, which enter hills on a slight upgrade, have a peculiar advantage—for ground water simply runs out of the tunnel by gravity flow.

Natural Waterways. Drift-mines often enjoy another peculiar advantage because their mine entrances, on valley sides, are adjacent to valley bottoms, some of which contain navigable rivers.

Water transportation routes, indeed, are sometimes the critical factor in transforming a region from a mineral reserve to a mining center. We have already encountered many contemporary examples of this point. The Great Lakes link the iron ore of the Lake Superior district with the coal of Appalachia. Who can tell what the status of Sweden's Kiruna would be were it not for the ocean highway that runs from Narvik to the coal belt of central Europe? Fortunately for Venezuela, her ore fields lie close to the Orinoco waterways and not far from the greatest waterway of all, the ocean. Quebec-Labrador iron ore moves up the St. Lawrence River to the manufacturing heart of Anglo-America and down that river to the Atlantic Ocean and eastern United States ports. For nearly three centuries before 1900, Great Britain was the world's leading coal producer, partly because, being surrounded by the sea, her mines were all close to ocean shipping. Three of her major coal

Figure 16-2 *This sketch diagrams the position of drift mines in horizontal rock strata in areas of hilly terrain.*

Figure 16-3 *This sketch suggests some of the difficulties in mining of rock formations which have been deformed by folding and faulting.*

fields—Northumberland-Durham, the Scottish Lowlands, and South Wales—actually front on tidewater. The ports of Newcastle in the first-named area and Cardiff in the third became the world's leading coal suppliers.

Climate. Climate relates to mining in two different ways. Historically, certain types of climate favored the formation of mineral deposits. Two examples are coal (vegetative growth of the type favorable to coal requires a warm moist climate) and bauxite (formed by weathering of feldspar rock in tropical moist climates).

Currently, climate affects both extraction and transportation. Obviously, surface mines have trouble operating in freezing temperatures. Moreover, there seems to be some correlation between stormy weather and mine explosions. For example, the air in shaft coal mines contains two compounds which are particularly prone to ignite: methane gas and coal dust. In a revealing article, C. B. McIntosh reports evidence that the passage of low pressure areas over mining regions correlates closely with increased methane in the air within the mines and that atmospheric *fronts* correlate with increased coal dust.[1]

Finally, severe winter climates block many waterways. As we saw, this is the main reason why Kiruna ore is exported through Narvik instead of Lulea. Transportation from Lake Superior's ranges is icebound four months of the year. And that which moves by rail in winter must be specially treated to keep it from freezing solid in the hopper cars.

Cultural Relationships

The relationships of mining and culture are reciprocal. Such relationships are discernible in population distribution, manufacturing, prices, technical discoveries, railroads and canals, mining settlements, economic bases, problems of land-use, political boundaries, and conservation problems.

[1]"Atmospheric Conditions and Explosions in Coal Mines," *Geographical Review*, Vol. 42, April, 1957, pp. 155–174.

Population Distribution. From the world viewpoint, regions of mining tend to be comparatively densely inhabited. Yet the correlation is not perfect since some populous areas have little mining; for instance, China and India. Other factors appear to be more strongly associated with mining, notably manufacturing.

Manufacturing. Since most minerals must be processed before man can use them, there is a rather close world-wide locational correlation between mining and manufacturing. This correlation holds particularly well if our unit of measurement is the nation: Frequently, countries that are the manufacturers are also the leading miners. (We shall elaborate on this relationship in Part Six.)

But on a finer areal scale, manufacturing correlates more closely with coal mining than with any other type of mining. This is because of coal's versatility as a fuel, as a source of power, and as a raw material. Consequently, many minerals are shipped toward coal-mining regions for final manufacturing. Some minerals, though, do go through preliminary stages of manufacturing in factories located near the mines, particularly low-grade metallic ores. Much of the dross can be separated by crushing the mined rocks and sorting out the mineral-bearing particles by washing, filtering, and precipitating. Such separation of dross by *mechanical* methods is termed *concentration*, and the factories that perform such operations are called *concentrators*. Mechanical methods however do not remove impurities in chemical union with the metal; such purification requires more elaborate techniques that are often applied in factories located far from the mines (see Chapters 19 and 20).

The significant fact for the geographer is that concentrators tend to locate in mining areas in order to avoid paying transport charges on dross. This tendency is well illustrated by the copper industry. Of every 100 tons of most copper ore, 98 tons are dross and only two tons are copper. Why pay freight on those 98 tons? Generally, the *lower* the percentage of metal contained in the ore, the *stronger* the tendency for concentrators to locate near mines. This principle holds for all ore mining, including iron ore and ferro-alloys. For some minerals, like copper, which average a very low percentage of metal, virtually every mining area has concentrators. But for other ores, like iron, which may yield high percentages (up to 70 per cent) of metal, relatively few mining areas support concentrators.

In some iron-mining localities man has proceeded to remove all the high-grade ores and is down to the low-grade ones. In the Lake Superior region, for example, most of the remaining ore is low grade. Taconite, which has a high silica content, is perhaps the most common low-grade ore. Traditional methods for processing are too costly to apply to taconite, so the Lake Superior iron region faced a dark future until technologists devised a process for crushing taconite and removing the silica, leaving a residue that is high in iron and can be profitably shipped to distant blast furnaces. Taconite processing mills (or concentrators) have been constructed in northeastern Minnesota and now account for a substantial portion of this region's output.

Prices. The value that factories place on minerals largely determines whether mining authorities judge a

rock to be an ore or not. The general situation is clear enough, though few precise details are available. Geographers need to do a good deal more research on the geography of prices not only for minerals but for all economic items.[2] But price alone is only part of the story; for mining soon ceases when production costs exceed prices (whether consumer payments or government supports). The point is emphasized here because the demand for minerals as expressed in *price* is such a clear-cut example of this force at work.

Technical Discoveries. For over three centuries western Europe was the unquestioned world leader in mining because it had a large number of people, extensive manufacturing, and a consequent demand for minerals reflected in high prices. But another force was at work too—discovery and invention. Human beings first learned to use iron about 1400 B.C. in China. If "early start" were the main factor in a region's economy, China should be a major market for iron ore today. But those early techniques were unable to process very large amounts of iron, which remained for many centuries a precious metal. It was in the minds of men in western Europe that the ideas unfolded for making large masses of iron available. Around 1300 A.D. Catalonian artisans in northeastern Spain developed the *Catalan Forge*, a furnace large and strong enough for developing high temperatures capable of separating large quantities of iron out from ore.

When the Moors invaded Spain, the ironmasters fled northward to the Meuse Valley in Belgium, a metal-working center. Here they developed the Catalan forge into a full-fledged blast furnace, using charcoal as the fuel. But charcoal supplies became scarce as oak and chestnut forests disappeared. A new fuel was needed. The process for making coke from coal finally solved the problem—another discovery of a European, this time an Englishman. (The first record of making coke from coal was in 1590 when a patent was granted to John Thornborough of York, England. Its first use was in the drying of malt.)

The idea for the steam engine, which unleashed a tremendous demand for both iron and coal, also flowered in Europe—in the mind of James Watt in 1776. It was in Europe also that the idea was born in the mind of England's Henry Bessemer for converting large amounts of iron into steel. Then in 1878 Sir William Siemens of England invented the electric furnace for making steel. That same year Gilchrist and Thomas (two Welshmen) discovered the technique for recovering iron from ores blighted with phosphorus.

These inventions strongly emphasize the truth that the origin and spread of ideas is as significant to the

This oil well on the grounds of the state capitol building in Oklahoma City vividly demonstrates the problem of land use associated with many types of mining. The high value of the oil enables it to be drilled in areas for which there is strong competition for land and in difficult physical environments. (*Courtesy Clair A. Shenk.*)

[2]A solid beginning is William Warntz's "The Geography of Prices and Spatial Interaction," The Regional Science Association, *Papers and Proceedings*, 1957, pp. 118–136, and his *Toward a Geography of Price* (Philadelphia, 1959), 117 pp.

geography of mining as is variation in the physical environment. For inventions played fundamental roles in Europe's development as the leading region in world mining.

Railways and Canals. Hand in hand with mining has gone the construction of railways and canals. Western Germany, northern France, and Belgium are interlaced with canals that carry heavy tonnages of coal, metallic ore, petroleum, sand, gravel, stone, and other minerals. A strong impetus in the construction of the Sault Saint Marie canals between Lakes Superior and Huron was the demand for ore shipment. For decades the St. Lawrence Seaway along the Ontario-New York boundary was proposed; yet time after time it was approved by the Canadian government only to be rejected by the United States. Then two developments in iron ore caused the United States government to change its mind: a decline in quality of Lake Superior ores and the opening up of the Quebec-Labrador field. America's steel mills in Chicago, Detroit, Cleveland, and Pittsburgh, long dependent on Superior ores, could still feed off rich ore if a waterway linked them to the St. Lawrence as the Great Lakes linked them to Superior.

One impulse for railroad-building, too, was the need to link mines with waterways. Witness the net of railways in northeastern Minnesota and in the Appalachian coal fields (Figure 24-1) and the 357-mile railway that links Quebec-Labrador iron with Seven Islands, its terminal port on the St. Lawrence. In Russia, too, prospects for coal and iron mining in the Karaganda, Kuznetsk, and Irkutsk areas played a potent role in the construction of the Trans-Siberian Railway.

For United States railways, minerals constitute 44 per cent of revenue tonnage and generate 16 per cent of freight revenues. Coal, the single most important commodity, accounts for 25 per cent of the tonnage and 10 per cent of the revenue.

Mining Settlements. Within mining regions distinctive settlements take root. The small ones contain the homes of a few miners who commute out to the mines just as fishermen and foresters commute out from fishing villages and forest communities. The large mining settlements include, in addition, company headquarters and railroad yards for joining loaded gondola and hopper cars (a few from each of many mines) to make complete trains. Beyond these bare statements, there is little we can add. For, as with fishing or forest villages, the geographer encounters a dearth of information. What are the characteristics of mining towns that distinguish them from other types of settlement? Do mining communities differ enough among themselves to distinguish coal towns from iron ore towns, or are they all essentially the same regardless of the mineral mined? The questions await careful analysis. What we need is a system of classification so that we can map the United States, and the world, showing regions by types of *mining settlement.* It should be possible to devise such a classification in

Clarkdale, Arizona, was built as a planned company town to accommodate workers in this large copper smelter. Although the smelter was closed in the mid-1950's, Clarkdale persists today as a center for retired people and workers employed elsewhere in the region. In 1950 the population here was 1600. In 1960 the figure was 1000—the same as it is today. (*Courtesy Ray Manley Photography.*)

terms of observable features, of functions in regional economic life, and of local problems.

We do know something about the simpler matter of location, though. Northeastern Minnesota is an excellent example of a region where mining makes a conspicuous impact upon the location of settlements. The over-all population density is low and there are few cities. But the Mesabi, Cuyuna, and Vermillion iron ranges have lured those few to locate in a pattern closely corresponding to the distribution of the ore. In the 60 miles from Grand Rapids at the southwest to Aurora in the northeast there are 30 settlements strung out like beads in a necklace. Hibbing (16,104 inhabitants) and Virginia (12,450) are the largest of these communities. To encounter another city at least as large as Hibbing one would have to travel 60 miles southeast (to Duluth), 160 miles south (to Minneapolis), 180 miles west (to Fargo), and 250 miles northwest (to Winnipeg).

Economic Base. This is a convenient point at which to illustrate the concept of *economic base*. A region's *economic base* consists of the activities that support the livelihood of its inhabitants.

The importance of mining in the economic base can be measured by means of a simple ratio, say, of the number of mining employees relative to the total number of workers. This ratio is one expression of the importance of mining in the economy of that area.

Data on mining employment that have been collected by the United Nations reveal considerable variation for most countries in the proportion of jobs in mining (see Table 16-3). In most political units, mining accounts for less than 5 per cent of total employment. The low percentages in highly industrialized nations are at first glance paradoxical, with such figures as 0.4 per cent in Japan, 0.6 in Sweden, 0.8 in the United States, 1.5 in Australia, and 2.4 in West Germany. Yet at least three of these five countries have high absolute employment in mining. What is the explanation?

There seems to be a tendency, at least in today's economy, for regions with an expanding mining economy to go through two stages: in the first stage, mining provides a large proportion of jobs; in the second, the proportion shrinks as other secondary and tertiary endeavors (manufacturing, trade, and services) expand more rapidly.

Within the United States we have enough information to measure the mining-employment ratio on three scales: by states, by counties, and by cities.

By *states*, the mining-employment ratio varies from a minimum of 0.1 per cent to a maximum of 9 per cent. The eight lowest and eight highest states are as follows:

Connecticut	0.1%	Alaska	2.6%
Delaware	0.1	Utah	3.0
District of Columbia	0.1	Arizona	3.1
Hawaii	0.1	Oklahoma	3.5
Maine	0.1	Louisiana	4.0
Massachusetts	0.1	New Mexico	5.6
New Hampshire	0.1	West Virginia	8.8
Rhode Island	0.1	Wyoming	9.0

The relationship between mining employment and total employment by counties is shown in Figure 16-4. On this basis, mining is plainly the foundation stone in the economic base of such counties as Harland and Letcher (Kentucky), and McDowell (West Virginia) with ratios of 43 per cent, 56 per cent, and 63 per cent, respectively.

Among the larger cities, mining employment varies from 0 to over 25 per cent (see Table 16-4). Within the

Table 16-4

Selected American Cities (over 10,000 Population) in Ratio of Mining Employment to Total Employment

City	Percentage
Carlsbad, N.M.	26
Midland, Texas	25
Hobbs, N.M.	23
Butte, Mont.	21
Rock Springs, Wyo.	19
Hibbing, Minn.	17
Virginia, Minn.	17
Duncan, Okla.	16
Snyder, Texas	16
Madisonville, Ky.	15
Odessa, Texas	15
Beckley, W. Va.	11
Casper, Wyo.	11
Bartlesville, Okla.	8

Source: U.S. Bureau of the Census, *1970 Census of Population* (1972).

Table 16-3

Economically Active Population in Mining and Quarrying

Place	Thousands of People in Mining and Quarrying	Percentage of Total Economically Active Population
South Africa	676	7.5
Hungary	156	3.1
Chile	75	2.9
West Germany	199	2.4
Australia	76	1.5
South Korea	100	1.0
Spain	124	1.0
United States	631	0.8
Sweden	19	0.6
India	923	0.5
Japan	216	0.4

Source: United Nations, *Demographic Yearbook* (1974).

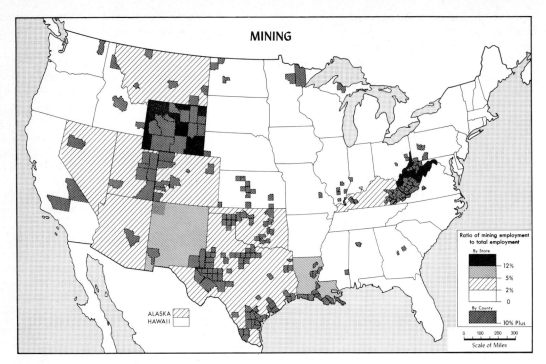

MINING

Ratio of mining employment
to total employment

By State
12%
5%
2%
0

By County
10% Plus

Scale of Miles
0 100 200 300

ALASKA
HAWAII

Figure 16-4

United States there are about 2,300 settlements having a population of at least 10,000 inhabitants, and their average ratio of mining employment is only 0.44 per cent.

When the mineral "downstairs" gives out or when the market price drops excessively, a city's economic base may collapse, causing employment to drop. People may even emigrate, causing the total population to decline. If collapse of the economic base is complete, a city may well-nigh disappear, becoming a ghost town. Many cities in the western United States that formerly had thousands of people are mostly empty now. For example, Silver City, Nevada, once had 35,000 people but now numbers only 100.

Problems of Land Use. Mining influences man's use of land in several respects. Strip-mines ruin the terrain for farming. This may not matter at Bingham, Utah, where the land being chewed up is too rough and rocky for cultivation. But a real problem develops in parts of Ohio, Indiana, Illinois, and elsewhere where coal and gravel pits are eating their way into farm land. Open-pit iron mines in Minnesota have bitten off not only farm land but also some urban land. Forty years ago the center of Hibbing, Minnesota, was moved two miles to the south to make way for the mines. Shaft-mines also blight the land by depositing *tailing* piles, cone-like hills of rock and other unsalable substances hauled up from the ground. Cave-ins of underground tunnels and mine rooms, years after mining has emptied them, cause the surface to sink and shift. The washing of coal at mine entrances fills streams with coal dust and mud. For example, the Schuylkill River, which drains the anthracite region of Pennsylvania into the Delaware

River at Philadelphia, was once a navigable river. But years of debris accumulating from coal mines filled the channel with black mud, spoiling its appearance and impeding navigation.

In recent years man has begun to combat some of these problems. As one remedy to blight he is planting trees in rough strip-mined areas. Although written off for traditional farming, they will eventually yield crops of trees, serve as habitat for wild life, and create a recreational area for hunting, fishing, and hiking.

This is an important question for any landowner who has legal control of subsurface rights to consider: In view of such adverse effects, is it worthwhile to sell mineral rights? A short-term gain may be realized, but in the long run the surface of the land may be ruined for further use.

Political Boundaries. Within mining regions, international boundaries sometimes impede mining activities. Europe's best coal (Westphalia) and one of her best iron ore fields (Lorraine) are only 200 miles apart. A single political boundary separates the two. America's best coal field (Appalachia) and her best iron-ore (Lake Superior) are 800 miles apart, with half a dozen state boundaries in between. Yet that lone boundary in Europe separates sovereign nations whereas those between Lake Superior and Appalachia delimit states that yielded their sovereignty to a federation. Had it not been for that boundary, Lorraine and Westphalia might have functioned together as do Superior and Appalachia. But the political boundary between France and Germany has cleft these two mining regions apart with severe repercussions. The new-born Germany, victorious in the Franco-Prussian war of 1870, occupied Lorraine, and for nearly 50 years both Westphalian fuel and Lorraine ore were controlled by a single political power which had the technological knowledge for processing, and the economic demand for consuming, large quantities of iron. During this period Germany made enormous strides as a world industrial leader.

With Germany's defeat in World War I, its western boundary was quickly pushed eastward, the Lorraine returned to France, and Europe's two main mineral regions were split asunder.

This cleavage was reflected in trade restrictions. German steel mills had to seek elsewhere than the Lorraine for ore and came to depend largely on Swedish ores, 1700 miles away. French steel mills were denied Ruhr coal. The relationships were more complex than this, of course, but essentially it was a case of neighboring, naturally complementary regions being sundered by man's political decisions.

A history-making experiment is now underway to erase the economic handicaps of these political boundaries. In 1953 six nations (Germany, France, Belgium, the Netherlands, Luxembourg, and Italy) launched the *Schuman Plan* whereby the sextet functioned as one areal unit insofar as the steel industry was concerned. There were no tariffs or trade restrictions on the movement of coal, coke, ore, limestone, scrap iron, pig iron, or steel between these countries. Moreover, the six states functioned as one in competing for sales on the world market. It was as if steel mills in Pennsylvania, Maryland, Alabama, and other American states once fought with one another for sales abroad, and then organized a United States of America for purposes of competing as a team on the world market. J.A. Coker analyzes the geography of the Schuman Plan region in an informative article, an excerpt from which is as follows:

> Nowhere else in the world do labor, capital equipment, raw materials, communications, and finishing industries coincide in such a small compass. France has the ore, Germany the coke, and Holland and Belgium the ports. The Schuman community has therefore a potential strength greater than the aggregate of the individual countries. It is a case of two and two making five.[3]

The Schuman Plan was so successful that subsequently its principles were applied to other phases of international trade among these six nations. Thus the European Common Market was formed (to be discussed in Chapter 25).

An ironic twist in the relationship of iron ore and political areas occurred after the Gilchrist-Thomas invention in 1878 of techniques for cheaply processing large volumes of phosphoric iron ores. Since the early 1700's, Britain had been the world's leading steel producer. Fortunately, her ores contained little phosphorus, and her supremacy in steel was unchallenged—until this discovery by two of her own scientists turned

out to be the very key to unlock the huge Lorraine field. Remember that Germany at that time had *both* the Lorraine and the Ruhr. So, aided by this English discovery, Germany rapidly rose to challenge England in steel production.

Problems of Conservation. Nature produces economic minerals very slowly—so slowly that man terms them *nonrenewable* resources. The only notable exception is water. Because minerals are nonrenewable they are also *exhaustible*. Some economically important minerals (for instance, coal) are so abundant that the supply will endure for hundreds of years. But others (such as copper) are rationed in small measures. This scarcity assumes political significance because the reserves of these minerals are unequally parcelled out among the nations. Take copper and petroleum in the United States, for instance. Known petroleum will be gone in perhaps 10 years, although new petroleum discoveries are being made every year. This process of depletion leads to a fundamental question: How should these limited resources be handled? Some persons advocate *preservation*. Under this policy a nation would seal up reserves and buy from abroad what she needs, withholding her own stores until a day when she may be unable to import. Others advocate *conservation*. This approach aims at extracting minerals with the least possible waste, processing them carefully, using the products fully, and then salvaging what remains after they have been used. (In forestry, this concept led to *tree farming;* but of course since minerals cannot be "grown," there can be no counterpart in commercial mining.) Still others seem to advocate neither preservation nor conservation; ignoring the obligation of the present generation to the future, they prefer whatever policy is "best" for today.

Ninety per cent of the world's mining today has come into existence within the past 150 years. This cannot be claimed for fishing, or forestry, or most bioculture. Indeed the Industrial Revolution has correlated with a mining revolution. Our tools, weapons, utensils, buildings, sewer systems, machines, ships, and trains: all are made now principally of minerals. Moreover, the *energy* that does our work is now mostly mineral in origin. For evidence, consider the astonishing developments in power within the last century. The wave of industrialization sweeping the earth today is calling for minerals at a rate unprecedented in all of human history.

But the *geography* of mining still wants a system for classifying by regions those many places where men are engaged in commercial mining. Extensive field work and research will be needed to get the answers from specific areas to specific questions: What is their mining like? How is it related to other phenomena there? And how does it link those areas with other regions?

---

[3]"Steel and the Schuman Plan," *Economic Geography*, Vol. 28, October, 1952, pp. 283–294.

Control of sulfur dioxide gas, generated by the converting operation of copper production, plays an important role in the air-quality program at the Ray Mines Division Smelter of Kennecott Copper Corporation. All three converter furnaces at the Kennecott Arizona facility are equipped with water-cooled hoods to prevent the sulfur dioxide from escaping. All three of the hoods are shown open in this photograph, but under normal operating conditions, each is tightly closed over the furnace mouth to collect the gas for use in the sulfuric acid plant. (*Courtesy Kennecott Copper Corporation.*)

SUGGESTED READINGS

CHAPMAN, J. D., "Natural Resource Developments in Canada, 1970–75," *The Canadian Geographer*, 1976, pp. 15–40.

DEASY, GEORGE F., and GRIESS, PHYLLIS R., "Effects of a Declining Mining Economy on the Pennsylvania Anthracite Region," *Annals of the Association of American Geographers*, 1965, pp. 239–259.

DOERR, ARTHUR, and GUERNSEY, LEE, "Man as a Geomorphological Agent: The Example of Coal Mining," *Annals of the Association of American Geographers*, 1956, pp. 197–210.

EARNEY, FILLMORE C., "Ocean Space and Seabed Mining," *The Journal of Geography*, 1975, pp. 539–547.

HAYNES, JAMES B., "North Slope Oil: Physical and Political Problems," *The Professional Geographer*, 1972, pp. 17–22.

McNEE, R. B., "Functional Geography of the Firm, with an Illustrative Case Study from the Petroleum Industry," *Economic Geography*, 1958, pp. 321–337.

SINCLAIR, ROBERT, "The Austrian Danube: A Central European Electric Power Bastion," *The Professional Geographer*, September, 1964, pp. 18–22.

WEBB, GEORGE W., "Factors Affecting the Location of Coal-Burning Steam-Electric Generating Plants," *The Professional Geographer*, 1967, pp. 171–174.

COMMERCIAL MANUFACTURING

Scarcely any of the products of commercial gathering or commercial bioculture are in usable form when they come from forests, fields, mines, or water. Logs must be converted into wood pulp, ores must be smelted, wheat must be milled, hides must be tanned. This conversion of commodities into a more useful form is called *manufacturing*.

For thousands of years manufacturing was conducted on a subsistence level in the homes of the consumers. The specialization of large numbers of people in commercial manufacturing is a phenomenon of the past 200 years.

As we shall use the term, *commercial manufacturing* includes all activities whereby man (a) assembles raw materials in an establishment (whether cottage workshop or factory building), (b) upgrades their usefulness by changing their form, and (c) ships out these more valuable commodities to other places. The focal point of this process is the factory, for it serves as a link between the source regions in which the raw materials originate and the market regions in which the products are consumed (see the accompanying figure). For convenience, we shall call every establishment that fulfills this function a *factory*.

In considering factories, we shall often take location factors into account. The term *location factor*, as used in the geography of manufacturing, is applied to any phenomenon that influences the location of a factory. Examples of location factors are source areas of raw materials, market areas, sources of labor supply, regions providing fuel and power, transportation lines, terrain, taxes, and city zoning codes.

The ideal manufacturing region provides its factories with four essential requirements: raw materials, fuel and/or power, labor, and customers. But since such ideal locations rarely exist, most factories must choose among locations that are well endowed in some but not all of these elements. The *orientation* of an industry determines which single requirement will be deemed most important in establishing the location of a factory. For example, a factory that is raw-material oriented tends to locate nearer to raw-material regions than to either markets or power sources; and if the raw-material region is sparsely inhabited, labor must be imported. A market-oriented factory places a premium on location nearer to customers than to the other factors. A power-oriented industry chooses a site near dams or supplies of mineral fuels even though it may be necessary to pay freight to bring in raw materials from afar, to ship products long distances to customers, and to lure labor from distant places. Finally, a labor-oriented industry responds primarily to the availability of an abundant or particularly skilled work force.

There are numerous ways in which we might answer the question, "How much manufacturing is there in a region?" We could reply in terms of number of people *employed* by manufacturing companies. This would include production workers (those engaged directly in manufacturing processes), supervisors, foremen, researchers, janitors, stenographers, and other personnel. Another criterion is number of *production workers* only. Still another is number of *factories* (or "establishments"). Value of *employee payrolls,* number of *production-worker man-hours*, value of *wages paid to production workers, value added* in the manufacturing process (that is, the differential between the value of a product as it leaves the factory and the value of raw materials, including purchased parts): All these are examples of criteria that might be used in quantifying the amount of manufacturing.

At this point we could indulge in a lengthy discussion of the question "Which criterion is best?" However, the authors have chosen to skip such comment here in favor of recounting a report which indicates that there is close correlation among all these criteria. A study was conducted in the United States in 1954 (a year in which a Census of Manufactures was taken); the objective was to see whether the several manufacturing criteria varied similarly or dissimilarly from place to place. The United States was divided into 166 metropolitan areas (each of which consisted of at least one county containing at least one major city), plus 2,791 other counties, making a total of 2,957 areal units in the entire nation. Of these, 811 counties had either no manufacturing or too little to be thoroughly tabulated in the Census. The remaining 2,146 areal units were quantified in terms of different manufacturing criteria. Coefficients of correlation (explained in Chapter 29) were then computed for several criteria as each varied from place to place among the

2,146 areal units. Table A indicates that every correlation in which the criterion *number of establishments* was involved had a rather high coefficient, over 0.90, but that all correlations involving the other six criteria had an astonishingly high correlation of 0.99, regardless of what pair of criteria were compared. A more recent study[1] indicates that the pattern of *number of establishments* is different from that of the other six variables. Nevertheless, differences are fairly subtle; these coefficients give considerable support to the belief that, when it comes to measuring manufacturing for purposes of an overall geographic pattern of the nation, it is immaterial which criterion we choose, since the probability is extremely high that we would get essentially the same pattern no matter which measurement we selected.

For this reason, we shall not take time in the following pages to quantify each manufacturing topic in terms of all possible criteria. Generally we shall adopt only one—number of employees—for the reason that it is readily comprehended and, in some instances, is the only criterion for which data are available.

Nobody knows for certain how many people in the world are engaged in commercial manufacturing, but the number lies somewhere in the vicinity of 125,000,000 to 150,000,000, approximately 4 per cent of the world's total population and probably no more than 10 per cent of the world's employed labor force. A breakdown of industrial employment by nations and regions such as that shown in Table B, demonstrates unmistakably that the world's outstanding manufacturing region is western Europe with almost 35,000,000 factory workers. This figure exceeds by almost 100 per cent the number of manufacturing employees in the United States.

Commercial manufacturing as a whole is highly concentrated within the middle latitudes of the Northern Hemisphere, especially in four rather clearly defined places: Europe, the Soviet Union, Anglo-America, and Japan.

Like the other economic activities we have studied, manufacturing exhibits regional variation. Our purpose is to identify the location, characteristics, and relationships of manufacturing regions. In doing so we shall adopt two approaches.

Table A

Coefficients of Correlation of Criteria for Measuring Manufacturing
of 2146 Areal Units (Metropolitan Areas and Counties) in the United States

	1 Number of Establish- ments	2 Number of Employees	3 Value of Payroll	4 Number of Produc- tion Workers	5 Number of Man- Hours	6 Value of Wages	7 Value Added
1. Number of establishments	1.00	0.94	0.92	0.94	0.93	0.91	0.92
2. Number of employees		1.00	0.99	0.99	0.99	0.99	0.99
3. Value of employee payroll			1.00	0.99	0.99	0.99	0.99
4. Number of production workers				1.00	0.99	0.99	0.99
5. Number of production man-hours					1.00	0.99	0.99
6. Value of wages paid						1.00	0.99
7. Value added							1.00

Source: John W. Alexander and James B. Lindberg, "Measurements of Manufacturing: Coefficients of Correlation," *Journal of Regional Science*, Vol. 3, Summer 1961, pp. 71–81.

[1]Joel L. Morrison, Morton W. Scripter, and Robert H. T. Smith, "Basic Measures of Manufacturing in the United States, 1958," *Economic Geography*, Vol. 44, No. 4, October 1968, pp. 296–311.

For the first few chapters, we shall deal with selected *industries* (for instance, vegetable canning and petroleum refining), considering *many areas* in which each *industry* appears. Then we shall investigate *selected areas* (such as New England and the Midwest), considering the many *industries* that exist in each area.

We begin with industries that process the products of farms and forests, whether they come from gatherers or bioculturalists; food manufacturing in

Table B

Employment in Manufacturing: Selected Leading Nations*

Region	Thousands of Employees
Africa	
Egypt	606
South Africa	1,073
North America	
Canada	1,677
United States	17,846
South America	
Brazil	1,648
Asia	
Hong Kong	626
India	4,500
Indonesia	1,011
Iran	531
Japan	10,786
South Korea	946
Pakistan	418
Turkey	555
Europe	
Austria	729
Belgium	1,128
Bulgaria	1,096
Czechoslovakia	2,425
Denmark	411
Finland	506
France	5,745
East Germany	2,818
West Germany	8,021
Hungary	1,540
Italy	3,291
Netherlands	1,063
Poland	3,857
Portugal	546
Romania	1,872
Spain	2,004
Sweden	877
Switzerland	800
United Kingdom	7,667
Yugoslavia	1,533
Oceania	
Australia	1,281
U.S.S.R.	28,465

Source: United Nations, *Statistical Yearbook* (1975).
*Employment estimates listed are for the most recent year for which figures are available.

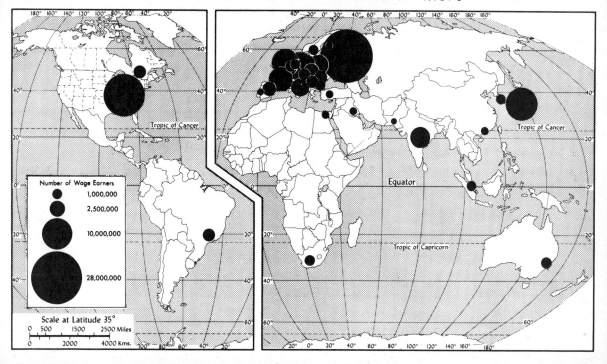

MANUFACTURING EMPLOYMENT: LEADING NATIONS

Chapter 17 and the processing of fiber and wood products in Chapter 18. Then, in Chapters 19 and 20 we cover industries that transform the products of mines. Now, these are instances of *primary manufacturing*, that is, industries that process raw materials from *primary* economic activities. In Chapters 21 and 22 we turn to selected types of *secondary manufacturing*, that is, factories that process materials produced by other factories. Finally, Chapter 23 is devoted to discussing manufacturing in the regions of the United States.

CHAPTER
17

commercial food manufacturing

When bakery products are produced for sale on the premises, the firm is classified as a retail establishment. Plants, such as this one in Oakland, California, however, act as suppliers to grocery stores and other retailers and are considered to be manufacturing operations. (*Courtesy Campbell Taggart, Inc.*)

Food processing was one of the last types of manufacturing to advance from the subsistence to the commercial stage, from home kitchen to business enterprise. The development of the industry has progressed rapidly, though, so that today, most of the food that the millions of people in the highly developed countries consume has passed through some sort of factory.

The eight food industries selected for individual discussion in this chapter illustrate different *types* of location in manufacturing. The *canning* industry exemplifies location that is determined almost entirely by nearness to perishable raw materials. In the second type, which is represented here by the *baking* industry and *soft-drink bottling* works, location is determined almost solely by proximity to customers. *Meat packing, flour milling,* and *sugar refining* are specimens of enterprises whose location is determined partly by the location of raw materials and partly by the location of markets. The distribution of the *brewing* and of the *distilling* industries illustrates the operation of still other forces which, for the present, can be termed "human factors."

COMMERCIAL CANNING AND FREEZING

Location and Characteristics

In the distribution of vegetable and fruit canneries in the United States, as Figure 17-1 shows, the chief region is the Northeast. Other concentrations have developed in central Florida, southern Texas, southern and central California, western Oregon, and Washington.

In terms of number of employees and value of production, the United States Census of Manufactures provides information which indicates that of the nation's total of 89,800 employees in the canned fruit and vegetable industry, Wisconsin has 7,800 and California has 24,500. Value of production of canned fruits and vegetables is about $4,050 million a year. California is again first with $1,253 million and Wisconsin is second with $315 million.

Regional specialties in canning reflect regional preferences in agriculture. There is a fat cluster on the map along the East Coast (Delmarva and the adjacent flanks of New Jersey, Pennsylvania, Maryland, and Virginia) which constitutes a leading area for its specialties, tomatoes and beans. In southern Maine the emphasis is on berries and beans. Western New York canners process both vegetables (tomatoes, cabbage, pickles) and fruits (grape juice, peaches). Their counterparts in western Ohio and eastern Indiana specialize in sweet corn and tomatoes. Factories in Wisconsin and neighboring states are the main centers for sweet corn, green peas, and cherries. Central Florida and southern Texas boast a huge volume of citrus fruit juices, and the Western states specialize in various fruits.

In all these areas canning tends to be a small-scale industry. Only about one-fourth of all canneries employ over 100 people, and few cover as much as 5 acres of land. Moreover, since the equipment required is comparatively simple, the capital investment is low. The industry is highly seasonal; most plants operate for only a few weeks each year. The technique of preserving food by heating it in airtight containers was discovered in 1795, but the technique of preserving food by freezing was discovered only about 1920. Yet despite its great headstart, canning is losing ground to freezing throughout the country. In 1937 the value of frozen fruits and vegetables was one-eighty-fourth the value of canned products; in 1954 it was one-fifth; and in 1972 the figures

Figure 17-1

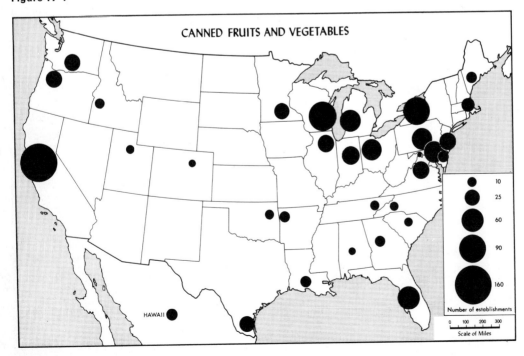

were almost equal! Many plants are now dual-process factories that engage in both canning and freezing.

Relationships

Sources of Raw Materials. The strongest influence on the location of the canning and freezing industry is the nearness of the perishable raw materials. Without exception, all the regions shown on Figure 17-1 are also notable for the cultivation of vegetables and fruits. Some of them are market-garden zones. There, the harvests are canned and consumed in the nearby markets. Many, however, are truck-farming areas, from which the canned goods must be shipped to distant markets. This relationship suggests a principle: If the raw materials that a factory processes are perishable, the factory will gravitate toward wherever the raw materials originate. We will encounter this principle again and again. Of course, another force also attracts factories to the source of raw materials: the desire to avoid shipping substances that will eventually be discarded (like corn cobs and pea pods). But perishability is the critical element. Any industry like canning that tends, for whatever reason, to locate mainly where its raw materials are is said to be *raw-material oriented.*

Contract Farming. Canneries do not, of course, simply take a chance on whatever produce might be available. They deliberately influence farmers' choices of crops. In fact, most farmers, before they put seed into the ground, make firm contractual arrangements with canneries for specified acreages of beans, tomatoes, sweet corn, and other crops.

Metal Can Factories. Canneries require still another basic material: metal cans. Because freight charges are higher on empty cans than on sheet steel, can factories locate where the canneries are. Geographers call such a relationship *symbiosis.* The term, borrowed from biology, applies here to the tendency of dissimilar factories to locate near one another for mutual advantage, in this case because the finished product from one serves as a raw material for the other. The regional pattern of can factories, as Figure 20-8 reveals, is in many places highly similar to that of canneries.

Small Settlements. Since the labor requirements of canneries are usually quite modest and cannery plants tend to gravitate toward the farms that supply them, they are often situated in small rural settlements. These settlements have the added advantage of relatively low tax rates, a decided advantage in an industry that pays taxes on installations that are idle much of the year. Canning is rarely an important activity in large cities. For example, in California, which has 24,500 workers in the canned fruit and vegetable industry, large metropolitan areas such as Los Angeles and San Francisco have only 1,200 and 3,400 workers, respectively, merely a fifth of the state total.

Sources of Labor. Since local labor forces often cannot meet the highly seasonal demand of canners, migrant laborers are employed by the thousands. Workers from Mexico and Puerto Rico find jobs not only in the harvest fields but also in the canneries as far north as New York and Wisconsin. Few other industries choose their locations with so little regard to labor supply.

Market Regions. The main market area is the northeastern United States. Scarcely any cannery goods are shipped abroad, and comparatively little canned food is imported.

Thus, canneries in the Lake Ontario lowland of New York, in New England, in Maryland, and other eastern locales are fortunate in being near both their customers and raw material sources.

COMMERCIAL BAKING

Bakeries provide jobs for over 230,000 people in the United States. Few industries are so ubiquitous, for commercial bakeries tend to follow population. Table 17-1 indicates that there is a strong tendency toward the following relationship: the more populous the settlement, the larger the employment in commercial baking.

Table 17-1

Population and Employment in Commercial Baking by Leading Metropolitan Areas

Metropolitan Area	1973 Population in Thousands	Employment in Bakeries 1972
New York, N.Y.-Northeastern New Jersey	16,075	21,500
Chicago, Ill.-Northwestern Indiana	7,643	16,400
Los Angeles-Long Beach	6,924	9,700
Philadelphia, Pa.-New Jersey	4,806	8,700
Detroit	4,446	5,000
San Francisco-Oakland	3,143	6,000
Washington, D.C.-Maryland-Virginia	3,020	1,500
Boston	2,898	3,400
Dallas-Ft. Worth	2,464	2,800
St. Louis, Mo.-Illinois	2,391	3,300

Sources: U.S. Bureau of the Census, *Statistical Abstract of the United States* (1975) and *1972 Census of Manufactures* (1975).

Bakers settle near their markets because of at least three considerations.

1. Their products are more perishable than their raw materials. Indeed, the stress some customers place

on the freshness of bread has led many bakeries to stamp on the loaf wrapping the day of manufacture. "Day-old" bread fetches a lower price than fresh bread.

2. The baking industry has a low *weight-loss ratio*. This ratio expresses the relationship between the weight of raw materials consumed by a factory and the weight of the finished products. In the case of commercial baking, these weights are roughly equal—that is, 1000 pounds of raw material (flour, salt, yeast, and so on) are transformed into approximately 1000 pounds of bread and pastry. There is little weight loss. Herein is another geographic principle: Other things being equal, the *lower* the weight loss the *stronger* the tendency for the industry to locate near its customers.

3. Transport costs for moving finished products are greater than those for moving raw materials. Flour, salt, sugar, and yeast can be handled in bulk form; consequently, freight charges are much lower per 100 pounds than are the charges on bakery goods, which must be handled more carefully and fill more shipping space. This leads us to still another geographic principle: Other considerations aside, the *higher* the transport costs on finished products (relative to transport costs on their raw materials) the *stronger* the tendency for the industry to locate near its customers.

SOFT-DRINK BOTTLING

Soft-drink bottling factories are dispersed in a pattern, which, like that of bakeries, reflects a high positive correlation with population (Figure 17-2). But the reasons in each case are somewhat different. In contrast to bakery goods, bottled drinks do not spoil quickly, so perishability is not a factor. But easy availability of raw materials is. One principal ingredient, fresh water, is virtually ubiquitous; so no matter what city a bottling factory selected, it would most probably find fresh water available locally. The other main raw material is the syrup, a sweetened, flavored, concentrated substance. Since it is usually manufactured according to a private formula, it is produced only in a few key places, so it does not affect the location of plants. For example, the Coca Cola Company manufactures its syrup in ten plants which supply the concentrate to its bottling works throughout the nation. With regard to an additional factor—relative transportation charges—baking and bottling are alike. The transport costs on a bottling works' products are much higher than those for drums of syrup. The principle observed with bakeries holds again. Factories tend to locate near their customers if transport costs on the product exceed those for raw material.

Correlation with Population

The association with population of both baking and bottling affords us an excellent opportunity to illustrate the principle of covariation. Two phenomena are said to covary positively if both reach their high values in the same places and their low values in the same places. Thus, when we observe that the soft-drink bottling industry or the bakery business tends to correlate positively with population, we can say that the higher the population the greater the amount of commercial baking or of soft-drink bottling.

Figure 17-2

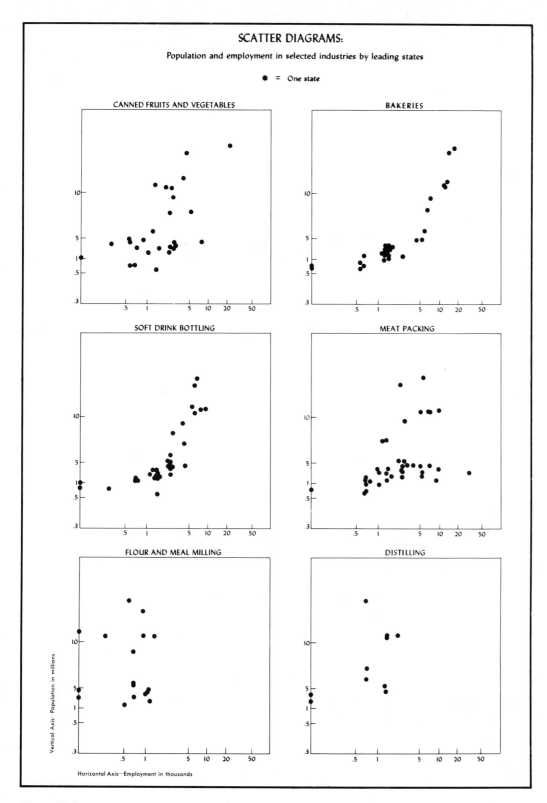

Figure 17-3

We can portray such correlations visually by means of a *scatter diagram*, a graphic device that depicts the variation of one phenomenon *in relation to* a second.

In Figure 17-3 there are six scatter diagrams, one for each of six industries. Each shows the correlation by states between *population* and *employees in the industry*.

Each state is represented on the diagrams by a single dot, the position of which is determined by the state's number of inhabitants and by the number of employees in the particular industry. Some diagrams in Figure 17-3 contain no dots for certain states because the Census of Manufactures failed to report any data.

If a *positive* correlation exists, the dots on a scatter diagram will tend to align along a sloping line that rises from left to right. If a *negative* correlation exists, the dots tend to align along a line that slopes downward from left to right. The line along which they tend to conform is known as the *regression line.* The closer the dots to this line, the *stronger* (or *higher*) the correlation. If the dots are widely diffused over a scatter diagram, the correlation is *weak* (or *low*) and it is difficult to discern any regression line.

Of the industries plotted on the scatter diagrams of Figure 17-3 the ones that reveal the highest correlation with population are baking and soft-drink bottling. For these two, the dots are most closely oriented along a clear line. Perhaps the weakest correlation with population is shown by the distilling industry; on that scatter diagram the dots are widely dispersed.

Mathematical formulas have been worked out for measuring the closeness of dots to the regression line. Such measurements, which permit a more accurate (or more scientific) appraisal of the strength of correlation, will be discussed in Chapter 29.

MEAT PACKING

Location and Characteristics

Historically, the meat packing industry was concentrated in the northeastern United States, and slaughter houses tended to cluster in the large cities, such as New York, Philadelphia, Cincinnati, Chicago, St. Louis, and Milwaukee. But since 1950 the industry's pattern has changed substantially, and the leading centers of activity are places such as Sioux City and Omaha. These centers are closer to the areas where cattle are fattened but less near to markets than were the previous leaders.

Meat-packing plants are disassembly plants in which animals are broken down into meats, hides, tallow, and waste products, some of which are used by other factories in making glue, fertilizer, and animal feed.

There is no typical size. Many small plants employ half a dozen people to make sausage, for example; some large plants employ 5000 people to process hogs, cattle, lambs, and horses into numerous products. But regardless of size, each slaughtering factory, or slaughter house, adjoins a *stockyard* where animals are penned, watered, and fed before being killed. Often these yards occupy as much land as the factory buildings themselves.

Meat-packing plants tend to specialize in processing one type of animal: hogs, cattle, calves, or sheep. And there are overall regional patterns of specialization, too. Hog slaughtering, for instance, is largely concentrated in the Midwest (Figure 17-4), from cities along the Missouri River to those in Illinois and Indiana. The center of cattle slaughtering is farther west (Figure 17-5), especially in the Missouri River Valley.

Relationships to Markets

Originally, meat-packing plants were located near their customers, because the salable product is more perishable than the live animals. Here is an obvious principle which we have already encountered with baking: Factories that turn out products *more perishable than the raw materials* gravitate toward their markets.

In the early days, livestock had to be driven over-

Figure 17-4

Figure 17-5

land to the slaughter houses. This was a costly maneuver because the animals walked off pounds of weight en route. Then, with the expansion of railroad service in the latter half of the nineteenth century, most of the animals were shipped in railway cattle cars. Not only did the journey take less time, but the animals also lost less weight in the process. But the influence of railways alone did not effect any great change in the location of the meatpacking industry. That came only with the invention of refrigeration.

Raw Materials

The refrigeration of perishable goods in railway cars was introduced around 1870. This innovation greatly increased the pull of the animal-producing areas upon the location of meat-packing plants. Transporting live animals has its drawbacks. For one thing, freight charges are high for shipping live beasts—they must be watered and fed by the carriers unless they are delivered within a certain time limit after departure. Then, in addition to some loss of weight by each animal, there often is some loss through injury. Moreover, in transporting live animals, freight charges are being paid on hides, skulls, hoofs, and other parts that, at the factory, become waste products at least and by-products at best. On all these counts, savings result if the slaughter house locates near the farms and ranges that raise the livestock. But such an arrangement was not feasible before refrigeration prevented spoilage en route to market.

To be sure, freight rates are higher per 100 pounds on refrigerated meat than on live animals. But the rates paid are for the moving of meat alone, not for meat plus half again as much weight in bones and waste.

Once it became possible to transport meat to the market from distant plants, another factor came into

play that further strengthened the lure of raw-material regions on the plants. This factor is the very high percentage of production costs that go into the purchase of raw materials—roughly 85 per cent. The other 15 per cent represents expenditures for such things as labor, fuel, and taxes. Now, a geographic principle tends to hold that, in the absence of other compelling considerations, the higher the ratio of raw-material costs to total production costs, the stronger the tendency of a factory to locate near its source of materials.

Still another factor is the increased consumption of *canned* meat in recent years—further enhancing the pull of the ranch and farm areas on the meat-packing industry. About 10 per cent of all meat packed is now put up in cans.

For all these reasons, meat-packing plants have abandoned the centers of population for communities within the stock-raising regions. The New York urban area, the nation's largest metropolis, with nearly 1 out of every 12 United States citizens, once led the nation in meat packing; but it has now fallen far behind western cities. The slaughtering of sheep and lambs is still important in New York and New Jersey, probably because of the large kosher market, but even this branch of the industry has gravitated to grazing regions. Hog packing and cattle packing are now largely clustered in the Corn Belt and along the eastern borders of the grazing regions, and calf packing is found largely in the Dairy Belt.

Some meat-packing factories are illustrative of *bridge industries*, factories that are located *between* their raw material and their market.

Transportation and Trade

For years, livestock moved to slaughter by rail, but today, almost all comes by truck. Trucks also are used to

A U.S. Department of Agriculture meat inspector examines carcass of a freshly slaughtered calf at a meat packing plant in Greencastle, Pennsylvania. In hot skinning, the hide is taken from the carcass immediately after slaughter. The carcass is then placed in a plastic bag to keep it clean to and preserve the tissue coloration existing at the time of slaughter. (*USDA Photo by Larry Rana.*)

carry meat from large packing centers to market. Most of the short-haul transport burden is carried by trucks, but meat destined for longer shipment moves by both truck and by rail, often in factory-owned refrigerator cars. These cars receive top priority from the railroads as they speed eastward from Omaha, Sioux City, and other great packing centers.

The United States engages in relatively little export or import of meat products. Western Europe is the largest world market for meat; a large proportion of its needs is satisfied by the packing plants of Argentina, Australia, and New Zealand.

COMMERCIAL FLOUR MILLING

Location and Characteristics

The United States flour-milling industry exhibits a complex locational pattern (Figure 17-6). Over 80 per cent of the value added by manufacture is in the eastern half of the country. Among the leading centers of production are Kansas City with 900 employees, Buffalo with 800, and Minneapolis with 600. If in delimiting

milling regions, however, we take into account the smaller plants in nearby communities, Buffalo quickly loses its position, for very little flour is processsed elsewhere in New York. Kansas City, on the other hand, is surrounded by a host of milling cities in nearby Kansas, Missouri, Nebraska, Oklahoma, and northern Texas. Together they form the nation's most productive zone of flour milling; they account for about 24 per cent of the employment in this industry and 27 per cent of the value added. Another ranking region is southeastern Minnesota, and significant concentrations are also found in southwestern Illinois and in Ohio.

Flour milling is so highly mechanized—several machines can be supervised by one man—that labor accounts for only about 7 per cent of total production costs. Operations of this sort lend themselves to large-scale enterprises carried on in enormous buildings. Indeed, the flour mills at Buffalo, Kansas City, and Minneapolis are visible for miles around. Adding to their size is the need to maintain tremendous storage facilities for the wheat that cascades out of the fields every harvest time.

Relationships

Raw Materials. Wheat-growing regions exert a strong pull on flour mills. For one thing, 75 per cent of the production costs go for grain purchases. Yet this alone would not necessarily lend the farming regions any particular attraction were it not that 40 per cent of the weight of the grain is "lost" in the manufacturing process: 100 tons of wheat make only 60 tons of flour. Thus the weight-loss ratio is high. Consequently, there is some correlation between the locations of flour milling and of commercial wheat farming—notice that many of the areas that stand out in Figure 17-6 appear also in Figure 11-3.

But some milling centers are located hundreds, even thousands, of miles from their raw-material sources. Buffalo and Liverpool are prime examples of how other relationships are operative in determining the location of this industry.

Figure 17-6

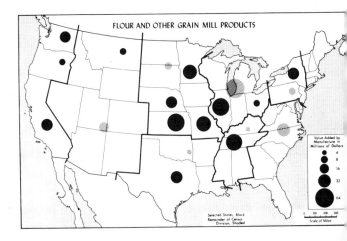

FLOUR AND OTHER GRAIN MILL PRODUCTS

Markets. The myriad of small mills and many of the medium-sized ones are located close to their markets. These are the old mills, relics of a bygone day when the nation's wheat regions and market areas were both situated in the eastern half of the country. These mills have lost their competitive advantage to newer and larger operations in the West, but they persist in processing local grain for local consumers. In terms of market relationships, mills in dairy and poultry regions have fared somewhat better because they suffer less from the weight-loss ratio—the 40 per cent waste can be sold as poultry and animal feed to nearby farmers. Of course, this does not bring as high a price as flour but the added revenue reduces the effect of the loss in weight.

The main milling centers in the West (especially in the winter and spring wheat belts) are far removed from their markets, and most of their flour is funneled off to the East. To avoid back-hauling, the mills in this area have been built on the eastern, marketward margin of the grain-growing zone—in Figures 17-6 and 11-3 notice, for instance, the position of Kansas City and Minneapolis relative to the two wheat areas for which they serve as milling capitals.

The prominence of Buffalo as a milling center illustrates the composite influence of several factors. It is located near the most populous market region of the nation. Although far removed from their major sources of wheat, Buffalo millers do enjoy extremely low transportation costs on the Great Lakes. Notice that Buffalo occupies a favored location at the eastern end of Lake Erie—the deepest penetration by the Great Lakes into the nation's main domestic market. At the other end of the Great Lakes chain, Lake Superior reaches almost to the edge of the spring wheat region and Lake Michigan almost halfway to the winter wheat region. Such easy access to different *kinds* of wheat gives Buffalo an advantage over other centers by enabling the millers to blend a variety of grain types into a variety of flours. A disadvantage for Buffalo, though, is that most Great Lakes shipping comes to a dead stop in winter; however, this drawback is partly offset in that, since the western ports freeze over before the harbor freezes over in Buffalo (if it freezes at all), the fully loaded freighters end up their last trip each season serving as storage bins in the Buffalo harbor, thus reducing the grain-elevator capacity needed there. This city is centrally located not only among urban markets but also among dairy and poultry farms that consume the by-products mentioned above.

Transportation Costs. Were proximity to markets and materials the only elements involved, flour mills would probably be either in the growing regions or in the consuming centers. There are, however, three considerations in transportation costs which help explain why certain places that are near neither one nor the other have achieved such eminence in the industry. These three considerations are bulk-break point, rate-break point, and milling-in-transit rate.

1. Bulk-break point: This term refers to any transportation center where commodities are transferred from one type of carrier to another. Wheat moves by truck from farms to railroad centers; there, numerous truck loads are consolidated into fewer rail carloads. A considerable volume of freight moves by rail to lake or sea ports where the wheat is further consolidated into shiploads. At the other end of the journey, ships deliver the wheat at ports where the bulk is broken down into carloads. It could even move by train to further destinations before being split up into truckloads. All these transportation centers are bulk-break points. Such centers punctuate the movement not only of wheat but also of petroleum and other bulky substances.

   In the flour business, the significance of a bulk-break point is that it could support considerable milling even though its immediate hinterland grew little wheat or consumed little flour. If such a point, Y, were on the line of movement between wheat-growing region X and flour market Z, it would be at no disadvantage, insofar as transport costs are concerned, compared with mills in X that ship flour through Y to Z or with mills in Z that receive wheat from X via Y. Buffalo and Toledo are examples of cities where flour mills enjoy the advantages inherent in location at bulk-breaking points.

2. Rate-break points: A principle of transportation economics is that charges increase with distance but at a decreasing rate. Thus, the charge for hauling wheat by rail 500 miles may be $25.00, while the charge for hauling it 1000 miles is $40.00. Although the distance is twice as great, the charge is less than twice as much. This would hold true even when no bulk-break is involved. Imagine a wheat region 1000 miles from a flour market; flour mills would tend to locate either with the wheat (and pay one through rate on flour) or with the customers (and pay one through rate on wheat), rather than at an intermediate point that would call for a joint rate—two separate lesser rates which, added together, would exceed either of the through rates. But in fact the system does not inevitably work so simply, for through rates may not always apply. To understand why, we must take into account freight-rate territories. (This topic is investigated more fully in Chapter 24.) These territories have arbitrary boundaries that are significant for this reason: The shipping cost from point X in territory A to point Y in adjoining territory B is not computed as one through rate but as the joint rate of the fee from X to the boundary and the fee from the boundary to Y. This practice applies even in situations where the same railroad company runs from the point of origination to the point of destination. Cities that are located where transport arteries cross rate-territory boundaries are called rate-break points. What matters here is that flour

mills located at rate-break points can often compete equally, insofar as freight rates are concerned, with mills located in the wheat lands and those in the markets.

3. Milling-in-transit: This is a privilege granted by railroads to milling centers that, although neither bulk-break points nor rate-break points, are located on the line of flow between raw material and market. Normally, the mills in such centers would be saddled with joint rates, but milling-in-transit permits them to pay through rates and yet stop the grain en route for milling purposes.

The Role of an Invention. As late as 1850, commercial flour mills were able to grind only soft wheat, for the mill stones wore out too rapidly when kernels of hard wheat were ground. Almost all the wheat grown in this country was of the soft variety produced in the humid East. Then in the latter half of the nineteenth century wheat lands opened up out West; although the new western producers enjoyed potential competitive advantages over their eastern brethren, the only variety they could grow was the unmillable hard wheat. Finally, though, in 1870, a design for steel *rollers*, instead of stone *discs*, was introduced from Hungary, and the hard-wheat flour-milling industry began to boom in Minneapolis. This city held first place in United States flour milling until it was surpassed by Buffalo in 1929.

The Sources of Power. In the early days of commercial flour milling, the mill stones were turned by power transmitted mechanically by waterwheels. Most of the small older mills in the eastern United States are still situated close to dams along small streams. This is one reason why, in the early 1800's, the leading flour city in New York was Rochester on the Genesee River rather than Buffalo on the Lake Erie lowland. Water power was also a factor in the early start of Minneapolis as a milling center on the St. Anthony Falls in the Mississippi. But water power no longer plays a significant role.

SUGAR MANUFACTURING

Sugar manufacturing involves three types of factory: sugar-cane *centrales*, cane-sugar refineries, and beet-sugar refineries.

Sugar-cane centrales are located right on the sugar plantations. Here the cane stalks are put through the initial stages of manufacturing in order to take advantage of a tremendous reduction in weight. For cane-sugar stalks consist of 74 per cent water, 10 per cent cellulose, and 2 per cent waste fibers; only 14 per cent is raw sugar. The other 86 per cent of the weight of the stalks can be eliminated right at the plantation. The cellulose (termed bagasse) serves as fuel on some *centrales* and, it has recently been discovered, is a usable material for paper pulp. Our mainland *centrales* (all in Gulf States, mostly Louisiana) produce only about 12 per cent of our needs.

Cane-sugar refineries are located in three general areas. The leading one, which extends from Boston to Philadelphia, refines one-third of the sugar processed in this country. These mills draw their raw sugar from *centrales* in Latin America, Puerto Rico, and other Caribbean islands. A second area along the Gulf Coast absorbs the raw sugar from domestic *centrales*, plus an even larger amount from the Caribbean. This region accounts for almost half of our domestic production. The third center is Crockett (California), whose refineries process Hawaiian raw sugar. Although we grow very little sugar cane in the continental United States, we

This sugar refinery in Raceland, Louisiana, processes sugar cane which is cut largely in local fields. Nearby, the port of New Orleans is a major center for importing semirefined sugar from countries in Africa, Central and South America, Asia, and the Pacific. Southern Louisiana thus provides the United States with a large portion of its sugar, and has come to be known as the nation's "sugar bowl." (*Courtesy Clair A. Shenk.*)

BEER AND OTHER MALT BEVERAGES

Number of Employees
- 500
- 1,000
- 2,000
- 3,000
- 7,500

Selected SMSAs, Black
Remainder in State, Shaded

0 100 200 300
Scale of Miles

Figure 17-7

refine most of the sugar we consume because (a) it is cheaper to ship raw sugar in bulk than to ship pure sugar in sacks, (b) there is very little weight lost in purifying raw sugar (a larger weight-loss factor would encourage the industry to locate near the plantation), and (c) the government protects domestic refineries by a rigid quota system that limits the volume of refined sugar that can be imported. In sum, imports of refined sugar account for only a small percentage of our total sugar consumption.

Beet-sugar refineries are located in California, Colorado, Idaho, Montana, Michigan, and the other northern states that grow sugar beets (Table 17-2). These factories locate near beet farms because (a) beets are of such little value per pound that transport charges quick-

ly exceed it on long hauls, and (b) beets are a perishable, seasonal crop that cannot be stored for very long. Beet-sugar mills, like vegetable canneries, tend to be small and numerous within the growing area. About 30 per cent of the sugar consumed in this country is refined from domestic beets.

The United States can be divided into three sugar market regions. The eastern part of the country (east of a line running from western Texas to Lake Superior—except for much of Michigan, which has its own beets) is served by cane-sugar refineries on the Eastern and Gulf Seaboards. The Pacific Coast states constitute a market served by both beet-sugar and cane-sugar refineries in California. Between these two regions is a large zone that extends from Canada to Mexico and is served by beet sugar refineries only.

COMMERCIAL BREWING

A comparison of the map of the brewing industry (Figure 17-7) with a population map suggests that, on a broad national scale, the brewing industry is *market-oriented*. Thus, the northeastern quadrant of the United States contains most of the nation's people, and a large share of the nation's breweries are there, too. Moreover, Wisconsin and New York are the nation's leading states and metropolitan Milwaukee, St. Louis, and New York are leading urban areas in brewing production. In a broad view of the nation, then, breweries tend to correlate in location with population. But the correlation tends to break down when we turn to a finer scale.

California, New York, Texas, Pennsylvania, and Illinois are the top ranking states in terms of population, but of these, only New York and Pennsylvania are ranking beer producers. At the SMSA scale, New York is clearly important but St. Louis, which has about the

Table 17-2

The Beet Sugar Industry, 1973, by Leading States

	Tons of Beets Harvested in Thousands
United States Total	24,499
California	6,447
Idaho	2,921
Washington	2,476
Minnesota	2,169
Colorado	1,851
Michigan	1,524
Nebraska	1,482
North Dakota	1,284
Wyoming	985
Montana	883
Kansas	605

Source: U.S. Department of Agriculture, *Agricultural Statistics, 1975* (1975).

same amount of employment in this industry as New York, ranks only 11th in population. The leading beer producer, Milwaukee, ranks 21st in population.

Here the location of a particular type of people who have both an unusual desire for the beverage and a peculiar aptitude for making it is a determining influence on the initial location of this industry. Germans have long been recognized as adept braumeisters, and many brewery companies bear German names. A large concentration of German immigrants and their descendants is a major reason why the business settled in New York, Milwaukee, and St. Louis rather than elsewhere. Few other industries in the United States have a locational pattern that illustrates so well the power of an ethnic factor in influencing location. The major raw material (by volume) is water; barley and hops, the other ingredients, can be grown widely in the Northeast.

DISTILLERIES OF ALCOHOLIC BEVERAGES

The last food industry we shall examine, the distilling business, is still something of a geographic conundrum. Its locational pattern suggests a slight correlation with population, since most of the production is in the northeastern states and on the West Coast. Yet New York and Pennsylvania are not the leading states; indeed, very little distilling is done in New York. Kentucky is unquestionably the leader, but Illinois, Ohio, Indiana, Maryland, and Pennsylvania are also important producers. The inordinate concentration of the industry in these states has puzzled analysts. Why here, instead of dispersed among the populous centers of the nation?

One suggestion is that distilling is a raw-material oriented industry, and therefore would naturally locate in the Corn Belt. But, Kentucky is not a leading corn state, and her distillers import the grain from states to the north. Moreover, the *weight-loss ratio* is so low that, on this count, there would be little advantage in a location near raw materials. Another suggestion is that Kentucky water possesses "unusual" qualities; but this claim has never been demonstrated, and Illinois distillers laugh at the suggestion.

Perhaps there is something in the costs of distilling liquor and of marketing it that gives states such as Kentucky and Illinois an advantage. But a glance at the relationship of selling price to production costs shows that federal *taxes* are a major component in the price of liquor. The federal government assesses a tax of $10.50 per gallon. Nearly every state adds an additional tax. The amount of state tax varies—in Alaska it is $4 a gallon, in Maryland it is $1.50, and in Montana it is 21 per cent of the retail price. The combined federal and state taxes in most cases make up between one- and two-thirds of the retail price of liquor.

Thus, the cost of actually distilling liquor is unusually low compared to its final value. Indeed, aging the product (including insurance and loss through evaporation) runs higher than raw materials, labor, and overhead combined. But taxes overshadow all other costs. Therefore, within the nation, Kentucky and Illinois would seem to have no particular advantage over other states.

Nobody has yet explained why the distilling industry is so highly concentrated in Kentucky rather than in say, Iowa. Perhaps it is a case of locational inertia—historically speaking, the industries got an early start in these places—and have maintained their position. But might it also be that distilling is a type of industry whose location is explained largely by the "reputation of an area"? Unless it can be demonstrated that Kentucky whiskeys are actually "better" than those distilled elsewhere, may it not be that clever national *advertising* which vaunts the rolling green pastures, the white rail fences, and the purebred horses of Kentucky has been able to weave an element of charm into the very name "Kentucky," and so has had a strong, though immeasurable, impact on the minds of whiskey drinkers? At first glance, this explanation may seem highly implausible, but social scientists may someday discover ways of measuring customer reaction accurately enough to put it to the test.

In this chapter we have dealt entirely with the United States, using it, in effect, as a case study area to illustrate how certain food industries have developed definite types of locational patterns. For the world as a whole, the regions of commercial food manufacturing conform to the same principles just observed within the United States.

CHAPTER

18

fiber, leather, and wood products

Aerial view of a pulp mill in Cosmoplis, Washington. Pulp mills commonly process both logs, such as those in the upper portion of the photo, and wood chips from lumber mills. (*Courtesy Weyerhaeuser Company.*)

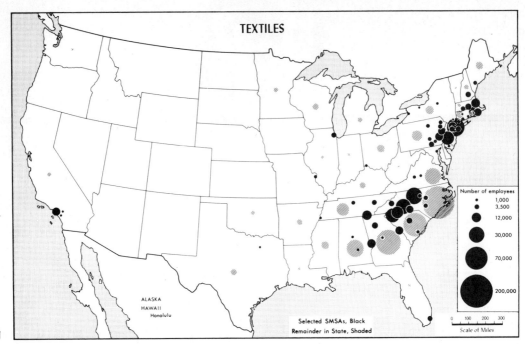

TEXTILES

Number of employees
· 1,000
· 3,500
● 12,000
● 30,000
● 70,000
● 200,000

Selected SMSAs, Black
Remainder in State, Shaded

Scale of Miles
0 100 200 300

ALASKA
HAWAII
Honolulu

Figure 18-1

The purpose of this chapter is two-fold: (a) to emphasize a special adaptation of the geographic method that is particularly appropriate to *manufacturing*, and (b) to consider the geography of a few selected industries that process the nonfood products of farm and forest.

A SPECIAL ADAPTATION OF THE GEOGRAPHIC METHOD TO MANUFACTURING

In Chapter 1 it was suggested that the third basic question in the geographic method (involving relationships) could be approached from four alternative viewpoints which considered (1) physical and cultural factors, (2) causes and consequences, (3) internal and external relationships, or (4) correlations. A fifth alternative is available when one studies manufacturing—he can choose to emphasize the relationships which link a factory (a) to areas which supply its raw materials, fuel and power, and (b) to areas which consume its product.

Recall that the basic function of a factory is to perform an intermediate function between raw-material producers and finished-product consumers. Thus, the role of a factory, which upgrades the value of existing items of wealth, is generally different from that of a farm, a forest, or a mine.

Now we will take up separately the textile, apparel, leather, lumber, furniture, pulp, paper, and printing industries. In each case the United States will serve as our case-study area, after which we shall trace the general world patterns.

TEXTILES

Location

There are two outstanding regions of textile manufacturing in the United States (Figure 18-1), both on the Altantic Seaboard. Few other industries are so concentrated in that part of the country. A southeastern strip, running from Virginia through the Carolinas and Georgia to Alabama, is the home of 68 per cent of the nation's textile industry, 29 per cent of it in North Carolina alone. Most of the textile mills here are located in the Piedmont, a transitional landform of rolling plains and hills between the Appalachian Mountains and the Atlantic Coastal Plain. A northeastern belt stretching from Pennsylvania to southern New England encompasses 22 per cent of United States textile production.

Characteristics

Textile workers spin fibers (plant, animal, or synthetic) into yarn, weave or knit the yarn into fabrics, and then finish the fabrics by bleaching, dyeing, and sometimes printing patterns.

It is a declining industry in the United States: Between 1947 and 1972 employment in textile factories dropped by almost 25 per cent, and the value added by manufacture figure grew by only 20 per cent, going from $5.3 billion to $11.7 billion. During this same period every other notable industry increased its value added by a much larger figure, and almost every other one increased the size of its labor force substantially. Yet for decades, the textile industry led the country in both categories, reaching its apex in 1920. But World War II, with its heavy demand for mechanized equipment, catapulted the machinery industries into the lead. Textiles now have also been surpassed by such industries as metals, apparel, and printing.

The textile industry has changed not only in size but also in situation. For over a century New England paced the nation. Then, shortly before the turn of the present century, textile mills began to spring up in the Piedmont, and in 1925 New England lost her supremacy to this new competitor. The older mills of New England were poorly equipped and poorly designed. Typically three- or four-story buildings, they required the vertical movement of materials during the manufacturing process. The new southern mills, by contrast, were equipped with modern machines and were efficiently designed so that all operations can be conducted on one level, the materials moving horizontally from step to step.

The two regions also differ in what they produce. The southeastern states support largely cotton manufacturers, whereas New England and the Middle Atlantic states (Pennsylvania, New Jersey, and New York) have more of a balance between woolens, cottons, and synthetics. Still, the southeastern states are increasing their share of all three fabrics. For example, they now account for about 95 per cent of the nation's employment in cotton weaving mills, for over 83 per cent of employment in manmade fiber and silk weaving mills, and for a third of the national employment in wool weaving and finishing mills.

External Relationships

What is the orientation of the textile industry? To raw materials? To markets? Or is its locational pattern deter-

mined by something else? Let's look first at the three principal raw materials—cotton, wool, and synthetics.

Raw Materials. Most of our raw cotton comes from the Mississippi Valley and Texas. In addition, small amounts originate near the factories in Georgia and South Carolina, and some cotton comes from California and Arizona (Figure 12-4). A very small quantity of long-staple cotton is imported for blending with the domestic variety, most of which is short-staple.

Most of our domestic wool originates in the western half of the country, particularly in Texas and the Rocky Mountain states (Figure 18-2), though a little is shorn from sheep in the Corn Belt. The United States also imports a considerable amount of wool, largely from Argentina, Australia, New Zealand, and South Africa.

Synthetic fibers originate almost entirely in chemical factories in the eastern United States, especially the Southeast.

Clearly, there is little correlation between the locational pattern of textiles and that of raw materials, otherwise Texas, the leading state in both cotton and wool shipments, would have a similar leading position in cloth manufacturing.

Markets. Markets are a more powerful draw than raw materials on textile mills, because little weight is lost in the manufacturing process and because transport costs on fabrics exceed those on fibers.

Figure 18-2

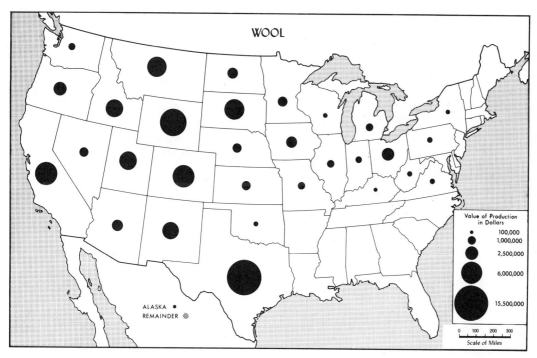

Since the cotton and synthetic-fiber mills produce both yarn and consumer goods, the market for these fabrics consists partly of apparel factories and partly of wholesalers. Both of these markets are also essentially eastern, the apparel factories being located according to the pattern in Figure 18-4 and the textile wholesalers corresponding generally with the distribution of population. Domestic demand takes care of most of the output of the mills. Foreign markets take scarcely any of it, because United States manufacturers cannot compete with the textile makers in Europe and eastern Asia where labor costs are markedly lower.

Notice New England's changing position relative to cotton markets. Does this provide us with a clue to the forces behind the region's decline? In the late 1700's and most of the 1800's New England had the core of the United States market near at hand. But for many years the center of population has been moving steadily westward and is now in southern Illinois. So the Piedmont is now somewhat closer than New England to the national market. In fact, though, the mills of neither New England nor the Piedmont are located very near the bulk of their customers. Other forces are apparently at work, as we shall see.

The market for woolen textiles is more restricted than that for cottons or synthetics, for it consists largely of apparel factories in New York and Philadelphia. This has been the strongest bulwark for New England and the Middle Atlantic states in retaining the woolen mills.

Relationships Within the Textile Regions

Within each of the areas shown in Figure 18-1, there are certain common relationships between textile manufacturing and labor supply, power supply, tax rates, and the economic base of settlements. Let us examine each in turn.

Labor Supplies. New England, with its early start in textile manufacture, developed a highly skilled work force. But the cost of labor there has always been higher than in the Piedmont. The gap was great in the early years of this century but has gradually narrowed so that today northern wage rates average only 10 per cent above those in the South. Moreover, the workers are less widely organized in the South, and are willing to work more hours per shift, more shifts per day, more days per week.

The resulting contrast in labor costs between New England and the South effected a competitive disadvantage to the northern mills. On this score, witness what an official commission appointed by the Commonwealth of Massachusetts had to say:

> The Commission finds that . . . probably the major factor in causing competitive disadvantage in the Commonwealth is wages and cost of labor.

> The Commission is of the opinion that a reduction of wages in the northern mills is no solution to the problem as it feels that any reduction would be followed by a similar reduction of wages in the South. Unionization in the southern industry is tending to narrow the gap in wage rates and will probably continue that trend in the future.

> The Commission finds that the differential in productivity is one of the two major factors causing competitive disadvantage to the textile industry in the Commonwealth. . . . The Commission finds that the individual work load of the northern worker is not as great in many instances as that of the southern worker. . . .

> The Commission finds that certain existing Massachusetts laws tend to prevent the most effective and economical use of machinery by rendering third shift operations difficult.[1]

This discrepancy in labor costs has been reflected in two developments. First, it has led New England textile companies to close their mills, move their supervisors south, and build new mills with modern machinery that southern workers have quickly learned to operate. Second, the mills that have remained in New England have begun to specialize in high-quality textiles for which their highly skilled and expensive workers may be used to better advantage.

Since woolen textiles, more than cotton, require more skillful workmen—largely because the patterns must be woven into the fabrics rather than simply stamped on them—the woolen industry has been slower than the cotton industry to leave New England's reservoir of expert labor. But improved machinery is now reducing this advantage, southern labor is developing the requisite abilities, and the woolen industry is shifting south, too.

Power Supply. In the 1700's and 1800's numerous textile mills were constructed along New England streams, for dams ten feet high developed enough fall to meet the power requirements of small factories. Besides a dam, a millrace (see Chapter 14) was necessary for waterpower. Any factory located downstream from the dam and between the millrace and the stream would be in a favorable position for generating waterpower. Then, if the dam were ten feet high, the factory could have the equivalent of a ten-foot waterfall turning a water wheel in its basement; water could be channeled into the factory from the upper millrace level on one side and be drained out on the other side into the lower stream below the dam. Thus, although the southern New England area got an early start in textiles because of closeness to market, specific sites were chosen primarily for water power.

Access to water power has also been an asset of the Piedmont area. By the time the textile industry began to develop there, though, the electrical revolution had

---

[1] The Commonwealth of Massachusetts, *Report of the Special Commission Relative to the Textile Industry and to Prevent Removal Thereof from the Commonwealth*, House Document No. 2590 (Boston, 1950), pp. 44–45.

dawned, and hydroelectric power became feasible. Therefore, there are few millraces in the Piedmont.

For the textile industry as a whole, power and fuel account for 2 per cent of the total cost of manufacture.

Taxes. Both municipal and state taxes on factories are lower in the South than in the North. Indeed, many southern communities have lured northern factories with the promise that no municipal taxes will be imposed for stipulated periods of time. Some mills have been built in rural areas outside the taxing limits of municipalities.

Economic Base of Settlements. Textile mills are important components of the economic base of many communities because they provide large percentages of the local jobs. In Fall River, Massachusetts, for instance, textile mills afford work to over a fifth of the urbanized area's employed residents; in Kannapolis, North Carolina, the figure is an astonishingly high 57 per cent. (For the nation's population as a whole the ratio of textile employment to total employment is 1 per cent.)

The overriding position of the textile industry in Kannapolis has made that community one of the nation's most industrialized cities: Manufacturing accounts for 66 per cent of all jobs in Kannapolis, nearly three times the national average.

The World Pattern

Four regions dominate the world production of textiles (Figure 18-3). They are, by percentage of world total: the Far East, mainly India (19 per cent) and Japan (10 per cent), Europe (25 per cent), the U.S.S.R. (15 per cent), and the United States (12 per cent). In Europe the top nations are France, West Germany, Italy, Belgium, and the United Kingdom.

As for raw materials, Europe and Japan import almost all their cotton and wool. The United States, as we saw, imports wool and some high-grade cotton but

has a tremendous surplus of short-staple cotton for export to Japan and Europe. The U.S.S.R. produces almost all of her own fibers.

The four leading manufacturing areas are the leading market areas as well. In addition, Europe, Japan, and India are the dominant exporters to the world market. Almost half the world's cotton textiles are exported from Europe, 37 per cent from the Far East, and only 8 per cent from the United States. Sixty per cent of all noncotton-woven textile exports originate in Eurpoean mills.

In general, the same basic factors are involved in the location of textile manufacturing in the other countries as have just been observed in the United States.

Hand weaving on a horizontal multiheddled loom in the city of Yazd, Iran. Factories such as this one are increasingly difficult to find as small producers turn to power-driven looms. (*Courtesy Michael Bonine.*)

Modern textile factory in Bayreuth, Germany. (*Courtesy German Information Center.*)

MANUFACTURE OF WOVEN FABRICS

Figure 18-3

Figure 18-4

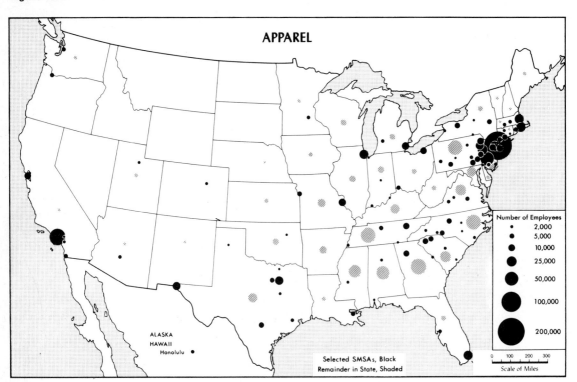

Location and Characteristics

The manufacture of clothing is highly concentrated in a small strip between metropolitan New York and Philadelphia, along with several communities in eastern Pennsylvania (Figure 18-4). Measured in terms of value added, about 40 per cent of the nation's apparel industry is in this small zone. Other conspicuous clothing centers are Chicago, St. Louis, Boston, Fall River, Baltimore, Miami, Dallas, Los Angeles, Detroit, and El Paso. Elsewhere, the distribution is spotty.

The apparel industry is a small-scale industry; in fact, the average number of employees in the nation's 24,438 clothing factories is only 56. Compare this with a national average of 132 in textile mills. One reason for this dissimilarity is differing degrees of mechanization; spinning machines and looms can manufacture the fabric, but no machine has yet been designed to make a suit of clothes. Another reason is that, by virtue of its tremendous variety in sizes, styles, and quality, clothing is difficult to mass-produce. Thus there is little advantage in large assembly lines manned by hundreds of workers. Factories that make women's clothing are much smaller than those that turn out men's. In keeping with the small scale of the operations, the machines themselves are small (for instance, sewing machines and cutting machines). A good deal of the work requires high skill. It takes years to learn the art of sewing neat seams and making trim shoulders on coats. Accordingly, labor costs account for 26 per cent of the value of the shipments that leave apparel factories.

Relationships

Raw Materials. The New York-Pennsylvania apparel region is close to the northern textile factories and 300 miles from those in the Piedmont. These are its chief sources of material. Comparatively small quantities of fabrics are imported from abroad. Thus, nearness to raw materials is a major consideration in the location of factories.

Market Regions. There is a rather close correlation between the location of garment factories and urban markets. Notice that virtually every large city appears on Figure 18-4 and that the main concentrations of clothing factories are generally in or close to large cities, where most of the consumers are. Very little apparel is exported to foreign markets, since the competition of European and Japanese clothing manufacturers (with their lower labor costs) is intense.

Labor Supply. The large labor pools of the nation's metropolitan areas are essential to an industry in which machines have augmented but not replaced the human hand. New York City had a particular advantage in this respect because, as the nation's main port of entry, it was able to tap the flow of European immigrants looking for work, many of whom had years of experience in European apparel factories. Even today, thousands of the New York area's 276,000 clothing workers are foreign-born.

Style Centers. All the leading designers of men's, women's, and children's clothes are in cities, principally New York. Since apparel manufacturers maintain constant contact with these designers, they are a powerful force in keeping clothing factories in New York. For this reason, the most expensive clothes are made in large cities while simpler garments (overalls, work shirts, and wash dresses), whose style is not so important, are made in smaller, distant communities, such as those in Ohio, Wisconsin, and, increasingly, the southern and southwestern states.

Central Business Districts within Cities. The garment business is one of the rare industries that tend to locate in the downtown sections of cities. In New York City, for example, there are 170,000 apparel workers in scores of small factories in Manhattan alone. In Chicago also, thousands of garment workers operate in the Loop and its periphery. Land in central business districts is expensive, and these factories cannot afford first-floor space. Often the ground floor in a building is occupied by a clothing retailer; sometimes the second floor is devoted to clothing wholesalers; while the clothing manufacturers occupy the upper stories, thereby winning the name of "loft" industries.

The main reason for the downtown concentration of garment manufacturing is labor supply. The downtown area, having a central location to the local population, is therefore in a good position for assembling a working force. In the case of New York City more workers can gather with less effort in Manhattan than in any other part of the city because most of the city's transportation arteries converge upon the island.

Metropolitan New York

The foregoing relationships all combine to make the New York metropolitan area the outstanding center of clothing production in the United States. This one urban area contains 40 per cent of the nation's garment factories, supports 20 per cent of the industry's employees, and accounts for 26 per cent of the value added (see Table 18-1). Rarely has any one industry become so highly localized.

Manhattan Island, containing New York City's central business district, can boast the greatest concentration of manufacturing of any area on the face of the earth, measured in terms of employment. And on the island, apparel-making is the leading type of manufacturing.

Table 18-1

Apparel Manufacturing: United States and the New York, N.Y.-Northeastern New Jersey Standard Consolidated Area

Criteria	United States	New York-Northeastern New Jersey	Percentage of U.S. Total
Number of establishments	24,438.0	9,779.0	40
Number of employees	1,368,300.0	276,100.0	20
Value added ($1,000)	$13,487.5	$3,484.3	26
Payrolls ($1,000)	$7,212.0	$1,704.0	24

Source: U.S. Bureau of the Census, *1972 Census of Manufactures* (1975).

The traditional core zone covers 150 acres in an area bounded by the Pennsylvania Railroad station on the south, Times Square on the north, Seventh Avenue on the east, and Ninth Avenue on the west. Here are the lofts that house the hundreds of small enterprises which constitute the garment business. In the neighboring streets are the buyers and sellers of high-style fabrics, feathers, furs, and other materials used in the manufacture of clothing. Though the following description was written in the 1930's, it is still remarkably applicable to the industry as it continues to function:

> Because it is built upon fashion and behaves accordingly, the district looks to the casual visitor more like a madhouse than anything else. To pass through its streets at lunch time is an unforgettable experience. Its sidewalks are so jammed with throngs of garment workers who have poured out of its buildings for a breathing spell that through traffic is virtually stopped. The buildings house a jumble of showrooms, workrooms, storerooms, and offices. Through them passes a stream of buyers looking for goods they can sell to the customers of the retail stores they represent. Boys push little carts around through from one workshop or showroom to another. In offices scattered throughout the section, employers and workers argue out their recurring disputes over wages. Throughout all these operations runs a high nervous tension.
>
> Madhouse though it may seem, the garment center and its way of doing business are a logical answer to the fundamental force which brought them into existence—fashion. It provides two fundamental needs: First, it enables everybody to keep in touch with what everybody else is making and with what the consumers of the country and the storekeepers who represent them in this market are buying. Second, it makes possible great speed in setting up facilities to produce a particular style while the demand for it is good, closing them down when demand falls off, dropping styles quickly before stocks have been accumulated if they fail to win demand, and copying immediately anything any competitor devises which consumers like.[2]

[2]Reavis Cox, *The Marketing of Textiles*, The Textile Foundation (Washington, D.C., 1938), p. 312.

The manufacture of garments for world export on a commercial basis is largely centered in western Europe. To be sure, considerable clothing is shipped from Japan, Hong Kong, and the United States: nevertheless, almost two-thirds of the apparel which moves through the arteries of international trade comes from factories in the United Kingdom, France, West Germany, Italy, Belgium, and the Netherlands. The same factors that have operated in the United States have likewise operated elsewhere, influencing the apparel industry to locate primarily in the more industrially advanced areas.

LEATHER

Location and Characteristics

The major region of leather manufacturing in the United States (Figure 18-5) runs from Pennsylvania to Maine. This region contains half of the employment in the leather and leather products industry. West of this region lies a lesser region, which runs from Ohio to Missouri, Iowa, and Minnesota and accounts for about 20 per cent of the nation's employment. The southeastern United States makes up a second minor region which also has 20 per cent of the national total employment.

Standard metropolitan statistical areas which are, in terms of employment, leading leather manufacturing centers inclitude: New York 23,000, Boston 20,000, St. Louis 5,500, Milwaukee 5,000, Los Angeles 5,000, Manchester (New Hampshire) 4,500, and Chicago 4,500.

Leather manufacture has two principal phases: *tanning* and *fabricating*. Each process has a different locational pattern.

Tanneries process hides and skins, first soaking them to remove the hair and flesh, then treating them with tannic acid and oils to preserve the leather. Within the United States there are 517 tanneries, which employ 25,700 people, an average of 50 workers per plant. The tanning phase has traditionally been heavily concentrated in Boston, Philadelphia, and other large centers in the Northeast: New England accounts for 30 per cent of the value of shipments from the nation's tanneries and Massachusetts alone supplies 16 per cent of that value. Wisconsin is the second ranking state with 14 per cent. Other important states are Maine, New York, New Jersey, and Pennsylvania.

The factories that fabricate the tanned leather into shoes, luggage, gloves, and belting employ 248,000 people and are much more widely distributed (Figure 18-5). The New York-New Jersey metropolitan complex is paramount in this stage with 40,000 leather workers.

Relationships

The United States imports and exports large numbers of hides and skins. Especially important are imports of

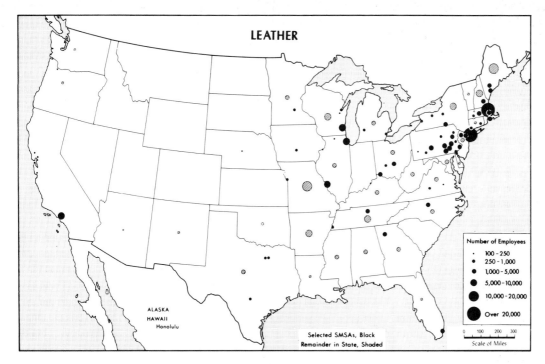

LEATHER

Number of Employees
· 100 - 250
· 250 - 1,000
● 1,000 - 5,000
● 5,000 - 10,000
⬤ 10,000 - 20,000
⬤ Over 20,000

ALASKA
HAWAII
Honolulu

Selected SMSAs, Black
Remainder in State, Shaded

0   100   200   300
Scale of Miles

Figure 18-5

sheep and lamb skins from Iran and New Zealand and exports of cattle hides to such places as Japan and Mexico. Tanneries located in coastal cities are particularly well located to participate in this active trade. But the tanneries in interior cities, such as Chicago, St. Louis, and Milwaukee, are also fortunately situated relative to raw materials, for they are near the large slaughter houses. Indeed, almost every large meat-packing center (Figures 17-4 and 17-5) is also a leather tanning center (Figure 18-5).

For centuries, the foremost source of tannin was the bark of oak trees, principally the cork oak. Since it was more expensive to ship bark than hides (considering the relative volumes of each required in the tanning process), tanneries tended to locate in regions with oak forests (Chapter 6) and the hides were shipped in from animal-raising areas elsewhere (Chapters 7 and 9). Then, in the late 1880's, it was discovered that tanning chemicals could be extracted from chrome-bearing minerals. These chemicals proved less expensive than oak bark, and tanneries began abandoning forest locations in favor of places closer to their sources of hides and skins. A few tanneries, however, have lingered on in some Piedmont and northern communities, which originally had nearby stands of oak trees. Their persistence demonstrates the power of an early start (or of subsequent *locational inertia*) in perpetuating an industry in a place which at one time promoted an association that is no longer predominant.

Markets. Today, the location of the leather industry is influenced more strongly by the pull of markets than of materials. It is much cheaper to ship leather to shoe, glove, and belt factories located near consumers than to ship shoes, gloves, and belts from factories located near tanneries. As the center of the nation's population has been shifting steadily westard, the leather industry in general and shoemaking in particular have also gradually moved westward from New England, which, as late as 1900, dominated the nation in the manufacture of shoes. Several New England firms subsequently moved their supervisors to St. Louis to train a new labor force. This was a planned regional shift in response to a moving market.

Labor Supply. Shoemaking and other forms of leather fabrication require considerable skill, and for years New England has had the nation's best reservoir of leather workers. This was a powerful factor in New England's long dominance in leather-working. But, as with the textile industry, labor rates there were higher than in other areas, so the shoe industry also tended to move away, in effect creating its own labor supply in its new locations.

Machinery-leasing Systems. The movement from New England was expedited by an unusual trend in mechanization begun in 1852 with the adaptation of sewing machines to shoemaking. Other inventions followed, as a result of which a new industry was born: the manufacture of shoemaking machinery. At first there were several small specialized companies, some making cutting machines, some stitching machines, and so on. Gradually these small companies began to merge, to evolve one giant firm, the United Shoe Machinery Corporation. This corporation originated the unusual policy of renting rather than selling machines. The geographic impact of this policy was that small shoe factories sprang up in Wisconsin, Illinois, Missouri, Ohio, and other states, for a large capital investment was no longer needed for purchasing machinery. The combination of mechanization and machinery leasing reduced New England's attraction because the role of skilled labor, though not eliminated, was substantially reduced in importance.

"Jobbing-Out" Practices. The large leather manufacturers in Boston, New York, Philadelphia, St. Louis, Chicago, and Milwaukee frequently "job out" some of their work to factories in smaller cities. Soles, inner soles, heels, and uppers are often cut in outlying communities and trucked into the parent factory for final assembly. This practice enables the parent factory to combine the distribution advantages of a large city with the lower wage rates prevailing in smaller cities. Sometimes children's shoes and less expensive brands of adult shoes are completely assembled in outlying towns and trucked for distribution to a central factory that itself specializes in more expensive footwear.

The World Pattern

Tanneries are widely distributed throughout the world, but they are concentrated in the industrial nations of Europe, the United States, the U.S.S.R., and Japan. To most of these countries comes a steady supply of hides and skins from Australia, South Africa, South America, and other ranching areas. All the industrial nations are large importers except for the U.S.S.R., which produces an adequate quantity of hides and skins to meet its demand.

Leather fabricators also tend to be located in Europe, the U.S.S.R., and the other industrialized regions of the world. For example, by percentage of world total, leading shoe manufacturing regions are Europe 46 per cent, the U.S.S.R. 20 per cent, and the United States 16 per cent (Figure 18-6). Producers of leather goods sell a large share of their product to customers within their own countries, but they ship some products, particularly shoes, back to the very nations from which they import hides.

LUMBER AND WOOD PRODUCTS

Location and Characteristics

Lumber manufacturing is one of the most widely distributed industries, as Figure 18-7 reveals, and one of the smallest in scale, averaging 20 employees per factory.

Two-thirds of the establishments fall in the category of *primary* manufacturing. This category includes all industries whose raw materials come from the primary forms of economic production—forestry, fishing, bioculture, or mining. In the lumber business, the typical primary manufacturers are logging camps, log contractors, sawmills, and veneer mills, which process logs

Figure 18-6

SHOE MANUFACTURING

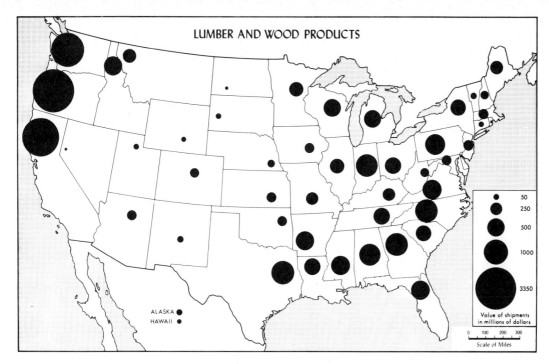

Figure 18-7

into boards, plywood, shingles, and excelsior. Some of the sawmills are actually portable factories that are moved about from week to week. But large sawmills are permanent. The *secondary* manufacturers, whose raw materials come from the primary ones, are typically mills that manufacture sash, doors, trim, wooden containers, kitchen cabinets, mobile homes, and prefabricated buildings.

Relationships

Raw Materials. Most lumber factories are located in forest regions as Figures 18-7 and 6-2 show. This is particularly true of the primary factories for two reasons: (1) Logs are difficult to transport, not only because of their bulkiness but also because of their low value compared with the cost of moving them, especially by truck or rail. (2) The weight-loss ratio is high; at least half of each log ends up as sawdust, bark, or odd-shaped boards—items for which there is often little use. This combustible waste matter presents a problem, since it cannot simply be dumped all over the countryside. The larger mills have so much that they build specially designed beehive furnaces to destroy it; this practice is becoming rare because of tighter laws designed to eliminate air pollution. In addition, in a few localities that are far from coal, the mills can sell sawdust and scrap for heating houses. Yet sawdust is not entirely a bother since the mills can burn some of it to meet their own fuel requirements. And some dust is chemically treated, heated, and compressed into salable sheets of "Prestwood."

Providing a large sawmill with raw materials requires several logging camps. These camps are usually moved from time to time through the forest as one area after another is harvested. Thus, a sawmill serves as a sort of nucleus for the numerous logging operations conducted in the region around it.

Frequently a similar relationship exists between a single planing mill and several sawmills that supply it with rough-sawn boards for planing and finishing down to precise measurements. Planing mills are not portable like some sawmills, so they tend to be larger than the sawmills that feed them.

Waterways. Permanent sawmills were traditionally often located at the confluences of rivers or along the coast. Because of the low costs of water transportation, mills at such sites could usually tap a vast source of logs upriver, so as to produce a steady flow of raw materials. By contrast, the small portable sawmills, which worked the interfluves, brought their logs overland. This is, of course, more expensive than floating them down watercourses; consequently, the overland hauls were comparatively short. That is why portable mills were moved close to where logging was going on. Today, logs usually move to the mill by truck, although water transport is, in some portions of the world, still important.

Markets. A large share of the products of United States lumber mills are destined for the northeastern part of the country. Until a few decades ago, this population heart of the nation was heavily forested. Indeed, lumbermen were in the vanguard as the pioneers moved through Ohio, Indiana, and Wisconsin. And the manufacture of wood products continues on in this great market region even though forests are severely depleted. One reason why the industry persists in the northeastern portion of the country is that freight rates on sash, door, and other wood products are higher than those on wood. Another reason is that the long-established mills enjoy an unusual freight-rate advantage, the fabrication-in-transit privilege. Under this arrangement, the railway companies permit lumber from the West Coast to be turned into doors in the Midwest and then shipped for sale into the East at a single through rate rather than at two joint rates. For example, Wisconsin is dotted with dozens of sash-and-door factories dating back to the 1800's, when Wisconsin was a forested state. These businesses would collapse if in-transit schedules were abolished. The fabrication-in-transit rates are to the wood-products industry what the milling-in-transit rates are to flour milling.

The World Pattern

Almost all of the world's lumber manufacturing is carried on in the industrial nations of the Northern Hemisphere. By percentage of world total, the leaders are as follows: United States 21 per cent, Canada 8, U.S.S.R. 27, Europe (mainly Scandinavia, France, and Germany) 20, and Japan 10. Principal exporters, however, are Canada 35 per cent, Sweden 17, and Finland 10.

FURNITURE

Location and Characteristics

The manufacture of furniture (including office and household furniture and partitions and fixtures) is highly

localized in the East (Figure 18-8). Over three-quarters of the employment in this industry is situated east of the Mississippi River; about half of these workers are north of the Ohio River and half are in the states to the south. When measured by states, furniture manufacturing shows a rather positive correlation with population, since the most populous states tend to be leaders in this industry. Measured in millions of dollars of value added, the top states are North Carolina 824, California 624, New York 396, Illinois 374, Michigan 363, Virginia 342, and Pennsylvania 314.

Furniture factories generally are small, averaging only 50 employees per plant, one of the smallest-scale industries in the nation. The main reason for the modest scale is that many styles of furniture require extensive hand work that can be performed in small establishments as efficiently as in large ones. Other styles, however, particularly the cheaper ones, can be mass-produced on assembly lines. Consequently, large-scale plants, averaging 150 employees, have recently come into being, particularly in North Carolina, which now leads the nation in making wood furniture.

Relationships

Markets. Although there has been a general shift to the Southeast, the furniture industry is still highly associated with populous regions, which would suggest that the industry is market oriented. This generalization is further supported by the amount of furniture-making in metropolitan areas. The New York-New Jersey metropolitan area alone has more employment in furniture manufacture than any state except North Carolina and California, and Los Angeles has more than any state except North Carolina and New York. These metropolitan areas, together with Greensboro, North Carolina, Grand Rapids, Michigan, and Philadelphia

Figure 18-8

account for almost a quarter of the nation's employment in the furniture industry.

In response to market, the furniture industry originally was settled in New England and along the Atlantic Seaboard. Then, as the center of the United States market moved westward, so, like the leather industry, did much of the furniture industry. However, some furniture companies moved south to the Piedmont where other powerful attractions were less-costly labor, lower taxes, and Appalachia's hardwood forests. The advantage of hardwoods is their strength; most softwoods make poor furniture.

Raw Materials. Today, most furniture factories are not located very close to their raw materials. Hardwoods, for instance, which are harvested and sawed into boards mostly in the South, are then shipped to northern factories. In recent years an increasing amount of furniture is being made of metal. For this material, the northeastern factories are somewhat closer to the source, since most metal-producing factories are in the same area.

The World Pattern

The manufacture of furniture as a commercial venture is widespread throughout the world. Small chairs, tables, and chests made from wood and woven fibers are made, at least in limited quantities, in a diversity of places such as the Philippines, Pakistan, India, South Africa, Colombia, and Britain. Yet most of the furniture that enters the channels of international exchange originates in the factories of Europe, Japan, and Anglo-America. This is particularly true for metal furniture, which has begun to account for an increasing, although still relatively small, proportion of the total output.

WOOD PULP

Location and Characteristics

Most of the United States' pulp mills, including some of the largest ones, are in Southern states, particularly along the Gulf of Mexico and the Atlantic Ocean and in the Appalachian highland. Elsewhere, northern New England, upper New York, the upper Midwestern states, and the Puget Sound-Willamette Valley region have sizable culsters of mills. Washington, Mississippi, and Wisconsin are all important states in the manufacture of wood pulp.

The transformation of logs into pulp requires both mechanical and chemical processes. These are diverse, depending on the type of paper desired. The logs are peeled to remove the bark and then, in the most frequently employed process, are chopped into small chips. The chips are boiled and treated with calcium bisulfite (or sometimes with caustic soda and sodium sulfide) to separate the woody fibers, which are discarded, from the cellulose fibers, which are sent through "beater

engines" that mix them into a homogeneous mass known as *wood pulp*.

Pulp-making establishments are large, covering several acres. Adjacent to the factory structures are storage spaces where logs are piled in huge stacks, 30 or 40 feet high. The average dimensions of pulpwood logs (termed "bolts" by people in the industry) are in lengths of from 6 to 8 feet, and in diameter of from 6 to 10 inches. There are 60 pulp mills in the country (not counting those grouped with paper mills), which employ 10,600 people, an average of 177 per plant. Pulp mills are thus one of the larger types of factory in the nation.

Relationships

Most pulp mills use softwood. Softwood is a term used by woodsmen to distinguish trees (such as the pine, larch, spruce, hemlock, and poplar) that are less dense and more easily worked than hardwoods (such as the oak, elm, maple, and walnut). It is possible to make paper from the cellulose material of hardwood, but the process is expensive and the resulting paper is unsatisfactory for many purposes. Pulp mills invariably locate in or near softwood forests for precisely the same reasons that sawmills locate near timber stands: a high weight-loss ratio.

In order to insure a steady supply of bolts, many a pulp company has gone into the business of tree farming. First it purchases vast tracts of land, often *marginal* farm land, with poor soil or some other handicap. These tracts are then planted with a specific type of tree good for pulping. The company then husbands the trees, protecting them against fire, insects, and diseases. Finally, the trees are harvested carefully by means of selective cutting—only the mature trees are cut for bolts, deformed and scraggly ones are thinned out, and only the promising saplings are permitted to remain.

One reason the southern states loom so large is that their mild humid climate permits trees to reach maturity more rapidly than in the North (see Chapter 6).

Another raw material pulp factories consume in tremendous quantities is water. Water is necessary for washing logs, boiling chips, and treating cellulose fibers. Since it must be fresh, most large-scale pulp mills are on rivers or lakes. In many instances the river or lake performs two additional functions: It provides a means of transportation (bolts are simply floated or towed to the mill) and it provides sorting ponds, in which bolts are classified in terms of size, or ownership, or any other criterion of significance at the moment.

Waste disposal is a problem. Liquid waste from pulp mills is abundant and smelly. Channeling such stuff into a municipal sewage system is usually discouraged by the community. In the past most mills have simply dumped the waste into the rivers from which they got their water. But this practice polluted many rivers, and in recent years several states have passed laws requiring pulp mills to treat their waste with

A roll of pulp, or sulphite, at the dry end of a pulp machine in Everett, Washington. (*Courtesy Weyerhaeuser Company.*)

chemicals to make it less obnoxious before dumping it into streams. Mills situated where streams enter salt water are often freed from these restrictions, however.

Pulp mills use great quantities of power in operating the machinery that removes bark, splinters the logs, and chips the splints. Large streams with rapids, falls, or enough of a drop to encourage dam construction can thus exert the added attraction of water power in the location of pulp mills.

The World Pattern

Most of the world's wood pulp is produced in those nations that are both highly industrialized and endowed with softwood forests. The leading manufacturing areas (Figure 18-9), by percentage of total world wood pulp manufacture, are the United States 38 per cent, Canada 16, Europe 26, U.S.S.R. 6, and Japan 9.

In international trade the leading exporting area is Scandinavia—Sweden, Finland, and Norway, in that order—37 per cent; Canada with 34 per cent is the largest exporting country.

PAPER AND ALLIED PRODUCTS

Location and Characteristics

Over half of the nation's paper, envelopes, bags, cartons, bread wrappers, stationery, decorations, and other paper products are made in the Northeast (Figure 18-10). The front-ranking states in order are New York, Pennsylvania, Illinois, Wisconsin, and Ohio. Leading cities are Chicago, New York, Philadelphia, and Los Angeles.

Paper factories convert pulp, waste paper, and rags into paper. The material is washed, soaked, and pulverized into a homogenerous fibrous mass which is then run through long machines—some a city block in length —which extract the water and roll the fibrous mixture into a uniform sheet. About half the solid raw material is

Figure 18-9

WOOD PULP PRODUCTION: LEADING COUNTRIES

PAPER & ALLIED PRODUCTS

Number of Employees
- 500
- 1,000
- 5,000
- 10,000
- 20,000
- 25,000

ALASKA
HAWAII
Honolulu

Selected SMSAs, Black
Remainder in State, Shaded

Scale of Miles
0   100   200   300

Figure 18-10

pulp, a third is waste paper, and much of the remainder consists of cotton and linen rags. But the proportion of these constituents varies, depending on the quality of paper being made. The best writing papers, for example, are made entirely from cloth rags. Coarser paper can be made from other fibers such as bagasse (sugar cane), straw, jute, and abaca.

Relationships

The paper industry as a whole is more market-oriented than raw material-oriented. Most of the paper mills in the United States are near their consumers, not only the manufacturers of stationery and printing paper but also those that make wrapping papers, decorating papers, and paperboard. The main reason for this pattern is that the value of most paper is low compared to its weight; consequently, it does not pay to ship it very far, since freight charges would eat up too large a percentage of its selling price. As a result, most paper factories are within 300 miles of most of their customers.

Many paper factories find it possible to locate near both their raw-material sources and their customers. This is particularly true for paper mills in the northeastern quarter of the country, for that is the foremost source region for waste paper (the main raw material used in making corrugated paper and packing boxes) and for rags (for stationery).

Factories that make newsprint and wrapping paper are exceptional. They tend to be raw-material oriented because they depend almost entirely on pulp, and it is usually more feasible to ship the papers than the pulp.

The World Pattern

The world pattern for paper and paperboard manufacture is similar to that for pulp. Leading areas by world share are the United States 36 per cent, Canada 8,

Europe 30 (with West Germany and Finland the leaders), the U.S.S.R. 5, and Japan 11. But the leading exporters are Canada 26 per cent and Scandinavia 29 per cent (with Sweden and Finland predominant).

PRINTING AND PUBLISHING

The locational pattern of the United States printing and publishing industry is portrayed in Figure 18-11. About two-thirds of the nation's printing is done in the Northeast: in order of importance the foremost states are New York, Illionis, California, Pennsylvania, and Ohio. New York, Chicago, and Los Angeles are the leading cities.

Printing and publishing make up a highly diversified industry: Some plants specialize in newspapers, others in periodicals, books, or telephone directories, while others concentrate on advertising materials. Newspaper factories employ a third of all those in the printing industry, but commercial print shops are the most numerous—and also the smallest—for the nation has 22,000 of them averaging only 15 employees each.

Printing is closely associated with urban settlements where most of the nation's readers live and where most of the businesses are located that need advertising brochures and letterheads. Most publishers of textbooks, novels, and trade journals tend toward large cities. The New York City vicinity is unquestionably the nation's capital for the printing and publishing industry; Table 18-2 clearly illustrates the stature of New York in various segments of the business. It is because the printed products are highly valuable in relation to shipping costs that they can bear transport charges over long distances and therefore can be marketed throughout the nation from publishers in a few large cities.

We can generalize, then, by saying that there is a high correlation between population and the printing

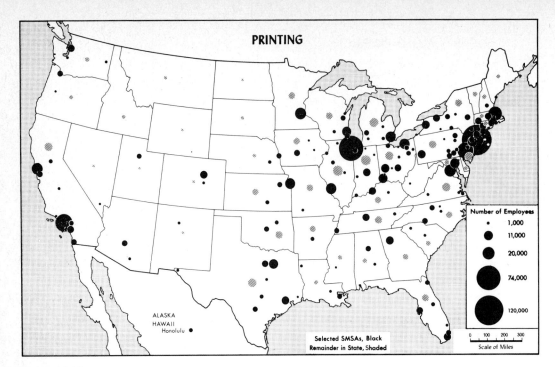

Figure 18-11

Table 18-2

Employment in the Printing and Publishing Industry

Type of Printing	United States in Thousands	New York-Northeastern New Jersey in Thousands	Percentage of U.S. Total
Newspapers	348.5	27.5	8
Periodicals	66.5	26.9	40
Books	98.1	26.1	27
Commercial printing	343.8	43.9	13
Bookbinding	25.1	7.0	28
Printing trade services	46.6	11.3	24
Greeting cards	23.5	2.0	9
Business forms	38.6	2.2	6
TOTAL	1,056.1	163.8	16

Source: U.S. Bureau of the Census, *1972 Census of Manufactures* (1975).

industry; as a whole, this endeavor tends to be market-oriented. There is one important additional relationship of daily newspapers with a raw material: If we consider "local news" to be a basic "raw material," then the same region that constitutes the newspaper's market has another function in generating one of the prime ingredients.

The World Pattern

On a world basis, the location of printing and publishing correlates closely with economic advancement and high rates of literacy. When reliable information is available for all parts of the world, it may be possible to measure a high correlation between the location of printing and publishing with that of commercial apparel production, number of telephones, educational level of the populace, and standard of living indices.

SUGGESTED READINGS

AIROV, JOSEPH, *The Location of the Synthetic Fiber Industry*, Cambridge, 1959.

American Paper Institute, *The Statistics of Paper* (annual), New York.

BARR, BRENTON M., "Regional Variation in Soviet Pulp and Paper Production," *Annals of the Association of American Geographers*, 1971, pp. 45–64.

——, and FAIRBAUN, KENNETH J., "Some Observations on the Environment of the Firm: Locational Behavior of Kraft Pulp Mills in the Interior of British Columbia," *The Professional Geographer*, 1974, pp. 19–26.

BURGY, J. HERBERT, *The New England Cotton Textile Industry: A Study in Industrial Geography*, Baltimore, 1932, 246 pp.

HARDWICK, WALTER G., "The Persistence of Vancouver as the Focus for Wood Processing in Coastal British Columbia," *The Canadian Geographer*, 1965, pp. 92–96.

SEIFRIED, NEIL R., "Locational Change in the Canadian Leather Footwear Industry," *The Canadian Geographer*, 1972, pp. 309–322.

STAFFORD, HOWARD A., JR., "Factors in the Location of the Paper-Board Container Industry," *Economic Geography*, 1960, pp. 260–266.

STEED, GUY P. F., "Centrality and Locational Change: Printing, Publishing, and Clothing in Montreal and Toronto," *Economic Geography*, 1976, pp. 193–205.

——, "Internal Organization, Firm Integration, and Locational Change: The Northern Ireland Linen Complex, 1954–1964," *Economic Geography*, 1971, pp. 371–383.

——, "The Northern Ireland Linen Complex, 1950–1970," *Annals of the Association of American Geographers*, 1974, pp. 397–408.

——, "Standardization, Scale, Incubation, and Inertia: Montreal and Toronto Clothing Industries" *The Canadian Geographer*, 1976, pp. 298–309.

WHEELER, JAMES O., "Location of Mobile Home Manufacturing: A Multidimensional Scaling Analysis," *The Professional Geographer*, 1976, pp. 261–266.

CHAPTER
19

mineral-processing industries

A 170-ton truck and a 225-ton truck (right) dump into a crusher at the Cyprus Pima Mine, south of Tucson, Arizona. The crushed ore is carried to storage piles by the conveyor system shown in the background. (*Ray Manley photo courtesy Cyprus Pima Mining Company.*)

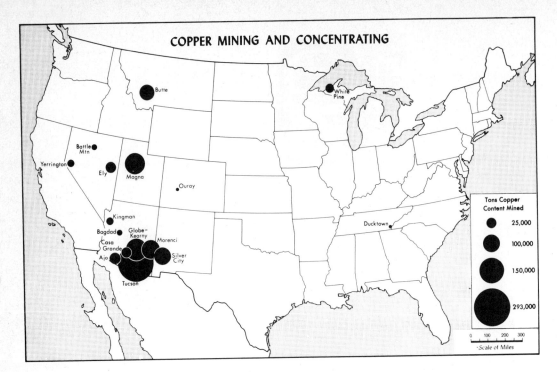

COPPER MINING AND CONCENTRATING

Tons Copper Content Mined

25,000
100,000
150,000
293,000

Scale of Miles
0   100   200   300

Figure 19-1

Few minerals are in usable form when they are dug out of the ground. Consequently, mining is closely related to manufacturing. In Chapters 19 and 20 we shall take up the industrial activities associated with several important minerals. Chapter 20 is concentrated largely on steel. But the present chapter deals with a trio of mineral-processing industries, chosen to illustrate different ways of upgrading the value of substances by changing their form. These industries are: copper processing, aluminum processing, and pertroleum refining. For each, the United States will serve as a case-study area, after which we shall take a look at the world pattern.

PRIMARY COPPER MANUFACTURING

Copper is not abundant in the earth's crust, and rarely does it occur in pure form. Usually the atoms of copper are chemically combined with other elements (particularly oxygen and sulfur), and these compounds in turn are mechanically mixed with numerous other substances. To extract usable copper metal from copper ore—*primary manufacturing*—generally requires three steps: concentrating, smelting, and refining.

Copper Concentrating

The first step in transforming ore to metallic copper is *concentrating*. The rocky mass excavated from mines is hauled to concentrating mills where it goes through the "froth-flotation process": The material is crushed, soaked in water, and mixed with oils. When that mixture is agitated, the copper-bearing materials float to the top and are separated. The discovery of the froth-flotation process in 1914 opened up many new regions of copper

mining by making it economically possible to process low-grade ores.

The location of copper concentrating mills in the United States is shown on Figure 19-1. From that map we learn that almost all this phase of copper manufacturing takes place in a copper belt running from Arizona to Montana. Several Arizona mills alone—the largest is near Tucson—perform 50 per cent of the country's copper concentrating. But the distinction of having the largest single mill in the nation belongs to Magna, Utah (a settlement about ten miles west of Salt Lake City), which shows up prominently on Figure 19-1.

The locational pattern of concentrating mills correlates closely with that of copper mining. Indeed, nearly all concentrating takes place within a few miles of the mines. The reason for such close affinity is a high weight-loss ratio: Of every 100 tons of copper ore processed, an average of approximately $97\frac{1}{2}$ tons is worthless waste. Even the remaining $2\frac{1}{2}$ tons consist of various impurities in chemical union with copper.

Thus, copper concentrating provides an excellent example of a raw-material-oriented industry, again illustrating the principle: The higher the weight-loss ratio, the stronger the tendency for the factory to locate near its raw material.

Copper Smelting

The purpose of smelting is to separate other elements, especially sulfur and oxygen, from the copper atoms. Chemically, the procedure is to convert copper sulfides (which survive the concentrating process) into oxides which are then reduced under great heat to relatively pure metal. Assuming that the weight-loss ratio for

Grinding of copper ore to a sandlike fineness is the first step in the reduction, or concentrating, of the ore to a point where the metallic copper can be recovered. The ore, mixed with water and chemicals, is fed into large rod or ball mills in which it is pulverized. (*Courtesy Kennecott Copper Corporation.*)

copper smelters is 60 per cent, the $2\frac{1}{2}$ tons of material which remain of the 100 tons that entered the concentrators are smelted into $1\frac{1}{2}$ tons of waste and one ton of "blister copper," which is 99 per cent pure metal. The impurities in blister copper are usually gold, silver, lead, and zinc, which cannot be smelted out. Since the weight-loss ratio is fairly high, smelters usually locate rather close to concentrators. Most of the 18 copper smelters in the United States (Figure 19-2) are so situated. Arizona alone has seven of the 18. All told, the copper-mining states contain 14 of the nation's 18 smelters and account for 90 per cent of its copper-smelting capacity.

Yet, since the smelting weight-loss ratio of 60 per cent is considerably lower than the 97 per cent ratio that prevails in concentrating, the location of smelters correlates less closely with the location of their raw-material sources (the concentrating mills) than does the location of the concentrating mills with the location of their raw-material sources (the copper mines). Accordingly, some smelters are hundreds of miles from concentrators. Both the Atlantic Seaboard (New York City area) and the Pacific Seaboard (Tacoma) boast copper smelters, though they have no concentrators. These coastal smelters depend on foreign supplies of copper concentrate.

Figure 19-2

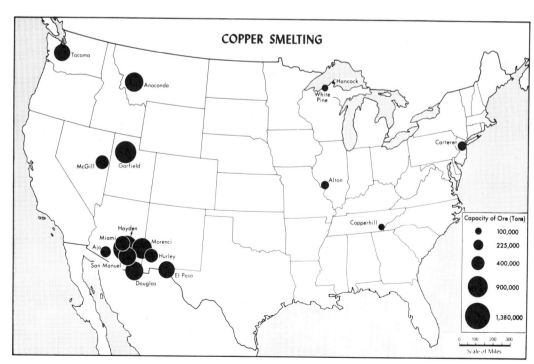

Copper Refining

Even though blister copper is 99 per cent pure metal, it is not suitable for manufacturing electric wires, cooking utensils, and other products. The gold, silver, lead, and zinc impurities must be extracted—and this must be done through electrolysis. In this process, blister copper is immersed in a bath of acidulated copper sulfate through which an electric current is passed. The ratio of weight loss in copper refining is extremely small, scarcely one per cent of the weight of the refinery's raw material.

Not only is the weight-loss ratio low, but what is "lost" is valuable. So, it is worthwhile to pay freight on it along with the copper. Consequently, the attraction of

copper-mining regions is substantially less for refineries than for smelters.

The nation has 21 copper refineries (Figure 19-3); the most productive are on the East Coast, with metropolitan New York and Baltimore the leading centers. One large refinery is located on Long Island (on an East River tributary), while four still larger ones are in the New Jersey suburbs of Perth Amboy and Carteret. The New York group accounts for 22 per cent of the United States total copper-refining capacity, whereas Baltimore's two refineries account for 21 per cent. When a small refinery at Reading, Pennsylvania is included, the combined capacity in the Northeast is 44 per cent of the nation's total. Seven refineries are located in or near the western copper belt; Arizona has two, and New Mexico one. Close by is El Paso, Texas, with two refineries, one of which is the largest refinery in the

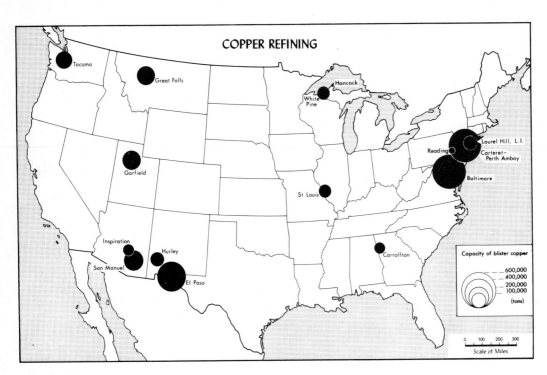

Figure 19-3

Figure 19-4

FLOW DIAGRAM: MANUFACTURE OF AMERICAN COPPER ORE

Some smelters are tied to a single mine, but this one, located in Douglas, Arizona, processes ores from several different mines in southern Arizona. (*Courtesy Phelps Dodge Corporation.*)

country. Utah has a refinery at Garfield, and Montana has one at Great Falls. The capacity of these seven copper-belt refineries is 42 per cent of the nation's total. The remainder of the country's capacity is in refineries located in Tacoma, Washington; St. Louis, Missouri (two refineries); Carrollton, Georgia; and Hancock and White Pine, Michigan.

The location of the copper-refining industry illustrates two principles: (a) Factories with low weight-loss ratios tend to be less raw material-oriented than factories with high ratios, and (b) if the weight lost consists of valuable substances (such as gold and silver, in this case), then the attraction of the raw material region for locating the factory is further weakened. For these reasons, in the matter of location, refineries correlate even less with their raw-material sources (the smelters) than smelters do with theirs. Smelters, in turn, correlate less closely with the source of their raw materials than do concentrating mills. These principles are illustrated by the data in Table 19-1.

Table 19-1

United States: Copper-Manufacturing Industries

Industry	Weight-Loss Ratio	Coefficient of Correlation*
Copper concentrating	97.5%	+0.98
Copper smelting	60 %	+0.35
Copper refining	1 %	−0.72

Source: Computed from data in *Minerals Yearbook* published by the United States Government, Department of the Interior, Bureau of Mines.

*Between tons of raw material produced and tons of product produced, on a state basis. A coefficient of correlation measures the strength of relationship between two variables. It will be discussed more fully in Chapter 29. In these computations, the figures employed to measure "tons of raw material produced" are as follows: For refineries, tons of smelter product were used; for smelters, tons of concentrate product were used; for concentrators, tons of copper ore mined were used. States with no production in any of these three items were omitted from the calculations.

Copper Market

With completion of the refining process, primary manufacturing is over. The copper has been brought to a form that is workable for fashioning many objects of utility. The production of these items constitutes *secondary* manufacturing. It occurs in the diverse factories that fabricate electric wire, electric generators, electric motors, hardware, cooking utensils, and so on. These industries, hence the market for the refineries, are located largely in the northeastern quadrant of the nation (Figures 20-6 and 20-7), particularly in Connecticut. In the early 1800's, that state became the nation's leader in brass and copper fabrication and indeed, for many decades, copper prices on the national market have been synonymous with prices in the Connecticut Valley, the "hardware heart" of the United States.

Primary Copper-Manufacturing Regions

When the regional patterns of concentrating, smelting, and refining are synthesized, two regional types emerge. One is close to copper-mining areas, the other on the margin of fabricating areas.

Within Mining Country Most regions of copper mining embrace all three stages of copper manufacturing. The western copper belt in particular contains 94 per cent of the concentrating in the country, 87 per cent of the smelting, and about half as much of the refining. In some places all three types of factories are close to the local mine as in northern Utah and upper Michigan. Some localities have only two factories: for instance, a concentrator and smelter in eastern Nevada, or smelter and refinery in El Paso. Elsewhere factories are isolated: In Montana the concentrator is at the mines in Butte, the smelter is at Anaconda 20 miles to the west, and the refinery is at Great Falls, 100 miles to the northeast on the Missouri River. Where the smelters and refineries are in different settlements from those of the concentrators but still within the general mining region, they tend to locate on the line of movement from mine to market. For instance, a large share of Arizona's and New Mexico's copper moves eastward, and much of it is refined at El Paso, which is on the eastern edge of the copper area and on a mainline railroad toward eastern fabricators.

Near Fabricating Regions Manufacturing regions far from copper mines account for 4 per cent of the nation's smelting and 45 per cent of its refining. Smelters in these areas are frequently alongside refineries (compare Figures 19-2 and 19-3). These refineries enjoy three favorable relationships: (1) They are close to their market, the fabricating mills. (2) They are close to foreign sources of copper. This is why a *port* location on the margin of the nation's main fabricating region is advantageous for a copper refinery in a nation whose mines do not meet all its copper needs. (3) They are close to scrap copper. In addition to blister, United States refineries also consume large amounts of scrap, most of which is "produced," so to speak, in northeastern states.

Relationships to Foreign Areas

Before 1939, the United States exported more copper than it imported. World War II, with its tremendous demand for electrical equipment, abruptly reversed that relationship. United States exports now total 200,000 to 300,000 tons of copper and her imports total 100,000 to 200,000 tons of which about 50 per cent is pure copper from foreign refineries, 40 per cent is blister copper from foreign smelters, and 10 per cent is "matte" (a product which has been only partially smelted). By percentage of total copper imports, these are the principal areas of supply: Canada 36 per cent, Peru 26 per cent, and Chile 12 per cent.

The World Pattern

Types of Region. The world can be divided up in exactly the same manner as the United States. One type of region refines more copper than it produces, and, therefore, must import semiprocessed materials. As Table 19-2 indicates, Japan, Belgium, West Germany, and the United States belong to this first type, since they refine considerably more copper (almost 50 per cent of the world's total) than they produce (less than 25 per cent). Europe, in fact, is largely devoid of copper ore.

A second type of area produces more ore than it refines. The Katanga district (straddling the Zaire-Zambia boundary), Canada, and Chile are of this type. Much of the former's copper moves to Europe; much of the latter's to the United States. Since central Africa possesses the greatest potential hydroelectric power on the globe, it will probably not be many years before

Table 19-2

Copper Production and Manufacturing: Percentage of World Total by Leading Areas

Area	Mine Production	Smelter Production	Refining Production
America	47%	38%	37%
United States	21	20	25
Canada	11	6	6
Chile	10	8	5
Peru	3	2	—
Europe	6	12	18
Yugoslavia	2	2	2
Poland	2	2	2
West Germany	—	4	5
Spain	—	1	1
Belgium	—	—	4
United Kingdom	—	—	2
Asia	6	15	14
Japan	1	13	11
Philippines	3	—	—
China	2	2	2
Africa	20	19	12
Zaire	7	6	3
South Africa	2	2	1
Zambia	10	9	8
Oceania	5	2	—
Australia	3	2	2
Papua New Guinea	2	—	—
U.S.S.R.	14	14	15

Source: American Bureau of Metal Statistics, *Year Book* (June, 1974).

enough dams are built to harness the power needed to feed refineries with adequate electricity to take care of Katanga's copper. Zambia is already a major producer of refined copper.

There is a third regional type, one where concentrating and refining are nearly equal. The U.S.S.R. and Australia fall into this category. They refine what they concentrate and neither export nor import very much concentrate or blister.

Control of the Copper Industry. The regions that consume the most copper are the home bases for the companies that control the mining and manufacturing. American firms oversee about half the world's production, principally in the United States, but also in varying degrees in Mexico and other Western Hemisphere nations. British companies control perhaps a quarter of the total with operations largely in Africa, Canada, and Australia. This pattern of control conforms with a principle of geography that investment capital and entrepreneurs tend to move from markets to areas of primary production. This pattern is changing, however, judging from actions in Mexico, Chile, and other countries, which have tended to greatly reduce the roll of foreign investors in developing nations.

PRIMARY ALUMINUM MANUFACTURING

Aluminum constitutes 8 per cent of the earth's crust, a larger proportion than that of any other metal or element except silicon and oxygen. However, it never occurs in pure form, always in combination with oxygen and often with other elements in a variety of minerals, only one of which—bauxite—contains enough aluminum to pay for the cost of extraction.

There are two types of plants engaged in the primary manufacturing of aluminum: (a) *alumina factories*, which separate out most impurities from bauxite, leaving aluminum oxide, or alumina, and (b) *aluminum factories*, which break down aluminum oxide into its two constituents. Because these two industries differ in both location and spatial relationships, each merits separate consideration. (A word about terminology: In the aluminum industry and the copper industry the terms *concentrate* and *refine* are used dissimilarly. Thus, alumina factories refine bauxite and aluminum factories concentrate alumina.)

Alumina Factories

Alumina factories are clustered in the south central part of the United States (Figure 19-5). Six are strung along the Gulf Coast, from Texas to Alabama, and two mills are in Arkansas. These factories consume three types of raw materials: bauxite, fuel, and caustic soda. The fuel is burned to supply heat in the mechanical

separation of impurities from bauxite, which is crushed and baked in rotating kilns. The aluminum-bearing residue is then soaked in caustic soda, which removes all other impurities with the exception of oxygen.

The weight-loss ratio is high enough—on the average it takes 100 tons of bauxite to make 40 tons of alumina—to discourage long hauls of bauxite by expensive forms of transportation, such as trucks and trains. Therefore, *inland* bauxite mines tend to have alumina factories close by, as in western Arkansas where 85 per cent of the nation's bauxite is mined. But the weight-loss ratio is still low enough to encourage long shipments of bauxite by water. The Gulf Coast mills feed on bauxite arriving by water, the main source regions being Jamaica, the Dominican Republic, and Surinam. In fact, for every ton of domestic bauxite mined, the United States imports 6 tons of Latin American ore, which helps explain the role of coast and river mills.

If importing aluminum ore to coastal mills is feasible, why isn't copper ore shipped to coastal concentrators? The answer lies in the ratio of dross to metal: 5000 tons of dry cargo would yield 1000 tons of metal from average bauxite but only 50 tons of metal from average copper ore.

From the standpoint of time of development, the East St. Louis mill was the first to be constructed in 1902. Not until 1938 was a second one built in Mobile, Alabama. Then, during World War II, three more were put up (Hurricane Creek, Arkansas; Baton Rouge, Louisiana; and Listerhill, Alabama). Since the war six more have been built, one in Arkansas, two in Texas, two

Figure 19-5

in Louisiana, and one on St. Croix, Virgin Islands. Thus, since its inception, alumina manufacturing in the United States has been a phenomenon of the south central portion of the country.

Aluminum Factories

These are located in three widely separated areas: the Pacific Northwest, the South, and the Northeast (Figure 19-5). The geography of aluminum manufacture may be understood more easily with an historical orientation, because different factors operated at different times to influence the location of aluminum production.

1895 to 1940. The nation's first aluminum mill was constructed at Niagara Falls in 1895; all the alumina processed was imported from Germany, and the electricity required was generated at the falls. In 1903 a second and smaller refinery was built at Massena, New York, adjoining a hydroelectric power plant on the St. Lawrence River. This was the year that the United States began to produce its own alumina (at East St. Louis, where Illinois coal and South American bauxite were brought together) which was then shipped to Niagara Falls. During World War I two additional concentrators (that is, aluminum factories) were constructed near hydroelectric plants in the southern Appalachians (Alcoa, Tennessee, and Badin, North Carolina). These four concentrators, operated by a single company, The Aluminum Company of America ("Alcoa"), supplied all the nation's aluminum until World War II broke out.

1940 to 1946 The sudden demand for lightweight metals in warplanes caused an intense shortage of aluminum. Alcoa hastily constructed a new mill at Vancouver, Washington; but the United States government, convinced that one lone company could not meet the nation's need, took a rare step—it itself hurried into the business. The government built and then operated seven new concentrators, one in Arkansas near bauxite, one in northern Alabama near hydroelectric plants on the Tennessee River, one in Massena, New York (a large new mill replacing the one built in 1903, which had been closed) and *four* in the Pacific Northwest where several power installations had been constructed in major river beds. During the war the aluminum industry consumed one-fifth of the electricity produced in the Pacific Northwest. These northwestern mills were far from alumina factories, and all the alumina they processed was hauled by rail from Arkansas and the Gulf—one of the longest rail hauls of bulk goods in the United States.

1946 to Present. Since World War II the federal government has either sold its concentrators to private companies, new competitors of Alcoa, or closed them. Alcoa dismantled its Niagara Falls plant, which was obsolete, and built a new one on the Texas coast. Other companies have constructed or are in the process of constructing new aluminum mills—generally in the South and the Ohio Valley.

Power Supply. To understand the locational patterns in these three periods, we must be familiar with the single dominant relationship in the placement of aluminum refineries: access to electric power. For electrolysis is the most feasible method for separating aluminum atoms from oxygen atoms in the alumina molecule. In this process, electricity is passed between carbon anodes and cathodes through the mineral cryolite. The mineral melts, forming a bath to which the alumina is added. Under these conditions, the oxygen in the alumina unites with the carbon in the anodes, forming carbon dioxide and leaving the aluminum to puddle at the bottom and be drained off as crude castings called "pigs." To produce one ton of aluminum requires 2 tons of alumina, $\frac{3}{4}$ ton of carbon anodes, and 20,000 kilowatt-hours of electricity—enough to service an eight-room house with six persons, electric washing machine, dishwasher, mangle, roaster, toaster, and other conventional electric gadgets for a full decade.

Because the power must be both electric and abundant, aluminum concentrators have tended to settle near the cheapest available source—thus, the mills at Niagara Falls, in the Tennessee River Valley, and in the Pacific Northwest: all areas of extensive hydroelectric power production. In the past three decades, however, improvements in techniques for manufacturing electricity from steam explain the birth of concentrators in the South, where natural gas serves as the fuel, and in the coal-rich upper Ohio Valley. Plans for future expansion call for increases in the East and South—near coal and gas. Apparently the era of supremacy of hydroelectric power sites for aluminum concentrating in the United States is over.

Market Regions for Aluminum. The market for refined aluminum consists of airplane manufacturers and a wide variety of fabricators—those who make storm windows, ladders, hardware, and a rapidly increasing number of other items. Indeed, the increase is so great that United States factories now use more aluminum than any other metal except iron. Most of these factories are located in the northeastern part of the country (see Chapter 20, Figures 20-6, and 20-7). Notice the contrast in locational pattern between aluminum concentrators and copper refineries: The former have displayed much less inclination than the latter to be near their market. Aluminum mills can afford to keep their distance, though, because the value of aluminum sheets, tubes, bars, and other forms is high relative to their weight, upon which freight rates are assessed. Besides, it is cheaper to ship aluminum from concentrator to market than to "ship" electricity (or tremendous tonnages of fuel for generating electricity).

Relationships with Foreign Areas. The United States exports only small amounts of aluminum and imports about 80 per cent of her bauxite requirements. Of her imports, approximately three-fifths come from Jamaica, and a fifth from Surinam. Before World War II we mined almost as much as we imported, but since then our degree of dependence on foreign regions has steadily increased.

The World Pattern

Four areas account for over 80 per cent of the world's aluminum manufacture (see Table 19-3): (1) Anglo-America produces over 40 per cent of the total. The United States is the world leader, and Canada accounts for a perhaps surprisingly large amount. (2) Western Europe refines about 20 per cent. (3) The Soviet Union and Japan together refine about as much as Western Europe.

Canada. Though lacking in bauxite, Canada has aluminum mills at the extreme eastern and western parts of the country. In 1901 a concentrator was built 60 miles southwest of Quebec City at Shawinigan Falls on the St. Maurice River, a few miles upstream from its confluence with the St. Lawrence River. Alumina was imported from Germany. This mill is still in operation, but limited water power restricts its expansion. In 1926, Aluminium Limited of Canada ("Alcan"), which operated the Shawinigan Falls concentrator, built a new plant in a forested wilderness 120 miles northeast of Quebec on the Saguenay River. The attraction of that remote spot was tremendous hydroelectric potential, for the water drops 300 feet between Lake St. John and the St. Lawrence River (Figure 19-6). At first, alumina was imported, but in 1928 an alumina mill was added. Bauxite arrives by ocean freighters from Jamaica and Guyana at Port Alfred, 40 miles up the Saguenay at the head of navigation; thence, it is taken by rail 20 miles to the mills. Personnel to operate the port facilities, the railroad, the refinery, and the concentrators were all brought in from elsewhere, and a new community, Arvida, displaced the forest surrounding the mills.

Western British Columbia also has a large aluminum mill, a development lured to a wet, rugged wilderness by potential water power resources. An initial

Table 19-3

Bauxite and Aluminum: Leading Nations by Percentage of World Total, 1972

Region	Bauxite	Aluminum
North America		
Dominican Republic	2	—
Jamaica	19	—
United States	3	34
Canada	—	8
South America		
Guyana	6	—
Surinam	10	1
Europe		
France	5	4
Greece	4	1
Hungary	4	1
U.S.S.R.	7	11
Yugoslavia	3	1
West Germany	—	4
Netherlands	—	2
Norway	—	5
United Kingdom	—	2
Africa		
Ghana	1	1
Guinea	4	—
Asia		
India	3	2
Indonesia	2	—
Malaysia	2	—
China	1	1
Japan	—	9
Oceania		
Australia	22	2

Source: U.S. Bureau of Mines, *Minerals Yearbook, 1972* (1974).

Figure 19-6

SAGUENAY ALUMINUM MILLING AREA

handicap was that most of the water drained along gentle gradients to the east, whereas the steep western slopes had very few streams. But by an ingenious plan, the Canadians reversed the direction of flow of a stream to fall down the precipitous western side of the mountains. This was accomplished by damming the Nechako River (which flows east) and creating a lake 120 miles long (Figure 19-7). At the lake's western end a 25-foot tunnel was drilled 10 miles to drain the lake *westward* to Kemano where a power house was constructed 2585 feet below the level of the lake. The potential for power development from a large volume of water with so great a waterhead exceeds the potential of that on the Saguenay. Electricity generated at Kemano is transmitted 50 miles to Kitimat (on the shores of Douglas Channel) which is accessible to ocean-going vessels delivering alumina and bauxite.

Canada is a prize demonstration of how a region with absolutely no native ore and scarcely any domestic market (she exports a large share of her aluminum to the United States and Europe) can be a dominant world figure in an industry that requires large amounts of power. The Canadian experience again illustrates the principle that aluminum production is a power-oriented industry.

Europe. The aluminum industry was born in Europe in 1886, France and Germany being the early leaders. Today, France, along with Greece, still supplies a large portion of the bauxite for western European mills. In the production of alumina and aluminum, Norway, France, and West Germany pace the continent. Germany is the largest link in a chain of aluminum nations that encircle the Alps. The largest single producer, however, is Norway, which, like Canada, lacks both ore and market but is blessed with power. All told, western Europe accounts for about 12 per cent of the world's bauxite and 20 per cent of the refined aluminum, so she does not figure nearly as much as Anglo-America in long ocean movements of materials.

U.S.S.R. Before World War II, the Soviet Union's largest aluminum factory was at Zaporozhye near the large dam in the Dnepr River at Dnepropetrovsk. This mill depended almost entirely on Hungarian bauxite. A smaller mill at Volkhov used low-grade ores that came from east of Leningrad. Both of these factories were destroyed by the German army in World War II. But just before the war started, at Kamensk on the eastern flanks of the southern Ural Mountains, the Russians built a third plant to take advantage of Ural bauxite and local lignite for thermal electricity. Later, far to the east in Stalinsk (Novokuznetsk) a fourth mill was constructed, equipped with machinery hastily evacuated from Volkhov, and based on bauxite from the Kuzbass field.

After the war the Russians rebuilt the Volkhov and Zaporozhye mills, using machinery expropriated from Germany. A large new mill was built at Krasnoturinsk in the northern Urals to process the bauxite there, some

Figure 19-7

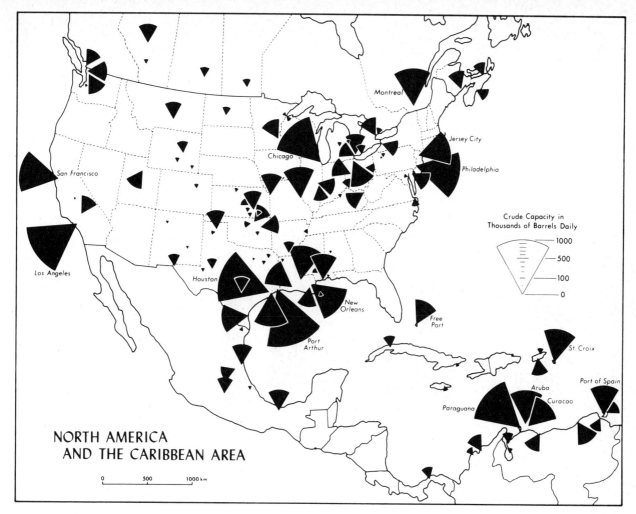

Figure 19-8

PETROLEUM REFINING

Location and Characteristics

The locational pattern of petroleum refining in the United States (Figure 19-8) reveals a few places with large refineries—Philadelphia, Houston, Los Angeles, Chicago, and Port Arthur—while numerous small refining centers are scattered elsewhere—in Texas, Oklahoma, Kansas, and the Rocky Mountain states in particular.

Refineries have several distinguishing characteristics that set limits on their location. They require a lot of land (particularly for storage tanks), they emit an obnoxious odor, and they present some danger of explosion. Accordingly, they are usually located on the outskirts of settlements or even in rural areas. Indeed, although many of the symbols on Figure 19-8 are identified by names of metropolitan areas, the refineries may

be actually in lesser-known suburbs such as Whiting (Chicago) and Marcus Hook (Philadelphia).

Petroleum refining is one of those rare industries in which the weight-loss ratio is zero. Besides, there is a volume-gain, for 1000 barrels of crude oil, when heated and distilled, yield more than 1000 barrels of kerosene, gasoline, fuel oil, or many other products that vaporize at different temperatures.

A petroleum refinery processes only one raw material, but over 100 products result. The steps for processing crude oil are so highly mechanized that few employees are needed. Indeed, labor accounts for only 6 per cent of the total value of payrolls and materials for the industry. On the other hand, payments for crude oil account for no less than 75 per cent of total cost of materials.

Relationships

Petroleum refineries can be classified by location into two types: those within (or on the margin of) resource regions and those within (or on the margin of) markets.

Refineries near Oil Fields. Here is a clear capsule description of the installations in the oil regions:

Many refineries are located on or near the oil fields. They are usually rather small. In Anglo-America inland refining centers of this type are numerous. They roughly outline the main oil field. Compare [on Figure 19–8] northern Texas, Oklahoma, and Kansas in the large Mid-Continent field [see Chapter 15] with the denser populated southeastern states which have virtually no oil production and very little inland refining capacity. Several . . . refining centers located on or near oil fields are . . . rather small compared to centers located in areas of maximum market potential or in shipping ports.[1]

In addition to the Mid-Continent field, refineries have been established in the oil fields of western Pennsylvania, Ohio, Michigan, Illinois, the Gulf Coast, the Rocky Mountain states, and the prairie provinces of Canada.

One reason that refineries within oil fields tend to be small is that the life of an individual oil pool tends to be short (approximately 25 years), discouraging companies from investing capital in the construction of large works. Besides, since transport costs on crude oil are slightly lower than those on petroleum products, firms are discouraged from establishing many large refineries within oil fields that have no large contiguous market. Most of the products of the small inland refineries move to market by truck or rail. Because of the expense this represents, their customers are principally in the immediate hinterland.

There are only a few enormous refineries within or on the edge of oil fields. Invariably, these few have three attributes. (1) They are in or near huge fields that produce large volumes of crude oil—volumes greatly exceeding the demands of local customers. (2) They are in port cities with access to deep-water shipping. Port Arthur, New Orleans, Baton Rouge, Houston, and Corpus Christi are examples of this type. (3) They are sustained by sales to numerous distant markets that lack oil resources and sufficient demand, as yet, to support a large refinery of their own. It is cheaper for such localities to import refined products from an efficient large refinery elsewhere than to run a less efficient small operation of their own.

Refineries within Market Areas. The northeastern quadrant of the United States is by far the nation's biggest market for petroleum products. Although the oil industry started there—in Pennsylvania—the Northeast today is relatively unimportant in oil production. Consequently it is an oil-deficit region and millions of barrels of petroleum are shipped in. Some of it arrives in processed forms, but most of it arrives as crude oil to be refined within the market region. The Delaware River estuary downstream from Philadelphia supports

[1]Gunnar Alexandersson, "The Oil Refineries of the World—A Case Study," *Proceedings* of IGU Regional Conference in Japan, 1957, p. 266.

one of the largest single concentrations of refineries in the world. Several other seaports between Massachusetts and Virginia stand out on Figure 19-8, and all receive crude oil by ocean-going tankers from such places as Texas, Louisiana, and Venezuela.

Within the northeastern market region a few centers are inland, however—Chicago, East St. Louis (Wood River), and Toledo. These places are served by pipelines from the Mid-Continent field; in addition, the first two cities, being on the Mississippi-Illinois waterway system, receive large volumes of crude oil by barge.

Elsewhere in the nation other refining centers have also come into existence to serve surrounding markets: for instance, Kansas City, Denver, Salt Lake City, and San Francisco. Los Angeles is unique in that it is endowed with both a substantial urban market and extensive oil resources; accordingly, Los Angeles is one of the nation's major refining centers.

There are four over-all reasons why large refineries are set up in large markets, even when such areas are barren of oil. First, it is easier to bring in one material and distill it centrally into 100 different products for subsequent distribution to surrounding consumers than to bring in 100 different products from refineries in distant oil fields. A second reason is the volume-gain factor mentioned earlier; it is cheaper to ship a small volume of crude oil than a larger aggregate volume of all its derivatives. Third, tanker shipping rates are lower on crude oil than on its products because "dirty" carriers can be used to haul crude oil whereas tankers carrying gasoline and kerosene must be clean. Fourth, there is a greater *evaporation loss* in transporting refinery products than in transporting crude oil. For example, for every 1000 barrels of crude oil shipped from the Gulf Coast to the Eastern Seaboard, the evaporation loss is approximately ten barrels, but for refinery products it averages about 50 barrels.

Products Demanded. For the United States as a whole, the demand for petroleum products breaks down as follows: gasoline 39 per cent, fuel oil 33 per cent, liquified gases 7 per cent, jet fuel 6 per cent, kerosene and other products 15 per cent. These figures reflect the ubiquity of the automobile. The demand for the foremost petroleum product is nationwide, so refineries are rather widespread throughout most of the country. We shall note a revealing contrast to this situation when we discuss refineries.

Transportation. Crude petroleum is moved to refineries by pipelines, tankers, barges, tank cars, and tank trucks. Refineries receive 77 per cent of their crude oil supply by pipeline, 22 per cent by water, and about 1 per cent by tank cars and trucks. When we consider total tonnage of both crude petroleum and petroleum products, however, the pattern is somewhat different: 47 per cent is moved by pipeline, 24 per cent by water carrier, 27 per cent by motor carrier, and 2 per cent by railroad.

Waterways play a critical part in the location of petroleum refineries because of the low cost of barge and tanker transport. Few commodities can be loaded and unloaded from ships as easily as crude oil. Water is a big factor in the success of large refineries near Galveston, Corpus Christi, and other port cities adjacent to large oil fields. One might suppose that only crude oil would move through these ports. Actually, however, these Gulf Coast refineries ship refined products by barge and tanker to a myriad of small market areas where demand, until now, has been too small to support a refinery. This is especially true of the southeastern portion of the United States, which is almost devoid of refineries. Some of the products move from Texas and Louisiana refineries by barge along rivers, but most of it moves along the coast by tanker to Tampa, Savannah, and other ports.

Clearly, the ideal locations for huge refineries are port cities, whether they are near oil fields or markets.

The World Pattern

By percentage of free world totals, the chief areas are Anglo-America 31 per cent, Western Europe 34, the Caribbean 8, and the Middle East 6. The world pattern of refining gives evidence of the same locational factors as we observed in the United States.

Markets and refining regions tend to coincide even though some yield no oil at all. The best example of this relationship is Europe. Figure 19-9 emphasizes the role of port cities encircling a region that consumes large quantities of oil, although it presently mines very little. Industrial Europe now depends on imports, most of which come from the Middle East (although development of the North Sea deposits is changing the traditional patterns). And Rotterdam, gateway to the industrial heart of the continent, is the foremost refining center, but the Thames estuary, Marseilles, Antwerp, and the Ruhr are not far behind. There is a closer locational correlation between refining and manufacturing in Europe than in the United States because much of Europe's refinery production is industrial fuel. Europe's refining is largely concentrated in her west central area, which is also her industrial heart. Likewise, northern Italy, another industrialized zone that possesses scarcely any crude oil, supports several market-oriented refineries (Figure 19-9).

As for other places, Figure 19-8 demonstrates that Canada's largest refineries (Montreal and Sarnia) are in the East—precisely where the majority of Canada's

Figure 19-9

1 Thames Estuary
2 Fawley
3 Le Harve
4 Antwerp
5 Koln – Bonn
6 Dusseldorff – Essen – Dortmund
7 Rotterdam

JAPAN

Osaka
Yokohama
Nagoya

Marseille
Milazzo
Ragusa – Augusta

Abadan
Ras Tanura

Crude Capacity in Thousands of Barrels Daily

1000
500
100
0

Selected Centers

Remainder in Nation

EUROPE AND THE MIDDLE EAST

0   500   1000km

The Strathcona refinery in Edmonton, Canada. The facility, which produces both oil and gas, is served by a large railroad yard. (*Courtesy EXXON Corporation.*)

population and market is. And Japan, an important buyer of crude oil, has refineries in several port cities (Figure 19-9).

Oil field regions of consequence that also contain refineries are the Middle East, Venezuela, and Indonesia. Virtually all the large refineries are in port cities close by the oil fields. Examples in the Middle East (Figure 19-9) are Abadan, Ra's Tannūrah, and Bahrein. In Venezuela (Figure 19-8) the principal refineries are in the ports of Amuay and Cardon. Indonesia's counterparts are Balikpapan (on Borneo) and Pladju (on Sumatra). Sarawak has a large refinery at Lutong.

A third type of refinery location is discernible: at intermediate *transport focal points* between oil fields and markets. Aruba and Curaçao (Figure 19-8), for instance,

refine considerable oil pumped up in the environs of Lake Maracaibo (see Chapter 15). The lake is too shallow for ocean tankers, but the ports of Aruba and Curaçao can handle large ships. Furthermore, these islands fly the Dutch flag, and Dutch investors preferred to install refinery equipment in a place that was under the protection of the Netherlands government. Refinery products from these small islands are exported to Brazil, Argentina, other Latin American countries and Europe.

In the eastern Mediterranean area (Figure 19-9) are several refining centers which conform to the intermediate location type, such as those on Sicily and Sardinia; they process oil from Africa and the Middle East en route to European and other customers.

SUGGESTED READINGS

CHAPMAN, K., "Corporate Systems in the United Kingdom Petrochemical Industry," *Annals of the Association of American Geographers*, 1974, pp. 126–137.

MELAMID, ALEXANDER, "Petroleum Refining and Distribution in Ethio-

pia," *The Professional Geographer*, 1968, pp. 388–391.

McNEE, ROBERT B., "Centrifugal-Centripetal Forces in International Petroleum Company Regions," *Annals of the Association of American Geographers*, 1961, pp. 124–138.

———, "Functional Geography of the Firm, with an Illustrative Case Study from the Petroleum Industry," *Economic Geography*, 1958, pp. 321–337.

RIMMER, PETER J., "The Australian Petrochemical Industry," *Economic Geography*, 1968, pp. 350–363.

CHAPTER
20

steel and fabricated-metal products

Blast furnaces at U.S. Steel's Fairless Works near Morrisville, Pennsylvania.

The purposes of this chapter are (1) to consider two classes of *location factors*, (2) to examine the primary manufacturing of iron, man's favorite metal, and (3) to investigate the geography of a few secondary manufacturing industries that fabricate steel products. As before, we shall examine the United States intensively before turning to survey world regions.

LOCATION FACTORS

There are two distinctly different types of location factors: initial and survival.

Initial location factors explain how a factory comes into existence in a particular place. Perhaps a local citizen invents a commodity and, wishing to abide in familiar territory, sets up his factory on home grounds. Perhaps available raw material convinces investors of the worth of processing it on the spot. Perhaps a local market, previously served by a distant factory, becomes prosperous enough to support a local outfit. Perhaps local power sources, such as the mill races in many New England cities, initially lure several factories to their sites. In some instances, a labor pool of skilled artisans gives birth to an enterprise. Such factors answer the question, "Why was the factory first located *there*?"

Survival location factors, which pertain to costs, explain how a factory continues to exist where it is. After it is in operation, a plant, to survive, must be favorably located relative to two kinds of costs: (a) *overhead costs* (such as real estate taxes), which continue regardless of whether the factory is operating full-time or half-time or is idle, and (b) *production costs* (such as labor, freight charges, and income taxes), which vary with the amount of manufacturing.

To answer the question, "Why is this factory where it is?" calls for inspection of both initial and survival factors. And that inspection requires extensive digging into the present and past relationships of individual factories—a task on which researchers have barely scratched the surface.

The problem is complicated because location factors may, of course, change with time. What was once a favorable factor in locating a plant may disappear. For instance midwestern sash-and-door mills were at first right in the middle of surrounding forests, but as the forests were cut over, the surviving mills had to draw lumber from distances as great as 2000 miles, as we said in Chapter 18. Thus an initial location factor is no longer a survival location factor.

THE STEEL INDUSTRY

Iron is an abundant element that constitutes 5 per cent of the earth's crust. Man uses iron in far greater quantities than any other metal—as Table 20-1 shows, over 40 times as much as the next-ranking element.

In the United States the iron-and-steel industry employs over half a million people, almost ten times the number engaged in the primary production of all other metals combined (Table 20-2).

Table 20-1

World Production of Metals

Metal	Tons
Pig iron	552,852,000
Aluminum	13,349,000
Copper	7,838,000
Zinc	5,795,000
Lead	3,801,000

Source: U.S. Bureau of Mines, *Minerals Yearbook* (1974).

Table 20-2

United States: Leading Industries in Primary Manufacture of Metals

Industry	Number of Employees in Thousands	Value Added in Millions of Dollars
Blast furnace and Basic steel production	552.9	12,116.1
Primary nonferrous metals	58.6	1,705.6
Copper	17.2	487.8
Lead	2.8	128.7
Zinc	6.3	121.6
Aluminum	25.6	816.0
Other primary nonferrous metals	6.7	151.5

Source: U.S. Bureau of the Census, *1972 Census of Manufactures* (1975).

Location

The Northeast dominates the nation in steel manufacturing. (Figure 20-1). Within this region just five states—Illinois, Indiana, Michigan, Ohio, and Pennsylvania—account for over two-thirds of United States employment in the manufacture of blast furnace and basic steel products. These same states produce almost three-fourths of United States tonnage of both pig iron and raw steel. The leading state is clearly Pennsylvania, which has 27 per cent of the nation's workers in the blast furnace and basic steel products industry and produces 22 per cent of our pig iron and steel.

The heart of this region is a triangular area, 250 miles on a side, that is marked off by Johnstown, Pennsylvania; Detroit, Michigan; and Buffalo, New York. Within this steel triangle are mills which account for over one-third of all United States steel production. The Pittsburgh metropolitan area alone has about 15 per cent of the nation's employment in this industry, but Detroit, Buffalo, and Cleveland, Youngstown and Canton (Ohio) are also major centers of production.

Elsewhere in the Northeast, the Middle Atlantic steel district contains several mills in various communities in eastern Pennsylvania and Maryland. The leading centers here are Bethlehem and Philadelphia, (Pennsylvania) and Sparrows Point (a suburb of Baltimore).

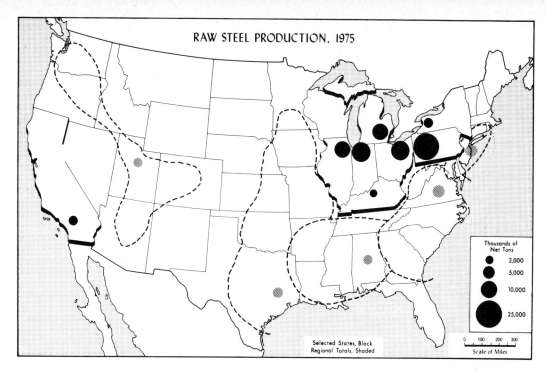

RAW STEEL PRODUCTION, 1975

Thousands of
Net Tons

· 2,000

● 5,000

● 10,000

● 25,000

Selected States, Black
Regional Totals, Shaded

0   100   200   300
Scale of Miles

Figure 20-1

Another concentration at the southern tip of Lake Michigan focuses on Chicago, Illinois and East Chicago, Hammond, and Gary, Indiana which together have almost a fifth of the nation's employment. Though the regional total is less than that of the steel triangle, these cities have wrested from Greater Pittsburgh the honor of being the nation's foremost urbanized area in steel production. Impressively enough, Chicago and its suburbs make almost as much steel as the entire United Kingdom.

All told, over 80 per cent of United States steel is made east of the Mississippi River and north of a line running from St. Louis to Baltimore. Elsewhere, steel districts are small and widely separated. The production of mills in southeastern states is about 8 per cent of the national total with Birmingham, Alabama, the leading center. The south central states account for a little, particularly at Houston. The West produces 7 per cent, mainly at Pueblo (Colorado), Provo (Utah), Fontana (California), and in the San Francisco area.

Characteristics

The manufacture of steel involves three general steps: smelting the ore into pig iron, refining the pig iron, and adding alloys.

Ore is smelted in blast furnaces. Four raw materials go into the process and three products result (see Figure 20-2). The solid raw materials—ore, coke, and limestone —are dumped in from above; then the coke is ignited, and a draft of forced hot air is introduced from the bottom. Gases (mostly carbon dioxide) are drawn off the top while molten iron and molten slag are drawn from the the bottom. The lighter slag floats on top of the heavier liquid iron. In addition to the four ingredients already mentioned, tremendous quantities of cold water (ten tons of water for every two tons of iron ore) are pumped through the jackets around the blast furnaces to keep them from melting.

Coke is the most common fuel in blast furnaces, although charcoal may be used. Coke itself is a manufactured product made from bituminous coal. The coal is heated in order to drive off volatile gases that are undesirable in smelting ore. The residue, the coke, is a light carbon substance that is still strong enough to bear the weight of ore and limestone in a blast furnace without being crushed. Were it not so strong, it would become so compact under the weight of rocky iron ore and rocky fluxing stone that passage of hot air upward through the burning charge would be obstructed. The function of coke in a blast furnace is two-fold: It provides heat to melt the iron-oxide ore with the fluxing stone, which unites with many of the impurities, and it provides carbon, which unites with much of the oxygen in the iron oxide to form carbon dioxide, thus releasing the iron. But in accomplishing these two objectives the coke unfortunately supplies an excess of carbon which combines with the iron. One of the main purposes of the next step—the refining process—is to separate iron and carbon atoms.

The locational pattern of smelters is shown in Figure 20-3. Notice that the general distribution conforms to that of steel mills. Many companies operate blast furnaces and steel furnaces side by side. But where only one plant exists, it is invariably a steel mill. For the United States as a whole, it can be said (1) that fewer places make pig iron than make steel, and (2) that most of the places that make steel but not pig iron are outside the prominent steel districts. For reasons which will be seen later, steel mills can thrive in places that lack blast furnaces, but blast furnaces can rarely subsist without the mills.

Pig iron is 95 per cent pure metal, but it contains certain other elements (mostly carbon and silicon) that must be eliminated before the iron is usable. These impurities are extracted by refining processes in special furnaces. Some furnaces (for instance, the open hearth or the Bessemer converter) burn them out under very

FLOW DIAGRAM: MANUFACTURE OF STEEL

1950 lbs. IRON ORE   370 lbs. LIMESTONE   1480 lbs. COAL   190 lbs. SCRAP, Etc.

BLAST FURNACE
uses
3990 lbs. of raw materials to produce

1215 lbs. PIG IRON

180 lbs. IRON ORE   130 lbs. LIMESTONE   960 lbs. SCRAP   30 lbs. FERRO-ALLOYS

STEEL FURNACE
uses
1215 lbs. of pig iron and
1300 lbs. of raw materials to produce ⟶ 2000 lbs. of INGOT STEEL

A total of 5290 lbs. of raw materials used to make one ton of ingot steel

Figure 20-2   (*After American Iron and Steel Institute.*)

high temperatures with jet streams of forced, superheated oxygen. Such furnaces are able to handle scrap iron as well as pig iron in one batch. Again, coke is the main fuel (although gas can be used). Typical proportions of these materials in refining operations are: 1 ton pig iron +1 ton scrap iron +1 ton fuel +2 tons steel +1 ton gas. The electric furnaces that have been perfected in recent years are now competing successfully with the other two types. Although more costly to operate, these electric furnaces can be controlled with more precision, so they are being used in making stainless steel and other high-quality products. United States raw steel production by type of furnace breaks down as follows: basic oxygen process 62 per cent, open hearth 19 per cent, and electric 19 per cent. The once important Bessemer converter is no longer significant in the production of raw steel in the United States.

After pure iron is obtained, certain alloys, such as carefully determined small quantities of carbon, manganese, nickel, and cobalt, are added to the refined pig iron to give specific qualities such as ductility, malleability, elasticity, and endurance under heat. The resulting product is *steel*.

Two other characteristics of steel manufacturing deserve citation: scale and nuisance.

Blast furnaces and steel mills are typically large-scale operations, averaging 570 employees per plant. Large tracts of land are required, not only for the structures (such as the blast furnaces, ovens for preheating air, refining furnaces, rolling mills, and soaking pits) but also for huge storage piles of ore, coal, and limestone.

Regardless of size, steel plants have certain nuisance attributes. All blast furnaces and most steel mills (except those that use electricity) are notoriously dirty and often smelly. Their belching smokestacks throw plumes of smoke into the atmosphere, and the fallout of dust particles over steelmaking centers is tremendous. When atmospheric conditions are favorable, the plume of reddish smoke from steel centers at the southern end of Lake Michigan can trail away to the east in a streamer 40 miles long. Some cities have passed antismoke measures requiring that all chimneys be equipped with devices to arrest escaping dirt particles. This scheme has worked with outstanding success in Pittsburgh. But perhaps the most significant step toward reducing pollution associated with steel manufacture came with the establishment of the Environmental Protection Agency. This federal agency is charged with controlling pollution from steel mills and from all other sources.

Relationships

The four principal relationships of steelmaking are (1) with sources of raw material, (2) with markets, (3) with transportation, and (4) with certain site features.

Raw Material. The steel industry consumes a number of materials in huge amounts (Table 20-3). In order of tonnage, important basic materials are iron ore, agglomerated products, coal, scrap iron, and flux.

1. Iron ore: When ore that is one-half iron is used in blast furnaces, there is a 50 per cent weight loss. This

Table 20-3

Consumption of Basic Materials Used in the Production
of Iron and Steel Products, 1975

Material	Net Tons	
	Subtotal	Total
Coal		78,615,888
For coke	75,514,838	
For steam	2,736,633	
Other	364,417	
Fluxes		29,470,518
Limestone	20,934,557	
Lime	7,110,001	
Other	1,425,960	
Iron ore		118,908,000
Agglomerated products		105,095,924
Pellets	69,816,461	
Sinter, briquettes, nodules and other	35,279,463	
Scrap		62,560,000
Nonferrous metals for coating		
Zinc		231,790
Tin		20,806
Aluminum		9,397
Copper		7,569
Lead		4,409
Nickel and chrome		694
Oxygen (*millions of cubic feet*)		230,477
Manganese ore		765,530

Source: American Iron and Steel Institute, *Annual Statistical Report, 1975*
(1976).

would tend to pull blast furnaces toward iron ore regions. But the strength of this attraction is neutralized by the pull of coal, since it takes about two-thirds of a ton of coke (which required a ton of bituminous coal) to make one ton of pig iron. The lower the percentage of iron content, of course, the stronger the drawing power of iron-mining regions on the location of ore-processing factories. In all likelihood, however, such factories will be concentrators (taconite mills) rather than blast furnaces (see Chapter 16).

2. Agglomerated products[1]: In the Great Lakes mining districts and elsewhere low-grade ores which once had little value are now being mined. But before they can be smelted they must be upgraded or improved. This process is called *beneficiation*. There are actually several steps involved in the beneficiation process. Crushing, grinding, and concentrating result in greatly improved ore, but this ore is in powdered form and cannot be used until it has passed through one more step, *agglomeration*. Several different methods are used to agglomerate iron ore concentrates: pelletizing, sintering, nodulizing, and briqueting are the most common.

Since the turn of the century, agglomerated products have been used in the manufacture of iron and steel. Sintering, for example, is still widely used to agglomerate flue dust and other blast furnace waste

[1]An excellent discussion of this topic is contained in: Fillmore C. F. Earney, "New Ores for Old Furnaces: Pelletized Iron," *Annals of The Association of American Geographers*, September, 1969, pp. 512–534.

Figure 20-3

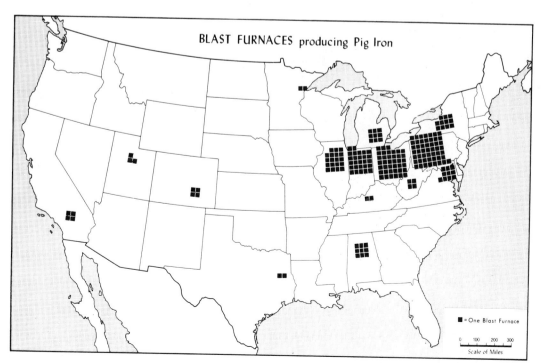

BLAST FURNACES producing Pig Iron

■ = One Blast Furnace

0   100   200   300
Scale of Miles

products, which are being recycled. But pelletization, which was only introduced in the United States in the mid-1950's, now accounts for about two-thirds of the agglomerated products.

3. Coal: There are several uses for coal in the iron and steel manufacturing process, but clearly the most important use is for coke. To manufacture a ton of coke requires $1\frac{1}{2}$ tons of bituminous coal. In the early days of coke manufacture, beehive ovens were used for heating the coal. The first beehive was built in the 1840's (before then, charcoal had served as the fuel for smelting ore and making steel). But beehive ovens had two shortcomings: They could handle only high-grade bituminous coal, and they lost all the volatile gases. Because Appalachian coal was the only satisfactory raw material for these ovens, and because so much weight was lost in the process, virtually all the nation's coke was made in the mining areas of western Pennsylvania, West Virginia, and eastern Ohio. Connellsville, Pennsylvania (40 miles south of Pittsburgh), was the unrivaled capital of coke production.

Then in the 1890's a new technique was devised —the by-product oven—which could use lower quality coal and salvage all the volatile gases. The gases, in turn, could be used not only as fuel in making more coke but also as raw materials for chemical factories. Now that there was no weight loss (the total weight of coal had value in one form or other) coke manufacturing quickly moved next door to the steel plants. Today, since the steel industry gobbles up most of the nation's coke the pattern of coke production coincides closely with that of steel.

4. Scrap iron: On the average, for every one ton of pig iron going into a steel furnace, there is almost one ton of scrap iron. Some small electric steel furnaces, however, subsist entirely off scrap. Most of this material comes from junkyards and secondary factories (for example, steel shavings and cuttings from machinery factories). Since these suppliers are chiefly located in the Northeast, that is the nation's major source region of scrap iron.

5. Fluxing stone: Limestone, lime, fluorspar, or other such materials are used in blast furnaces to attract and combine with impurities that are mechanically mixed with iron in the ore; the resulting mixture is called slag. Some slag can be used as a raw material in cement factories or as a surface on rural roads. Yet much of it is useless, and disposing of it is an appreciable cost item for steel plants because it must be transported, sometimes considerable distances, to dumping grounds.

Limestone and other fluxes are widely distributed. Mills in western Pennsylvania procure the stone from limestone quarries a few miles to the east. Mills along Lake Michigan and Lake Erie receive some of theirs in lake freighters. Certain plants need no limestone, for some ores contain enough lime to be almost entirely self-fluxing.

In addition to the materials already discussed, the iron and steel industry uses alloy and coating metals,

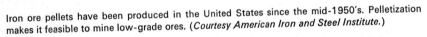

Iron ore pellets have been produced in the United States since the mid-1950's. Pelletization makes it feasible to mine low-grade ores. (*Courtesy American Iron and Steel Institute.*)

oxygen, water and large amounts of fuel. Each year iron and steel manufacturers purchase huge quantities of fuel oil, natural gas, and electricity, as well as using coke oven and blast furnace gases.

Water is used to cool furnaces, to generate steam, and to quench coke. Since water is so important, most mills select sites along rivers or lakes. Where several plants are clustered in one valley, the river water, being used and reused repeatedly, absorbs so much heat that its temperature rises. Water in the Mahoning River, for instance, below the final mill in Youngstown has registered temperatures above 90°F. Obviously, thermal pollution of this sort has had a dramatic impact on the plant and animal life in this area. Sometimes, other considerations take precedence over the availability of fresh water in locating a plant. In such cases, clever solutions have been devised to supply the necessary coolant. The Sparrows Point mill (near Baltimore, Maryland), for one, has adapted its cooling system to permit the use of sea water. And in the semiarid Los Angeles basin, the Fontana steel mill has set up an elaborate and complex water reclamation system.

Oxygen is also used in great quantity. To make a ton of steel it is necessary that air be heated to 1500°F and that it be blown up through the coke and ore in the furnace. Some blast furnaces swallow 50,000 cubic feet air a minute. Although air is free, *hot forced* air must be manufactured. So every blast furnace is flanked by a series of tall ovens (usually more conspicuous than the furnace itself) in which the air is warmed under pressure.

Although air and water are items used in great quantities by blast furnaces and steel mills, the industry cannot be said to be "air-oriented" or "water-oriented." For these materials—the one worldwide and the other widely available—are less costly to assemble than other raw materials that are consumed in smaller amounts.

Comparison of Steel Centers in Their Relationships to Raw Materials. At this point it is possible to appraise the several steel regions in terms of their relationships to the source areas of raw materials. The steel triangle is well off vis-à-vis coal; indeed, to the south it coincides with a portion of the Appalachian coal field. But for iron ore, the triangle must depend entirely on distant sources—mostly Minnesota, to a lesser degree upper New York, and increasingly the Quebec-Labrador fields.

Southern Lake Michigan mills are far from coal, coking coal, that is, for the nearby Illinois and Indiana coal is not of good coking quality. Consequently, the big mills in Gary and Chicago depend on Appalachia for much of their fuel. Lake freighters transport ore to these mills, which depend on Lake Superior mines.

The Middle Atlantic steel region gets its coal from West Virginia and other Appalachian states by way of rail to Newport News, thence coastal waterways up Chesapeake Bay and the Delaware River. For its iron ore this region is becoming increasingly dependent on foreign imports, notably from Venezuela and Canada; some

domestic ore, though, comes from eastern Pennsylvania, and upper New York.

The blast furnaces in Alabama are unique among United States mills in that their immediate environs have abundant natural resources of coking coal, iron ore, and fluxing stone. The Pueblo, Colorado, mill subsists on coal from western Colorado and ore from eastern Wyoming, and the one in Provo, Utah, keeps going on coal from the eastern part of the state and ore from Cedar City in the southwestern part.

All told, United States blast furnaces, steel furnaces, and agglomerating plants consume about 120,000,000 tons of iron ore annually. As can be seen from the following breakdown, the Great Lakes states of Minnesota, Michigan, and Wisconsin are the leading suppliers:

United States	
Great Lakes states	56%
Northeastern states	2
Western states	6
Southern states	3
Canada	
Ontario	3
Other eastern provinces	12
All other foreign countries	18

Canada is our biggest foreign source, and it is followed by Venezuela, with Brazil a poor third. These three countries provide the United States with over four-fifths of her iron ore imports.

Considering the importance of ores from the Great Lakes region, it is not surprising that lake ports ship over 80,000,000 tons of iron ore annually (Figure 20-4). Duluth is the leader, but several others also stand out.

If steel were a raw material-oriented industry we might expect it to be concentrated more heavily near coal fields or ore fields, for these are the raw materials that cost the most to assemble. But only a small percentage of the nation's steel is made in coal-mining regions and an even smaller share in iron-mining regions. Notice how little steel is made in Kentucky, the leading coal-mining state, and in Minnesota, which mines almost three-fourths of the country's iron ore. Clearly, other relationships are operative that influence the location of the steel industry.

Relationships to Market Regions. Over 95 per cent of the steel made in the United States is sold domestically. Domestic customers are (1) secondary fabricators who purchase ingot steel and pig iron (to make castings) or steel sheets, tubes, wires, and bars for use in further manufacture, and (2) direct consumers who use I-beams, pipes, and rails as they come from the mill without further fabrication.

Figure 20-4

Molten steel being teemed into ingots. Once these ingots have cooled on the outside, they will be stripped of their molds by a stripper crane and placed in soaking pits to be brought up to uniform temperature prior to rolling. (*Courtesy American Iron and Steel Institute.*)

By percentage of steel they take, the leading domestic consumers are listed in Table 20-4. The significance of this table to the geographer is that most of the secondary manufacturers who process the steel, most of the warehouses that distribute steel sheets and other forms of the metal, and a large share of the contractors who use I-beams and other construction materials are located in the northeastern quadrant of the nation. We shall develop this point later in this chapter and in the chapters on urban economic activity.

It is in market relationships then that the leading steel regions have their advantage. The steel triangle, for example, provides steel to a market consisting of thousands of foundries, hardware factories, plumbing-equipment producers, and automotive manufacturers in Pittsburgh, Cleveland, Detroit, Buffalo, and scores of other places in the Northeast.

Chicago, too, is centrally located within a large market, in her case the midwestern steel-using industries. Middle Atlantic steel mills are close by manufacturers dispersed all the way from Baltimore to Boston. Alabama mills supply southern markets. And steel mills have sprung up in Texas, California, and the Pacific Northwest to meet local needs for steel.

Thus, it appears that within the United States, steel is essentially a market-oriented industry, since all the largest markets have steel mills close by and all the large-scale steel mills are close to substantial markets. This fundamental relationship explains why Birmingham, Alabama, with supplies of all three major raw materials, has less of a steel industry than either Chicago or Baltimore with none of the three. And even though the cost of making steel is less in Alabama than in many other

Table 20-4

Net Shipments of Steel Products by Market, 1975

Market		Percentage of U.S. Total
Steel service centers and distributors		19.5
Oil and gas supply houses	3.6	
All other	15.9	
Construction		11.0
Contractors' products		4.9
Automotive		19.0
Vehicles, parts, etc.	18.4	
Other	0.6	
Rail transportation		3.9
Locomotives and cars	2.3	
Rails and other	1.6	
Shipbuilding and marine equipment		1.8
Oil and gas drilling		0.8
Mining and quarrying		0.7
Agriculture		1.8
Agricultural machinery	1.3	
Other	0.5	
Machinery, industrial equipment, and tools		6.5
Electrical equipment		2.7
Appliances, utensils, and cutlery		2.1
Other domestic and commercial equipment		1.7
Containers, packaging, and shipping		
Materials		7.6
Cans	6.0	
Barrels and drums	0.8	
Other	0.8	
Ordnance and other military		0.5
Export		2.2
All other markets		13.3
TOTAL		100.0

Source: American Iron and Steel Institute, *Annual Statistical Report, 1975* (1976).

places in the United States, that state produces less than 4 per cent of the national total.

A by-product market is frequently provided by cement mills that settle near steel mills, for they can use slag from blast furnaces as a raw material. In fact, the same general region that takes most of our steel also uses much of our cement. This is another example of *symbiosis*.

Transportation. Steel companies select plots of land along water bodies for blast furnaces and steel furnaces not only for access to cooling water but also for cheap water transportation to link the mills to iron mines, to coal fields, to limestone quarries, and to customers. An ideal situation exists where waterways penetrate deeply into market regions, thus permitting water transport of the bulky raw materials into the middle of the steel-consuming area. Mills at the southern end of Lake Michigan have just such a setting as do the Sparrows Point Mill of Bethlehem Steel Corporation on Chesapeake Bay and the Fairless Hills mill that the

United States Steel Corporation constructed in 1956 in the rural countryside of eastern Pennsylvania. This mill is alongside the Delaware River, convenient for bringing in raw materials, and on the main lines of railways and highways to Philadelphia, New York, and other eastern customers.

Site Features. The most desirable topography for blast furnaces and steel mills is expansive flat land. Such terrain facilitates the construction of buildings and allows for future expansion. In this respect western Pennsylvania and eastern Ohio, despite their other attractions, faced a handicap. The terrain is rough and valley bottoms are narrow. Even so, the mills were located in the valley bottoms, not only for access to water for coolant and for barge transportation but also because the railroads follow the rivers. Other industries subsequently flocked to these valley bottoms, which are now built up solidly around the mills.

Quite the opposite is the setting of mills at the edge of Lake Michigan. There the land is flat and swampy, undesirable for residential areas but ideal for steel mills which need elbow room for expansion and vast dumping grounds for slag that cannot be used in cement milling or road building.

A hot saw cuts a heavy wide-flange beam at U.S. Steel's Homestead, Pennsylvania, facility. This product is rolled in a mill which can produce 6- to 36-inch structural shapes, varying in weight from 8.5 to a maximum of 730 pounds per lineal foot.

Steel Regions of the World

Worldwide, steel production is highly concentrated in four places—Anglo-America, western Europe, the Soviet Union (and her European satellites), and Japan. Together, these regions account for over 85 per cent of the world's pig iron and steel. Outside the four main regions, China is the most conspicuous. Tonnage and percentages by nation are given in Table 20-5; the locational pattern is shown in Figure 20-5.

Table 20-5

World Production of Pig Iron and Raw Steel, 1975

Area	Pig Iron		Raw Steel	
	Millions of Tons	Percentage of World Total	Millions of Tons	Percentage of World Total
WORLD	515.8	100	718.2	100
North America				
Canada	10.1	2	14.4	2
Mexico	3.5	1	5.9	1
United States	79.9	15	116.6	16
South America				
Brazil	7.7	1	9.2	1
Europe				
Austria	3.4	1	4.5	1
Belgium-Luxembourg	14.4	3	17.9	2
Czechoslovakia	10.3	2	15.7	2
France	19.8	4	23.7	3
East Germany	2.7	—	7.2	1
West Germany	33.2	6	44.6	6
Italy	12.6	2	24.1	3
Netherlands	4.4	1	5.3	1
Poland	8.6	2	16.6	2
Romania	7.1	1	11.0	2
Spain	7.6	1	12.2	2
Sweden	3.5	1	6.2	1
United Kingdom	13.3	3	21.9	3
U.S.S.R.	112.8	22	156.5	22
Africa				
Republic of South Africa	5.6	1	7.5	1
Asia				
China	24.3	5	33.1	5
India	9.0	2	8.8	1
Japan	95.5	19	112.7	16
Australia	8.4	2	8.7	1

Source: American Iron and Steel Institute, *Annual Statistical Report, 1975* (1976).

The world pattern of steel gives evidence of the same relationships that we observed in the United States: The steel industry tends to locate where the demand for steel products is vigorous, and of all the raw materials coal exerts the most powerful lure. Indeed, most of the individual foreign areas that are outstanding for steel manufacture have already been identified in Chapter 14 as major coal-producing zones: In Western Europe, Germany's Ruhr, northeastern France, the Midlands of Britain centering on Birmingham, and the Scottish Lowland; in the Soviet Union, Donetsk in the Donbass, Magnitogorsk and Chelyabinsk (in the Urals), and Kuznetsk, 1000 miles east of the Urals; and in Japan, the Yawata district of Kyushu Island.

METAL-FABRICATING INDUSTRIES

Before reaching the final consumers, most of the steel that primary factories produce is fabricated by a large number of secondary factories into machinery and an extensive variety of consumer goods. We shall now make a few comments on the manufacture of fabricated-metal goods, and give a closer look to the manufacture of machinery in Chapter 21.

As revealed in Figure 20-6, which shows the locational pattern of the fabricated metal industry, leading centers are Chicago, Detroit, Los Angeles, Cleveland, and a whole series of cities between Philadelphia and Boston. A principal reason for this pattern is that it is cheaper to ship steel sheets, bars, and ingots to these centers of population than to make hardware grills, stampings, and so on, in the steel regions and then pay high freight rates on them to the wholesale centers. Thus, fabricated metal factories are near their customers and many steel mills have been drawn to these fabricators.

Metal fabricating is a big business: There are 29,000 factories employing almost 1.5 million people (Table 20-6); only four industries in the United States employ more people, and only three have a larger annual

Table 20-6

Fabricated Metal Products

Industry	Number of Employees (Thousands)	Value Added (Million Dollars)
Metal cans	78.6	2,004.6
Cutlery, handtools, and hardware	159.2	3,253.4
Plumbing and heating equipment	60.7	1,131.6
Fabricated structural metal products	394.8	6,742.9
Bolts, nuts, screws, etc.	100.6	1,845.3
Metal forgings and stampings	263.5	5,057.3
Plating, coating, etc.	82.1	1,120.3
Ammunition, small arms, etc.	109.5	1,507.3
Springs, wire, valves, fittings, etc.	244.3	4,283.0
TOTAL	1,493.3	26,945.7

Source: U.S. Bureau of the Census, *1972 Census of Manufactures* (1975).

Figure 20-5

Figure 20-6

payroll. Space does not permit us to discuss the geography of all the different types of fabricated metal products, but we can provide maps of some of them along with a few brief comments.

Hardware

Most hardware (Figure 20-7) is produced in large cities, but a good deal comes from smaller settlements, such as New Britain and Hartford, Connecticut, Grand Rapids, Michigan, and Rockford, Illinois. The surprising thing about such places is that they produce no steel, so all face *backhauls* on freight, shipping most of their hardware back in the very same direction from which their steel came! This peculiar situation can be explained in terms of three factors. (1) Tools, cutlery, and other hardware items are highly valuable relative to their weight (on which freight charges are assessed) so that a few extra miles does not price factories in these cities out of competition with hardware producers who have the locational advantages of being near steel mills or markets. (2) Many of these towns, those in the Connecticut Valley in paritcular, got an early start in making not only tools but also firearms, clocks, and many other kinds of hardware. Local entrepreneurs in these settlements recognized the hardware market and risked some capital in starting hardware factories. This force, which might be termed "whim," is one of the most difficult influences to study scientifically, but there is no doubt that it is operative. Surely it is a strong reason why Rockford and Grand Rapids—instead of Fort

Wayne and Indianapolis or Saginaw and Dayton, or Peoria and Pittsburgh—are outstanding centers of hardware production in the Midwest. An early start provides a powerful impulse in perpetuating manufacturing in any region. (3) Finally, production costs—expenses for labor, rent, municipal taxes—are slightly lower in small cities than in large ones, an advantage that helps neutralize the possible drawback of higher freight costs.

Metal Cans

The pattern of metal can factories (Figure 20-8) correlates strongly with the market for metal cans, which consists, of course, of the packers of vegetables, fruit, beer, and a host of other perishable items. Compare Figure 20-8 with Figure 17-1, which shows the location of the fruit and vegetable *canning* industry. Rarely do metal can factories locate near the steel mills that make metal plate, since it is much cheaper to ship the plate from mills to can factories than to ship cans from steel mills to the agricultural area. Take New York for example: There are more canneries and more can factories in the vegetable and fruit area south of Lake Ontario than in steelmaking Buffalo. Similarly, New England, which produces hardly any steel, has more can factories than does the steel district straddling western Pennsylvania and eastern Ohio. There are many can factories in California, a state which produces scarcely 3 per cent of our nation's steel but has the largest number of canneries, putting up a third of our canned fruits and vegetables.

Within canning regions, can factories locate in large cities for easy distribution to the myriad canneries in the hinterland. Most packing plants are too small to support

Figure 20-7

Figure 20-8

Figure 20-9

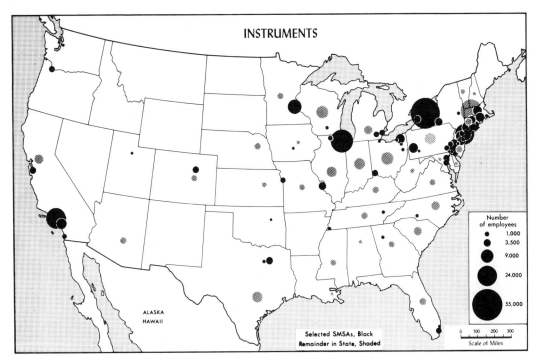

a can factory individually, hence can factories locate at transport centers. Thus Illinois' can factories are in Chicago, California's are in the San Francisco and Los Angeles areas.

Instruments

The manufacture of photographic equipment, measuring instruments, medical instruments, scientific instruments, and ophthalmic equipment has an unusual pattern (Figure 20-9). It is extremely localized in just a few cities and states; the leaders are listed in Table 20-7. It is not unexpected that Chicago, New York, and Los Angeles, the nation's largest metropolitan centers with longstanding reputations as centers of learning and scientific development should dominate the map. The surprises are Rochester, New York (not listed in Table 20-7 because the *Census* does not disclose exact figures when only one or two firms dominate) and several communities in southern New England. Here is an industry that is neither power-oriented nor raw material-oriented. To be sure, it does tend to develop within the broad framework of its market, and linkages with other industries do exert some influence; but the precise location of a factory seems to be due to chance. It was merely coincidence, for instance, that a particular invention, George Eastman's *Kodak* camera, was the prime stimulus to the development of manufacturing in the particular city of Rochester. One cannot help but speculate whether, if George Eastman had lived in Columbus, or Erie, or any one of dozens of cities in the populous heart of the nation, that city would not loom as conspicuously as Rochester in fact does.

Table 20-7

United States: Manufacture of Instruments and Related Products by Leading States and Selected Metropolitan Areas

Area	Number of Employees (Thousands)	Value Added (Million Dollars)	Percentage of U.S. Value Added
UNITED STATES TOTAL	454.1	10,583.7	100
Massachusetts	37.0	877.5	8
Boston	(26.4)	(710.9)	(7)
New York	96.4	3,535.8	33
New York, N.Y.-N.J.	(22.4)	(368.0)	(3)
New Jersey	22.6	505.0	5
Pennsylvania	32.7	601.5	6
Philadelphia (Penn.-N.J.)	(17.7)	(315.5)	(3)
Illinois	44.5	848.9	8
California	48.1	927.3	9
Los Angeles	(23.0)	(409.4)	(4)

Source: U.S. Bureau of the Census, *1972 Census of Manufactures* (1975).

SUGGESTED READINGS

AMERICAN IRON and STEEL INSTITUTE, *Steel Facts*, Washington, D.C. (annual).

EARNEY, FILLMORE C., "New Ores for Old Furnaces: Pelletized Iron," *Annals of the Association of American Geographers*, 1969, pp. 512–534.

GIBSON, LAY JAMES, "An Analysis of the Location of Instrument Manufacture in the United States," *Annals of the Association of American Geographers*, 1970, pp. 352–367.

HEAL, DAVID W., *The Steel Industry in Postwar Britain*, North Pomfret, Vt., 1974, 224 pp.

Iron Age (the national metalworking weekly) New York.

ISARD, WALTER, and CUMBERLAND, JOHN, "New England as a Possible Location for an Integrated Iron and Steel Works," *Economic Geography*, 1950, pp. 245–259.

MASON, PETER FRANK, "Some Changes in Domestic Iron Mining as a Result of Pelletization," *Annals of the Associa-tion of American Geographers*, 1969, pp. 535–551.

SHARER, CYRUS J., "The Philadelphia Iron and Steel District: Its Relation to the Seaways," *Economic Geography*, 1963, pp. 363–367.

UNITED STATES BUREAU OF MINES, *Minerals Yearbook* (published annually) and *Mineral Trade Notes* (published monthly).

CHAPTER

21

transportation machinery

Japanese automobiles being unloaded from a vessel in Los Angeles harbor. (*Courtesy Nissan Motor Corporation in U.S.A.*)

Machines are power-driven instruments that perform work for man. Machines are both savers of work and makers of work, since the manufacture of machines provides employment to millions of people. In the United States more than 5,200,000 people are at work making machinery—a larger number than in any other type of manufacturing (a breakdown of the machinery industry into its component parts is given in Table 21-1). Never

Table 21-1

United States: Leading Machinery-Making Industries

Type	Number of Employees (Thousands)	Value Added (Millions of Dollars)
Transportation equipment	1,719.0	39,799.4
Motor vehicles and equipment	807.5	22,056.2
Aircraft and parts	438.7	9,123.6
Ship and boat building and repairing	185.2	2,398.2
Railroad equipment	50.8	1,113.3
Motorcycles, bicycles, and parts	17.6	315.2
Guided missiles and space vehicles	160.1	3,969.2
Other	59.1	823.7
Machinery (except electrical)	1,827.7	37,562.9
Electric and electronic equipment	1,662.2	30,583.6

Source: U.S. Bureau of the Census, *1972 Census of Manufactures* (1975).

before has man had so many labor-saving devices at his command, and never before have so many workers earned their livelihood by making them.

Since different machinery industries conform to different locational patterns, we shall direct our attention separately to particular industries, beginning with those that make machines for transporting people and freight.

More persons (1,700,000) are employed in making equipment to save man time in transporting himself and his goods than in any other industry (except machinery manufacturing) in the United States. Nearly half of these workers are in the motor vehicle industry with aircraft manufacture a poor second (Table 21-1).

AIRCRAFT

Location and Characteristics

The aircraft industry is concentrated in a few widely separated places in the United States (Figure 21-1), mostly in large metropolitan areas. Leading centers in terms of employment include Los Angeles, California, 101,000; Hartford, Connecticut, 36,000; Wichita, Kansas, 22,000; and Dallas-Fort Worth, Texas, about 30,000.

Notice the position of Los Angeles (Figure 21-1), which provides jobs for one of every five persons employed by aircraft plants. By state, California accounts for 24 per cent of the national total of jobs in this industry, followed by Connecticut with 11 per cent, Ohio and Texas with 7 per cent each, and New York and Washington with 6 per cent each.

A Few Large Companies. In the early days of the airplane industry there were numerous small com-

Figure 21-1

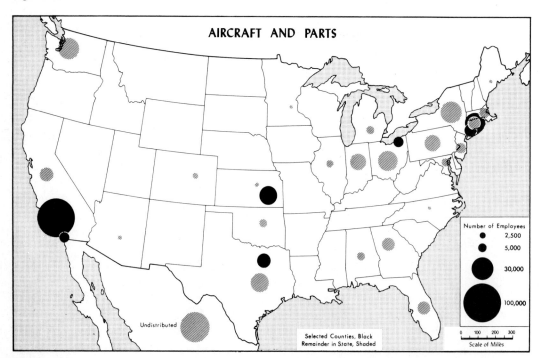

AIRCRAFT AND PARTS

Number of Employees
- 2,500
- 5,000
- 30,000
- 100,000

Undistributed

Selected Counties, Black
Remainder in State, Shaded

0 100 200 300
Scale of Miles

panies, but they gradually merged or faded from the picture, so that today there are only a few companies which manufacture aircraft. By far the largest are the trio of McDonnell Douglas, Lockheed, and Boeing.

Limited Mass-Production Methods. Plane makers have adopted some of the mass-production methods typical of the automotive industry but with only partial success. Several characteristics of airplane production limit the applicability of such methods: Many models are produced in small numbers, designs change rapidly, and over-all airplane production is sporadic. Still, during periods of large output—as in the later years of World War II—mass production can be highly successful indeed.

Subcontracting. Airplane companies purchase engines, propellers, instruments, and parts from many other firms. So an airplane plant is usually a combination of (a) an air-frame factory where aluminum sheets and other metal forms are manufactured into wings and fuselages, and (b) an assembly plant where engines, radios, compasses, wheels, and a host of other parts are brought together from far-flung factories. The manufacture of frames usually occurs in the same locality (often the same factory) as the final assembly. Yet there have been instances in which fuselages have been shipped long distances from factory to assembly plant. In 1953, for example, fuselages (or "hulls") for giant "Albatross" seaplanes were manufactured in Evansville, Indiana, and hauled on huge trailers 1,000 miles to the Grumman Aircraft Engineering Corporation at Bethpage, Long Island.

Generally speaking, there are two basic patterns. First, there are the centers which specialize in the production of aircraft. Some employment will be located in firms which produce engines, engine parts, and other equipment, but a majority of the employees will work in assembly plants. In Los Angeles, for instance, 72 per cent of all employment in this industry is located in plants primarily engaged in manufacturing or assembling complete aircraft, 10 per cent in plants making engines, engine parts, and propellers and 18 per cent in establishments making other types of aircraft equipment. In Wichita, Kansas, 65 per cent of the industry employment is devoted to manufacturing complete aircraft.

The second pattern is well developed in the Northeast. Here we find many centers which produce engines or other equipment but not complete aircraft. Hartford, Cleveland, and Detroit are not known as producers of aircraft, but rather for their production of aircraft engines, propellers and other equipment. In Hartford, there are 29,000 workers engaged in the manufacture of engines and engine parts, and in Cleveland, there are over 5,000.

Size. Aircraft factories have enormous payrolls. The industry as a whole has payrolls that exceed

$5,000,000,000 annually! Slightly over half of the total payroll and half of the employment in this industry is in just 140 aircraft plants. The average plant will typically employ between 1500 and 2000 workers. Plants making engines and other equipment tend to be smaller and more numerous. Airplane factories are also large in terms of acreage, for they require huge parcels of land for hangars and adjoining airstrips where planes are flight-tested.

Intense Fluctuations. Aircraft production is a highly fluctuating industry, which experiences its greatest booms in wartime. Before World War I the industry scarcely existed; but by the time of the Armistice, the nation's factories were making planes at the rate of 20,000 a year and employing 200,000 people. Then the industry (based entirely on military demands) collapsed overnight as peace dawned. Lindbergh's flight across the Atlantic in 1927, however, stimulated interest in commercial aviation, and rearmament in the late 1930's revived orders for military planes. By 1940 the industry employed 100,000 people making 5000 planes a year. In the next four years the production skyrocketed to a wartime peak of over 2,000,000 employees and 96,000 planes a year.

The experience of Los Angeles epitomizes these fluctuations in aircraft employment (Table 21-2). In

Table 21-2

Aircraft and Parts Manufacturing: Employment, Los Angeles and United States

Year	Los Angeles Metropolitan Area (Thousands)	United States Total (Thousands)	Los Angeles (Percentage of Total)
1940	40	148	27
1943	262	1,345	19
1946	74	237	31
1949	65	264	25
1951	109	423	26
1953	174	825	21
1956	197	793	25
1959	156	762	20
1962	112	677	17
1965	107	619	17
1968	142	846	17
1970	118	697	17
1971	93	531	18
1972	103	498	21
1973	101	501	20

Source: 1940–46 data compiled by Research Department, Security First National Bank, Los Angeles; 1949–73 data are from *County Business Patterns.*

three short years (from 1940 to 1943) Los Angeles plane makers created 222,000 new jobs as their payrolls leaped from 40,000 to 262,000. The pendulum then swung back almost as sharply, and by 1949 there were 65,000 on the payrolls. From the late 1950's through the early 1970's Los Angeles' share of national employment has been fairly stable, but the number employed in a given year has varied by over 100,000 workers.

Change in Location. The aircraft industry has been characterized by an unusual change in locational pattern. In the early days it grew up largely on the East Coast and in the Midwest; New York, Dayton, Buffalo, and Detroit were the focal points. After World War I the industry began to move west—San Diego, Seattle, Wichita, Dallas, and Fort Worth now loomed up large, and Los Angeles soon became the airplane capital of the country. With this locational change there developed the regional specialization already noted. Some assembly plants remained in the East, particularly those making small planes, for both private and military purposes (for instance carrier-based Navy planes).

Relationships

Raw-Material Source Regions. Since aircraft are often not assembled in areas where aluminum, engines, propellers, radar, electronic devices, and other materials are produced, those components are shipped long distances. Therefore, we may conclude that the pull of raw-material source regions upon the location of aircraft assembly plants is weak.

Market Regions. The market for airplanes is threefold: military, commercial, and private. In 1975, the United States Armed Forces purchased 1357 planes,

and private firms and individuals bought 15,236 including 315 transport planes, 864 helicopters, and 14,057 "private planes." Private planes produced by firms such as Beech, Piper, Cessna, and Gates Learjet are generally smaller and less complex than transport or fighting craft, so that by value the private plane market is relatively small. In 1975, the value of civil aircraft shipments was $5.1 billion, including $3.8 billion for transport aircraft, $0.3 billion for helicopters, and $1 billion for private or general aviation aircraft. The flyaway value of military aircraft produced in the United States was $2.9 billion.

To some degree, the location of customers does affect the location of plants. The military market is nationwide, of course, for air bases occur in all parts of the country; however, since there are more large air bases in the West and South than in any other part of the nation, factories in Los Angeles, Wichita, and Dallas have an advantage. Then too, the civilian market for commercial and for private planes, being largely in the Northeast has served to attract factories there. And a considerable factor in the growth of Wichita's industry was the demand of oilmen in Kansas and Oklahoma for small planes with which to visit their oilfields. But for the nation as a whole it does not appear that market is the dominant influence upon the location of airplane manufacturing.

Climate. For one, a warm, dry climate, as in southern California, is ideal for airplane manufacture, for it enables substantial savings in costs of storage, assembly, and testing. Engines, propellers, aluminum, and other parts can be stockpiled outdoors; much of the assembly work can be done outdoors; the heating requirements for what few hangar buildings are required is small; and the assembled planes can be flight-tested nearly every day of the year. But the importance of the aircraft industry in such places as Dallas, Wichita, and Seattle serves as a reminder that a warm, dry climate is more a "bonus" than a requirement.

Production of Northrop Corporation's F-5E International Fighter aircraft at the company's manufacturing facilities in California. (*Courtesy Northrop Corporation.*)

Entrepreneurs. The term "entrepreneur" here stands for all the intangible factors that have motivated enterprising men to start manufacturing. In Seattle a wealthy lumberman named Boeing operated a private plane as a hobby during World War I. After a minor accident he himself repaired the damage to the plane and became so interested in its construction that he decided to build a new one himself. The experiment was a success, and from this chance event grew the nation's largest single airplane factory. May we not wonder as with Eastman and Rochester: if Boeing had lived in Portland (or in San Francisco, or in any other town) would it instead of Seattle be the conspicuous dot on Figure 21-1?

Similarly, Donald Douglas was a Los Angeles citizen and an airplane fan. In 1923, backed by local capital, he set up a small factory to make planes. His ideas worked, his operation succeeded, and from this chance start emerged the largest airplane factory in Los Angeles.

Risk Capital. "Risk capital" applies to the supply of money in the hands of investors who are willing to invest in new enterprises. It was the juxtaposition of risk capital and men with ideas in Seattle, Los Angeles, and Wichita that led to the start of aircraft making there.

Labor. But ingenious enterprises and daring capital cannot develop a large industry by themselves. Thousands of productive workers are needed to turn out the items designed. All the steps in the manufacture of airplane frames (cutting aluminum sheets, riveting, and so on) and the assembly of engines, propellers, and wires can be performed in large measure by semiskilled labor. Even so, the assembly plants that sprang up during World War II in Los Angeles, Fort Worth, Dallas, Wichita, and Seattle were hopelessly unable to procure labor from local sources. But the nature of the work was such that farmers, salesmen, schoolteachers, and housewives could be recruited from all parts of the nation and quickly trained in large numbers to augment a few highly skilled technicians and supervisors.

Noticeably different is the manufacture of engines, propellers, radar devices, compasses, and various electronic equipment. This requires highly skilled workers who cannot be quickly recruited and trained. Skilled machinists in particular must serve long apprenticeships. Now, one of the principles of labor location is that skilled labor tends to be more immobile than unskilled labor. This offers a persuasive explanation of why assembly plants dispersed (or sprang up) widely whereas engine production plants remained rooted in the northeastern states where most of the nation's skilled machinists are.

"Security". During World War II the government encouraged aircraft plants to expand less in coastal cities and more in inland centers. Boeing set up a branch in Wichita, and eastern producers moved to Dallas and Fort Worth. Defense contracts were awarded to producers in the interior—such as the contract for "Albatross" hulls, mentioned earlier, that was awarded to an Evansville company. With the advent of missile production, the government is even establishing factories in barren western deserts.

World Regions

Because aircraft have such strategic significance, data on world production are almost as difficult to procure as those for uranium. There is no doubt, however, that the United States and the U.S.S.R. make the most planes. Still, Germany, the United Kingdom, France, and Japan each produce quite a large number of aircraft.

MOTOR VEHICLES AND EQUIPMENT

Location

The manufacture of automobiles, buses, and trucks is highly concentrated within a midwestern region we might well call "the automotive triangle" (Figure 21-2). If we drew three imaginary lines from Buffalo to Cincinnati to Janesville (Wisconsin) and back to Buffalo, we would delimit an area containing some two-thirds of the nation's automotive employees. The southern half of Michigan alone accounts for almost 40 per cent of the employees in this industry. Few other large industries are so highly concentrated in a single state. And on an even finer scale, Detroit and its suburbs can boast 20 per cent of the automotive jobs in the country.

The automotive triangle is a virtually continuous cluster of large cities: Detroit, Flint, Lansing, Saginaw, Grand Rapids, Pontiac, Jackson—all in Michigan—and Cleveland, Buffalo, Toledo, South Bend, Chicago, Milwaukee, Indianapolis, and Cincinnati in neighboring states. But the triangle also contains numerous smaller settlements, such as Janesville and Kenosha (Wisconsin) and Belvidere (Illinois).

Outside this triangle, automotive manufacture is widely scattered. It appears in such places as Los Angeles and Fremont, California; Wilmington, Delaware; Atlanta, Georgia; and Arlington, Texas.

Characteristics

Two Factory Types. The automotive industry has two types of plants: factories where *parts* are made (engines, transmission systems, axles, wheels, and frames) and factories where *assembly* takes place. The regional patterns of these two components are somewhat different.

Nearly all parts are manufactured within the automotive triangle or on the Middle Atlantic Seaboard. This region contains about 85 per cent of those engaged in the manufacture of motor vehicle parts and accessories (Figure 21-3). Elsewhere employment is modest,

MANUFACTURING: MOTOR VEHICLES AND EQUIPMENT

Number of Employees

- 1,500
- 5,000
- 15,000
- 40,000
- 115,000

Undistributed

Selected Counties, Black
Remainder in State, Shaded

0 100 200 300
Scale of Miles

Figure 21-2

Figure 21-3

MANUFACTURING: MOTOR VEHICLE PARTS AND ACCESSORIES

Number of Employees

- 1,000
- 3,000
- 8,000
- 25,000
- 70,000

Undistributed

Selected Counties, Black
Remainder in State, Shaded

0 100 200 300
Scale of Miles

with only a few states such as California (especially Los Angeles), Missouri, and Tennessee showing significant numbers.

Assembly plants, on the other hand, are scattered in a number of spots throughout the nation (Figure 21-4). Detroit still assembles more cars than any other city, Michigan than any other state; the automotive triangle is still the main assembly area. But more and more assembling is being done elsewhere: on the East Coast, in the South, and on the West Coast. Examples of such assembly points are South Gate and Van Nuys (California), Wilmington (Delaware), Atlanta and Doraville (Georgia), Baltimore (Maryland), Kansas City and St. Louis (Missouri), and Arlington (Texas).

Invariably, each assembly plant has a body-making factory close by because transportation costs on long-distance shipments of bodies can often exceed their value.

Large Scale. There are nearly 3400 factories in the United States that make motor vehicles and parts; they average 238 employees apiece. Large corporations predominate. In 1973, the United States produced 9,667,000 passenger cars; in 1974, the figure was 7,324,000; and in 1975, it was 6,717,000—all of them the output of just five companies (Table 21-3). And of that group, General Motors alone produced about as many automobiles as the other four combined. About the individual make of car, the names Chevrolet and Ford identify almost half of the cars that roll off factory lines in the United States. Clearly, the tendency is toward gigantism.

Mass-Production Methods. The manufacture of automobiles is an excellent example of the mass-production method. Thousands of engines, pistons, bearings, shafts, and wheels are produced by specially designed tools with such precision that craftsmen can fit any one of a thousand axles with any two of a thousand wheels and achieve a smoothly functioning unit. These multitudes of parts are then assembled along complex assembly lines on which each of dozens of workers specializes in a comparatively simple task, such as affixing a wheel, welding a joint, or securing a few screws. The result of this system, developed to a large extent by Henry Ford, is greater aggregate production

Table 21-3

United States: Passenger Car Production by Companies and Selected Leading Makes, 1973–1974 Average

Company and Make	Amount	Percentage of Total
UNITED STATES TOTAL PASSENGER CARS	8,495,824	100
American Motors Corporation	353,971	4
Chrysler Corporation	1,366,519	16
Plymouth	672,781	8
Dodge	528,428	6
Chrysler	165,310	2
Ford Motor Company	2,350,548	27
Ford	1,813,092	21
Mercury	426,975	5
Lincoln	110,481	1
General Motors Corporation	4,419,122	52
Chevrolet	2,118,987	25
Pontiac	684,340	8
Oldsmobile	733,388	9
Buick	613,234	7
Cadillac	269,173	3
Checker	5,664	<1

Source: Motor Vehicle Manufacturers Association, *1975 Automobile Facts and Figures* (1975).

Figure 21-4

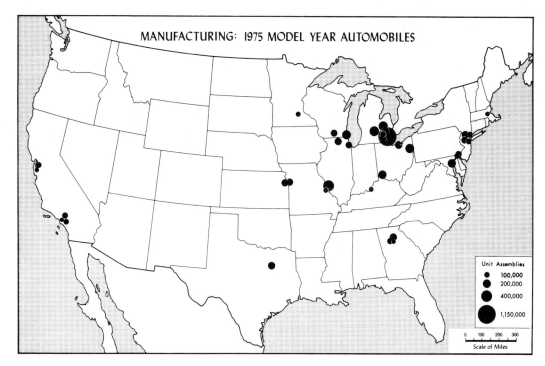

MANUFACTURING: 1975 MODEL YEAR AUTOMOBILES

Unit Assemblies
- 100,000
- 200,000
- 400,000
- 1,150,000

0 100 200 300
Scale of Miles

than would be possible if each worker endeavored to assemble a complete car by himself.

The latest development in the mass-production technique is *automation*, whereby machines turning out the manufactured product are operated, not by human operators, but by other machines. In not only the automotive industry but many other industries as well, automation is accounting for a slowly increasing percentage of output.

Changing Location. The automotive industry today has a very different pattern than it had 30 or 40 years ago. Michigan in general and Detroit in particular play a much smaller role than they once did. In 1949, the United States had 682,000 people employed in the motor vehicle and equipment industry. Michigan had 380,000 or 56 per cent of this number, and Detroit had 273,000 or 40 per cent. By 1973, the United States total had grown substantially to 900,000, but Michigan's share had dropped to 37 per cent. Michigan and Detroit may be associated with automobile manufacture in the minds of many people, but the fact is that only one-third of all 1975 car assemblies were produced in Michigan, and only about 7 per cent came from Detroit.

Relationships

Market Regions. Today, assembly plants are located primarily in cities that are centrally situated among customers. Originally, though, this was not true; automobiles were made mostly in Michigan and shipped throughout the country. But shipping costs on an automobile are extremely high. It is much less expensive to ship carloads of engines, transmissions, wheels, and other parts to Los Angeles, Dallas, Atlanta, and Boston for assembly there. Although an assembly plant on, say, the West Coast might send cars to places throughout the nation, most of its output will probably stay within its local market area. This principle holds not only for distant cities but also for assembly points close to the automotive triangle, such as Minneapolis, Janesville, St. Louis, and Tarrytown. From these points, finished automobiles have shorter, cheaper distances to travel to dealers. They are usually carried on specially designed trailer trucks that, rolling along the highways, are notable features of the landscape throughout southern Michigan and on the roads radiating outward from other assembly plants.

The location of the market corresponds closely with that of population. In 1975, Americans purchased over 10,000,000 motor vehicles. The leading buying states, as indicated in Table 21-4, are generally those where most assembly work is now performed.

It is in this relationship of the automobile to markets that we find part of the explanation for Michigan's losses in automotive job opportunities. To be sure, Michigan has a rather good location relative to the

Table 21-4

New Car and Truck Registrations by State, 1974–1975 Average

State	Amount
UNITED STATES TOTAL	11,008,634
California	1,007,790
New York	739,544
Texas	719,096
Illinois	669,690
Michigan	617,214
Pennsylvania	600,586
Ohio	570,560
Florida	466,849
New Jersey	370,267
Indiana	288,248

Source: Motor Vehicle Manufacturers Association, *Motor Vehicle Facts and Figures '76* (1976).

domestic market, but her position in this respect is probably less favorable than that of Ohio, Indiana, or Illinois.

The foreign market buys a small portion of total United States motor vehicle production; the value of exports is only about 10 per cent of the total value of production. Nevertheless, the value of motor vehicles is such that they constitute one of our top-ranking exports! In 1974 United States motor vehicle exports were over $3,700,000,000. The foreign market consists chiefly of Canada, Latin America, and Asia. Major customers in terms of value of vehicles purchased are Canada $2,570,900,000; Mexico $161,200,000; Venezuela $79,700,000; Japan $75,900,000; and Saudi Arabia $71,900,000. Some producers are recognizing the attraction of the foreign market by locating assembly plants in foreign nations. In many cases, United States producers are required to operate a plant in a foreign country in order to do business there. Some countries have laws which specify "local content," that is, the amount of locally produced material that must be used to keep the vehicle from being designated an import. United States firms usually establish subsidiaries in order to avoid taxes and tariffs which would make them uncompetitive.

The pull of market areas on the location of parts factories is weaker than its effect on assembly, because parts can be shipped much more economically than can finished vehicles. Of the many parts that go into an automotive vehicle, only one is usually manufactured near the assembly plant: the body. This is by far the bulkiest component of the vehicle and it is costly to transport. Therefore, sheet steel is shipped to assembly centers and manufactured into bodies in factories that often adjoin the assembly plant. Notice the similarity in this respect between airplane frames and automobile bodies.

Raw-Material Regions. Assembly plants are evidencing less and less of a tendency to locate where the parts they assemble are made. But factories that make engines, carburetors, and gears show a definite disposition to settle near steel centers. Compare the pattern of the automobile industry (Figure 21-2) with that of the steel industry (Figure 20-1). Admittedly, Pittsburgh has scarcely any automotive manufacturing; but, on the other hand, many of the leading automotive areas do have steel mills: for instance, Detroit, Chicago, Cleveland, and Buffalo. No part of the automotive triangle is very far from sources of steel.

Up to this point it seems logical to expect that the heart of the automotive industry would naturally be somewhere in the Midwest, a region that has the advantage of being centrally located both to the bulk of the market and to the principal raw material—steel. But why should Detroit rather than Pittsburgh, Chicago, or a dozen other midwestern cities have become the automotive capital of the world?

An Early Start. Part of the answer lies in Detroit's early start. Even before the day of the large corporation, in the late 1890's and early 1900's when cars were made by numerous small companies, Detroit was the leading center. (This statement applies only to gasoline-burning vehicles; in 1900 the United States produced 4000 horseless carriages, about half of which came from New England shops. But over 3000 of these vehicles were powered by either steam or electricity—types of motive power that soon disappeared. It was the gasoline burners that won the competition, and by 1900 southern Michigan was ahead of all other regions in this phase of the industry.)

But the concept of "early start" is only a partial answer to the query and, in a sense, begs the question. It certainly leads to others. Why did Detroit get such an early start? Moreover, why has Detroit persisted for so many years as the outstanding automotive center? Many an industry has started in one region and subsequently moved to another which outstripped the original site. What other advantages did Detroit have to begin with, and which ones have persisted?

Favorable Environment. Many authorities point out that since southern Michigan has a comparatively flat and gently rolling topography, horseless carriages did not encounter discouraging gradients in the early days. Moreover, the glacial soil with a high proportion of sand and gravel made for more "navigable" roads in inclement weather; though horse-drawn vehicles can make their way through mud roads, horseless ones cannot. Then, too, Detroit's location along the Detroit River, a major link in the Great Lakes thoroughfare, supposedly stimulated the development of factories to make internal combustion engines for boats, a factor which then combined with the manufacture of carriages to give natural birth to the automobile industry. All this is true and unquestionably played a part in the early start of automobile making in Michigan. But these conditions are essentially true for eastern Wisconsin and northern Ohio. What did Michigan have that these other states lacked?

Inventive Genius. The birth of the automotive industry occurred in 1886 with the invention (by Gottlieb Daimler in Germany) of the first internal combustion engine using petroleum. But several years elapsed before anybody successfully harnessed the engine to a wheeled vehicle. By 1895 though, several inventors had built experimental vehicles, with Ford, Hanes, and Duryea each claiming to have built the first successful one in the United States. By 1900 there were a large number of manufacturers making cars. The products were somewhat like houses in that very few were exactly alike. Each manfacturer made a variety of vehicles at a variety of prices.

Then Henry Ford conceived three ideas that were to catapult his company to fame and give his home town, Detroit, a tremendous lead over all other places in the manufacture of automobiles. First, he designed an extremely simple internal combustion engine that was also unusually durable and easy to operate. The vehicle built around this power unit was called "the model T," and it immediately caught the fancy of the American buyer. Ford's second idea was to abandon the strategy of many models at many prices and concentrate on one model in order to produce the most efficient car at the lowest price, "a motor car for the multitude." The third idea was to manufacture these cars, not piece by piece as one builds a house, but by mass-production methods whereby all parts of the car were standardized and produced by extremely specialized machine tools and then fitted together on assembly lines. These two technical innovations combined with the marketing innovation were so successful that in 1909 Ford turned out 10,000 vehicles. By 1923 production hiked past 2,000,000. At the same time, selling prices dropped steadily in response to efficiencies of the mass-production system, from $950 per car in 1909, to $295 in 1922.

Now, Henry Ford had been born on a farm a few miles from Detroit. We can only speculate, of course, about where the automobile industry might have taken root had this inventive genius resided in Pittsburgh or in Chicago. But if he had, might not Pennsylvania or Illinois instead of Michigan have dominated the geography of the automotive industry this past half-century?

Ford was not the only maker of automobiles, of course. Numerous other companies were in the business, but most of them followed Fort's basic ideas, and most of them were started in Michigan. Lansing was the home town of R.E. Olds, a young mechanic who launched the Oldsmobile company in 1901. Flint was the home town for a carriage producer, W.C. Durant, who founded Buick.

Just as Iowa was blessed by a natural endowment of rich soil for corn agriculture, Michigan was blessed by an unusual group of bright, inventive minds.

Risk Capital. Henry Ford had the ideas but not the money for launching an automotive factory. And most people who had the money lacked the disposition to risk it on so novel a venture as manufacturing a horseless carriage. But Detroit investors were willing to gamble their dollars on Ford's ideas. Again we can wonder: If Detroit money had said "no" to Ford and Milwaukee money or Cleveland money had said "yes," would the mass of black circles on Figure 21-2 be hovering over southern Wisconsin or northern Ohio instead of southern Michigan?

Productive Labor. We have exposed Michigan's advantageous relationships to market, environment, human inventiveness, and so on. What about that other essential, an adept work force? Southern Michigan in the early days had a flock of carriage factories, wagon factories, and machine shops where mechanically trained men had gathered experience which fitted them well for making automobiles. And yet the whole agricultural heart of the Midwest, from Ohio to Iowa, had just as many wagon factories and machine shops—enough to supply a labor pool as wide and deep as that in southern Michigan. Without question, Michigan's labor force was fundamental to her automotive industry, but this relationship in itself scarcely explains why Michigan instead of Ohio should have become so prominent.

Indeed, not many years elapsed before the new industry exhausted Michigan's supply of labor and began attracting workers from other states, from as far distant as Alabama and Mississippi. Thousands of Southerners, many of them Negroes, flocked to Michigan, primarily Detroit, to work for General Motors, Ford, or Chrysler. Regardless of origin, race, or sex, these workers did not have to be highly skilled; the widespread use of machinery on the production line enabled semi-skilled labor to turn out acceptable cars.

Highly developed skills are required, however, in the design and manufacture of the machinery, in its supervision and maintenance, and in the organization of a production line. The highly trained mechanics required for these jobs take years to develop; they are a fruit of the Midwest's long experience in producing machines, and they are a powerful force in perpetuating the boundaries of the automotive triangle.

Wage Rates. The automotive industry pays one of the highest wage rates of any manufacturing industry. The Bureau of Labor Statistics, which publishes data on the average hourly earnings of production workers in over 200 different types of manufacturing industries, shows that the motor vehicle and equipment business accounts for three of the ten highest wage industries (Table 21-5). Consequently, Michigan leads all other

Table 21-5

Average Hourly Earnings of Production Workers in Manufacturing, November, 1975 (by Industry)

Leading Industries	Average Hourly Earnings
1. Passenger car bodies	$7.61
2. Blast furnaces and steel mills	7.49
3. Malt liquors	7.31
4. Petroleum refining	7.17
5. Motor vehicles	6.98
6. Primary aluminum	6.91
7. Hydraulic cement	6.82
8. Soap and other detergents	6.62
9. Motor vehicle parts and accessories	6.61
10. Metal cans	6.60

Source: U.S. Bureau of Labor Statistics, *Employment and Earnings* (February, 1976).

heavily industrial states in the hourly earnings of factory workers, and several of Michigan's cities enjoy a high rating among cities for their average hourly earnings of production workers in manufacturing; indeed, of the top ten cities in Table 21-6, seven are in the automotive triangle and five are in Michigan.

"Agglomeration". As used in geography, "agglomeration" means the tendency for enterprises to locate near one another. Automotive factories have shown a strong tendency to do this in Michigan, particularly in Detroit. At first glance this may seem surprising; one might expect that a new company would locate in a different region from the seat of an already existing company in order to get away from the competition. Yet in any mass-production industry, large factories have an advantage over small ones, and a city that has attributes attractive to one large producer may be equally attractive to another. Thus, apart from competing for the same labor pool, there is no particular disadvantage in two or more manufacturers locating in the same state—or city. Indeed, there are certain advantages, such as nearness to local trained technicians; the combined influence of two or more companies in turn can lure even more potential technicians from other places. Besides, the interests of other establishments in the region (such as banking, financing, vocational schools) become geared to the industry. And other industries that specialize in servicing the agglomerated one also cluster round.

Unionization. The automobile business is one of the most highly unionized industries in the country; furthermore, its union, the United Auto Workers, is one of the most powerful labor organizations. At this point we encounter a phenomenon about which there is violent difference of opinion. Some persons believe that the strength of the U.A.W. in Michigan is one reason for the exodus of the industry from Michigan. Others

Table 21-6

Average Hourly Earnings of Production Workers in Manufacturing, November, 1975 (by State and Area)

Ten Highest States Reporting		Ten Highest Areas Reporting	
1. Alaska	$8.56	1. Saginaw, Mich.	$7.38
2. Michigan	6.40	2. Flint, Mich.	7.12
3. Washington	5.99	3. Waterloo-Cedar Falls, Iowa	6.91
4. Ohio	5.76	4. Galveston-Texas City, Texas	6.89
5. Oregon	5.73	5. Ann Arbor, Mich.	6.79
6. Indiana	5.66	6. Detroit, Mich.	6.78
7. Montana	5.62	7. Lansing-East Lansing, Mich.	6.70
8. Illinois	5.56	8. Youngstown-Warren, Ohio	6.70
9. Iowa	5.52	9. Dubuque, Iowa	6.66
10. Wisconsin	5.48	10. Kenosha, Wis.	6.60

Source: U.S. Bureau of Labor Statistics, *Employment and Earnings* (February, 1976).

reply that the industry is inevitably destined to become more evenly dispersed through the northeastern quadrant of the nation, and that only the momentum of Michigan's early start has kept her ahead this long.

The Economic Base. Employment in automotive factories constitutes a large segment of the economic activity in several places. Michigan's jobholders in the automotive industry make up about 30 per cent of her employment in manufacturing and 12 per cent of her total employment. In Detroit those percentages are about the same. In Flint they are unbelievably high: 75 per cent, manufacturing employment and 40 per cent, total employment. Think what it means to the economic life of Flint and Detroit—and Michigan—when the automotive industry is in trouble.

The World Pattern

The great majority of the world's automotive vehicles are manufactured in Anglo-America and western Europe. Over 33,000,000 passenger cars, trucks, and buses rolled off the world's factory lines in 1975, and about a quarter of this number came from United States producers. Table 21-7 suggests that there are two types of areas in terms of emphasis on passenger car and truck output. One type produces a high percentage of trucks and buses: India 58 per cent, Brazil 44, and the U.S.S.R. 39. The other type emphasizes passenger cars more than trucks: Italy 92 per cent, West Germany 91, and France 89. There may be a correlation between such variation and standard of living, so we might hypothesize that the higher the standard of living, the higher the ratio between output of passenger cars and output of trucks. Although there appears to be a general relationship between affluence and emphasis on truck and bus or passenger car production it should be noted that such affluent nations as the United States and the United Kingdom fall between the two extremes with 27 and 23 per cent, respectively, in truck and bus production. What does this do to our original hypothesis?

Table 21-7

World Motor Vehicle Production by Leading Nations, 1975 in Thousands

Region	Passenger Cars	Trucks and Buses	Total
North America			
United States	6,717	2,265	8,982
Canada	1,054	389	1,443
Mexico	239	122	361
South America			
Brazil	524	406	930
Argentina	201	61	262
Europe			
France	2,953	347	3,300
West Germany	2,908	278	3,186
United Kingdom	1,268	381	1,649
Italy	1,349	110	1,459
Spain	696	118	814
Sweden	316	50	366
Poland	174	85	259
Belgium	197	25	222
Czechoslovakia	175	36	211
U.S.S.R.	1,201	763	1,964
Asia			
Japan	4,568	2,374	6,942
India	31	43	74
Others			
Australia	335	65	400
WORLD TOTAL	25,192	8,002	33,194

Source: Motor Vehicle Manufacturers Association, *Motor Vehicle Facts and Figures '76* (1976).

International trade in motor vehicles is a somewhat different story from that of production. Western Europe is by far the leading source region of vehicles that figure in international trade. France and West Germany are far ahead of all other European countries. But the United States and Canada are also important, and in recent years, Japan's growth as an exporter has been spectacular. For the leading exporters and importers, see Table 21-8.

Table 21-8

Motor Vehicles: Exports and Imports by Leading Nations, 1974

Leading Exporters* (Thousands)		Leading Importers (Thousands)	
Japan	2,618	United States	2,573
France	1,949	Canada	665
West Germany	1,881	West Germany	590
Canada	1,063	Netherlands	409
United States	816	France	376
Belgium	772	United Kingdom	375
United Kingdom	735	Italy	335
Italy	734	Belgium	277
Sweden	195	Switzerland	198
Spain	141	Sweden	177

Source: Motor Vehicle Manufacturers Association, *Motor Vehicle Facts and Figures '76* (1976).

*Includes vehicles imported from other countries and reexported.

Imports are a still different story since the United States imports more than three times as many vehicles as any other nation—and about three times as many as she herself exports. Thousands of Americans have come to prefer the smaller, more economical European and Japanese cars.

SHIPBUILDING

Only one-quarter the number of persons are engaged in the manufacture of ships and boats in the United States as are employed in the motor vehicle industry (Table 21-1); the employment figure is about equal to the number making motor vehicles in Detroit alone.

The main region of watercraft manufacture is a belt along the Middle Atlantic Coast. Places which predominate include Newport News, Sparrows Point, Chester, Camden, and Quincy. Other tidewater producers are found in Pascagoula, Port Arthur, San Diego, San Francisco, and Seattle. Leading states, by employment, are Virginia and Maryland 19 per cent, Louisiana and Texas 17 per cent, Alabama and Mississippi 17 per cent, and California 8 per cent.

The location of shipbuilding has gone through a pronounced change. For nearly two centuries before 1900 the industry was centered in New England. During colonial days New England had all the requirements for shipbuilding: a location at one end of a major avenue of ocean shipping, a thriving maritime trade, a brisk whaling industry which demanded ships, a resourceful people with the ingenuity and productivity for making ships, rich stands of timber for making hulls, masts, spars, and decks, and satisfactory harbors along which "ways" (for building ships) could be constructed. The industry thrived and the United States led the world in launching ships until 1860. The famous "Yankee Clippers" designed and built in American yards were the world's fastest ships; numerous foreign shippers bought and operated them in all the world's major seas. Then American shipbuilding ran into stormy weather which changed both its location in the United States and this nation's position in world production.

A technological revolution saw steel displace wood as the material for construction and steam replace wind as the propelling force. New England, rich with trees,

Shipbuilding at the Avondale Shipyards near New Orleans. The two vessels being constructed are of the LASH (lighter aboard ship) type, which are designed to transport floating containers. Computer-operated machinery is used to cut and bend many of the metal structures used in the construction. (*Courtesy Avondale Shipyards, Inc.*)

had scarcely any steel mills, so it quickly lost out to harbor cities farther south that were close to the steel mills in Pennsylvania and Maryland. Indeed, Baltimore developed shipyards immediately adjoining a steel mill at Sparrows Point. The change from wood to steel also played a role in America's loss of first place to the United Kingdom. Although severely limited in timber resources, Britain was well-endowed with coal and iron ore; indeed she led the world in coal mining, iron ore mining, and steel manufacture. She had a 50-year head start on the United States in the large-scale production of steel.

Even more important in the decline of the United States in shipbuilding, though, was a rise in this nation's wage rates. The average hourly wage in our shipyards is over $5.00 per hour, which is high compared with other shipbuilding nations. Such discrepancies can be overcome by industries that are adaptable to mechanization. But shipbuilding is the antithesis of mechanized production. Small boats can be mass-produced, but ships are simply too large to produce on assembly lines; the demand is too small to justify mass production, and the few orders that do come in are from shippers who stipulate different specifications. For these reasons, shipbuilding—in peacetime—defies mass production and simply does not fit into the present scheme of American manufacturing. The nation that manufactures a quarter of the world's automobiles makes only 2 per cent of the world's launched tonnage of ships (Table 21-9).

Table 21-9

Tankers and Other Seagoing Merchant Vessels, Launched Tonnage, 1973 in Thousands of Tons

Country	Vessels	Percentage of Total	Tankers only
TOTAL	30,561	100	18,008
Japan	15,571	51	11,442
Sweden	2,517	8	1,383
West Germany	1,875	6	—
Spain	1,568	5	1,012
France	1,134	4	650
Norway	1,071	4	573
United Kingdom	963	3	360
Denmark	920	3	725
Netherlands	897	3	740
Italy	754	2	379
United States	734	2	315
Poland	550	2	—
Yugoslavia	354	1	30
East Germany	287	1	—
Canada	234	1	129
Belgium	225	1	76
Finland	209	1	41

Source: United Nations, *The Growth of World Industry* (1975).

Things are different in wartime, however. During World Wars I and II the call for military and merchant ships was tremendous. Orders for large numbers of similar ships permitted the use of a few mass-production methods. Steel mills, for instance, turned out beams and plates cut to specification for Victory ships, Liberty ships, and destroyers. Overnight, during the second war, the United States became the world's leading shipmaker again. In 1943 our yards turned out ships totaling 12,499,000 tons. But just as quickly, with peace, the industry collapsed; in 1948 our production was down to 164,000 tons! Still, the government recognizes that for defense purposes shipyards must not close completely and the labor force must not be allowed to disappear. A nucleus must be maintained around which wartime production—if necessary—may be quickly rallied. Accordingly, the government is now heavily subsidizing the construction of not just men-of-war but also merchant tankers, freighters, and liners. Even so, American yards still launch less than 800,000 tons of ships a year.

American coastal shipyards are concentrating on tankers, which constitute over two-fifths of the annual launched tonnage of merchant vessels. Great Lakes yards make ore and coal carriers and barges; inland centers limit themselves to barges, yachts, and small craft.

The world picture (Figure 21-5) shows that Japan, Sweden, and West Germany now lead in the construction of merchant vessels (Table 21-9).

RAIL VEHICLES

A large share of the United States' transportation machines with flanged wheels are manufactured in the northeastern quadrant of the country. For decades steam locomotives came mostly from Philadelphia, Schenectady, and Lima (Ohio) where, in early railroad history (the mid-1800's), designers of locomotives got a head start, just as Henry Ford did later in Michigan in automobile production. But the steam locomotive industry is dead now, having been replaced by electric-diesel engines. It was not the steam engine makers who made the change, however, but competitors from quite different industries, such as the Electro-Motive Division of General Motors in La Grange, Illinois, and Fairbanks Morse in Beloit, Wisconsin. Today there are several firms which specialize in rebuilding used locomotives, but only a handful of companies which build new ones. Perhaps the best known builder of new locomotives is the Electro-Motive Division of the General Electric Company. This Erie, Pennsylvania based firm has been building locomotives since 1895.

Almost all of the nation's railway cars come from just 18 car builders, Chicago, Illinois; St. Charles, Missouri; and Bethlehem and Altoona in Pennsylvania are all well-known centers. Ten of the 18 car builders are located in Illinois and Pennsylvania and 4 others are located in nearby Ohio, Michigan, and Missouri. Such locations have the dual advantage of being near steel

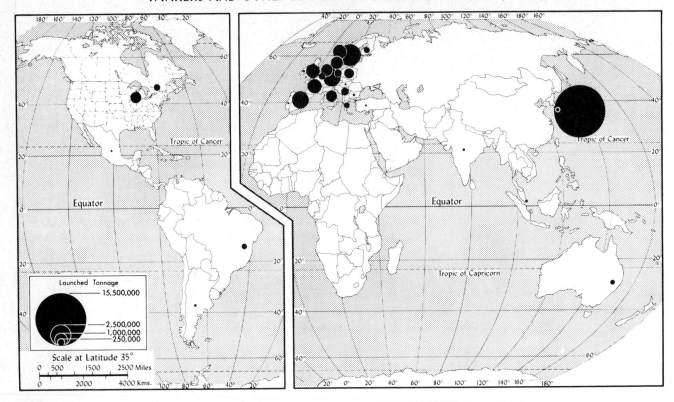

Figure 21-5

mills and in the most densely trafficked railway region of the country. The northeastern quadrant does not, however, hold a monopoly in car building. Important producers are also found in Oregon, Washington, Texas, Minnesota, and Georgia.

The world pattern of the manufacture of railway equipment is familiar, since there is a very close correlation by nations between the production of steel and the production of railway equipment. So the steel regions indicated in Figure 20-5, page 271, are approximately those where vehicles are produced.

SUGGESTED READINGS

Automobile Facts and Figures, Motor Vehicle Manufacturers Association of the United States (annual).

Boas, Charles W., "Locational Patterns of American Automobile Assembly Plants, 1895–1958," *Economic Geography*, 1961, pp. 218–230.

Cunningham, William Glenn, *The Aircraft Industry: A Study in Industrial Location*, Los Angeles, 1951, 247 pp.

Goodwin, William, "Relocation of the British Motor Industry," *The Professional Geographer*, July, 1962, pp. 4–8.

Steed, G. P. F., "The Changing Milieu of a Firm: A Case Study of a Shipbuilding Concern," *Annals of the Association of American Geographers*, 1968, pp. 506–525.

CHAPTER

22

electrical equipment and machinery

Although the electrical equipment industry is exceedingly sophisticated, many operations are labor intensive. (*Courtesy Honeywell Information Systems, Inc.*)

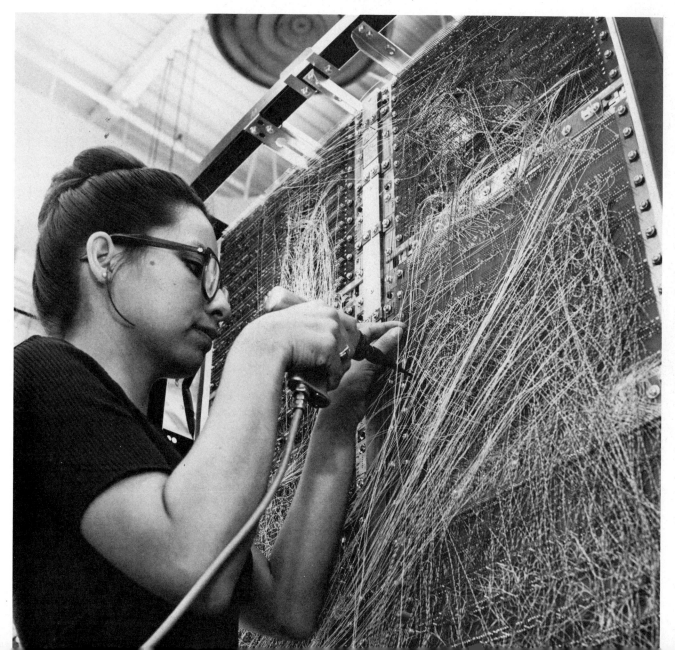

Since the Industrial Revolution began, inventive individuals have devised machines to perform so many different jobs, and the demand for such machinery has become so great that in the United States today there are 3,500,000 people who earn their living by manufacturing engines, motors, lathes, typewriters, televisions, and a host of other items. Another 1,700,000 workers produce the transport machines that we discussed in the previous chapter. The machinery industries we shall examine in this chapter are extremely diverse, so for better understanding, we shall separate them into two broad groups: electric and electronic equipment and nonelectrical machinery. A breakdown of the number of jobs provided by these industrial groups is listed in Table 22-1 according to the classification system of the Bureau of the Census.

Table 22-1

United States: Leading Machinery Manufacturing Industries

Type	Number of Employees (Thousands)	Value Added ($ Millions)
Machinery (except electrical)	1,827.7	37,562.9
Engines and turbines	116.0	2,899.5
Farm and garden machinery	125.3	2,701.2
Construction and mining machinery	275.4	5,962.2
Metalworking machinery	268.1	4,901.7
Special industry machinery	190.1	3,731.9
General industrial machinery	262.0	5,019.7
Office and computing machinery	208.4	4,904.5
Refrigeration and service machinery	197.9	4,426.7
Other	184.5	3,015.5
Electric and electronic equipment	1,662.4	30,583.4
Electric distributing equipment	116.0	2,060.3
Electrical industrial apparatus	188.3	3,224.4
Household appliances	162.8	3,562.2
Electric lighting and wiring equipment	179.3	3,302.0
Radio and TV receiving equipment	106.9	2,183.4
Communication equipment	453.6	8,453.1
Electronic components	335.6	5,310.9
Other	119.9	2,487.1
Transportation equipment	1,719.0	39,799.4

Source: U.S. Bureau of the Census, *1972 Census of Manufactures* (1975).

ELECTRIC AND ELECTRONIC EQUIPMENT

As Table 22-1 shows, approximately 1,660,000 people are at work making generators, transformers, motors, appliances, bulbs, lamps, telephones, radios, electronic tubes, storage batteries, X-ray apparatus, and other categories of electrical machinery. And as Figure 22-1 indicates two-thirds are in the northeastern part of the

country, within an area delineated by Boston, Philadelphia, St. Louis, and Milwaukee. The two outstanding centers are Chicago and the greater New York area, which between them account for almost a sixth of the nation's makers of electric equipment. Other focal points of this industry in the Northeast are Boston, Philadelphia, and Milwaukee. Los Angeles is the most noteworthy spot outside of the Northeast; indeed, when figures for Anaheim and other centers are combined with those for metropolitan Los Angeles, this region ranks with New York and Chicago.

By either state or metropolitan area, there seems to be a correlation between the manufacture of electric equipment and size of population (see Table 22-2).

Table 22-2

United States: Leading Areas of Employment in Electric and Electronic Equipment Manufacture and Population

Area	Employees in Electric and Electronic Equipment Manufacture		Population Percentage of U.S. Total	
	Number in Thousands	Percentage of U.S. Total		
New England states	151.9	9	6	
Middle Atlantic states	374.1	23	18	
New York	161.0		10	9
Pennsylvania	116.5		7	6
East North Central states	483.2	29	20	
Ohio	110.2		7	5
Indiana	116.4		7	3
Illinois	171.4		10	5
West North Central states	86.4	5	8	
South Altantic states	157.0	9	15	
East South Central states	98.2	6	6	
West South Central states	90.6	6	10	
Mountain states	37.2	2	4	
Pacific Coast states	183.8	11	13	
California	176.9		11	10
U.S. TOTAL	1,662.4	100	52	100	38

Source: U.S. Bureau of the Census, *1972 Census of Manufactures* (1975) and *Statistical Abstract of the United States: 1975.*

California is the most populous state and also the leading maker of electric equipment. The 14 northeastern states do contain the bulk of the nation's population as well as the bulk of employment in electric equipment production. But the correlation is very gross, for those 14 states contain 61 per cent of the industry's employment but only 44 per cent of the population.

Similarly with metropolitan areas: The correlation between population and employment in the electric equipment industry tends to hold, but there are striking exceptions. San Francisco, 6th in population, does not appear among leading electric equipment makers, whereas San Jose, 50 miles to the south and 30th in population does (Table 22-3, page 291). But perhaps the most glaring exception is Detroit, the 5th largest American metropolitan area. It has over 4,400,000 inhabitants but only about 7,000 electric equipment workers. Why this major manufacturing city should have so small a proportion of the electric equipment industry is, so far, a mystery. Milwaukee, by contrast, ranks higher in making electrical devices (9th) than it does in population (21st).

Such concentration in the Northeast suggests that this region is still riding on the momentum of an early start in this industry. Manufacturers in the region could get an early start because the Northeast early had four qualifications essential for industrial development: (1) the nation's largest group of potential customers; (2) the nation's most abundant supply of steel (as we saw in Chapter 20), copper (Chapter 19), and other required raw materials; (3) the nation's biggest supply of adaptable labor; and (4) abundant supplies of electricity.

As Figure 22-1 shows, there is an unusually heavy concentration of plants along the Atlantic Seaboard (particularly New York, Philadelphia, Boston, Baltimore, and other cities in the New England and Middle Atlantic states). Now, this area is favorably located with regard to one additional factor: the export trade. Since over $5 billion dollars worth of electrical apparatus is exported from the United States annually, a value exceeded only by that of grains, nonelectrical machinery, motor vehicles, and chemicals, the foreign market is not an inconsiderable influence. And for this export trade the Atlantic Coast states in general and their coastal cities in particular have historically had a tremendous locational advantage.

Communication Equipment

One subtype of electric equipment is particularly outstanding for the payroll it supports: communication

equipment. This industry provides jobs for over 450,000 people (Table 22-1). In its broad locational pattern (Figure 22-2), it resembles that of all electrical machinery, but it is more highly localized in fewer places; for example, the two main centers (Chicago and the New York-northeastern New Jersey area) together account for a fifth of the nation's total employment in the industry. Greater New York (with about 52,000 employees) has more people producing telephone apparatus, burglar alarms, highway signals, laser sys-

Table 22-3

Selected Leading Metropolitan Areas in Electric and Electronic Equipment Employment and in Population

Thousands of Employees in Electric Equipment (1972)		Thousands of Inhabitants (1973)	
New York, N.Y.-northeastern N.J.	142.7	New York, N.Y.-northeastern N.J.	16,075
Chicago	131.6	Chicago	7,002
Los Angeles	78.1	Los Angeles-Long Beach	6,924
Philadelphia, Pa.-N.J.	48.8	Philadelphia, Pa.-N.J.	4,806
Dallas	37.0	Detroit	4,446
Boston	36.8	San Francisco-Oakland	3,143
Anaheim-Garden Grove	33.1	Washington, D.C.-Md.-Va.	3,020
San Jose	32.7	Boston	2,898
Milwaukee	32.3	Dallas-Ft. Worth	2,464
Baltimore	21.8	St. Louis, Mo.-Ill.	2,391

Source: U.S. Bureau of the Census, *1972 Census of Manufactures* (1975) and *Statistical Abstract of the United States: 1975.*

Figure 22-1

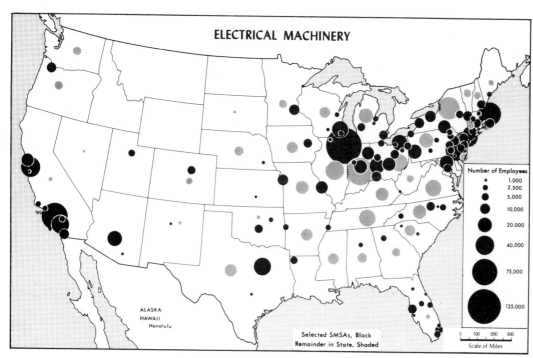

ELECTRICAL MACHINERY

Number of Employees
- 1,000
- 2,500
- 5,000
- 10,000
- 20,000
- 40,000
- 75,000
- 135,000

ALASKA
HAWAII
Honolulu

Selected SMSAs, Black
Remainder in State, Shaded

0   100   200   300
Scale of Miles

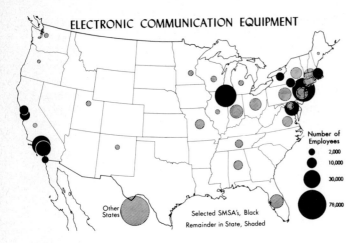

ELECTRONIC COMMUNICATION EQUIPMENT

Number of Employees
• 2,000
● 10,000
● 30,000
● 78,000

Other States

Selected SMSA's, Black
Remainder in State, Shaded

Figure 22-2

tems, radar equipment, television monitors, and other communication equipment than any other metropolitan region. Chicago with 45,000 employees is almost as important as Greater New York. It is interesting to note that the communication equipment industry is not especially well developed in the Pittsburgh-Youngstown-Cleveland-Toledo zone. Manufacturers in this region have tended to concentrate on making electrical industrial apparatus, such as generators, motors, and batteries.

On the state scale, California is clearly the leader with 75,000 employed in the communication equipment industry. Since 1950, the westward shift of this industry has been substantial, with such centers as Los Angeles and Anaheim in California and Phoenix in Arizona leading the way. Today there are 60 per cent more communication equipment employees in California than in either Illinois or New York, the second and third ranking states.

NONELECTRICAL MACHINERY

More than 1,800,000 people are involved in producing machines that are neither electrical nor for transportation: steam engines, turbines, tractors, grain combines, corn pickers, milking machines, bulldozers, road graders, steam shovels, mining machinery, oil-drilling equipment, lathes, drills, looms, printing presses, power saws, pumps, elevators, conveyors, typewriters, scales, washing machines, and dozens of other mechanical devices. (To be sure, some of these machines are driven by electric motors, but their distinction lies in their use rather than their motive power.) This myriad of machinery industries, which supports more wage earners than the transportation-equipment industry (compare Tables 22-1 and 21-1), is located according to the pattern drawn on Figure 22-3.

Six general areas stand out: (1) The Atlantic Seaboard from Maryland to southern New England.

(From the consistency with which this area looms up in almost every industry studied so far, it would seem to be the nation's number-one manufacturing region.) (2) Middle New York State, from Albany to Buffalo. (3) The Detroit-Cleveland-Pittsburgh belt. (4) The Middle Ohio Valley, especially Dayton and Cincinnati. (5) Chicago and environs bounded by Milwaukee, Moline, Peoria, South Bend, and Muskegon—this is the machinery heart of the country, principally because of Chicago's prominence. (6) Los Angeles, which leaps out strikingly as the principal center west of Chicago.

As is true for electrical machinery, so for the non-electrical, there seems to be an over-all similarity between the location of people and the location of factories, as Figure 22-3 reveals. Another view of this correlation (see Table 22-4) also supports the conculsion that the northeastern states (consisting of the three groups of states, East North Central, Middle Atlantic, and New

Table 22-4

United States: Leading Regions in Machinery Manufacture and Population

| Region | Employees in Manufacture of Machinery | | Population |
	Number in Thousands	Percentage of U.S. Total	Percentage of U.S. Total
New England states	152.3	8	6
Middle Atlantic states	320.1	18	18
New York	135.1	7	9
Pennsylvania	122.7	7	6
East North Central states	698.1	38	20
Ohio	198.6	11	5
Illinois	196.7	11	5
Michigan	136.9	7	4
Wisconsin	97.4	5	2
West North Central states	165.4	9	8
South Atlantic states	117.6	6	15
East South Central states	75.9	4	6
West South Central states	108.0	6	10
Mountain states	34.4	2	4
Pacific Coast states	155.9	9	13
California	135.0	7	10
U.S. total	1,827.7	100 / 55	100 / 41

Sources: U.S. Bureau of the Census, *1972 Census of Manufactures* (1975) and *Statistical Abstract of the United States: 1975.*

England) are the nation's main machine shops. In fact, the northeastern states are credited with 64 per cent of the employment in this industry, although they support only 44 per cent of the population.

The Question of "Leading Region"

At this point, we want to direct our gaze at a question that often confronts the student of geography: "How does one determine the location of the leading region of an economic endeavor?" The machine industry can be used to illustrate this problem. If we take a map, say, Figure 22-3, and the measurements of employment in individual states (or metropolitan areas), as in Tables 22-4 and 22-5, we can discern at least five general ways

Table 22-5

Leading Metropolitan Areas in the Manufacture of Machinery

Area	Employees (Thousands)
Chicago, Ill.-northwestern, Ind.	110.6
New York, N.Y.-northeastern, N.J.	75.7
Detroit	72.9
Los Angeles	66.7
Milwaukee	49.4
Philadelphia, Pa.-N.J.	45.4
Minneapolis	42.7
Cleveland	42.5
Dayton	38.4
Boston	30.0

Source: U.S. Bureau of the Census, *1972 Census of Manufactures* (1975).

of proceeding to answer our question. Let's see what we find in this particular case. (1) By individual metropolitan areas, Chicago is the unrivaled leader, accounting for 6 per cent of the national total. (2) By groups of neighboring metropolitan areas, the leading region surrounds southern Lake Michigan and extends into northern Illinois. This region consists not only of Chicago

but also of Milwaukee, Peoria, Moline, Rockford, Beloit, South Bend, Muskegon, and Grand Rapids. Some 15 per cent of the nation's employment in nonelectrical machinery is here. (3) By single states, Ohio ranks first, slightly ahead of Illinois. (4) If we choose groups of neighboring states as our basis, the leading region consists of five midwestern states—Ohio, Michigan, Indiana, Illinois, and Wisconsin. This quintet accounts for over one-third of the nation's machinery fabrication. (5) By major segments of the country, the northeastern quadrant (east of the Mississippi River and north of the Ohio River) accounts for 64 per cent of the jobs in this industry.

So, to answer the question, "What is the leading region of economic activity?" we must first select the *scale* in which we want the answer given. *Coarse* scale involves large areas, such as the northeast quadrant of the United States; *fine* scale involves small areas, such as metropolises. Between these two extremes are transitional magnitudes of scale from which we may choose, and the choice depends upon the degree of accuracy which we desire. For some purposes, a "coarse" generalization will suffice; for other purposes, a "fine" scale answer may be required.

To understand the locational pattern of the machinery industry as a whole it will help to look at the location of leading regions in a few individual industries: metal-working machinery, refrigeration and service machinery, farm and garden equipment, construction machinery, office and computing machines, engines and turbines, and special industry machinery.

Figure 22-3

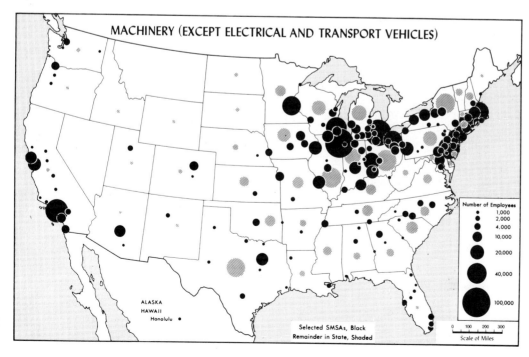

MACHINERY (EXCEPT ELECTRICAL AND TRANSPORT VEHICLES)

Number of Employees
1,000
2,000
4,000
10,000
20,000
40,000
100,000

ALASKA
HAWAII
Honolulu

Selected SMSAs, Black
Remainder in State, Shaded

0   100   200   300
Scale of Miles

Metal-Working Machinery

"The Metals Revolution."   Until very recently in the long span of history, man used metals to a severely limited degree. He made his boats of skin or wood, his wagons of wooden bodies and wooden wheels; he built his shelters of skins, timber, stone, or other earth materials, and the furniture in them mainly of wood; he even fashioned plows, rakes, hoes, and tools from wood. Metals were always scarce enough to be precious. But in the last century and a half man has unlocked the earth's metallic storehouse and discovered methods for cheaply producing steel, aluminum, copper, zinc, and lead. As a result, metals have displaced wood as the most prominent raw material in the manufacture of consumer and producer goods.

Consumer goods are items that we use directly, in satisfying our needs—such personal items as watches, fasteners on clothing, furniture, automobiles, toys, washing machines, refrigerators, stoves, and such public ones as rails, bridges, and buildings, whether they be cottages or skyscrapers. Today all of these are exclusively or partly made of metal.

Producer goods are items that manufacturers use in making consumer goods or other producer goods. Nearly all producer goods are made of metal: looms and spinning machines in textile mills, cutting and sewing machines in apparel factories, milling machines in flour mills, ovens in bakeries, bottling machines in beverage plants, machines that convert sheets of steel into automobile fenders, and machines that form steel or aluminum panels for new office buildings.

"The Power Revolution".   Concomitant with the *metals revolution* was a *power revolution* in which steam and then electricity displaced animal power in doing our work for us. Without an abundance of cheap metals, this power revolution would have been impossible since no nonmetallic substance can withstand the tremendous pressures of steam or transmit electricity in large quantities.

Inventions of Metal-Working Machines.   The combined effect of the metals revolution and the power revolution enabled man to invent many different machines to perform a hitherto unbelievable number of jobs, from heating his house in winter to cooling it in summer, from transporting wheat to transmitting voice, from plowing soil to baking his bread, from grading his roads to balancing his ledgers. Whether the goods he manufactures be consumer or producer, whether they be for generating power or using it, man needs machines that will take metal in the shape of sheets, bars, rods, or plates, and change its form by cutting, drilling, boring, planing, grinding, or pressing it. Machines that do such work are known collectively as *metal-working machinery*. To be sure, man can perform these steps manually, but the cost of such effort is excessive. A high economic standard of living is utterly dependent on machines that can process metals (a) in large quantities, (b) in short time, and (c) with high accuracy.

This third point—accuracy—is of central importance, for metal-working machines exceed by far what the human hand can do. Forges and stamping machines rapidly process thousands of automobile fenders with such accuracy that any one of them fits the auto body for which they were designed. Some metal-working machines are so precise that they can cut and form metal to within one ten-thousandths of an inch (0.0001 inch), which is about $\frac{1}{20}$ the diameter of a human hair. This interchangeability enabled by accuracy is the secret of mass production in which thousands of parts are formed to precisely the same dimensions and then assembled into finished products. And mass-production, of course, is a foundation stone of our prosperous industrial economy.

Machine-tool manufacturers, observing the high standard of living made possible by mechanization, declare proudly, "We make not only the machinery used in all metal-fabricating factories; we also make the machine tools that make machine tools."

A note on nomenclature is in order here. Sometimes the general public uses the term "machine tool" to identify these machines that process metal. But the men in the industrial world restrict the term to those machines that perform six basic jobs in shaping metal: turning, drilling, planing (when cutting is done by a fixed cutting tool), milling (when cutting is done by a rotating cutter), grinding, and shearing.

Location of Metal-Working Machinery Factories.   More than a quarter of a million people are now engaged in making metal-working machines in the United States; Figure 22-4 shows their locational pattern. Detroit stands head and shoulders above all other cities; the leading *region* can be bounded by a line encircling Detroit, Milwaukee, Rockford, Cincinnati, Pittsburgh, and Cleveland. Over one-half of American metal-working machinery comes from this region. Nearly another third comes from New England, New York, New Jersey, and eastern Pennsylvania. Elsewhere, however, very little metal-working machinery is made.

The industry is essentially market-oriented. Now, the market for lathes, drills, dies, and other metal-working machines consists entirely of factories, most of which are in the northeast quadrant of the country. Therefore, the western half of that quadrant is an ideal location for three reasons: (1) The five states of Ohio, Michigan, Illinois, Wisconsin, and Indiana are themselves the nation's biggest market. They contain thousands of factories that produce metallic products and therefore require metal-working machinery. Since the automotive industry is the single largest buyer of metal-working machinery, Detroit is prominent in both (note the cor-

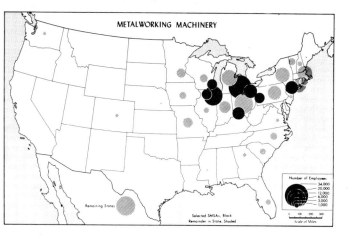

Figure 22-4

relation between Figures 22-1 and 22-4). (2) The Midwest is centrally located for shipments to metal-working factories in the East, South, and West. (3) The Midwest is well-endowed with steel. Compare the map of steel production, Figure 20-1, with 22-4, noting visually the correlation between midwest steel centers and midwest centers in the production of metal-working machinery.

On the East Coast the metal-working machinery factories of New England and New York may not have the fortunate location of those in the Midwest but they are advantageously situated for the foreign market. Machine tools are a lucrative export of the United States ($636,000,000 worth in 1974), some machine-tool companies selling over 25 per cent of their production to foreign buyers.

As the regional pattern portrayed by Figure 22-4 evolved, these leading regions assumed critical significance in the military strategy of the nation, for they produce the machines that make airplane engines, radar units, guns, tanks, ammunition, ships, and torpedoes. Indeed, one of the most paralyzing blows that can be dealt a nation's industrial life is to knock out its machine-tool factories.

Metal-Working Machinery and the Level of Industrial Development. This is an opportune time to introduce a vital principle in the relationship between a region's level of manufacturing in general and its level of machinery-making in particular. *The higher the level of industrial development, the greater the production of metal-working machinery.* We can examine this principle in several ways: first in terms of time-periods within a given region. Let us continue to use the northeastern United States as our example.

Four periods are discernible in the development of *commercial* manufacturing. First comes the *handicraft* period in which manufacturing processes are performed by hand with aid of simple equipment. At this stage in the United States, furniture, cloth, clothes, whale oil, ships, harnesses, nails, and numerous other items are

made essentially by machines. In stage two, which can be called the *imported-machinery* period, thread is spun, cloth is woven, garments are sewn, and many other items are made essentially by machines—but by machines imported from a region that is industrially advanced. The northeastern United States entered this second stage in the latter years of the eighteenth century, and imported its machines from Europe. Stage three is the *machinery* period. In the northeastern United States, manufacturers began to make their own spinning jennies, weaving looms, sewing machines, and an increasing number of machines that had previously been imported. But Americans made these products with machine tools and other metal-working machinery that they purchased across the Atlantic. The United States entered stage three early in the nineteenth century. The fourth and final stage is the *metal-working machinery* period. The northeastern United States, since the late 1800's, has not been dependent on other regions for machine tools but has made its own—plus a surplus for export. Maturity in a region's industrial development is attained when it becomes capable of making the tools that make the machines that fill its factories. Table 22-6 portrays this sequence in diagrammatic form.

Table 22-6

Periods in Development of a Major Manufacturing Region

Period	Items Made by Hand	Items Made by Imported Machinery	Machinery Made by Imported Machine Tools	Machine Tools Made
4	Very few	Yes	Yes	Yes
3	Few	Yes	Yes	No
2	Yes	Yes	No	No
1	Yes	No	No	No

The principle we are discussing also applies at any one time to different regions. Take the world pattern today. Four types of manufacturing regions are discernible. The first includes those countries whose manufactures are largely handmade from materials produced by their farms, forests, mines, and fisheries. Very few countries are still completely in this stage, although substantial portions of China, India, Indonesia, the Philippines, much of Africa, parts of Latin America, and Greece are located in its latter phases. The second type of region is more dependent on mechanization than on handiwork, but machinery is largely imported. Venezuela, Brazil, Argentina, South Africa, Australia, Iceland, and Austria fall in this category. The third stage has been reached by Canada and the Netherlands.

Sweden, France, Spain, and the U.S.S.R. might be considered advanced stage-three countries. Their machine tool imports are substantial, and imports exceed exports by a sizable margin. The fourth and final stage has been attained by West Germany, the United States, Switzerland, and to a lesser extent by Italy, Japan, and the United Kingdom. In the case of the latter group, imports are considerable, but exports are greater than imports. Japan is, perhaps, the country that has come up fastest in recent years. And the U.S.S.R., which shot up rapidly from stage one to stage three in just 40 years, is probably nearing stage four, although she still produces only a tiny exportable surplus of machine tools.

Refrigeration and Service Machinery

The manufacture of vending machines, laundry and dry-cleaning equipment, vacuum cleaners, garbage grinders, refrigeration machinery, pumps, and a wide diversity of household and service mechanisms supports approximately 200,000 employees. In Figure 22-5, which shows the locational pattern of employment, we see again the familiar prominence of the northeastern states that has distinguished all our maps of machinery production.

Note, however, that the manufacture of refrigeration and service machines does not coincide very closely with large metropolitan areas. There are many factories that turn out this equipment in cities not even identified in the *Census of Manufactures*. Consequently, it has been necessary on Figure 22-5 to represent a rather sizable component of this industry by means of shaded rather than black circles, with one shaded circle per state standing for the employment that remains after available metropolitan area employment is subtracted. Even so, the East North Central states dominate the map.

Ohio is the leading state with 17 per cent of the nation's employment in the refrigeration and service machinery industry. New York is next with 13 per cent, followed by Illinois with 8 per cent. Elsewhere the pat-

Figure 22-5

Figure 22-6

Figure 22-7

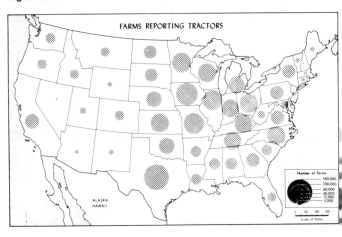

tern is spotty. Although the northeastern states together have about two-thirds of the employment in this industry, no one state really seems to dominate the map.

Farm and Garden Machinery

The manufacture of no other type of machinery is so highly concentrated in the Midwest—or in just two states, Iowa and Illinois—as is that of farm and garden machinery (Figure 22-6). From Ohio to Iowa there are a group of communities that constitute the farm machinery heart of the nation. Iowa, the leading state, has 24,000 employees—19 per cent of the nation's total. Close behind is Illinois with 22,000 employees; Wisconsin, the only other conspicuous producer, has 13,000 employees. Figure 22-6 maps one of the rare machinery industries in which the East Coast in general and Greater New York City in particular are insignificant. Several factors have operated to produce this midwestern dominance.

Markets. One cannot miss the obvious locational correlation between makers and users of farm machines.

For instance, compare Figure 22-6 with Figure 22-7, which shows the distribution of tractors on farms. A common sight on freight trains outbound from Milwaukee, Chicago, Beloit, Rockford, Peoria, and the Tri-Cities are flat cars loaded with tractors, corn-pickers, and other brightly painted farm machines bound for customers in diverse parts of the nation. Many of them are too large to be shipped bodily and are shipped knocked-down from the factory for assemblage by the hundreds of dealers who are located in a widely dispersed pattern through the farming regions of the nation.

The nearness of midwestern cities to mechanized farms has long attracted manufacturers from other parts of the country. For example, it was in the Shenandoah Valley of Virginia that, around 1830, Cyrus McCormick invented the reaper, the first successful device for mechanically harvesting grain; but McCormick constructed his first factory in Chicago in order to be near the greatest number of reaper-using farms.

Today, new markets for both farm and garden machinery are growing on the West Coast and in the South, yet the demand in these areas, being relatively recent, is still not great enough to overcome the head-start that the midwestern manufacturing region enjoys. Nevertheless, a few companies have responded to the pull of the new market areas and have opened plants that make small items, such as (a) attachments to farm machines, (b) some of the simpler machines (for instance, harrows, discs, and some lawn and garden machines), and (c) special machines to meet local needs (special hay balers or cotton-picking machines are examples). North Carolina, Georgia, Tennessee, Mississippi, Texas, and California each have 2,000 to 3,000 employed in the farm and garden machinery industry and many of these employees are working to meet the needs of their local market.

Inventions. The Midwest has not only had the nation's best market for farm machines but also an abundant supply of human inventiveness, from the time in 1855 when a citizen of Moline, Illinois—John Deere—designed a plow with a steel moldboard. The significance of this invention to midwestern America cannot be overemphasized.

For centuries farmers had successfully used *wooden* plows to turn furrows in the soil of their fields. But throughout those ages they were cultivating soils in humid regions where *trees* had been the native vegetation; wooden plows were capable of turning over forestland soils once the trees and stumps were removed. The world's great clusters of population up until 1800 (China, India, and western Europe) coincided with areas of native forest vegetation, and the first populous belts in the United States were in forested New England, the tree-covered Middle Atlantic states, and the wooded southeastern states. But grasslands have a different history. Through the centuries they had been used for grazing, not for cultivating. The tough sod of heavily interwoven grass roots is too tight for wooden plows to cut. Accordingly, the first settlers in the Mississippi Valley, lower Ohio Valley, and other midwest areas clung to the ribbons of woodland along streams or to the pockets of trees on the interfluves. One reason for this was that tree-cleared land could be worked by the only earth-turning tool they had. Grassland soils, although they are richer than forest soils, were avoided.

Then came Deere's invention. Steel moldboards easily sliced through grassland turf, exposing the dark rich face of prairie soils that, when sown with wheat or planted in corn, delivered abundant yields. There followed, simultaneously, a boom in homesteading and sales of prairie land and a demand for plows with steel moldboards. Deere set up production in Moline, not only because it was his hometown, but also because it was situated so near the center of the American prairie. Moline boomed and, along with neighboring Rock Island and Davenport, became one of the world's foremost centers of farm machinery as other items were

Motorola semiconductor plant in Phoenix, Arizona. The manufacture of electronic equipment is considered a clean industry and is frequently found in a suburban setting adjacent to residential areas. (*Courtesy Motorola Inc.*)

added to the Deere company's production line and other companies moved into the area.

There were other midwestern inventions, too. In the late 1840's a Rockford machinist, John H. Manny, invented a reaping machine that won numerous medals and cups in contests with other reapers. By the early 1850's the city's factories were turning out hundreds of these machines, earning for Rockford the nickname, "Reaper City." Another Rockford industrialist, Marquis L. Gorham, invented three agricultural machines—a seeder, a corn cultivator, and a binder. In Beloit, Wisconsin, just north of Rockford, John Appleby designed the first twine binder, which freed farmers from the use of wire binders. Nearly all the farm machinery industry in the Midwest can be traced to inventions by local designers of tractors, harrows, drills, cultivators, harvesters, pickers, and binders.

The invention of farm machines in this region was stimulated by three concurrent conditions during the 1800's and early 1900's when the Midwest was being settled: (a) land was abundant, (b) labor was scarce, and (c) the market for agricultural products was large, particularly in Europe and the eastern United States where the Industrial Revolution was increasing the purchasing power of thousands of people who were leaving the farms for higher-paying jobs in cities. The thrust of American invention, therefore, was toward labor-saving devices. By contrast, very few farm machines were invented in Europe because (a) farm population remained so large that there continued to be an abundance of labor, and (b) agricultural land was scarce. Accordingly, the ingenuity of European inventors was directed more toward land-saving devices such as weed control, improved fertilizers, better strains of seeds for crops, and scientific breeding of animals.

Raw Materials. In addition to their central location (relative to markets) and the supply of inventive minds, the midwestern farm machinery centers are close to the steel mills that manufacture their main raw material. Much of the steel is produced in Gary and Chicago itself, although some comes in from Youngstown and Pittsburgh.

Size. Farm machinery companies tend to be large, each making a diversity of implements. A strong reason for this diversity is the competitive advantage in selling a *complete line* of implements. And this advantage in turn encourages the development of a few large companies that manufacture for a nationwide market instead of a host of smaller companies each specializing in one implement. Thus, if he chooses, a farmer can get his tractor, plow, disk, drill, and harrow in one package deal from a single company.

Construction and Mining Machinery

Construction and mining machinery will be considered together mainly because statistics on their location are lumped together in census publications. Earth-moving equipment, bulldozers, oil-drilling equipment, and coal-loaders are typical examples. As Figure 22-8 shows, much of this industry is also in the Midwest, with Illinois the leading state. The principal cities in this business are Milwaukee, Chicago, and Cleveland. This rather diverse industry seems to conform with two principles: (1) that machinery factories tend to locate near their markets, and (2) that if the machines are manufactured in relatively small numbers but used throughout the country, the factories tend to settle in a central location.

The latter principle happens to apply particularly to earth-moving and construction machinery, whereas the former principle holds for equipment used in iron-ore mining, coal mining, and oil drilling, the markets for which are highly localized. Consequently, the location of factories correlates well with the location, respectively, of iron ore in Wisconsin and Minnesota (Figure 14-4), of coal in Ohio, Pennsylvania, and West Virginia (also Figure 14-4), and of oil mining in Texas, Oklahoma, and California (Figure 15-7). Texas manufactures more construction and mining machinery than any state except Illinois; indeed, Houston has the second largest solid circle on Figure 22-8. From Houston factories, oil-drilling machinery is shipped not only to Gulf Coast states but to Venezuela, Mexico, the Middle East, and other foreign oil-mining areas.

Office and Computing Machines

Typewriters, scales, balances, adding machines, bookkeeping machines, and computers are manufactured largely in the northeastern quadrant of the nation and in California. Unfortunately, cities that are important in this industry usually have one or two big employers, which dominate activity there. And since the Census of Manufactures does not disclose data on individual firms, we are unable to include these cities on Figure 22-9.

Figure 22-8

CONSTRUCTION AND RELATED MACHINERY

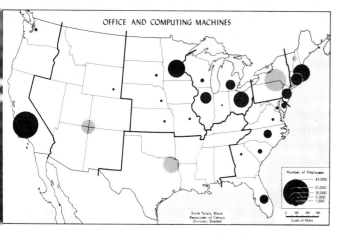

Figure 22-9

regions where it is used. It is there that fuel and power-making machinery converge; it is there that most of that machinery is manufactured.

Special-Industry Machines

There are 190,000 persons in the United States who make textile machines, printing machines, and other equipment designed specifically for particular trades (see Table 22-7).

Table 22-7

United States: Manufacture of Special Industry Machinery

Type	Number of Employees (Thousands)	Value Added ($ Millions)
Food products machinery	31.9	605.2
Textile machinery	32.7	487.9
Woodworking machinery	13.7	285.1
Paper industries machinery	15.3	254.0
Printing trades machinery	23.9	503.6
Other	72.6	1,596.1
U.S. TOTAL	190.1	3,731.9

Source: U.S. Bureau of the Census, *1972 Census of Manufactures* (1975).

Nevertheless, we can note that prominent cities are Chicago, New York, Dayton (home of National Cash Register), and Binghamton-Endicott, New York (home of International Business Machines).

This industry serves a nationwide market, therefore it has benefited historically from being located in the Midwest, which now has 25 per cent of industry employment. Even so, the New England and Middle Atlantic states (with 32 per cent of the employment) stand out in Figure 22-9, in part because the most intense use of office and store machines in the nation coincides with the highly commercialized belt running from Boston through New York, Philadelphia, and Baltimore to Washington, D.C. In no other comparable portion of the earth do so many commercial and government offices and stores use office machinery. In recent years, this industry has shifted to the West, because of both local market demands and easy access to national markets. California with 43,000 employees (21 per cent of the total) leads the nation in employment in the office and computing machine industry.

Engines and Turbines

Steam engines, turbines, and internal combustion engines are produced largely in those states east of the Mississippi and north of the Ohio rivers; this region contains about 85 per cent of this industry's employment. Half of those engaged in the manufacture of engines and turbines are found in just five states—Ohio, Indiana, Illinois, Michigan, and Wisconsin. Elsewhere, New York, Pennsylvania, and Massachusetts are all important states.

These places are within the very region that demands most of the nation's power and so uses the power-production machines. Logically enough, the machines that convert energy from fuels (coal, petroleum, gas) into usable power are made there. To be sure, there is a demand for turbines at hydroelectric power dams, but only 4 per cent of the power generated in the United States is hydroelectric; 96 per cent is generated from the burning of fuel that is transported into the

The familiar Northeast again stands out fittingly, for the publishing capital of the country, printing presses and other printing trades machinery are made in and around New York. New England and the Middle Atlantic states still produce textile machinery, although southern factories, especially in the Carolinas, are increasingly important. Paper industry machines come from Wisconsin, New York, and Washington and woodworking machines are made in Illinois, Ohio, and Michigan. To a significant extent, firms making special industry machines are market oriented.

United States Machinery Manufacturing: Conclusions

Inspection of the foregoing series of maps leads to the conclusion that the United States contains *one* single outstanding *machinery zone*, a region extending from the Mississippi River to the Atlantic Coast. The northern boundary of this belt roughly coincides with a line from Milwaukee through Buffalo to Boston, while the southern margin runs from St. Louis through Cincinnati to Baltimore. The significance of this machinery belt in the nation's economic life can scarcely be overemphasized, for in it we make most of (a) our transportation machines for both freight and passengers, (b) the machines that perform work for us in our kitchens and living rooms, forests and mines, farms and building projects, (c) the machines that perform most of the work in the nation's factories making shoes, clothes, tires, chemicals, flour, and a host of other consumer commodities which stream from factories in massive quantities thanks to mechanized methods of manufacturing, and (d) the machines that make all the machines just mentioned.

Within this main machinery belt, three clear subregions are conspicuous: a western area dominated by Chicago and Milwaukee; a central area led by Detroit, Cleveland, and Cincinnati; and an eastern one highlighted by New York, Philadelphia, and Boston.

Access to Customers. The single most important reason for the prominence of this great region is its nearness to machinery users. A basic principle prevails here that pertained to other industries discussed in previous chapters: For any given factory, if transport charges on its finished product *exceed those on its raw materials, that factory will tend to locate near its customers.* Freight rates on machinery are half again as much as those on the steel from which machines are made. Moreover, very little weight is lost in the conversion of steel to machinery. Therefore, users lure makers to their regions.

The customers who constitute the market for machinery are diverse indeed, but whether they be trucking companies, railroad companies, private automobile operators, whether they be housewives using vacuum cleaners and washing machines or business firms using typewriters and comptometers, whether they be factories using machines to make consumer goods or factories that manufacture machines—a large share of these customers are located in the northeastern part of the nation. This is chiefly why most machinery factories are there.

Access to Ideas. New machines and improvements on old machines are conceived not only by designers in machinery-making factories but also by operators who use those machines, whether in factories, mines, farms, or homes. Close association between maker and user stimulates inventions and improvements— another reason for the Northeast's prominence.

Time Lag Principle. In recent years new markets for machinery have developed in other parts of the country, notably the southeastern states for textile machinery, and California for a diversity of equipment. These new markets are relatively small compared with the Northeast; they have fewer people to buy the consumer machinery and fewer factories to buy the producer machinery. Consequently, as yet they have attracted few machinery-making factories. We can explain this by the *time lag principle; A maker of machines tends to locate in the same region as the industry that uses those machines; but when that industry moves elsewhere, the machinery maker lags behind.* Take textiles for example. For decades New England and the eastern parts of the Middle Atlantic states manufactured nearly all of this nation's textiles, and Massachusetts and Pennsylvania became the leading producers of textile machinery. Then the textile industry moved south, so that today almost three-fourths of its workers are in southern states. Yet these southern factories operate with machinery that is often northern-built; over half of United States textile machines are still made in the North.

In such situations there is a conflict between (a) the lure of the new market region where transport charges on finished machinery would be less, and (b) the lure of the established region where, due to its *early start*, companies have built up an experienced labor force. Sometimes the hold of an established region is termed *industrial inertia*; it is a psychological factor, very difficult to measure scientifically, but nonetheless real in maintaining *momentum* in a region where factories continue to operate for awhile, sometimes long after one would expect.

Access to Steel. Customers may have been the chief initial attraction, but the machinery belt has within its borders the world's most productive steel mills to supply the basic ingredient for its factories. If we compare the map of steel production (Figure 20-1) with the machinery maps in this chapter we can see how centrally located the Pittsburgh-Youngstown-Cleveland steel district is for supplying the factories of the machinery belt.

Measurement of Geographic Association

The machinery industry was chosen as the "laboratory specimen" in a research project that is noteworthy as the first systematic attempt (as far as the authors know) to measure association in industrial geography. This analytical effort is so significant that we shall reserve it for careful treatment in Chapter 30, which deals with *methods of measuring* the location of manufacturing and the association of manufacturing with other phenomena.

The World Pattern

Most of this chapter has dealt with locational patterns and locational principles of machinery-making in the United States.

But the same basic principles are observable in the world pattern, that machinery-making tends to locate primarily within its main market region and secondarily near steel centers. The leading nations in machinery production are the countries in which there is both a great demand for machines and considerable production

Table 22-8

International Trade: Machinery (Millions of U.S. Dollars)

Leading Exporters		Leading Importers	
West Germany	20,578	United States	9,909
United States	17,303	France	6,887
Japan	9,043	West Germany	6,594
United Kingdom	7,894	Canada	5,844
France	6,504	United Kingdom	5,816
Italy	5,282	Italy	3,930
Switzerland	3,036	Belgium	3,276
Sweden	3,005	Netherlands	2,839
Netherlands	2,522	Japan	2,622
Canada	2,516	Sweden	2,345

Source: United Nations, *Yearbook of International Trade* (1974).

of steel. Specifically, the foremost machinery-makers are the United States, West Germany, the United Kingdom, France, Japan, and the U.S.S.R.

International trade in machinery displays a distinctive pattern: the world's major exporting regions are likewise its major importing regions (see Table 22-8). This contrasts rather markedly with the patterns of international trade for wheat, wool, wood, iron ore, fish, and most other commodities—for which the leading export nations are rarely the leading import nations.

CHAPTER

manufacturing regions:
anglo-america

This iron ore transport vessel carries ore to Great Lakes blast furnaces. U.S. iron and steel manufacture is heavily concentrated in close proximity to the Great Lakes. (*Courtesy American Iron and Steel Institute.*)

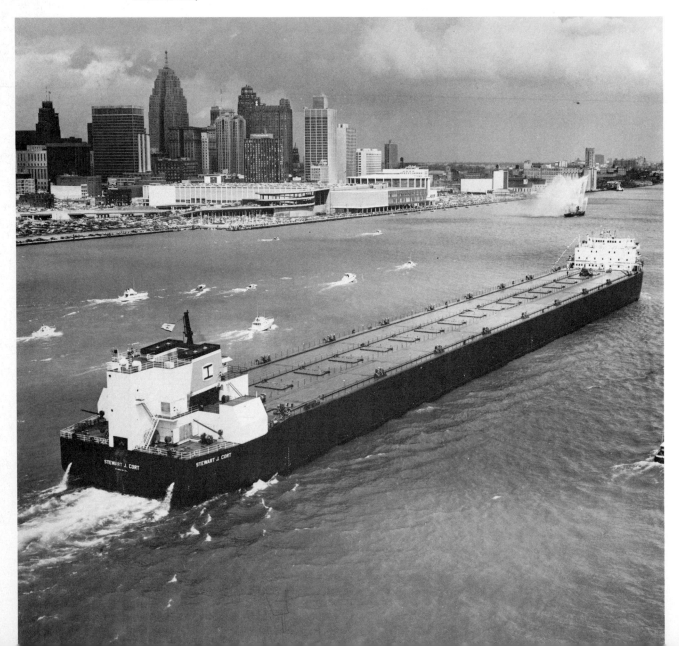

In the last six chapters we have taken an industry approach to the geography of manufacturing. That is, taking individual industries one by one, we have identified the many different areas in which they are located. In this chapter we shall adopt a *regional approach*. Taking regions one by one, we shall consider the many different industries that they contain. For an example, southern New England as a type of manufacturing region is different from northeastern Ohio; for another, the Midwest thrives on a different industry mix than does the Pacific Coast.

THE UNITED STATES

All told, the United States has over 400 different types of manufacturing industries, according to the classification system devised by the Census of Manufactures. Together these industries employ 19,000,000 people, who are tabulated by industry in Table 23-1 and are distributed geographically according to the pattern shown in Figure 23-1. Each circle on this map represents either the manufacturing in one metropolitan area, which may consist of several counties, or the manufacturing in a state's nonmetropolitan areas. For example, New York state has 170,000 manufacturing employees scattered throughout its small communities; New Jersey has 34,000. But the largest concentrations are in the metropolitan areas, especially the one centered on New York City. The single circle for the New York metropolitan area represents nine counties, eight in New York State and one in New Jersey.

In terms of employment in manufacturing, the United States can be split in two along a line running from the southern tip of Texas northward to the Minnesota-Dakota border. East of this line, manufacturing centers are numerous and even nonmetropolitan counties have some manufacturing. West of this line major centers are few and far between, and rural areas frequently have little or no manufacturing activity.

The industrialized eastern half of the country, in fact, supports almost 90 per cent of the nation's employment in manufacturing. And a large share of these jobs—over 50 per cent of the total—are in the northeastern states (east of the Mississippi and north of the Ohio rivers). A closer inspection of the Northeast reveals that all but three—California, Texas, and North Carolina—of the nation's ten leading manufacturing states are located there, as are all of the ten major industrial metropolises except for Los Angeles (Table 23-2).

Actually there are several clearly identifiable manufacturing areas: the New York metropolitan area, New England, the Middle Atlantic states, middle New York State, the Midwest, the South, and the Pacific Coast. We shall pursue our investigation of the national pattern in those regional categories.

Before inspecting these regions, it will be helpful to consider four concepts that shed light on the industrial

Table 23-1

United States Industrial Structure, 1972

Census Code Number	Industry	Number of Establishments	Thousands of Employees	Annual Payroll ($ millions)	Value Added by Manufacture ($ millions)	1958 Thousands of Employees
20	Food	28,184	1,569	$ 12,922	$ 35,617	1,781
21	Tobacco	272	66	502	2,637	92
22	Textiles	7,203	953	6,052	11,718	919
23	Apparel	24,438	1,368	7,212	13,487	1,188
24	Lumber and wood	33,948	691	4,983	10,309	591
25	Furniture	9,232	462	3,202	6,089	357
26	Paper	6,038	633	5,992	13,064	574
27	Printing and publishing	42,102	1,056	9,827	20,197	872
28	Chemicals	11,425	836	8,730	32,414	784
29	Petroleum and coal	2,016	139	1,637	5,793	247
30	Rubber and plastics	9,237	618	5,165	11,653	356
31	Leather	3,201	273	1,589	2,917	358
32	Stone, clay, glass	16,015	623	5,547	12,586	575
33	Primary metal	6,792	1,143	12,166	23,258	1,129
34	Fabricated metal	29,525	1,493	13,821	26,946	1,090
35	Machinery (except electrical)	40,792	1,828	18,523	37,563	1,386
36	Electric equipment	12,274	1,662	15,200	30,584	1,219
37	Transportation equipment	8,802	1,719	19,880	39,799	1,642
38	Instruments	5,987	454	4,296	10,584	294
39	Miscellaneous	15,188	446	3,184	6,777	569
TOTAL	(including administrative and auxiliary establishments)	320,710	19,029	174,205	353,994	16,025

Source: U.S. Bureau of the Census, *1972 Census of Manufactures* (1975).

MANUFACTURING

Number of
Employees

• 10,000 or less

• 10,000 – 25,000

• 25,000 – 50,000

● 97,000

● 173,000

● 640,000

● 900,000

● 1,700,000

Selected SMSAs, Black
Remainder in State, Shaded

0 100 200 300
Scale of Miles

ALASKA %
HAWAII %
Honolulu •

Figure 23-1

Table 23-2

United States Manufacturing: Leading States and Metropolitan
Areas (Thousands of Employees)

States		Standard Metropolitan Statistical Areas	
New York	1679	New York, N.Y.-N.J.	951
California	1546	Chicago, Ill.	909
Pennsylvania	1418	Los Angeles-Long Beach, Cal.	780
Ohio	1346	Detroit, Mich.	556
Illinois	1306	Philadelphia, Penn.-N.J.	498
Michigan	1076	Boston, Mass.	273
New Jersey	836	Newark, N.J.	271
North Carolina	744	Cleveland, Ohio	269
Texas	736	Pittsburgh, Penn.	262
Indiana	704	St. Louis, Mo.-Ill.	256

Source: U.S. Bureau of the Census, *1972 Census of Manufactures* (1975).

characteristics of a region and help one to distinguish
between regions: *location quotient, light industry and heavy
industry, industrial structure,* and *index of diversification.*

Location Quotient

The *location quotient* measures the degree to which a
specific region has more or less than its share of any
particular industry. Using the Greater New York metropolitan area[1] as the illustrative region and the number of

[1]In this example we will be using data for the New York-
Northeastern New Jersey Standard Consolidated Area. This region
includes the New York, New York-New Jersey Standard Metro-
politan Statistical Area (SMSA), the Nassau-Suffolk, New York
SMSA and four New Jersey SMSA's: Newark, Jersey City, Paterson-
Clifton-Passaic, and New Bruswick-Perth Amboy-Sayreville.

manufacturing employees as the illustrative criterion, we
can derive the quotient as follows.

1. Compute New York's employment in manufacturing
   (1,623,300) as a percentage of the national total
   (19,028,700). The answer is 8.5 per cent.
2. Compute New York's share of the national employment in each individual industry. For example, here
   are the New York and national figures for certain
   leading industries:

Industry	A Employment in New York (Thousands)	B Employment in the United States (Thousands)	Percentage of A/B
Apparel	276.1	1,368.3	20.2
Printing	163.8	1,056.1	15.5
Foods	82.8	1,569.4	5.3
Chemicals	102.1	836.5	12.2
Textiles	67.8	952.7	7.1
Primary metals	36.1	1,142.8	3.2
Toys and sporting goods	20.7	132.7	15.6
Grain mill products	1.2	111.4	1.1

3. Compare the above percentage for each industry
   with 8.5 per cent (New York's share of the national
   total). If the percentage exceeds 8.5 per cent, New
   York has more than its share. To express this relationship precisely, divide 8.5 per cent into the percentage value for each industry. The results will be
   the New York Metropolitan area's *location quotients*
   for those industries. Here are the figures and computations for our selected industries:

Industry	A New York's Percentage Share of National Employment in Each Industry	B New York's Percentage Share of Nation's Total Manufacturing Employment	New York's Location Quotient: A/B
Apparel	20.2	8.5	2.4
Toys	15.6	8.5	1.8
Printing	15.5	8.5	1.8
Chemicals	12.2	8.5	1.4
Textiles	7.1	8.5	0.8
Foods	5.3	8.5	0.6
Primary metals	3.2	8.5	0.4
Grain mill products	1.1	8.5	0.1

The maximum a location quotient could be in the New York metropolitan area is 11.8 if this region (which contains 8.5 per cent of the nation's manufacturing) had all (100 per cent) of any given industry. The minimum a location quotient could be anywhere is, of course, zero.

A location quotient of 1.0 means that a region has neither more nor less of the national industry than its over-all volume of manufacturing would suggest. A quotient over 1.0 indicates a high particular concentration in that locality, relative to local industrial development. A quotient less than 1.0 suggests that an industry is less developed in that region than is manufacturing in general.

Location quotients can be computed for any region and for any industry, not only for metropolitan areas but for cities, counties, states, or any other areal unit one cares to investigate. They are useful in comparing different industries with one another in the same region and in comparing different regions with one another.

Light Industries and Heavy Industries

Another frequently useful approach to studying industrial regions is to categorize industries as light and heavy.

Light industry is a rather loosely defined term applied to factories that use comparatively light-weight machinery, or that consume small quantities of raw material, or that are free of nuisance qualities such as offensive odors, noise, or dirt. *Heavy industry* is also loosely defined but, in general usage, is applied to factories that use bulky machinery and consume copious quantities of raw materials, thus necessitating water or rail transport. Accordingly, heavy industries are often located along railroads, canals, rivers, or ocean inlets and often have their own docks and/or railway sidings with conspicuous piles of raw materials adjoining factory buildings. Furthermore, heavy industries often have severe nuisance qualities, emitting dirt, noise, or unpleasant odors.

Industrial Structure

A region's *industrial structure* can be defined as the aggregate of individual industries that account for all the manufacturing in the region ranked by magnitude. The magnitude of each industry is measured proportionately in terms of some given criterion. For instance, if employment is the criterion we choose, and we want to measure the significance of the printing industry in the New York metropolitan area's industrial structure, we divide 1,623,300 (the total number of manufacturing employees in New York factories) into 163,800 (the number employed there in the printing and publishing industry), giving us a quotient of 10.1, which is one measure of the relative importance of the printing industry in New York. If we proceeded to make similar computations for each industry, we would arrive at a measure of New York's *industrial structure*. In other words, a region's industrial structure is a proportionate listing of all industries, rated according to a given criterion. Table 23-5 illustrates this concept.

Index of Diversification

If most of a given region's manufacturing employees are in just one industry, then obviously that region is much less diversified than a region where employment is spread rather evenly among many different industries. The one region has all its money on one horse, industrially speaking; the other is playing the field. In an effort to measure such differences, the *index of diversification* has been devised.

This index was developed by Allan Rodgers and is computed as follows, using United States Census data:

1. For each industrial region being studied, Rodgers constructed a table that ranks all manufacturing industries in terms of employment, by number and percentage, as in columns 1 and 2 in Table 23-3, which uses Indianapolis, Indiana, as an example. There are 22 entries in the table, the number of major manufacturing categories recognized by the Census.
2. Computation was made of "progressive totals" of the percentages that appear in Table 23-3, column 2. These were then entered in column 3.
3. The progressive totals were added. The result was termed the *crude diversification index*. In the illustration, Indianapolis has a crude index of 1698. The highest possible crude index would be 2200, which would pertain if 100 per cent of a region's manufacturing employment were in one industry. Under such circumstances the first industry listed in Table 23-3 would show 100 in column 2 and 100 in column 3; thereafter each entry would show zero in column 2 and 100 in column 3. The lowest possible crude index would be approximately 1150. This would result if there were *absolute diversification*, that is, if employment were equally divided among the 22 industries so that each entry in column 2 would be 4.54.

At this point, the graphs in Figure 23-2 illustrate the principle involved in computing the crude diversification index. Flint had a very steep curve because her leading industry accounted for over 90 per cent of all her employment in manufacturing. Binghamton's

Table 23-3

Computation of Index of Diversification (Example: Indianapolis)

Manufacturing Industries	Employees in Manufacturing		
	(1) Number	(2) Percentage	(3) Progressive Totals
TOTAL	76,945	100.00	—
Electrical machinery	10,256	13.33	13.33
Other machinery	9,596	12.47	25.80
Foods	8,712	11.32	37.12
Motor vehicles	7,488	9.73	46.85
Chemicals	6,300	8.19	55.04
Fabricated metals	6,256	8.13	63.17
Printing and publishing	5,101	6.63	69.80
Transport equipment (except motor vehicles)	4,444	5.78	75.58
Primary metals	4,092	5.32	80.90
Paper	2,262	2.94	83.84
Rubber	2,210	2.87	86.71
Textiles	1,996	2.59	89.30
Miscellaneous durables	1,571	2.04	91.34
Apparel	1,524	1.98	93.22
Stone, clay, glass	1,200	1.56	94.88
Furniture	1,085	1.41	96.29
Lumber and wood	831	1.08	97.37
Not specified	744	0.97	98.34
Professional equipment	636	0.83	99.17
Petroleum and coal	424	0.55	99.72
Leather	173	0.22	99.94
Tobacco	43	0.06	100.00
Sum of progressive totals (Crude Diversification Index)			1697.71

Source: Allan Rodgers, "Some Aspects of Industrial Diversification in the United States," *Economic Geography* (January, 1957), pp. 16–30.

curve is much less steep since her leading industry accounted for 46 per cent of her manufacturing total. Curves for a few other cities are shown, as well as a curve for the United States as a whole and one for a hypothetical area in which *absolute diversification* prevailed.

4. The next step was to convert the crude index into the *refined index of diversification.* The aim was to express the crude index in relationship to an average or norm. The norm Rodgers selected was the totality of employment for all metropolitan areas with at least 20,000 manufacturing workers. There were 93 such places, and the crude diversification index for the group was 1553. The formula he devised for computing the refined index for Indianapolis was as follows:

$$\frac{1698 - 1553}{2200 - 1553} = \frac{145}{647} = 0.224$$

In the above formula, the numerator represents the *difference* between the crude index of the city being measured and that of the norm; the denominator represents the *difference* between the crude index for the least possible diversity and the index for the average.

The refined diversification indexes for several American cities computed by the Rodgers formula are listed in Table 23-4.

Table 23-4

Refined Diversification Indices of Selected American Cities

Philadelphia	.039	Columbus (O.)	.298	Fort Worth	.580
St. Louis	.090	Cleveland	.301	Pittsburgh	.600
Los Angeles	.114	Des Moines	.355	Fort Wayne	.606
Boston	.118	Milwaukee	.363	Birmingham	.615
New Orleans	.152	Grand Rapids	.369	Wichita	.629
Cincinnati	.167	Toledo	.372	South Bend	.641
New York	.173	Miami	.383	Binghamton	.651
San Francisco	.173	Salt Lake City	.388	Galveston	.652
Memphis	.215	Houston	.393	New Britain	.655
Dallas	.218	Racine	.397	San Diego	.689
Chicago	.224	Providence	.402	Detroit	.700
Indianapolis	.224	Syracuse	.416	Youngstown	.709
Atlanta	.229	Chattanooga	.456	Akron	.717
Baltimore	.235	Seattle	.458	Fall River	.742
Denver	.238	Erie	.462	Peoria	.773
Buffalo	.243	Hartford	.462	Durham	.793
Kansas City	.257	Rochester	.498	Lansing	.848
Louisville	.261	Kalamazoo	.575	Flint	.934

Source: Allan Rodgers, *op. cit.*

Two generalizations can be drawn here: (1) The higher the percentage of manufacturing employment accounted for by a region's leading industry, the higher is its refined index of diversification. (2) Large cities tend to have lower indices than do small cities, because they tend to have more diversification.

The New York Metropolitan Area

With 1,623,000 industrial workers, the Greater New York metropolitan area (consisting of the New York, New York Standard Metropolitan Statistical Area [SMSA]; the Nassau-Suffolk, New York SMSA; and four New Jersey SMSA's) comprises the world's single largest concentration of manufacturing employees, a group that makes up 8.5 per cent of the manufacturing labor force of the United States. This one metropolitan area contains the astonishing total of 41,700 factories. (Unless otherwise indicated, the name "New York" will be used in this section to identify this whole great metropolitan area.)

Manufacturing is the largest single endeavor in New York's economic life, providing jobs for almost 30 per cent of her employed labor force. And New York's *industrial structure* is dominated by the apparel industry. As Table 23-5 shows, clothing factories provide nearly one out of every six manufacturing jobs in New York, more than half of them in the making of women's clothing. Printing (including publishing) runs second. News-

Table 23-5

New York Metropolitan Area Industrial Structure

Manufacturing Industries	Employees Number (Thousands)	Per-centage	Percentage of National Total	Location Quotient
TOTAL	1,623.3	100.0	8.5	
Apparel	276.1	17.0	20.2	2.4
Printing	163.8	10.1	15.5	1.8
Electric equipment	142.7	8.8	8.6	1.0
Chemicals	102.1	6.3	12.2	1.4
Fabricated metals	94.2	5.8	6.3	0.7
Food	82.8	5.1	5.3	0.6
Machinery	75.7	4.7	4.1	0.5
Textiles	67.8	4.2	7.1	0.8
Transportation equipment	63.0	3.9	3.7	0.4
Paper and allied products	48.5	3.0	7.7	0.9

Source: U.S. Bureau of the Census, *1972 Census of Manufactures* (1975). Data describe the New York-Northeastern New Jersey Standard Consolidated Area.

paper, periodical, and book publishers as well as thousands of commercial printers, lithographers, bookbinders,

and greeting card printers provide New York with over 160,000 jobs. This combination of apparel and printing is unique.

Other major industries are electrical equipment (especially communication equipment), which supports a payroll of 142,000 individuals; chemicals (notably the manufacture of drugs and medicines); fabricated metal products (with structural steel items, a leading product); food (especially bakery products), machinery (with an emphasis on printing and other special industry machinery); textiles (knitting mills); and transportation equipment (aircraft and aircraft parts). Numerous other industries are represented in some degree, but a few are noted for their absence. For example, New York has almost no steel industry; scarcely any farm machinery is manufactured; and the region does comparatively little flour milling. Nevertheless, New York is one of the most diversified manufacturing metropolises in the nation.

Factories are located in many parts of New York. The greatest concentration is on lower Manhattan Island as was discussed in Chapter 18. Numerous factories have sprung up on the Jersey side of the Hudson River. Many are light industries that were originally located in New York City but have migrated to the

Figure 23-2 *(Courtesy Allan Rodgers and Economic Geography.)*

INDEXES OF INDUSTRIAL DIVERSIFICATION

suburbs to the west in search of space for expansion, lower taxes, room for parking lots, and the chance to build new factory structures designed for their particular needs. Printing, textile, apparel, and light-machinery makers are in this category. But New Jersey also has much of metropolitan New York's heavy industry, for example, copper smelters, petroleum refineries, shipyards, chemical plants, and meat-packing establishments.

The New York metropolitan area also spreads eastward onto Long Island, which contains a large volume of industry in its western third, especially in Brooklyn and the suburbs. Industry here is highly diversified, both light and heavy, from factories that produce electrical machinery (gyroscopes, radios, and computers) to airplane plants.

This great metropolis can offer numerous advantages to a manufacturer. Foremost is the tremendous population and concomitant purchasing power that make it the largest domestic market for bread, dresses, books, radios, pencils, telephones, and almost every other consumer item you can name. In addition, New York is the headquarters for numerous businesses that "consume" typewriters, computing equipment, and printed material in greater volume than their counterparts in any other city. Besides its desirability as a market, New York City's huge labor force is an attraction for factories. Thousands of individual immigrants during the great influxes in the late nineteenth and early twentieth centuries brought their industrial skills with them from Europe; and New York, functioning as the port of entry, had an initial advantage over the rest of the nation in bidding for their services. Yet there are also some industries that do not need and cannot afford highly skilled labor; for them New York contains thousands of people, many just arrived from nonindustrial areas, with as yet few skills developed. Moreover, New York, being the monetary nerve-center of the Western Hemisphere, is crammed with large amounts of the investment capital so necessary before a factory can even begin operations. As a transportation center, too, New York City provides its factories with excellent inland

The New Jersey portion of metropolitan New York contains many industrial developments. This view (looking south) shows the Port Newark and Elizabeth-Port Authority Marine terminal. This area has several advantages: diversity of transportation (ocean shipping, railways, highways, and even airways), open flat land, and location near Manhattan, the primary commercial center in the world. (*Courtesy the Port Authority of New York and New Jersey.*)

facilities and with superb ocean shipping not only to foreign countries but also to other coastal ports of the United States. Its excellent harbor system is lined with miles of docks along the Hudson River, East River, Upper Bay, and Newark Bay. And the Hudson River lowland leads to the Mohawk Valley, which provides New York with the easiest access of any eastern port to the interior of the continent.

On the other hand, New York has two pronounced drawbacks for manufacturing; it lacks both power and raw materials. Scarcely any water power is generated along its rivers and all its fuel (coal, petroleum, gas) must be imported from far away. Likewise, the territory encircling New York produces very few raw materials for factories. The wool, cotton, paper, food, and metals they require originate hunderds (and sometimes thousands) of miles away.

New York is the prime example of the principle that market and labor are more powerful than raw material and power in determining the location of factories.

The New York metropolitan area is the pivotal zone of a large manufacturing region that extends along the Atlantic Coast from Maryland to Maine (Figure 23-1). For clarity in our discussion, however, we shall examine the remainder of this region under two headings: New England and the Middle Atlantic states.

New England

In the six *New England* states (Connecticut, Rhode Island, Massachusetts, Vermont, New Hampshire, and Maine) there are about 1,360,000 factory employees—a figure somewhat less than that for metropolitan New York. The hub is Boston (Figure 23-1), which is, in fact, the nation's sixth-ranking industrial metropolis (see Table 23-2). Within New England the bulk of manufacturing is located toward the south, in Connecticut, Massachusetts, and Rhode Island with a northern fringe extending along coastal Maine.

The chief components of New England's *industrial structure* are shown in Table 23-6. Since the two leading industries each make up only 11 per cent of the indus-

trial structure, we can say that New England's structure is more *diversified* than that of metropolitan New York, where the single leading industry accounts for 17 per cent of all factory jobs.

Eastern New England. There are two zones of manufacturing within New England: an eastern area and a western area. The eastern section focuses on Boston and includes the Merrimac Valley, Providence, Fall River, New Bedford, and Brockton, with an extension into Maine. Textiles, for a long time were the dominant industry. Leather industries, such as tanning and shoe making, also figured heavily in the economy of the region. But both of these have slumped in New England, and in the last 50 years many textile and shoe factories have moved south and west. Their places have been taken though, by others—electrical machinery and plastics plants. In addition, much of our domestic jewelry and silverware is made in Providence.

Eastern New England got a head start in manufacturing on all other parts of the nation. In the late 1700's and early 1800's her population made up one of the chief markets in the Western Hemisphere; the supply of capital, reaped from exports of timber and from successful operation of ships, both commercial vessels and fishing boats, was good. Numerous streams flowing over the rocky terrain were easily dammed to provide scores of water power sites and millraces. Entrepreneurs flocked there to build factories. Another advantage of eastern New England lay in its location near the sea and its several good harbors which facilitated the import and export trade. Then, too, Yankee settlers had either a background of industrial experience in Europe or else displayed a quick propensity for grasping factory skills.

A key development was Samuel Slater's choice to emigrate from England to Providence, Rhode Island, in 1789. What is significant is this: Since New England was a lucrative market for textiles, England had banned the export of textile machinery and blueprints of textile machinery as well as the emigration of textile workers—lest consumer regions such as New England establish textile factories of their own. But Slater, born in 1768 in Derbyshire, England, was apprenticed in 1782 in a textile mill and became a skilled mechanic—and he memorized the design of textile machines! In 1789 he left England disguised as a farm youth, migrated to America, settled in Rhode Island and contracted with a Providence firm to build and operate cotton-spinning equipment. A site near a waterfall on the Blackstone River (in Pawtucket, five miles northeast of Providence) was selected. A factory housing 72 spindles was built and began operations in 1790. Slater is generally acknowledged as the father of the American cotton industry.

As time elapsed, however, eastern New England lost much of its competitive advantage. As the nation's

Table 23-6

New England: Industrial Structure

Industry	Employees (Thousands)	Percentage	Percentage of National Total	Location Quotient
Machinery	152	11.2	8.3	1.2
Electric equipment	152	11.2	9.1	1.3
Fabricated metal	117	8.6	7.8	1.1
Transportation equipment	101	7.4	5.9	0.8
Printing and publishing	79	5.8	7.5	1.0
TOTAL	1363	100.0	7.2	—

Source: U.S. Bureau of the Census, *1972 Census of Manufactures* (1975).

population grew and moved west, New England manufacturers found themselves an increasing distance from the center of the national market, though they were still ideally situated relative to foreign markets. In cutting over their forests, too, New Englanders exhausted the supply of their one abundant raw material. With the development of electricity, the numerous small water power sites lost their advantage because electrically driven motors were cheaper to operate and easier to control. Moreover, electricity is more economically produced at large water power installations than at small ones. But unfortunately, most New England sites for high dams in sizable streams are far from industrial cities. The regional problem was compounded by inventions that generated thermal-electric power (in power plants driven by steam) at less cost than most hydroelectric plants. Coal was the most desirable fuel for such steam plants—but New England has no coal. Most of industrial New England's power is now produced with imported coal, most of the factories depend on raw materials that are shipped in from other parts of the nation, and the market is now largely to the west. Consequently, New England industrialists face the handicap of *backhauls*. The major assets of New England's factories today are enterprising directors, skilled labor, access to ocean shipping, and local capital.

Western New England. In western New England, manufacturing is located largely in the Connecticut Valley. No large city dominates this zone as Boston does to the east. Springfield, Hartford, Bridgeport, New Haven, and New Britain-Bristol are the main industrial centers. Metal products make up over one-half of all manufacturing. Machinery, aircraft parts and equipment, hardware, tools, guns, screws and bolts are typical commodities. This is one of the nation's "copper belts"; finished copper goods, such as electric wire, cooking utensils, and decorative hardware are produced here.

The Middle Atlantic States

Eastern Pennsylvania, southern New Jersey, Delaware, and Maryland support extensive manufacturing (Figure 23-1). Philadelphia and Baltimore are the dominant cities here, although smaller places such as Allentown-Bethlehem and Reading provide a substantial number of factory jobs.

Diversity is the hallmark of this region. Virtually every industry is present in at least small amounts, from the heaviest industries (blast furnaces at Sparrows Point) to the lightest (the apparel plants and optical instruments factories in Philadelphia). Shipyards and petroleum refineries line the Delaware River below Philadelphia, yet Baltimore and Camden are also known as major food-processing centers.

The Middle Atlantic area has several advantages for manufacturing. As one of the country's thickest concentrations of population and purchasing power, it provides a ready market for its own factories. It produces some raw materials—coal and iron ore, for instance, although neither in adequate amounts for the region's factories. Consequently, coal for industry must be brought in; but fortunately the bituminous coal fields of western Pennsylvania and West Virginia are not far away. Eastern Pennsylvania coal is closer, but being mostly anthracite it is more costly and so little used by factories. Iron ore is still mined in eastern Pennsylvania. Originally, local mines supplied the steel mills in this region, but today most of the ore comes from Canada and Venezuela. For such imports, the Delaware River and Chesapeake Bay serve as convenient waterways for ocean vessels. Frontage on the Atlantic Coast combined with good harbors along the Chesapeake and Delaware estuaries give this region easy access to foreign markets. Equally effective transportation, via the Pennsylvania and the Baltimore and Ohio railroads as well as the Pennsylvania Turnpike, links these states with the markets in the interior of the continent.

Middle New York State

A band of manufacturing runs through New York State from Troy to Buffalo. Rochester, Syracuse, and Utica, all good-sized towns, along with Binghamton and several smaller places in the south-central portion of the state, are the chief points of concentration (Figure 23-1).

This is a transitional zone. The range is between Troy, whose industrial structure resembles that of New England, and Buffalo, whose structure resembles that of Cleveland and Pittsburgh in its emphasis on heavy metal industries. In between lies Rochester, one of the most unusual industrial cities in the nation. Of its 140,000 manufacturing employees, about one-third make instruments (cameras, optical equipment, thermometers, and so forth). Indeed, for the instrument industry, Rochester's location quotient is estimated to be an astounding 18. This is attributable in large measure, of course, to the Eastman Kodak Company.

Buffalo's prominence stems basically from its location at the eastern end of Lake Erie; it is a vital point of trans-shipment for goods flowing from Atlantic ports, through the Mohawk-Hudson Valleys to the interior of the continent, and vice-versa. Prior to 1825 the westbound traffic moved along the Hudson River to Albany, then overland via the Mohawk Valley and Ontario Lowland to Buffalo. Then in 1825 the Erie Canal was opened to link Lake Erie with the Hudson River. In 1851 a railway route was completed, which is now the main line of the New York Central Railroad running from New York City to Chicago. In the early 1900's highways were threaded through this same route, climaxed today by U. S. Route 20 and the New York State Thruway. The line of industrial cities through middle New York is one of the nation's best examples of alignment of manufacturing centers along a transportation route.

Another appreciable manufacturing region (Figure 23-1) extends from western Pennsylvania to southeastern Wisconsin and from central Michigan to the Ohio River. An imaginary line connecting Pittsburgh, Louisville, Rockford, Green Bay, Flint, Detroit, and Cleveland would encircle what is, in fact, the industrial heart of the nation. The counties within this boundary share an unusual industrial consistency; manufacturing is an important part of the economic structure of nearly every one of them. Manufacturing activity is especially well developed in Ohio, northern Indiana, southern Michigan, northern Illinois, and southeastern Wisconsin. Somewhat detached from, but essentially part of, the core of the Midwestern area are St. Louis, Minneapolis, St. Paul, Kansas City, and smaller manufacturing centers sprinkled throughout Iowa and southern Minnesota.

The Midwest is a conglomeration of a few huge industrial centers (such as Chicago and Detroit) and scores of highly industrialized small cities, such as Hamilton (Ohio), Anderson (Indiana), Midland (Michigan), and Kenosha (Wisconsin), where the proportions of jobs in manufacturing reach the unusually high figures of 49, 61, 64, and 48 per cent respectively. The Midwest has a diverse mixture of industries. Nearly every type of manufacturing is represented, from the blast furnaces of Pittsburgh and Chicago to the auto factories of Detroit and the paper mills of the Miami Valley.

Within the Midwest, several zones stand out clearly. From Pittsburgh to Cleveland, including Youngstown, Akron, Canton, Wheeling, Steubenville, and Weirton, runs a band of heavy industry—the steel center of the nation. Metal industries dominate the industrial structures here, accounting for an astonishing 60 per cent of the industrial jobs in Pittsburgh, 60 per cent in Cleveland, and 85 per cent in Youngstown. *Primary* metal works (where metallic ores are converted into metal and where the product is refined) account for 35 per cent of all manufacturing jobs in Pittsburgh, whose location quotient for primary metal factories exceeds 5.

This metal works zone has an ideal setting for manufacturing. First of all, it possesses an excellent location relative to the domestic market;[2] Cleveland, for example, is central to markets located both to the east and to the west. In addition, this zone has excellent transportation advantages: the Great Lakes, all the major railroads running from the Middle Atlantic (including New York City) to the Midwest, major highways, and a network of pipelines and air routes (Chapter 24). Furthermore, the area is rich in coal. Notice that the manufacturing belt does not run northeast-southwest as does the coal field; rather it runs

[2]Access to market is a very difficult concept to measure. An excellent analysis of market influence in Cleveland is by Chauncy D. Harris, "The Market as a Factor in the Localization of Industry in the United States," *Annals* of the Assoiation of American Geographers (December 1954), pp. 315–348.

northwest, forming a bridge between the Appalachian coal region and the Great Lakes.

A second subzone is made up of Detroit and southeastern Michigan, the automotive capital of the United States. Detroit, the fourth-ranking industrial metropolis in the country, has a very asymmetrical (in contrast to diversified) industrial structure; it is dominated by the production of motor vehicles and parts (Table 23-7).

Table 23-7

Detroit: Industrial Structure

Industry	Employees (Thousands)	Percentage	Percentage of National Total	Location Quotient
TOTAL	555.6	100.0	2.9	—
Transportation equipment	240.0*	43.2	14.0	4.8
Fabricated metals	74.6	13.4	5.0	1.7
Machinery	72.9	13.1	4.0	1.4
Primary metals	43.0	7.7	3.8	1.3

Source: U.S. Bureau of the Census, *1972 Census of Manufactures* (1975).
*Estimate.

The leading industries (after motor vehicles) are fabricated metal products and machinery. Located along the Detroit River, this metropolis is on the main stream of Great Lakes shipping with easy access to iron ore from Lake Superior ports and coal from Lake Erie ports. But location alone was not enough to produce an industrial giant the size of Detroit in eastern Michigan, especially since it is considerably north of the main land routes (rail and highway) between Chicago and Atlantic port cities. Surely another major factor was the presence of the automotive inventors in Detroit (Chapter 21).

There is some correlation between the locational pattern of wage levels and the industrial structure of the Midwest since the automotive, machinery, and steel industries are, comparatively speaking, industries that pay high wages and so raise the pay level of the Midwest to the top spot in the nation (see Figure 23-3).

The third important subregion is the *Southern Lake Michigan Hinterland*, a horseshoe-shaped industrial area wrapped around the lower end of Lake Michigan. The greater Chicago metropolitan area (comprising 6 counties in Illinois and 2 in Indiana) and Milwaukee dominate the area, but there are several other highly active cities close by, such as Green Bay (Wisconsin), Rockford (Illinois), South Bend (Indiana), and Muskegon (Michigan).

Machinery is unquestionably the foremost industry for the region as a whole. In the metropolitan areas of Chicago (Table 23-8) and Milwaukee, electric equip-

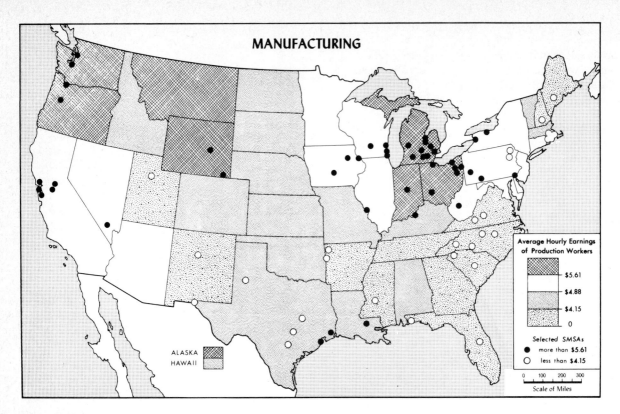

MANUFACTURING

Average Hourly Earnings of Production Workers

$5.61
$4.88
$4.15
0

Selected SMSAs
● more than $5.61
○ less than $4.15

0 100 200 300
Scale of Miles

ALASKA
HAWAII

Figure 23-3

Table 23-8

Chicago: Industrial Structure

Industry	Employees (Thousands)	Percentage	Percentage of National Total	Location Quotient
TOTAL	1,009.1	100.0	5.3	—
Electric equipment	132.2	13.1	8.0	1.5
Primary metals	124.7	12.4	10.9	2.1
Fabricated metal	118.5	11.7	7.9	1.5
Machinery	110.6	11.0	6.1	1.2
Printing	86.3	8.6	8.2	1.5
Food	75.7	7.5	4.8	0.9

Source: U.S. Bureau of the Census, *1972 Census of Manufactures* (1975). Data describe the Chicago-Northwestern Indiana Standard Consolidated Area.

ment and other metal-using industries are especially well developed.

In Milwaukee 40 per cent of the factory workers are employed in making many different types of machinery and electric equipment. The cities of this region produce a major portion of the nation's machine tools, farm machinery, and industrial appliances.

But the most spectacular factories are the steel mills lined up along a twelve-mile strip of Lake Michigan shoreline from Gary, Indiana, to southern Chicago. Towering above flat plains, the blast furnaces, coke ovens, gas ovens, and rolling mills (with associated stock

piles of black coal, rust-brown iron ore, and gray limestone) give a striking impression of *heavy industry*. Plumes of reddish smoke from the rows of chimneys draw attention from miles around.

Elsewhere in Chicago there is considerable activity in food processing and printing. Baking, candy manufacture, and meat packing are all important although meat packing has declined substantially in recent years. As a printing center, Chicago built its reputation on telephone directories, mail-order catalogs, and weekly magazines. Manufacturing is prominent in the Lake Michigan hinterland for four basic reasons: (a) This being the most productive agricultural region in the nation, there is plenty of purchasing power, engendered by agricultural surpluses, for manufactured commodities; (b) this being a densely populated area, there are not only numerous customers but also a numerous labor supply for factories; (c) being toward the center of the entire United States, this region is well-served by rail and highway transportation; and (d) this is conveniently the point of deepest penetration by the Great Lakes into the densely populated interior of the nation. These factors combined advantageously with another: the favorable coincidence of level terrain, fertile soils, and favorable climate which supported successful ventures in commercial agriculture as soon as peoples with the cultural potential for such an economy moved in. Another, if less vital, consideration was the coal field underlying Illinois, Indiana, and Kentucky. Actually, though, the manufacturing region is on the edge of, rather than atop, this resource (compare Figure 23-1 with Figure 14-4), which is not adequate for making coke; coking coal comes largely from Appalachia.

Southwestern Ohio (notably Cincinnati, Hamilton, Middletown, and Dayton), east central Indiana particularly Indianapolis, Anderson, and Fort Wayne), and Louisville constitute a fourth area of diversified manufacturing, with machinery, aircraft, and paper among the most conspicuous products. Cincinnati is a national leader in making machine tools, the Miami Valley in paper, and Dayton and Indianapolis in household machinery, office machinery, and airplane parts.

Outliers of the Midwest region are the Tri-Cities (Moline, Rock Island, Davenport), famous for farm machinery; Minneapolis and St. Paul, where machinery manufacture prevails; Omaha, where meat packing is a major employer (Omaha is now one of the nation's foremost meat-packing centers); and St. Louis, whose structure is well diversified. An outlier on the southeast is the Kanawha Valley and adjacent stretches of the upper Ohio River where the chemical industry has taken root. (Some people may question the inclusion of West Virginia in the midwestern manufactural region. Granted, West Virginia is considered by some to be a southern state, but on the basis of the pattern portrayed in Figure 23-1, its manufacturing is generally located in those counties nearer to northern than to southern industrial areas.)

There is one portion of the Midwest which serves to illustrate a principle of manufacturing geography. The area in question is the Rock River Valley, and the principle involves the relationship between labor costs and transportation costs. The Rock River Valley extends in a north-south direction from southern Wisconsin into northern Illinois and includes several cities in which manufacturing constitutes the main component of the economic base; Rockford, Illinois, is probably the best known.

The Rock Valley stands out somewhat conspicuously on Figure 23-1 and might be said to mark the western margin of "the manufacturing parallelogram"— a region bounded by four imaginary lines connecting Portland (Maine), Green Bay (Wisconsin), St. Louis, and Baltimore—which constitutes the industrial heart of the nation. At first glance the Rock Valley seems to be a conundrum insofar as manufacturing is concerned: Its major industries produce machinery, but the Valley mines no metals, smelts no ores, and must therefore call upon other areas (principally Chicago and Pittsburgh) for the raw materials used by its machinery makers. Neither does the Valley have, nor has it ever had, any peculiar power resource. In the late 1800's, small dams in the river generated a little waterpower, but for years its power requirements have been met by local thermal electric plants burning coal hauled in from Illinois mines to the south. Nor has it ever been a major transportation corridor, like the Mohawk Valley in New York. Finally, the region has no major market. Its machinery output is shipped to diverse parts of the nation and even abroad, with a large share of it moving to the *east*, the very direction from which come most of its raw materials. The question thus becomes: How can Rock Valley manu-

facturers pay freight on steel shipments of 90 miles from Chicago steel mills, then pay freight on machinery moving back the 90 miles to Chicago, and still quote a price—to eastern buyers—which is competitive with that charged by Chicago firms? Historically, the answer has been that there are savings on other items, principally labor costs. The explanation of this factor is presented in Chapter 30 under the general heading "A Theory of Labor Differentials and Transport Costs."

The South

The South contains 28 per cent of the nation's employees in manufacturing. There are no large agglomerations of workers and factories comparable with those in the North. The largest concentrations are Houston (163,000 manufacturing employees), Dallas (160,000), Greensboro (119,000), and Atlanta (115,000). These figures are surpassed in a number of localities in the Northeast. Nevertheless, in Figure 23-1, the South presents a rather continuous display of manufacturing with a broad swath of counties blanketing the territory from southern Virginia through the Carolinas into northern Georgia, Alabama, and Tennessee. A second belt, rather fragmented, can be discerned running northward from Houston to Wichita.

In the *Southeast* (from Virginia to Mississippi), three industries stand out—textiles, apparel, and food processing—but others, including lumber, furniture, tobacco, and electric equipment, are also important. The role that textiles plays in the industrial structure of this region is illustrated by the example of North Carolina (Table 23-9), where this industry provides 37 per cent of factory jobs. Few states have so skewed an industrial structure.

Table 23-9

North Carolina: Industrial Structure

Industry	Employees (Thousands)	Percentage	Percentage of National Total	Location Quotient
Textiles	276	37.1	29.0	7.4
Apparel	79	10.6	5.8	1.5
Furniture and fixtures	70	9.4	15.2	3.9
Food	37	5.0	2.4	0.6
Electric equipment	35	4.7	2.1	0.5
TOTAL	744	100.0	3.9	—

Source: U.S. Bureau of the Census, *1972 Census of Manufactures* (1975).

The Southeast has several valuable attributes for manufacturing. Its moderately large population offers a potential labor force. Although originally the skills of the people were directed largely to agriculture, mining, and other nonindustrial pursuits, in recent years they have quickly learned the industrial arts. A related advantage is that the wage rates here are generally lower than in the North. Numerous factories have transferred operations from North to South in order to realize savings in wages. The average hourly earnings received by factory workers are $3.66 in North Carolina, $3.69 in Mississippi, and $4.06 in Tennessee. Compare these figures with $5.11 in New York, $4.62 in Massachusetts, and $5.16 in Pennsylvania (Figure 23-3). Living costs and usually, municipal and state taxes are lower in the South. The milder climate means less factory overhead expense than in the North for winterizing and heating. The Southeast has many raw material advantages too. Some cotton is grown; it has the nation's most vigorous forests; most of the nation's tobacco is produced here; and a few minerals are mined (such as iron ore in Alabama, phosphate in Florida, and kaolin in Georgia). Moreover, the Southeast has two excellent power resources: water and coal. Two important hydroelectric locations are the Piedmont and the Tennessee Valley. Waterpower sites are abundant in the Piedmont, and in the late 1800's men started building factories by them. On the other side of the Appalachian highlands, the Tennessee River and tributaries have been dammed, mostly by the Tennessee Valley Authority—a gigantic experiment in regional planning launched by the federal government for the purpose of upgrading the economy of a region. In addition to controlling floods, reducing soil erosion, and providing recreational environments, the T.V.A. generates a tremendous amount of electricity.

The Southeast also has coal; two-thirds of the great Appalachian coal field lies in West Virginia, Kentucky, Virginia, Tennessee, and Alabama. But notice that the southeastern manufacturing belt does not coincide with this, the world's major coal field. Indeed, the coal area is amazingly devoid of manufacturing! Obviously, the relationship to coal—although very important in some regions—is not the major factor determining the location of factories either in the Northeast (else West Virginia, a leading coal mining state, would be a leader in manufacturing) or in the Southeast.

The recent industrialization in the Southeast has had an impact on life there in two significant ways: (a) The standard of living has increased, and (b) the rate of both white and Negro emigration to the North has declined.

The *Southwest*, from the Mississippi River to Texas and Oklahoma, including southern Kansas, reveals a different locational pattern and a different industrial structure. There is no extensive industrial zone, but rather a series of nodes, such as Houston, Beaumont, Dallas, Fort Worth, and Wichita. The region as a whole has 1,239,000 industrial employees, roughly comparable to the number in New England.

The industrial structure is highly diversified; food processing is the leading industry in this region, but

Table 23-10

Texas: Industrial Structure

Industry	Employees (Thousands)	Percentage	Percentage of National Total	Location Quotient
Food	77	10.5	4.9	1.3
Machinery	71	9.6	3.9	1.0
Apparel	67	9.1	4.9	1.3
Fabricated metal	67	9.1	4.5	1.2
Transportation equipment	67	9.1	3.9	1.0
TOTAL	736	100.0	3.9	—

Source: U.S. Bureau of the Census, *1972 Census of Manufactures* (1975).

machinery and fabricated metal products are not far behind. In Texas (Table 23-10), which has about 60 per cent of the region's manufacturing employment, apparel and transportation equipment (especially aircraft) join the three regional leaders. Although not exceptional in terms of employment, petroleum refining and the manufacture of chemicals are also important elements in this region's economic structure.

The Southwest does not have as abundant a labor pool as the Southeast, nor as much water power or coal. But it does have a sound agricultural base plus most of the petroleum in the country. Astute industrialists moving onto such a scene quickly linked this region (via Gulf Coast shipping, the Mississippi River traffic, railways, and pipelines) with the nation's main market to the north and east.

The main drawback for manufacturing in both Southeast and Southwest has been the lack of a local market. This stems from the low population in the Southwest and the low purchasing power (in spite of rather high population) in the Southeast. But other attributes are drawing manufacturers so that the South, at least in certain well-favored localities, is currently going through a period of rapid industrial growth.

The Western Void

A vast, nearly blank area on Figure 23-1 occupies much of the western half of the United States. The eastern margin of this void runs generally from Minneapolis through Omaha to Houston. Its western margin runs parallel to, and 100 miles inland from, the Pacific Coast. Within this enormous space there probably are not more than 550,000 manufacturing employees, or about triple the number in Arkansas and equal to that in Detroit. Denver's 91,000 industrial workers form the one outstanding concentration.

The absence of manufacturing in this large realm is due basically to the dearth of population. With little local market to be served, factories often depend on processing local raw materials for distant consumers. Foods, lumber, and primary metals are a distinctive trio. Specifically, meat products are processed from beef cattle and

Baytown refinery, Texas. (*Courtesy EXXON Corporation.*)

sheep; sawmills and planing and veneer mills convert mountain stands of timber into lumber and plywood; and copper, lead, zinc, silver, and gold ores are put through primary processing. In recent years, electronics and other industries have moved into places like Phoenix and Denver, but manufacturing employment is still modest by national standards.

The Pacific Coast

A spotty pattern of small industrial developments characterizes many portions of Washington, Oregon, and California. But the Los Angeles and San Francisco metropolitan areas are prominent on not only the regional but also the national manufacturing scene. They are, in fact, the largest industrial centers outside the northeastern quadrant of the nation. Factory employment in major West Coast urban areas is Los Angeles 775,000 (ranking third in the nation, see Table 23-2); San Francisco 190,000; San Jose 125,000; Anaheim 118,000; and Seattle 108,000. For the West Coast's industrial structure, see Table 23-11.

Table 23-11

Pacific Division: Industrial Structure

Industry	Employees (Thousands)	Percentage	Percentage of National Total	Location Quotient
Transportation equipment	327	16.5	19.0	1.8
Food	219	11.0	14.0	1.3
Lumber and wood	187	9.4	27.1	2.6
Electric equipment	184	9.3	11.1	1.1
Machinery	156	7.9	8.5	0.8
TOTAL	1983	100.0	10.4	

Source: U.S. Bureau of the Census, *1972 Census of Manufactures* (1975).

The advantages of the Pacific Coast for aircraft production have already been outlined in Chapter 21. The large lumber industry is based on the most voluminous stands of timber in the nation; West Coast mills ship boards, shingles, veneer, millwork, pulpwood, and paper to nationwide markets utilizing rail, highways, and even the Panama Canal for reaching eastern customers. The foods industry is represented largely by the canning or freezing of the myriad of fruits and vegetables that flourish in the mild Pacific Coast climates.

The Pacific Coast is a rapidly growing manufacturing region because of a relatively new factor—the emergence of the West Coast as a substantial market in its own right. This growth of course correlates directly to the population boom in western states. The emergence of this market has led to the appearance of machinery and fabricated metals in the Pacific Coast's industrial structure.

Conclusion

The United States Census Bureau recognizes nine arbitrary regions in publishing data on industrial structures. Figure 23-4 outlines these regions and identifies the three leading manufactures in each region. Notice that the map graphically illustrates the characteristics of regions discussed in this chapter and depicts such regional differences as degree of diversity and distinguishing industries.

Relation to Total Employment. In Figure 23-1 we mapped manufacturing in the United States in terms of one variable, number of employees. In Figure 23-5, we present still another view, showing the location of manufacturing employees as related to total nonfarm employment. For the nation as a whole, the ratio is one in four. The range for all 50 states is 34.1 (the lowest percentage being Nevada, where only 4.7 of all nonfarm employees are in manufacturing; the highest in North

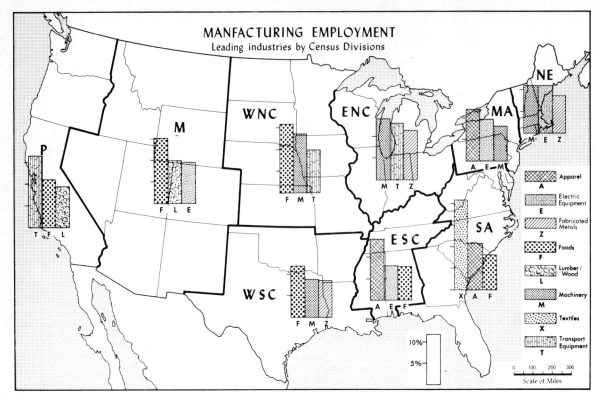

Figure 23-4 *Census divisions are: Pacific, Mountain, West North Central, East North Central, West South Central, East South Central, New England, Middle Atlantic, South Atlantic.*

Figure 23-5

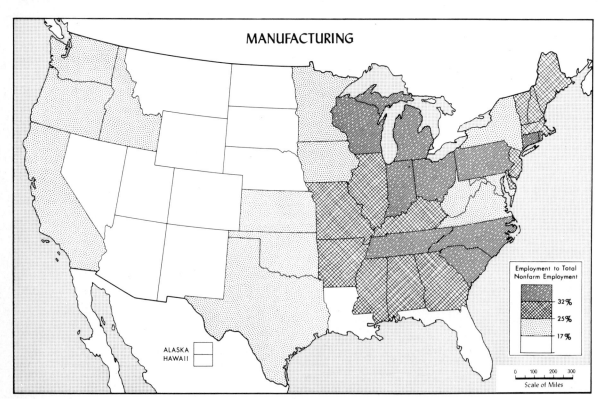

Carolina, where the figure is 38.8). It is interesting to note that states with large numbers of employees in manufacturing (Figure 23-1) are not always those where manufacturing employment is exceptionally important in *relative* terms (Figure 23-5).

Changes in the Location of Manufacturing Between 1947 and 1972

During this period, manufacturing employment in the United States increased by 26 per cent, from 14,294,000 to 18,034,000 people. But this growth was not uniformly distributed throughout the nation. Some areas enjoyed healthy gains, some had moderate increases, and some suffered losses. Of the 48 contiguous states, 5 experienced a reduction in manufacturing jobs.

Figure 23-6 shows the location of change in employment by state. All five of the losing states are in the Northeast, and two suffered severe declines: Massachusetts 14 per cent, and Rhode Island, 20 per cent. Fortunately for this region, gains by the states west of Pennsylvania were enough to offset losses in the New England and Middle Atlantic states. Still, the nation's foremost industrial region stands out as its foremost region of loss of manufacturing job opportunities. Most western and some southern states enjoyed vigorous gains, with Arizona (up 561 per cent), Florida (up 336 per cent), and Nevada (up 270 per cent) leading the way. It should be remembered, however, that sizable percentage gains can be achieved by adding only a few thousand more jobs in states with small 1947 payrolls.

Clearly, manufacturing is moving west and south. One reason for the western growth—beginning roughly at the Mississippi River—is that there are now relatively

more people in these states than in 1947 and factories have followed them. Another reason is the somewhat popular policy of *decentralization* by which some companies decide to build branch plants in less-developed areas. Another factor, especially in the booming southern states, is increased use of local labor, power, and materials—as well as Southern purchasing power.

CANADA

Canada has about 1,600,000 people who earn their livelihood in manufacturing, about as many as metropolitan New York, and a bit more than California.

Location

The locational pattern of Canadian manufacturing is, in some respects, similar to that of the United States. The preponderance of activity is in the eastern half of the country, and within the eastern half, it is concentrated in a few outstanding zones. Furthermore, Canada's chief manufacturing cities are also her principal ports.

The main manufacturing zone of Canada runs through the St. Lawrence Valley and southern Ontario (Figure 23-7), between the two cities of Quebec and Windsor. Probably 85 per cent of Canadian manufacturing takes place in this zone; this is where the country's two largest industrial concentrations and all but four of her cities with at least 10,000 industrial workers are

Figure 23-6

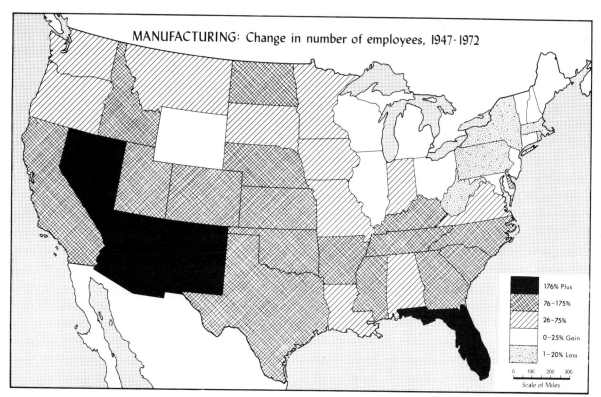

MANUFACTURING: Change in number of employees, 1947-1972

176% Plus
76 - 175%
26 - 75%
0 - 25% Gain
1 - 20% Loss

0   100   200   300
Scale of Miles

317

located. The exceptions are Winnipeg, Edmonton, Calgary, and Vancouver.

The two principal metropolitan areas far outrank all others: Toronto with 334,000 manufactural employees, and Montreal with 297,000. Vancouver, the third ranking center, only supports 70,000 industrial workers, and Hamilton has about 69,000. Toronto is in the same general category as Boston, and Montreal in the same category as Cleveland.

Characteristics

Canada's industrial structure is headed by two groups of industries: foods and beverages, and transportation equipment. Food factories process a broad diversity of Canadian products, notably dairy goods, meat, and flour. Fruit, vegetable, and fish canneries are numerous. Canadian transportation equipment factories produce a wide line of merchandise: motor vehicles and motor vehicle parts, aircraft and parts, railroad equipment, and boats. Two traditional leaders, wood and paper, are still important even though they have been surpassed in terms of employment by several industries. The sawmill is one of the most common factory types. Thousands of them dot the forested countryside, especially on the southerly margin of the great forest zone (see Chapter 6), extending from British Columbia to Quebec. Although individual sawmills frequently employ few persons, their total payroll in Canada classes them as a major industry. Pulp mills are more important than sawmills in terms of employment, payrolls, and value of shipments, although they tend to be far fewer in number and less widespread.

Other industries are numerous and diverse. Virtually every type of manufacturing is represented: metal smelting and refining, petroleum refining, chemicals, textiles, clothing, rubber goods, furniture, printing, publishing, metal fabricating, electrical products, and so on.

Relationships

The location of all these industries harmonizes with the same set of forces as operate in the United States. Correlation with markets is the most apparent relationship, since most Canadians with purchasing power live in the peninsula of southern Ontario and along the St. Lawrence lowland. Similarly, this area provides the largest labor force. Raw material supplies, however, are meager in many respects and this region must import a lot: coal from the Appalachian field to the south; iron ore from the Lake Superior ranges to the west and the Labrador-Quebec field to the east; and wheat mostly from the Prairie Provinces to the west (Chapter 11). On the other hand, Ontario farms yield a surplus of dairy produce, fruits, vegetables, and tobacco. Without this successful agricultural base, there would be considerably less population and much less industry there today.

Canada has been signally well endowed in forests and potential water power, resources that lured certain types of manufacturing to the Pacific Coast and to the northern fringe of the main manufacturing belt. The presence of nickel, copper, and other metallic ores have favored the development of primary metal manufacturing industries in the sparsely settled zone lying between Lake Huron and Hudson Bay; here the settlements of Sudbury, Cobalt, Kirkland, Cochrane, and Noranda are cities whose manufacturing to a large degree is of this type. The name of the settlement of Asbestos (75 miles east of Montreal) identifies its mineral resource. Discoveries of petroleum in Alberta have stimulated the location of refineries not only in this province, to serve hinterland markets, but also in the manufacturing belt to which the crude oil is passed by pipeline and tanker.

The role of the Great Lakes and the St. Lawrence

Figure 23-7

MANUFACTURING IN CANADA

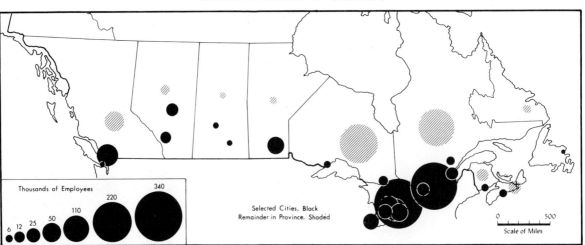

Thousands of Employees

6 12 25 50 110 220 340

Selected Cities, Black
Remainder in Province, Shaded

0   500
Scale of Miles

River cannot be overemphasized in the industrial development of Canada. Indeed, where good agricultural land borders these water bodies, population is heavy, and that is where we find the great preponderance of Canadian manufacturing. These water bodies function as a sort of main street for Canadian industry, linking

her industrial zone with not only the rest of the country but also with foreign sources of many raw materials and with foreign markets.

SUGGESTED READINGS

ALEXANDER, JOHN W., "Location of Manufacturing: Methods of Measurement," *Annals of the Association of American Geographers*, 1958, pp. 20–26.

ALEXANDERSSON, GUNNAR, *Geography of Manufacturing*, Englewood Cliffs, N. J., 1967, 148 pp.

CROSSLEY, J. C., "The Location of Beef Processing," *Annals of the Association of American Geographers*, 1976, pp. 60–75.

DE GEER, STEN, "Delimitation of the North American Manufacturing Belt, *Geografiska Annaler*, 1927, pp. 247–258.

DILLMAN, C. DANIEL, "Brownsville: Border Port for Mexico and the U. S.," *The Professional Geographer*, 1969, pp. 178–183.

ESTALL, R. C., "The Electronics Products Industry of New England," *Economic Geography*, 1963, pp. 189–216.

FOUST, J. BRADY, "Ubiquitous Manufacturing," *Annals of the Association of American Geographers*, 1975, pp. 13–17.

GILMOUR, JAMES M., "Some Considerations of Spatial Separation Between Linked Industries," *The Canadian Geographer*, 1971, pp. 287–294.

———, and MURRICANE, KENNETH, "Structural Divergence in Canada's Manufacturing Belt," *The Canadian Geographer*, 1973, pp. 1–18.

GOODWIN, WILLIAM, "The Management Center in the United States," *Geographical Review*, 1965, pp. 1–16.

HARRIS, CHAUNCY D., "The Market as a Factor in the Localization of Industry in the United States," *Annals of the Association of American Geographers*, 1954, pp. 315–348.

HARTSHORN, TRUMAN A., "The Spatial Structure of Socioeconomic Development in the Southeast, 1950–1960," *Geographical Review*, 1971, pp. 265–283.

HELLMAN, DARYL A., "Agglomeration Economics: A Model of Regional Export Activity," *Growth and Change*, January 1974, pp. 12–17.

JOHNSON, LANE J., and TEUFNER, WALTRAUD E., "Industry Combinations in the Central United States: An Application of Weaver's Method," *The Professional Geographer*, 1968, pp. 297–302.

LONSDALE, RICHARD E., and BROWNING, CLYDE E., "Rural-Urban Locational Preferences of Southern Manufacturers," *Annals of the Association of American Geographers*, 1971, pp. 255–268.

MORRISON, JOEL L., SCRIPTER, MORTON W., and SMITH, ROBERT H. T. "Basic Measures of Manufacturing in the United States, 1958," *Economic Geography*, 1968, pp. 296–311.

PRED, ALLAN, "The Concentration of High-Value-Added Manufacturing," *Economic Geography*, 1965, pp. 108–132.

———, "The Intrametropolitan Location of American Manufacturing," *Annals of the Association of American Geographers*, 1964, pp. 165–180.

———, "Toward a Typology of Manufacturing Flows," *Geographical Review*, 1964, pp. 65–84.

RAY, D. MICHAEL, "The Location of United States Manufacturing Subsidiaries in Canada," *Economic Geography*, 1971, pp. 389–400.

RODGERS, ALLAN, "Some Aspects of Industrial Diversification in the United States," *Economic Geography*, 1957, pp. 16–30.

SHEAR, JAMES A., "A General Measure of Diversity," *The Professional Geographer*, March 1965, pp. 14–17.

STEED, GUY P. F., "Centrality and Locational Change: Printing, Publishing, and Clothing in Montreal and Toronto," *Economic Geography*, 1976, pp. 193–205.

———, "Intrametropolitan Manufacturing: Spatial Distribution and Locational Dynamics in Greater Vancouver," *The Canadian Geographer*, 1973, pp. 235–258.

STRUYK, RAYMOND J., "Spatial Concentration of Manufacturing Employment in Metropolitan Areas: Some Empirical Evidence," *Economic Geography*, 1972, pp. 189–192.

PART

SEVEN

TRANSPORTATION AND TRADE

Transportation is quite simply the movement of goods and people from place to place. Some persons also hold that communication, the movement of ideas from place to place, is a type of transportation.

From the standpoint of value, there are two types of transportation. The first is *economic* transportation by which goods and people are carried for the purpose of economic profit. The economist sometimes says that such transportation is a change in *place utility*—that is, the value of a commodity is worth more after it has been transported from its region of production to that of consumption. Grain pouring out of harvesting machinery in Kansas wheat fields has a certain value, but that wheat is worth more after it has been transported to Kansas City flour mills. Flour streaming from the milling machines in those factories has a certain value, but it is worth more after being transported to Chicago bakeries. Transportation accounts for such increase in value by moving commodities to locations of demand.

Noneconomic transportation includes all movements which are carried on for some purpose other than economic profit. Recreational travel and military logistics are two examples.

The significance of transportation in economic geography cannot be over-emphasized. In its own right transportation is an important *geographic element*— a spatial variable by which regions can be delimited and their characteristics studied, and in terms of which relationships can be analyzed, such as relationships among route location, traffic flow, and other phenomena. In addition, organized transportation is a *geographic factor*—an *influence* on the location of other economic activities; for without means of transport there would be no commercial coal mining, no production of surplus wheat, and no commercial lumbering. Without commercial transportation, in fact, the world's economy would remain at a subsistence level and regional specialization yielding exchangeable surpluses would be impossible.

We are all familiar with transportation in a practical way, but in Part Seven we shall consider the topic in terms of the basic categories of geographic method— location, characteristics, and relationships. Chapter 24 deals with the various means of transportation—railways, roads, waterways, airways, and pipelines. Chapter 25 covers international trade. Transportation hubs, however—places where routes converge that function as the nerve centers of trade—are reserved for Part Eight, which deals with service centers.

CHAPTER
24

means of transportation

Containerized freight transport is becoming increasingly important as more ports and transshipment centers in the world establish the facilities and equipment needed to take advantage of this modern and efficient system. The vessel shown here at the Port of San Francisco can load and unload the prepacked containers in a much shorter time than is required by more conventional methods of shipping. The containers are designed to fit onto flatbed railroad cars and trucks, further cutting transshipment time. (*Courtesy Southern Pacific.*)

In a sense, the transportation system of the world is analogous to several vital systems within the human body. One might say that the body keeps functioning by virtue of the finely adjusted co-ordination of several different transportation media, each with its own network: The nervous system conveys electrical impulses from the brain to the spinal cord and other parts of the body; the circulatory system keeps the blood cells moving; the lymph system circulates lymph; the alimentary system passes food and wastes along; and the respiratory system exchanges air between the lungs and the atmosphere.

The world's economy likewise depends on the interplay of several transportation systems: railways, roads, waterways, airways, and pipelines, plus the communication media—radio, telephone, telegraph, postal systems, and publications.

Because of this analogy with the human body, some economic geographers refer to transportation as the *world's circulation system.*

RAILWAYS

Location

Distributed very unevenly over the surface of the earth are 750,000 miles of commercial railways. By the standard of *railway tracks*, we can readily discern two major regions and six minor ones. (See a map of world railways in almost any economic atlas.)

In Europe a remarkably dense network spreads eastward from the Atlantic shores through the middle of the continent, gradually thinning out in the Soviet Union. Approximately 235,000 miles of track (nearly

one-third of the world total) make up this European network (*railnet* for short). In terms of track density (miles of line per unit of land, for instance, per every 100 square miles), Europe is the foremost railway region of the world. Belgium, most notably, is interwoven with an average of 22 miles of railway line for every 100 square miles of area; comparable average ratios in other countries are 20 for Switzerland, 17 for Luxembourg and Czechoslovakia, and 15 for West Germany. On the outer edges of this railnet, the national ratios drop to 1 in Albania, 2 in Norway, and 3 in Finland and Greece. Although her overall ratio is less than one, the U.S.S.R. has approximately 80,000 miles of railway, far more than France's 23,000; Poland's 17,000; or West Germany's 15,000.

Over 250,000 miles of railway (34 per cent of the world total) stretch westward across North America from the Atlantic, thinning out abruptly along the 100th meridian. With approximately 210,000 miles of track, the United States (Figure 24-1) has 28 per cent of the world total, or over six times the density of the U.S.S.R. In the continental United States, there are 6 miles of track per 100 square miles of area, but by state this ratio varies widely. Canada's network of 44,000 miles is surpassed in size only by those of her neighbor to the south and of the U.S.S.R.

The rest of the world has about one-third of the total, roughly 265,000 miles. This track is distributed for the most part in six places. (1) In southern Asia, railways appear almost exclusively in India and Pakistan. The combined mileage is that of Canada, and the ratio of 2.8 approximates that of Finland. (2) Railways are congested in eastern Asia (Japan, Korea, and China). Japan has only 17,000 miles of line, but the area of the country is so small that the density exceeds 11. (3)

Figure 24-1 (*From Association of American Railroads.*)

RAILWAY MAP OF THE UNITED STATES: 1960

Unit oil train winding its way through the Sierra Nevadas of California. Unit trains generally run a regular schedule between a particular production and market point and are less expensive than shipping by more conventional rail methods. (*Tom Brown Photo Courtesy Southern Pacific.*)

Australia's 25,000 miles of track are almost entirely confined to the eastern and southern fringes of the continent. (4) The southern tip of Africa is crisscrossed by a network about as dense as that of southeastern Australia. (5) Eastern Argentina stands out with the densest railway pattern in the Southern Hemisphere. (6) Finally, a small but thick mesh of railway tracks spreads inland from coastal Brazil.

Elsewhere, railways are few and far between. The tropics have comparatively few rail lines and the Equator itself is crossed by less than half a dozen railroads. Most of South America, Africa, inner Asia, northern Asia, inner Australia, and northern North America are literally trackless.

Characteristics

We could refine our picture of world railway lines *if* we could introduce into our maps information on such matters as: number of tracks (whether a line is four-track, double-track, or single-track makes a huge difference in its capacity for traffic), gauge of track (that is, the distance between the rails, which varies from six feet in a few countries to two-and-one-half feet in others), weight of rail (heavier rails can support heavier carloads), type of traffic control (more traffic can move over an automatic central traffic control system than over one with few signal devices), and type of motive power (whether electric, coal-fired steam, wood-fired steam, or

Figure 24-2

VOLUME OF RAILWAY FREIGHT TRAFFIC

diesel-electric). Unfortunately, such data, and the maps derived from them, are extremely hard to come by.

Rights-of-way, however, are not the principal objects of analysis; at best they make up only the anatomy of the world's railways system. What we might call the physiology of the system is traffic, the flow of commodities and passengers. This constitutes the life of the railway. Fortunately, good maps can be made to show us some of the regional differences in freight and passenger traffic.

Freight Traffic. Figure 24-2 portrays the regional pattern of freight traffic quantified by means of annual ton-miles of freight. Ton-mile figures are determined by multiplying the tons of freight in each shipment by the mileage over which that shipment moves. As Table 24-1 and Figure 24-2 show, the Soviet Union is far ahead of any other nation, more than 2,000,000 million ton-miles of freight traffic annually move along her railways. This astonishing volume reflects the large number of manufacturing areas separated by vast distances. The Soviet Union also has high *freight density* (ton-miles divided by miles of route). The figure for the U.S.S.R. is more than six times that of the United States. One reason for this is the Soviet railway pattern of several main lines but few branch lines; thus the traffic is concentrated on fewer miles of *route*. It is a principle of railway geography that in regions of comparable economic activity, the areas with a *fine* railway pattern (many lines close together) tend to have lower traffic densities than areas with a *coarse* pattern (few lines far apart). China does not have many railways, considering her size, but if recent estimates are accurate, freight now moves there with an intensity exceeding that of every nation except the U.S.S.R. and the United States (Table 24-1).

Most European nations report freight volumes of over four billion ton-miles per year. The highest volumes

Table 24-1

World Railroad Traffic Volumes (Selected Nations)

Rail System	Millions of Passenger-Miles	Millions of Freight Ton-Miles	Rail System	Millions of Passenger-Miles	Millions of Freight Ton-Miles
Africa			Pakistan	6,256	5,211
Angola	196	4,178	Sri Lanka	2,001	223
East Africa (Kenya,			Thailand	2,917	1,418
Uganda, Tanzania)	—	3,043	Turkey	3,243	4,657
Egypt	4,540	2,039			
Mauritania	—	4,662	*Europe*		
Nigeria	642	940	Austria	4,197	7,183
South Africa	—	41,027	Belgium-Luxembourg	5,197	6,128
Rhodesia	—	4,537	Bulgaria	4,394	11,398
			Czechoslovakia	11,979	44,486
North America			Denmark	1,987	1,467
Canada	1,599	131,771	Finland	1,723	4,800
Mexico	2,521	17,977	France	27,782	50,569
United States	9,299	851,809	East Germany	12,957	36,287
Amtrak	(3,807)	—	West Germany	24,729	46,070
Eastern District	(3,762)	(245,022)	Hungary	8,630	14,171
Southern District	(574)	(157,879)	Italy	22,593	12,038
Western District	(1,156)	(448,908)	Netherlands	5,079	2,272
			Poland	24,636	79,763
South America			Portugal	2,551	561
Argentina	7,664	8,602	Romania	13,191	39,116
Brazil	7,139	12,385	Spain	9,725	7,708
Chile	2,159	1,792	Sweden	3,044	12,508
			Switzerland	5,904	4,917
Asia			United Kingdom	21,875	17,477
Burma	1,910	410	Yugoslavia	6,573	14,006
China	—	206,185			
India	81,683	81,999	*U.S.S.R.*	184,316	2,026,220
Iran	1,332	3,036			
Japan	193,196	40,058	*Australia*	—	18,209
South Korea	6,661	5,750			

Source: United Nations, *Statistical Yearbook, 1974* (1975) and Association of American Railroads, *Yearbook of Railroad Facts* (1976).

(outside the U.S.S.R.) occur in Poland, whose surprisingly high figure exceeds even those of France and West Germany. The main reason for this is that waterways carry more of the traffic burden in western Europe than in eastern Europe. Volume in Canada is exceeded only by that of the United States, China, and the U.S.S.R., the only other nations with more than 100,000 million ton-miles of freight.

Within the United States, data are readily available to describe freight volumes in three large districts. The Eastern District generally conforms to the area identified as the nation's major manufacturing area in Part Six. It includes southern Wisconsin and all states east of the Mississippi River and north of the Ohio River. An imaginary line continues east of Ohio to include West Virginia and most of Virginia. South of this line and east of the Mississippi River is the Southern District. The remainder of the nation forms the Western District. Freight volumes in the districts vary strikingly as can be seen in Table 24-1. The Western District is the largest in both area and freight volume. It is interesting to note that Figure 24-1 shows a fairly sparse railway network in this region where long hauls of heavy raw materials are common.

Passenger Traffic. Spatial variation in passenger traffic is as striking as that in freight traffic. Passenger traffic is represented here in terms of the total number of miles traveled by rail passengers in a 1-year period. Thus, one passenger taking a 1,000-mile trip would account for 1,000 passenger-miles; 20 persons each taking

a 50-mile trip would also produce 1,000 passenger-miles. Passenger traffic volumes quantified in this manner range from a low of two million in Lebanon to an astounding 193,196 million in Japan. The figure for the United States is 9,299 million, and this number is exceeded by 11 countries. Of these 11, the 3 largest are Japan, the U.S.S.R., and India; the remaining 8 are all European nations.

A somewhat different picture of passenger traffic is provided by estimating railway passenger traffic densities. Such estimates are produced by dividing the total number of passenger-miles traveled in a region by that region's miles of right-of-way. If we were to make a map of densities and compare it with Figure 24-3, the general patterns would be similar, but a few significant differences could be noted. Japan, with a passenger traffic density figure of over 11,000,000 million, would still head both lists. Hong Kong with relatively low volume but high density (about 8 million) would take over the number two position. Elsewhere there would be some shifting of position, but for the most part, the high-volume countries, such as the U.S.S.R., India, and those elsewhere in Europe and the Far East, are also the high-density countries.

Perhaps the most conspicuous dropout from the list of high-passenger traffic densities would be the United States. Although volumes are high, so are the miles of railway. As a result, the density figure for the United States is a low 45,000. This figure is lower than figures

Figure 24-3

VOLUME OF RAILWAY PASSENGER TRAFFIC

for places such as Greece and Ghana and similar to densities found in Finland, Iran, and Israel. There are several reasons for the low density figure found in the United States: Commuter traffic, which helps inflate density figures, is confined to only a small fraction of the railway network; the railway network covers large underpopulated stretches; and finally, well over half of the railway tracks in the United States no longer carry passenger trains. But perhaps the most significant factor is that alternative modes, e.g., the automobile, are readily available to a large share of the American people. The number of passenger miles traveled in the United States reached its peak during World War II. From the mid-1940's until the early 1970's passenger traffic steadily declined. Since Amtrak operations began in May, 1971, there has been a slight increase in passenger miles traveled, but there is little indication that rail passenger densities will return to levels established in the 1950's and 1960's.

Railway Rates. One might suppose that the price paid by customers for shipping freight would be commensurate with mileage. Although no worldwide study has been made to test the validity of this assumption, studies within the United States reveal that freight rates themselves are remarkably variable and that they do not vary consistently with either length or direction of shipment. Five aspects of freight rates illustrate this point: freight-rate territories, the rate-group principle, class rates, commodity rates, and in-transit rates.

1. Freight-rate territories: The freight rates charged by railways in the United States are regulated by the Interstate Commerce Commission. This agency divided the nation into five regions (see Figure 24-4). For several decades before 1937, when this map was constructed, the Commission authorized lower rates in the Eastern (or Official) Territory than anywhere else. The map shows prices were highest in the Mountain-Pacific Region, averaging 90 per cent more than those in Eastern Territory. The Interstate Commerce Commission defended this policy on the grounds that traffic was so heavy in the Eastern Territory that lower operating costs (per ton-mile) produced by the efficiencies of mass movement should be passed on to shippers in the form of lower rates. But this policy came under increasing attack from traffic agents in other parts of the nation arguing that the rate structure of Figure 24-4 was discriminatory in favor of the Eastern Territory. In response to such pressure, spearheaded by the governors of the southern states, the federal government in 1940 began gradually to reduce the differentials among the five regions. By 1952, all regions east of the Rockies were on equal footing.

The map of freight-rate territories, as they are defined today, is similar to the original with one important exception. The Mountain-Pacific Region's

Figure 24-4 (*Source: U.S. Government, 75th Congress, First Session. The Interritorial Freight-Rate Problem of the United States, House Document number 264, 1937, Chart 4.*)

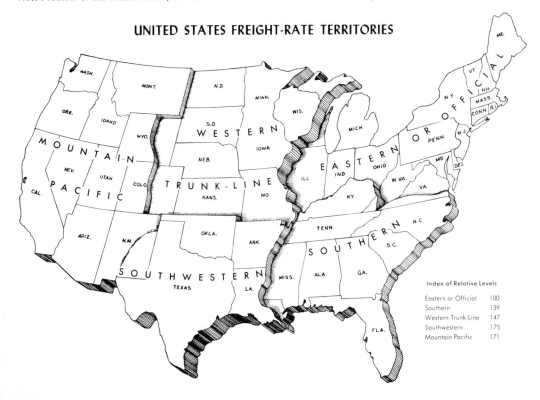

UNITED STATES FREIGHT-RATE TERRITORIES

Index of Relative Levels

Eastern or Official	100
Southern	139
Western Trunk-Line	147
Southwestern	175
Mountain Pacific	171

Figure 24-5

boundary has been shifted slightly and its name has been changed to Trans-Continental Territory. Because it is so large, two subregions—the North Pacific Coast and the Pacific South Coast—have been recognized. Committees within each of these territories meet periodically to discuss rate changes and to make recommendations which are then reviewed and passed upon at the national level.

2. The rate-group principle: One might suppose that, along a railway radiating outward from a transportation center, rates would gradually increase with distance. But this is not true. Instead, the places along each route are divided into groups, all the points in one group having the same rate. Consequently, profiles of freight-rate structures follow a stair-step pattern (Figure 24-5), not a curve.

3. Class rates: The Interstate Commerce Commission authorizes two types of rates: *class rates*, which apply to all items that move in small quantities, and *commodity rates*, which are applicable to a few items that move in large quantities. The rate-group principle is usually applied to class rates in such a manner that there is at least a loose correlation with distance. Consequently, class-rate structures tend to be somewhat symmetrical; this is illustrated by Figure 24-6, which shows the pattern of class rates between Milwaukee and all points in Wisconsin. The lines on this map that connect points with equal freight rates are called *isophors*.

4. Commodity rates: Where the tonnage of a particular item is consistently large, the Commission permits a commodity rate that is lower than the class rate would be. For instance, in the Wisconsin rate structure (Figure 24-7) loads of coal from Milwaukee (Appalachian coal that has come in by ship) enjoy a more favorable position in the northern part of the state than in the western part because of competition from railroads which link the northern area with other ports on Lakes Michigan and Superior.

Clearly, railway freight charges do not always increase at the same rate in all directions around a shipping terminal (isophors are not circular) nor do they increase consistently with distance in any one direction.

5. In-transit rates: These are privileges granted by the I.C.C. to factories located between the origin and destination of a commodity. Sash and doors sold on the East Coast at one time were manufactured largely in Wisconsin factories from local pine. When Wiscon-

Figure 24-6 (*Courtesy* Economic Geography.)

Figure 24-7 (*Courtesy* Economic Geography.)

329

sin's pine forests were cut away 50 years ago, these factories began buying raw material from saw mills in Oregon and Washington. But this resulted in two separate rates, one from the Pacific Northwest to Wisconsin and another from Wisconsin to the East. *Since freight costs tend to increase with distance but at a decreasing rate*, the through charge on a 3000-mile trip is less than the combination of one fee on the first 2000 miles plus a second on the final 1000 miles. The "in-transit" privilege permits a stop-over of raw material for processing before being shipped on to market—all at a *single through rate*. Such privileges are granted by the I.C.C. in only a few instances, but they spell the difference between life and death for factories located midway between raw materials and markets by enabling them to compete with factories located within the market areas. Most of Wisconsin's sash and door factories, for example (Chapter 18), would have vanished with the pine forests but for in-transit rates.

Advantages and Disadvantages of Railways.
The transportation advantages of railroads lie in their capacity for carrying *large volumes* of *heavy items* in comparatively *short time* at rather *low cost*. A four-person crew and a locomotive can haul a load of 100 or more cars averaging 40 tons per car. A drawback, however, is that it takes a good long time to assemble cars in a freight yard and then to link them together in proper sequence to form a train. Still, once underway, such a train moves at a relatively high speed. Again at the end of the journey it takes time to disconnect the cars and switch them around to the proper sidings for consignees. Consequently, railways are much better fitted for handling long shipments than they are for short hauls.

Relationships to Other Phenomena

The relationships between rail transportation and other phenomena are essentially the same as those involving road, water, air, and pipeline transport. For this reason, we shall postpone a discussion of them until we have taken a look at the locations and characteristics of other media.

ROADS AND HIGHWAYS

Location

It is difficult to find or work up a map of the world's roads because concepts of just what constitutes a road vary so widely. In some places roads are wide and well-paved; elsewhere they are narrow and poorly, if at all, surfaced. One thing is sure, though, most roads are unsurfaced—mere ribbons of dirt track over the landscape. And yet such tracks constitute the major "highways" in

vast underdeveloped regions. In general, though, the world pattern of surfaced roads resembles that of railroads, the main difference being that the road network covers a larger area, penetrating into areas where traffic is insufficient to demand a railway. The regions with the most highly developed road systems are Anglo-America, Europe, India, Pakistan, eastern Asia, southern Africa, and southeastern South America. At the other extreme are the great stretches of the earth's surface that are virtually unmarked by any semblance of a road: the vast northern expanses of North America and Eurasia, inner South America, inner Asia, inner Australia, and the islands of New Guinea and Borneo.

Within the United States the density of roads averages almost exactly one mile of road for one square mile of land area. The highest ratio—5.28 to 1—obtains in Rhode Island, where 1049 square miles of land are interlaced with 5540 miles of rural and municipal roads. The thinnest density—0.02—is in Alaska, where 9043 miles of road serve 566,432 square miles of land.

Characteristics

We can use numerous criteria to reveal differences among roads: width in feet, number of lanes, type of surface, sharpness of curves, and whether they are toll or free. Depending on our objective, we could suggest other criteria. But the most significant variable for economic geography is traffic. In the United States the volume varies from scarcely any on some rural routes to an almost constant stream of cars and trucks in some metropolitan centers. Traffic on the highway network in the United States is shown in Figure 24-8. Again we are using the density concept: Annual vehicle miles of travel have been divided by total highway mileage. Within the United States the highest densities are reached in a belt that runs from Maryland to Massachusetts. Notice the close correlation between states with large urban populations and high traffic densities. Traffic thins out rather abruptly west of the 90th meridian.

The role played by highways in the movement of freight in the United States is shown in Tables 24-2 and 24-3. The shortest hauls (Table 24-2) are those made by motor carriers and private trucks (*private trucks* are

Table 24-2

Average Length of Haul*

Means of Transport	Straight-Line Miles
All means of transport	389
Rail	577
Motor carrier	306
Private truck	166
Air	850
Water	507

Source: U.S. Bureau of the Census, *1972 Census of Transportation* (1975).
*Excludes petroleum shipments.

Table 24-3

Means of Transport*

Means of Transport	Percent of All Tons Shipped		Percent of Total Ton-Miles	
	1972	1967	1972	1967
Rail	37.8	44.4	55.9	61.5
Motor carrier	35.7	33.5	28.2	24.2
Private truck	21.3	17.6	9.0	7.0
Air	0.1	—	0.2	0.1
Water	4.6	4.1	6.1	6.5
Other and unknown	0.5	0.4	0.6	0.7

Source: U.S. Bureau of the Census, *1972 Census of Transportation* (1975).
*Excludes pipeline and parcel post shipments.

motor carriers which are owned by the shipper or the customer). Over half of all freight tonnage that is moved in the United States is transported on her highways, and judging from the figures given in Table 24-3, highway traffic is increasing at the expense of the railroads. In terms of ton-miles moved, railroads are still in the lead because they can carry heavy loads great distances at relatively low cost. But even in this category, the railroads' share of the market seems to be declining.

The comparative advantage of motor carriers lies in the fact that they are particularly adapted to moving *light* loads *short* distances in a brief *time*. On short hauls, road transport actually costs less than rail. In countries where the government builds and maintains roads (but not railroads), shippers sometimes find it cheaper also to send long shipments by truck. The contrasting advantages of the road for short hauls and of the railroad for long ones has led to the *piggyback* practice, which combines the advantages of both forms. When the origin of a shipment is several hundred miles from its destination and neither is at a railway terminus (thereby necessitating transfer between truck and rail at both ends), it is practical to load the shipment into a truck, drive the truck to the nearest railway terminal, load the trailer onto a railway flatcar which carries it to the railway terminal nearest its destination, and drive the truck off the flatcar to complete the journey to the consignee. Long trainloads of scarcely anything but piggyback flatcars are daily sights on railways between pairs of traffic centers such as Los Angeles and San Francisco, and Chicago and New York.

The Interstate Highway System. A new era in highway transportation was opened in 1956 when the United States Government passed the Federal Aid Highway Act which made provision for construction of a 42,500 mile network of high-speed, limited access, divided super-highways threading throughout the 48 contiguous states (Figure 24-9).

The concept of the Interstate System dates back a number of years prior to implementation in 1956. Previous federal highway policy has resulted in the

Figure 24-8

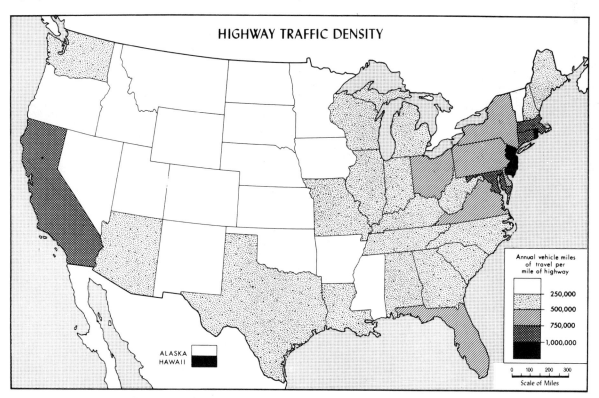

federal aid primary system of about a quarter of a million miles, the federal aid secondary system (the farm to market system), and certain national parks and forest roads. The result of this previous policy is a relatively fine-scale network linking urban centers of all classes with each other, and linking urban centers with their tributary areas. The Interstate System is more gross in scale—in a sense it lies on top of previous highway systems and it emphasizes linkages within and between major cities.

Perhaps two things may be gleaned from this brief statement. First, the Interstate System may be thought of as a large-city or metropolitan system of highways since it provides links between (and within) metropolitan areas. This represents a marked shift in federal policy because previous highway policy might be characterized as catering to rural areas and small urban centers. Another notion is that the Interstate System may be thought of as a new highway network. In many ways it is more comparable to networks of airline and railroad routes than present highway networks.

How far-reaching will be the location shifts following construction of the Interstate Highway System? The writer is inclined to the view that these changes will be as significant as those induced by other major technological changes in transportation systems— railroad developments or paving of rural roads. . . .

The Interstate Highway System is inducing changes in the relative location of urban centers and, thus, the success of activities within these centers. Locations of cities relative to each other are changing, city tributary areas are shifting, and the relative location of sites within cities is changing.[1]

[1]William Garrison, "Connectivity of the Interstate Highway System," *Papers and Proceedings*, The Regional Science Association (1960), pages 122–124.

Location

Two major types of waterway can be distinguished for purposes of regional analysis: the ocean and inland waterways. Most commercial ocean transport involves international trade, which is the main topic in the next chapter. We shall concentrate on inland waterways here. Inland waterways carry tremendous tonnages in four parts of the world.

1. The rather flat plains of Europe and western Russia are laced with numerous rivers and canals, from Britain's Manchester Ship Canal on the west to Russia's Volga River on the east. The densest pattern of waterways in the world is in west central Europe, between the Seine River of France and the Oder River of Germany, a network that includes the world's most heavily trafficked river, the Rhine.
2. The American waterway system consists of two parts: the Great Lakes and the inland waterways. The Great Lakes are unique in that tremendous vessels, larger than most ocean freighters, are able to navigate deep inside the continent. In 1959 these lakes were opened to large ocean vessels with the completion of new locks and deeper channels in the St. Lawrence River. The inland waterway system consists largely of the Mississippi and its tributaries as well as the intracoastal waterway which is a medley of canals and protected channels skirting the Gulf Coast and Atlantic Coast.
3. Vessels are much smaller but more numerous on the rivers and canals of Asia, particularly in eastern China (the Yangtze River and its canal connections with the North China Plain) and in northeastern India (where the Ganges River carries a heavy load).
4. Considerable tonnages of freight in the Soviet Union

Figure 24-9

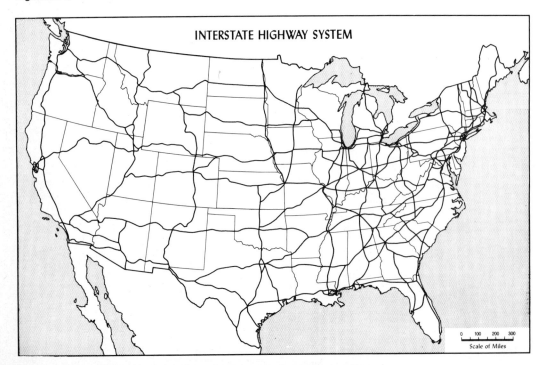

INTERSTATE HIGHWAY SYSTEM

0   100   200   300
Scale of Miles

Tugs and barges await the filling of the locks, which allow river traffic to pass between Lake Ponchartrain and the Mississippi River at New Orleans. This is an important link in the Intracoastal Waterway, which provides an avenue for transport along both the Gulf and Atlantic coasts. (*Courtesy Clair A. Shenk.*)

move on the Volga and Don rivers (which were linked in the late 1950's by a canal), and on the Caspian and Black seas.

Elsewhere, as in the great Amazon valley and many valleys of Africa, waterways provide virtually the sole means of getting about. Although in traffic tonnages, they are dwarfed by the systems already mentioned, their relative significance to their regions is probably greater.

Characteristics

Depth of channel; duration of ice-free, high-water, and low-water seasons; frequency of locks—these are some of the criteria by which we could construct informative maps of the world's waterways. Even more useful would be a map of traffic. Although such maps are not available

on a worldwide scale, they exist for some countries. To illustrate, Figure 24-10 portrays the movement on inland rivers and canals within the United States. In the whole western half of the country there is no commercial traffic on inland waters except for the Columbia, Willamette, Sacramento, and San Joaquin rivers. And on the East Coast there is only one noteworthy water route to the interior: the Hudson River-New York State Barge Canal. Clearly, the heart and arteries of the nation's inland water system (apart from the Great Lakes) are the Mississippi River and three major tributary systems: (a) the Ohio River, including *its* tributaries, especially the Monongahela and Tennessee rivers; (b) the Illinois Waterway, which runs from Chicago to the Mississippi River; and (c) the Intra-Coastal waterway from Texas to Florida. Freight movement on the entire Mississippi system is much greater upstream than downstream, since large

Figure 24-10

quantities of petroleum, sulfur, chemicals, timber, and paper are shipped northward and eastward to the economic heartland. The second ranking inland waterway system is the Atlantic Intracoastal Waterway, which runs from Norfolk, Virginia to Miami, Florida. This waterway carries considerable traffic, but even more important are several navigable rivers which feed into it—the James, the Delaware, and the Potomac rivers and, of course, Chesapeake Bay. The nation's inland waterways carry six billion tons of freight annually, a volume which is about three times as great as that of United States freight carried on the Great Lakes.

A number of commodities move on the Great Lakes. Some of the more important items are iron ore from Duluth-Superior, and coal from Toledo and Chicago. Three generalizations can be made about the nature of traffic on the Great Lakes. First, most of the tonnage which moves on the lakes moves *between* lake ports. Even though the St. Lawrence Seaway has opened the lakes to the ports of the world, over four-fifths of all shipping activity is *lakewise*. Second, trade between lake ports is usually one-sided. The five largest Great Lakes ports are Chicago, Duluth-Superior, Detroit, Cleveland, and Toledo. Chicago, which receives almost twice the tonnage that she ships, is the closest to being in balance. But the other four—and this is often true of smaller ports too—tend to emphasize either shipments or receipts. In the Duluth-Superior harbor, 93 per cent of the total freight tonnage handled is shipped out; the figure for Toledo is 70 per cent. In Cleveland and Detroit, on the other hand, much more comes in on the Great Lakes than goes out. In both cities almost 20 times as much tonnage is received as is shipped. Finally, most Great Lakes ports specialize in just one or two commodities. For example, over three-fourths of the tonnage handled in the Duluth-Superior harbor is iron ore and concentrates. Over 80 per cent of the port of Detroit's tonnage is iron ore, coal, and limestone—inputs for the steel industry. And in Toledo, almost 60 per cent of the total tonnage is coal which is shipped to other Great Lakes ports

The advantage of inland waterways is cheapness. The disadvantages are that they often flow in the "wrong" direction (for example, the Mississippi and the Ohio), freeze over in winter (Great Lakes shipping is halted for four winter months), and are incapable of moving goods swiftly.

Coastal Shipping. Although most ocean shipping is involved in international trade, there is one type that carries domestic traffic. The term *coastal shipping* sometimes is used to identify such movement. United States coastal shipping carries more tonnage than Great Lakes shipping, with the heaviest traffic, by far, consisting of tanker loads of crude oil and refined products from the Gulf Coast to the Middle Atlantic Coast. Considerable tonnage of domestic traffic moves between the Atlantic

Table 24-4

Principal Commodities Carried by Water in the United States

Commodity	Percentage
Total domestic waterborne traffic	100.0
Coal and lignite	14.8
Residual fuel oil	11.3
Gasoline	9.2
Crude petroleum	8.5
Distillate fuel oil	8.5
Iron ore and concentrates	8.1
Sand, gravel, crushed rock	7.7
Limestone	3.7

Source: U.S. Army, Corps of Engineers, *Waterborne Commerce of the United States* (1975).

and Pacific Coasts via the Panama Canal—a waterway movement termed *intercoastal*.

United States Domestic Waterborne Traffic. Of all the tonnage moving in United States' domestic waterborne traffic, petroleum and petroleum products are unquestionably the foremost commodity, accounting for 42 per cent of the total; other important items, with their percentages, are coal 15 per cent, sand-gravel-stone 11 per cent, iron ore and steel 9 per cent, and chemicals 4 per cent. (Table 24-4).

Domestic waterborne traffic constitutes over 55 per cent of all the tonnage moving in and out of United States ports. The leading ports are ranked in Table 24-5, which reveals that for all Great Lakes ports and all but three of the leading coastal ports (Philadelphia, Baltimore, and Norfolk), domestic traffic exceeds foreign. For the port of New York, domestic traffic is twice that of foreign. Table 24-5 also indicates the somewhat surprising fact that over half of the nation's busiest ports are on the Gulf of Mexico. This is because a large share of our waterborne traffic is domestic, and much of our domestic waterborne tonnage is petroleum and its products. In Chapter 15 we saw that the Gulf Coast is one of the world's foremost regions of surplus petroleum, and such ports as Houston, New Orleans, and Beaumont-Port Arthur ship tremendous quantities of petroleum to other domestic ports, especially Philadelphia, Baltimore, New York, and Boston. New Orleans is the nation's foremost exporter—12 per cent more than Norfolk and over twice as much as our third ranked exporter, Houston.

AIRWAYS

An airway simply extends from one point to another with all the intervening air theoretically available for travel. Actually, of course, airplanes usually follow charted routes marked by beacons and radio beams.

Air routes form a more extensive pattern across the globe than any other transport medium. They penetrate

Table 24-5

Waterborne Commerce at Leading United States Ports
in Millions of Tons

| Port | Total | Foreign | | Domestic |
		Imports	Exports	
UNITED STATES				
TOTAL	1,746.8	497.3	266.8	982.7
Coastal ports				
New York	195.5	58.7	7.9	128.9
New Orleans	144.2	13.5	37.2	93.5
Houston	89.1	18.8	15.9	54.4
Baltimore	59.9	25.2	12.9	21.8
Philadelphia	59.9	33.1	6.0	20.8
Baton Rouge	59.1	12.4	7.7	39.0
Norfolk	55.3	8.9	33.3	13.1
Tampa	40.1	5.8	12.9	21.4
Beaumont	33.5	6.2	4.2	23.1
Mobile	33.2	9.4	4.0	19.8
Corpus Christi	32.8	11.1	4.6	17.1
Great Lakes ports				
Chicago	45.9	2.6	2.7	40.6
Duluth-Superior	40.3	0.3	4.7	35.3
Detroit	27.5	3.2	0.7	23.6
Cleveland	21.9	4.0	0.2	17.7
Toledo	21.6	1.1	4.4	16.1

Source: U.S. Army, Corps of Engineers, *Waterborne Commerce of the United States* (1975).

to some of the most remote portions of the world. No longer, in fact, are any extensive regions devoid of air transportation—a generalization that cannot be made for railways, roads, or waterways. Nevertheless, most of the world's air routes serve Anglo-America, Europe, western Russia, and the Far East.

We can map airway traffic according to traditional techniques, as in the preceding maps of traffic flow. But since there are so few points of access to air routes (as compared to roads and railways), it is feasible to describe air traffic in terms of *airport* business. In the United States, excellent data on both passenger and freight traffic are collected by a number of governmental agencies. One of the most basic ways of showing air traffic volumes is by number of passengers boarding aircraft. Table 24-6 indicates that just nine communities handle over 40 per cent of the passenger traffic in the United States.

Another technique has been adopted in Figure 24-11, which portrays the airway traffic between *leading pairs* of cities. Since it is possible to purchase a ticket (or ship a package) between any two commercial airports in the nation, the theoretical number of pairs of stations is tremendous. As it turns out, however, a large share of the traffic is handled by a relatively small share of the total number of airports. A study by E.J. Taaffe determined that 99 leading pairs of stations accounted for half of all commercial passenger-mileage. New York and Miami constituted the busiest pair. The next heaviest

traffic was between New York and Los Angeles. In third place were New York and San Francisco, slightly ahead of New York and Chicago. Air traffic in the United States converges so intensely on a handful of cities that four of them (New York, Chicago, Los Angeles, and Miami) were involved in 87 of the 99 leading pairs. And the remaining 12 pairs involved either Washington,

Table 24-6

Enplaned Revenue Passengers at Selected Large Air Traffic Hubs, 1975

Community (Airport Name)	Enplaned Passengers	Percentage of United States Total
Chicago		
(O'Hare International)	15,904,449	
(Other airports)	85,530	
Community total	15,989,979	8.3
New York		
(Kennedy International)	6,627,695	
(La Guardia)	6,723,069	
(Wall Street Heliport)	12,451	
Community total	13,363,215	6.9
Atlanta		
(Hartsfield International)	12,294,599	6.4
Los Angeles-Orange County		
(Los Angeles International)	8,782,950	
(Other airports)	330,522	
Community total	9,113,472	4.7
Dallas-Fort Worth		
(Dallas-Fort Worth Regional)	7,068,238	
(Love Field)	37,910	
Community total	7,106,148	3.7
Miami-Fort Lauderdale		
(Miami International)	4,683,269	
(Fort Lauderdale-Hollywood International)	1,701,637	
Community total	6,384,906	3.3
San Francisco-Oakland		
(San Francisco International)	5,971,444	
(Other airports)	367,085	
Community total	6,338,529	3.3
Washington, D.C.		
(Washington National)	5,220,197	
(Dulles International)	1,073,998	
Community total	6,294,195	3.3
Denver		
(Stapleton International)	5,383,894	2.8

Source: Civil Aeronautics Board, *Airport Activity Statistics* (1976).

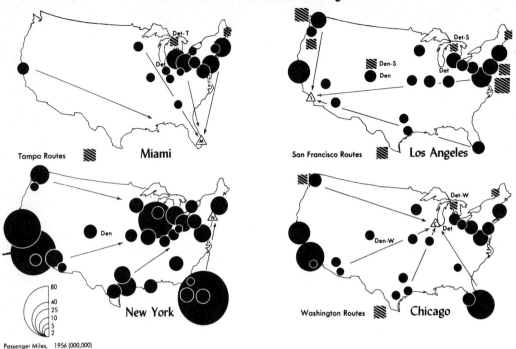

THE 99 CITY PAIRS in Airline Passenger Traffic

Figure 24-11 (*Source: Edward J. Taaffe, "A Map Analysis of United States Airline Competition," The Journal of Air Law and Commerce, Vol. 25, 1958, pp. 123–124.*)

D.C., Tampa, or San Francisco. As Figure 24-11 shows, long-haul traffic is dominant. Most of the symbols stand for trips of at least 500 miles, and the largest ones represent flights exceeding 1000 miles.

Traffic Shadow Concept. The number of cities with airports is small enough, and the government publishes enough data on air passenger travel, so that a scholar can readily analyze certain locational aspects of commercial air passenger traffic. In a study which compared cities in terms of the ratio between the number of airline passenger departures and population, E. J. Taaffe found a *traffic shadow* existing around New York, Boston, Pittsburgh, Cleveland, Detroit, Chicago, San Francisco and a few other large cities. Traffic shadow occurs wherever (a) several cities are located close together, and (b) the largest city in the cluster acts as both the receiving and generating point of air traffic for the entire cluster. Evidence of traffic shadow appears where the ratio for the largest city in the cluster is above normal while the ratios for surrounding cities are below normal. Here are the reasons for traffic shadow: (a) In any cluster of cities the largest city tends to have the most frequent service and the fastest flights to distant terminals, and (b) to travel by air from an outlying member of a cluster to the major airport is likely to involve more time than to drive or take a taxi or bus directly to the airport. New York's traffic shadow extends over most Connecticut airports, over Albany, Scranton, Reading, Newark—and even Philadelphia! Washing-

ton's extends over Baltimore, Cleveland's over Akron and Canton, Detroit's over Toledo, and Chicago's over Milwaukee and South Bend.[2]

PIPELINES

Most of the world's pipelines are threaded through three regions; the United States, Europe, and the Middle East. The United States network has expanded at a phenomenal rate. The petroleum pipeline network alone is over 225,000 miles long, and the natural gas pipeline network is four times as large. The American network is actually composed of four entirely different systems: (1) The gas system, which conducts only natural gas, is the most extensive and runs mostly from the gas fields in Texas and adjacent states to the markets in the Northeast (from Nebraska to New England) and to those in California. Although California produces some gas, the state is becoming increasingly dependent on imports from New Mexico, Oklahoma, and Texas. The maximum diameter of these pipes is normally 42 inches. However, new pipelines carrying gas from Alaska's North Slope are specified as being 48 inches or larger! (2) The petroleum network carries crude oil and the numerous liquids refined from it. Its locational pattern

[2]Interesting analyses of traffic shadow and other aspects of air traffic appear in E. J. Taaffe's "Air Transportation and United States Urban Distribution," *Geographical Review*, 1956, pp. 219–38, and "The Urban Hierarchy: An Air Passenger Definition," *Economic Geography*, 1962, pp. 1–14.

is similar to that of gas pipelines except that the gas network is much more extensive and penetrates more remote places. Canadian petroleum from Alberta is piped across the continent to refineries in Toronto, Ontario. (3) A third type of cross-country pipeline has been developed to move solids, such as coal. The solid is powdered and suspended in water; this mixture (called slurry) enters the pipeline. The slurry is then pumped (or carried by gravity) to its final destination where it is dewatered and used as an energy source. An early example of this process is a 108-mile pipe, 10 inches in diameter, which was completed in 1947 to move coal from strip mines around Cadiz, Ohio, to a lakeshore thermal-electric power plant on the outskirts of Cleveland. More recently, a 275-mile slurry line has been built to carry coal from Black Mesa, Arizona, to an electric generating plant located south of Las Vegas, Nevada. The dewatered coal is used to generate electricity which is used in southern California. (4) Some large-scale water transfer projects use pipelines. For example, a pipeline and aqueduct system for moving fresh water extends from reservoirs in the Catskill mountains to New York City, and from Owens Valley to Los Angeles.

European pipelines distribute refined petroleum products from seaport plants to inland markets. Recently, however, the demand for oil derivatives in inland markets of Europe has skyrocketed and stimulated the development of inland refineries. At first these were supplied by crude oil barged up from seaports such as Rotterdam. In 1957 and in 1958 two pipelines were constructed from Wilhelmshaven and from Rotterdam to refineries in the Ruhr. July 1961 saw the beginning of construction of the longest pipeline in Europe, a 475-mile stretch of 34-inch pipe connecting Marseilles with Karlsruhe. This line serves as a shortcut for Middle Eastern oil which otherwise would have to be shipped around Portugal to North Sea ports.

Pipelines in Russia move crude oil and derivatives from the two great oil fields (the Caucasus and the Volga) to the Industrial Center and the Ukraine and along the Trans-Siberian Railway.

The Middle East network functions primarily as a link between wells in the desert and the refineries and tanker docks located on the Persian Gulf and Mediter-

ranean Sea (Figure 24-13). Notice how many national boundaries these lines cross. The number of disputes that could and do arise among the nations involved is considerable.

In concluding this discussion of the location and characteristics of the main means of transport, we must point out that economic geographers need a map of world transportation based on some system of classification by areal associations (or combinations) of transportation media. Such a classification system will enable us to plot world circulation by types of regions comparable to the mixed-farming areas that we touched upon back in Chapter 9.

RELATIONSHIPS BETWEEN TRANSPORTATION AND OTHER PHENOMENA

Numerous forces interact to influence the flow of goods and people from place to place. Conversely, transportation has an influence on many other phenomena. The relationship is reciprocal.

The discussion that follows will mainly concentrate on relationships involved in *economic* transportation; little will be said about *noneconomic* transportation, a distinction we made in the opening paragraph of the introduction to Part Seven.

General Factors

In general, six factors (or prerequisites) must be operative if economic transportation is to occur between any two points. We will illustrate these factors with North Dakota and Illinois as examples.

1. There must be a *surplus product*, such as wheat in North Dakota.
2. Illinois must *desire* the surplus product. The intensity of desire depends on the culture of the inhabitants of Illinois (that is, their "taste" for wheat flour and its products) and the insufficiency of their own wheat production. Illinois matches up with Dakota since it

The Kharg Island terminal in the Persian Gulf is capable of loading 2.6 million barrels of Iranian crude oil daily. (*Courtesy EXXON Corporation.*)

NATURAL GAS PIPELINES

14-inch diameter or greater

Less than 14-inch diameter

0 100 200 300
Scale of Miles

Figure 24-12

Figure 24-13 (*After* World Oil.)

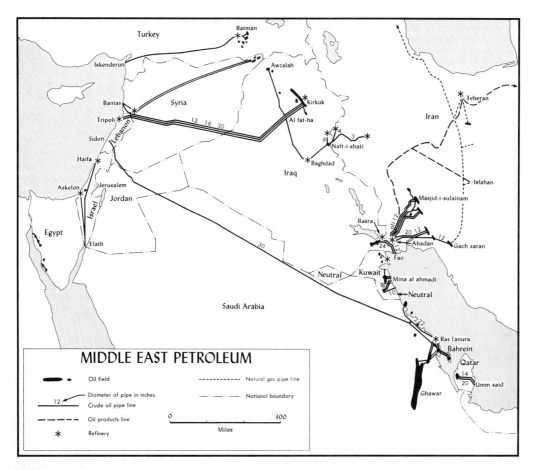

Turkey
Batman
Iskenderun
Awzalah
Banias
Syria
Kirkuk
Tripoli
Al fat-ha
Sidon
12 16 30
Iran
Teheran
Haifa
Naft-i-shati
Baghdad
Iraq
Isfahan
Askelon
Jerusalem
Jordan
Masjid-i-sulainam
Israel
Basra
Egypt
Elath
20 12
Abadan
Gach saran
24
Fao
Neutral
Kuwait
Mina al ahmadi
Neutral
Saudi Arabia
Ras Tanura
Bahrein
Qatar
14
20 Umm said
Ghawar

MIDDLE EAST PETROLEUM

Oil field

12 Diameter of pipe in inches

Crude oil pipe line

Oil products line

* Refinery

----- Natural gas pipe line

-·-·- National boundary

0   300
Miles

has millions of citizens who desire bread, pastries, and spaghetti made from wheat flour but who have insufficient grain to satisfy that desire. Where such a relationship exists between two places, they are said to be *complementary*.

3. North Dakota must have a *competitive advantage* in the production of her surplus. No matter how much wheat she produces beyond her own needs, she may fail in her bid for sales of wheat (or flour) to Illinois customers if other wheat growing regions produce wheat at less cost. From our preceding analyses of agriculture, mining, forestry, and other productive activities, we have seen that competitive advantage is the result of a more favorable natural environment, or a more favorable cultural endowment, or both. The advantages of North Dakota in both of these respects for wheat production were spelled out in Chapter 11.

4. Illinois must have the *ability to pay* for Dakota wheat. Ability to pay may take the form either of available currency or of a surplus of some commodity desired by Dakota people (for instance, corn starch, clothing, machinery, and telephones). Such a surplus and a competitive advantage in *its* production depend also on physical environment and cultural traits within Illinois as per 1 and 3.

5. There must be an absence of *intervening opportunity*. Complementariness alone does not bring about trade between two areas; only where there is no nearer complementary source to each will trade be encouraged between Dakota and Illinois.

6. Both ability to pay and absence of intervening opportunity are, in turn, influenced by *transferability*, that is, the *cost* of transportation measured by (a) the time required for the trip, and (b) money, or its equivalent in credit. No matter how perfectly complementary the two areas, no matter how complete the absence of intervening opportunity, there would be no trade in wheat from Dakota to Illinois if transfer costs exceeded the ability and the desire to pay.

The foregoing sextet of factors may operate through complex linkages involving several "third parties"; that is, the wheat need not necessarily go directly from Dakota to Illinois and machinery need not necessarily pass directly from Illinois to Dakota. For example, Dakota wheat might go to Minneapolis millers. the revenue thus received then being spent for shoes and gasoline purchased from Minneapolis distributors. The millers in turn might sell flour to Chicago bakeries, the revenue from such sales being paid out to the flour mills' labor force who use some of it to buy radios made in Chicago.

Selected Specific Factors

Several relationships involving railways, highways, waterways, airways, and pipelines apply to the group as a whole and are involved with the operation of the foregoing general factors.

Location of Population. There is a moderate locational relationship between transportation and

population; that is, the larger the population, the greater the transportation. The two glaring exceptions to this rule are China and India, which have most of the world's people but relatively little of the transportation facilities. Still, the two regions that stand out most boldly in the world patterns of railways, roads, waterways, airways, and pipelines are Europe and Anglo-America, which *are* two thickly peopled continents.

Correlation between population and transportation is closer as the scale becomes finer; that is, within the United States, within Europe, within India, within nearly every nation, the most densely populated areas throb with the greatest amount of transportation.

Other things being equal, an area with large numbers of people tends to have more circulation than one with fewer people. Conversely, transportation has had an influence on location of population. The great migrations of recent times (eastward into Siberia and westward into Anglo-America) have been expedited and even stimulated by transportation facilities. Here then is a reciprocal relationship, a "chicken-and-egg" matter. Which comes first is difficult to say, but it is certain that each influences the other and a chain reaction sets in.

Location of Surplus Production. A still closer correlation exists between production and transportation. Areas that generate a surplus of any commodity in economic demand also foster transportation media, often constructed in the face of stiff impediments, to move that surplus to potential customers. Iron ore lured railways into both Arctic Labrador and tropical Venezuela; coal drew railways up steep gradients of the winding valleys of the Appalachians; forests attracted railways into the Cascade Mountains. And conversely, once the transport arteries begin functioning, the volume of surplus production mounts.

The location of surpluses depends on interaction between the physical environment and cultural forces. An area cannot possibly have a surplus of coal unless nature endowed it with coal resources and unless the inhabitants possess cultural characteristics enabling them to transform the natural resource into an economic surplus. In chapter after chapter we have seen this principle at work—in the discussion of areas characterized by surplus wheat, or lumber, or milk, or machinery.

Location of Markets. As production can determine one end of transportation routes, consumption can fix the other end. Consumption is, in fact, the major cause for the intense development of transportation in Europe and Anglo-America, the world's two main markets. Those large markets, in turn, are due to the presence of large populations and large purchasing power per capita. In turn, a good circulation system has enabled these areas to develop a high standard of living with high purchasing potentials.

Industrialization and Urbanization. These two processes go hand in hand, influencing the spread of economic exchange. Many a railway spur and siding have been built in response to the construction of new factories. Cities invite roads, railways, pipelines, and airways. Whether on a world, nation, state, or county basis, the correlation between transport development and industrial urban development is high, as visual comparisons of the world pattern of manufacturing and of major cities with atlas maps of world railways, highways, waterways, pipelines, and airways will reveal. Unquestionably cities attract transportation.

Conversely, transportation is a maker of cities. A focus of routes is a favorable location for a city, and cities with the heaviest traffic tend to grow most rapidly. Furthermore, a decline of traffic can cause cities to shrivel. To illustrate: U.S. Highway 20 through New York State runs through many settlements; when the New York State Thruway was constructed, bypassing these settlements, it drained off so much traffic that many business districts suffered, and several gas stations, eating establishments, and other businesses along Route 20 experienced a sharp decline in trade.

A sizable settlement may even disappear from the face of the earth if transportation ceases to nourish it, as illustrated in the case of Grand Detour, which, in the early part of the 19th Century, was one of the major cities in the Rock River Valley of northwestern Illinois.

> A grist mill was completed at Grand Detour in 1839, and from 1840 to 1855 it was the largest trade and industrial center in the county and one of the most important in the valley. Its ferry vied with Dixon's. . . . The great mistake made by the citizens of Grand Detour was to oppose the coming of the railroad under the mistaken idea that its business and manufactures would thereby be dissipated among various upstart towns. So the railroads all passed her by, and left her almost a deserted village. . . . Even the local post office was eventually discontinued and Grand Detour received its mail by rural delivery from Oregon [Illinois][3]

Culture. Occidental culture has had a positive influence on the evolution of transportation. The invention of most of the machines and devices used for transportation today (other than the wheel itself) took place in the Western World. With inventions, the principle holds that improvements in carriers tend to precede improvements in route facilities. Better highways are built only after better vehicles are invented—and usually there is a noticeable time lag separating the two events.

Variation in culture from place to place is most important in explaining the kinds of surpluses that typify

[3]Way, R.B., *The Rock River Valley* (Chicago) 1926, p. 571.

areas. North Carolina produces a surplus of tobacco not only because the climate and soils are favorable to this crop but because the men occupying that area have decided to be tobacco specialists. In nearly every chapter of Parts Three through Six we have seen the importance of the cultural factor in explaining the surpluses of given areas. Were it not for spatial variation in the cultural factor, all areas with similar natural environments would tend to have identical surplus commodities.

Spatial variation in culture also explains certain types of consumption that typify areas. For example, peoples in different countries have developed different tastes; notice that the inhabitants of the United Kingdom and the United States have developed tastes for such nonindigenous beverages as tea and coffee. Every coffee bean and every tea leaf must be imported from distant lands, and considerable transportation is required to meet the demand. But the tastes are different in these two lands: the British are primarily tea drinkers, while Americans are mainly coffee drinkers. These tastes are associated with a brisk tea trade between the Far East and the United Kingdom and a lively business in coffee between Latin America and the United States.

Vulnerability to Economic Cycles. Improved linkage between regions unquestionably has raised the over-all level of economic development, but it probably has accentuated the variation between depressions and booms. Or, to put it another way, the less dependent an area is on trade with other areas, the less likely that it will be affected by economic fluctuations in those places. Any cyclical variation in the economy of a subsistence realm, for example, will depend solely on factors within its region. But when linkages are interwoven among many areas around the world, economic depression in one is likely to trigger destructive blasts in others.

Government. Government and politics, both national and international, strongly affect the location of transportation. Here are a few examples.

Figure 24-14 presents the pattern of railway lines in an area sharply divided into two sections—not by a mountain range, nor by a deep canyon, but by an arbitrary boundary between Canada and the United States marked off on the flat lands of America's Great Plains.

In the last century the land-grant policy of the United States government was a powerful incentive to railway construction across the western grasslands. Prior to this encouragement there was scarcely any occupancy of these lands except along rivers—the arteries of transportation. But in subhumid lands, navigable waterways are few and far between. Hence, vast areas remained unsettled. Moreover, railway companies did not possess enough risk capital to engage in road building through expansive stretches of unpopulated land. But the federal government believed these lands should be occupied and adopted the policy of donating portions of the public domain to railway companies who would build. For 21 years, beginning in 1850 the government gave away 131,000,000 acres to railway companies, promising a minimum of one square mile and a maximum of six square miles for every one mile of route laid down. The companies then could sell the land to settlers, thereby realizing earnings to pay for the road building.

Largely because of military as well as economic strategy, the government of Russia built the world's longest railway—the famous Trans-Siberian Railway—from Leningrad through Moscow and Novosibirsk to Vladivostok.

Government policy was also resposible for the construction from 1947 to 1951 of the Arabian railway (from Damman on the Persian Gulf to the capital at Riyadh, 366 miles to the west). Since there was no compelling economic demand for train transportation between these two points, the most plausible conclusion is that Ibn Saud, the Saudi Arabian monarch, had the road built for "status"—since in many underdeveloped parts of the world the presence of a railroad carries a certain amount of prestige.

Whether they are actively involved in the construction of canals and highways or offering inducements to the builders of railways, governments have been positive forces encouraging the growth of transportation. On the other hand, governments can play a role in stopping the circulation of goods. Tariffs and quotas are well-known techniques for this purpose. Less familiar, perhaps, is the type of influence exerted by the government of Iran in nationalizing the oil industry in the early 1950's. During 1950, over 240,000,000 barrels of oil passed through Iranian pipelines to ocean tankers for delivery to foreign markets. But Premier Mossadegh's government expropriated the oil business (whose facilities were largely owned by European and American companies), and the flow trickled down sharply to a mere 9,000,000

barrels in 1953. Traditional customers simply boycotted Iranian oil.

Land Values. The relationship between land values and transportation is a fascinating one that apparently varies, depending on the transport medium and the stage of a region's development. Being near to railways tended to raise the value of land during the last century when Land Grant railroads were built. In the early 1850's the federal government had found no takers at $1 per acre for its public domain in the Midwest. But as soon as railways were built a brisk sale developed in land adjacent to the railways at the price of $3 an acre.

In urban areas, however, the relationship between railways and land values is more complex. As one travels out from a major rail center (say, Chicago) along a suburban railroad, he discovers that, as the miles go by, land values gradually rise and fall like giant waves at sea. The crests correspond with outlying settlements possessing a railway station while the troughs correspond with the rural areas between the station settlements. Moreover, the pitch of this imaginary wavy line is downward as one travels outward. Or in different words, as distance from the metropolis increases, the land value for each successive crest decreases. Similarly, each successive trough is slightly lower than the next one nearer the main city.

In addition, there is a relationship between land values and distance from the railroad measured at right angles to the right-of-way. For the first quarter mile, land values are low; beyond that distance they tend to rise and remain high for some distance (which may stretch as much as two miles) before values drop down

Figure 24-14 (*Adapted from August Lösch,* Die Räumliche Ordnung der Wirtschaft, *Jena, 1940, p. 292. Solid lines are railway lines.*)

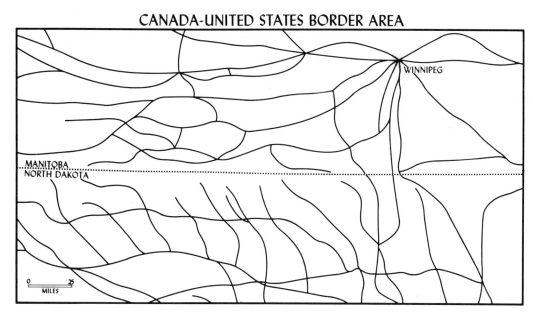

CANADA-UNITED STATES BORDER AREA

to the level of those near the railroad. With further distance away from the tracks, values continue to drop. In other words, a suburban railroad can be said to run within a minor valley of land values which reposes within a much broader ridge of land values.[4]

The relationship between land values and highways indicates a strong tendency for land values (a) to vary directly with nearness to the highway, and (b) with passage of time, to rise more rapidly in proportion to nearness to the highway. Table 24-7 indicates (with data from several cities in diverse parts of the nation) that the value of land near a freeway tends to rise more sharply than that of land farther from the thoroughfare.

A similar relationship tends to exist between land values and pedestrian traffic. In cities where the sidewalk is the artery and the individual human being the "carrier," the greater the number of pedestrians, the higher the land value in dollars per front foot. Figure 24-15 illustrates the correlation between these two variables as measured along a portion of Halsted Street in Chicago.

The Influence of Transportation Media on One Another. Railway freight volumes are sometimes lower in western Europe than in eastern Europe partly because the numerous canals and rivers in the former

[4]For further analysis of this relationship see Charles R. Hayes, "Suburban Residential Land Values Along the C.B.&Q. Railroad," *Land Economics*, 1957, pp. 177–181.

region carry so much traffic. For example, freight volumes in Poland exceed those of France and West Germany. In the United States, passenger travel on railways is low largely because of competition from highways and airways. Deep within Amazonia, boat traffic on the Medeira River (near the Bolivian border) was heavy enough to cause the construction of a 100-mile railway to function as a bypass around rapids and falls in the Madeira itself. Similarly isolated railways within the Congo perform the same function as did many routes within the United States during the early days of railroading.

Problem of Integration. When transportation develops to the point that the government is involved either in regulating private enterprise or in constructing and operating facilities itself, the complex problem arises of how the railways, highways, waterways, airways, and pipelines can be integrated most efficiently. In the United States this problem is at the root of such questions as these: How free should railways and trucking companies be in setting their rates? Should the government build rights-of-way for trucks, boats, and airplanes but not for railways or pipelines? In the socialistic nations the problem is the same but the question becomes: What share of the national budget should go toward operations of railways, of canals, of roads, and of other transport media?

Physical Factors

Thus far, most of this discussion has dealt with relationships between transportation and cultural matters.

Table 24-7

Change in Land Values and Proximity to Highways

City	Freeway	Period	In Strip on Either Side of Freeway a Distance of 2 Blocks	In Entire Ward	In Entire Borough
New York	Shore Parkway	1939–1953	+ 76%	+ 19%	+ 14%
New York	Henry Hudson Parkway	1935–1953	+ 102%	− 23%	+ 5%
New York	Grand Central Parkway	1925–1953	+2038%	+501%	+232%
			Group A Contiguous to Freeway	Group B Separated from Freeway by Group A	
Houston	Gulf Freeway	1940–1955	+585%	+242%	
Dallas	Central Expressway	1941–1955	+431%	+100%	
			Industrial Subdivisions		
			Fronting Freeway	Not Fronting Freeway	
Oakland	Eastshore Freeway	1941–1953	+8600%	+5100%	

Source: Garrison, William L. and Marts, Marion E., *Influence of Highway Improvements on Urban Land: A Graphic Summary*, Highway Economic Studies, University of Washington, 1958, pp. 8–19.

Figure 24-15 *These two profiles suggest a close correlation between pedestrian traffic and land values within a city.* (*Courtesy Brian J. L. Berry from* Comparative Studies of Central Places, *Project Report NONR 2121-18, NR389-126, February, 1962.*)

Several physical factors are also important. The location of mineral resources such as coal in the Ukraine and iron ore in Quebec have been causal factors influencing railway construction. Forest resources discussed in Chapter 6 have stimulated construction of railways, roads, and flumes.

Oases providing water and forage are key points determining the location of caravan routes across deserts. The Oregon Trail, over which thousands of migrants trekked between 1840 and 1870 with their oxen and horses, was located (at least in its stretches from Nebraska to Oregon) mainly according to the availability of three physical elements: water, grass, and firewood (for campsites). The Trail followed a winding rather than a straight course through Wyoming as men chose to go up and down gradients in the wooded foothills of the Laramie Range, the Rattlesnake Range, and the Green Mountains, rather than choosing to take the straighter, flatter route through southern Wyoming's desert. But when engines replaced oxen, the Oregon Trail faded from the scene (indeed, today it can scarcely be identified in much of Wyoming) because railway builders were more interested in straight routes with low gradients;

the absence of grass and campfire wood was no hindrance to the railway which was built through southern Wyoming. Water shortage, though, was a handicap; so wells had to be dug at points along the route to supply locomotive tenders.

Topography is probably the physical factor most obviously related to the location of a land transport route. Other things being equal, the builders of transportation routes tend to select the lower gradients, as illustrated by the Hudson-Mohawk route through the Appalachians. Boston and New York probably would be more comparable in size and importance if the Berkshire Mountains were oriented east-west instead of north-south, so as to block off New York instead of Boston from the Mohawk Valley. If the prospects of economic gain are bright enough or the need of the military services strong enough, roads (such as the Burma Road), railroads (for example, several in Switzerland and Peru), airports (Dutch Harbor, Alaska), and pipelines are built in extremely rugged terrain. Men go to great expense in constructing transportation routes through inhospitable environments—if they are sure it will pay to do so.

SUGGESTED READINGS

ALEXANDER, JOHN W.; BROWN, S. EARL; and DAHLBERG, RICHARD E. "Freight Rates: Selected Aspects of Uniform and Nodal Regions," *Economic Geography*, 1958, pp. 1–18.

FRANCAVIGLIA, RICHARD V., "Some Geographical Implications of the Vanishing American Passenger Train in 1969," *The Professional Geographer*, 1971, pp. 333–336.

GARRISON, WILLIAM L., *The Benefit of Rural Roads to Rural Property*, Washington State Council for Highway Research, Seattle, 1956, 107 pp.

———, BERRY, BRIAN J. L.; MARBLE, DUANE F.; NYSTUEN, JOHN D.; and MORRILL, RICHARD L. *Studies of Highway Development and Geographic Change*, Seattle, 1959, 291 pp.

GUEST, B. ROSS, "Soviet Gas Pipeline Development During the Seven-Year Plan," *The Professional Geographer*, 1967, pp. 189–192.

KENYON, JAMES B., "Elements in Inter-Port Competition in the United States," *Economic Geography*, 1970, pp. 1–24.

MAYER, HAROLD M., "Some Geographic

Aspects of Technological Change in Maritime Transportation," *Economic Geography*, 1973, pp. 145–155.

MELAMID, ALEXANDER, "Petroleum Product Distribution and the Evolution of Economic Regions in Iran," *Geographical Review*, 1975, pp. 510–525.

RIMMER, PETER J., "The Changing Status of New Zealand Seaports, 1853–1960," *Annals of the Association of American Geographers*, 1967, pp. 88–100.

ROBINSON, ROSS, "Modelling the Port as an Operational System: A Perspective for Research," *Economic Geography*, 1976, pp. 71–86.

SIDDALL, WILLIAM R., "Railroad Gauges and Spatial Interaction," *Geographical Review*, 1969, pp. 29–57.

TAAFFE, EDWARD J., "Trends in Airline Passenger Traffic: A Geographic Case Study," *Annals of the Association of American Geographers*, 1959, pp. 393–408.

————, "The Urban Hierarchy: An Air Passenger Definition," *Economic Geography*, 1962, pp. 1–14.

————, and GAUTHIER, HOWARD L. JR., *Geography of Transportation*, Englewood Cliffs, N. J., 1973, 226 pp.

————, MORRILL, RICHARD L.; and GOULD, PETER R. "Transport Expansion in Underdeveloped Countries: A Comparative Analysis," *Geographical Review*, 1963, pp. 503–529.

WALLACE, IAIN, "Containerization at Canadian Ports," *Annals of the Association of American Geographers*, 1975, pp. 433–448.

WALLACE, WILLIAM H., "Railroad Traffic Densities Patterns," *Annals of the Association of American Geographers*, 1958, pp. 352–374.

YASEEN, DAVID W., "Transferability: Economic Regulation of Motor Carriers of Property," *The Professional Geographer*, November 1964, pp. 14–19.

CHAPTER

international trade

LASH (lighter aboard ship) vessels at Bremerhaven, Germany, represent one of the newest systems of ocean transport. This ship can carry a total of 73 lighters, or floating containers, which measure approximately 61.5 × 31.2 × 13.0 feet. The lighters, each of which can carry up to 376 tons of freight, are loaded and unloaded from the stern of the vessel by means of an onboard movable crane. Here, tugs are taking lighters to a holding area where they await further shipment or unloading. Obvious advantages of this type of shipping are that it has less dependency on dock facilities and space availability than more conventional methods and that the ship need spend very little time in port. (*Courtesy German Information Center.*)

International trade is of such significance to the world's political and economic life that it is worth being singled out for special consideration.

Approximately 150 countries submit reports on foreign trade to the United Nations, which publishes a valuable and informative *Yearbook of International Trade Statistics*. This source provides data on commodities exported, commodities imported, destinations of exports, sources of imports, and other aspects of trade. The annual value of exports from these nations is approximately $842 billion; the value of imports is $845 billion. The difference between these figures represents for the most part the value added in transport, for obviously a commodity is worth more at the end of its journey than at the start because of the charges assessed for moving and insuring it. The few countries that do not submit data to the United Nations account for a relatively small volume of exports and imports.

Location and Characteristics

We shall consider the where and what of international trade under the following headings: amount of trade, destination of exports, types of commodities exported, source of imports, types of commodities imported, balance of trade, balance of payments, and major ocean shipping routes.

Amount of Trade. Western Europe and Anglo-America account for over half of the world's international trade. Western European nations together generate $720 billion worth of trade (exports plus imports), about 40 per cent of the world total. Of the 11 leading trading nations, 6 are western European (Table 25-1). West Germany is involved in the exchange of more goods than any other nation except the United States, and only Japan and the United States exceed the trade volumes of France and the United Kingdom. The Netherlands, Belgium, and Italy are also high on the list. Anglo-America accounts for about 12 per cent of all exports and imports. A $204 billion volume marks the United States as the world's foremost trading country. Canada does about one-third the volume of her southerly neighbor, which places her in seventh position and ahead of the U.S.S.R.

If we think in terms of integrated economic regions, this picture of international trade alters somewhat. Thus, among western European nations international trade is, to a large extent, a matter of traffic with one another. For instance, iron ore shipped from Sweden to Germany figures in the foreign trade of both. In contrast, iron ore shipped from Minnesota to Pennsylvania is counted as domestic trade within the United States. Now, if we take the position that intra-European trade (approximately $480 billion worth) is essentially domestic and therefore subtract it from the $720 billion total, we arrive at the figure of $240 billion for western Europe's trade with other regions. Similarly, since Canada and the United States are important trading partners, if we subtract their mutual traffic from their

Table 25-1

International Trade, 1974, in Billions of U.S. Dollars

Place	Imports	Exports
Anglo-America		
United States	107.1	97.1
Canada	32.3	32.8
Latin America		
Brazil	14.1	7.4
Mexico	6.5	3.4
Europe		
West Germany	70.2	90.6
France	52.2	45.1
United Kingdom	54.1	38.6
Italy	40.9	30.3
Netherlands	32.6	32.8
Belgium-Luxembourg	29.7	28.3
Sweden	16.5	15.9
Switzerland	14.4	11.8
Spain	15.3	7.1
Poland	10.5	8.3
East Germany	9.6	8.7
Denmark	9.9	7.7
Austria	9.0	7.2
Norway	8.4	6.3
Czechoslovakia	7.5	7.1
Finland	6.9	5.5
Yugoslavia	8.0	4.1
Hungary	5.6	5.1
U.S.S.R.	24.9	27.4
Africa		
Nigeria	2.7	9.6
South Africa	7.2	5.0
Libya	3.3	7.7
Asia		
Japan	62.1	55.5
Saudi Arabia	3.5	37.2
Iran	5.6	23.8
China*	8.7	6.0
Singapore	8.3	5.8
Kuwait	1.5	11.2
Hong Kong	6.7	5.9
South Korea	6.8	4.5
Indonesia	3.9	7.4
Oceania		
Australia	11.1	10.8
New Zealand	3.7	2.4

Source: United Nations, *Yearbook of International Trade Statistics, 1974* (1975).
*Includes Mongolia, North Korea, and North Vietnam.

$269 billion total, we have $180 billion left as the Anglo-America volume of trade with the rest of the world.

The remaining volume of world trade is widely dispersed. Asian countries that submit data to the United Nations together account for only slightly more trade than does Anglo-America. Japan, which ranks 3rd among the world's traders, generates 37 per cent of Asia's total. The Middle East, which includes 11th-ranked Saudi Arabia, generates one-third. The Soviet Union trades $52 billion worth, which is a figure smaller than that of Canada. Soviet European satellites, led by Poland and East Germany, report $78 billion. The Latin American total is about half that of West Germany. Of the places with appreciable trade figures, Brazil has a considerable margin over Mexico and Venezuela. The sum for all of Africa slightly exceeds that of Italy. Australia and New Zealand are comparable with the lesser European nations.

Figure 25-1 portrays the locational pattern of international trade by presenting each nation's trade turnover. More strikingly than words, this map illustrates the prominence of Europe and Anglo-America in international commodity exchange.

Destinations of Exports. Where do exports go? Of the world's 12 leading trading regions (Figure 25-2 and Table 25-2), 5 have western Europe as their primary destination for exports, and 4 others have western Europe as a secondary destination. In fact, western Europe is either the first or second leading customer for every exporting region in the world except for those in Asia. The United States is next; it is the leading customer for 3 regions and the second leading customer for ship-

ments from 3 others. Japan is the leading customer for 2 regions.

Two generalizations can be made about export patterns. First, leading customers are usually the affluent, highly industrialized regions. Second, proximity often promotes trade. For example, European countries emphasize trade among themselves, as do Canada and the United States and the countries of Asia. Japan is the leading customer of Australia and New Zealand. Many of the trade patterns shown in Figure 25-2 were established during the period of active colonization by the nations of Europe.

Types of Exports. A map of the world in terms of what commodities are exported (Figure 25-3) reveals five regional types.

1. *Machinery and transport equipment* are the leading shipments from Anglo-America, the major traders of western Europe, eastern Europe and the U.S.S.R., and Japan; these two classes of commodities account for 30 to 40 per cent of the total exports of these regions by value. Japan is an exception; machinery and transport equipment account for an astonishing 49 per cent of her exports.

Figure 25-1

TRADE TURNOVER: MAJOR TRADING NATIONS

Turnover in Billions of U.S Dollars

5
10
20
50
100
200

Scale at Latitude 35°

0   500   1500   2500 Miles

0   2000   4000 Kms.

Countries with trade turnover under .8 billion dollars omitted

INTERNATIONAL TRADE: EXPORTS

Figure 25-2

Shipments are mainly:
- To Western Europe
- To U.S.S.R. and Eastern Europe
- To United States
- To "Other Asia"
- To Japan

Scale at Latitude 35°
0 500 1500 2500 Miles
0 2000 4000 Kms.

Figure 25-3

INTERNATIONAL TRADE: EXPORTS

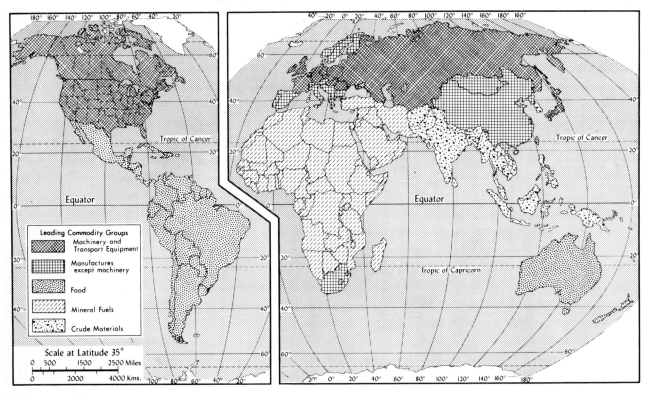

Leading Commodity Groups
- Machinery and Transport Equipment
- Manufactures except machinery
- Food
- Mineral Fuels
- Crude Materials

Scale at Latitude 35°
0 500 1500 2500 Miles
0 2000 4000 Kms.

Table 25-2

Ch. 25 / International Trade

Exports to Leading Customers as a Percentage of Total Exports

Region	Percentage of Exports to Its Leading Customers
Western Europe	69% to Western Europe 7% to United States
South Africa	56% to Western Europe 14% to Africa
Canada	68% to United States 15% to Western Europe
United States	29% to Western Europe 21% to Canada
Japan	26% to United States 24% to other Asia
Australia and New Zealand	29% to Japan 25% to Western Europe
Africa (except South Africa)	64% to Western Europe 11% to United States
Latin America	38% to United States 29% to Western Europe
Middle East	47% to Western Europe 19% to Japan
China (including Mongolia, North Korea and North Vietnam)	31% to other Asia 20% to Japan
Other Asia	22% to Japan 22% to United States
Estern Europe and the U.S.S.R.	57% to Eastern Europe and the U.S.S.R. 22% to Western Europe

Source: United Nations, *Yearbook of International Trade Statistics, 1974* (1975).

2. A second type of region exports large quantities of *manufactures* but not much machinery and transport equipment. Most of Scandinavian and Mediterranean Europe fits in this category as do China and South Africa. Notice how these regions are either near major machinery- and transport equipment-producing regions or, in the case of South Africa, have long been culturally and economically tied to them.

3. Countries whose leading export is *foods* are more numerous than those in any other category. Moreover, in such lands, foods attain phenomenally high percentages (and usually one or two crops dominate the structure) of total exports. However, when we group countries into major regions, as has been done in Figure 25-3, foods are usually overshadowed by some other more valuable commodity group. On a regional basis foods dominate the export structure of only two regions: Latin America, and Australia and New Zealand. In both of these areas, foods account for 36 per cent of the total value of exports.

4. and 5. *Crude materials* and *mineral fuels* lead the outbound parade from almost as many countries as do foods. Also, as in food-shipping countries, these items —usually one or two, such as metal ores and crude petroleum—reach very high percentages. In Africa, mineral fuels (largely from Libya and Nigeria) account for 38 per cent of the export traffic, and in the Middle East the figure is 86 per cent. In Asia (except China and Japan), crude materials are the leading category, but they account for only 22 per cent of this region's export value.

The variation in exports according to these five categories is given in Table 25-3 for regions and selected nations.

Sources of Imports. Where do imports come from? The answer is fairly obvious—from industrialized regions. Four regions stand out as sources of imports:

The tanker Esso Fuji. Oil has become an extremely important commodity in international trade in recent years, seriously altering the balance of trade of some nations. (*Courtesy EXXON Corporation.*)

Table 25-3

Export Structures of Selected Regions and Nations

	Percentages of Total Exports Accounted For by Five Major Categories				
				Manufactures	
Place	Foods	Crude Materials	Mineral Fuels	Machinery and Transport Equipment	Other
Anglo-America	17	16	4	38	17
Canada	13	23	10	31	20
United States	18	13	2	40	16
Latin America	36	15	27	4	13
Brazil	50	24	2	5	13
Mexico	36	12	—	20	12
Venezuela	3	3	90	—	—
Western Europe	11	5	4	34	35
West Germany	4	2	3	47	31
France	15	5	2	32	31
United Kingdom	4	3	3	38	35
Italy	6	2	6	35	41
Sweden	2	19	1	41	33
Spain	21	4	4	21	37
Eastern Europe	10	9	11	33	23
Poland	13	5	13	30	20
Hungary	20	4	2	33	29
Czechoslovakia	3	5	3	50	33
U.S.S.R.	1	13	18	23	14
Africa	21	19	38	1	18
Nigeria	6	6	85	—	—
South Africa	23	26	3	6	34
Libya	—	—	99	—	—
Middle East	4	6	86	1	3
Saudi Arabia	—	—	91	—	—
Iran	3	5	89	—	3
Kuwait	—	—	92	3	3
China (includes Mongolia, North Korea and North Vietnam)	27	20	2	2	43
Other Asia	8	11	5	31	40
Japan	2	2	—	49	39
Singapore	6	25	19	22	19
Hong Kong	4	4	—	14	75
South Korea	6	6	—	13	72
Australia-New Zealand	36	35	5	7	12
Australia	31	35	6	8	13
New Zealand	53	34	—	4	8

Source: United Nations, *Yearbook of International Trade Statistics, 1974* (1975).

western Europe, the United States, eastern Europe and the U.S.S.R., and Japan. These industrial regions supply imports to underdeveloped regions, to other industrialized regions, and, in the case of western Europe and eastern Europe, to the individual countries within these areas.

The location of the import-from-western Europe realm is shown in Figure 25-4 (constructed by the same method as was Figure 25-2); it blankets the countries of western Europe, Africa, the United States, the Middle East, and Australia and New Zealand. In 6 of the world's 12 major trading regions, imports are mainly from western Europe. Next most visible is the United States. Imports to Canada, Japan, and Latin America are mainly from the United States. Finally, imports to much of Asia are mainly from Japan; the eastern Europe and U.S.S.R. region trades extensively with its member countries and with China.

Similarity of Trade Linkages. One principle of international trade is this: A nation's leading trading partner tends to be both the leading consignee for its exports and leading source of its imports. This is generally true whether viewed on a nation-to-nation basis or on a region-to-region basis, as a visual comparison of Figures 25-2 and 25-4 indicates.

Type of Imports. Machinery, transport equipment, and other manufactured goods are the leading imports of most of the world's nations (Figure 25-5). Fifteen of the top trading nations are described in Table 25-4; manufactured items account for 50 per cent or more of the imports for all but two. It is interesting to note that manufactured imports are important for both highly developed and lesser developed nations. We should also recognize, however, that manufactured goods are usually more valuable than foods and unprocessed

items. In some cases, nonmanufactured items might be the most *critical* imports for a nation, even though their *value* is less than that of manufactures.

Imports of nonmanufactured items vary in importance from country to country, depending on a particular nation's resource base and the demands of its producers and consumers. Nigeria and Saudi Arabia are both lesser developed nations that export petroleum. They import food and manufactured goods but not much else. Similarly, Australia and the U.S.S.R. have a substantial resource base which requires that only modest amounts of food and raw materials be imported. Japan and South Korea, on the other hand, are resource poor countries, which are heavy importers of foods, crude materials, and mineral fuels.

Balance of Trade. Some nations have an even or nearly even flow of commodities in and out; for instance, Canada's exports in 1974 were valued at $32.8 billion, her imports at $32.3 billion. For most countries, however, there is a substantial discrepancy in the value of inbound and outbound goods. On the one hand are those countries that buy more than they sell, Japan, for instance, whose purchases abroad exceeded her sales abroad by $6.6 billion in 1974. At the other extreme are such nations as Saudi Arabia and West Germany, whose exports greatly exceed imports. Countries with

Figure 25-4

INTERNATIONAL TRADE: IMPORTS

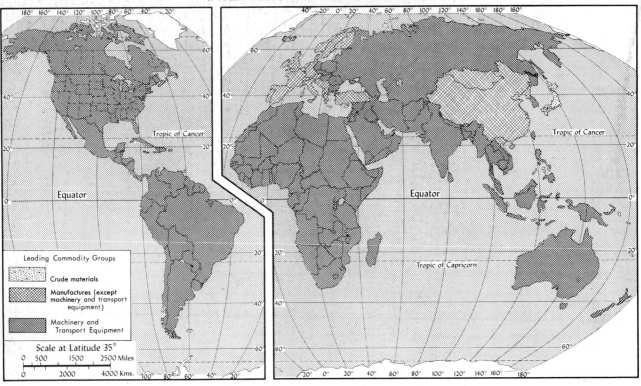

Figure 25-5

Table 25-4

Import Structures of Selected Nations

| Place | Percentages of Total Imports Accounted For by Five Major Categories | | | | |
| | | | | Manufactures | |
	Foods	Crude Materials	Mineral Fuels	Machinery and Transport Equipment	Other
Canada	8	5	6	51	24
United States	12	7	12	30	31
Brazil	10	3	16	33	21
Mexico	10	7	7	44	17
West Germany	15	11	11	18	34
France	11	9	12	26	30
Sweden	8	5	11	32	33
Spain	13	16	13	27	18
Hungary	8	13	10	30	25
U.S.S.R.	6	4	3	34	20
Nigeria	11	—	—	37	32
Saudi Arabia	18	—	—	27	27
Japan	15	32	22	8	17
South Korea	14	21	7	29	21
Australia	4	7	4	37	34

Source: United Nations, *Yearbook of International Trade Statistics, 1974* (1975).

an excess of imports over exports are termed *trade debtor nations;* those in the reverse condition are called *trade creditor nations.*

The astonishing fact is that of the largest trading countries, a large share are debtors. The size of the negative differentials varied in 1974 from the $15.5 billion of the United Kingdom to a modest $0.6 billion for Sweden; smaller traders often have tiny negative differentials. The nations with a large commodity debt are listed by dollars of difference in Table 25-5, column A. In such a list, the United Kingdom would seem to be in a desperate position. But the size of the debt by itself may not be too meaningful without reference to total trade. Therefore, it is useful to look at negative differentials from another perspective, *the export/import index.*

If 100 is the index of perfect balance between inbound and outbound shipments, the greater the excess of imports over exports, the lower the index will be. On this basis, the countries with the most severely imbalanced trade are listed in Table 25-5, column B.

The locational pattern of *trade debtor nations* is portrayed in Figure 25-6. Were it not for West Germany and the Netherlands, Western Europe would be a solid mass of debtor nations. In Eastern Europe, only the U.S.S.R. and Romania report favorable trade balances. Elsewhere in the world, the pattern of debtors and creditors is mixed.

Table 25-5

Nations with Large Negative Differentials between Exports and Imports, 1974

(A) Negative Differential in Billions of U.S. Dollars		(B) Export-Import Index	
United Kingdom	15.5	Panama	25
Italy	10.6	Israel	40
United States	10.0	Jordon	40
Spain	8.2	Turkey	41
France	7.1	Greece	45
Brazil	6.7	Lebanon	46
Japan	6.6	Spain	46
Yugoslavia	3.9	Kenya	50
Mexico	3.1	Yugoslavia	51
Switzerland	2.6	Egypt	65
Israel	2.5	New Zealand	65
Greece	2.4	Pakistan	65

Source: United Nations, *Yearbook of International Trade Statistics, 1974* (1975).

On the other side of the balance are the minority of *trade creditor nations;* there are almost twice as many

Figure 25-6

INTERNATIONAL TRADE: BALANCE OF TRADE

Index of trade balance
$$\frac{\text{Exports}}{\text{Imports}} \times 100$$

118 — median of indices above 100
100 — 100
80
0

Scale at Latitude 35°

0   500   1500   2500 Miles
0   2000   4000 Kms.

debtors as creditors. The leading trade creditors are listed by dollars of differential in Table 25-6. The sizes of the

Table 25-6

Nations with Large Positive Differentials between Exports and Imports, 1974

Positive Differential in Billions of U.S. Dollars		Export-Import Index	
Saudi Arabia	33.7	Saudi Arabia	1,063
West Germany	20.4	Kuwait	747
Iran	18.2	Iran	425
Kuwait	9.7	Nigeria	356
Nigeria	6.9	Iraq	278
Libya	4.4	Libya	233
Indonesia	3.5	Venezuela	224
Venezuela	3.1	Indonesia	190

Source: United Nations, *Yearbook of International Trade Statistics, 1974* (1975).

positive differentials range fantastically from small surpluses of just a few million dollars to the $33.7 billion of Saudi Arabia. Other nations with copious credits are West Germany, Iran, and Kuwait. The size of the sur-

pluses quickly drops after the first three countries, however. The distribution of positive differentials shows a heavy concentration in the petroleum-producing countries.

The sharp spatial variation in trade differentials is a prominent feature of the geography of international trade; recognition of this condition is fundamental to understanding the economic problems of western Europe, Japan, the United States, and other nations.

For an illustration of all the foregoing characteristics of international trade in a single nation, see Table 25-7 and Figure 25-7, which identifies the leading exports, imports, consignees, and sources in the foreign trade structure of the United States. Inspection of Part A raises such questions as: What explains the contrast between United States trade with Venezuela and with Brazil? Between trade with the Netherlands and with Spain? Between trade with Israel and with Saudi Arabia? The sum of United States imports and exports with the U.S.S.R. is $0.9 billion (roughly comparable to the trade between the United States and the Dominican Republic)—Is this a surprisingly large amount, a surprisingly small amount, or not surprising at all? Why? Most of the above questions can be answered at least partially by considering Part B of Table 25-7 and material encountered elsewhere in this book.

Balance of Payments. International trade is only one component (albeit a major one) of economic

Figure 25-7

TRADE RELATIONS OF THE UNITED STATES

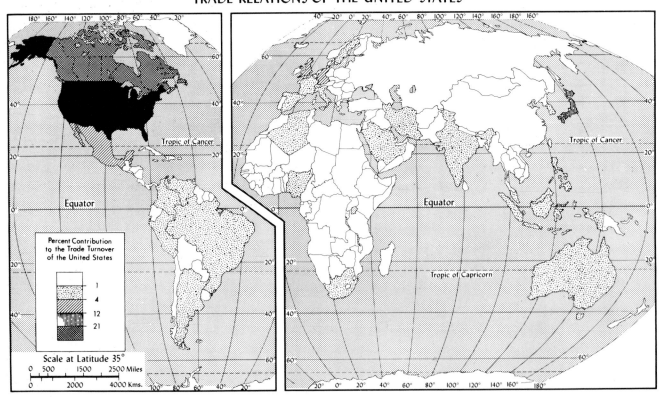

Table 25-7

United States: International Trade, 1974
(Value in Billions of Dollars)

Total Imports 101.0
Total Exports 98.5

Part A: Leading Trading Areas			Part B: Commodities			
Nation	Imports	Exports	Imports		Exports	
Canada	22.3	19.9	Food	9.4		14.2
Latin America			sugar	2.3	unmilled wheat	4.4
Mexico	3.4	4.9	coffee	1.6	unmilled maize	3.8
Venezuela	4.7	1.8	fish	1.5	animal feeds	1.3
Brazil	1.7	3.1	meat	1.3	fruits and vegetables	1.2
Neth. Antilles	2.0	0.2	*Beverages and tobacco*	1.3		1.3
Western Europe			alcoholic beverages	1.0	tobacco and products	1.2
West Germany	6.4	5.0	*Crude materials*	5.9		11.0
United Kingdom	4.0	4.6	metalliferous ores		soybeans (except flour)	3.5
Netherlands	1.5	4.0	and scrap	1.8	metalliferous ores	
Italy	2.6	2.8	lumber	1.1	and scrap	1.5
France	2.3	2.9	pulp and waste paper	1.1	cotton	1.4
Belgium-Lux.	1.7	2.3	*Mineral fuels*	25.3		3.4
Spain	0.9	2.0	crude petroleum	16.5	coal	2.4
Switzerland	0.9	1.1	petroleum products	7.7		
Middle East			*Chemicals*	4.0		8.9
Iran	2.1	1.7	*Machinery and transport*			
Saudi Arabia	1.7	0.8	equipment	24.7		38.5
Israel	0.3	1.2	road motor vehicles	11.8	nonelectric machinery	16.8
Asia			nonelectric machinery	6.4	road motor vehicles	7.9
Japan	12.5	10.7	electrical machinery	5.4	electrical machinery	7.2
South Korea	1.5	1.5			aircraft	5.8
Hong Kong	1.6	0.9	*Other manufactured goods*	27.5		17.1
Indonesia	1.7	0.5	iron and steel	5.4	iron and steel	2.6
Africa			nonferrous metals	3.9	instruments, watches,	
Nigeria	3.3	0.3	clothing	2.3	and clocks	2.4
South Africa	0.6	1.2	paper and paperboard	1.8	yarn and fabrics	1.8
Algeria	1.1	0.3	yarn and fabrics	1.6	nonferrous metals	1.6
Australia	1.0	2.2	instruments, watches,		paper and paperboard	1.5
			and clocks	1.3		
			footware	1.2		

Source: United Nations, *Yearbook of International Trade Statistics, 1974* (1975).

interaction between nations. Nations sell not only goods but also services to one another, services such as insurance, capital loans, and transportation rendered by ocean vessels. Accordingly, economic geographers interested in economic interaction among nations should give attention not only to the flow of commodities (international trade) but also to the total flow of money (and credit) between them. In other words, the balance of payments covers much more than just the balance of trade. A statement explaining the balance of payments concept is in order.

A balance of international payments is a record of a nation's total economic transactions with the rest of the world during a given period of time. It is not a balance sheet since it does not show a nation's total assets abroad or its total liabilities to foreigners, but rather provides a summary of its total receipts from foreign individuals, corporations, governments and international organizations, and its payments to them. It includes transactions related to the supplying of goods and services, the lending and investing of short- and long-term funds and the granting of aid.[1]

Unfortunately, it is not possible to define a single balance which can adequately represent the underlying balance of payments position of the United States. Some of the regularly computed balances are given in Table 25-8. The first figure of interest is the *balance on goods and services*, which is the difference between exports of goods and services and imports. This figure covers not only trade of merchandise but also passenger fares and other transportation fees, payments for private services, investment interest and dividends, and royalty payments. A second balance covers goods and services and certain other payments, such as social security or other pension

[1]Federal Reserve Bank of Chicago, "What Is a Balance of International Payments?" *Business Conditions*, August, 1962, p. 14.

Table 25-8

Summary of United States International Transactions,
1975 (Millions of Dollars)

merchandise trade balance	9,045
services	7,455
Balance on goods and services	16,500
remittances, pensions, and other transfers	− 1,764
Balance on goods, services, and remittances	14,736
U. S. Government grants	2,820
Balance on current account	11,916
U. S. Government capital flows	− 1,726
long-term private capital flows	− 8,789
Balance on current account and long-term capital	1,401

Source: U.S. Department of Commerce *Survey of Current Business* (March, 1976).

payments, research grants, cash transfers by money order, and cash and goods donated abroad by religious

These logs are being shipped from Longview, Washington, to Japan where they will be made into lumber and plywood. Through efficient processing, Japanese manufacturers can afford to import bulky raw materials, such as these logs, and then ship products made from them to distant markets. (*Courtesy Weyerhaeuser Company.*)

and charitable organizations. Still another balance is produced when United States Government grants (excluding military grants) are subtracted from the second balance figure. The result is a new balance of payments estimate—the balance on current account. Finally, by adjusting this third balance to account for capital flows, we can produce a balance on current account and long-term capital. United States Government capital flows would include such things as long-term loans to foreign governments and income from repayment of such loans. Private capital flows include funds used for direct investment abroad, funds used to purchase foreign securities, direct investment in the United States by foreigners, and foreign purchase of securities.

Our discussion of the balance of payments has been brief, and we have not explored all of the various ways in which we might define this complex concept. Nevertheless, materials presented in Table 25-8 clearly show that while imports and exports of commodities are significant, there are many other items which contribute to a nation's international transactions.

Ocean Shipping Routes. The location of ocean shipping routes (maps of which can be found in almost any economic atlas) provides an additional perspective on the geography of international trade.

1. The North Atlantic route runs from eastern Anglo-America to west central Europe. London, Liverpool, Hamburg, Rotterdam, Antwerp, and Le Havre are the leading ports at its eastern terminus, and New York, Philadelphia, Boston, Baltimore, and Montreal do most of the business at the western end. Most of the traffic on this route consists of dry goods, particularly machinery, automobiles, clothing, and other manufactured items; wheat is a major foodstuff; there is relatively little tanker traffic. Along most of the length of this route there are no ports of call.
2. For years a major route ran through the Mediterranean to the Indian Ocean; it ran from west central Europe, around Spain, through the Straits of Gibraltar, then eastward for 2000 miles to the Suez Canal, and thence an additional 5000 miles to Singapore. Along this route are numerous ports of call, principally the oil shipping ports on the Persian Gulf and at the eastern end of the Mediterranean. At Singapore the route fans out in several directions, primarily northeastward toward Hong Kong and Japan.

   This route is still important but has undergone a major reorientation since the closing of the Suez Canal in June of 1967. The Suez Canal was closed until January, 1975. During this period, much of the traffic which had gone through the Suez Canal was routed around the southern tip of Africa. Because this route is longer and more costly, some petroleum shippers have turned to the giant *super-tankers* (which are too large for the Suez Canal) in an effort to become more efficient. Now that the Suez Canal is again open, it will be interesting to see how much of its once brisk traffic it can recapture. In either case, however, few of the world's ocean routes are as busy as those connecting the petroleum ports of the Persian Gulf with Europe.

3. Linking western Europe with the Caribbean is a heavily traveled artery over which petroleum, bananas, coffee, and other tropical products move eastward while manufactured goods flow westward.

4. Between Europe and eastern South America, particularly the ports of Rio de Janeiro, Santos, Montevideo, and Buenos Aires, there is heavy traffic.

5. A short but busy artery connects Caribbean America with Anglo-American ports—especially New Orleans and Galveston—in addition to the ones mentioned in paragraph 1. Petroleum, iron ore, bauxite, coffee, and bananas are major northbound commodities; automobiles and diverse machinery predominate in the southbound flow.

6. Considerable traffic moves between the West Coast of the United States and the Panama Canal, where contact is made with routes mentioned earlier. But even more important, perhaps, is the flow of traffic between the Panama Canal and Asia, especially Japan.

7. A major trade flow has developed between North America and Asia to accommodate increased demands for both raw materials and manufactured goods by industrialized Asian nations such as Japan. Manufactured goods make up a large share of the reverse flow from Asia to Anglo-America.

8. A noticeable volume of traffic flows between western Europe and southern Africa and between western Europe and southeastern Australia. Flows between Australia and Japan are also substantial.

9. Elsewhere, ocean trade routes are dispersed widely over the oceans between latitudes 60° North and 50° South. Most of these routes are not particularly important, but a few, such as domestic routes along the coasts of the United States or the one that connects Tokyo Bay with northern Kyushu, carry substantial volumes of tonnage.

Relationships of International Trade with Population

To understand the location and the characteristics of international trade, we need to recall several relationships that apply to transportation in general, as presented in Chapter 24, and then go on to certain relationships that involve international trade particularly.

The world's total international trade of $1,700,000,000,000 (the sum of all imports and exports) averages out to around $425 per inhabitant of the earth. But the regional variation in this ratio is striking. The highest ratio prevails in the Bahamas, a tax haven, that serves as the nominal origin or destination for over three billion dollars worth of commodities. Not far behind the figure of $16,750 for the Bahamas is the Netherlands Antilles, where concentrated heavy traffic (largely the refining of Venezuelan crude oil for the

American and European markets) brings it up to $14,880 per inhabitant. Other countries with high values of foreign trade per capita are Kuwait $12,777; U.S. Virgin Islands $8790; Singapore $6143; Belgium-Luxembourg $5739; Libya $4978; and Saudi Arabia $4779. The United States ratio is above average but not as high as these nations; the figure is $966.

At the opposite extreme are countries whose per capita foreign trade is far below the world average: India $15, China $17, Pakistan $41, Sudan $58, Zaire $61, Sri Lanka $83, Philippines $87, Indonesia $88, and Thailand $94.

A world map based on this relationship would show western Europe standing head and shoulders above most other regions. Eastern Europe and much of the Middle East are at a lower level, followed by most of the Asian, African, and Latin American nations. (Interesting questions arise at this point: Is there any correlation between an area's economic health and its per capita foreign trade? Other things being equal—especially level of economic development—does per capita trade tend to shrink with large population?)

Trade and Political Alliances

National governments influence trade in numerous ways, one of the most important being by means of legislative controls in the form of tariffs, quotas, and embargoes. Most countries also show favoritism to others with which they share some sort of political attachment. We can illustrate this point by six case studies: OPEC, LAFTA, Benelux, the Schuman Plan, EEC, and EFTA.

OPEC. The Organization of the Petroleum Exporting Countries (OPEC) was organized in 1960 to coordinate the petroleum policies of member countries and to safeguard their interests. The 13 members are Algeria, Ecuador, Gabon, Indonesia, Iran, Iraq, Kuwait, Libya, Nigeria, Qatar, Saudi Arabia, United Arab Emirates, and Venezuela. These countries produce a good portion of the world's oil and hold a large share of the world's reserves. OPEC policies, however, had little effect on world petroleum supplies until the early 1970's. In 1967, OPEC called for an embargo on oil exports to the United States and the United Kingdom, but the embargo was lifted in short order. The first truly significant act of OPEC came in 1970 when the conference, which is OPEC's governing body, decided to raise the tax on the income of oil companies to 55 per cent. Since 1970 OPEC has emerged as a major force in both international trade and international relations. The constant threat of price increases and embargos has had a significant influence on the foreign policies of the United States and other major petroleum importers, and it has stimulated the search for petroleum reserves in non-OPEC countries.

LAFTA. The Latin American Free Trade Association (LAFTA) was established in 1960 to promote cooperation between major Latin American nations, thus stimulating the economic and social development of member countries. Mexico and all South American countries except Guyana, Surinam, and French Guiana are members. LAFTA is probably best known for efforts to reduce and eliminate tariffs and other trade barriers so as to encourage trade between members. But it has also worked to facilitate the transfer of investment capital from one LAFTA member to another and to otherwise support intergovernmental agreements which are beneficial to two or more of its members.

Benelux. On January 1, 1948, Belgium, the Netherlands, and Luxembourg inaugurated the Benelux Customs Union. The provisions of this agreement were (a) that there should be no tariff barriers on any commodities moving among the three (this meant that shipments of any commodity among them began moving as freely as between New York and Ohio), and (b) that the three should have one common set of tariffs on commodities imported from elsewhere (this meant that the trio functioned as a single region in world economic agreements). Immediately, the Benelux plan proved successful. Foreign trade as well as the over-all economy of the three countries advanced vigorously and stimulated speculation about the feasibility of expanding the idea to adjacent countries.

The Schuman Plan. This was a cautious experiment for applying the Benelux scheme to more countries but on fewer commodities. In 1952, six nations (the Benelux trio plus West Germany, France, and Italy) launched a plan for their *steel* industries with these provisions: (a) all tariffs between the six countries were abolished on coal, iron ore, and scrap iron and, (b) on the world market for steel, the six nations were to act as a single competitor. In 1954 refined steel was added to their list of tariff-free goods. Known as the European Coal and Steel Community (ECSC), these six nations enjoyed a pronounced increase in production in all items covered by the Schuman Plan.

European Economic Community. So successful was the Schuman Plan that in January, 1958, the six nations launched the *European Economic Community* (known more popularly as the "European Common Market" or EEC) which called for (a) gradual removal of all barriers to trade among the member countries, (b) the establishment of a common external tariff, (c) the formulation of common policies for agriculture, transportation, and the development of all resources of the six states, and (d) provision for free movement of workers and capital.

Between 1958 and 1968, the EEC established a customs union covering the exchange of all goods, and both eliminated customs duties on exports and imports between member states and adopted a common external tariff for relations with non-EEC countries. Although tariff barriers have been removed some nontariff barriers, such as national regulations on health and safety, still remain to retard the free movement of some goods. Since 1968, free movement of workers between member countries has also become a reality, but the free movement of services is being held back by differing standards for certification of lawyers, doctors, and other professionals. Similarly, policies designed to promote the free movement of capital and a uniform fiscal policy for members have not been fully implemented. Such changes have far-reaching implications and do not come easily.

By almost any measure, the EEC has been a tremendous success. Most of the original objectives of the Common Market have either been met or are in the process of being accomplished. Integration of the six original members is becoming a reality, and much progress has been made toward incorporating Denmark, Ireland, and the United Kingdom—countries which joined the EEC in 1973.

European Free Trade Association. Seven countries (Great Britain, Austria, Denmark, Norway, Portugal, Sweden, and Switzerland) endorsed a plan in July, 1959, for a trade association among themselves. In May of 1960 the new organization, *European Free Trade Association* (EFTA), officially came into existence. The members covenanted to gradually abolish tariffs among themselves, with 1970 being the deadline for tariff extermination. Each country, however, remained free to decide its own external tariff policies. The first tariff reduction occurred in July, 1960 (less than two months after the EFTA was launched), and was a full 20 per cent. The next cut (10 per cent) came in July, 1961—six months ahead of schedule. The third cut—scheduled for July, 1963—was accomplished in March, 1962. The fourth cut (leaving tariffs at 50 per cent of their starting level) was voted in June of 1962. There were four more stages, which, by the end of 1966, resulted in the removal of import duties within EFTA.

In 1961, steps were taken extending to Finland the privileges of EFTA. By 1967, import duties between Finland and EFTA had been removed; Finland is an associate member of EFTA.

From both camps (EEC and EFTA) the evidence unanimously indicates that as the trade barriers are going down, the economic health is going up.

Thus, Europe has been split into several trading zones. The two major associations (originally dubbed "the sixes and sevens") have become the "nines and sevens" (Denmark and the United Kingdom left EFTA for the EEC in December of 1972, but the addition of Iceland and Finland maintains the membership number of EFTA at seven). A third major block, the eastern European nations, has remained rather tightly enmeshed in the Soviet zone.

For a diversity of reasons which relate to differences in both physical endowments and cultural aptitudes, nations in the world engage in a lively exchange of commodities. Certain areas enjoy a much brisker trade than others. The North Atlantic "axis" (United States, Canada, and western Europe) constitutes the heart of the world's international trading pattern.

Even among these nations, human-made barriers still impede the circulation of commodities. Nevertheless, vigorous steps are now being taken to remove these restrictions, and it seems likely that within a decade much of the world's trade will encounter greatly curtailed obstacles, provided, of course, that new barriers are not erected and that the basic stimuli to trade continue to function.

SUGGESTED READINGS

BERGMAN, EDWARD F., "The Multinational Corporation," *The Professional Geographer*, 1973, pp. 255–260.

DOYAL, EDISON, "The Changing Pattern of India's International Trade," *Economic Geography*, 1968, pp. 240–269.

GROTEWOLD, ANDREAS, "The Growth of Industrial Core Areas and Patterns of World Trade," *Annals of the Association of American Geographers*, 1971, pp. 361–370.

HARKEMA, ROLL C., "Zambia's Changing Pattern of External Trade," *The Journal of Geography*, 1972, pp. 19–27.

KELLOGG, J. E., "A Tale of Two Ports: Seward and Whittier, Alaska," *The Journal of Geography*, 1976, pp. 454–458.

LEWTHWAITE, GORDON R., "Commonwealth and Common Market: The Dilemma of the New Zealand Dairy Industry," *Geographical Review*, 1971, pp. 72–101.

RIMMER, PETER J., "The Problem of Comparing and Classifying Seaports," *The Professional Geographer*, 1966, pp. 83–91.

THOMAN, RICHARD S.; and CONKLING, EDGAR C. *Geography of International Trade*, Englewood Cliffs, N. J., 1967, 186 pp.

WARNTZ, WILLIAM, "Transatlantic Flights and Pressure Patterns," *Geographical Review*, 1961, pp. 187–212.

WONDERS, WILLIAM C., "Japan's Role in Land Resource Development in the Canadian Northwest," *The Journal of Geography*, 1976, pp. 200–208.

PART

EIGHT

TERTIARY ECONOMIC ACTIVITY

The five major categories of production we have discussed so far (subsistence economies, commercial gathering, commercial bioculture, manufacturing, and transportation) employ approximately 90 per cent of the workers of the world. The remaining 10 per cent includes persons in a wide diversity of occupations: retail merchants and clerks, wholesale distributors, government employees, doctors, teachers, lawyers, bankers, insurance salesmen, real estate salesmen, carpenters, plumbers, electricians, telephone operators, radio announcers, garage mechanics, household servants, hotel maids, bellhops, actors, professional athletes, musicians, and many others. The term *tertiary activity* embraces all such economic pursuits, pursuits that do not qualify as primary activities, since they do not involve the harvesting of naturally produced commodities, or as secondary activities, because they do not entail any change in the *form* or the *location* of commodities—pursuits, in short, that involve services.

Each tertiary activity is a spatial variable just as surely as food manufacturing,

361

textile manufacturing, and machinery production are. In truth, we might devote a chapter each to retail trade, wholesale trade, banking, and so on, applying the geographic method of analysis to all. The number of chapters would be large indeed. Fortunately, though, there is a relationship among tertiary activities that permits of an alternative approach. *Tertiary activities tend to agglomerate.* That is, retail stores are likely to be in the same places that garages, law offices, dental offices, and other services are. As a result, we do not find a pattern of specilization in large areas—one part of the world in retail trade, another in wholesale trade, another in education, another in medical treatment, and so on. Therefore, because of the high degree of intercorrelation, it is possible to distinguish regions of agglomeration of tertiary activities. And it is through these agglomerations that we shall approach the geography of tertiary activity.

Many geographers prefer the term *trade center* (covering all commercial activity, not just retailing or wholesaling), or *service center*, or *central place*, or *urban place*, for such settlements. These centers vary in size from the character-istically American *roadside*, which may have only one business, say a gasoline station, to the *metropolis*, which consists of thousands of service establishments. In traditional nomenclature, the words *urban* and *city* apply to these clusters after they reach a certain size. Unfortunately, there is no agreement about just how big a settlement must be before it can qualify as a city. Nevertheless, tertiary regions are so distinctive and important economically that we must do our best to analyze them.

One further point needs to be made. Rarely do *tertiary agglomerations* consist *solely* of tertiary activities. At least in the larger settlements a modicum of manu-facturing is usually present as well as some commercial transportation. Indeed, there are some settlements where employment in the secondary endeavors (manu-facturing and transportation) exceeds that in the tertiary ones. And in some parts of the world there are even settlements where most of the inhabitants earn their living in the commercial primary industries (for instance, mining, fishing, forestry, farming). Still, tertiary activity does tend to occur in agglomerated settlements.

Some textbooks in economic geography do not devote even a chapter to tertiary economic activities or to the service centers in which they chiefly occur. Sometimes the role of cities is recognized in chapters dealing with manufacturing or with trans-portation, but cities themselves are usually not deemed worthy of a chapter, or one at best. In this book three full chapters are devoted to service centers for the following reasons: They are the nerve centers of the world's commercial economy; the proportion of city dwellers is rapidly expanding throughout the world; and in the United States particularly that proportion is now three-fourths of the nation's people.

In Chapter 26, we will deal with location of tertiary, or service, centers—first on a worldwide basis, afterwards in the United States alone, with considerable attention to the one characteristic of size. Then in Chapter 27 we shall narrow the focus down to consider individual urban areas, observing the characteristics that distinguish one from another, including relationships to other areas. Finally in Chapter 28 we shall apply the geographic method to regions *within* a city.

CHAPTER
26

service centers: location and size

The skyline of Dallas, Texas, a typical large city profile, distinguished by the central business district. There, demand for land has caused the obliteration of the natural landscape, which is now replaced by close-packed tall buildings. In the foreground, on the fringe of the CBD, is the circular auditorium and convention center. (*Courtesy Dallas Chamber of Commerce.*)

Figure 26-1

WHERE SERVICE CENTERS ARE

The World Pattern

Information on the location of service centers is inadequate for constructing a satisfactory world map. The most serious difficulty is that we lack data for the thousands of small centers scattered over the face of the earth. Moreover, scores of fairly good-sized settlements (those containing a few hundred or even a few thousand inhabitants) in some parts of the world are not service centers at all but *farm villages* composed primarily of farm domiciles rather than clusters of commercial establishments.

Yet rather complete figures are available for cities of 200,000 or more inhabitants. Since it is a pretty safe bet that a settlement of this size is too large to be merely a collection of farm dwellings, we can take it for granted that the locational pattern of such cities will shed light on the world pattern of tertiary activity, and on this assumption we have constructed Figure 26-1. On this map, shaded areas indicate the presence of cities of at least 200,000 inhabitants. All told, there are about 800 cities in this size category. Rather than plot points for each, however, we have simply drawn a line to enclose all points within 100 miles of a city exceeding 200,000 people. And we have made a further distinction, delimiting areas containing "super," or "millionaire," cities, that is, those with 1,000,000 or more inhabitants. This mapping technique reveals four great urban regions

in the world. (Later on, we shall make an attempt to define *urban* more accurately.)

1. The foremost area covers almost all of western Europe to the Mediterranean shores and even includes the Mediterranean fringe of Morocco, Algeria, and Tunis. Eastward prongs extend beyond the Urals and over the Caucasus as far as the Persian Gulf. A southern extension penetrates Turkey and reaches Egypt and Israel. Within this vast zone are over 45 cities of a million or more people. Great Britain alone has 6, Germany has 4, Italy 4, Russia 9, and the Iberian peninsula 4. In 1935 Europe had 23 of the world's 56 millionaire cities; today it contains 41 of the world's 142.

2. In eastern Asia the zone of urbanism extending from Manchuria, Korea, and Japan to Indonesia contains 22 millionaire settlements including 2 which have over 10,000,000 in population. The striking thing about this region is the number of *new* supercities; two-thirds of them have passed the million mark since 1935. The tropical portion of this realm is particularly noteworthy in that every one of its supercities assumed millionaire status within the past 45 years.

3. India and Pakistan likewise are experiencing rapid growth in both the population of large cities and the number of supercities. Less than half a century ago only Bombay and Calcutta were in the one-million-

or-more category. Today Madras, Delhi, Hyderabad, Bangalore, Ahmedabad, Karachi, Lahore, Kanpur, and Poona have joined the ranks.

4. North America has a cluster of large cities in its eastern portion, from the St. Lawrence Valley on the north to Cuba on the south. There are several detached areas on the West Coast, in central Mexico, and along the Pacific side of Central America. All told there are 29 millionaire cities in this part of the world.

Elsewhere, urbanism appears in nodes or short belts. The pattern in South America is peripheral, resembling a giant horseshoe with one point in Venezuela and the other in eastern Brazil. Of this continent's 11 millionaire settlements, 7 have more than 2,000,000 people. Africa has no extensive urban belts; 5 of her 8 super settlements (Cairo, Alexandria, Casablanca, Cape Town, and Johannesburg) are at her antipodes. Spotted around in numerous parts of the continent are places that have passed the 200,000 mark. Four of the 5 metropolises of Australia front on her eastern and southern coasts (Figure 26-2).

Population Ratio. The foregoing discussion has been based on the location of cities exceeding 200,000 inhabitants with little being said about the relative importance of such settlements in the total population picture. Additional light on the relative significance of such settlements will be shed if we ask the question: What proportion of a nation's total population resides in urban centers? The answer is expressed as a ratio, or as a percentage, and ranges from maxima of 97 per cent (Macau) and 94.3 per cent (Malta) to a minimum of 2.2 (Burundi). Table 26-1 lists selected nations in terms of this ratio.

Figure 26-3 shows the general location of urbanism

Table 26-1

Percentage of Total Urban Population

Nation	Total Population in Millions	Percent Urban
Macau	0.2	97.1
Malta	0.3	94.3
Belgium	9.8	87.1
Australia	12.8	85.6
New Zealand	2.9	81.4
Denmark	4.9	79.9
England and Wales	49.0	77.9
Netherlands	13.4	77.4
Canada	21.7	76.1
Chile	8.9	76.0
Venezuela	10.4	75.7
United States	203.2	73.5
Japan	104.7	72.1
Scotland	5.2	70.9
France	49.7	70.0
Mexico	54.3	61.2
Cuba	8.7	60.5
U.S.S.R.	249.7	59.2
Brazil	101.7	58.3
Finland	4.7	57.1
Poland	33.1	52.9
Austria	7.5	51.9
South Africa	23.0	47.9
Egypt	35.6	43.2
Iran	32.1	42.6
Turkey	37.9	38.6
West Germany	60.8	38.4
Zambia	4.6	34.3
Pakistan	44.1	26.8
Zaire	23.6	25.1
Sri Lanka	12.7	22.4
India	563.5	20.2
Haiti	4.2	19.4
Indonesia	124.6	17.5
Nepal	11.6	4.0
Burundi	3.5	2.2

Source: United Nations, *Demographic Yearbook* (1974).

according to this ratio; it presents a markedly different pattern from that of Figure 26-1, which shows a more place-specific distribution.

The United States Pattern

Figure 26-4 shows the location of major urban regions in the United States. Dark shading covers areas in which no point is more than 30 miles from a city of 50,000 people. Metropolitan areas with a million or more people are shown by a black circle with a 30-mile radius.

The western half of the country is much less urbanized than the eastern; most of it is blank on Figure 26-4. Nevertheless, there are several metropolitan areas with over 1,000,000 people: Seattle, Portland, San Francisco, Los Angeles, San Diego, Denver, Dallas, and

Figure 26-2

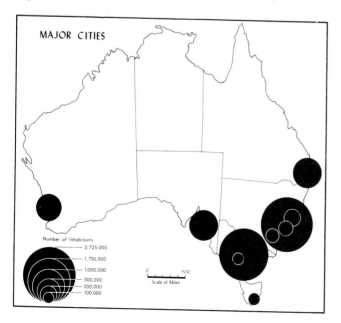

MAJOR CITIES

Number of Inhabitants
2,725,000
1,750,000
1,000,000
500,000
200,000
100,000

Scale of Miles
0   500

Figure 26-3

Figure 26-4

URBAN REGIONS

SMSA exceeding
1,000,000 inhabitants.

Major urban region—
within 30 miles of SMSA
central city of 50,000 inhabitants or more.

0   100   200   300
Scale of Miles

Houston. Texas and California are well supplied with major urban regions, and concentrations in Oregon, Washington, and Utah are also to be seen.

The eastern half of the country unquestionably is more highly urbanized. The foremost urban region of the country is the northeastern parallelogram, bounded by Boston, Washington, St. Louis, and Milwaukee. Within this quadrangle are no fewer than 15 millionaire settlements, most of which define two straight lines, one from Detroit through Cleveland to Pittsburgh, the other through 5 supercities: Washington, Baltimore, Philadelphia, New York, and Boston.

Besides having most of the nation's large cities, the East also contains most of its small service centers. A map of hamlets (Figure 26-5) emphasizes eastern Kentucky, West Virginia, Pennsylvania, and Maryland; in these states, the frequency of hamlets is unusually intense.

SIZES OF TERTIARY SETTLEMENTS

Before considering the various size categories of service centers it must be emphasized again that service centers are primarily centers of tertiary functions. Consequently it is possible for a settlement to be quite large and still not be a service center. For example, on the populous plains of the Far East are hundreds of settlements (ranging in size from 100 to 5000 persons) whose main function is residential; in this capacity they serve farmers and their families. Most of the working population are tillers of the soil who commute to their farms in the morning and return to the settlement at night. Such settlements may, at first glance, appear large enough to qualify as service centers, but their role is that of *farm village* because inhabitants produce scarcely any surplus rice, wheat, or poultry to engage in commerce. Regardless of size, a settlement clearly cannot qualify as a service center if most of its residents are engaged in subsistence economies. China, India, Pakistan, and the tropical countries of Asia and Africa have numerous settlements of the farm-village type.

Function varies considerably from one service center to another. Take these samples: London is highly diversified because it serves as the home of the British Parliament, of several universities, and of numerous banking and insurance offices as well as being the center of wholesaling, retailing, and many professional services; Singapore and Hong Kong owe their growth mainly to trade; Washington, D.C., and Delhi, India, are essentially government centers. The number of functions in any service center varies with size; that is, the larger the place, the more the types (as well as the volume) of services rendered. This principle will be observed more closely in the next chapter which is devoted largely to spatial variation in economic functions of service centers.

Common Size Categories

By size, service centers range from *roadside* to *megalopolis*. A rather complex nomenclature identifying many different categories has come into existence and merits comment here. Some of the terms are only loosely defined, but some (particularly those adopted by the United States Bureau of the Budget and employed by the Bureau of the Census) are very precise.

Roadside. A roadside is an isolated establishment, such as a lone gasoline station, drive-in eating place, small general store, or motel, situated along a highway. Frequently the operator of such a business resides on the floor above or in a house next door. (On

Figure 26-5

DISTRIBUTION OF HAMLETS
(Selected Group 20-150 Population)

About 1938

Each Dot Represents One Hamlet

all sides this embryonic settlement is flanked by rural uses of land such as farms, forests, or desert.) Roadsides are restricted almost entirely to the United States, Canada, and Europe—regions of dense highway traffic. Before the automobile age, roadsides were few and far between (except for the "wayside inn" which has been a fixture of the road ever since man ventured to travel more than a day's journey).

Hamlet.   A hamlet is larger than a roadside and consists of a few buildings some of which are residential and some commercial.

> . . . the unincorporated hamlet represents the first hint of thickening in the settlement plasm. It is neither purely rural nor purely urban, but neuter in gender, a sexless creation midway between the more determinate town and country.

What attributes qualify a settlement for the hamlet category? Glenn Trewartha has proposed the following:

> Defined quantitatively I propose that there must be a minimum of, (1) *four* active residence units, at least two of which are non-farm houses; (2) a total of at least *six* active functional units—residential, business, social or otherwise; and (3) a total of at least *five* buildings actively used by human beings. [In hamlets a building often houses more than one functional unit.] According to the above minimal requirements four farmsteads each located at one corner of a cross-roads could not comprise a hamlet even though, as far as residence units are concerned, four are all that is required. Counting four or five people to a residence this minimum of four residence units in a hamlet establishes a minimum population of 16 or 20. Spacing of buildings in a hamlet must be such as to give an appearance of compactness exceeding that of ordinary farmstead spacing. In a hamlet composed of the minimum number of buildings, the maximum linear distance between the outermost buildings should not exceed one-quarter mile.

> For a number of reasons a population of approximately 150 (not more than 38 residences) was adopted as the maximum for hamlets, and therefore the limit separating them from villages. When settlements reach about that size it was found that there existed a distinct tendency for them to incorporate. Apparently they become conscious of their contrast with the countryside in general, and, as a community, desire more services than the county or township in which they are located is willing to provide. It was found also that in communities with over 150 inhabitants there was a marked tendency for a distinct business core to develop, a feature that is not conspicuous in most hamlets. Teachers and preachers are not so uncommon even in hamlets.

One of the major factors in the birth of hamlets was the presence of small post offices.

> A fairly common center of accretion, having sufficient centripetal power to induce minor coagulation within the open-country settlement plasm, was the fourth-class post office. One of the first requirements in a frontier region of new settlement was some center from which mail could be sent and received. Frontier post offices were established in farm homes, and occasionally in cross-road general stores, blacksmith shops, or similar establishments. From over a wide neighborhood farmers and miners were drawn frequently to a post office center and as a consequence business and service units were attracted to these focal points forming the nuclei of settlement.

> In fact, of all the functions represented in hamlets prior to 1900, postal service was the most universal and appears to have been one of the most common reasons for the origin and growth of small cross-roads settlements.[1]

[1]Glenn T. Trewartha, "The Unincorporated Hamlet," *Annals of the Association of American Geographers*, 1943, pp. 32–40.

Gorden City is a moderate-size service community in the southwestern portion of Kansas. In it a variety of services are provided for the townspeople and for the farmers and ranchers residing in the surrounding agricultural region. (*Courtesy Clair A. Shenk.*)

Wellsford, Kansas, is a small community, which, like many others, found it increasingly difficult to compete with the larger, more attractive regional centers owing to the greater mobility of local consumers. Other small centers in the same area have remained viable but are generally characterized by a decreasing number of functions. (*Courtesy Clair A. Shenk.*)

Village. A village, in turn, is larger and has more functions than a hamlet; we shall adopt population limits of 150 to 1000 for the village category. To qualify as a village, a settlement should have at least ten business establishments. In addition to those functions found in a hamlet, a village should have such other types as an automobile dealer, a farm implement distributor, a lumber yard, a hardware store, a livestock feed dispensary, and an auto repair shop. Many villages have a graded school and several churches. (NOTE: The use of *village* in geography is not to be confused with its use in political science where it denotes a specific form of government. In that sense a service center could have a population of 50,000 and still be a "village.")

Town. A town, in this sequence, loosely ranges in population from around 1000 to 2500 and has additional functions beyond those of a village. Usually there are at least 50 service units, the additional types being a bank, a high school, and a representative of at least one of the professional services (a physician, dentist, veterinarian, or lawyer). Sometimes a weekly newspaper is published. (Like village, *town* means different things to different people. In New England and Wisconsin, for instance, *towns* are governmental subdivisions of counties. In some parts of Europe, *towns* refer to service centers of considerable size.)

City. In this book, we shall apply *city* to service centers that have 2500 or more people, simply and practically because that is the figure chosen by the United States Bureau of the Census to separate *urban* from *rural* settlements, as will be discussed more fully in later paragraphs. Again, a city has a larger number, and greater diversity, of service functions than a town. (On the other hand, some state constitutions declare that a village can incorporate as a *city* if it has only 1000 residents. As with *village* and *town*, the definition given to the word *city* is not everywhere the same.)

Conurbation. In this book we shall apply the term *conurbation* to a group of cities that have coalesced, that is, grown together economically while remaining politically independent, as in New York-northeastern New Jersey where New York, Newark, Jersey City, Paterson, Clifton, and Passaic and suburbs constitute an urbanized cluster of over 16,000,000 people.

Metropolis. This is a loose term for a large city. Popular usage seems to imply that a metropolis contains at least 500,000 people, although again this notion is not at all universal.

The term *millionaire city* is self-evident. There are now more than 140 urban settlements with over 1,000,000 inhabitants in the world, a phenomenal increase over the 56 in 1935. In 1900 there were only 11. The world's largest service centers (those with 3,000,000 or more inhabitants—there are 32) are listed in Table 26-2.

Megalopolis. This term applies to the most massive concentration of urbanized settlement on the face of the earth—a 600-mile stretch of towns, cities, and supercities, many of which have coalesced (see Figure 26-6). Here is "a phenomenon unique by its size not only in America but in the world. It resulted obviously from the coalescence, recently achieved, of a chain of metropolitan areas, each of which grew around a substantial urban nucleus. The super-metropolitan character of this vast area, the greatest such growth ever observed, called for a special name. We chose the word *megalopolis.*"[2]

The Question of "Urban." All the terms mentioned thus far, from *roadside* to *megalopolis*, are still

[2]So writes Jean Gottmann in "Megalopolis: Or the Urbanization of the Northeastern Seaboard," *Economic Geography*, Vol. 33, 1957, pp. 189–200.

Table 26-2

World's Largest Urban Settlements

Rank	Urban Agglomeration	Population in Millions
1.	Tokyo	11.6
2.	New York	11.6
3.	Shanghai*	10.2
4.	Mexico City	10.2
5.	Buenos Aires	8.4
6.	Paris	8.2
7.	Peking*	7.6
8.	Moscow	7.4
9.	London	7.3
10.	Los Angeles	7.0
11.	Calcutta	7.0
12.	Chicago	7.0
13.	Bombay*	6.0
14.	Seoul	5.4
15.	Sao Paulo*	5.2
16.	Cairo*	5.0
17.	Philadelphia	4.8
18	Jakarta*	4.6
19.	Tientsin*	4.3
20.	Rio de Janeiro*	4.3
21.	Detroit	4.2
22.	Hong Kong	4.2
23.	Leningrad	4.1
24.	Tehran*	3.9
25.	Delhi	3.6
26.	Karachi*	3.5
27.	Berlin*	3.2
28.	Madras	3.2
29.	Lima	3.2
30.	Madrid	3.1
31.	Istanbul	3.1
32.	San Francisco	3.1

Source: United Nations, Demographic Yearbook (1974).
*Population of "city proper," rather than "urban agglomeration."

loosely defined and have not been adopted by all scientists. Indeed there is still no general agreement as to what the term *urban* stands for. Consequently it is very difficult to compare urban population from census data of one nation with that of another nation if their opinions differ as to what qualifies as *urban*. Look at the spread among the following: Denmark tabulates as urban every settlement with 200 inhabitants; a 1000 minimum applies in Canada and Venezuela; 1500 is the requirement in Panama, Colombia, and Ireland; in East Germany it is 2000. The 2500 basis holds in Mexico, as well as the United States. Austria counts as urban only those places with 5000 inhabitants, Switzerland only those with 10,000.

United States Census Classifications

The United States Census publications employ a series of definitions which define rather precisely several categories of urban settlements: *urban place, urbanized area, standard metropolitan statistical area, central city,* and *standard consolidated area.*

Urban Place. An urban place is any settlement (whether incorporated or not) with 2500 or more inhabitants. Incorporated urban places can be referred to as *municipalities* (but this term also includes some incorporated places of less than 2500 people).

Any settlement that does not qualify as urban is considered by the United States Census to be *rural.* Table 26-3 indicates the structure of United States population, in terms of urban and rural components, by size categories of settlements. All told, the nation contains almost 21,000 service centers of which 7000 are in the urban category. Their aggregate population is 150,000,000. The nearly 14,000 rural centers have around 10,000,000 people. The remaining 43,000,000 Americans reside on farms or in various types of rural but nonfarm homes.

Figure 26-6

MEGALOPOLIS

Scale of Miles
0 20 40 60

Table 26-3

United States Population in Groups of Places Classified according to Size

Classification	Population in Millions	Percentage of Total	Number of Places
TOTAL	203.2	100.0	20,768
Urban places	149.3	73.5	7,062
Places of 1,000,000 or more	18.8	9.2	6
500,000 to 1,000,000	13.0	6.4	20
250,000 to 500,000	10.4	5.1	30
100,000 to 250,000	14.3	7.0	100
50,000 to 100,000	16.7	8.2	240
25,000 to 50,000	17.8	8.8	520
10,000 to 25,000	21.4	10.5	1,385
5,000 to 10,000	12.9	6.4	1,839
5,000 or less	8.8	4.4	2,922
other urban	15.2	7.5	—
Rural	53.9	26.5	13,706
Places of 1,000 to 2,500	6.7	3.3	4,191
1,000 or less	3.8	1.9	9,515
Other rural	43.4	21.3	—

Source: U.S. Bureau of the Census, *Census of Population: 1970*, United States Summary, Table 7 (1971).

The population structure of urban places by size category varies considerably from state to state. Table 26-4, for instance, shows that in California the major size category (over 100,000) accounts for 37 per cent of the state's inhabitants; in Arizona and Nevada the largest percentage also resides in the "over 100,000" size category; in Wyoming the 25,000 to 50,000 category predominates.

Urbanized Area. Many an urban settlement has experienced so great a population expansion (resulting from its own *natural increase*—that is, excess of births over deaths—and also *migration increase*—that is, excess of in-migration over out-migration) that it has spilled over its city limits. In such instances the population of the official *urban place* is actually less than the number of people residing in that particular urban agglomeration. Frequently this kind of growth involves the coalescing of several incorporated suburbs encircling the main municipality. It also includes urban settlement which has crept out into the country, beyond even the corporate limits of the suburbs. In order to provide a single population figure for this single agglomeration (of diverse areas of

Table 26-4

United States: Percentage of Population in Groups of Places Classified, by Regions and States, according to Size, 1970

Regions and States	Urban Population								Rural Population
	Total Urban	Over 100,000	50,000 to 100,000	25,000 to 50,000	10,000 to 25,000	5,000 to 10,000	Less than 5,000	Other Urban	
U.S. TOTAL	73	28	8	9	11	6	4	7	27
Northeast	81	31	7	8	9	7	4	15	19
Vermont	33	0	0	9	7	13	4	0	67
Massachusetts	85	21	19	11	3	2	2	27	15
New York	86	50	4	6	9	6	3	8	14
North Central	72	27	8	10	12	6	5	4	28
Iowa	57	11	13	11	6	9	6	1	43
North Dakota	44	0	9	17	12	5	1	0	56
South	65	24	6	7	10	7	5	6	35
West Virginia	39	0	8	10	8	5	6	2	61
North Carolina	45	13	5	8	7	5	4	3	55
Florida	81	25	7	9	13	10	6	11	19
Mississippi	45	7	0	13	11	8	5	1	55
Texas	80	38	11	6	11	6	5	3	20
West	83	32	13	11	12	5	4	6	17
Wyoming	60	0	0	24	14	12	10	0	40
Nevada	81	26	15	7	22	7	3	1	19
New Mexico	70	24	0	19	12	8	6	1	30
Arizona	80	48	11	5	4	6	4	2	20
California	91	37	17	13	12	5	2	5	9

Source: U.S. Bureau of the Census, *Census of Population, 1970*, United States Summary, Table 19 (1971).

government) the term *urbanized area* has been coined. Today, the concept of urbanized area is probably the best for distinguishing between rural and large urban settlements.

As viewed by the United States Census, an urbanized area consists of at least one urban place having 50,000 or more inhabitants (termed *central city*) or twin cities, that is, cities with contiguous boundaries with a combined population of at least 50,000 and with the smaller of the two having a population of at least 15,000. Also included is surrounding closely settled territory, including the following: (a) incorporated urban places, (b) other incorporated settlements having at least 100 dwelling units, (c) unincorporated parcels with a population density of at least 1000 people per square mile, and (d) other similar small areas in unincorporated territory with lower population density, provided that they serve to eliminate enclaves, close indentations, or link outlying enumeration districts of qualifying density that are not more than 1.5 miles from the main body of the urbanized area. The map of the Syracuse Urbanized Area (Figure 26-7) illustrates this concept.

Central Cities. There are a few urbanized areas having "twin central cities," neither of which has a population of 50,000 but which are contiguous and have a combined population of at least that amount. Where several contiguous cities each exceed 50,000, the definitional criteria become more complex. The "central city" category consists of the population of the cities

named in the title of the urbanized area. The title is limited to three names and normally lists the largest city first and the other qualifying cities in size order. For the other cities to be listed in the title they must have (a) 250,000 inhabitants or more or (b) at least one-third the population of the largest city and a population of 25,000 or more (except in the case of twin cities). Examples of twin central cities are San Bernardino-Riverside, Seaside-Monterey, Seattle-Everett, Newport News-Hampton, and Nashville-Davidson. Examples of triplet central cities are Davenport-Rock Island-Moline, Allentown-Bethlehem-Easton and Albany-Schenectady-Troy.

Altogether, there are 248 urbanized areas in the United States, ranging in size from Harlingen-San Benito, Texas (50,469 inhabitants), to the New York-Northeastern New Jersey Urbanized Area (16,206,841 inhabitants). Their aggregate population is 118,446,566 (over half the nation's 1970 total of 203,000,000). Twenty-five urbanized areas have over 1,000,000 people each with a combined total of 71,000,000. The largest of these are listed in Table 26-5.

Figure 26-8 shows where the nation's population is, with the larger symbols portraying urbanized area. Note the prominence of the parallelogram mentioned earlier (that is, the area bounded by Boston, Milwaukee, St. Louis, and Washington).

Ratio of Populations of Urban Area and Central City. Inspection of Table 26-5 reveals that there is not a perfect correlation between size of urbanized area and size of the nucleus, that is, the largest central city. For example, the City of Chicago is greater

Figure 26-7

URBANIZED AREA OF SYRACUSE, NEW YORK

Table 26-5

Population in Millions of Largest U.S. Urbanized Areas, Their Largest Central Cities, and Their Standard Metropolitan Statistical Areas

Area	Urbanized Area	Largest Central City		SMSA's	
New York-northeastern New Jersey	16.2	New York	8.8	Jersey City	0.6
				Newark	1.9
				New York	11.6
				Paterson	1.4
Los Angeles-Long Beach	8.4	Los Angeles	2.8	Anaheim	1.4
				Los Angeles	7.0
Chicago-northwestern Indiana	6.7	Chicago	3.4	Chicago	7.0
				Gary	0.6
Philadelphia	4.0	Philadelphia	1.9	Philadelphia	4.8
Detroit	4.0	Detroit	1.5	Detroit	4.2
San Francisco-Oakland	3.0	San Francisco	0.7	San Francisco	3.1
Boston	2.7	Boston	0.6	Boston	2.8
Washington	2.5	Washington	0.8	Washington	2.9
Cleveland	2.0	Cleveland	0.8	Cleveland	2.1
St. Louis	1.9	St. Louis	0.6	St. Louis	2.4
Pittsburgh	1.8	Pittsburgh	0.5	Pittsburgh	2.4
Minneapolis–St. Paul	1.7	Minneapolis	0.4	Minneapolis	1.8
Houston	1.7	Houston	1.2	Houston	2.0
Baltimore	1.6	Baltimore	0.9	Baltimore	2.1
Dallas	1.3	Dallas	0.8	Dallas	1.6

Source: U.S. Bureau of the Census, *Census of Population: 1970,* United States Summary, Tables 20 21, and 32 (1971).

than the City of Los Angeles, but the reverse is true for their urbanized areas. The same can be said for St. Louis and Houston. The explanation of this condition is that some central cities are tightly ringed by large suburbs and unincorporated fringes; this may result in a large urbanized area population encompassing a relatively small central city.

For the same reason, the ratio between central city population and urbanized area population ranges from a minimum of 19.9 per cent in West Palm Beach, Florida, to 100 per cent in five places; Amarillo, Bryan-College Station, Wichita Falls, and Galveston, Texas; and Ponce, Puerto Rico. Central cities snugly hemmed in by suburbs have low ratios (Boston 24.2, Providence 22.5, Pittsburgh 28.2), whereas central cities with vigorous annexation policies have maintained ratios of 100 by continually pushing their municipal boundaries out into the countryside ahead of the advancing wave of urban settlement.

Standard Metropolitan Statistical Area. For many types of economic analysis it is necessary to compare data which are collected on a county basis—for example, the Census of Manufactures, and the Census of Population. To facilitate such comparison the Census publishes urban population figures for certain counties and groups of counties identified as *Standard Metropolitan Statistical Areas* (SMSA's).

An SMSA is a *county* (or a group of contiguous *counties*) containing at least one central city of at least 50,000 inhabitants or twin central cities with an aggregate of 50,000 or more people. In addition to this "core" county (or counties) contiguous counties are included in the SMSA if, according to criteria listed below, they are metropolitan in character and are integrated economically with the central city.

If two or more adjacent counties each have a city meeting specifications for a central city and located within 20 miles of one another (measured between city limits), the counties are included in the same SMSA unless evidence indicates that the central cities are not economically integrated.

The criteria for measuring the *metropolitan* character of any other contiguous county for possible inclusion in the SMSA are as follows:

1. At least 75 per cent of the labor force working in the county must be in nonagricultural endeavor.
2. The county must also meet at least *one* of the following requirements if it is to qualify as "metropolitan":
   a. At least half of its population must reside in contiguous minor civil divisions (in most states these

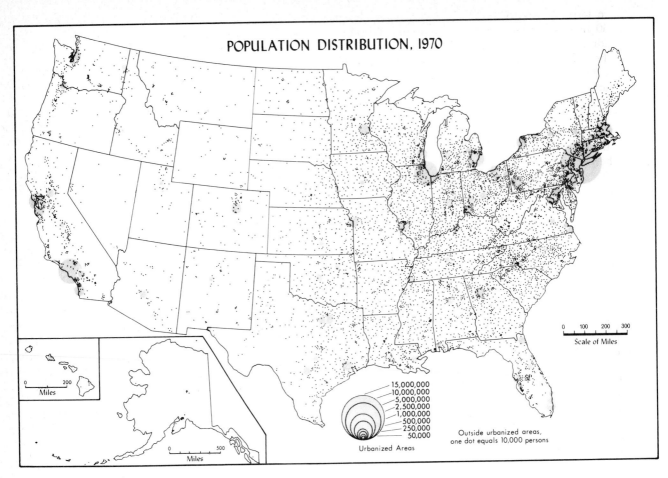

POPULATION DISTRIBUTION, 1970

Scale of Miles
0 100 200 300

Miles
0 200

Miles
0 500

15,000,000
10,000,000
5,000,000
2,500,000
1,000,000
500,000
250,000
50,000

Urbanized Areas

Outside urbanized areas,
one dot equals 10,000 persons

Figure 26-8

Figure 26-9

STANDARD METROPOLITAN STATISTICAL AREAS
in Northeastern United States, 1970

DULUTH-SUPERIOR (Pt.)

APPLETON-OSHKOSH
GREEN BAY
LA CROSSE
MADISON
MILWAUKEE
MUSKEGON-MUSKEGON HEIGHTS
BAY CITY
LANSING-EAST LANSING
SAGINAW
GRAND RAPIDS
FLINT
KENOSHA
RACINE
BATTLE CREEK
DETROIT
ROCKFORD
GARY-HAMMOND-EAST CHICAGO
JACKSON
ANN ARBOR
DAVENPORT-ROCK ISLAND-MOLINE (Pt.)
CHICAGO
SOUTH BEND
TOLEDO
LORAIN-ELYRIA
CLEVELAND
ERIE
PEORIA
BLOOMINGTON-NORMAL
LAFAYETTE-WEST LAFAYETTE
FORT WAYNE
LIMA
MANSFIELD
AKRON
CANTON
YOUNGSTOWN-WARREN
WILLIAMSPORT
PITTSBURGH
SPRINGFIELD
DECATUR
ANDERSON
MUNCIE
DAYTON
STEUBENVILLE-WEIRTON
ALTOONA
HARRISBURG
SPRINGFIELD
INDIANAPOLIS
COLUMBUS
CINCINNATI
JOHNSTOWN
YORK
BALTIMORE
TERRE HAUTE
HAMILTON-MIDDLETOWN
WHEELING
EVANSVILLE
HUNTINGTON-ASHLAND
PARKERSBURG-MARIETTA
WASHINGTON
RICHMOND
LOUISVILLE
LEXINGTON
CHARLESTON
LYNCHBURG
OWENSBORO
ROANOKE
PETERSBURG-COLONIAL HEIGHTS-HOPEWELL
NEWPORT NEWS-HAMPTON
NORFOLK-VIRGINIA BEACH-PORTSMOUTH

LEWISTON-AUBURN
PORTLAND
UTICA-ROME
SYRACUSE
ALBANY-SCHENECTADY-TROY
MANCHESTER
NASHUA
LAWRENCE-HAVERHILL
ROCHESTER
PITTSFIELD
BOSTON
BUFFALO
BINGHAMTON
POUGHKEEPSIE
BROCKTON
ELMIRA
WILKES-BARRE-HAZLETON
SCRANTON
FALL RIVER
PROVIDENCE-WARWICK-PAWTUCKET
NORWICH-GROTON-NEW LONDON
MERIDEN
NEW HAVEN
BRIDGEPORT
NORWALK
STAMFORD
NEW YORK
JERSEY CITY
LONG BRANCH-ASBURY PARK
PHILADELPHIA
ATLANTIC CITY
VINELAND-MILLVILLE-BRIDGETON
WILMINGTON
NEW BEDFORD

374

are termed *townships*) with a density of at least 150 persons per square mile, such civil divisions radiating from a central city in the area.

b. The number of nonagricultural workers *employed* in the county must be at least 10 per cent of the number of nonagricultural workers employed in the core county.

c. The number of nonagricultural workers *residing* in the county must be at least 10 per cent of the number of nonagricultural workers residing in the core county.

d. The county must be the place of *employment* for at least 10,000 nonagricultural workers.

e. The county must be the place of *residence* for at least 10,000 nonagricultural workers.

3. The county must meet one of the following requirements if it is to qualify as being "integrated" with the core county:

a. At least 15 per cent of the workers residing in the county must work in the core county (or counties) containing the central city (cities).

b. At least 25 per cent of those working in the outlying county must reside in the core county (or counties) containing the central city (cities).

If data for criteria 3a and 3b are inconclusive, Census authorities then consider such measures of integration as average telephone calls per subscriber per month from the outlying county to the core counties, newspaper circulation reports, and analysis of charge accounts by retail stores in the central cities.[3]

In total, there were 243 SMSA's in the United States in 1970 ranging from Meriden, Connecticut (55,959 inhabitants) to New York (11,571,899). Table 26-5 indicates the population for some of the larger SMSA's. Notice that there is not a perfect correlation between population of urbanized area and of SMSA. Two reasons explain this discrepancy. Counties are not of uniform size; thus, two central cities of equal size in two counties of unequal size would tend to show different SMSA populations. Secondly, a central city whose urbanized area has filled in most of the county would tend to be augmented by less in SMSA calculations than would a central city whose urbanized area has filled in far less of a county of the same size.

Most SMSA's contain more people than do their urbanized areas (see Table 26-5). New York is the glaring exception. This monstrous urban mass is now so large that economic integration is no longer able to make it cohere into one SMSA, in terms of Census SMSA criteria. The Newark SMSA and the Paterson-Clifton-Passaic SMSA are contiguous to, but not sufficiently integrated with, the New York SMSA.

[3]For a more detailed discussion see Bureau of the Budget, *Standard Metropolitan Statistical Areas* (1967).

Standard Consolidated Areas. Around the nation's two largest *urban places* (New York and Chicago), several contiguous SMSA's and additional counties which do not meet the formal requirements for economic integration but do have considerable interrelationships of other types, have been given a new regional designation: *Standard Consolidated Areas.* The New York-Northeastern New Jersey SCA has a population of 16,178,700 while the Chicago-Northwestern Indiana SCA has 7,612,314.

Rank-Size Hypothesis

Some scholars, viewing population structure of major regions by sizes of service centers (such as that for the United States in the last column of Table 26-3) have been impressed with the fact that as the size category increases, the number of settlements per size category decreases. They have formulated the *rank-size hypothesis*. According to this, as a region advances from subsistence into commercial stages, two developments will occur. (1) One service center will tend to outstrip all others in size and become the main city for the entrie region. Such a center is termed a *primate city.* (2) Each remaining city will assume a size roughly equal to the population of the primate city divided by that city's rank in the region. This is expressed by the following formula:

$$P_x = \frac{P_l}{R_x}$$

in which P_l is population of the region's largest urban agglomeration, P_x is the population of any other urban agglomeration, and R_x is the rank of that other agglomeration.

To illustrate (referring to data on urbanized areas in Table 26-5): The population of New York is 16.2 million, that of Philadelphia is 4 million. Dividing the latter into the former figure gives a quotient of almost 4 which should be the rank of Philadelphia according to this hypothesis. A few moments inspection of Table 26-5 will enable the reader to comment on whether this hypothesis holds more firmly when applied to central cities or to urbanized areas or to SMSA's.

This chapter has dealt with general locational patterns of tertiary settlements and has considered one selected characteristic, that of size. The next chapter continues our train of thought by considering other characteristics and then moving into a discussion of relationships.

SUGGESTED READINGS

BERRY, BRIAN J. L., *Geography of Market Centers and Retail Distributions*, Englewood Cliffs, N. J., 1967, 146 pp.

BOAL, F. W., and JOHNSON, D. B., "The Rank-Size Curve: A Diagnostic Tool?" *The Professional Geographer*, September 1965, pp. 21–23.

BORCHERT, JOHN R., "America's Changing Metropolitan Regions," *Annals of the Association of American Geographers,* 1972, pp. 352–373.

BURTON, IAN, "A Restatement of the Dispersed City Hypothesis," *Annals of the Association of American Geographers,* 1963, pp. 285–289.

CHANG, SEN-DOU, "The Changing System of Chinese Cities," *Annals of the Association of American Geographers,* 1976, pp. 398–415.

CHEN, CHENG-SIANG, "Population Growth and Urbanization in China, 1953–1970," *Geographical Review,* 1973, pp. 55–72.

GONZALEZ, ALFONSO, "Population Growth and Socio-Economic Development: The Latin American Experience," *The Journal of Geography,* 1971, pp. 36–46.

GOTTMAN, JEAN, "Megalopolis or the Urbanization of the Northeastern Seaboard," *Economic Geography,* 1957, pp. 189–200.

———, *Megalopolis: The Urbanized Northeastern Seaboard of the United States,* New York, 1961, 810 pp.

HAAKE, JOHN H., "Do Cities Grow in Isolation?—Metropolitan Expansion and Urban Corridors," *The Journal of Geography,* 1972, pp. 285–293.

HARRIES, KEITH D., "Population Change Trends in Large U. S. Metropolitan Areas, 1960–70: A Review," *The Journal of Geography,* December 1973, pp. 19–30.

HART, JOHN FRASER, "Urban Encroachment on Rural Areas," *Geographical Review,* 1976, pp. 1–17.

———, SALISBURY, NEIL E., and SMITH, EVERETT G., JR., "The Dying Village and Some Notions about Urban Growth," *Economic Geography,* 1968, pp. 343–349.

HOLZNER, LUTZ, "World Regions in Urban Geography," *Annals of the Association of American Geographers,* 1967, pp. 704–712.

JORDAN, TERRY G., "On the Nature of Settlement Geography," *The Professional Geographer,* 1966, pp. 26–28.

LEWIS, ROBERT A., and ROWLAND, RICHARD H., "Urbanization in Russia and the U.S.S.R.: 1897–1966," *Annals of the Association of American Geographers,* 1969, pp. 776–796.

MAYER, HAROLD M., and KOHN, CLYDE F., editors, *Readings in Urban Geography,* Chicago, 1959, 625 pp.

MITCHELL, JAMES K., "Adjustment to New Physical Environments Beyond the Metropolitan Fringe," *Geographical Review,* 1976, pp. 18–31.

MOOKHERJIE, DEBNATH, "Urbanization Pattern in India: 1951–1961," *The Professional Geographer,* 1969, pp. 308–314.

NORTHAM, RAY M., "Declining Urban Centers in the United States: 1940–1960," *Annals of the Association of American Geographers,* 1963, pp. 50–59.

PHILLIPS, PHILLIP D., "The Changing Standard Metropolitan Statistical Area," *The Journal of Geography,* 1976, pp. 165–173.

PILCHER, WILLIAM W., "The Dispersed Urban Community: The Case of the Portland Longshoremen," *Growth and Change,* July 1972, pp. 3–10.

PRED, ALLAN, "Diffusion, Organizational Spatial Structure, and City-System Development," *Economic Geography,* 1975, pp. 252–268.

———, "Industrialization, Initial Advantage, and American Metropolitan Growth," *Geographical Review,* 1965, pp. 158–185.

STEWART, CHARLES T., JR., "The Size and Spacing of Cities," *Geographical Review,* 1958, pp. 222–245.

WINID, B., "Problems of Towns: Patterns in Developing Countries," *The Professional Geographer,* 1967, pp. 15–16.

CHAPTER

cities: characteristics and relationships

The town of Eldora is situated in the glacial drift plains of central Iowa. It is primarily an agricultural service community, one of many in this part of the country. The central business district displays the most intensive land use and is surrounded by lower density residential land, which in turn is encircled by agricultural land used for mixed farming. (*Courtesy USDA, Soil Conservation Service.*)

Economic progress from subsistence to commerce has spawned thousands of service centers of various sizes. If all service centers were essentially alike, except for size, the story could end there. But even settlements of equal size can be markedly different in many respects and can be differently related to the regions around them. Because of the really sharp variations, and because cities are playing an ever-increasing role in human life, we should know something about their characteristics and relationships. The present chapter deals with these topics, observing them in one selected area—the United States. The main reason for this selection is that the United States Bureau of the Census collects and publishes the world's most detailed data on economic endeavor in cities of all sizes.

ECONOMIC ATTRIBUTES OF CITIES

Service centers differ from one another in many ways, some social, some physical, and some economic. It is the latter category of attributes that are of immediate interest to us, particularly volume of business, employment structure, and personal income.

Volume of Business

Beginning with the 1967 censuses, the United States Congress authorized that economic censuses be taken at five-year intervals. Economic censuses cover a variety of topics, but those of most interest in this chapter cover *retail trade*, *wholesale trade*, and *selected services*. These censuses describe trade and service activities in terms of number of establishments, value of sales, number of employees, and value of payroll.

Retail Trade Illustrative of the kind of information presented in the *Census of Retail Trade* is Table 27-1. Note that of the ten top retailing centers, only five are within that familiar northeast quadrant. This represents a significant departure from the long-standing tendency for the Northeast to dominate the retail trade picture. As we might expect, however, New York still constitutes the foremost retail trade market in the nation.

Ratio of Retail Sales per Capita Another useful indicator of retailing activity is the measure of volume of sales per inhabitant. For example, one would expect New York to rank first in Table 27-1 for the simple reason that it contains the largest number of customers who demand groceries, clothing, furniture, and gasoline. But does New York likewise rank first in terms of the retail sales/inhabitant ratio? The latest published data for this ratio appear in the *1972 Census of Retail Trade*. For the nation as a whole this ratio varies sharply among the cities and states. The ten cities with the largest volume of sales (Table 27-1) show considerable variation in sales per inhabitant. Detroit is well below the United States average, whereas Atlanta, a major retail trade center in the Southeast, is about 60 per cent above the national average. Even New York City is below the United States average. Reasons for variations of this sort are explained by a variety of factors, such as (a) competition from nearby retailing centers, (b) variations in personal income from region to region, and (c) the amount of tourist business or other outside income that comes into an area. This final point is illustrated by Nevada, which is not a large retailing state in absolute terms but is a leader in sales per inhabitant, in part because of its considerable tourist business (Table 27-2).

Table 27-1

Retail Trade: Selected Places Counted among the 250 Largest Cities Ranked by Volume of Sales, 1972

Place	1970 Population (Thousands)	Sales per Inhabitant	Sales (Millions)	Percentage of U.S. Total
U.S. TOTAL	203,211	2,258	459,040	100.0
The 250 largest cities	—	—	167,871	36.6
Ten largest cities				
New York	7,894	1,901	15,014	3.3
Chicago	3,366	2,226	7,494	1.6
Los Angeles	2,816	2,447	6,891	1.5
Houston	1,232	3,051	3,760	0.8
Philadelphia	1,948	1,835	3,575	0.8
Detroit	1,511	1,802	2,724	0.6
Dallas	844	3,010	2,541	0.6
Indianapolis	744	2,702	2,011	0.4
San Francisco	715	2,788	1,994	0.4
Atlanta	496	3,653	1,812	0.4

Source: Bureau of the Census, *1972 Census of Retail Trade* (1975).

Table 27-2

Retail Trade: States with Highest and Lowest Sales

State	Number of Establishments (Thousands)	Sales (Millions) of Dollars)	Percentage of Total U.S. Sales	Sales per Inhabitant
States with highest sales				
California	178	48,893	10.7	2,450
New York	158	39,173	8.5	2,148
Illinois	94	25,922	5.6	2,332
Texas	123	25,833	5.6	2,307
Pennsylvania	113	25,182	5.5	2,135
Ohio	91	22,890	5.0	2,148
Michigan	72	20,630	4.5	2,324
States with lowest sales				
Nevada	6	1,600	0.3	3,278
Delaware	5	1,480	0.3	2,700
South Dakota	8	1,316	0.3	1,978
North Dakota	7	1,275	0.3	2,066
Vermont	5	1,103	0.2	2,484
Wyoming	5	816	0.2	2,457
Alaska	3	772	0.2	2,573
U.S. TOTAL	1,913	459,040	100.0	2,258

Source: U.S. Bureau of the Census, *1972 Census of Retail Trade* (1975).

South Dakota, on the other hand, (a) is not an affluent state, (b) is not a major destination for tourists, and (c) has no ranking retail trade centers. Not surprisingly, South Dakota's sales per inhabitant are below the national average.

The *Census of Retail Trade* indicates for cities, counties and states not only the total amount of retail trade but also the level of individual types of business, such as grocery stores, gasoline service stations, eating places, and drug stores. Detailed data are now reported for major retail centers in SMSA's. Table 27-3 describes the sort of data which are available for SMSA's, individual cities within SMSA's, central business districts, and major retail centers with 100 or more retail establishments.

Wholesale Trade. The variation among cities in wholesale trade is not very different from that of retail trade. Table 27-4 indicates that of the 12 leading wholesaling centers only 6 are in the familiar northeast parallelogram. Remember that 5 of the 10 leading retailers were here. Clearly, a large number of wholesaling centers, such as Atlanta, Dallas, Minneapolis-St. Paul, San Francisco, and Los Angeles, achieve national prominence by supplying retailers in their parts of the nation.

A major difference between wholesaling and retailing is that the large metropolitan areas tend to concentrate more on wholesaling. For example, the New York SMSA has 5 per cent of the national population, does

4 per cent of the nation's retailing, but accounts for an astonishing 12 per cent of wholesale merchandising. However, if we compare Tables 27-2 and 27-5 we can observe that with progressively smaller states the disproportion between wholesaling and retailing tends to shrink until at last, among the smallest states, the sales of wholesalers are less than those of retailers. In other words, the economic activity of wholesaling is highly concentrated in a relatively few large states dispersed at great distances throughout the country, whereas retailing is less concentrated, appearing in many states, both large and small.[1]

Services. The *Census of Selected Service Industries* contains information on a host of service enterprises, such as hotels, laundries, beauty shops, barber shops, photography studios, funeral services, shoe repair ships, advertising offices, credit bureaus, auto repair garages, parking facilities, movie theaters, bowling alleys, and many others.

The Census shows that the service function differs considerably from one place to another. One might think, for example, that expenditures for amusement and recreation would vary from city to city in about the same fashion as population; that is, that New York would

[1] A suggested method for classifying cities in terms of the ratio between wholesale and retail functions appears in William Siddall's "Wholesale-Retail Trade Ratios as Indices of Urban Centrality," *Economic Geography*, 1961, pp. 124–132.

Table 27-3

Retail Trade Activity in the Los Angeles-Long Beach SMSA, 1972

Type of Business	Number of Establishments	Sales (Thousands of Dollars)
Retail stores, total	53,062	16,770,524
Building materials, hardware, garden supply, and mobile home dealers	1,757	540,850
Hardware stores	555	130,335
Other	1,202	410,515
General merchandise group stores	1,162	2,482,918
Department stores	216	2,210,082
Variety stores	416	152,910
Miscellaneous general merchandise stores	530	119,926
Food stores	5,703	3,643,167
Automotive dealers	3,185	3,409,354
Gasoline service stations	5,763	1,118,661
Apparel and accessory stores	4,975	981,504
Women's clothing, specialty stores, and furriers	2,195	413,335
Women's ready-to-wear stores	1,720	368,758
Men's and boys' clothing and furnishings stores	887	254,046
Family clothing stores	430	112,049
Shoe stores	881	165,388
Other apparel and accessory stores	582	36,686
Furniture, home furnishings, and equipment stores	4,143	856,230
Furniture stores	1,342	401,662
Home furnishings stores	1,228	151,781
Household appliance, radio, television, and music stores	1,573	302,787
Eating and drinking places	12,514	1,672,585
Eating places	9,453	1,451,589
Drinking places (alcoholic beverages)	3,061	220,996
Drug stores and proprietary stores	1,506	678,803
Miscellaneous retail stores	12,354	1,386,452
Liquor stores	2,142	541,725
Miscellaneous shopping goods stores	5,026	542,808
Florists	672	46,676

Source: Bureau of the Census, *1972 Census of Retail Trade* (1975).

do about 5 per cent of the nation's business, somewhat more than four times as much as Washington, which in turn would slightly exceed Boston and so on. But as Table 27-6 shows, New York accounts for 10 per cent of the motion picture receipts in the United States, two times its percentage of the nation's population, and Washington does three-quarters as much business of this type as does Boston. A still different pattern unfolds for other specific types of entertainment. For example, receipts from bowling alleys are noticeably higher in Chicago than anywhere else in the country, one-third

again as much as in New York. Detroit, in second place, is considerably ahead of third ranking Los Angeles.

Employment Structure

The term employment structure, as we have seen, refers to the way that the working population of a place is divided among the various categories of economic activity. The employment structure for the United States urban populace as a whole, given in the first column of Table 27-7, is a "datum plane," or criterion,

Table 27-4

Wholesale Trade: Selected Leading Standard Metropolitan Statistical Areas

Place	Thousands of Establishments	Sales (Millions of Dollars)	Percentage of National Sales
UNITED STATES TOTAL	370	$695,224	100
New York, N.Y.-N.J.	27	86,030	12
Chicago, Ill.	13	42,406	6
Los Angeles-Long Beach, Cal.	13	32,511	5
Detroit, Mich.	6	18,594	3
Philadelphia, Pa.-N.J.	8	18,493	3
San Francisco-Oakland, Cal.	6	17,818	3
Dallas-Fort Worth, Tex.	6	15,157	2
Boston, Mass.	6	14,907	2
Atlanta, Ga.	4	14,738	2
Houston, Tex.	4	12,805	2
Minneapolis-St. Paul, Minn. Wis.	4	11,726	2
St. Louis, Mo.-Ill.	4	11,314	2

Source: Bureau of the Census, *1972 Census of Wholesale Trade* (1975).

Table 27-5

Wholesale Trade: States with Highest and Lowest Sales

Place	Thousands of Establishments	Sales (Millions of Dollars)	Percentage of National Sales
UNITED STATES TOTAL	370	$695,224	100
States with highest sales			
New York	40	100,414	14
California	32	68,562	10
Illinois	21	52,805	8
Texas	24	42,189	6
Ohio	17	33,680	5
Pennsylvania	18	32,374	5
States with lowest sales			
Alaska	0.5	604	0.1
Vermont	0.7	670	0.1
Wyoming	0.8	718	0.1
Nevada	0.8	917	0.1
New Hampshire	1.1	1,145	0.2
New Mexico	1.8	1,515	0.2

Source: Bureau of the Census, *1972 Census of Wholesale Trade* (1975).

with which individual cities can be compared. The employment structures of 15 selected cities are also given in Table 27-7. Notice how they deviate from the national average and from one another.

For cities in general, manufacturing provides the most jobs, 25 per cent. Retail trade trails in second place

with 17 per cent of the jobs. Education accounts for 8 per cent.

The proportions are strikingly different from city to city, however. In Brawley, California, almost as many people work on farms as in retail establishments. Gloucester, Massachusetts, has a high percentage of population in fishing; nevertheless, its structure is dominated by manufacturing and retailing. In Hibbing, Minnesota, mining provides almost as many jobs as retailing, while in Kannapolis, North Carolina, the textile mills and other factories account for an amazing 66 per cent of all job opportunities. Conneaut, Ohio, is a leading transport city if we go by its employment structure. Downey, California, has twice the national percentage for wholesaling and Durant, Oklahoma, and Hollywood, Florida are both notable retailing centers. Notice the importance of finance in Hartford, entertainment and service employment in Las Vegas, medical employment in Rochester, educational employment in State College (termed "University Park" by some), Pennsylvania, and government workers in Washington, D.C.

Retail trade is the most universally important economic activity, ranking first in the employment structure of most cities. In those communities where some other line of endeavor ranks first, retailing almost invariably ranks second (except in rare instances such as Conneaut). Figure 27-1, part A, illustrates how employment structures can be portrayed graphically,

Table 27-6

Motion Picture Theaters: Receipts from Customers in the 12 Largest Standard Metropolitan Statistical Areas

Place	Number of Establishments	Receipts (Millions of Dollars)	Percentage of National Receipts
UNITED STATES TOTAL	11,670	$1,816	100
New York	457	180	10
Los Angeles-Long Beach	323	85	5
Chicago	220	74	4
Philadelphia	154	41	2
Detroit	131	34	2
San Francisco-Oakland	196	47	3
Washington	122	27	1
Boston	153	38	2
Pittsburgh	104	19	1
St. Louis	97	22	1
Baltimore	94	15	1
Cleveland	82	16	1

Source: Bureau of the Census, *1972 Census of Selected Service Industries* (1975).

Table 27-7

Employment Structures: Selected Service Centers with 10,000 or More Inhabitants

$\dfrac{\text{Employment}}{\text{Population}}$ Ratio (as a Percentage)	United States Urban 39	New York (SMSA) 58	Brawley, Calif. 32	Gloucester, Mass. 39	Hibbing, Minn. 35	Kannapolis N. Car. 51	Conneaut, Ohio 36	Downey, Calif. 46
Percentage employed in								
All activities	100	100	100	100	100	100	100	100
Agriculture, forestry, and fisheries	1	—	17	5	—	—	—	1
Mining	1	—	—	—	17	—	—	—
Construction	5	4	5	7	6	3	4	5
Manufacturing	25	21	7	25	9	66	41	31
Transportation, communications, and utilities	7	9	10	6	6	5	18	8
Wholesale trade	4	5	4	7	5	2	2	8
Retail trade	17	15	18	19	18	11	13	17
Finance, insurance, and real estate	6	9	2	3	4	2	3	5
Business and repair services	3	5	4	2	3	2	2	4
Entertainment and recreation services	1	1	1	1	1	—	—	1
Medical services	6	6	5	7	10	2	3	6
Education	8	7	11	6	8	3	6	5
Public administration	6	6	4	5	3	1	3	4
Other services	10	12	12	7	10	3	5	5

$\dfrac{\text{Employment}}{\text{Population}}$ Ratio (as a Percentage)	Durant, Okla. 38	Hartford, Conn. (SMSA) 43	Opelika, Ala. 42	Hollywood, Fla. 36	Las Vegas, Nev. (Urbanized Area) 40	Rochester, Minn. 44	State College, Penn. 38	Washington, D.C. 44
Percentage employed in								
All activities	100	100	100	100	100	100	100	100
Agriculture, forestry, and fisheries	2	1	1	1	1	1	1	—
Mining	1	—	—	—	—	—	—	—
Construction	6	6	4	12	8	5	2	5
Manufacturing	13	29	42	11	4	16	6	5
Transportation, communications, and utilities	6	4	5	8	7	4	2	6
Wholesale trade	6	4	3	4	2	2	1	2
Retail trade	20	15	15	21	17	18	12	12
Finance, insurance, and real estate	3	12	3	7	4	3	2	5
Business and repair services	2	3	2	4	7	2	3	4
Entertainment and recreation services	1	1	—	2	6	1	1	1
Medical services	7	6	3	6	3	27	2	6
Education	19	8	7	5	5	7	44	8
Public administration	5	5	3	4	6	3	2	27
Other services	9	6	12	15	30	11	22	19

Source: Bureau of the Census, 1970 Census of Population, *Characteristics of the Population* (1973).

using the urban United States, New York, and Hartford as examples.

Classification by Total Employment. In terms of employment structure, cities can be classified in many ways. One system employs letter symbols for the various types of economic activity—M for manufacturing, R for retail trade, T for transportation, N for mining, E for education, D for medical, and so forth—and lists the two (or more) leading categories for each city. According to this system, New York would be classified

MR, indicating that manufacturing and retailing provide, in that order, the most jobs. Hibbing would be classified RN, since retailing and mining are its leading sectors. (Some Swedish geographers have prepared an ingenious map showing both the size and function of cities in Europe in terms of total employment structures. Printed in four colors on a very large scale with intricate symbols, the map is not amenable to black-and-white reproduction. Yet, this wall map produced by William-Olsson and entitled *Economic Map of Europe*, is so noteworthy an example of the mapping of urban settlements by size and employment structure that every economic geographer should be familiar with it.)

Differentials from National Average. But what if we inquire into the activities that are distinctive in a city, that is, the endeavors in which it exceeds the national average by the widest margin? Downey, California, for example, in the system described above, would be classified MR, since manufacturing and retail trade account for 31 and 17 per cent, respectively, of the jobs in town. Now, when we compare Downey's percentages in the several employment categories (Table 27-7) with the national averages, we discover a positive differential of 6 in manufacturing (31 per cent against the national average of 25 per cent) and no differential in retail trade (17 per cent minus 17 per cent). Wholesale trade, however, has a positive differential of 4 and is, in relative terms, more conspicuous than retail trade. Downey would be classified according to the *positive differential system* as MW, the leading activities in terms of positive differentials being manufacturing and wholesaling. On the same basis, Hartford, Connecticut, would be FM (finance and manufacturing), whereas by total employment it would be MR (manufacturing and retailing).

Part B of Figure 27-1, which uses as examples the employment structures of Hibbing, New York, and Hartford, strikingly reveals the contrast between structures built up in terms of differentials and those founded on total employment.[2]

Standard Deviations. Still another perspective on employment structures is provided by use of the statistical technique of *standard deviation.* Standard deviation is a measure of the average variability of a group of values from the average value, or mean. A detailed explanation of *standard deviation* can be found in any elementary textbook on statistics, but for our purposes here we can say that it is computed by adding up the squares of the *differences* of all values from the mean, dividing that sum by the number of those values, and determining the square root of that quotient. Or, in algebraic symbols,

$$SD = \sqrt{\frac{\Sigma\,d^2}{N}}$$

in which Σ = sum, d = difference between each value and the mean, and N = number of values.

Geographer Howard Nelson, applying this device to 1950 Census data on employment structures, found, for example, that the standard deviation[3] of employment in retail trade in the United States is 3.63. If a city's percentage of employment in retail trade is equal to the national average plus 3.63, then Nelson classified the city in the R category. If its percentage exceeds the

[2]Further treatment of this method appears in Leigh Pownall's "Functions of New Zealand Towns," *Annals of the Association of American Geographers*, 1953, pp. 332–350.

[3]To be truly "standard" the standard deviation should refer to areas under the normal curve. Of the distributions used by Nelson, only retail trade was normally distributed.

Figure 27-1 *Symbols: A agriculture, forestry, and fishing, MI mining, MA manufacturing, T transportation, communications and utilities, W wholesale trade, R retail trade, FI finance, insurance and real estate, EN entertainment and recreation services, ME medical services, ED education, C construction, BR business and repair services, PA public administration, OS other services.*

EMPLOYMENT STRUCTURES

A. TOTAL EMPLOYMENT

B. DIFFERENTIAL EMPLOYMENT ABOVE THE AVERAGE

national average by 7.26 (two standard deviations—2×3.63) then it is classified R2; if by 10.89 or more (three or more standard deviations), then the city is classified R3. In sum, a single letter symbol indicates an excess of at least one deviation but less than two; the arabic numeral 2 following the letter indicates at least 2, but not 3, deviations; the numeral 3 indicates 3 or more deviations; and more than one letter symbol indicates the city exceeds the average by more than one deviation in more than one category.

Accordingly, Hartford is classified F3 because employment there in the financial category exceeds the national average by more than three standard deviations and because in no other activity does it top the average by as much as one standard deviation. A city that exceeds the national average in no activity by so much as a single deviation is put in the D category—diversified. Selected examples of cities classified by the Nelson system are given in Table 27-8.

Actually, we can construct maps (like Figure 27-2) based on the Nelson classification system. Remember, though, that the appearance of a city on any one map does *not* mean that the indicated activity is the city's principal source of jobs. For instance, Trinidad, Colorado, is on the mining map, but mining is *not* its foremost endeavor (actually retail trade was first). It means, in this case, that Trinidad's percentage of miners exceeds the average by more than one standard deviation.[4]

Personal Income

Annual personal incomes vary considerably from place to place. The average per capita income in the United States is about $5400, but the figure is highly variable, from $7479 in Washington, D C., and $7023 in Alaska to $3764 in Mississippi. The highest per capita income in any large American urban area is $7800 in Bridgeport, Connecticut. Other ranking centers are Nassau-Suffolk, New York ($7200); Newark, New Jersey ($7000); and San Francisco-Oakland, California ($6900). Large centers with low incomes are Charleston, South Carolina ($4000); Mobile, Alabama ($4100); and $4200 in both El Paso and Corpus Christi, Texas. In general, manufactural cities tend to have a distinctly higher per capita income than any other type of city.

Whether the economic character of tertiary centers be appraised in terms of retailing, wholesaling, services, employment structure, or personal income, it is clear that urban settlements vary considerably. But research needs to be done to extract geographic principles from the wealth of data available in United States Census volumes. More on this later under the *economic base concept*.

[4]An interesting method for classifying towns in terms of a "functional index" and a "specialization index" has been presented by John Webb in "Basic Concepts in the Analysis of Small Urban Centers of Minnesota," *Annals of the Association of American Geographers*, 1959, pp. 55–72.

Table 27-8

Economic Classification of Selected American Cities: Nelson System

New York	F2
Chicago	F
Los Angeles	F
Philadelphia	F
Detroit	Mf
Boston	F
San Francisco, Oakland	F2
Pittsburgh	D
St. Louis	Ps
Cleveland	D
Washington	Pb3, F
Baltimore	D
Minneapolis-St. Paul	F2, W
Milwaukee	D
Cincinnati	D
Buffalo	D
Houston	F
Kansas City	F
New Orleans	T, W, F
Seattle	F2
Alisal, California	W3
Asbury Park, New Jersey	Ps3, R, Pb
Atlanta, Georgia	F2
Brockton, Massachusetts	Mf
Butte, Montana	Mi3
Cheyenne, Wyoming	T3, Pb2
Conneaut, Ohio	T3
Dallas, Texas	F3, W
Denver, Colorado	W, F
Durant, Oklahoma	R2
Hanford, California	R3
Hartford, Connecticut	F3
Hibbing, Minnesota	Mi3
Hollywood, Florida	Ps3, F3
Kannapolis, North Carolina	Mf2
Kearney, Nebraska	R3, Pf2, Ps2, W
Las Vegas, Nevada	Ps3
Madison, Wisconsin	Pf2, Pb, F
Minot, North Dakota	R, T, W
State College, Penn.	Pf3, Ps

Source: Howard Nelson, "A Service Classification of American Cities," *Economic Geography*, 1955, pp. 205–210.

D	diversified	Pf	professional services
F	finance	Ps	personal services
Mf	manufacturing	R	retail trade
Mi	mining	T	transportation
Pb	public administration	W	wholesale trade

3—City employment exceeds national urban average by 3 or more standard deviations

2—City employment exceeds national urban average by 2 standard deviations

Absence of numeral indicates the excess is at least 1 standard deviation

ASSOCIATIONS OF TERTIARY ACTIVITY WITH OTHER PHENOMENA

Internal Relationships

As tertiary endeavor takes root and proliferates in a place, several other phenomena flourish too, and, because of their variation from place to place, add distinctive qualities to service centers.

Six of these phenomena will be discussed in the pages to follow: numbers of inhabitants, changes in numbers of inhabitants, amount of land occupied by the service center, shape of the land occupied, types of usage to which that land is put, and morphology of the settlement.

Number of Inhabitants. Generally speaking, there is a strong correlation between job opportunities and population; the larger the number of jobs, the larger the population. It is not surprising therefore to find that the number of jobs in New York (the nation's largest trade center) exceeds the number in Los Angeles, which slightly exceeds that in Chicago. Yet the covariance is not exact. If it were, the labor force of every city would equal 39 per cent of its populace—the national average. The remaining 61 per cent fall in various classes, such as housewives, school pupils, retried persons, or inmates of penal institutions. But this ratio, known as the *E/P ratio* (employment/population), varies from city to city. Computation based on a sampling of cities indicates that ratios vary widely from place to place (see Table 27-7). On the high side are New York (58) and Kannapolis, North Carolina (51), whereas Brawley, California's ratio is only 32, and Hibbing, Minnesota's is 35.

A minority of Americans are free to choose their place of residence quite apart from the question of job opportunities. Retired pensioners, for example, can often settle anywhere since their income follows them. Many choose communities with amenable climates, such as Santa Cruz, California. One might suppose,

then, that these communities would have an extremely low E/P ratio. But what happens is that the pensioners create a demand for grocery stores, clothing stores, barber shops, and other businesses. The E/P ratio of 34.0 for Santa Cruz, for instance, is lower than the average but not as low as might be supposed.

Changes in Number of Inhabitants. Tertiary settlements differ in their population changes. For example, in 1970 the three urban places of Johnstown, Pennsylvania; Rockville, Maryland; and Newark, Ohio, each had about 42,000 inhabitants. By size alone, they would appear to be three of a kind. But by population *change* they are three entirely different breeds, as shown in Table 27-9; Johnstown is shrinking, Newark is holding rather steady, and Rockville is gaining.

Figure 27-3 illustrates one type of mapping that can be done on the basis of change. Wisconsin had 514

Table 27-9

Population Change: Selected Cities

Place	Number of Inhabitants 1970	1960	Change
Johnstown, Pa.	42,476	53,949	−21.3%
Rockville, Md.	41,583	26,090	+59.4%
Newark, Ohio	41,822	41,790	+ 0.1%

Source: U.S. Bureau of the Census, *County and City Data Book* (1974).

Figure 27-2

CITIES DISTINGUISHED BY EMPLOYMENT IN SELECTED ACTIVITIES

MANUFACTURING

MINING

WHOLESALE TRADE

FINANCE, INSURANCE, REAL ESTATE

· EXCEEDS AVERAGE BY 1 STANDARD DEVIATION

● EXCEEDS AVERAGE BY 2 OR MORE STANDARD DEVIATIONS

tertiary centers of which 112 lost population between 1940 and 1950, and 402 gained. The gainers are depicted with circles proportional to their increments. Two large gainers stand out—Milwaukee and Madison. The smaller gainers are widely dispersed throughout the state. The 112 losers show an entirely different pattern. Nearly all of them are in the northern and western parts of the state. This pattern is consistent with what we have learned in previous chapters about Wisconsin: the southeastern portion is a region of intense manufacturing, high-value agriculture, high railway traffic density, low freight rates, and a high degree of urbanism; the northwestern section tends to be just the opposite on all of these counts.

There is some correlation between rate of population change and the distinctive economic activities of cities. Manufactured cities are experiencing much smaller growth rates than are cities whose characteristic employment categories are retail trade, finance, and professional and other services. This has been the case since the 1940's, as can be seen by inspection of Table 27-10 in which the vertical columns are identified by symbols in the Nelson system.

Amount of Land. One might suppose that the more people in a service center, the greater its acreage. This correlation tends to hold for urbanized areas, since the largest urbanized area (New York with over 16,000,000 people) also covers the most land (2425 square miles). But a study of all urbanized areas reveals that the least population does not correlate with the least land. In the former case Harlingen-San Benito, Texas, has 50,469 people on 34 square miles of land; in the latter Owensboro, Kentucky, harbors 53,133 residents on 12 square miles of land.

If land and population covaried closely, service centers of the same population should cover the same amount of land, and places the same size should have similar populations. Yet the Oshkosh and Sherman-Denison urbanized areas, each with 55,000 people, cover 13 and 35 square miles, respectively; and Muncie, Indiana, and Simi Valley, California each encompass 25 square miles of land, yet their populations are 90,000 and 57,000, respectively.

One way to express this relationship is by the ratio of population per square mile. Put together, all the nation's urbanized areas have 118,446,566 people on 35,081 square miles of land, or a ratio of 3,376 people per square mile. At one extreme is New York with a density of 6,683, at the other is Vineland-Millville, New Jersey, with 863.

The question now becomes: Is there any relationship between area and population density? For example, do larger cities tend to be more densely or less densely occupied?

We can portray such covariation in a *scatter diagram* (see page 000 for an explanation of this device), as in Figure 27-4. Each city is represented by a dot, the position of which is determined by the two variables—area in square miles and inhabitants per square mile.

If both population and area increased consistently with size of cities, then the dots in Figure 27-4 would lie in a *straight* line, and that line would be *horizontal* at whatever level prevailed as the urban density per square

Figure 27-3

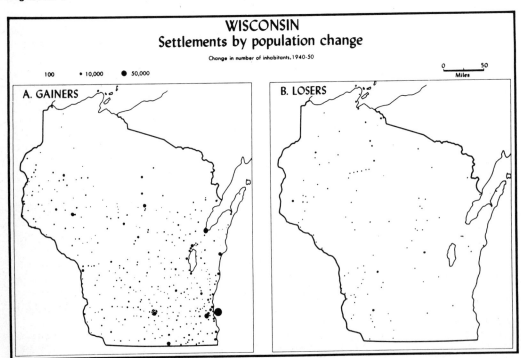

WISCONSIN
Settlements by population change
Change in number of inhabitants, 1940-50

100 •10,000 ●50,000

0 50
Miles

A. GAINERS

B. LOSERS

Table 27-10

Averages of Various Criteria by Economic Classification of Cities

Criteria	All Cities	Mf3 & Mf2	R3 & R2	Pf3 & Pf2	T3 & T2	Mi3 & Mi2	Pb3 & Pb2	Ps3 & Ps2	W3 & W2	F3 & F2
Percentage increase in population, 1940–50	27.9	2.2	39.4	65.0	17.5	31.1	40.0	61.0	30.4	35.6
Percentage 65 years old or older	8.6	7.6	9.0	7.6	9.7	7.4	7.3	9.2	7.7	10.0
Average years of school completed	10.0	8.9	10.5	12.3	10.4	9.7	10.8	11.0	9.9	11.1
Participation in labor force, percentage of males	77.8	82.8	77.1	55.8	78.0	79.2	77.8	73.2	80.0	75.6
Participation in labor force, percentage of females	32.8	35.9	30.3	34.1	29.2	27.1	33.0	33.3	33.0	34.6
Median income	$2643	$3134	$2560	$1674	$2733	$2822	$2658	$2227	$2566	$2780

Source: Howard J. Nelson, "Some Characteristics of the Population of Cities in Similar Service Classifications," *Economic Geography* (1957), page 97.

mile. But this is not the case. If, however, though population and land both increased with city size, but population did so at a faster rate, then the dots on the scatter diagram would conform with a line that trended upward from left to right. That no such line emerges on

Figure 27-4

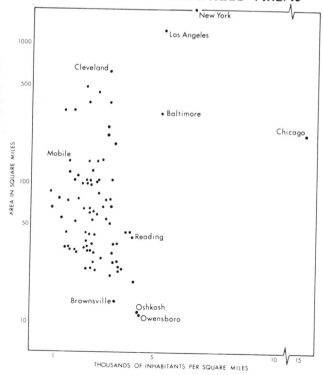

SCATTER DIAGRAM UNITED STATES URBANIZED AREAS

Figure 27-4 leads to the conclusion that population and amount of land in urbanized areas do not covary spatially at as high a degree as might be supposed.[5]

Types of Land Usage. Service centers clearly differ markedly in the use of land, though data on this point are scanty. The United States Census, for instance, contains very little on land usage. Still, a sample investigation of American cities by Harland Bartholomew and Jack Wood for the Harvard Planning Studies reveals some interesting correlations between this variable and city size (see Table 27-11). Multiple-family dwellings (residences with three or more families) occupy an increasing percentage of land as size of city increases. Other uses that tend to covary positively with population are parks and playgrounds, heavy industry, light industry, and commercial uses. Conversely, some uses shrink relatively as size increases: single family residential areas, public and semipublic uses (such as schools and churches), streets, and vacant land.

Notice the high percentages in streets. Few realize that, in most cities, streets occupy over 20 per cent of the land whereas commercial structures rarely take up more than 4 per cent. On a national average, housing spreads out over approximately two-fifths of a city's territory.

But all these uses vary spatially. As a result of a policy of unusually wide streets in St. Petersburg, Florida, 57 per cent of the city is composed of streets; at the opposite pole is Bar Harbor, Maine, with only 16

[5]See Chester Smolski, "A Study in Sampling: City Size and Population Density," *The Professional Geographer*, March 1962, pp. 8–10, for further analysis of this relationship.

per cent in streets. Bartholomew and Wood indicate ranges in other uses as follows:

Commercial usage varies from 1.7 per cent in St. Petersburg to 6.5 per cent in West Palm Beach. Residential use covers 64 per cent of Bar Harbor, and only 24 per cent of Utica, New York. Heavy industry spreads over 14 per cent of Newark but is entirely absent in Santa Fe, New Mexico.

The Shape (Outline) of Service Centers. Cities assume a variety of shapes which are related to both physical and cultural factors.

The *strassendorf* (or shoe-string) type is much longer on one axis than the other and usually appears in valleys —numerous towns in Switzerland and West Virginia are examples. West Palm Beach, Florida (Figure 27-5), has a tendency toward linear shape.

Rectangular communities generally occur where the terrain is rather flat *and* where cultural attitudes have decreed that the land be divided into rectangular "blocks." as in Des Moines, Iowa (Figure 27-5).

Circular shapes are often found in old cities that were once surrounded by a wall, or where the main streets all converge on the settlement's center, like spokes on a wheel.

The star shape appears in large cities that are major transport centers; settlement tends to creep out along the transport routes, as in Lexington, Kentucky.

Crescent-shaped cities sometimes develop around the end of a body of water.

In addition to these simple types there are complex or irregular shapes that indicate responses to a combination of influences. Figure 27-5 shows how different the shapes of several selected urbanized areas are. The particular shape of any specific city is explained by its relationships to both physical features (for instance, the ocean front at Atlantic City and St. Petersburg, rugged terrain at Wilkes-Barre, waterways at Huntington-Ashland) and cultural features (main line railways and highways and annexation policies at Phoenix).

The *morphology* of a city is its "anatomy," the physical form and structure—including street layout, spacing of buildings, size and architectural design of buildings, types and color of building materials, presence or absence of an encircling wall, and so forth. Surely, cities vary enough in these respects from one part of the world to another to enable us to classify them scientifically on the basis of morphology. Such a classification, were it available, might well serve as a basis for delimiting urban regions of the entire world.[6]

In addition to numbers of people, changes in population, amount of land, uses of land, shapes of the settlement, and morphology, service centers differ in other ways, such as (a) percentage of population that is foreign-born white, (b) percentage of population that is nonwhite, and (c) median school years completed by persons 25 years of age and older.

All these internal variables need to be investigated before we can understand their relationship to the economic life of a service center. But even that will not

[6]Illustrative of what can be done in this direction for one part of the world is Robert Dickinson's book, *The West European City*, Routledge and Kegan Paul, Ltd., London, 1951.

Table 27-11

Mean Percentage of Land Usage in Selected Cities by Size

Land Use	Under 50,000	50,000 to 100,000	100,000 to 250,000	Over 250,000
Number of cities studied	28	13	7	5
All land (percentage)	100	100	100	100
Mean percentage in following uses:				
Residential, one family	34.0	31.0	36.0	28.0
Residential, two families	3.7	4.1	3.6	6.8
Residential, three plus	1.7	2.1	2.2	4.9
Commercial	3.1	2.6	2.9	4.3
Light industry	2.8	2.1	2.4	3.8
Heavy industry	2.9	2.7	3.5	4.7
Railways	5.0	4.9	5.4	4.4
Parks, playgrounds	5.1	6.5	5.7	8.6
Public and semipublic	13.3	10.9	11.2	9.6
Streets	28.3	33.3	27.6	24.8
Vacant	47.0	38.9	21.9	20.4

Source: Harland Bartholomew and Jack Wood, *Land Uses in American Cities*, Harvard Planning Studies, Vol. XV, 1955, Tables 1, 2, 3, and 4.

be enough. We also need to know how a city is related to other places.

External Relationships

The external relationships of a service center link it to areas of surplus production of some sort. And the link is accomplished by means of transportation arteries over which people travel and surplus goods are shipped. We shall take up these linkages first insofar as they relate to primary production, transportation routes, and topographic features.

Primary Production. Cities ultimately depend for their life upon the surplus production of farmers, miners, foresters, and fishermen. But before surpluses of wheat, iron ore, logs, and salmon can be consumed, they must be processed, or manufactured. This need gives birth to service centers whose residents (a) assemble surpluses, (b) change the form of some of the commodities, or (c) ship them on to other service centers, and, in either case, (d) in return distribute tractors, overalls, shoes, flour, and so on to the farmers and other primary producers. Thus, a chain is welded together whereby primary production, transportation,

manufacturing, and servicing are all interrelated. If we synthesized the information presented in preceding chapters we would discover a striking correlation between the urban regions on Figure 26-3 and regions of commercial agriculture, mining, forestry, fishing, manufacturing, transportation, and international trade. But the foundation of the whole complex is a solid base of surplus primary production. "Cities do not grow up of themselves. Countrysides set them up to do tasks that must be performed in central places." So wrote Mark Jefferson over forty-five years ago. And the people in these countrysides must be generating an excess before they can pay for the services performed for them in tertiary service centers.

A strong correlation also exists between the *mechanization* of primary production and urbanization. The more highly mechanized the agriculture, forestry, and mining of a region, the greater its tendency to urbanize. Not only does mechanization enable the production of a greater surplus, which leads to increase of city services, it also unshackles numerous rural laborers for city jobs. As a result, mechanized primary production stimulates migration from rural to urban places.

Figure 27-5

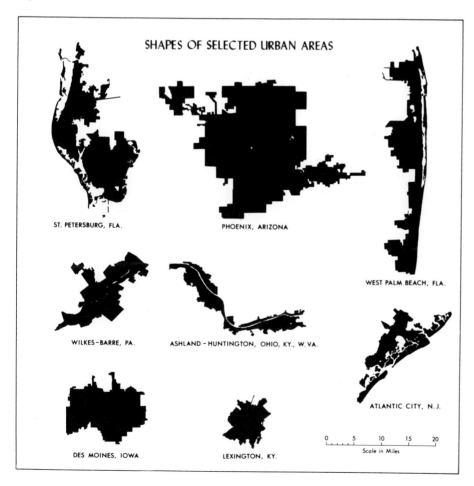

SHAPES OF SELECTED URBAN AREAS

ST. PETERSBURG, FLA.

PHOENIX, ARIZONA

WEST PALM BEACH, FLA.

WILKES-BARRE, PA.

ASHLAND - HUNTINGTON, OHIO, KY., W. VA.

ATLANTIC CITY, N.J.

DES MOINES, IOWA

LEXINGTON, KY.

0 5 10 15 20
Scale in Miles

Transportation Routes. Service centers normally develop at junctions of transportation routes. Typical examples are *road crossings* (as illustrated by thousands of hamlets at rural crossroads), road *junctions* with railways (as in numerous villages and towns), road crossings of nonnavigable streams (as at fords, which so frequently lent their names—Rockford, Oxford, and Brantford), *river ports* where roads or railways cross navigable streams (Cincinnati, St. Louis, and Duisburg), *railheads* where a railway line ends and roads or water routes converge upon it (as at Faith, South Dakota), *railway junctions* (Kansas City), and *heads of navigation* where waterways make their deepest penetration of a land mass in convergence with roads and railways (London and Chicago). Finally, the world's greatest cities tend to be near the heads of navigation for ocean vessels.

Generally, the greater the convergence of traffic, the larger the service center. Chicago illustrates this point well. Located at the ultimate intrusion by the Great Lakes into the productive interior of America (which had a surplus first of furs and timber and then of agricultural products), Chicago quickly shot out roads and then railroads in all directions from its waterfront. As it happened, the railroads building eastward from Chicago soon linked up with those heading westward from New York. This is the real explanation of Chicago's position as a railway center, not the widely held fallacy that railroads had to bend around Lake Michigan as they penetrated westward from the East Coast.

In some places, service centers are lined up along the busiest transport routes like beads on a string. Witness, for example, the string of cities from Buffalo to Albany along a route that contains a canal, a railway, a highway, and a thruway. A chain of smaller cities stretches in almost a straight line from St. Louis to Indianapolis along the old national turnpike of the 1800's and the present-day main line of the Pennsylvania Railroad as well as U.S. Highway 40.

Topography. There is scarcely any correlation between topography and the location of service centers on a world scale. Most city builders have preferred flat sites, so most cities are on plains. Still there are vast plains with no cities, and many hilly areas that do have large settlements. Even the flat-sites principle needs qualification; for centuries, hilltop sites were preferred for protective reasons. After all, assailants could sack a valley town more readily than one built on an impregnable hilltop. Even today in Italy and numerous countries of southern Europe and the Middle East (where urbanism first became extensive) the typical location for villages and many towns is the summit of a hill.

But with the transportation revolution, railways, highways, and canals snaked their way through valleys more readily than across hilltops; and, with improvements in social mores and in law and order, the value of hilltops for protection began to shrink while the value of valley sites for access to transportation rose. Consequently, urban centers that have developed since 1800 have tended to be located in valleys. Urban New York State, Pennsylvania, and California illustrate the tendency of modern cities to attach themselves to valley sites.

The actual movement along transportation routes between a center of tertiary economic activity and other areas is reciprocal with both outbound and inbound phases.

Outbound Movements

Commodities. How a city is linked to other places through the outward movement of a particular commodity (say, the circulation, by counties, of a Chicago daily newspaper) is shown in Figure 27-6. Even a casual inspection of this map raises several questions. For example, why the sharp break in circulation at the Missouri border? Why does the *Tribune* penetrate farther into Iowa than into Minnesota? Why the particular pattern in Michigan? Why is the penetration into southwestern Indiana greater than into southeastern Indiana? Since nearly every daily newspaper releases information on its circulation, we can make fascinating maps of the areas tied to a city through this medium.

Service centers large enough to have post offices can also provide accurate maps showing the exact boundaries of rural delivery. Similarly, we can easily map regions that receive gas, electricity, and telephone service from an urban center.

Concept of Nodal Regions. The circulation of newspapers is a good example to illustrate the concept of nodal regions. *A nodal region is a portion of the earth's surface that is homogeneous in relationship to a node, or central point.* In a sense, Figure 27-6 is the pattern of one nodal region, specifically the one tied by circulation of the *Tribune* to the focal point of Chicago.

Figure 27-7 illustrates how a different criterion—that of *dominance* of newspaper circulation—can be used to delimit nodal regions. Lines are drawn, not around the entire area into which a newspaper circulates, but only around the area in which that paper outsells every other competitor. Accordingly, the Milwaukee nodal region on Figure 27-7 is not the area within which Milwaukee newspapers circulate but rather the area in which they dominate the newspaper market. Thus, even though Chicago papers circulate widely in Wisconsin, the Chicago nodal region as shown on Figure 27-7 is restricted to an extremely small area in the southeast corner of the state tucked in behind the nodal regions of Milwaukee, Racine, Kenosha, and Beloit.

As this map illustrates, most nodal regions contain the city they focus on; however, it is possible for a nodal region to exist without containing its node. Note that one small detached segment of the Milwaukee nodal region is on the tip of Door Peninsula (northeast of the Green Bay Region), and a large detached piece occupies the north-central part of Wisconsin.

Nodes by no means need occur in the center of their regions. Notice how far off-center Madison is in its nodal area, LaCrosse, Chippewa Falls, and Superior in theirs. A principle holds that a city's nodal region will extend farther on the side of weaker competition; for instance, Madison's area extends only 20 miles to the east because of intense competition from Milwaukee papers, but it spreads out 80 miles to the west and northwest where there is much weaker competition. Similarly, the Milwaukee region protrudes much farther to the northwest than to the west (where Madison heads it off) or to the north where several sizable cities (Green Bay, Appleton, Oshkosh, and Fond du Lac) all bid successfully for local readers.

Although the foregoing illustration of nodal regions has been cast in terms of outward movements, the concept could be shown to apply equally well to inbound traffic.

People. Cities, towns, villages, and even hamlets are linked with other places through the travels of their residents: commuters who go elsewhere to work, citizens who go to nearby towns to shop, young folks who go to school in other settlements, traveling salesmen whose work sends them ranging over territories of varying sizes.

For one of these types of movement we have the useful concept of the *employment field*, that is, the area to which the residents of a settlement commute to work. Illustrative of this concept is Figure 27-8, which shows the location of the Natick, Massachusetts, employment field (or labor field), as mapped by Vance in 1960.

Money. Money (including credit) flows out from service centers for numerous reasons. At present it is impossible to measure the total outflow from a city without going directly to every individual and agency

Figure 27-6

WISCONSIN: NODAL REGIONS OF DAILY NEWSPAPER CIRCULATION

- Nodal city in Wisconsin

— Boundary of nodal region

▨ Milwaukee nodal region

Figure 27-7

Figure 27-8

NATICK, MASSACHUSETTS, LABOR FIELD

NEW HAMPSHIRE

BOSTON

CONN.

R.I.

Natick residents move to work by
- Auto
- Auto and/or bus
- Auto and/or bus and/or rail
- Natick

within the place to ask them how much money they send out of the city each year, for what purposes, and where they send it. Such a task is formidable; however, the research staff of *Fortune* magazine did exactly that in Oskaloosa, Iowa, in the late 1930's. They discovered that the 10,000 inhabitants of the town sent out $9,093,000 in one year. Most of this ($8,549,000) was sent out by business firms in payment for the merchandise

that stocked their shelves. Only a small amount ($391,000) was spent elsewhere by Oskaloosa customers. A still smaller amount left Oskaloosa through government agencies—for instance, the United States Post Office and several county offices.

Inbound Movements

Commodities. Goods stream into a city, some for local consumption, some for distribution throughout the hinterland, and others for processing in factories before shipment elsewhere. Comparatively little research has been done on such movements; however, some information is available. Figure 27-9 shows the location of the area from which milk moved into Madison, Wisconsin—that is, the "Madison milk shed."

People. Inbound human traffic consists of three major streams: those going *through* the city, those going *to* it in order to work, and those going *to* it to shop. To be sure, there are other categories, but they are mere trickles compared to these three.

Inbound *through* traffic is relatively insignificant for large cities. Even the most hurried tourist tends to stop for at least some purchases in a metropolis. As investigations of highway traffic have revealed, the correlation between the size of a city and the percentage of inbound highway traffic that is just going through is inverse (or negative); the *smaller* the city, the more cars will simply pass on.

Commuters link a city to a surrounding area that may extend outwards for a surprising distance. A survey of the General Motors Automotive Division in La Grange, Illinois, revealed that laborers commuted from as far away as the city of Dwight, 67 miles to the southwest. (Workers residing in Dwight drove a total of 33,500 miles a year just travelling to and from work.) A map of automobile commuting to this one factory would have shown workers driving as far as 60 miles from the north, 45 miles from the northwest, 46 miles from the west, 67 miles from the southwest, 52 miles from the south, and 35 miles from Indiana to the east. Railway commuters to some service centers travel even further.

The term *labor shed* is commonly applied to the area from which a city draws commuting labor. A great deal of study has been given to this concept in recent years, largely because consideration of journey-to-work patterns is such an important part of the "trip making" studies produced by transportation planners and other urban analysts.[7] Many of the research reports on this topic use data from the special *Journey to Work* reports which are published by the Bureau of the Census.

The concepts of labor shed and employment field

---

[7]Excellent examples are studies by James E. Vance, Jr., "Labor-shed, Employment Field, and Dynamic Analysis in Urban Geography," *Economic Geography*, 1960, pp. 189–220; Richard E. Lonsdale, "Two North Carolina Commuting Patterns," *Economic Geography*, 1966, pp. 114–138; and Brian J. L. Berry, *Growth Centers in the American Urban System*, Cambridge, Mass., 1973.

are useful in distinguishing, on a *functional basis*, two types of settlements that develop in the countryside surrounding a large city. One type is the *satellite*, which can be defined as a settlement whose labor shed exceeds its employment field. The other type is the *suburb*, in which the relationship is reversed. Notice that these definitions of suburb and satellite are based on their functional relationship to other places and not on their political status or on popular terminology. That is, the general public may consider some specific settlement to be a suburb when in terms of function it is actually a satellite.

BART (Bay Area Rapid Transit) commuters board a three-car train in Oakland. The specially designed cars now serve much of the East Bay region, connecting the urban centers there with each other and with the city of San Francisco by means of elevated and subway tracks, as well as by a tunnel beneath the Bay itself. The system is almost entirely computer-operated. (*Courtesy Bay Area Rapid Transit.*)

AN URBAN MILK SHED

Figure 27-9

Figure 27-10

HOMETOWNS OF PATIENTS
AT JACKSON CLINIC
Madison, Wisconsin

The inbound flow of *customers* to a city is sometimes as great as that of commuters and may link a city to an enormous area. In Figure 27-10 we illustrate this relationship by portraying the places with which Madison, Wisconsin, is connected by virtue of patronage of one of its medical institutions.

Money. Customers bring money into a city when they arrive to shop. Additional sums arrive by mail or wire for commodities that are shipped out or for services rendered. In the Oskaloosa project mentioned earlier, the investigators discovered that $9,432,000 poured into Oskaloosa in one year. Of this amount, $8,223,000 resulted from sales outside the town by trade, service, and manufacturing firms; $820,000 was taken in by citizens either through investments elsewhere or through labor on farms or in other service centers; and $389,000 was released locally by government agencies.

Tourism. In recent years, the economy of many service centers has been geared to the intake of money from tourism; today many a settlement renders services not so much to people in the immediate hinterland as to travelers from afar. Many communities in Arizona, Nevada, Montana, and northern Wisconsin, and such overseas localities as Lourdes, France, and Positano, Italy, thrive on an increasing number of tourists. Tourism is such a new phenomenon that only in recent years have scientific studies been made of it. But research that has been done turns up some surprises. In Arizona, for example, tourism is a leading industry in bringing money

393

into the state. Tourists and other travelers, including large numbers of winter visitors from the northeastern United States, annually spend an estimated $680,000,000 as follows:

Food and beverages	$195,000,000
Lodging	128,000,000
Gas, oil, and repairs	130,000,000
Other retail	97,000,000
Public transportation	53,000,000
Amusement, recreation	45,000,000
Personal and other services	32,000,000
	$680,000,000

Tourism has been the salvation of a number of Arizona communities that came into being as mining centers and then faced extinction when these activities were discontinued. Tombstone, Jerome, and Bisbee are all one-time mining towns which are now heavily dependent upon tourist dollars.

A similar story could be told for northern Minnesota, northern Michigan, upper New York, and northern New England where the residents of a host of small service centers earn a living from tourists from Boston, New York, Philadelphia, and other cities to the south.

Trade Area. The region from which a business establishment's customers come or from which it gets money for its goods and services is the *trade area* of that particular business. Rarely do any two types of business in a city have exactly the same trade area. Therefore, there is no such thing, strictly speaking, as *the* trade area of a service center. Rather, a city is surrounded by numerous *trade areas*, one for each service. In popular usage, though, we say a city has *a trade area* from which most of its business comes.

Economic-Base Concept. The money that comes into a city enables us to formulate its *economic base*. Nearly every city depends for its life on the revenue from its trade areas for its services. And yet, some of its business must be formed to meet the needs of its own inhabitants. The former component is termed *basic* economic activity; without revenue from such services the city would probably cease to exist. The component that meets the needs of the city itself is termed *nonbasic*, not because it is unnecessary (for it is most assuredly as necessary for an efficient city as the other) but because it feeds off money that has been brought in already by the basic component.

The *basic* component of a city's economic life consists of such activities as the following: sales by local stores to farmers in the surrounding countryside or to tourists passing through, sales by local wholesalers to retailers in other cities, sales by local factories to buyers located elsewhere, pensions received by local citizens from outside sources, interest received by local residents on capital they have invested in other cities, payments to local government agencies from government offices situated elsewhere. These and other similar endeavors are *basic* to a city's economy.

It is extremely difficult to measure all the money that makes up the basic support of a city's economic life. But we can achieve a partial measurement by means of the employment structure of a city. If a city is not too large, it is possible in a reasonable amount of time to contact every business in town and determine the total number of people employed, and the percentages of the business that meet both local and nonlocal demand. By this system, a store that employs 30 people and does two-thirds of its business with local customers would be credited with 20 nonbasic employees and 10 basic em-

In 1950, mining activity in Jerome, Arizona supported 1200 people. Discontinuation of mining caused the population to drop to 250 in 1960. Today, the population of 450 is supported largely by tourist expenditures. (*Courtesy Ray Manley Photography.*)

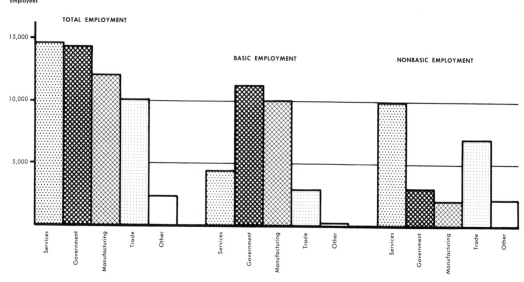

Figure 27-11

ployees. In any city there are some businesses that are mostly *nonbasic:* indeed, neighborhood groceries are entirely so. Some factories on the other hand are strictly *basic*. Most establishments, though, fall somewhere in between these two extremes. In any event, we can make a tally of every business in town, and then determine the size of basic employment. The result can be expressed as a percentage of the city's total employment. This percentage is the *index of basic activity*.

The foregoing method of analysis has been applied to the employment structures of several different cities with some interesting results. For instance, in one well-known study Alexander found the leading economic activity in Madison, Wisconsin, in terms of *total* employment, was the general class of *services*, which employed 14,500 persons. But under the method outlined above, it turns out that 10,000 of those service employees belong in the *nonbasic* category, which means that only 4500 service employees can be classified as basic (Table 27-12). In *basic* employment (Table 27-12 and Figure 27-11), government and manufacturing rank much higher than services. Madison's economy was founded, therefore, on

government and industry more than on services. In *nonbasic* employment, however, service and trade outranked manufacturing and governmental employment by a substantial margin. Evidence seems to indicate that for many cities the structure of *basic* employment is considerably different from that of nonbasic employment and that each may be obscured in the single composite view of total employment.

Clearly, knowing the total employment structure of a city is not enough. To understand that city's economic functioning we should know what keeps it going, what sustains it. The economic base is one concept for revealing this force. It also gives a criterion by which urban regions could be mapped and by which types of cities could be determined.[8]

[8]Further discussion of the concept appears in Lay James Gibson, James L. Barr and Terrence B. O'Keefe, "Measuring the Community Economic Base: A Comparative Analysis," *American Industrial Development Council Journal*, July 1975, pp. 7–35; and Charles M. Tiebout, *The Community Economic Base*, Supplementary Paper No. 16, Committee for Economic Development, December 1962, 86 pages.

Table 27-12

Employment Structures: by Total, Basic, and Nonbasic Categories: Madison. Wisconsin

Category	Total Employment		Basic Employment		Nonbasic Employment	
	Number	Percentage	Number	Percentage	Number	Percentage
Services	14,500	27	4,500	8	10,000	18
Government	14,300	27	11,300	21	3,000	6
Manufacturing	12,100	23	10,100	19	2,000	4
Trade	10,200	19	3,000	6	7,200	13
Others	2,400	4	300	1	2,100	4
	53,500	100	29,200	55	24,300	45

Source: John W. Alexander, "The Basic-Nonbasic Concept of Urban Economic Functions," *Economic Geography* (1954), pp. 246–261.

Balance of Movements

When we take into account both inbound and outbound movements, we discover some interesting observations. For example, it would seem that every city, to survive, must have a *balance* in the flow of money, a balance between revenues and expenditures. Precisely in order to investigate this relationship the research staff of *Fortune* magazine conducted their now classic investigation of Oskaloosa, Iowa. They introduced their report with these provocative statements:

A traveler through the American countryside from place to place often comes unexpectedly on a little city spread out on a flat plain or settled in a valley between the hills. He has perhaps never seen it before, and will never see it again: people living there for some reason he cannot explain, a community doing things that are essentially the same things every community does, and yet—by reason of the mere fact that it is where it is—different.

The traveler will very likely ask himself who lives in this town, and why? What keeps it going? What is it there for?

Without pausing to reflect upon the profundity of his question, he will drive on. But his question deserves pause. It is a question that cannot be answered, any more than the meaning of life can be answered. Yet if the traveler were to stop over in the town he could learn some of the answer . . .

Set down in the middle of a continent, perhaps a thousand miles or more from the sea, it is the prey of vast and distant industrial regions, whose purpose is to draw from it as much money as they possibly can, in exchange for the necessities, near-necessities, luxuries, and adjuncts of civilization. The little city pours out its money year after year to those industrial regions for automobiles, ice-boxes, clothes, canned food, and diamond rings, which it very much wants, and thus builds up a huge *negative* factor in what international commerce calls the balance of trade. And this it can very readily do. For small as it is and perhaps almost entirely devoid of manufacturing, the little city itself is an economic beast of prey. To supply itself with money to send to the industrial regions, it sucks money from all the immediately surrounding countryside. There the farmers climb into their automobiles (which they purchased in the little city years ago) and clatter in at comfortable speeds to park slantwise on the main street and buy clothes and tools and diamond rings and legal advice and new sets of teeth. The result of this business with the farmer is what international commerce calls the balance of trade. And if the little city is to live it must see to it that this favorable balance at least equals, if it does not exceed, year after year, the unfavorable balance with the industrial regions.

How the money that the farmers spend in the little city gets back to the farmers to be spent again in the little city, is another story that does not concern us here. The brief and basic fact of that segment of the economic circuit is that the industrial regions must eat, and so they pay the farmers a great part (but never all) of the money that they get from the little city for the products of civilization.[9]

The Oskaloosa investigation revealed that the inbound money flow slightly exceeded the outbound money flow, thus yielding a small surplus of $339,000 (Table 27-13). This surplus averaged out at around $140 for each of the city's 2700 families that year.

Table 27-13

Balance of Money Flow, Oskaloosa, Iowa

	Inflow	Outflow	Net
Business	$8,223,000	$8,549,000	−$326,000
Government	389,000	153,000	+ 236,000
Consumers	820,000	391,000	+ 429,000
TOTAL	$9,432,000	$9,093,000	+$339,000

Source: "Oskaloosa Versus the United States," *Fortune,* April, 1938.

TYPES OF LOCATIONAL PATTERNS

All these many types of interaction of tertiary settlements with other areas have been influential in determining the locational pattern of hamlets, villages, towns, and cities in the parts of the earth where commercial activity prevails. At least four types of patterns are discernible: dispersed, linear, clustered, and random (Figure 27-12).

Dispersed Pattern, or Central Place Theory

According to a theory advanced by a German geographer, Walter Christaller, there is a tendency for service centers to be dispersed over the countryside in a uniform pattern. The strength of this force is best observed in regions where two conditions prevail: (a) the topography is uniform so that no site has any advantage in terms of slope or of physical influences on transport routes, and (b) the economy is such that no site has an advantage in producing such primary products as grain, timber, or coal. Granted these conditions, Christaller postulates that three developments will transpire:

1. Service centers will spring up evenly spaced over the region at a distance equivalent to two hours of nonmechanized travel time. Most service centers predate the automobile era. So since a man could walk or drive a team about three-and-one-half kilometers in one hour (if service centers were so situated that no farmer would be more than one hour from the nearest one), the centers would be about seven kilometers from one another. Theoretically, the trade area around each nucleus, where the rural people who patronize the service center lived, would be a circle with a three-and-one-half-kilometer radius. Because

[9]Quoted by courtesy of *Fortune* from "Oskaloosa Versus the United States," April, 1938.

SETTLEMENT PATTERNS

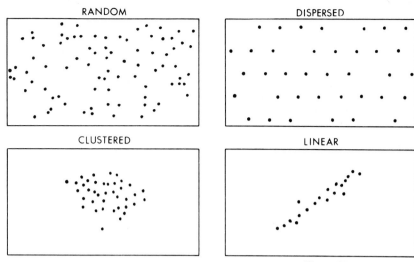

Figure 27-12

this theory postulates that service centers tend to be located in the center of their area served, it is frequently termed the *central place theory*.

2. But contiguous trade areas circular in shape would, of course, produce either overlaps or voids. Of all geometric shapes, hexagons come the closest to circles, and still neither overlap nor leave voids when packed together. Therefore, Christaller postulated, trade centers would be located in hexagonal patterns

and their trade areas would be hexagons instead of circles (see Figure 27-13).

3. A hierarchy of trade centers would develop in this hexagonal framework. The most numerous would be the smallest, mere hamlets, each serving a rural population. The denser the rural population, the *larger* the hamlets would be; but the hamlets would *not* be *closer* together. Hamlets would stay seven miles apart. A second order of settlement would come into

CHRISTALLER HYPOTHESIS

Figure 27-13

Hamlet ○	Trade area boundary of hamlet - - - -
Village ◉	Trade area boundary of village ────
Town ●	Trade area boundary of town ─────
City ⬤	Trade area boundary of city ━━━━

existence to render services demanded so infrequently that the trade area of no one hamlet could support them. But if the composite demand from several trade areas could support such a business, it would locate in one of the hamlets. Such a hamlet would begin to grow larger than the others and achieve the status of a village. Accordingly, villages would be larger in size, fewer in number and farther apart than hamlets, and their trade areas would be bounded by six hamlets (Figure 27-13).

By the same process, a third order of service center, towns, would unfold with each town having a hexagonal trade area bounded by six villages. Fourth-order centers would be cities, each of which would service a region whose margins connected six towns.

Unfortunately, the two conditions requisite for this pattern (uniform economy and uniform topography) rarely exist in reality. Two factors in particular (transportation routes and irregular land forms) disrupt the regular hexagons of the Christaller hypothesis. Main transportation routes either nourish hamlets to grow into villages and towns and cities or kill them off. The transportation revolution has left many a fossil hamlet, its former customers having begun to trade in larger settlements now accessible by automobile.

How a few large service centers and many small ones in southwestern Wisconsin have dispersed in fashion somewhat like Christaller's hypothetical pattern is illustrated in Figure 27-14. Notice how the larger centers tend to have more services (that is, more spokes on the hub) and more business in each service (that is, longer spokes).

The Linear Pattern

This arrangement prevails where service centers, instead of being dispersed, as in the Christaller hypothesis, are strung out along transport routes, often in valleys, or along seacoasts like the resort cities of southern California and New Jersey. The line of agglomerated settlements in northeastern Minnesota correlates with a belt of iron ore mines. Lines of cities in Utah and Idaho coincide with irrigated farm land at the bases of mountain ranges.

The Clustered Pattern

This pattern is usually associated with mining, as in the agglomeration of cities in southern Illinois, where the landforms are not very rough, and in West Virginia, where local relief is pronounced. One type of clustered pattern is *the dispersed city.*

The Dispersed City. Under certain conditions, a cluster of cities may actually function as a single *dispersed city.* Oliver Beimfohr first applied this term to what

Figure 27-14

he observed in southern Illinois where a total of 14 urban places were clustered unusually close together in the four counties of Perry, Franklin, Jackson, and Williamson.

The spacing of these cities was unusual in that the larger ones did not have several smaller ones in their hinterlands. In fact, the larger ones tended to be rather close together. For example, Carbondale (population 15,000) was only 7 miles from Murphysboro (population 9,000). Marion (population 11,000) was only 11 miles from West Frankfort (population 9,000). It is rare to find settlements as large as those just described so close together *unless* they are part of some metropolitan area, parts of Chicago, say, or St. Louis.

On this basis, some analysts believe that such a cluster of discrete cities actually function as a single large city, only fragmented into component parts. From this viewpoint, the dispersed city in southern Illinois was estimated to have a population of 157,000.[10]

In terms of function, particularly retail trade, no one of the 14 larger settlements had any clear dominance over the others; that is, the dispersed city had no clear counterpart to a "downtown shopping center." One might suppose that the most populous settlement in this dispersed city would have the largest volume of

[10]Burton, Ian, "Retail Trade in a Dispersed City," *Transactions of the Illinois State Academy of Science,* 1959, pp. 145–150. See also Howard A. Stafford, Jr., "The Dispersed City," *The Professional Geographer,* July, 1962, pp. 8–10.

retail trade; the fact is that the second-, third-, fourth-, and fifth-ranking settlements (in population) all do more business than the largest one. Some of the settlements do appear to have specialized in types of trade; for example, some do a disproportionately large volume of business in furniture, household, and radio goods, while others are disproportionately high in general merchandise—all of which suggests that each settlement is comparable to a specialized business district within an urbanized area.

A random sample taken in West Frankfort revealed that 68 per cent of the inhabitants make habitual purchases of retail goods outside the settlement. Of these individuals, 82 per cent reported the "outside place" to be some other settlement within the dispersed city. The remaining 18 per cent identified their place of purchase as follows: St. Louis 14 per cent, Chicago 2 per cent, and Evansville 2 per cent.

The foregoing information lends support, in the minds of some scholars, to the hypothesis that the discrete cities of southern Illinois really function as a single metropolitan area—with a few miles of open countryside interspersed between the many fragments that compose it.

The Random Pattern

The random pattern is more difficult to explain but it may be related to a number of different factors. It is often found in the arid western United States, where population densities are light and settlements are few and far between. In ranching areas where settlements are associated with shipping points or available water, this pattern is frequently produced. Similarly, mining regions or areas of rough topography might also have a settlement pattern which is best described as random.

In any case, it must be remembered that the pattern of settlement within a region will very likely depend upon how the researcher defines the region in the first place. Even so, few regions will conform perfectly with any one of these basic patterns. But this does not negate the fact that the forces behind these patterns are at work; rather each area's pattern results from the interplay of those forces, each of which is stronger in some places and weaker in others.

SUGGESTED READINGS

ALEXANDER, JOHN W., "The Basic-Nonbasic Concept of Urban Economic Functions," *Economic Geography*, 1954, pp. 246–261.

APPLEBAUM, WILLIAM, "Teaching Marketing Geography by the Case Method," *Economic Geography*, 1961, pp. 48–60.

———, and COHEN, SAUL B., "The Dynamics of Store Trading Areas and Market Equilibrium," *Annals of the Association of American Geographers*, 1961, pp. 73–101.

BARTHOLOMEW, HARLAND, and WOOD, JACK, *Land Uses in American Cities*, Cambridge, 1955, 196 pp.

BERRY, BRIAN J. L., "Commuting Patterns: Labor Market Participation and Regional Potential," *Growth and Change*, October 1970, pp. 3–10.

———, "The Impact of Expanding Metropolitan Communities Upon the Central Place Hierarchy," *Annals of the Association of American Geographers*, 1960, pp. 112–116.

———, and GARRISON, WILLIAM L., "Alternate Explanations of Urban Rank-Size Relationships," *Annals of the Association of American Geographers*, 1958, pp. 83–91.

———, and ———, "The Functional Bases of the Central Place Hierarchy," *Economic Geography*, 1958, pp. 145–154.

———, and ———, "A Note on Central Place Theory and the Range of a

Good," *Economic Geography*, 1958, pp. 304–311.

BLOUNT, STANLEY F., "The Spatial Distribution of Shoppers Around the Valley Shopping Center, St. Charles, Ill.," *The Professional Geographer*, September 1964, pp. 8–17.

BROWN, LAWRENCE, A., ODLAND, JOHN, and GOLLEDGE, REGINALD G., "Migration, Functional Distance, and the Urban Hierarchy," *Economic Geography*, 1970, pp. 472–485.

BRUSH, JOHN E., "The Hierarchy of Central Places in Southwestern Wisconsin," *Geographical Review*, 1953, pp. 380–402.

———, and BRACEY, HOWARD E., "Rural Service Centers in Southwestern Wisconsin and Southern England," *Geographical Review*, 1955, pp. 559–569.

BURGHARDT, ANDREW F., "A Hypothesis About Gateway Cities," *Annals of the Association of American Geographers*, 1971, pp. 269–285.

CARTER, H., STAFFORD, H. A., and GILBERT, M. M., "Functions of Welsh Towns: Implications for Central Place Notions," *Economic Geography*, 1970, pp. 25–38.

CHRISTIE, ROBERT M., "The City in the American Industrial System," *Growth and Change*, January 1976, pp. 39–44.

CLARK, W. A. V., "Consumer Travel Patterns and the Concept of Range,"

Annals of the Association of American Geographers, 1968, pp. 368–396.

COHEN, SAUL B., and LEWIS, GEORGE K., "Form and Function in the Geography of Retailing," *Economic Geography*, 1967, pp. 1–42.

GESSAMAN, PAUL H., and SISLER, DANIEL G., "Highways, Changing Land Use, and Impacts on Rural Life," *Growth and Change*, April 1976, pp. 3–8.

GIBSON, LAY JAMES, and REEVES, RICHARD W., "The Roles of Hinterland Composition, Externalities, and Variable Spacing as Determinants of Economic Structure in Small Towns," *The Professional Geographer*, 1974, pp. 152–158.

GREEN, HOWARD L., "Hinterland Boundaries of New York City and Boston in Southern New England," *Economic Geography*, 1955, pp. 283–300.

HAGERSTRAND, TORSTEN, "Migration and the Growth of Culture Regions," *Lund Studies in Geography*, 1951, No. 3, pp. 33–36.

HAGGETT, P., and GUNAWARDENA, K. A., "Determination of Population Thresholds for Settlement Functions by the Reed-Muench Method," *The Professional Geographer*, July 1964, pp. 6–9.

HECHT, A., "The Journey-to-Work Distance in Relation to the Socio-Economic Characteristics of Workers," *The Canadian Geographer*, 1974, pp. 367–378.

HUGHES, JAMES W., editor, *Suburbanization Dynamics and the Future of the City*, New Brunswick, N. J., 1974, 286 pp.

JANELLE, DONALD G., "Central Place Development in a Time-Space Framework," *The Professional Geographer*, 1968, pp. 5–10.

JOHNSON, LANE J., "The Spatial Uniformity of a Central Place Distribution in New England," *Economic Geography*, 1971, pp. 156–170.

JOHNSTON, R. J., "Central Places and the Settlement Pattern," *Annals of the Association of American Geographers*, 1966, pp. 541–549.

KENYON, JAMES B., "On the Relationship Between Central Function and Size of Place," *Annals of the Association of American Geographers*, 1967, pp. 736–750.

LENTNEK, BARRY, LIEBER, STANLEY R., and SHESKIN, IRA, "Consumer Behavior in Different Areas," *Annals of the Association of American Geographers*, 1975, pp. 538–545.

LONSDALE, RICHARD E., "Two North Carolina Commuting Patterns," *Economic Geography*, 1966, pp. 114–138.

MARSHALL, JOHN U., "Model and Reality in Central Place Studies," *The Professional Geographer*, January 1964, pp. 5–8.

MOORE, CRAIG L., "A New Look at the Minimum Requirements Approach to Regional Economic Analysis," *Economic Geography*, 1975, pp. 350–356.

MORIARTY, BARRY M., "Population and Employment Shifts Within Regional Hierarchies of Cities," *Proceedings of the Association of American Geographers*, 1975, pp. 155–159.

MORRILL, RICHARD L., "The Development of Spatial Distribution of Towns in Sweden: An Historical Predictive Approach," *Annals of the Association of American Geographers*, 1963, pp. 1–14.

NELSON, HOWARD, "A Service Classification of American Cities," *Economic Geography*, 1955, pp. 189–210.

————, "Some Characteristics of the Population of Cities in Similar Service Classifications," *Economic Geography*, 1957, pp. 95–108.

PRATT, RICHARD T., "An Appraisal of the Minimum-Requirements Technique," *Economic Geography*, 1968, pp. 117–124.

PRESTON, RICHARD E., "The Structure of Central Place Systems," *Economic Geography*, 1971, pp. 136–155.

ROWLEY, GWYN, "Central Places in Rural Wales," *Annals of the Association of American Geographers*, 1971, pp. 537–550.

RUSHTON, GERARD; GOLLEGE, REGINALD G.; and CLARK, W. A. V. "Formulation and Test of a Normative Model for the Spatial Allocation of Grocery Expenditures by a Dispersed Population," *Annals of the Association of American Geographers*, 1967, pp. 389–400.

RUSSWURM, LORNE, H., "The Central Business District Retail Sales Mix, 1948–1958," *Annals of the Association of American Geographers*, 1964, pp. 524–536.

SPARICIO, FRANK J., "Trading Area Variations for Different Goods Sold in the Same Store," *The Professional Geographer*, 1966, pp. 5–8.

STAFFORD, HOWARD A., JR., "The Dispersed City," *The Professional Geographer*, July 1962, pp. 8–10.

SYMANSKI, RICHARD, and NEWMAN, JAMES L., "Formal, Functional and Nodal Regions: Three Fallacies," *The Professional Geographer*, 1973, pp. 350–352.

VANCE, JAMES E., JR., "Cities in the Shaping of the American Nation," *The Journal of Geography*, 1976, pp. 41–52.

————, *The Merchant's World: The Geography of Wholesaling*, Englewood Cliffs, N. J., 1970, 167 pp.

WALZER, NORMAN, and SCHMIDT, DAVID, "Population Change and Retail Sales in Small Communities," *Growth and Change*, January 1977, pp. 45–49.

WOLPERT, JULIAN, "Distance and Directional Bias in Inter-Urban Migratory Streams," *Annals of the Association of American Geographers*, 1967, pp. 605–616.

WHEELER, JAMES O., "Commuting and the Rural Nonfarm Population," *The Professional Geographer*, 1971, pp. 118–122.

————, "The Transportation Model and Changing Home-Work Location," *The Professional Geographer*, 1967, pp. 144–148.

WHITE, STEPHEN E., "Action Space, Human Needs and Interurban Migration," *The Professional Geographer*, 1977, pp. 47–52.

WILLIAMSON, ROBERT B., "Regional Growth: Predictive Power of the Export Base Theory," *Growth and Change*, January 1975, pp. 3–10.

CHAPTER
28

spatial variation within a service center

The New Jersey Turnpike approach to Lincoln Tunnel with the New York skyline in the background. Streets and highways typically account for between one-quarter and one-third of the land usage in American cities. (*Courtesy the Port Authority of New York and New Jersey.*)

Variation from place to place *within* a service center gives rise to distinctive areas; through studying the subdivisions we can better understand the large economic entities. And because in their internal natures service centers differ one from another, analyzing such spatial variation offers a useful geographic approach. Moreover the study has an urgent practical value, for areal variation within a city lies at the root of many a problem bothering today's urbanites. The discussion to follow will be organized around several individual elements whose locational patterns contribute particularly to our understanding of service centers. These are employment, population, types of people, and types of land use. A presentation of theoretical patterns within cities will close the chapter.

EMPLOYMENT

Places of employment are concentrated in comparatively few areas within any city. This principle is illustrated by Figure 28-1 which locates all organizations that employ 100 or more persons in Madison, Wisconsin. The size of each circle is proportionate to the number of employees; the division of each circle is proportionate to the degree to which each organization is *basic* to Madison's economic life. Remember that *basic* endeavor is not a priori more or less important than *nonbasic*; it's a matter of bringing money in. The map shows how highly concentrated employment is in the central and northeastern parts of the city. Except for a few enterprises to the

south of Lake Mendota, the western part of the city is devoid of large job-makers as is the southern part of the city.

Since places of work are not uniformly spread out, the journey to work for most persons entails considerable movement, all of which converges on those few places where jobs are concentrated. Traffic analysts refer to such areas as *zones of convergence*.

Convergence of traffic would not be so bad were it not for a second matter: nearness to work usually ranks low on the scale of values by which the city dweller chooses his residence. Look at Figure 28-2: If workers tended to live close to their work, the dots would be liberally sprinkled in the vicinity of the Oscar Mayer factory in east Madison; instead, they are widely dispersed, which means that employees are heading for the Oscar Mayer plant from every part of the city. Dozens of them travel clear across town. This situation—which exists in all cities—has a tremendous impact on the problems of urban traffic.

POPULATION

"Where are the people?" The question has always been pertinent in locating schools and stores, but in recent years it has taken on new significance due to (a) the automobile revolution with its consequent intense traffic congestion and (b) the growing acceptance of comprehensive planning in metropolitan regions.

In selecting locations for facilities the regional

Figure 28-1

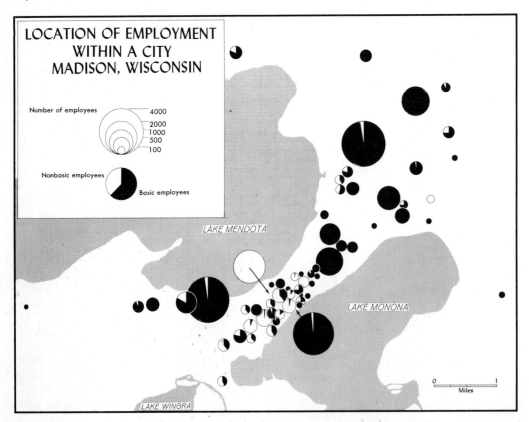

LOCATION OF EMPLOYMENT
WITHIN A CITY
MADISON, WISCONSIN

Number of employees — 4000 / 2000 / 1000 / 500 / 100

Nonbasic employees / Basic employees

LAKE MENDOTA

LAKE MONONA

LAKE WINGRA

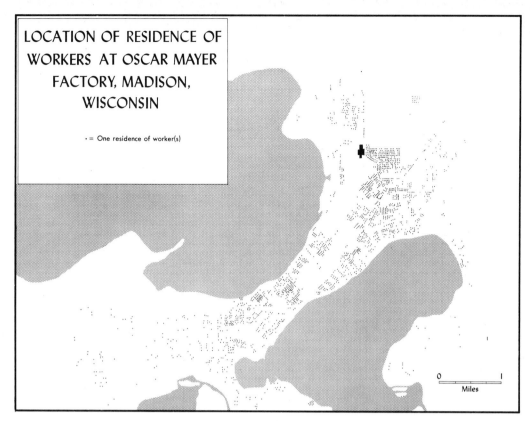

LOCATION OF RESIDENCE OF WORKERS AT OSCAR MAYER FACTORY, MADISON, WISCONSIN

· = One residence of worker(s)

0   1
Miles

Figure 28-2 *(After George P. Stevens.)*

planner must be able to read the message of at least *two* maps: one a map of where people *reside*, and another of where they *work* and *shop*, or do anything else away from home. The traffic engineers should be familiar with these same patterns if they are to locate thoroughfares effectively.

Unfortunately, research methods have yet to be discovered for feasibly gathering data for such maps of all cities. The best published information is that contained in the United States *Census of Population*, "Census Tract Statistics." This is a valuable source of information that tabulates information for small areal units (*census tracts*) within cities. This source clearly makes remarkably detailed mapping possible. Yet the Census has certain disadvantages, principally that it presents information for comparatively few cities (approximately 275 SMSA's in 1977) and locates people by residence only.

Population Patterns

Nighttime Population Pattern. The type of map that *can* be constructed from Census information is exemplified by Figure 28-3, which shows the locational pattern of the people of Tucson, Arizona, *when they are at home*. Even though Tucson is a sprawling city with a weak central business district, certain features that seem to be characteristic of most large service centers still stand out clearly. First, there is a relatively hollow core coinciding with the central business district (see page 404). Not too many people reside here, so the center of

town is comparatively deserted at night. Immediately surrounding the core is a ring where residential density is high, indeed some of the highest densities in town are found here. This juxtaposition can be understood, in part at least, when relationships with land use are considered, as we shall see later in the chapter. Beyond this ring there are a couple of other high density islands, but generally speaking, the density of population tends to taper off gradually until finally, near the edge of the city, densities lower than those in the commercial core are encountered.

But this pattern is essentially that of the city at night when it is asleep, rather than when it is awake and performing the functions that sustain its life. Unfortunately, the Bureau of the Census does not (and probably could not) publish anything on the *daytime* location of all a city's people.

Daytime Population Pattern. Even so, for large cities the Census does publish data on work destinations for commuters, and field studies of daytime population have been made for a few cities; they provide some stimulating suggestions. On a typical weekday in Winnipeg, Manitoba, it was found that the "downtown" area (the central business district plus several adjacent blocks containing governmental institutions, several factories and wholesaling establishments, and some residences) contained 102,000 people, which was 27 per cent of the entire population of Winnipeg and its suburbs. Over half (63,000) were employed in the downtown area, 6000 reside there, and 33,000 were in the downtown area for shopping or other purposes. Within the core of the business district, densities ranged from 400 to 4000 per acre. On the fringe of the business district they varied from 125 to 500 per acre. In the encircling wholesale-industrial zone they ranged from 400 to 1500 per acre. In the surrounding residential ring the daytime densities were 30 to 90 per acre. But the nighttime pattern for downtown Winnipeg was entirely different. Density in the commercial core was down to almost zero except for a very few isolated blocks, in every instance containing hotels, where it rose abruptly to 200 to 800. The fringe of the business district likewise was nearly deserted except for a few low-class hotels and rescue missions. The wholesale-industrial zone had scarcely any population at night. But surrounding these three parts of the downtown area was the first ring of continual housing where nighttime densities were up to 100 to 200 per acre.[1]

[1]Several revealing maps with analytical comment on the Winnipeg study appear in Thomas R. Weir's "Land Use and Population Characteristics of Central Winnipeg," *Geog. Bull.*, 1957, Number 9, pp. 5–21.

A study of Chicago's central business district (an area 10 blocks long from north to south and 9 blocks wide from east to west, and bounded on the west and north by the Chicago River) showed that between 7:00 A.M. and 7:00 P.M. on a June weekday a total of 950,000 people enter as passengers in some sort of vehicle. Those who come in on foot are difficult to tally, but number somewhere between 150,000 and 200,000. By percentages, passengers arrive by the following means: automobiles 25 per cent, street cars 26, elevated railways 23, buses 9, and railways 17. The peak hour of arrival is from 8:00 to 9:00 A.M. when 192,000 arrive; the slowest hour is from 3:00 to 4:00 A.M. when only 2,342 people enter. The total daytime population (shoppers, workers, sightseers, and so on) in so congested an area as downtown Chicago is extremely difficult to measure; however, employment alone is estimated to account for 373,000 people—several blocks contain 5,000 working persons each, and one has 10,000 employees. The biggest rush for the exits comes between 5:00 and 6:00 P.M., when 197,000 people leave the district.[2]

[2]For a vast amount of information about Chicago's daytime population and for a thorough description of research methods for tackling such a topic, see Gerald Breese's *Daytime Population of the Central Business District of Chicago*, University of Chicago Press (Chicago), 1949.

Figure 28-3

POPULATION DENSITY, TUCSON, ARIZONA

Figure 28-4

Similarly, transportation planning agencies in most metropolitan regions have produced maps of places of work. The map of Tucson (Figure 28-4) is not a complete map of daytime population because it does not show the location of shoppers, school children, or many others. Nevertheless, the pattern shown is probably fairly typical of the actual daytime population on a typical weekday.

Change in Population Pattern. The locational pattern of people is in flux in cities that are growing. The changes are most pronounced in the three inner areas: the center, the ring encircling the center, and the territory encircling that second zone. Consider, for example, Table 28-2A, which reveals the spread of the residential void in the center of Frankfurt, Germany where, in the four decades between two field studies made in 1890 and 1933, density dropped from 200 to 121 persons per acre. The adjacent ring also lost people, but the drop was only from 76 to 69 persons per acre. The same principle is illustrated by Chicago and Cleveland (see Table 28-2B). In Chicago the innermost zone lost 23 per cent of its residents during the decade 1910–1920; outer zones had not yet been whittled away by the exodus of residents; indeed, the second zone showed

a gain, albeit only one per cent. But in the next decade not only did the inner zone lose an additional 22 per cent but the second zone also succumbed to outmovement and lost 11 per cent. The same story holds for Cleveland although the timing was a bit later. Cleveland's inner zone did not report a loss until 1930, but when loss did set in, it went swiftly (27 per cent) and widely (for both inner zones had been hit by 1930).

A change in the intensity of daytime convergence upon a city's center is revealed by the Chicago study previously cited; the daytime population (arriving by some sort of vehicle) in Chicago's central business district increased from 870,000 in 1926 to 950,000 in 1946. Notice in Table 28-1 how this number did not rise steadily but moved in waves which reflected economic and political events. Thus, with the passage of years it appears that, in some cities at least, the innermost zone is throbbing with increasing numbers of people during the daytime, but is spreading ever outward as a population void at night.

A second area of change is the next outward ring. Instead of being deserted at night, this ring has the densest nighttime population in town and, insofar as it changes, experiences the greatest *absolute* gains of any area within a city. As Table 28-2A shows. this ring in Frankfurt's third zone had an increment of 35 residents

Table 28-1

Number of Passengers Entering the Central Business District of Chicago, 1926–1946, 7:00 A.M.–7:00 P.M.

1926	870,000	1939	840,000
1928	893,000	1940	824,000
1929	923,000	1941	823,000
1931	843,000	1942	803,000
1935	755,000	1943	814,000
1936	801,000	1944	796,000
1937	845,000	1945	817,000
1938	812,000	1946	950,000

Source: Gerald Breese, Daytime Population of The Central Business District of Chicago, University of Chicago Press (Chicago), 1949, pp. 114–115.

Table 28-2

Changes in Location of People by Residence Within Cities

Part A. Absolute Change in Density, Frankfurt, Germany

Zone	Kilometers from Town Center	Number of People Per Acre 1890	1933	Change
1	0–½	200	121	−79
2	½–1	76	69	− 7
3	1–2	33	68	+35
4	2–3	7	25	+18
5	3–4	3	12	+ 9
6	4–5	1	7	+ 6

Part B. Relative Change in Density, Chicago and Cleveland

Zone	Miles from Town Center	Chicago 1910 to 1920	1920 to 1930	Cleveland 1910 to 1920	1920 to 1930
1	0–2	−23%	− 22%	0%	− 27%
2	2–4	+ 1%	− 11%	+ 29%	− 4%
3	4–6	+40%	+ 13%	+117%	+ 49%
4	6–8	+76%	+ 51%	+290%	+103%
5	8–10	+77%	+112%	+ 69%	+ 95%

Source: Robert E. Dickinson, City, Region and Regionalism, Routledge and Kegan Paul, Ltd. (London), 1947, pp. 129 and 135.

per acre. No other zone approached this figure. The Frankfurt study reveals several corollaries of this principle which seem to apply in most cities: (a) outward from the ring of greatest increment, every circle grew, (b) the amount of increase diminished with distance from the ring of maximum growth, and (c) all areas that grew were outside of this ring.

The third type-area consists of rings with only modest increments but high percentage gains. Such areas are on the sparsely settled fringe of cities. Thus, the percentage gains in Chicago *rose steadily with increasing outward distance*, from one to 77 per cent (1910–1920) and from 13 to 112 per cent (1920–1930).

These generalized patterns of change result largely from the outward movements of numerous residents. The *outer* fringes, though, are settled by two kinds of "immigrants": those who come from inner portions of the city in a flight to the suburbs and those who move to town from elsewhere and settle on its margins. The innermost ring of densest residential population is growing for several reasons, the principal one being the influx of outsiders who move to town and are able to afford only cheaper rooms and apartments; thus, this ring is the port of entry to most large cities.

Another criterion for considering changes in location of people is residential mobility. A study of this factor in St. Louis revealed that, in concentric rings increasing in radius by one mile around the city center, residential mobility *decreased* as distance from the center *increased*. An index of mobility designed for the study attained a peak of 45 in the city center and dropped progressively with each zone, through indexes of 43, 39, 31, 29, and 27 to 24 in the seventh zone. In other words, the closer to the center of a city, the higher the rate of turnover in residential occupancy.

TYPES OF PEOPLE

Not only do numbers of people differ spatially within a city, but types of people do also. Of course, the criteria for determining types are legion, but among the more frequently considered classifications are race, nativity, education, age, sex, marriage rates, death rates, and median income.

Race, Nativity, and Ethnicity

Granted, the validity of the concept of "race" is suspect in many quarters. Certainly it is emotionally explosive. Still, within the United States, two major racial types are clearly identifiable, Negroes and whites. And the distribution of these groups falls into definite patterns. In some parts of the country, Indians and Orientals form distinct racial enclaves, too. The Negro districts of most large American cities, Chinatown in San Francisco, and the white section of Jackson, Mississippi, are examples of this obvious phenomenon. The principle holds almost universally that in the United States nonwhite races tend to locate in pockets within the innermost ring of highest residential density, only gradually spreading out through the ring and into the next one. Much of New Orleans is virtually devoid of black people, but near the center of town they make up from 85 to 100 per cent of the residents of some neighborhoods. In South African cities, however, nonwhite people reside in areas on the fringe of the city, areas with the highest density. The foreign-born also tend to cluster together in regions that stand out conspicuously on city maps.

The notion of ethnicity is related to race and nativity but is clearly more difficult to define in consistent terms. Figure 28-5 shows minority ethnic composition in Tucson, Arizona. What does this mean? As it turns out, the ethnic population described on Figure 28-5 is composed of Negroes, whites, Indians, members of *other races*, plus all those who either have a Spanish surname or who claim Spanish as their first language. In this case, at least, the term *ethnic* covers race, nativity, heritage, and language. Would ethnic be used the same way if we were making a similar map for Boston?

Education

Even years of schooling are reflected in residential distribution. For persons 25 years or older, the median number of school years completed is almost always lowest in the center of town; in fact, most large cities have at least one census tract where the median is less than an eighth-grade education. There is frequently a fairly strong relationship between educational levels and such variables as income, race, and ethnicity.

Age

There is a general tendency for the median age of residents to be highest in the center of town and gradually drop toward the fringes. In the center of Tucson elderly people (65 or more years of age) make up over

25 percent of the population in several census tracts (Figure 28-6). This outward decline in median age with distance from city center is frequently explained by several factors: Many families with young children move to the suburbs; many single adults prefer to live near job opportunities and shopping facilities in the center; many adult couples move back from the suburbs to apartments near the center to be near libraries, theaters, and stores. In the case of Tucson, the aged population is generally associated with an area which has modestly priced housing and ready access to shopping and public services; high youth populations are found in areas with large minority populations or in areas with modestly priced suburban-type housing (Figure 28-7).

Being aware of age distributions can be highly practical. Mapping a city on the basis of persons under age 19, for instance, would be valuable to members of the Board of Education and others responsible for allocating funds for school maintenance and construction.

Other Criteria

Sex Ratios. In most cities the male/female ratio tends to reach a pronounced peak in the center of town and drop off sharply toward the fringes.

MINORITY ETHNIC COMPOSITION, TUCSON, ARIZONA

Figure 28-5

Persons per square mile

- Over 69
- 23–69
- 12–22
- 8–11
- Under 8

AGED POPULATION, TUCSON, ARIZONA

Persons 65 years or older
per square mile

Over 678
328 – 678
156 – 327
46 – 155
Under 46

Figure 28-6

Figure 28-7

TUCSON: YOUTH POPULATION

Persons 7 – 18 Years
Per Square Miles

Under 614
614 – 889
890 – 1,245
1,260 – 1,715
Over 1,715

Marriage Ratios. Married people ordinarily constitute a very low percentage of residents in the central business district but an ever-increasing percentage toward the edge of town.

Median Income. Income is generally lowest in the center, rising toward the fringe, of a city. The fringe is never a continuous belt of high incomes, however; instead, the wealthy cluster in certain sectors. On a map of Tucson (Figure 28-8), for instance, the lowest median family incomes (less than $5845) appear in the central part of the city and on the city's north side. High incomes (those over $10,056) are found in two islands near the center of town, but for the most part, high-income families are found on the city's east side in newer areas of suburban-type housing.

Death Rates. Death rates are usually higher in the center of town and grade off slowly toward the fringe. This of course reflects to a large extent the age pattern mentioned above.

TYPES OF LAND USE

Even the most casual observer of large cities knows that men use land for different purposes in different parts of town. Stores, houses, factories, and apartments are not sprinkled ubiquitously throughout the city. Areas tend to be specialized.

This is not so for hamlets, the smallest (except for roadsides) category of service center. As Figure 28-9 shows, hamlets have farmsteads, nonfarm residences, stores, garages, schools, and churches intermixed along the roadway in no particular pattern and often at considerable distances from one another.

As soon as a hamlet begins to grow several things begin to happen, however. A process of separation between the commercial and residential area sets in. And the concentration of business establishments gives rise to a *commercial core.* Within that core, structures are built ever closer together. Then, with continued growth, buildings in the commercial core begin to grow *up,* as businesses begin to use floors above the ground level. Further growth usually brings the development of distinct industrial zones and certain types of residential areas as well. We can examine each of these three main use categories individually.

Commercial Areas

There are at least four principal types of commercial use of land in large cities: centralized commercial areas, com-

MEDIAN FAMILY INCOME, TUCSON, ARIZONA

Figure 28-8

*Families and unrelated individuals

mercial strips, dispersed businesses, and shopping centers.

Centralized Commercial Areas: the CBD.
Centralized commercial areas are clusters of diverse business establishments usually at intersections of major thoroughfares. The outstanding example of such an area is the Central Business Destrict, termed CBD for short.

The central business district is the economic heart of nearly every city. There are exceptions, though, such as factory towns that grew up around a manufacturing plant in the middle of the countryside, such as Kannapolis, North Carolina, which developed around the Cannon textile mills (Chapter 18); or the castle towns in Europe that sprang up around a lord's residence (such as Touraine, France); or cathedral towns (such as Rochester, England, and numerous towns in north-central France) which encircled some religious structure; or garrison towns (such as Aberystwyth, Wales) which began as military posts. But the vast majority of service centers have grown around a retail trading district. The site of origination is called the *point of attachment*, and for most contemporary cities the point of attachment is somewhere within the CBD.

Certain general characteristics of a CBD are well known: the greatest concentration of stores in town (from single proprietorships to huge department stores), the greatest concentration of offices and services (medical, insurance, real estate, banking), the most expensive land

and the tallest buildings (to get the most out of such expensive land). Other characteristics are less obvious, however. Vertical zoning, for instance. Ground floors are often given over to retailing, upper levels to offices or manufacturing. In the CBD's of small settlements second floors are often put to residential use. There are also lateral gradations within a CBD, from the *commercial core*, the area of most intense commercial use, to the CBD *fringe*, where commercial use fades out and some other becomes dominant.

The most significant point within the *core* is the *peak land-value intersection* (PLVI), which is the street intersection where land values are higher than at any other in town. This point also has the greatest concentration of pedestrians and, often, the worst automobile congestion. In small cities, land values decrease sharply in all directions as one begins to move away from the PLVI; however, the decrease begins to slacken off toward the edge of the CBD. A curve of land values thus would be concave, in harmony with the principle that *land values decrease at a decreasing rate with distance from the PLVI*. If the CBD is elongated, the rate of decline is less along the axis than at right angles to it.

However, in the CBD's of large urban agglomerations (such as New York's Manhattan Island) the land values appear to have an undulating profile, dropping with distance from the PLVI and then rising again to secondary peaks as other concentrations of business activity—still within the central part of the metropolis—are encountered.

The edge of the CBD is a transition zone, not a sharp line of demarcation. In most instances it is a peculiar combination of *high land values* and of *low building values*. The land values are high because of the antici-

Figure 28-9 (*Courtesy Glenn T. Trewartha, from* Annals of the Association of American Geographers.)

Downtown Tucson, Arizona, looking east. In 1960 when this photo was taken, downtown Tucson was still the center of activity in trade, finance, and government in southern Arizona. The Tucson metropolitan area had a population of 266,000. (*Courtesy Cooper Aerial Survey Co., Tucson, Arizona.*)

By 1976 the metropolitan population had grown to 455,000. Most of this growth occurred on the margins of the urbanized area, and most retail activities shifted to outlying shopping centers. Today, downtown Tucson is like the downtown areas in many growing American cities where parking lots and modern office buildings dominate the scene. In the late 1960's and early 1970's an urban renewal project (middle of photo) led to the creation of a massive governmental complex and convention center. Office buildings have replaced hotels and stores. (*Courtesy Cooper Aerial Survey Co., Tucson, Arizona.*)

pated *invasion* into the still essentially residential area by the expanding CBD. Usually this expansion begins with the conversion of residential properties to business use. Sometimes a new front is constructed to give the appearance, from the street, of a store or office building; but from the alley (or the sides) the structure still looks like a house. The building values remain low, though, mainly because the structures that have not yet been taken over are invariably the oldest buildings in town, the most obsolete in design, and the most deteriorated in condition. Owners of structures so obsolete on land so valuable are understandably reluctant to make improvements on monstrosities that may soon be sold either to be demolished or remodeled. So deterioration sets in; thus the edge of the CBD is, in many cities, a genuine eyesore.

Delimiting the CBD. In spite of the transitional nature of the CBD's margin, city dwellers still need to be able to define it in order to understand their city and handle effectively its many problems. One of the most scientific systems for delimiting the CBD is the Murphy-Vance method. In this system, a block is considered part of the CBD if it fulfills three requirements:

1. A Central Business Height Index of 1. The *Central Business Height Index* (CBHI) of a block is a ratio in which the numerator is the square footage of floor space devoted to typical CBD activities (retail stores and offices; excluded are wholesale outlets, storage warehouses, manufacturing plants other than those of newspapers, churches, and residences), and the denominator is the *ground* area in square feet.
2. A *Central Business Intensity Index* (CBII) of 50 per cent. This is also a ratio; in this one, the numerator is the same as in the Central Business Height Index, but the denominator is the square footage of all floor space in the block.

   Table 28-3 illustrates how these two indexes may be computed. The inventory of land and floor space for a block on the edge of the Tulsa, Oklahoma CBD is itemized. The ground area (identical with first floor space—since this block has no vacant land) is 2100 units of measurement. The total floor space regardless of usage is 7070 units of measurement, but of this there are 2135 units in the non-CBD types, leaving 4935 devoted to CBD purposes. Notice that this block contains fourteen parcels of land, none of which is vacant, eleven of which are only one story tall.

$$\text{Central Business Height Index} = \frac{4935}{2100} = 2.4$$

$$\text{Central Business Intensity Index} = \frac{4935}{7070} = 69.8 \text{ per cent}$$

Accordingly, this block merits inclusion within the CBD boundary.

3. A block that meets the above requirements must also be part of a contiguous group of blocks surrounding the PLVI. In addition, a block is included in the CBD even though it fails to meet the first two required indexes if: (a) it is surrounded by blocks that do qualify, or (b) if it is devoted to government buildings and is adjacent to a block that does meet these CBD qualifications.

Changes in the CBD. CBD's are not static; they are dynamic. They are constantly changing in profile, in shape, and in internal composition. Most people assume that if a city grows, its CBD will get larger. This is essentially true, but the statement needs to be qualified. In the first place, CBD's probably grow less rapidly than cities as a whole do—that is, in growing cities, outlying business districts increase at a faster rate than does the CBD. In the second place, expanding CBD's do not advance on all fronts. Indeed, activity is distinctly different on two different fronts; on one the CBD is advancing, on another it is receding. The advancing front rolls toward high-quality residential areas. This may seem surprising at first, since the land there is likely to be more costly than in poor-quality residential zones, but when businessmen choose to invest in CBD structures, they tend to shy away from skid rows and slums. A shift in the CBD usually occurs "at the expense of the better residential areas, areas that have . . . already begun to retrogress as the CBD's advancing shadow of blight falls over them." So write Raymond Murphy and James Vance. The retreating front is usually pulling away from three repelling phenomena: slums, railways, and rivers. As the CBD withdraws, the vacated space adjoining railways and waterfronts tends to be filled up by wholesaling or manufacturing establishments or low-class housing.

The advancing front produces a *zone of assimilation* within the CBD, the receding front a *zone of discard*, each with its own distinctive composition. Assimilation spawns specialty shops, drive-in banks, professional offices, headquarters offices of large corporations, newer hotels, and businesses with a "prestige" factor, such as clothiers with a high reputation for quality merchandise. Discard produces pawn shops, bars, low-grade restaurants, bus stations, cheap movie houses, and businesses with little prestige. Figure 28-10 shows the CBD's analyzed by Murphy and Vance, indicating boundaries, location of zones of assimilation and discard, and also the shift of the PLVI.

The movement of the PLVI can be summed up in

Table 28-3

Measurements and Calculations for a Selected Block on the Edge of the CBD in Tulsa, Oklahoma

First Floor		Second Floor		Upper Floors		Adjusted Value	Block Inventory	
Use	Space	Use	Space	Use	Space		Use	Space
C*	0.350**	C	0.350	C	0.350 × 4	1.400	C	4.935
C	0.385	C	0.315	C	0.315 × 5	1.575	X	2.135
X†	0.665	X	0.665	X	0.665	0.665		
C	0.050							
C	0.050							
C	0.050							
C	0.050							
C	0.050							
C	0.050							
C	0.050							
C	0.140							
X	0.070							
X	0.070							
C	0.070						Total	
Total	2.100		1.330			3.640	Space = 7.070	

Source: Raymond E. Murphy and James E. Vance, Jr., "Delimiting the CBD," *Economic Geography*, 1954, p. 207.

*C = Floor space used for typical CBD purposes.

**Measurements are in square inches at a scale of 1 inch to 200 feet on Murphy's and Vance's maps.

†X = Floor space used for untypical CBD purposes.

NINE SELECTED CENTRAL BUSINESS DISTRICTS

Tacoma

Grand Rapids

Worcester

Sacramento

Salt Lake City

Roanoke

Phoenix

Tulsa

Mobile

////// ZONE OF ASSIMILATION
▨▨▨ ZONE OF DISCARD
○ PEAK LAND VALUE INTERSECTION
+ GEOGRAPHIC CENTER OF CBD

N

0   900
FEET

Figure 28-10   (*Courtesy Raymond E. Murphy and James E. Vance, Jr., and* Economic Geography.)

two tendencies: It goes in the same direction as the advancing front but lags behind it. As is shown clearly on Figure 28-10, the PLVI stays closer to the receding front. This lag is due principally to the inertia of investment policy. For as the CBD moves, although its traffic pattern will change (the busiest intersection shifting a block or two from the PLVI), financiers and businessmen are at first reluctant to abandon the investments around that original point. "The pull toward a newer site must build up slowly" (Murphy and Vance). Ultimately, the pull overpowers the inertia, and speculators pour funds into new construction at the new intersection of greatest traffic. As we might expect, then, derelict PLVI's are typical of cities whose *point of attachment* was on a waterfront or railroad.

Problems and Future of the CBD.[3]   Today the chief problems of CBD's are traffic congestion and park-

[3]For further discussion of CBD's see Larry S. Bourne, ed., *Internal Structure of the City*, New York, 1971, 528 pp. Also see Raymond Murphy and J. E. Vance, "Delimiting the CBD," and "A Comparative Study of Nine Central Business Districts," *Economic Geography*, Vol. 30, 1954, pp. 189–222 and pp. 301–336; with Bart Epstein, these authors present the internal nature of CBD's in "Internal Structure of the CBD," *Economic Geography*, Vol. 31, 1955, pp. 21–46.

ing facilities. Some urban observers are convinced that these problems are so severe that the CBD is doomed to extinction, especially when they see business fleeing the CBD for outlying business areas.

CBD's are not really fading away, though. Indeed, their very congestion is a sign of their powerful attraction. In New York City, for example, the 1950's alone saw at least 75 tall buildings thrown up on Manhattan Island, adding 26,000,000 square feet of office space—an *increment* that exceeded the total *existing* office space in any other city of the world except Chicago: More recently, projects such as the World Trade Center in lower Manhattan, a project which consists of six buildings including two 1350-foot tower buildings, gives additional evidence that the CBD is still very much alive.

Admittedly, the CBD's are losing some businesses. Yet for each firm that leaves, another takes its place, though often of a different type. Grocery stores, meat markets, and general stores are being replaced by specialty stores and services. The growth of governmental employment has also been a major force in maintaining many CBD's.

Thus, CBD's are frequently growing but usually at a much slower rate than outlying business districts; concomitantly, the CBD's are becoming more highly specialized.

Other Centralized Commercial Areas. Large cities usually have several secondary clusters of commercial activity that somewhat resemble the CBD but are smaller in size and less specialized and less diversified in types of businesses. The larger a metropolis the more and the larger the subsidiary centers. Indeed, many such areas today were originally genuine CBD's of separate small cities. Subsequent growth has caused these settlements to coalesce with the expanding metropolis.

Commercial Strips. Commercial strips, sometimes called *commercial ribbons*, are composed of stores and services strung along main thoroughfares. Usually strips are only one block wide, with residential property (or land given over to some other use) coming right up to the rear of each business tract. In villages and small towns, the CBD itself is often a commercial strip. In length, these strips attain astonishing distances. A mile is common. But in Tucson (Figure 28-11), Los Angeles, Chicago, New York, and many other cities, some are several miles in length. With few exceptions, commercial strips develop along traffic arteries, radiating out from the CBD (as the Tucson map clearly shows).

A problem peculiar to every commercial ribbon is the friction between two types of traffic: (a) *through* traffic enroute to and from other parts of the city, often the CBD, and (b) local traffic enroute *to* businesses on the artery. This conflict produces tensions and turmoil; on the one hand there is the demand to prohibit curb parking "to let the traffic through," on the other, the demand from merchants and customers to use the curbs for stowing cars. The general consensus of experts today seems to be that commercial strips are an inefficient use of land, that through traffic and local traffic should be separated into different arteries, and that businesses, rather than being strung out in a ribbon several miles long, should be bunched together so that customers would be able to reach them more easily.[4]

Dispersed Businesses. Lone grocery shops, or drug stores, perhaps even pairs of stores, sprinkled throughout the older portions of many cities—these are dispersed businesses. Their *raison d'être* is that they are within walking distance for customers. The only kinds of businesses in such minute commercial developments are those that meet the daily needs of people. In the motor-

[4]Fascinating discussions of commercial strips are available in F. W. Boal and D. B. Johnson, "The Functions of Retail and Service Establishments on Commercial Ribbons," *Canadian Geographer*, Vol. 9, 1965, pp. 154–169; Gerard Foster and Howard Nelson, *Ventura Boulevard: A String-Type Shopping Street*, University of California Press (Los Angeles), 1958; and Brian J. L. Berry, "Ribbon Developments in the Urban Business Pattern," *Annals of the Association of American Geographers*, Vol. 49, 1959, pp. 145–155.

ized parts of the world, we can easily tell which areas within a city predate the automobile age: Such areas have corner groceries about six blocks apart. But the automobile unshackled citizens from having to walk to the store; now they could drive to stores located much farther than six blocks away; this development, coupled with a public demand for purely residential areas free of commercial zoning, has led to the prohibition of dispersed businesses in new regions within most cities.

Shopping Centers. The new look in urban development calls for both commercial strips and dispersed businesses to give way to shopping centers. Whereas the other types of commercial areas sprang up at random, shopping centers are planned in advance. The objective is to gather businesses in outlying areas in such a way that the advantages of CBD's can be enjoyed without the disadvantages. Accordingly, a large variety of stores are brought close together so that, in one stop, a customer can make many purchases. Such centers are always located so as to be accessible to large numbers of people. Therefore, they occur either near intersections of main arteries, off to *one* side of a busy thoroughfare, or at a major commuter station. The size of such centers is startling. Many are 50 to 100 acres in size and have parking lots which can accommodate over 6000 cars. In contrast to CBD's, shopping centers devote land adjoining major thoroughfares—not to store buildings—but to vast parking lots. In their relatively short life to date, shopping centers are doing more business per square foot of floor space than even the central business districts; moreover, land costs and operating costs are generally lower.

Numerous outlying business districts do not fall clearly into any of the foregoing categories; nevertheless, on closer inspection, they usually turn out to be deviant specimens of either a centralized commercial area, a commercial ribbon, a dispersed establishment, or a shopping center.

Industrial Areas

Industry in most cities includes both wholesaling and manufacturing, and the two branches gravitate toward specific places within a city.

Within the CBD there often are considerable manufacturing and some wholesaling of light items on the upper floors of commercial buildings. The advantage of the location for industry is proximity to labor, for the very centrality of the CBD, which makes it accessible to customers, simultaneously makes it accessible to large numbers of workers. Light manufacturing can take advantage of this. Where the first floor serves as a retail outlet, upper floors can be devoted to making the items sold below: For example, hosiery factories in downtown New York. And in towns that sprang up around mill races, factories often remain still on the ground level within the CBD or on its edge.

The margins of CBD's usually contain a city's chief wholesaling district, often threaded through by railway sidings (tracks adjoining buildings for loading purposes), "team tracks" (railway tracks where trucks can load and unload in truck-load lots), freight terminals, and warehouses. A good many truck depots are here, too.

Elsewhere, industrial use is usually related to one or more of the following: (a) access to transportation (canal, railway, or highway) for moving inbound raw materials and outbound products, and (b) relatively cheap land. Notice how the pattern of industrial land in Tucson invariably conforms to the pattern of railways or highways (Figure 28-11). In some cities, swamps or valley bottoms are often filled and devoted to industrial uses (for instance, the Menominee Valley, which splits Milwaukee into a northern and southern half, or the Cuyahoga Valley, which bisects Cleveland, or the Monongahela Valley in Pittsburgh).

Industrialists must frequently fight public opinion in selecting a site on which to build. Many cities in the United States have zoning laws that prohibit them from much of the city's acreage. In a sense, then, they get what is left after commercial and residential interests have had their pick. But two concepts are changing this: (a) planned industrial tracts, and (b) zoning tolerance for light industries.

Planned Industrial Tract. This is to industry what a planned shopping center is to retailing. A large piece of land is set aside for industry and all other uses are zoned out. Streets are laid out, water mains and sewers installed, power lines designed, railway spurs and roads are positioned—all from the standpoint of the needs of factories and warehouses. Five miles east of the CBD of Dallas, Texas, is an example of just such a scheme: "Brook Hollow," a 1200-acre stretch of former farm land, has been developed solely for industry. With attractive factories so positioned as to reduce traffic congestion and with enough land devoted to parking to accommodate the cars of everyone who drives, the tract is turning out to be an appealing place for people to work.

Zoning Tolerance. The premise here is that certain light industries, small in size, should not be banned from residential neighborhoods but should actually

Figure 28-11

LAND USE: TUCSON, ARIZONA

Commercial
Industrial
Other Uses
Railroad
Major Highway

0 1 2 3
MILES

DAVIS MONTHAN
AIR FORCE BASE

TUCSON
INTERNATIONAL
AIRPORT

be welcomed. Workers can then go home for lunch. This is no small factor in a culture where so many mothers of school-age children work in industry. Cross-town travelling can thereby be reduced, thus easing the city's traffic pains.

Residential Uses

We can usually discern two broad residential regions on a land-use map of a city. *Multiple-family housing* (structures with two or more families) tend to cluster in the center of town. Occasionally they appear within the CBD itself or within the industrial ring that sometimes encircles the CBD. Usually, though, they crop up in the next outer ring, immediately beyond the warehouses and factories. Multiple-family structures correlate closely with the zone of maximum population density (in the nighttime pattern). Most of these residences were built originally as apartment houses; but many a house at the edge of the CBD has either been converted into a rooming house (recall the dwelling pattern of single persons within a city) or subdivided into two or more apartments. The unit rents here are rather low, but the number of apartments is often so high that the rental income per house is great. Landlords have tradionally met the continuing demand from the poor for housing by further subdividing these houses into an ever-increasing number of ever-smaller dwelling units. The result is the cheapest housing *and* the most severe overcrowding. Thus, slums are born. It is in just such areas that *planned housing tracts* have recently been launched. Applying the basic concept behind the shopping center and the industrial tract, proponents of the housing-tract philosophy try to design large chunks of land for the optimum residential use. Some of these schemes resort to remedial surgery, whereby slum buildings are razed and replaced by modern apartments—for instance, Stuyvesant Town on the Lower East Side of Manhattan and Lake Meadows on the near South Side of Chicago.

Multiple-housing tracts are becoming common now in outlying areas, too. No longer is it surprising to find apartments being built on the urban fringe where city meets country.

Anyone building a *single-family* house tends to avoid the CBD, the industrial areas, and the multiple-housing area. In most cities, single-family residences cover more acres than any other type of structure, generally in the city's outer reaches. Most American citydwellers today place high values on such land use and strongly resist invasions by any other type.

Other types of land use concern geographers, too, of course. Are there any principles that operate in the location of schools, churches, parks, playgrounds, cemeteries, airports, and golf courses? Such questions are of great moment to economic geographers. And what about the location of freeways, of one-way streets, of streets where parking is banned, of parking lots, of bus routes,

and of subways? These are problems of practical and theoretical concern to city planners. And they can be attacked by the same techiniques of geographic analysis we have adopted here.

URBAN PATTERN

Descriptive Theories

Analysis of the several locational patterns we have just observed supports the conclusion that there are three basic types of designs, or patterns, which seem to be woven into the fabric of any given city: the concentric-ring pattern; the sector, or wedge, pattern; and the multiple-nuclei pattern.

In the *concentric-ring pattern*, the CBD is in the center surrounded by at least four concentric rings. The first is a zone of *transition* where old residential structures are being taken over by business and light manufacturing, and where slum conditions are frequent. The next ring is residential, with multiple-family structures predominant. The third ring is also residential, but given over to single-family houses; in this zone, lots are wider than in the inner rings. The final ring is also dominated by single family residences on still wider lots; usually, a city's highest-class homes are in this ring. The idea of concentric rings is often termed the *Burgess hypothesis* after its author, the noted sociologist E. W. Burgess.

The *sector, or wedge, pattern* pertains when different types of land use and different population densities are located within areas that either taper toward the CBD like pieces of pie or taper outward like the points of a star (as do the prongs of some CBD's or the high-class residential areas of some cities). Sometimes the idea of sectors or wedges is called the *Hurd-Hoyt hypothesis* after R. M. Hurd and Homer Hoyt.

In the *multiple-nuclei pattern*, besides the CBD, several points within the city draw traffic and stimulate development around them nearly as much as does the CBD. Examples of such nuclei are big-scale industrial installations, large public institutions (universities or hospitals), government office centers, or major military establishments. Occasionally this idea is termed the *Harris-Ullman hypothesis* after the two geographers who first formulated it, Chauncy Harris and Edward Ullman.[5]

The Colby Hypothesis

The foregoing are useful *descriptive* theories. The *Colby hypothesis* offers a *dynamic* explanation of urban development. According to this theory (formulated by Charles Colby) the pattern of any city at any given moment is the result of two great forces at work: centripetal and centrifugal. *Centripetal* forces are of two types: (1) Residents and businesses are lured into a city from else-

[5]More thorough discussion of these three patterns appears in Chauncy Harris and Edward Ullman, "The Nature of Cities," *Annals of the American Academy of Political and Social Science*, 1945, pp. 7–17.

where by the amenities and economic advantages of being in town. (2) Within the city itself, both people and businesses on the fringe are drawn towards the CBD because the central point provides the best access to either customers or labor or simply its characteristic institutions, such as stores, theatres, or libraries. Some parents who have reared their children in the suburbs, for instance, are beginning to respond to this pull by moving back into town. *Centrifugal* forces, on the other hand, drive people and businesses out of the CBD into outlying areas and out of the city into the suburbs; in some instances the power is strong enough to drive them clear out of the service center. Flight from congestion and a yearning for open space are the major motives.

Urban Fringe. As a result of these two opposing forces, there develops at the fringe of a city a zone of transition which in some respects resembles the one encircling the CBD. The *urban fringe* is a stretch of land that is in the process of changing from rural to urban use. Typically, population density becomes too high for rural classification but too sparse for urban, as the vanguard

of the urban army of settlement proceeds outward, often ahead of surfaced streets, and of city services such as water and sewerage. Many an urban fringe, indeed, is dotted by hand pumps and septic tanks. With too many children for country schools yet too few to warrant a city school, and with a location far from existing city schools, the fringe areas are a problem to education authorities. Strange juxtapositions develop as the wave of new residences (usually one-floor houses but sometimes multistory apartments) sweeps up to and encircles an old farm house and barn. The latter are sometimes converted into retail outlets—for instance a furniture store—or some other urban use. Occasionally, too, a farm will resist the invasion and stand islanded by the urban wave.[6]

[6]For further information on this unique zone of transition see George Wehrwein, "The Rural-Urban Fringe," *Economic Geography*, Vol. 28, 1942, pp. 217–228 and Peter Fielding, "Dairying in Cities Designed to Keep People Out," *The Professional Geographer*, January, 1962, pp. 12–17.

SUGGESTED READINGS

ADAMS, JOHN S., "Residential Structure of Midwestern Cities," *Annals of the Association of American Geographers*, 1970, pp. 37–62.

APPLEBAUM, WILLIAM, and COHEN, SAUL B., "The Dynamics of Store Trading Areas and Market Equilibrium," *Annals of the Association of American Geographers*, 1961, pp. 73–101.

ARCHER, J. CLARK, "Occupational Rank and Residential Association: Testing a Hypothesis," *Proceedings of the Association of American Geographers*, 1975, pp. 29–32.

BERRY, BRIAN J. L., "The Economics of Land-Use Intensities in Melbourne, Australia," *Geographical Review*, 1974, pp. 479–497.

———, "Ribbon Developments in the Urban Business Pattern," *Annals of the Association of American Geographers*, 1959, pp. 145–155.

BELL, THOMAS L., LIEBER, STANLEY R., and RUSHTON, GERARD. "Clustering of Services in Central Places," *Annals of the Association of American Geographers*, 1974, pp. 214–225.

BOEHM, WILLIAM T., and POND, MARTIN T., "Job Location, Retail Purchasing Patterns, and Local Economic Development," *Growth and Change*, January 1976, pp. 7–12.

BOURNE, L. S., "Comments on the Transition Zone Concept," *The Professional Geographer*, 1968, pp. 313–316.

———, "Urban Structure and Land Use Decisions," *Annals of the Association of American Geographers*, 1976, pp. 531–547.

BRITTON, JOHN N. H., "The Influence of Corporate Organization and Ownership on the Linkages of Industrial Plants: A Canadian Inquiry," *Economic Geography*, 1976, pp. 311–324.

BRODSKY, HAROLD, "Land Development and the Expanding City," *Annals of the Association of American Geographers*, 1973, pp. 159–166.

CAREY, GEORGE W., "Land Tenure, Speculation, and the State of the Aging Metropolis," *Geographical Review*, 1976, pp. 253–265.

CARLSON, ALVAR W., "Recent Immigration, 1961–1970: A Factor in the Growth and Distribution of the United States Population," *The Journal of Geography*, December 1973, pp. 8–18.

CHANG, SEN-DOU, "Some Observations on the Morphology of Chinese Walled Cities," *Annals of the Association of American Geographers*, 1970, pp. 63–91.

CLARK W. A. V., "Migration in Milwaukee," *Economic Geography*, 1976, pp. 48–60.

———, and RUSHTON, GERARD, "Models of Intra-Urban Consumer Behavior and Their Implications for Central Place Theory," *Economic Geography*, 1970, pp. 486–497.

DOEPPERS, DANIEL F., "'Ethnic Urbanism' and Philippine Cities," *Annals of the Association of American Geographers*, 1974, pp. 549–559.

EPSTEIN, BART J., "Geography and the Business of Retail Site Evaluation and Selection," *Economic Geography*, 1971, pp. 192–199.

ERICKSON, RODNEY A., "The Filtering-Down Process: Industrial Location in a Nonmetropolitan Area," *The Professional Geographer*, 1976, pp. 254–260.

FORD, LARRY R., "The Urban Housetype as an Illustration of the Concentric Zone Model: The Perception of Architectural Continuity," *The Journal of Geography*, February 1974, pp. 29–39.

FORWARD, CHARLES N., "Waterfront Land Use in the Six Australian State Capitals," *Annals of the Association of American Geographers*, 1970, pp. 517–532.

FOSTER, GERARD J., and NELSON, HOWARD J., *Ventura Boulevard: A String-Type Shopping Street*, Los Angeles, 1958, 63 pp.

FOWLER, GARY L., and DAVIES, CHRISTOPHER SHANE, "The Urban Settlement Patterns of Disadvantaged Migrants," *The Journal of Geography*, 1972, pp. 275–284.

GRIFFIN, DONALD W., and PRESTON, RICHARD E., "A Restatement of the 'Transition Zone' Concept," *Annals of the Association of American Geographers*, 1966, pp. 339–350.

HARRIES, KEITH D., "Ethnic Variations in Los Angeles Business Patterns," *Annals of the Association of American Geographers*, 1971, pp. 736–743.

HARTSHORN, TRUMAN A., "Industrial/

Office Parks: A New Look for the City," *The Journal of Geography*, March 1973, pp. 33–45.

——, "Inner City Residential Structure and Decline," *Annals of the Association of American Geographers*, 1971, pp. 72–96.

HECHT, ALFRED, "Exploring the Urban Industrial Relocation Process," *The Journal of Geography*, 1977, pp. 15–18.

HILTNER, JOHN, and SMITH, BRUCE W., "Intraurban Residential Location of the Elderly," *The Journal of Geography*, April 1974, pp. 23–33.

HOLMES, JOHN H., "External Commuting as a Prelude to Suburbanization," *Annals of the Association of American Geographers*, 1971, pp. 774–790.

HURST, M. E. ELIOT, "An Approach to the Study of Nonresidential Land Use Traffic Generation," *Annals of the Association of American Geographers*, 1970, pp. 153–173.

KENYON, JAMES B., "Land Use Admixture in the Built-up Urban Waterfront: Extent and Implications," *Economic Geography*, 1968, pp. 152–177.

LAKSHMANAN, T. R., "An Approach to the Analysis of Intraurban Location Applied to the Baltimore Region," *Economic Geography*, 1964, pp. 348–370.

LEIGH, ROGER, "Analysis of the Factors Affecting the Location of Industry Within Cities," *The Canadian Geographer*, 1969, pp. 28–33.

LEY, DAVID, *The Black Inner City as Frontier Outpost: Images and Behavior of a Philadelphia Neighborhood*, Association of American Geographers Monograph Series No. 7, Washington, D. C., 1974, 282 pp.

LOGAN, M. I., "Locational Behavior of Manufacturing Firms in Urban Areas," *Annals of the Association of American Geographers*, 1966, pp. 451–466.

LORD, J. DENNIS, "Locational Shifts in Supermarket Patronage," *The Professional Geographer*, 1975, pp. 310–313.

MCDERMOTT, PHILIP J., and TAYLOR, MICHAEL J., "Attitudes, Images, and Location: The Subjective Context of Decision Making in New Zealand Manufacturing," *Economic Geography*, 1976, pp. 325–347.

MAHER, C. A., "Spatial Patterns in Urban Housing Markets: Filtering in Toronto, 1953–71," *The Canadian Geographer*, 1974, pp. 108–124.

MANNERS, GERALD, "The Office in Metropolis: An Opportunity for Shaping Metropolitan America," *Economic Geography*, 1974, pp. 93–110.

MATTINGLY, PAUL F., "Delimitation and Movement of CBD Boundaries Through Time: The Harrisburg Example," *The Professional Geographer*, November 1964, pp. 9–13.

MURPHY, RAYMOND E., and VANCE, J. E., JR., "A Comparative Study of Nine Central Business Districts," *Economic Geography*, 1954, pp. 301–336.

——, and ——, "Delimiting the CBD," *Economic Geography*, 1954, pp. 189–222.

——, and ——, and EPSTEIN, BART J., "International Structure of the CBD," *Economic Geography*, 1955, pp. 21–46.

PORTEOUS, J. DOUGLAS, "Social Class in Atacama Company Towns," *Annals of the Association of American Geographers*, 1974, pp. 409–417.

PRESTON, RICHARD E., "A Detailed Comparison of Land Use in Three Transition Zones," *Annals of the Association of American Geographers*, 1968, pp. 461–484.

——, "The Zone in Transition: A Study of Urban Land Use Patterns," *Economic Geography*, 1966, pp. 236–260.

RAY, D. MICHAEL, and BREWIS, THOMAS N., "The Geography of Income and Its Correlates," *The Canadian Geographer*, 1976, pp. 41–71.

ROEDER, PHILLIP G., and MITCHELL, RICHARD A., "The Importance of Type of Business in Junk Yard Location," *Proceedings of the Association of American Geographers*, 1975, pp. 182–185.

ROSENBURG, TERRY J., *Residence, Employment and Mobility of Puerto Ricans in New York City*, Univ. of Chicago, Dept. of Geography, Research Paper No. 151, Chicago, 1974.

SARGENT, CHARLES S., JR., "Toward a Dynamic Model of Urban Morphology," *Economic Geography*, 1972, pp. 357–374.

STERNLIEB, GEORGE, and HUGHES, JAMES W., editors, *Post-Industrial America: Metropolitan Decline & Inter-Regional Job Shifts*, New Brunswick, N. J., 1975, 267 pp.

STRUYK, R. J., and JAMES F. J., *Intra-metropolitan Industrial Locations*, Lexington, Mass. 1975.

WARD, DAVID, "The Industrial Revolution and the Emergence of Boston's Central Business District," *Economic Geography*, 1966, pp. 152–171.

WEAVER, DAVID C., "Changes in the Morphology of Three American Central Business Districts, 1952–1966," *The Professional Geographer*, 1969, pp. 406–410.

WISEMAN, ROBERT F., and VIRDEN, MARK, "Spatial and Social Dimensions of Intraurban Elderly Migration," *Economic Geography*, 1977, pp. 1–13.

YOUNG, WILLIAM J., "Distance Decay Values and Shopping Center Size," *The Professional Geographer*, 1975, pp. 304–309.

NINE

MEASUREMENT, THEORY, AND PLANNING

In Parts One through Eight of this book we have dealt with population and specific types of economic endeavor, attempting to show their general locational pattern, their distinguishing characteristics, and some of the relationships pertinent to them. The strategy has been to proceed from the less complex to the more complex categories of economic pursuits; accordingly, we began first with *primitive* gathering then moved "upward" through *subsistence* grazing, subsistence cultivation, *commercial primary* production (fishing, forestry, bioculture, and mining), commercial *secondary* production (manufacturing and transportation), and finally into commercial *tertiary* endeavors.

Now we turn attention to some ideas that are pertinent to the entire array of economic activities. In Chapter 29 we tackle the problem of measurement, specifically, the measurement of a single economic endeavor (for example: How much manufacturing is there in Sweden?) and then the measurement of association between an endeavor and some other phenomenon (for instance, how strong is the correlation, or association, between the location of cash-grain farming and the location of flat land?).

In Chapter 30 we deal with location theory—attempts to formulate statements that express principles governing the location of economic activity. Some theories endeavor to state cause-and-effect relationships; other theories express relationships that are more matters of "associations" than of causal or consequential connections.

In the final chapter, 31, we shall essay a few summarizing comments about the current levels of areal development, first on a world scale and then on a national scale. We shall direct our attention toward a few problems that demand solution, problems with which spatial analysts (whether they be beginning students in geography, advanced geographic researchers, or professional regional planners) should be concerned. In the process, we shall make mention of specific efforts that have been made to improve the economic health of areas, some on a large scale and some on a small scale.

CHAPTER

29

measurement of location and association

A portion of the port of New York—the Brooklyn and Queens shoreline on the right, Manhattan in the center, and New Jersey to the left. Employment in some industries is associated with city size. What are some industries that appear to be positively correlated with population ? (*Courtesy Port Authority of New York and New Jersey.*)

Figure 29-1 (*After John Weaver, from* Economic Geography.)

Knowledge of the amount and kind of economic endeavor in any given place, understanding of the comparison of places in amount and type of economic activity, and comprehension of the way an economic activity is related to some other phenomenon—all these goals of scientific investigation require accurate *measurement* of economic activity.

We shall be concerned here with two types of measurement. One is the measurement of a single economic activity, the second the measurement of the association between two phenomena: an economic activity and another variable—for example, manufacturing and population. In a sense, the former provides answers to the first two questions (on location and characteristics) of the geographic method we have been following, while the latter serves the third question (on relationships).

MEASURING A SINGLE ECONOMIC ACTIVITY

How much manufacturing is there in India? What is the leading manufactural industry in France? What is the leading industrial nation in Europe? How much agriculture is there in the U.S.S.R.? What is the leading type of agriculture in Guatemala? Where are the major agricultural areas of China? What is the most important mining activity in the United States? What nations lead the world in harvesting forest products? How important

is fishing in the economic life of Japan? How important is wholesale trade in the economy of Winnipeg?

Answering such questions of where and what requires quantification of individual economic activities. Such quantification is necessary in order to study those endeavors by themselves or in relation to one another.

Choosing Criteria

All very well to know that we must measure, but how do we select the relevant elements for measurement? At the outset of any scientific investigation, we must formulate our objectives as clearly as possible. This done, we must make a choice of the criteria that will be the most useful measuring-sticks in working toward those objectives. If we are analyzing the geography of cotton production, for instance, should we measure that activity in terms of the number of cotton-growing farms, the number of acres devoted to cotton production, the number of bales of cotton produced, the value of cotton crops, or something else?

Or again, suppose we are analyzing the locational pattern of agriculture to determine the "leading" state in the United States. In terms of *acres of land in farms*, Texas, with 143,000,000 acres, is the nation's leading agricultural state. But when we adopt *value of farm products sold* as our criterion, then California, with $3.9 billion, ranks for ahead of any other state. If *average value of farms* be the criterion, Arizona is the front runner, since the average farm value there is $452,000. Examples could be cited not only from agriculture, but also from all other classes of economic endeavor to illustrate the fact that different locational patterns of an activity may be revealed by different criteria. Clearly, we must be careful to select the right criterion in tracing the aspect we want to study.

Figure 29-1 portrays an example of a pattern produced when a "leading" (or "first-ranking") element is taken as the mapping unit. In this map of 12 contiguous midwestern states, counties are the areal units of measurement, and the "first-ranking" type of livestock on farms is the criterion for measurement. This map reveals the location of several agricultural regions, particularly those specializing in dairy farming and in mixed farming.

Clearly, then, regardless of the economic activity being investigated, the choice of criteria is a fundamental problem every analyst must face.

MEASURING GEOGRAPHIC ASSOCIATION

In Chapter 1 we pointed out that relationships between geographic phenomena can be approached from four different perspectives: from the standpoint of physical and cultural conditions, or of intraregional and extraregional relationships, or of cause and effect, or of covariation. Advocates of this last approach emphasize the importance of the *geographical association* of phenomena as they vary from place to place. The term has a precise meaning: That is, if two phenomena reach high values

in the same places and low values in similar other places, they are said to have a close geographical association.

The question naturally arises: How does one determine whether two phenomena are geographically associated? There are numerous possibilities for determining such association, nine of which will concern us here. These are: the visual comparison of maps, the ratio map, the location quotient, the coefficient of geographic association, index of concentration, analysis of rank, scatter diagrams, the coefficient of correlation, and the mapping of residuals from regressions.

Visual Comparison of Maps

Suppose we were interested in understanding the geographic relationship between labor force (measured in terms of total number of people employed) and manufacturing (measured in terms of number of manufactural employees) in the state of Ohio. Now, first we might select *counties* as our areal unit of measurement and proceed to construct two maps, one based on *number of employees in manufacturing*, the other on the total *number of employed people*. For the first, in each county we would plot the number of manufactural employees. Then we would apply in each county a visual symbol (say, a circle), the size of which would be proportionate to the number of employees (Figure 29-2). Similarly, for the labor force,

Figure 29-2

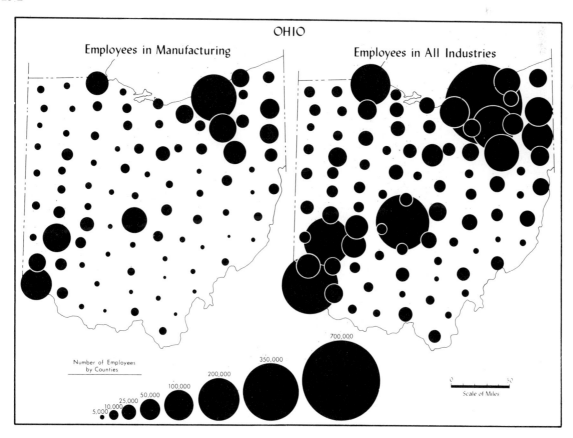

county by county, for the second map. The next task would be to compare the two maps. If each portrayed the *same pattern*, we could conclude that the two phenomena have a close geographic association.

The difficulties of the visual inspection method are twofold. First, an enormous amount of time would be required to construct a series of such maps for any large region. For the United States, which contains more than 2000 counties, data would have to be plotted in each county, the size of symbols would have to be computed mathematically, and the symbols would have to be put on the maps. The second difficulty is more serious: Even when the maps are done, visual comparison is subject to human differences. Various scholars inspecting the results might arrive at different conclusions. One analyst might conclude that the two maps revealed essentially *the same* pattern, another that the two patterns were *almost* the same ("rather similar"), and a third, impressed with the differences between the two maps, might conclude that in his opinion, their patterns should not even be termed "similar." In other words, *visual inspection alone permits little scientific quantification of the similarity in locational patterns portrayed by different maps.*

In a scientific analysis of the visual comparison method, Harold McCarty and Neil Salisbury of the State University of Iowa ran several experiments with geography scholars to determine the reliability of this method in appraising the degree of association between isopleth maps.[1] Here are some of their findings and conclusions.

It is easier for the eye to measure the degree of association between two maps if their correlation is highly positive (see Chapter 1 and later in this chapter) than if it is weakly positive. Appraisal of correlation by this method becomes highly erratic where the correlation is negative.

> In brief, the findings do not support the contention that visual comparisons of isopleth maps provide an effective means of determining or demonstrating the degree of association that exists between sets of spatially distributed phenomena. Only in cases in which the degree of association is very high does the process produce results which approach the standards of accuracy generally demanded in present-day research and teaching. In situations involving lesser degrees of association, the visual-comparison procedure must be viewed as an inadequate substitute for measurement where a determination of the extent of such an association is required.
>
> On the other hand, visual methods produce generally satisfactory results, even among untrained students, when the sole object is to select pairs of maps whose distributions are most highly correlated when several alternative choices are available. . . .

---

[1]An isopleth is a line on a map and connects points of equal value. On one side of the line is an area of higher values; on the other side of the line is an area of lower values. For an example of isopleths, see Figure 29-5, page 435.

If the degree of association is very high, and if the direction of that association is positive, map comparison may be expected to produce reasonably good results, provided the maps are comparable with respect to colors and intervals. In cases involving lesser degrees of association, however, there is no assurance that the desired effect will be created.[2]

The Ratio Map

In drawing a ratio map, a geographer endeavors to show the degrees of relationship between two variables as they differ from place to place. The method for constructing a ratio map is to show in each areal unit, not the value of each of the two elements separately, but rather the *ratio* between the two. For example, the varying relationship from county to county between the number of manufacturing employees and number of persons in the labor force can be expressed in terms of *the percentage of employed persons in manufacturing.*

If two phenomena vary *similarly* from county to county, the ratio between them will tend to be *constant*, in which a close geographic association exists. But if they vary dissimilarly from place to place, so will the ratio. And the greater its variation, the weaker the geographic association between the two elements.

In the state of Ohio, the ratio between number of manufactural employees and total number of workers varies from a maximum of 49 per cent in Trumbull County to 13 per cent in Athens County. For the state as a whole the figure is 36 per cent. From such variation relative to the state percentage, we can discern four categories of counties. Of Ohio's 88 counties, 48 are above the state percentage and 40 below. The median percentage for the 48 above-average counties is 41.1 per cent. The median refers to the midpoint, and designating it splits the group into two halves. Of the 48 counties, 24 are *above* 41.4 per cent, 24 are *below* 41.4 per cent, but all are above the state percentage of 36. The median for the 40 below-average counties is 30.2 per cent—20 counties below, 20 above, yet all below the stage average percentage. Our first category, then, consists of 24 counties that are not only above the state percentage but are also above the median of the above-average counties. The second category consists of 24 counties, which are above the state's ratio but less than the above-average median; the third category consists of 20 counties whose ratios are between 30.2 and 36 per cent; and the fourth category also consists of 20 counties, those with ratios of less than 30.2 percent. The last step is to present the four different categories on the map by means of distinctive shading.

Spatial variation in the relationship between manufactural employment and total employment in Ohio on a county basis is shown in Figure 29-3, where each county is shaded with a symbol indicating to which of the four categories it belongs.

Ratio maps are useful in showing how closely any

---

[2]Harold H. McCarty and Neil E. Salisbury, *Visual Comparison of Isopleth Maps as a Means of Determining Correlations Between Spatially Distributed Phenomena* (Iowa City), 1961, 81 pp.

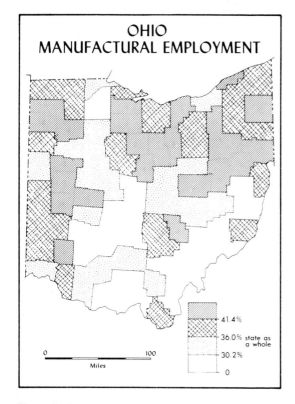

OHIO
MANUFACTURAL EMPLOYMENT

41.4%

36.0% state as a whole

30.2%

0

0   100
Miles

Figure 29-3

Iowa $\dfrac{512,371}{2,824,376} = 18.1$

Missouri $\dfrac{359,319}{4,676,501} = 7.7$

Wisconsin $\dfrac{415,206}{4,417,731} = 9.4$

Illinois $\dfrac{428,726}{11,109,935} = 3.9$

The location quotient of farm population for each state is determined by dividing its percentage by the national percentage of 4.1. If a state has a location quotient exceeding 1.0 it has "more than its share" of the nation's farm population; a quotient of under 1.0 (the quotient can never be less than zero) indicates "less than its share."

In brief, the formula for the location quotient in this illustration is as follows:

$$\dfrac{\dfrac{\text{state's farm population}}{\text{state's total population}}}{\dfrac{\text{United States farm population}}{\text{United States total population}}}$$

Accordingly the location quotients for these nine states in terms of their total population and farm population are as follows:

North Dakota $\dfrac{24.6}{4.1} = 6.00$

South Dakota $\dfrac{24.5}{4.1} = 5.98$

Nebraska $\dfrac{16.1}{4.1} = 3.93$

Kansas $\dfrac{10.6}{4.1} = 2.59$

Minnesota $\dfrac{11.9}{4.1} = 2.90$

Iowa $\dfrac{18.1}{4.1} = 4.41$

Missouri $\dfrac{7.7}{4.1} = 1.88$

Wisconsin $\dfrac{9.4}{4.1} = 2.29$

Illinois $\dfrac{3.9}{4.1} = .95$

The foregoing methods have proved highly useful for many purposes of geographic analysis. However, some geographers believe that more fruitful results can be obtained from methods that are mathematically more sophisticated. We shall now examine six such methods. All endeavor to apply the techniques of mathematics to the problem of measuring the association

two variables—whether they be manufactural employment and total employment, or wheat yields and rainfall, or value of retail trade sales and number of inhabitants —are associated as they differ from place to place.

Location Quotient

The *location quotient* concept was introduced in Chapter 23 where we described its computation in a manufacturing example, but it can be used for any other economic endeavor. In brief, the location quotient is a ratio of ratios. To illustrate: The ratio of farm population to total population for the United States as a whole is

$$\dfrac{\text{farm population}}{\text{population}} = \dfrac{8,292,150}{203,212,877} = 4.1$$

The ratios of these two variables for selected midwestern states are as follows:

North Dakota $\dfrac{152,261}{617,761} = 24.6$

South Dakota $\dfrac{162,730}{665,507} = 24.5$

Nebraska $\dfrac{237,978}{1,482,412} = 16.1$

Kansas $\dfrac{237,944}{2,246,578} = 10.6$

Minnesota $\dfrac{454,516}{3,804,971} = 11.9$

between two phenomena as they vary from place to place. Each of them, in its own way, can shed some light on the degree to which the two locational patterns are alike, in terms of *geographic association*.

Coefficient of Geographic Association

We shall illustrate the computation of the *coefficient of geographic association* in terms of three categories of employment: (1) all manufacturing, (2) food manufacturing, and (3) electrical machinery manufacturing. Our areal units will be the 50 states and Washington, D.C.

First construct a table of values as in Table 29-1. List each areal unit in the left-hand column; in columns to the right (2 and 4 in Table 29-1), enter each areal unit's *percentage* of the national total of whatever phenomena are under investigation. Obviously, to establish these values, other numerical data must be available. To illustrate, Iowa has 1.1 per cent of the nation's total manufacturing, 3.2 per cent of the nation's food manufacturing, and 1.2 per cent of the nation's electrical machinery manufacturing (all measured in terms of employment).

The next step is to compute for each state the *difference* between its percentage in each industry and its percentage in total manufactural employment. For Iowa the difference for the food industry would be determined as follows: Food industry percentage (3.2) minus total manufactural employment percentage (1.1) yields a *difference* of +2.1. If a state's percentage in any particular manufacturing is *less than* its percentage in all manufacturing, then its difference is a negative figure; Minnesota's differential for the electrical machinery industry is −0.5.

Now compute the *sum of either* the positive differences *or* the negative differences. (It makes no difference which is chosen since their totals will be exactly the same.) Divide that figure by 100 and subtract it from unity (1.000). The result is the coefficient of geographic association for the industry in question.

Now for the food industry in our example, the sum of the positive (or negative) differences is 17.9 (column 3). Divide that by 100, which gives 0.179. Subtract that figure from 1 to find the coefficient, in this case, 0.821.

For employment in electrical machinery manufacturing, add the differences recorded in column 5 of Table 29-1. Since the sum is 16.7, the coefficient is 0.833 (16.7 ÷ 100 = 0.167; 1.000 − 0.167 = 0.833).

The higher the figure, of course, the closer the correlation. Accordingly, we can conclude that within the United States, electrical machinery manufacturing varies from place to place in slightly closer association with all manufacturing than does the food industry.

The coefficient of geographic association may reach 1.00, if two phenomena are perfectly associated geo-

graphically, varying from place to place in exactly the same manner and degree. At the other extreme the coefficient may reach 0.000 if two activities are located so dissimilarly that *all* the persons engaged in such activity are in locales containing *no* one engaged in the other. In this instance, the sum of the differences would be 100.

Sometimes the coefficient of geographic association is called the *coefficient of linkage* or the *coefficient of similarity*. Although illustrated above with manufacturing, this device, whatever the name, can be used for measuring the association of any pair of phenomena.

Index of Concentration

The index of concentration is a measure of the degree to which an activity is concentrated regionally. It is based on a comparison between the distribution of two phenomena—in the illustration to follow we shall use employment in the transportation equipment industry and number of inhabitants. The index of concentration is computed as follows:

1. Determine the total population of the United States and the total employment in the transportation equipment industry.

   United States population
   (1972 census estimate)   208,230,000
   Employment in transportation
   equipment industry   1,719,000

2. Take one-half the employment figure in the industry (the significance of the half will be apparent later). Transportation equipment employment: 1,719,000 ÷ 2 = 859,500

3. For each state compute the employment/population ratio in terms of the number of transportation equipment workers per 1000 persons. For example, the ratio for Michigan is as follows:

   Population in thousands: 9013
   Employees in transportation
   equipment: 310,000
   Ratio: transportation equipment
   employees per 1000 population: 34.4

4. List the states in descending order according to the above ratio (see Table 29-2, columns A and B).

5. For each state in the array, indicate the number of employees in the transportation equipment industry (Table 29-2, column C) and the population, in thousands (column D).

6. Beginning with the state that has the highest *ratio* (for the transportation equipment industry, this state is Michigan), add the *number of employees* by state until a cumulative figure equal to *half* the national total is reached. (The last state listed may bring the cumulative sum to more than one-half; therefore, it must be prorated). The states that contribute to this cumulative figure constitute the *areas of concentration* of the industry being measured. As

Table 29-1

Table of Values for Computing Coefficients of Geographic Association in Selected Industries

Areal Unit	All Manu- facturing	Food Industry	Difference (Column 2 minus Column 1)		Electrical Machinery Industry	Difference (Column 4 minus Column 1)	
			Employment by Percentage of United States Totals				
Maine	0.5	0.8	+0.3		0.2		−0.3
New Hampshire	0.5	0.2		−0.3	0.7	+0.2	
Vermont	0.2	0.1		−0.1	0.2		
Massachusetts	3.3	2.1		−1.2	4.7	+1.4	
Rhode Island	0.6	0.3		−0.3	0.5		−0.1
Connecticut	2.1	0.7		−1.4	2.4	+0.3	
New York	8.8	5.9		−2.9	9.8	+1.0	
New Jersey	4.4	3.4		−1.0	5.8	+1.4	
Pennsylvania	7.4	6.2		−1.2	7.0		−0.4
Ohio	7.1	4.7		−2.4	6.6		−0.5
Indiana	3.7	2.4		−1.3	7.0	+3.3	
Illinois	6.9	7.2	+0.3		10.4	+3.5	
Michigan	5.6	3.1		−2.5	2.2		−3.4
Wisconsin	2.6	3.6	+1.0		2.9	+0.3	
Minnesota	1.6	2.9	+1.3		1.1		−0.5
Iowa	1.1	3.2	+2.1		1.2	+0.1	
Missouri	2.3	2.7	+0.4		2.0		−0.3
North Dakota	0.1	0.2	+0.1				−0.1
South Dakota	0.1	0.5	+0.4		0.1		
Nebraska	0.4	1.6	+1.2		0.6	+0.2	
Kansas	0.7	1.2	+0.5		0.2		−0.5
Delaware	0.4	0.5	+0.1		0.1		−0.3
Maryland	1.3	2.0	+0.7		1.7	+0.4	
Washington, D.C.	0.1	0.1			0.1		
Virginia	2.0	2.1	+0.1		1.7		−0.3
West Virginia	0.6	0.4		−0.2	0.3		−0.3
North Carolina	3.9	2.4		−1.5	2.1		−1.8
South Carolina	1.8	0.8		−1.0	0.8		−1.0
Georgia	2.5	2.9	+0.4		0.7		−1.8
Florida	1.8	2.8	+1.0		2.0	+0.2	
Kentucky	1.4	1.4			2.1	+0.7	
Tennessee	2.5	2.1		−0.4	2.1		−0.4
Alabama	1.7	1.6		−0.1	0.8		−0.9
Mississippi	1.1	1.1			0.9		−0.2
Arkansas	1.0	1.6	+0.6		1.1	+0.1	
Louisiana	0.9	1.8	+0.9		0.4		−0.5
Oklahoma	0.8	0.9	+0.1		0.7		−0.1
Texas	3.9	4.9	+1.0		3.3		−0.6
Montana	0.1	0.2	+0.1				−0.1
Idaho	0.2	0.9	+0.7		0.1		−0.1
Wyoming		0.1	+0.1				
Colorado	0.7	1.4	+0.7		0.4		−0.3
New Mexico	0.1	0.2	+0.1		0.2	+0.1	
Arizona	0.5	0.4		−0.1	1.4	+0.9	
Utah	0.3	0.4	+0.1		0.2		−0.1
Nevada	0.1	0.1			0.1		
Washington	1.2	1.7	+0.5		0.2		−1.0
Oregon	0.9	1.4	+0.5		0.2		−0.7
California	8.1	9.8	+1.7		10.7	+2.6	
Alaska		0.2	+0.2				
Hawaii	0.1	0.8	+0.7				−0.1
TOTALS	100.0	100.0	17.9	17.9	100.0	16.7	16.7

Source: Computed from *Census of Manufacturers* (1975).

Table 29-2

Computation of Index of Concentration

TRANSPORTATION EQUIPMENT INDUSTRY

United States population:	208,230,000
United States employment in manufacture of transportation equipment:	1,719,000
Half of the total employment in the industry is:	859,500

Column A	Column B Number of Transportation Equipment Employees per 1,000 Population	Column C Employees in Transportation Equipment Industry	Column D Population in Thousands
Michigan	34.4	310,000	9,013
Connecticut	22.5	69,400	3,080
Indiana	18.0	95,000	5,286
Ohio	15.0	161,400	10,722
Washington	15.0	51,200	3,418
Missouri	14.6	69,400	4,747
Kansas	13.2	29,900	2,268

Cumulative total of above seven states: 786,300

Additonal number of employees required to equal half the national total: 73,200

Total: 859,500

27.3%

California 13.1 268,300

5,572 (27.3% of California's population of 20,411,000)

44,106 Total which is 21.2% of total United States population

Index of Concentration (100 minus 21.2) is 78.8

Table 29-2 reveals, for the transportation equipment industry, the areas of concentration are Michigan, Connecticut, Indiana, Ohio, Washington, Missouri, Kansas, and part of California.

7. Compute the percentage of employment in this industry in California required to bring the cumulative employment to 859,500 (half the national total in this industry).

California: (a) total employment in transporation equipment: 268,300
(b) required for cumulative total: 73,200
Percentage (b)/(a) 27.3%

8. Apply this percentage to California's population.

$$20,411,000 \times 27.3\% = 5,572,000$$

9. Enter 5572 (27.3% of California's population in thousands) in column D of Table 29-2.
10. Add the entries in column D. The total is 44,106.
11. Convert this figure (44,106) to a percentage of the nation's total population.

(a) United States population: 208,230,000

(b) Population total in column D: 44,106,000
Percentage (b)/(a): 21.2%

This step reveals that one-half of the nation's transportation equipment workers are concentrated in an area that contains only 21.2 per cent of the nation's people. (This is obviously a highly concentrated industry since half of its employment is packed into just eight states.)

12. Subtract the percentage figure just computed (21.2) from 100. The result, 78.8, is the *index of concentration* for the transportation equipment industry. In 1954 the index was 82.8; the difference today indicates that this industry has become less concentrated.

The higher this index, the greater the geographic concentration of the industry, the lower the index, the more widespread or scattered the industry. A truly ubiquitous industry would have an index of 50, if by *ubiquitous* we mean that the industry is located in direct proportion to the population, that the two are perfectly *associated geographically* with each other. The index could never reach 100, for that would mean that all of the

Table 29-2—_Continued_

BAKERY PRODUCTS INDUSTRY

United States employment in manufacture of
   bakery products: 234,600

Half of the total employment in the
   industry is: 117,300

Column A	Column B	Column C	Column D
North Carolina	1.9	9,800	5,221
Georgia	1.7	7,900	4,733
Pennsylvania	1.6	19,400	11,905
Illinois	1.6	18,200	11,244
New Jersey	1.6	11,800	7,349
Tennessee	1.6	6,500	4,072
Maine	1.5	1,500	1,026
Rhode Island	1.4	1,400	969
Ohio	1.4	14,800	10,722
Colorado	1.4	3,200	2,364
Missouri	1.3	6,300	4,747
Connecticut	1.3	3,900	3,080
North Dakota	1.3	800	634
Oregon	1.2	2,600	2,185
Massachusetts	1.2	6,800	5,796

Cumulative total of the
   above fifteen states: 114,900 ⎫

Additional number of   ⎬ Total:
   employees required to equal   117,300
   half the national total: 2,400 ⎭

Maryland   1.2   4,700 ⎫   51.1%

                                         2,069
                                       (51.1% of Maryland's
                                       population of
                                       4,048,000)

                         Total which is 37.5%   78,116
                         of total United States
                         population

Index of Concentration (100 minus 37.5) is 62.5.

---

employment in an industry exists in an area containing no people. Neither could the index drop below 50. (If a person did arrive at an index of 40, for example, it would indicate an error in calculation—probably that he failed to array the states properly and entered in his table in steps 3 and 4 some states which did not belong so high in the ranking.)

In Table 29-2 we also show computations for determining the index of concentration for the bakery products industry. That this is a far more ubiquitous business than the transportation equipment industry is revealed by the following characteristics: (a) 16 states are required to make the cumulative half of the national total employment, (b) there is little difference in _ratio_ (column B) among these 16 states, and (c) the index of concentration is only 62.5. In 1954 the index was also 62.5.

In general, high indexes indicate that various combined relationships give competitive advantages to only a few locations; low indexes indicate that interacting relationships favor numerous places, none of which has a markedly superior competitive advantage.

Although the foregoing discussion of the _index of concentration_ was based on data for individual states and for manufacturing, the concept can be applied to counties, cities, or any other areal unit one chooses and to any type of economic activity.

Analysis of Rank

Another method for quantifying relationships is _correlation of rank_. By this technique, which can be applied to any criteria or any areal units, places are first simply arrayed according to their rankings in terms of whatever phenomena are under study. Suppose, for example, that we are interested in observing the relationships among population, employment in the baking industry, and employment in meat-packing plants as they vary from state to state in the United States. Our first step would be to construct three lists, each ranking the states in descending order in terms of one of the criteria. How such a list would be constructed is shown in Table 29-3, which gives the ten leading states in each category.

If we compare the three columns we find that the rankings are not exactly the same in any two lists. Even so, the first two columns are considerably more alike than are columns 1 and 3 or columns 2 and 3. Therefore, we can conclude that there is a closer relationship between *population* and *employment in the bakery industry* than between any other pair of variables appearing in this table. The more similar the rankings, the closer the relationship as revealed by the rank-analysis method.

The rank-analysis method presents some severe difficulties, however. One is the matter of *differences between rank values.* Ten states (as in Table 29-3) might conceivably have exactly the same rankings in two listings, but their relative values in the two might be vastly different from one another. Measuring them by rank alone would not reveal such differences. Another difficulty is the question of *ties*: If two states have exactly the same value, what ranking is ascribed to each?

To help overcome this difficulty, statisticians have developed formulae for computing *rank correlations*, which are mathematical measurements of the similarity between two lists of rankings. However, these are beyond the scope of this volume and are best reserved for more advanced courses in economic geography.

Scatter Diagram

A relatively simple yet very helpful device for visually portraying the relationship between different phenomena is the *scatter diagram,* a graph on which one plots dots, each one representing an areal unit (e.g, a state, a county, or a city). This technique has already been touched upon in Chapter 17. In the paragraphs to follow, we shall illustrate the scatter diagram technique in terms of number of inhabitants, employment in retail trade, and agricultural employment expressed as a percentage of total population. For convenience, we have created nine hypothetical states as our areal units. And in demonstrating the steps in the construction of a scatter diagram, we shall use the data given for the nine states in Table 29-4.

Table 29-4

Selected Data for Nine Hypothetical States

State	Population	Employees in Retail Trade	Employment in Agriculture as a Percentage of Total Employment
A	10,081,158	463,808	2.5
B	3,951,777	164,030	7.5
C	4,319,813	192,596	6.5
D	2,757,537	118,429	10.6
E	3,413,864	145,954	8.1
F	2,178,611	92,480	7.5
G	1,411,330	64,723	11.2
H	680,514	26,374	13.8
I	632,446	25,053	14.8

Now, a scatter diagram portrays the relationship between any *two* phenomena, so we can deal with only two of these elements at a time. Therefore, Figure 29-4, Part A, relates to *population* and *employment in retail trade,* Part B to *population* and *percentage of population employed in agriculture* (page 431).

The vertical axis of a scatter diagram is scaled for plotting one variable, the horizontal axis for plotting a second. The scales need not be the same. Thus, each areal unit can be represented by means of a single dot, whose position is fixed by that place's value on each of the two scales. For example, on Figure 29-4, Part, A

Table 29-3

Ranks of Leading States in Terms of Selected Criteria

Rank	Population	Rank	Employment in Bakery Products	Rank	Employment in Meat Packing
1	California	1	California	1	Iowa
2	New York	2	Pennsylvania	2	Texas
3	Pennsylvania	3	Illinois	3	Minnesota
4	Texas	4	New York	4	Nebraska
5	Illinois	5	Ohio	5	Ohio
6	Ohio	6	New Jersey	6	Illinois
7	Michigan	7	Texas	7	Wisconsin
8	New Jersey	8	North Carolina	8	California
9	Florida	9	Michigan	9	Kansas
10	Massachusetts	10	Georgia	10	Tennessee
				10	Colorado

Sources: U.S. Bureau of the Census, *1972 Census of Manufactures* (1975) and *Statistical Abstract of the United States* (1975).

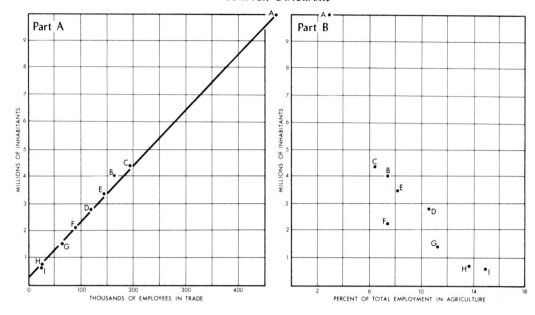

SCATTER DIAGRAMS

Figure 29-4

state E is represented by a dot opposite 3.4 on the vertical scale (because its population is 3,413,864) and opposite 1.4 on the horizontal scale (because 145,954 of its inhabitants are employed in trade).

After we have plotted all the dots on a scatter diagram, we can answer the following:

First, do the dots tend to align? If they do *not*, there is little correlation between the two variables. Dispersion of dots suggests scarcely any covariation of the variables in the areas being plotted, If the dots *do* tend to align, then correlation exists (unless the line is exactly horizontal or exactly vertical, either of which indicates that one of the two measurements is a spatial constant, and does not vary from place to place). And the nearer the dots lie to a line, the closer the relationship between the two.

Second, *if the dots do align, in what direction is the line oriented?* If the line slants *upward*, from left to right, it indicates positive (or direct) correlation. That is, as one variable *increases*, the other variable *increases* also, as illustrated by Part A of Figure 29-4. If the line slants *downward* from left to right it indicates *negative* (or inverse) correlation. That is, as one variable *increases*, the other variable *decreases*, as illustrated by Part B of Figure 29-4. The name given to this hypothetical line is *regression line*.

We can discern quite a bit about the correlation of two variables by inspecting a scatter diagram. But we can be far more precise if we go on to compute the regression line mathematically. We shall examine this operation in connection with Figure 29-4, Part A.

Regression Line. Three major steps are involved in computing a regression line: construction of a Table

of Values, computation of the *a* value of the regression line, and computation of the *b* value of the regression line.

1. Construction of a Table of Values: A Table of Values contains data for the two relevant phenomena (in our example, population and employment in trade) in five columns (see Table 29-5). Column 1 lists values in each areal unit for one of the phenomena being studied, the one plotted on the horizontal axis or the scatter diagram; column 2 contains the *squares* of the values in column 1; column 3 shows values for the second phenomenon being studied, the one plotted on the vertical axis; column 4 has the *squares* of those in column 3; the entries in column 5 are *products* of the values in column 1 and those in column 3. Each areal unit being studied has one entry in each of the five columns.

   Statisticians have adopted certain symbols for each of the various components of Table 29-5: Thus, x for the phenomenon quantified in column 1, y for that in column 3, and Σ for the total of any column.

2. Computation of the *a* value of the regression line: The *a* value is the point of origin of the regression line on the vertical axis, that is, it is the point from which the line moves from left to right across the scatter diagram.

   The value of *a* is computed by determining a ratio, both the numerator and denominator of which are built up from the totals appearing at the bottom of columns in the Table of Values, as shown below. (The reader should not attempt to memorize this formula but rather read through it endeavoring to see how each part of it relates to the Table of Values.)

Table 29-5

Table of Values: Selected Criteria for Nine Hypothetical States

State	Column 1 (Value Graphed on Horizontal Axis of Scatter Diagram) Employment in Trade (Thousands)	Column 2 Square of Value in Column 1	Column 3 (Value Graphed on Vertical Axis of Scatter Diagram) Population (millions)	Column 4 Square of Value in Column 3	Column 5 Product of Values in Columns 1 and 3
A	463	214,369	10.0	100.00	4630.0
B	164	26,896	3.9	15.21	639.6
C	192	36,864	4.3	18.49	825.6
D	118	13,924	2.7	7.29	318.6
E	145	21,025	3.4	11.56	493.0
F	92	8,464	2.1	4.41	193.2
G	64	4,096	1.4	1.96	89.6
H	26	676	0.6	0.36	15.6
I	25	625	0.6	0.36	15.0
TOTALS	1,289	326,939	29.0	159.64	7220.2
Statistical symbols for items in above columns:	x	x^2	y	y^2	xy
Symbols for totals:	Σx	Σx^2	Σy	Σy^2	Σxy

ORIGIN of the regression line on vertical axis } equals {

RATIO

Numerator which consists of:

$\begin{bmatrix}\text{Column 2 total}\\ \textit{multiplied by}\\ \text{Column 3 total}\end{bmatrix}$ minus $\begin{bmatrix}\text{Column 1 total}\\ \textit{multiplied by}\\ \text{Column 5 total}\end{bmatrix}$

Denominator which consists of:

$\begin{bmatrix}\text{Number of areal units}\\ \textit{multiplied by}\\ \text{Column 2 total}\end{bmatrix}$ minus $\begin{bmatrix}\text{Square of}\\ \text{Column 1}\\ \text{total}\end{bmatrix}$

The above equation can be expressed tersely, in the language of statistical symbols, thus:

$$a = \frac{(\Sigma x^2 \cdot \Sigma y) - (\Sigma x \cdot \Sigma xy)}{(N \cdot \Sigma x^2) - (\Sigma x)^2}$$

The solution to the equation for our example is accomplished by substituting in the proper places the entries from Table 29-5:

$$a = \frac{(326,939 \cdot 29.0) - (1,289 \cdot 7,220.2)}{(9 \cdot 326,939) - (1,289)^2}$$

$$a = \frac{9,481,231.0 - 9,306,837.8}{2,942,451 - 1,661,521}$$

$$a = \frac{174,393.2}{1,280,930.0}$$

$$a = 0.13$$

The figure just reached must be read in millions, since that is the unit of measurement used in calibrating the vertical axis on Figure 29-4A. Thus, the regression line on Figure 29-4A intersects the vertical axis at the value of 0.13 million.

3. Computation of the *b* value of regression line: The *b* value is the average change in *y* with a given change change in *x*. That is, for every one unit of measurement marked off on the horizontal axis, the regression line moves *vertically* the number of units indicated by the

b value. The b value is computed by solving this equation:

$$b = \frac{(N \cdot \Sigma\, xy) - (\Sigma x \cdot \Sigma\, y)}{(N \cdot \Sigma\, x^2) - (\Sigma x)^2}$$

When the appropriate entries from the Table of Values are inserted in the above equation, it reads as follows:

$$b = \frac{(9 \cdot 7{,}220.2) - (1{,}289 \cdot 29.0)}{(9 \cdot 326{,}939) - (1{,}289)^2}$$

$$b = \frac{64{,}981.8 - 37{,}381.0}{2{,}942{,}451 - 1{,}661{,}521}$$

$$b = \frac{27{,}600.8}{1{,}280{,}930.0}$$

$$b = 0.021$$

This figure must be read in millions of population per thousand of trade employees, since these are the units in which the vertical and horizontal axes of Figure 29-4A are calibrated. The regression line, then, moves *upward* at the rate of 0.021 million vertical units for each horizontal unit; for every 100,000 employees in retail trade (horizontal axis) the regression line will rise 2.1 millions on the population scale (vertical axis). The regression line on Part A of Figure 29-4 does this.

The regression line on Figure 29-4, Part B has not been constructed—in hopes that the reader might want to try his hand at constructing it himself. (NOTE: The *a* value will be positive, the *b* value will be negative.)

What do the two scatter diagrams in Figure 29-4 tell us? Part A (on the relationship between *population* and *employment in trade*) shows a positive correlation—as population increases, there is a tendency for employment in trade to increase.

Part B (on the relationship between *population* and the *agricultural percentage of total employment*) shows a negative correlation—as population increases from state to state (at least for these nine states), there is a tendency for the relative importance of agriculture in the employment structure to decline.

We can discern something about the relationship

between two spatial variables if we construct a scatter diagram to show their variation through different areas. We can learn more about their relationship by plotting their regression line, and still more if we compute their *coefficient of correlation*.

Coefficient of Correlation

One of the best-known and most frequently used methods for measuring the relationship between two phenomena is the *Pearson Product Moment Coefficient of Correlation*.

If two phenomena vary similarly from place to place (that is, if both tend to reach their high values in the same places and their low values in other, similar, places), under the Pearson formula they have a coefficient that is a *positive* number.

If such covariation is perfect, their correlation is said to be complete, and by the Pearson formula the coefficient would be +1.00. (This would occur, for instance, if the dots on a scatter diagram conformed to a straight line slanting upward.)

On the other hand, if two criteria vary oppositely (that is, if one reaches a high value in those places where the other is low, and vice versa) the coefficient is a *negative number*, which indicates a *negative* (or *inverse*) *correlation*. The more unlike the two patterns, the closer their coefficient approaches −1.00, a figure that indicates complete inverse variation. (This would occur if the dots on a scatter diagram conformed to a straight line slanting downward.)

If two things vary from place to place with absolutely no relationship between them (neither *positive* nor *negative*) the coefficient is 0.00. (This would occur if the dots on a scatter diagram were uniformly dispersed.)

Plainly, then, the closer to +1.00 the coefficient of correlation between two spatial variables, the stronger their positive geographic association; the closer to −1.00, the stronger their negative geographic association.

The formula for computing the coefficient of correlation between two variables is a scientific device that is a useful aid to understanding of relationships in physical science and in social science. Unfortunately, the first

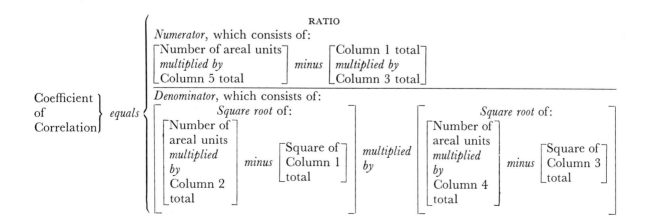

Coefficient of Correlation *equals*

RATIO

Numerator, which consists of:

[Number of areal units *multiplied by* Column 5 total] *minus* [Column 1 total *multiplied by* Column 3 total]

Denominator, which consists of:

Square root of: [Number of areal units *multiplied by* Column 2 total] *minus* [Square of Column 1 total] *multiplied by* *Square root* of: [Number of areal units *multiplied by* Column 4 total] *minus* [Square of Column 3 total]

encounter with this formula is apt to be dismaying, partly because its symbols may be new and partly because the process requires slow and careful study. The basic steps in its application are as follows:

1. Construct a Table of Values in exactly the same fashion as in computing the *a* and *b* values of the regression line.
2. Compute the value of the coefficient of correlation by solving the equation at the bottom of this page—a ratio in which both the numerator and denominator are built up from the totals of columns in the Table of Values.

This equation is expressed as follows in statistical symbols (*r* stands for *coefficient of correlation*):

$$r = \frac{(N \cdot \Sigma xy) - (\Sigma x \cdot \Sigma y)}{\sqrt{(N \cdot \Sigma x^2) - (\Sigma x)^2} \cdot \sqrt{(N \cdot \Sigma y^2) - (\Sigma y)^2}}$$

We can figure the coefficient of correlation between population and employment in trade as they vary through the nine hypothetical states listed in Table 29-4 by transposing to the above formula the appropriate totals from the Table of Values (Table 29-5):

$$r = \frac{(9 \cdot 7,220.2) - (1,289 \cdot 29.0)}{\sqrt{(9 \cdot 326,939) - (1,289)^2} \cdot \sqrt{(9 \cdot 159.64) - (29.0)^2}}$$

$$r = \frac{64,981.8 - 37,381.0}{\sqrt{2,942,451 - 1,661,521} \cdot \sqrt{1,436.76 - 841.0}}$$

$$r = \frac{27,600.8}{\sqrt{1,280,930} \cdot \sqrt{595.76}}$$

$$r = \frac{27,600.8}{1,134 \cdot 24.4} = \frac{27,600.8}{27,669.6}$$

$$r = 0.99.$$

A coefficient of 0.99 is extremely high and indicates that there is an uncommonly close geographic association between population and employment in retail trade in these nine states. (The coefficient of correlation for Figure 29-4, Part B, is not presented here in hope that the reader may want to work it out for himself. NOTE: It will be a negative number and will be somewhere between −0.60 and −0.90.)

Correlation between Cash-Grain Farming and Flat Land.   The objective in one research project conducted by John Hidore at the State University of Iowa was to see whether there was any correlation between cash-grain farming and flat land in the midwestern United States. The definitions adopted for the two phenomena are as follows: A cash-grain farm is one on which at least 50 per cent of the value of all farm products sold comes from the sale of grains. *Flat land* is land with slopes of less than three degrees.

Hidore first constructed two maps to show the locational pattern of these two phenomena in eight contiguous states—North Dakota, South Dakota, Nebraska, Kansas, Minnesota, Iowa, Missouri, and Illinois: Figure 29-5 (left) shows the pattern of cash-grain farming, and Figure 29-5 (right) shows that of flat land, both maps being on a county basis.

Visual comparison of these two maps (as in the method mentioned earlier in this chapter) suggests that there is some association between these two variables. Both attain their highest values in three regions (northeastern Illinois, the spring wheat region of the Dakotas, and the winter wheat region of Kansas). Furthermore, they both attain their lowest values in similar regions (northern Nebraska, southern Missouri, and a belt along the Mississippi from Minnesota to Illinois).

Still, the visual inspection method, useful as it is, provides no method for measuring the degree of similarity between the two patterns. But since both maps were constructed on the same areal unit basis, it was possible to compute coefficients of correlation between these two phenomena as they varied among the 730 counties in the case study area. The resulting coefficient is +0.652, a figure that, being much closer to +1.00 than to 0.00, indicates a positive geographic association.

When coefficients were run for counties in separate states, it was found that the association between these two variables is strongest in the counties in Illinois and Kansas, and weakest through the counties of Missouri and South Dakota (see Table 29-6). In other words, the

Table 29-6

Coefficients of Correlation between Percentage of Flat Land and Percentage of Cash-Grain Farms in Selected States on a County Basis

State	"r"	State	"r"
Illinois	+0.690	Minnesota	+0.581
Kansas	+0.671	North Dakota	+0.552
Nebraska	+0.652	Missouri	+0.398
Iowa	+0.644	South Dakota	+0.303

Source: John J. Hidore, *The Relationship Between Cash-Grain Farming and Flat Land in the Western Midwest,* unpublished Master's thesis, Department of Geography, State University of Iowa (1958), p. 32.

states in which cash-grain farming is most important tend to be the states in which this type of agriculture is most closely associated with flat land.

It must be emphasized that such high correlations do *not* suggest that flat land *determines* the degree to which cash-grain farming develops. Two hundred years ago the land in this region was essentially as flat as it is now—but it supported no cash-grain farming. In short, high correlations do not prove cause-and-effect relationship. But they *are* a quantitative *measurement of association*. Further research can build upon such measurement, however, and subsequently *may* prove that flat land is one of several factors that *influence* the location of cash-grain farming—after cultural forces have given birth to the type.

Correlations Involving the Machinery Industry. If we should compare a map of the machinery industry with that of blast furnaces and steel mills, or with that of petroleum and coal products, or of food manufactures, or of any other industry, we could—by the method of visual inspection—arrive at some general statement about whether there seemed to be any similarity (or *association*) between any pair of patterns.

But the computation of coefficients of correlation for employment in such industries (as they vary from state to state among all states in the United States) reveals that the machinery industry is far more nearly associated geographically with certain industries than with others, as in Table 29-7. Specifically, it is most closely related, spatially, with nonferrous foundries, but shares virtually no relationship, spatially, with the lumber and wood products industries.

In a research project (conducted by Harold Mc-Carty, John Hook, and Duane Knos) at the State Univiersity of Iowa, the coefficient of correlation method was applied in testing three hypotheses on the machinery industry.

The first hypothesis was that the number of workers in the machinery industry will vary directly with the percentage of manufacturing workers in the total employment structure. For each state in the United States, the researchers computed the percentage of the total labor force accounted for by manufacturing. Coefficients were then calculated, showing the correlation between this percentage and employment in the machinery industry. The resulting coefficient of $+0.564$ indicates a definite positive association.

The second hypothesis was that the machinery industry was more market-oriented than raw-material-oriented. This was tested by computing correlations between the machinery industry and (a) "earlier stages" industries (that is, industries that process metal before it is shipped to other factories), and (b) "later stages" industries (those that process metal goods in a stage that may be sold to the general consumer public, to non-manufacturing business users, or to other factories). If the hypothesis is sound, then the coefficients measuring the correlation of machinery with earlier-stages industries should be lower than those for later-stages industries. Part A of Table 29-7 shows that this is the case.

The third hypothesis was that the machinery industry is more closely associated with metal-consuming industries than with nonmetal-consuming industries. This was tested by computing coefficients between numbers of workers in the machinery industry and those in the industries listed in Part B of Table 29-7. If the hypothesis is valid, then the coefficients in Part B should be lower than those in Part A. This is seen to be true; indeed, the highest coefficient in Part B, $+0.778$, is exceeded by no fewer than seven of the entries that appear in Part A.

Figure 29-5 (*After John Hidore.*)

Table 29-7

Coefficients of Correlation between Employment in the Machinery Industry and in Selected Industries, by States

Part A Other Metal-Consuming Industries	r	Part B Nonmetal-Consuming Industries	r
(Earlier-stages industries)		Paper and allied products	+0.778
Blast furnaces, steel mills, etc.	0.657	Food products	+0.775
Primary nonferrous metals	0.145	Furniture and fixtures	+0.753
(Later-stages industries)		Printing and publishing	+0.749
Iron and steel foundries	0.879	Rubber products	+0.707
Nonferrous foundries	0.959	Chemical industries	+0.662
Other primary metals industries	0.927	Leather products	+0.512
Hardware, cutlery, hand tools	0.741	Apparel manufactures	+0.471
Heating and plumbing equipment	0.896	Petroleum and coal products	+0.467
Metal stamping and coating	0.954	Textile products	+0.176
Fabricated wire products	0.842	Lumber and wood products	−0.009
Electrical machinery	0.876		
Motor vehicles and equipment	0.514		

Source: Harold H. McCarty, John C. Hook, and Duane S. Knos, *The Measurement of Association in Industrial Geography,* Department of Geography, State University of Iowa (Iowa City, 1956), pp. 82 and 123.

Mapping of Residuals from Regression

One of the better systems for portraying the spatial relationships of two (or more) variables is the mapping of residuals from regression. This system will be illustrated by an example involving nine hypothetical counties which are listed in Table 29-8 in terms of their values for two variables: percentage of population that is urban and

Table 29-8

Nine Hypothetical Counties

County	Average Family Income
Jackson	$6000
Howe	5500
Gray	5000
Florence	4500
Essex	4000
Dunkirk	3500
Calhoun	3000
Ballert	2500
Adams	2000

County	Urban Population as a Percentage of Total Population
Gray	80
Jackson	75
Dunkirk	70
Florence	65
Howe	60
Essex	55
Adams	50
Calhoun	45
Ballert	40

average family income. Note that Jackson County tops the list in income and that Gray leads the array in urban percentage.

Comparison of the county rankings in the two parts of Table 29-8 reveals that the sequences are somewhat similar. Thus, we conclude that there is at least a weak positive correlation. But let's look at the locational pattern of these two variables.

Figure 29-6, Part 1 shows the location of the nine counties. Map 2 of that series shows the location of average family income among the nine counties and reveals that the higher incomes are in the northern portion of the map. Notice that the three middle-value counties (Dunkirk, Essex, and Florence) are shaded alike as are the three highest-value counties (Gray, Howe, and Jackson) and the three lowest-value counties (Adams, Ballert, and Calhoun).

When percentage of the population that is urban is considered, counties Essex, Howe, and Florence have the middle values and are shaded alike on Figure 29-6, Part 3; counties Ballert, Calhoun, and Adams have the lowest values and are shaded alike as are the three highest values in counties Dunkirk, Jackson, and Gray.

Map 3 in the series indicates that the lowest urban percentages appear in the south so that the locational pattern is somewhat similar to the pattern in Map 2, but the patterns are not precisely the same. The scatter diagram in Figure 29-7 indicates that there is a definite positive correlation between these two variables—as visual inspection of Maps 2 and 3 suggests.

The regression line clearly slopes upward from left to right—revealing the average areal relationship between these two variables. The question now is this: Is there any way to measure the degree to which counties are "above average"—relative to this regression line and which counties are "below average." And if so, is it possible to map counties in terms of their departures or differentials from that regression line, that is, from the average relationship?

Residuals provide the answer, and these can be mapped.

Suppose we decide to map the nine counties (a) in terms of *dollars of family income* greater than would be the case if there were a perfect relation between the two variables—as defined by the regression line, that is, the average relationship, or (b) in terms of *dollars of family income* less than the average relationship. Take county B

(Ballert) for example. In Table 29-8 it appears as one of the *lowest*-ranking counties in terms of income. But its income *relative to its percentage of urban population* is rather high as indicated by its dot on the scatter diagram being above the regression line. For a county with 40 per cent urban population it would be expected (insofar as relationships among the nine counties are concerned) to have

Figure 29-6

Figure 29-7

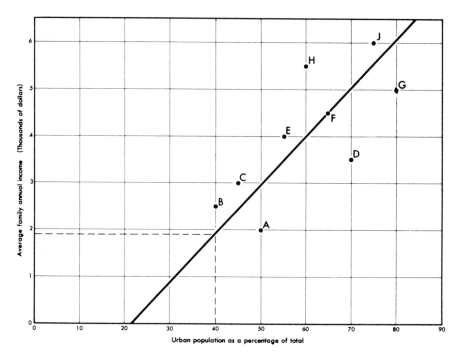

Table 29-9

Residuals for Nine Hypothetical Counties

County	Actual Average Family Income	Computed Average Family Income on the Regression Line	Residuals from Regression
Howe	$5500	$4000	+$1500
Ballert	2500	1900	+ 600
Calhoun	3000	2430	+ 570
Essex	4000	3480	+ 520
Jackson	6000	5550	+ 450
Florence	4500	4500	0
Adams	2000	2950	− 950
Gray	5000	6200	− 1200
Dunkirk	3500	5000	− 1500

an average family income of $1900 (that is, the 40 per cent population value intercepts the regression line opposite 1900 on the vertical axis).

The next step is to determine the difference between the *actual income* ($2500) and the *computed income* ($1900) which would obtain if the county's dot (with 40 per cent urban population) were on the regression line. This difference is the residual value—$600 in this instance. In formula form:

Residual = Actual Value minus Computed Value.

If the actual value is greater than the computed value, the residual is a *positive* value; if the actual value is less than the computed value, the residual is a *negative* value.

The residuals for the nine counties are shown in Table 29-9.

In Table 29-8 Jackson ranks first in income; but in terms of residuals from regression with urban percentage, Table 29-9 shows that Howe ranks first and that three other counties outrank Jackson. Part 4 of Figure 29-6 shows each county in terms of its residual family income.

A residual from regression is defined as that part of the magnitude which a phenomenon reaches within a given unit area which is independent of the areal association between the given phenomenon and the other factors included in the investigation.[3]

In this chapter we have dealt with several methods for analyzing the relationship, or association, between phenomena as they differ spatially. Although most of our examples were drawn from manufacturing and agriculture, the methods are nevertheless equally valid for measuring the geographic associations of any economic endeavors.

[3]Edwin N. Thomas, *Maps of Residuals from Regression: Their Characteristics and Uses in Geographic Research* (Iowa City) 1960, p. 12.

SUGGESTED READINGS

ALEXANDER, JOHN W., and LINDBERG, JAMES B., "Measurements of Manufacturing: Coefficients of Correlation," *Journal of Regional Science*, Summer, 1961, pp. 71–81.

BANNISTER, GEOFFREY, "Population Change in Southern Ontario," *Annals of the Association of American Geographers*, 1975, pp. 177–188.

McCARTY, HAROLD H., HOOK, JOHN C., and KNOS, DUANE S. *The Measurement of Association in Industrial Geography*, Iowa City, 1956, 143 pp.

——, and Lindberg, James B., *A Preface to Economic Geography*, Englewood Cliffs, N. J., 1966, 261 pp.

——, and SALISBURY, NEIL E., *Visual Comparison of Isopleth Maps as a Means of Determining Correlations Between Spatially Distributed Phenomena*, Iowa City, 1961, 81 pp.

GIBSON, LAY JAMES, and REEVES, RICHARD W., "The Role of Hinterland Composition, Externalities, and Variable Spacing as Determinants of Economic Structure in Small Towns," *The Professional Geographer*, 1974, pp. 152–158.

GRIFFITH, DANIEL A., "A Note on Spatial Autocorrelation," *The Professional Geographer*, 1975, pp. 470–474.

HIDORE, JOHN J., "The Relationship Between Cash-Grain Farming and Landforms," *Economic Geography*, 1963, pp. 84–89.

MONMONIER, MARK S., and SCHNELL, GEORGE A., "Interstate Migration of Physicians in the United States: The Case of 1955–1959 Graduates," *The Professional Geographer*, 1976, pp. 29–34.

MULLER, JEAN-CLAUDE, "Associations in Choropleth Map Comparison," *Annals of the Association of American Geographers*, 1975, pp. 403–413.

OLSON, JUDY M., "Autocorrelation and Visual Map Complexity," *Annals of the Association of American Geographers*, 1975, pp. 189–204.

ROBINSON, ARTHUR H., LINDBERG, J. B., and BRINKMAN, L., "A Correlation and Regression Analysis Applied to Rural Farm Population Densities in the Great Plains," *Annals of the Association of American Geographers*, 1961, pp. 211–222.

SCHNELL, GEORGE A., and MONMONIER, MARK S., "U. S. Population Change 1960–70: Simplification, Meaning, and Mapping," *The Journal of Geography*, 1976, pp. 280–291.

THOMAS, EDWIN N., *Maps of Residuals from Regression: Their Characteristics and Uses in Geographic Research*, Iowa City, 1960, 60 pp.

YEATES, MAURICE, *An Introduction to Quantitative Analysis in Human Geography*, New York, 1974, 300 pp.

YOUNG, WILLIAM J., "Distance Decay Values and Shopping Center Size," *The Professional Geographer*, 1975, pp. 304–309.

CHAPTER

30

location theory

This unit coal train transports 11,000 net tons of Wyoming coal per trainload to a San Antonio, Texas, public utility company. What factors might account for the fact that this coal is being hauled a great distance for use in the nation's leading petroleum and natural gas producing state? (*Courtesy Southern Pacific.*)

With the amazing growth in population in the last 300 years has come an associated increase in economic interaction as the peoples of different areas exchange their surpluses. This orderly exchange of commodities and services between places, some of which are thousands of miles apart, has produced a worldwide pattern of *geographic organization*. Through his economic and political decisions, man has organized a series of interrelated areas, each with its own distinctive role in the world's economy. To be sure, some parts of the world have remained virtually untouched by changes in human society, but most of the world today is dominated by societies that, at an ever accelerating rate, are coming into closer and closer association with one another. Areas specialize in producing distinctive products, and many areas now consume an ever greater variety of products coming from an ever larger number of source areas. Economically, the world is constantly becoming more complex. Faced with this complexity, the student of economic geography naturally aspires toward a set of principles by which he can understand the *areal organization of economic activity*—the manner in which the diverse areas of the earth are interrelated.

A *location theory*, as we shall use the term herein, is an endeavor to account in a consistent, logical way for the locational pattern of economic activity and for the manner in which economic areas are interrelated. A theory need not be all-encompassing, of course, but may cover only one aspect of economic activity.

> If we are to accept the idea that economic geography is becoming the branch of human knowledge whose function is to account for the location of economic activities on the various portions of the earth's surface, it seems reasonable to expect the discipline to develop a body of theory to facilitate the performance of this task.
>
> At the outset it seems desirable to inquire into the most probable and desirable characteristics of such a body of theory, if one were to come into existence. Certainly it would consist, in essence, of a large number of interrelated and noncontradictory principles each of which would account for the location of some type of economic activity. With such a group of principles the geographer would be able to provide satisfactory explanations of the location of the world's agricultural regions, manufacturing industries, and all other types of economic occupance. These principles would be essentially similar to those developed by other physical and social sciences, except that they would be concerned with locations rather than with those physical and social processes which are the main concern of the systematic sciences.[1]

With all the material presented in preceding chapters to drawn on, we could mention many location theories that have been proposed; however, we shall discuss only eight of them, eight which have been comparatively well conceived: (1) the von Thünen theory, (2) a weight-loss and transportation-cost theory, (3) a

[1]H. H. McCarty, "An Approach to a Theory of Economic Geography," *Economic Geography* (1954), p. 95.

labor-differential and transportation-cost theory, (4) the Weber theory, (5) the Fetter theory, (6) the interaction theory, (7) the theory of intervening opportunity, and (8) the nested-hierarchy theory. There is one other theory that would deserve discussion in association with this other group—the Christaller, or *central-place* theory. But since we presented it in Chapter 27, we shall not elaborate further on it here except to say that it was one of the first theories dealing with the results of the influences of transportation, interaction, and intervening opportunity on the location of cities, and other trading centers, and that it was formulated by Walter Christaller, German economist and economic geographer born in 1893. It has been one of the most widely discussed theories on economic location.

Most theories consist of two main components: premises and propositions (or postulations). A *premise* (as the term is used in this context) is a statement that, for the purposes of the theory, is accepted as being true. Now, a premise may be either a statement of proven fact, or it may be an assumption or presupposition. In any case, all theories are built upon one or more such premises. A *proposition* (or *postulation*) is a statement that is likely to be true in the light of the premises. In phrasing a theory, one can usually introduce *premises* by the words "since" or "if," *postulates* by the word "then."

"*If* a factory has a weight-loss ratio of 90 per cent, and *if* all other factors are equal, *then* the factory will tend to locate near its raw material."

"*If* a factory has a weight-loss ratio of zero, and *since* freight rates on finished products usually exceed those on raw materials, and *if* all other factors are equal, *then* the factory will tend to locate in its market area."

THE VON THÜNEN THEORY

Apparently, the very first attempt to devise a scientific theory explaining the location of an economic activity can be credited to Johann Heinrich von Thünen, who lived in Germany from 1783 to 1850. Both a scholar and a farm operator, von Thünen formulated his famous theory on the basis of 40 years' experience in managing an agricultural estate near the city of Rostock in Mecklenburg.

The von Thünen theory tries to account for the types of agriculture that will prosper around an urban market. It rests upon several premises.

Premises

Von Thünen theorized that *if* a "laboratory" could be constructed according to seven conditions, *then* agriculture would tend to locate in a specific determinable pattern. These are the conditions proposed:

1. There is an isolated area consisting of just one city and its agricultural hinterland. Such an area could be called "an isolated state," for example, feudal states in the Middle Ages.
2. The city is the market for surplus products from the

hinterland and receives products from no other area.

3. The hinterland ships its surpluses to no other market except its city.

4. The hinterland has a homogeneous physical environment favorable to the production of mid-latitude plants and animals.

5. The hinterland is inhabited by farmers *desiring* to maximize their profits and *capable* of adjusting their type of farming to the demands of the market.

6. The hinterland is traversed by only one means of land transportation. (In von Thünen's day this was the horse and wagon, not counting, of course, pedestrians.)

7. Transportation costs are directly proportional to distance and are borne entirely by the farmers who ship all food "fresh."

Postulates

Given this controlled laboratory system, then different types of agriculture would develop around the city in discrete concentric rings.

The greatest distance from the city at which any given type of farming *could* be conducted depended on selling price at the market, production cost on the farm, and transport cost between the two. Any profit a farmer realized depended on the relationship of these three variables, as expressed in the following formula: $P = V - (E + T)$. This means that profit (P) equals the value of commodities sold (V) minus both total production expenses (E) such as labor, equipment and supplies, and transportation costs (T) in getting the commodities from farm to market.

In the light of this formula, look at Table 30-1. In this table the data are based on von Thünen's observa-

tions that the costs expended and prices received *per acre* (or per any other *unit of land area*) vary with commodity. Take wood and grain. The product from an acre of wood commands a higher market price than does that from an acre of grain; but the greater volume of wood requires more trips to market, hence it costs more to move to market the wood harvest of an acre than the grain harvest.

The three factors of market price, production cost, and transfer cost, are given hypothetical values in columns 1, 2, and 3 of Table 30-1 to demonstrate how a farmer's profit (column 4) decreases with increasing distance from the market.

The farthest distance at which farmers could profitably cultivate wood would be within 3 units of distance from the town. Beyond that distance, transport costs would be so great as to eat up all profit. Grain, however, as Table 30-1 shows also, *could* be produced at a profit as far out as $4\frac{1}{2}$ distance units. In other words, the farmers close to the city would have a wide range of selections in deciding which commodities to produce for sale. The distant farmers had fewer choices. One principal theme in the von Thünen theory is that *the number of profitable options decreases with distance from the city market.*

At the other extreme, there is no least distance within which a farmer *could not* make a profit on any given commodity. Yet there is a minimum distance within which he *would not* choose to produce a given commodity because some other commodity yielded a greater profit.

From these two principles—that an outer distance for each type of farming would be determined by declining profits depending principally on transport costs and

Table 30-1

Von Thünen Theory: Prices, Costs, and Profits per Acre for Selected Commodities by Distance from Market

Rings: Units of Distance from Market	WOOD				GRAIN			
	(1) Market Price (MP)	(2) Production Costs (PC)	(3) Transport Costs (TC)	(4) Profit (P)	(1) MP	(2) PC	(3) TC	(4) P
$\frac{1}{2}$	200	140	10	50	80	50	3	27
1	200	140	20	40	80	50	6	24
$1\frac{1}{2}$	200	140	30	30	80	50	9	21
2	200	140	40	20	80	50	12	18
$2\frac{1}{2}$	200	140	50	10	80	50	15	15
3	200	140	60	0	80	50	18	12
$3\frac{1}{2}$	200	140	70	0	80	50	21	9
4	200	140	80	0	80	50	24	6
$4\frac{1}{2}$	200	140	90	0	80	50	27	3
5	200	140	100	0	80	50	30	0

Source: Adapted from Andreas Grotewold, "Von Thünen in Retrospect," *Economic Geography* (1959), pp. 346–355.

that an inner distance would be determined by more lucrative alternatives—von Thünen postulated that six concentric zones of agriculture would develop around the market city.

Zone #1. The land nearest the market would be used to produce *perishable* items, principally milk and vegetables (that is, market gardening) as in Figure 30-1A. These activities would be concentrated in the inner zone because of the slowness of transportation and the absence of food-preserving techniques, such as refrigeration or canning. Zone #1 would extend outward in proportion to the city's need; the greater the demand for milk and vegetables, the greater the radius of Zone #1. Moreover, since city dwellers would insist on a certain volume of milk and vegetables, they would pay prices high enough to make it more profitable for farmers in Zone #1 to produce these items than wood, grain, or other commodities.

Zone #2. The inhabitants of the second concentric zone would specialize in producing *wood*, with firewood in much greater demand than lumber. (In von

Thünen's day, firewood was the main type of fuel, and the heating of houses provided the main market for fuel.) Von Thünen demonstrated, from accurate accounts kept on his Mecklenburg estate, that forestry yielded greater returns to the farmer near the city than did any other type of production except fluid milk and vegetables. The outer limit of Zone #2 would depend on the amount of wood demanded by the market.

As to the advantage of growing wood or grain, however, Table 30-1 indicates that farmers as far out as 2 distance units would prefer to grow wood instead of grain.

Zones #3, #4, and #5. These areas would tend to be devoted mainly to grains and other crops. The distinctions among these zones need not be spelled out here, except to note that with distance from the city the intensity of cultivation would decrease. This is indicated by the proportion of fallow land—zero in Zone #3, 14 per cent in Zone #4, and 33 per cent in Zone #5.

Although wood commanded (in von Thünen's day) a higher market price than grain, it would be grown only for subsistence needs beyond Zone #2. For there was a critical distance ($2\frac{1}{2}$ units of distance in Table 30-1) beyond which a farmer realized greater profits in grain. Indeed, beyond 3 units of distance his profits in commercial wood production would be zero. Conversely, farmers in the second ring would grow grain for subsistence purposes, and although they *could* realize a profit on commercial grain sale (indeed a greater profit on grain sales than the grain farmers in Zone #3), they would choose to specialize in sales of wood.

Zone #6. This would be the region of livestock farming. Marketed products would be of two types: livestock, which could be driven to market, hence cutting transport costs almost to zero; and cheese, which is not highly perishable, and which is valuable enough to be able to stand rather high transport costs.

How the von Thünen theory would be modified by the presence of a navigable river and a smaller market city, is illustrated in Part B of Figure 30-1. The river would provide cheaper transportation, hence its effect would be to lengthen out the zones along its course. The smaller city would serve zones around itself on a smaller scale than those around the larger city and extending farther on the side away from the main city.

Although the basic forces von Thünen tried to explain in his theory are still operative, it is difficult to find examples today, and for several reasons. Numerous new forms of transport (truck, barge, railway) are cheaper than horses and wagons. Moreover, transportation costs are neither directly proportional to distance nor do they increase similarly in all directions. Perishable goods can be moved long distances under refrigeration, in air-tight cans, or by other means of preservation. Finally, firewood is no longer the major domestic fuel. Even so, the von Thünen theory was a pioneering step

Figure 30-1 (*After Andreas Grotewold, in* Economic Geography.)

THE LOCATION OF AGRICULTURAL PRODUCTION AFTER VON THÜNEN

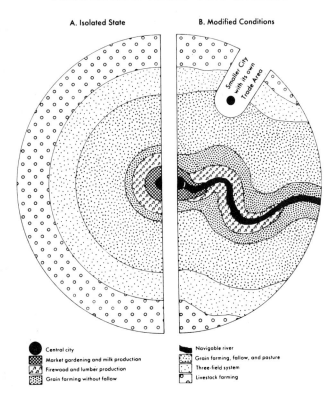

A. Isolated State   B. Modified Conditions

Central city
Market gardening and milk production
Firewood and lumber production
Grain farming without fallow
Navigable river
Grain farming, fallow, and pasture
Three-field system
Livestock farming

in developing a theory of location of certain economic activities.[2]

A THEORY OF WEIGHT LOSS AND TRANSPORT COSTS

A theory that expresses the relationship between weight-loss and transport costs is pertinent to understanding the location of manufacturing.

The first four cases cited illustrate how this theory can be applied in an attempt to understand the location of manufacturing. We shall cast the illustrations in terms of a single factory that processes raw materials (R) from a single source area (SR) into a single finished product (P) for sale at a single market (MP) which is in a different location from that of the source of raw materials. The weight-loss–transport-cost theory is useful

[2]See A. Grotewold, "Von Thünen in Retrospect," *Econ. Geog.,* 1959, pp. 346–355, and H. B. Johnson, "A Note on Thünen's Circles," *Annals of the Assoc. of Amer. Geog.,* 1962, pp. 213–220.

in answering the question: "Where will the factory tend to locate?"

In the four illustrations to follow, the two variables are *weight-loss ratio* and *transportation costs*. All other factors are considered invariable. Obviously, in reality other things are *not* equal, but to observe the interaction of any two variables, all other elements must be held constant. The transport costs cited in the illustrations conform to the well-known principle that freight rates are usually higher per ton of finished product than per ton of raw material from which the product is made (Table 30-2).

In Case A of Table 30-2, the factory would tend to locate at the market because the burden of transport costs would be less than if the factory located at the source of raw materials. In Case B the factory would again tend to locate at the market. But in Cases C and D, the factory would tend to locate at the source of raw

Table 30-2

Weight Loss and Transport Costs in Four Hypothetical Cases

Illustrative Cases	Weight-Loss Ratio	Transport Costs	
		If Factory Locates at Source of Raw Materials:	If Factory Locates at Market:
Case A. 1000 tons of R are processed into 1000 tons of P	0%	1000 tons of P must be shipped to MP $20 per ton is the transport cost on P from SR to MP Transport cost: $20,000	1000 tons of R must be shipped from SR $10 per ton is the transport cost on R from SR to MP Total transport cost: $10,000
Case B. 1000 tons of R are processed into 600 tons of P	40%	600 tons of P must be shipped to MP $20 per ton Transport cost: $12,000	Transport costs are the same as in Case A: $10,000
Case C. 1000 tons of R are processed into 400 tons of P	60%	400 tons of P must be shipped to MP $20 per ton Transport cost: $8,000	Transport costs are the same as in Case A: $10,000
Case D. 1000 tons of R are processed into 500 tons of P	50%	500 tons of P must be shipped to MP $17 per ton is the transport cost on P from SR to MP Transport cost: $8,500	1000 tons of R must be shipped from SR $9 per ton is the transport cost on R from SR to MP Transport cost: $9,000

material. In Case D, transport costs are listed as different than in Cases A, B, and C. Were transport costs for D the same as the previous trio, then the answer would be inconclusive—and the factory's location would be determined entirely by other relationships.

Here is the theory that synthesizes the relationships between weight-loss ratio and transportation costs shown in these cases: The greater the percentage of weight loss in a manufacturing process, the stronger the tendency for a factory to locate at a source of raw material. All other things being equal, though, a market location may be preferable, depending on the transport charges on raw material and on finished product relative to the weight-loss ratio; the greater the spread between the total charges (*not* the per-unit rate, which will inevitably be lower on raw material), the stronger the pull of the market on factory location.

Numerous industries discussed in Part Six illustrate the applicability of the foregoing theory; for instance, copper concentrating, copper refining, farm machinery manufacturing, automobile assembly, and baking.

What about intermediate locations between market and raw material? For example, in Case B where the weight-loss ratio is 40 per cent, why wouldn't the factory tend to locate at a point two-fifths of the distance from market to raw material? Suppose the weight-loss ratio were 50 per cent. Wouldn't the factory entrepreneurs do well to choose a site midway between their customers and their source of raw materials?

The answer is to be found in the *tapering principle* of freight-rate structures. As we saw in Chapter 24, freight charges, generally speaking, do not increase directly with distance; rather they increase *at a decreasing rate* with distance. That is, the charge for hauling a commodity 500 miles is usually less than 5 times that for hauling it 100 miles. Figure 30-2 illustrates this principle; the dashed line shows the rate on a ton of raw material moving from SR. The rate on a ton of raw material from *SR* to *MP* is $80, whereas the rate from *SR* to *Y* is $55 even though the distance from *SR* to *Y* is only one-half the distance from *SR* to *MP*. If the factory builders chose to locate at *X*, they would pay transport charges of $30

Figure 30-2 (*After E. M. Hoover.*)

AGGREGATE TRANSPORT CHARGES AT FIVE SELECTED PLACES

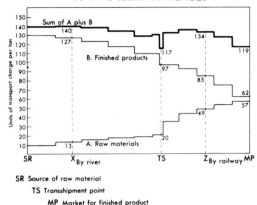

Figure 30-3 (*After E. M. Hoover.*)

AGGREGATE TRANSPORT CHARGES AT FIVE SELECTED PLACES

per ton of raw material, while a location at *Z* would necessitate payments of $72 on such shipments.

The gradient of transport charges on finished products is shown by the dotted line. Accordingly, if a factory located at SR the transport charges per ton of finished product moving to *MP* would be $120. If the factory located at *Y*, charges would be $88.

The significance of these two gradients is to be seen in the pattern of the solid curve which connects the summation values of the raw material curve and the finished product curve. Thus, in Case A from Table 30-2, where the weight-loss ratio is zero, if the factory is located at *Y*, the freight charges will be $55 per ton of raw material received and $88 per ton of product shipped, for a total of $143.

Because of the tendency of freight rates to taper off with distance, intermediate locations are at a competitive disadvantage with points of origin or destination. This principle holds true regardless of the weight-loss ratio and regardless of relative freight rates.

Still, intermediate locations *can* enjoy a favorable position under certain conditions: (a) if in-transit rate privileges are granted (Chapter 24), or (b) if transshipment (such as transfer from water carrier to rail carrier) is necessitated at the intermediate point, or (c) if there is some other departure in freight-rate structures from the curve shown in Figure 30-3. In Figure 30-3, we see how a trans-shipment point would be a favorable location for a factory in a region where freight-rate structures were of the stair-step rather than the gradient type. A factory that processed raw materials from *SR* for sale in *MP* would (given a weight loss of zero) face a total transport burden of $138 per ton if it located at *SR*, $140 if it located along the river at *X*, $117 if it located at the point of trans-shipment (*TS*), and $139 if it located at *MP*.

A THEORY OF LABOR DIFFERENTIALS AND TRANSPORT COSTS

One enormous influence on the location of any economic activity is the cost of labor. This is a matter not only of hourly wages but also of hourly production. Other things being constant, worker A at $2.50 per hour is actually cheaper labor than worker B at $2.40 if A produces 50 units in an hour to B's 40. In the case of A, the cost of labor per unit of output is $2.50 ÷ 50 = 5¢ whereas the cost for B is $2.40 ÷ 40 = 6¢. The principle can be drawn that *all other things being equal*, a factory will tend to locate in an area where unit labor costs are lowest, *irrespective of hourly wage rates*.

Immediately this question arises: Can factories in an area with low unit labor costs compete successfully if that area is far from both markets and raw materials? Would not a competing factory located at either the market or at the raw material be better off? For example, Chicago has both steel mills and factories that require machinery. Accordingly, a lathe manufacturer located in Chicago would be in the same metropolitan area with his main source of raw material and with many customers. Could a lathe manufacturer in Rockford, Illinois, 90 miles to the west, dependent for steel on those Chicago mills, compete successfully for sales to those Chicago customers? At first thought one might reply negatively, since the Rockford plant would have to bear transport charges on a 90-mile shipment of steel and a 90-mile backhaul of lathes, both of which would be unnecessary for the Chicago factory.

But the problem merits further consideration. Let's examine two cases, in one of which (Case A) the two cities have similar labor productivity but different wage rates, and in the other of which (Case B) the variables are reversed, as follows:

Hourly Wage Rates

	Chicago	Rockford
Case A:	$2.20	$2.10
Case B:	$2.30	$2.30

Man-Hours of Labor to Produce a Lathe

	Chicago	Rockford
Case A:	1000	1000
Case B:	1000	960

Assuming that all other costs are equal, we can solve the above case problems by means of the work-sheet (Table 30-3), in which we list the figures for the various conditions.

In both instances, a Rockford lathe-maker could compete successfully with a Chicago competitor despite the drawbacks in his location.

We can sum up this location theory as follows:

All other things being equal, the greater an area's savings in labor costs (attributable to either low hourly wage rate or high productivity per hour, or both) the greater the distance handicap that can be overcome in processing materials from far-away sources for sale to far-away markets.[3]

THE WEBER THEORY

The first person to work up a comprehensive theory accounting for the location of manufacturing was Alfred Weber. Weber was a German economist who taught at the University of Prague from 1904–1907 and the Univer-

[3]The preceding pair of theories dealing with weight-loss ratios, labor differentials, and transportation costs are discussed at length and at a much higher level of sophistication in several publications such as those by Edgar M. Hoover and Walter Isard which are cited at the end of this chapter.

Table 30-3
Work-Sheet of Comparative Production Costs

Components	Case A		Case B	
	Chicago Lathe Factory	Rockford Lathe Factory	Chicago Lathe Factory	Rockford Lathe Factory
Transport charges on steel from Chicago steel mill	$15	$40	$15	$40
Number of man-hours required to make identical lathes	(1000)	(1000)	(1000)	(960)
Hourly wage per hour	($2.20)	($2.10)	($2.30)	($2.30)
Total labor cost per lathe	$2200	$2100	$2300	$2208
Transport charges on lathe to Chicago customer	$35	$100	$35	$100
All other costs are assumed to be equal	——	——	——	——
	$2250	$2240	$2350	$2348

sity of Heidelberg from 1907–1933. In 1909 he published his famous *Theory of the Location of Industries* incorporating several ideas that had been partially formulated by Wilhelm Launhardt in the 1880's.

Premises and Postulates

Weber began with several *premises*:

1. The unit of analysis is a single, isolated country that is homogeneous in terms of climate, topography, race of people, technical skills of the population, and is under one political authority.
2. Some natural resources (for instance, water and sand) are ubiquitous whereas others (such as coal and iron ore) occur only in "fixed" locales.
3. Available workers are not ubiquitous; rather, they are "fixed" in specific places.
4. Transportation costs are a function of *weight* and *distance*, increasing in direct proportion to length of shipment and weight of cargo.

Weber *postulated* that, given the controlled laboratory just described, manufacturing plants would be located in response to three forces: relative transport costs, labor costs, and something he called "agglomeration," which will be defined in a moment.

Role of Transport Costs

Weber theorized that the transport costs would operate in distinctively different ways in different cases. We shall examine a couple of situations to see how.

Case A: One Market and One Raw Material. If just one locale demands the product, and if only one raw material is involved in the process, then there are three possible locations for manufacturing.

1. If the raw material is *ubiquitous*, then the factory will locate at the market, since at this point the lowest transport costs would prevail on both material and product.
2. If the raw material is *fixed* (that is, localized in a specific place) and if it is *pure* (that is, its weight-loss is zero), then the factory can locate in either the market or at the source of materials.
3. If the raw material is *fixed* and *gross* (by gross, Weber meant that weight was lost in the manufacturing process), then the industry would locate at the source of material. Remember that it was one of his premises that transport charges were directly proportional to weight of cargo, whether it was raw material or finished product.

Case B: One Market and Two Raw Materials. If customers for a product are in only one place and the

product is manufactured from two raw materials (R_1 and R_2), then manufacturing will tend to locate in one of the following several ways:

1. If both R_1 and R_2 are ubiquitous, then manufacturing will be at the market for the same reason as in Case A-1.
2. If R_1 is ubiquitous and R_2 is *fixed* elsewhere than at the market, and if both are *pure*, then manufacturing will be at the market. Transport charges will have to be paid on only R_2. Were the factory at the source of R_2, transport charges would have to be paid on the finished product, which, since both materials are pure, would equal their combined weights.
3. If both raw materials are *fixed* and *pure*, the factory will be at the market. Both components would be sent directly to the consumption area for processing since this would give the lowest aggregate transportation cost (Figure 30-4). Otherwise, if the factory located at either the source of R_1 or the source of R_2, additional transport charges would have to be paid on that leg of the journey on which the product moved to market (M). Any manufacturing using pure materials from two sources will always locate at the place where finished products are consumed. The only exception would be if one of the raw materials, in being shipped to the market area, passed through the place where the other raw material was produced. This locale would be equally attractive as the factory site.
4. If both raw materials are *fixed* and *gross*, the solution is complex. To solve it, Weber introduced his famous *locational triangle*. One point is the market (M), another is the source of R_1 (SR_1), and the third is the source of R_2 (SR_2); Figure 30-4 (Case B-4) shows how the locational triangle is constructed.

To illustrate: Suppose that both R_1 and R_2 lose 50 per cent of their weight in the manufacturing process, and that 2000 tons of each are required a year. If the factory were located at M, the total transport cost for a year would be (a) 2000 tons × 100 miles = 200,000 ton-miles on R_1 from SR_1 to M, plus (b) 200,000 ton-miles

Figure 30-4

THE WEBER THEORY

CASE B-3   CASE B-4

SR1   Source of one raw material
SR2   Source of another raw material
M   Market

on R_2 from SR_2 to M, or 400,000 ton-miles in all. If the factory were located at SR_1 the burden would be (a) 2000 tons $\times$ 100 miles = 200,000 ton-miles on R_2 from SR_2 to SR_1 plus (b) 2000 tons $\times$ 100 miles = 200,000 ton-miles on the finished product from SR_1 to M, also 400,000 ton-miles. However, if the factory were located at point X, midway between SR_1 and SR_2, the transport burden would be as follows: (a) 2000 tons $\times$ 50 miles = 100,000 ton-miles on R_1 from SR_1 to X, plus (b) another 100,000 ton-miles on R_2 from SR_2 to X, plus (c) 2000 tons $\times$ 87 miles = 174,000 ton-miles on finished product from X to M, or a total of 374,000 ton-miles. This is less than the burden facing an enterprise located at either M or SR_1 or SR_2.

If the two raw materials do not have the same weight-loss ratio, and if different amounts are required, the factory would tend to locate nearer one of the raw material sources so as to lessen the burden of transportation costs.

We could analyze many other cases, such as two markets and two raw material sources, or three of one and two of the other, and so on, applying Weber's locational triangle, or variations of it (such as a *locational quadrilateral*) to any situation.

Critics have assailed Weber's locational triangle concept on two major counts: Freight rates are not directly proportional to distance, and they are not, ton for ton, the same on finished products as on raw materials. But in spite of these criticisms, Weber's locational figure can be adjusted to realistic transport charges, and it surely was a major step forward in the advancement of location theory. He laid bare the fact that transportation costs are theoretically the most fundamental element determining the location of manufacturing.

Role of Labor Costs

Weber went on to recognize that labor costs too vary spatially and therefore could wield an influence on the location of a factory. Conceivably, a locality handicapped by high transport costs might be able to offset that disadvantage through savings in wages. Hence, this dual question as an entrepreneur decides on location for a factory: In any given place, how much would a firm have to pay in transport costs and how much would it have to pay in labor costs?

To help answer the question, Weber introduced the concept of the *isodapane*. This is a line connecting the locus of points of equal total costs. Since this statement calls for some elaboration and illustration, let us examine Figure 30-5 in detail. It represents a very simple problem involving a single market, M, and a single raw material source, SR. Behind the construction of Figure 30-5 are certain assumptions: (1) Transport costs are the same per ton-mile for raw materials and finished products. The concentric circles around M portray transport charges from all points to M; those around SR portray transport charges to all points from SR. Both sets of circles are spaced to represent one unit of transport cost *per ton*. (2) The raw material is gross and loses 50 per cent of its

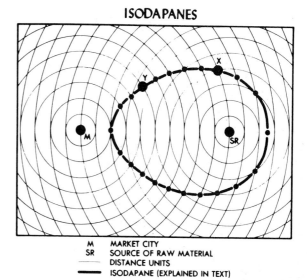

ISODAPANES

M	MARKET CITY
SR	SOURCE OF RAW MATERIAL
	DISTANCE UNITS
▬	ISODAPANE (EXPLAINED IN TEXT)

Figure 30-5

weight, which means that two tons of material enter the factory for every ton of product that leaves it.

Now, if the factory were located at SR, every ton of product shipped from SR to M would bear 10 units of transport cost. If the factory were located at M, the amount would be 20 units of transport cost, since two tons of material would have to move the ten distance units from SR to M for every ton of product made at the factory.

Suppose the factory were at X. The aggregate transport cost would consist of eight units on raw materials (two tons to the fourth concentric circle around SR), plus ten units on product (one ton to M from the tenth concentric circle around M), or 18 units in all. The heavy solid line in the figure is an isodapane connecting all points at which transport cost would total only 18 units. Point Y, for instance, would bear 13 transport cost units on two tons of raw material moving six and one-half units of distance plus five cost units on one ton of product.

This type of isodapane has very little value if transport costs are the sole determinant in the location of industry. But as soon as any other variable is introduced, it may well be that some place other than SR or M would have a great advantage. Isodapanes reveal how great the advantage in that other place would have to be in order to offset its disadvantage in terms of transport costs, thereby luring industry to that location.

As Figure 30-5 shows, all points on the isodapane bear a transport cost burden of 18, a handicap of eight cost units compared to SR. Accordingly, all points on that line would have to possess an advantage of at least eight units in labor cost (per ton of finished product) in order to lure a factory in this enterprise. Weber's contribution of isodapanes provided a technique for the systematic introduction of a new variable (such as labor) into a theoretical scheme.[4]

THE FETTER THEORY

Another theory deals with the location of the boundary between trade areas around two trade centers and derives its name from one of the first scholars to give it expression, F.A. Fetter. We shall see how the theory applies by considering three cases involving two trade centers, X and Y. It will become evident that the theory is applicable whether X and Y are two factories competing for sales to the hinterland or whether they are two wholesalers or two retailers or two competitors in any other kind of business who are concerned with both transport costs and production costs.

Sample Cases

Case A. Assume that X and Y are similar in terms of both production costs and transport costs, the latter being exactly the same per ton-mile in all directions from each place, and increasing with distance at the same rate. Each circle and arc on Figure 30-6 represents a given distance from its own center. Points D, E, and F mark the boundary line separating the trade area of X from that of Y since they bear the same transport-cost burden to both places. Notice that the values of the places on a boundary line need not be identical, only that they are equal in each case with respect to the trade centers.

Accordingly, all other things being equal, if production costs and transport costs surrounding two centers are identical, the boundary between their trade areas will be a straight line that is at right angles to a line connecting the two centers. This is shown by line 2 on Figure 30-6.

Case B. If transport-cost structures around two centers are similar, but if production costs are dissimilar, the trade-area boundary will be a curved line that is *closer to* and *bends around* the center with the higher production costs. This is shown on Figure 30-6 by line 1, which connects all points with equal total costs (production plus transport) in relation to X and Y.

To illustrate: Suppose that both X and Y are wholesaling centers for a product that is manufactured far to the right of Y. Suppose also that through transportation routes are so laid out that consignments from the factory destined for the wholesaler at X must pass through city

[4]More detailed discussion of the Weber theory, particularly his suggestion regarding *agglomeration* (the advantages inherent in factories locating near to each other) is presented in David Smith, *Industrial Location, An Economic Geographical Analysis*, New York, 1971, 553 pp.; and C. J. Friedrich, *Alfred Weber's Theory of the Location of Industries*, Chicago, 1928, 256 pp.

FETTER'S THEORY

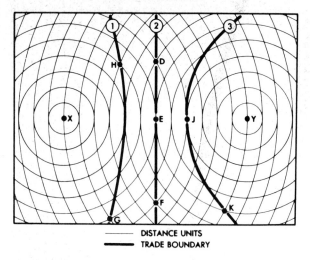

Figure 30-6

Y first; and that wholesale prices in X are therefore higher per commodity unit than those in Y (say, $50 in Y and $54 in X). Assume that transport charges on shipments from X and from Y are $1 per distance unit as stepped off by the concentric circles. Under these conditions, point G is on the trade-area boundary line, because the aggregate costs there are $61 from Y ($50 plus $11 of shipping charges) and $61 from X ($54 plus $7). Point H is also on the boundary line since its aggregate costs are $59 from both Y ($50 plus $9) and X ($54 plus $5).

Case C. If the conditions in the foregoing case are reversed, so that production costs are constant but transport costs vary, the trade-area boundary will be a curved line that is *closer to* and *bends around* the center with the higher transport costs. This is shown on Figure 30-6 by line 3, which connects all points of equal aggregate costs (production plus transport) for both X and Y.

To illustrate: Assume that production costs per unit of commodity are $50 in both X and Y but that transport charges around Y increase at the rate of $2 per distance unit while those around X increase at the rate of $1. Point J lies on the trade-area boundary line since its combined costs in trading with X and Y are $58. Point K also lies on the line since its costs relative to both X and Y are $62.

Another theory that deals specifically with the location of trade-area boundaries is Reilly's Law of Retail Gravitation. We shall take it up below under the general topic of the interaction theory.

THE INTERACTION THEORY

The interaction theory is that the strength of the economic connections between two places varies positively according to their size and negatively according to the intervening distance. The larger the populations of the two places, the greater their economic interaction, but the greater the distance between them, the less the interaction. For example, suppose there are three cities, X (with 20,000 people), Y (with 10,000), and Z (with 30,000), located as in Figure 30-7, with Y in the middle, 50 miles from X and 100 miles from Z. How would the amount of business contacts between Y and X compare to that between Y and Z? The interaction theory suggests an answer; namely, that the amount of business will vary *directly* with the *product* of the two populations and *inversely* with the distance between them.

The theory is expressed in the following formula:

$$i = \frac{P_1 P_2}{d}$$

In this equation, i = interaction, P_1 = population of one of the places, P_2 = population of the other place, and d = distance between them. Accordingly, the index of business between X and Y would be computed as follows:

$$\frac{10,000 \cdot 20,000}{50} = \frac{200,000,000}{50} = 4,000,000$$

The index number between Y and Z as follows:

$$\frac{10,000 \cdot 30,000}{100} = \frac{300,000,000}{100} = 3,000,000$$

Thus, the interaction between Y and Z would tend (other things being equal) to be only three-fourths as strong as that between X and Y.

Other evidence in support of this theory shows that the interaction theory holds for number of telephone messages, for number of bus passengers, for weight of railway express shipments, and for other types of interaction that generally occur between numerous pairs of cities.[5]

Sometimes the *interaction* concept is called the *gravity* or *potential* concept because of similarity with Newton's law of gravitation which postulates that the potential power of attraction between two bodies increases with the product of their masses and decreases with distance between them. The formula cited above is the simplest, most elementary expression of the interaction theory. Some economic endeavors appear to have spatial relationships that truly conform to this formula. But the interaction of other phenomena seems to correlate

INTERACTION FORMULA

CITY X
20,000 pop.
50 miles
CITY Y
10,000 pop.
100 miles
CITY Z
30,000 pop.

Figure 30-7

more closely with some modification of the formula, such as $ixy = (PxPy)/d^2$ in which ixy = interaction between place X and place Y, P = population, and d = distance. Such interaction varies positively with product of populations but negatively with the *square* of the distance.[6] In a word, the *interaction* theory and its derivatives declare that the strength of economic linkage between two places varies *positively* with some exponent of the product of their populations and *negatively* with some exponent of their intervening distance. This will be apparent in two variations of gravity theory: the breaking-point theory and the law of retail gravitation. Let us look at each of these.

The Breaking-Point Theory

The first modification of the interaction theory is the *breaking-point theory*, which is an endeavor to provide a way to predict the location of the boundary line separating trade areas around two cities unequal in size. Referring to Figure 30-7 again, where would the boundary line run separating the trade area of City Y from that of City Z? Would it be halfway between the two cities, or closer to one of them? And if the latter, how close would it be?

The breaking-point theory endeavors to predict the location of this line by means of the following formula:

RATIO

Distance of breaking point from the smaller trade center } equals {
Numerator: distance between the two trade centers
———————————
Denominator: 1 plus the square root of { Population of larger city *divided by* Population of smaller city }

---

[5]See G. K. Zipf, *Human Behavior and the Principle of Least Effort*, Cambridge, Mass., 1949.

[6]For an illustrative study of this modification see Edward J. Taaffe, "The Urban Hierarchy: An Air Passenger Definition," *Economic Geography*, 1962, pp. 1–14.

In symbols, the ratio is:

$$\frac{d}{1 + \sqrt{Pop\ Z/Pop\ Y}}$$

From Figure 30-7 the appropriate values can be inserted in the formula as follows:

$$\text{Distance from } Y = \frac{100}{1 + \sqrt{\dfrac{30,000}{10,000}}} = \frac{100}{1 + \sqrt{3}}$$

$$= \frac{100}{1 + 1.73} = \frac{100}{2.73} = 36.6 \text{ miles}$$

In reality, of course, the position of a trade area boundary is influenced not only by the forces of *distance* and *size* of trade centers (as considered in the interaction theories just cited) but also by the forces explained by Fetter's Law as well as by variations in landforms, by location and nature of transportation routes, by political boundaries, and so on. But when these are equalized, interaction theories tend to hold for retail trade.

Law of Retail Trade Gravitation

A second modification of interaction theory is W. J. Reilly's *Law of Retail Trade Gravitation*, an attempt to provide a way to predict the volume of retail trade patronage that a city's residents will give to other cities. For example, in Figure 30-7, what are the relative volumes of patronage that inhabitants of City *Y* will give to businesses in City *X* and to those in City *Z*?

Reilly's theory can be stated as follows:

$$\frac{\text{Volume of Y's patronage to X}}{\text{Volume of Y's patronage to Z}}$$

$$= \frac{\text{Population of X}}{\text{Population of Z}} \cdot \left(\frac{\text{Distance Y-Z}}{\text{Distance Y-X}}\right)^2$$

From Figure 30-7, we can insert values in the above formula, thus:

$$\frac{\text{Volume of Y's patronage to X}}{\text{Volume of Y's patronage to Z}} = \frac{20,000}{30,000} \cdot \left(\frac{100}{50}\right)^2$$

$$= \frac{2}{3} \cdot (2)^2 = \frac{2}{3} \cdot 4 = \frac{8}{3}$$

Thus, for every three dollars of goods that *Y's* inhabitants purchase in *Z*, they will tend to purchase eight dollar's worth in *X*. The principle can be summed up this way:

The degree to which the residents of a city patronize another city is directly proportional to the other city's population and inversely proportional to the square of the distance between them.

Fertility Rings

For a final example of the interaction theory at work, consider the following remarks on the *fertility rings* in the agricultural hinterlands around Chinese cities.

An important tie between countryside and city is the fertilizer in the form of night soil which the latter provides. Since the amount of night soil is most abundant in the vicinity of cities and large towns it is the land closest to the urban centers which is most heavily fertilized and yields the largest returns. Thorp writes: "Every large city and town which I have observed in China is surrounded by a more or less irregular ring of very fertile soils which usually extends at least as far as a man may walk and return in one day." The fertility rings around cities are most concentrated just outside the city walls where market gardens occupy much of the land. Here the soils are as black and rich as typical chernozems. On the North China Plain one can often tell when he is approaching a city by the improved appearance of the crops. Thorp suggests, as a rule of thumb, that for the first few kilometers around each city the fertility of the soil roughly varies inversely with the distance, or perhaps the square of the distance from the city.[7]

A THEORY OF INTERVENING OPPORTUNITIES

The movement of people and goods from place to place has long been an interesting topic of investigation by social scientists. Why do people go *where* they go—to work, to play, to shop, to worship—why don't they select some alternative place that can likewise meet their needs? One endeavor to describe at least one "law" governing such movements is the *theory of intervening opportunities*, formulated by sociologist Samuel Stouffer thus: "The number of persons going a given distance is directly proportional to the number of opportunities at that distance and inversely proportional to the number of intervening opportunities."

The theory was tested in a case study of residential mobility in Cleveland, Ohio. Moves by Cleveland families during a three-year period were tabulated and classified in terms of (a) the linear distance between the old home and the new, and (b) the number of intervening opportunities. To qualify as an *intervening opportunity*, a dwelling had to meet four requirements: (1) It had to be vacant so that it was available to receive a family. (2) Its price had to be comparable to that of the dwelling into which the family actually moved. (3) It had to be located in a neighborhood free of racial or ethnic barriers that would bar the family from selecting it. (4) It had to be located closer to the original dwelling than was the place actually chosen. Stouffer found that there was a definite tendency for the number of family moves of a given distance to be directly proportional to the number

[7]Glenn T. Trewartha, "Chinese Cities: Origins and Functions," *Annals of the Association of American Geographers* (1952), p. 86.

of opportunities at that distance and inversely proportional to the number of intervening vacant homes in the same price range and available for occupancy.[8]

THE NESTED-HIERARCHY THEORY

To understand this theory, we must define certain terms.[9]

Human occupance encompasses all human activities that are conducted in any type of establishment. Examples of *units of occupance* are farm fields, domiciles, farms, mines, stores, and factories. It is out of these units that the pattern of human occupance of the earth has been woven. This pattern, whatever its design, is not haphazard; it has been formed by the application of creative choice and by the application of energy to the processes of meeting man's economic needs. As a result, man's various occupance units become *interconnected*.

The nested-hierachy theory is built around three major postulates. The first is that some of these interconnections are between *uniform* areas, which are homogeneous in terms of occupance. Examples of small *uniform* areas are an oat field, or a corn field. A larger

[8]For a full explanation of this theory see Samuel Stouffer, "Intervening Opportunities: A Theory Relating Mobility to Distances," *American Sociological Review* (1940), pp. 845–867.

[9]See Allen K. Philbrick's "Principles of Areal Functional Organization in Regional Human Geography," *Economic Geography* (1957), pp. 299–336.

example of a uniform area would be a farming region containing hundreds of occupance units, individual farms in this case.

The second postulate is that other interconnections between occupance units give rise to *nodal* areas. A *nodal* area consists of several different uniform areas that are connected to a focal point. An example of a small nodal area is a single farm that consists of several unlike fields (each of them a uniform area) which are organized around the farmstead, which functions as the node. A large nodal area would be the trade area of a village, which consists of diverse uniform areas (farms, residential areas, commercial areas) all tied to the village as a trading center.

Thus, according to the second postulate, human occupance is focal in character. That is, the activity of any occupance unit focuses on some nodal place. This is true of an oat field on a farm, a farm in a village trading area, a village in the trading area of a larger city, and a large city in the trading area of a metropolis. Sometimes this concept is termed the principle of *focality*.

A nodal area, regardless of magnitude, has three distinct components: a node, an internal area, and an external area. We can stay with the example of a village trade area to illustrate these three components. The village itself is the *node*; the *internal area* consists of the hinterland from which rural occupants come to patronize

Figure 30-8 *(Courtesy Allen K. Philbrick and* Economic Geography.*)*

TRADE AREAS OF BOSWELL, INDIANA

Trade Areas of Establishments	Area Served by	Cultural Features
—1— MAIN POULTRY & EGG CO. (60% of total)	1 ESTABLISHMENT	INCORPORATED PLACES (TOWNS)
—2— RESTAURANT (75% of total)	2 ESTABLISHMENTS	US. HIGHWAY SYSTEM
—3— GRAIN ELEVATOR	3-6 ESTABLISHMENTS	MAJOR STATE & COUNTY HIGHWAYS
—4— GRAB-IT-HERE GROCERY STORE	7 ESTABLISHMENTS	RAILROAD SYSTEM
—5— CAMPBELL'S SERVICE STATION	8-10 ESTABLISHMENTS	STATE BOUNDARY (IND. & ILL.)
—6— DRUG STORE		COUNTY BOUNTARY
—7— CORN BELT FEED COMPANY		HALF WAY POINT TO TOWNS WITH
—8— FARMERS & MERCHANTS BANK		SIMILAR ESTABLISHMENTS
—9— LUMBER YARD & JOB PRINTING		
—10— CAMPBELL'S CAR SALES (CHEVROLET)		

Figure 30-9 (*Courtesy Allen K. Philbrick and* Economic Geography.)

establishments in the village; the *external area* consists of all the interconnections that link the village to larger cities from which village retailers get their supplies and to which the villages forward surplus farm produce from the farms in the internal area.

The third postulate in this particular theory is that occupance units are arranged in a nested hierarchy of functional areas, the hierarchy being characterized by alternate shifts from uniform relationship to nodal organization as the size and complexity of the units of occupance progress from smaller to larger portions of the earth's surface. In other words, as we shift our attention from small areas to large areas, we encounter *successive alternation* in type of areal organization: from uniform to nodal to uniform to nodal, and so on. A farm, for example, contains homogeneous fields, each of which is a uniform area; but the farm unit as a whole is a nodal region containing several unlike fields organized around the farmstead. This plus neighboring farms forms a higher-order uniform region.

Accordingly, man's occupance of the earth can be classified in terms of seven orders of magnitude, each of which contains two types of areas: uniform and nodal. Thus:

Order Number	Area Type	Example
7	nodal	Primate city (for instance, New York). Different seventh-order uniform areas focus on the primate city.
7	uniform	A group of contiguous sixth-order nodal areas.
6	nodal	Major metropolis and its trade area (for example, Chicago). Different sixth-order uniform areas focus on a great metropolis.
6	uniform	A group of contiguous fifth-order nodal areas.
5	nodal	Metropolis and its trade area (say, St. Louis, Missouri). Different fifth-order uniform areas focus on a metropolis.
5	uniform	A group of contiguous fourth-order nodal areas.
4	nodal	Large city and its trade area (South Bend, Indiana). Different fourth-order uniform areas focus on a large city.
4	uniform	A group of contiguous third-order nodal areas.
3	nodal	City and its trade area (Kankakee, Illinois). Different village trade areas focus on a city.
3	uniform	A group of contiguous village trade areas.
2	nodal	Village and its trade area (Boswell, Indiana). Different second-order uniform areas focus on a village.
2	uniform	A group of contiguous farms.
1	nodal	Farm. Different fields focus on a farmstead.
1	uniform	Individual field on a farm.

We have already shown how a farm and its fields are examples of *first-order* nodal and *first-order* uniform areas respectively.

An area of *contiguous* first-order nodal areas constitutes a uniform area of the *second order*. A group of contiguous farms, a group of contiguous residences, and a group of contiguous stores compose, respectively, agricultural, residential, and commercial uniform areas of the second order.

A group of second-order homogeneous areas that differ from one another but in which life is organized around a focal point constitute a second-order nodal area. Homogeneous areas of residences, of farms, of stores, of institutions (each area homogeneous within itself) make up a quartet of different yet uniform areas which focus upon Boswell, Indiana, as illustrated in

Figure 30-10 (*Courtesy Allen K. Philbrick and* Economic Geography.)

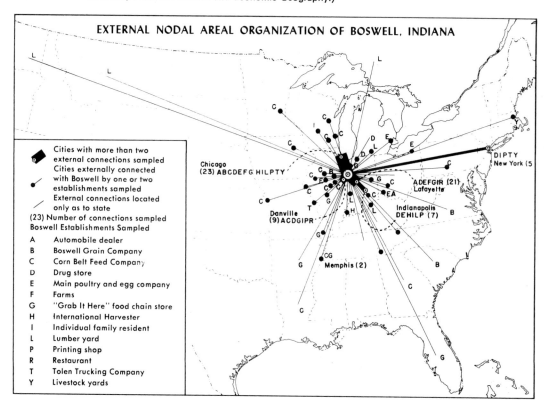

Figure 30-8. That figure shows the location of the *node* and some of the *internal* portion of the Boswell nodal area; Figure 30-9 shows the rest of that *internal* portion, and Figure 30-10 shows *external* components of the Boswell nodal area.

Overlap begins to set in with second-order nodal areas; that is, the periphery of Boswell's internal area overlaps with those of neighboring second-order nodal centers.

Third order and all succeeding orders proceed upward, each encompassing an increasingly larger number of interconnections with other places.

Each unit of occupance regardless of size—provided it is involved in commercial life—functions as a component of two types of areas *simultaneously*: a uniform area that consists of other components similar to it, and a nodal area in which these similar components plus several dissimilar components focus on a node.

SUGGESTED READINGS

GETIS, ARTHUR, and GETIS, JUDITH, "Some Current Concepts, Techniques, and Recent Findings in Urban Geography," *The Journal of Geography*, 1972, pp. 483–490.

GRIFFIN, ERNST, "Testing the Von Thünen Theory in Uruguay," *Geographical Review*, 1973, pp. 500–516.

HOOVER, EDGAR M., *An Introduction to Regional Economics*, New York, 1971, 395 pp.

——, *The Location of Economic Activity*, New York, 1948, 310 pp.

HORVATH, RONALD J., "Von Thünen's Isolated State and the Area Around Addis Ababa, Ethiopia," *Annals of the Association of American Geographers*, 1969, pp. 308–323.

HUFF, DAVID L., and JENKS, GEORGE F., "A Graphic Interpretation of the Friction of Distance in Gravity Models," *Annals of the Association of American Geographers*, 1968, pp. 814–824.

ISARD, WALTER, *Introduction to Regional Science*, Englewood Cliffs, N. J., 1975, 506 pp.

——, et al., *Methods of Regional Analysis: An Introduction to Regional Science*, Cambridge, 1960, 784 pp.

LÖSCH, AUGUST, *The Economics of Location*, New Haven, 1954, 520 pp.

McCARTY, H. H., "An Approach to a Theory of Economic Geography," *Economic Geography*, 1954, pp. 95–101.

PARR, JOHN B., and DENIKE, KENNETH G., "Theoretical Problems in Central Place Analysis," *Economic Geography*, 1970, pp. 568–586.

PHILBRICK, ALLEN K., "Principles of Areal Functional Organization in Regional Human Geography," *Economic Geography*, 1957, pp. 299–336.

SINCLAIR, ROBERT, "Von Thünen and Urban Sprawl," *Annals of the Association of American Geographers*, 1967, pp. 72–87.

SMITH, DAVID M., *Industrial Location, An Economic Geographical Analysis*, New York, 1971, 553 pp.

——, "A Theoretical Framework for Geographical Studies of Industrial Location," *Economic Geography*, 1966, pp. 95–113.

STOUFFER, SAMUEL, "Intervening Opportunities: A Theory Relating Mobility to Distances," *American Sociological Review*, 1940, pp. 845–867.

WAGNER, WILLIAM B., "An Empirical Test of Reilly's Law of Retail Gravitation," *Growth and Change*, July 1974, pp. 30–35.

WARNTZ, WILLIAM, "Geography of Prices and Spatial Interaction," *Regional Science Association, Papers and Proceedings*, 1957, pp. 118–129.

CHAPTER

31

levels of areal development; regional planning

Akalla, one of the most recent of Stockholm's new suburbs. A shortage of housing in the 1940's led to the creation of a series of suburbs in the undeveloped areas around Stockholm. New suburbs contain single-family housing and multiple family units such as those shown here. Even though these communities contain work places and a variety of social, commercial, and cultural services, there is a substantial volume of commuting traffic to Stockholm. (*Courtesy Swedish Information Service.*)

Throughout this book our goal has been to understand spatial variation in economic activity around the world. As a means to that end, we have used the regional (or areal) method of analysis as a framework around which to organize knowledge of spatial differentiation. Beginning with a view of the world's population pattern we have gone on to consider the individual activities by which people meet their economic needs. With all this as background, we can now survey the totality of economic activity and make some concluding observations about the delimitation of regions, about general world regions of economic development and areal (or regional) planning.

DELIMITATION OF REGIONS

Throughout this book our attention has been drawn to numerous maps showing boundary lines around regions. Frequently the area inside the line has been solid black while that outside the line has remained untouched. Sometimes the area inside has been shaded, or lined, or dotted—but in such instances the boundary line is a conspicuous feature.

Such a device is helpful in presenting an initial view of spatial variation—but it has one pitfall. It gives the impression that the difference is abrupt from one side of the boundary to the other. Rarely is such abruptness found in reality. Rather, spatial variation of most phenomena is gradual; consequently the most important

part of a region is not its boundary but its core, or heart. A region in reality is rarely a homogeneous area separated from a different region by a *boundary line*, but rather a homogeneous area surrounded by a *transition zone* in which characteristics of one *core area* blend with those of the next. This is a very important principle of geography to keep in mind whenever one studies a map of regions of economic activities.

GENERAL WORLD AREAS OF ECONOMIC DEVELOPMENT

We can attempt to sum up what we know about world economic activity from two standpoints: *level* of economic development, and *interregional connections*.

Level of Economic Development

In Figure 31-1 we see the locational pattern of five major types of economic regions as determined by progress up the ladder of economic advancement. Areas of Type 1 have a predominantly exchange (or commercial) economy with a relatively high level of productivity. Areas of Type 2 are also mainly exchange economies but still contain large sectors of subsistence economy and have only a moderate level of productivity. Areas of Type 3 are distinguished, for the most part, by subsistence economies, though they do contain some elements of exchange economy; in general, activity in this type is at

Figure 31-1 (*Courtesy Richard Hartshorne and University of Chicago Department of Geography*, Essays on Economic Geography. *Symbols explained in text.*)

KINDS AND LEVELS OF ECONOMIC DEVELOPMENT

1
2
3
4 and 5

0   1000   2000 Miles
Scale at Latitude 35°

Figure 31-2 *This map is one example of how spatial variation in level of economic attainment can be portrayed by a composite of patterns of several variables; per capita income, 1958; increase in per capita income, 1950–1957; average unemployment, 1949–1958; percentage of growth of total employment, 1947–1956; percentage of population in the 20- to 59-year age group in 1950; percentage of population growth, 1950–1956; percentage increase in value added by manufacturing, 1947–1954; increase in annual average weekly wage and salary earnings, 1950–1958; percentage of growth in retail sales, 1948–1958. (Map courtesy John H. Thompson and* Annals of the Association of American Geographers.)

a relatively low level of productivity. Type 4 consists of areas that are almost entirely subsistence in nature and have a low productivity level. Type 5 areas contain few people and are largely undeveloped. If we compare Figure 31-1 with the front endpaper (world population) and with the back endpaper (population density) we can bring out several important truths that are basic to many of the world's economic and political problems. For example, most of the world's people are located in areas where the level of economic development is exceedingly low; on the other hand, the regions where the level of development is high are small in extent and they support a minority of the world's inhabitants. Clearly, the stage is set for reaction on the part of the masses in areas 3 and 4 as information trickles through to them about the differential between their level of living and that in areas 1 and 2. These three maps are probably the most important to keep in mind in trying to understand the significance of current events involving the political aims and stratagems of nations.

In recent years, increasing attention has been directed by an increasing number of scholars in all the social sciences toward problems of *underdeveloped* and *stranded* areas.

Underdeveloped Areas. Here is a concise statement of some of the problems facing underdeveloped areas:

Economic progress is measured by a rising standard of consumption of goods and services, which involves changes in the character and also the location of production. Different regions do not advance at the same rate, and serious locational problems are raised by these differences.

In a primitive region, the high costs of transport prevent the development of much specialization of production and require that each locality produce nearly the whole range of commodities it consumes. Local self-sufficiency is the rule, and the only known ways to live on this basis are by hunting, fishing, grazing, or cultivation of the soil. Products not essential to existence have little place in such primitive economies.

An advance to higher living standards requires more trade. Such trade permits each locality to share, to some extent, the production advantages of other localities and to attain a better consumption standard by concentrating on the lines of production in which it has the greatest relative advantage. The essentials for increasing trade are reduction of transfer (i.e. transport) costs and increased specialization of production, involving shifts of resources to new uses.

To secure a continually larger income from the same area, there must be continually increasing intensity of land use. Gradations of intensity in agriculture run from range grazing through cereals and other extensive crops through fruit and dairy farming to poultry keeping and truck gardening. A few fortunately situated agricultural countries like Denmark have kept increasing populations well abreast of advancing world standards of living by following this sequence of increasingly intensive forms of agriculture.

Much more generally, however . . . economic progress depends eventually on industrialization, i.e., the development of manufacturing. This is a commonly accepted generalization, though the reasons behind it are not well understood.[1]

The analysis of underdeveloped areas is a study in itself and the subject of an increasing body of literature, some items of which are identified in the bibliography of this chapter. One of the questions receiving frequent attention is this: What are the criteria by which an underdeveloped area is identified? Is comparative standard of living a valid criterion? That is, is an area underdeveloped if that standard is lower than the one prevailing in a so-called "developed area," say Germany, or Britain, or the United States? If such comparison is

[1]Edgar M. Hoover, *The Location of Economic Activity*, McGraw-Hill, 1948, pp. 187–188.

not valid, is comparison with some abstract standard more meaningful? For instance, are Germany, Britain, and the United States underdeveloped because they are all in process of raising their living standards to some higher level? In a word, how does one determine whether an area is developed or underdeveloped? The answer is still being worked out.

Stranded Areas.   A stranded area is a comparatively small region that at one time kept abreast of contiguous areas in economic development but then suffered a curtailment of opportunity. Consequently, as the surrounding territories moved ahead, they left the stranded area as an island of relatively lower production and income. In size, stranded areas are rather small, even as small as a single city. Domestic examples of stranded areas are the southern Appalachian coal mining area from West Virginia to Tennessee, the anthracite-mining area of northeastern Pennsylvania, the old Cotton Belt from South Carolina to Alabama, the cut-over area of upper New England and of northern Michigan, Wisconsin, and Minnesota, several copper mining settlements in upper Michigan, and several gold mining towns in the western United States.

The causes for becoming stranded are diverse. One common factor is the depletion of natural resources. Mineral deposits (such as gold, copper, oil, and gas) may be used up. Forests may be cut over, fish stocks depleted, or soil seriously damaged—as when wheat farming invaded the grazing lands of America's subhumid Great Plains.

A second powerful influence involves changes in relationships with other places that may leave an area stranded even when its natural resources are still in good supply. Such changes are expressed as a drop in demand for the stranded area's products. A drop in demand may be attributable to declining incomes in the markets the stranded area supplies, or to obsolescence of product, or to increasing competition from other areas, or to new trade restrictions.

The Trans Alaska Pipeline System extends 800 miles from Prudhoe Bay to southern Alaska. The impact of this project on both human and natural environments has been massive. Geographers can play an important role in the analysis of the environmental impacts which are associated with a project such as this one. (*Courtesy EXXON Corporation.*)

Some areas become stranded because of the interplay of both factors, as happened to the copper mining industry in upper Michigan—not only did the copper reserves diminish but stiff competition was offered by newer, richer and more productive copper mining ventures in the western United States and central Africa.

Area Redevelopment Administration

In early 1961 the United States Congress passed, and on May 1 the President signed into law, the Area Redevelopment Act (ARA) designed to help underdeveloped areas recoup their economic strength. The background for this Act is described as follows.

> One of the anomalies of our modern society is the continuing existence, even during periods of national prosperity, of geographic pockets in which chronic unemployment and underemployment are excessively high.
>
> These areas regardless of the national rhythm of recession and recovery have been unable to develop local economic strength. These are the areas that, in a manner of speaking, never really recovered from the Great Depression of the 30's.
>
> The victims of changing times and changing technologies, these areas pockmark our nation. And as long as they exist, they constitute a drag on the national, state, and local economies.
>
> Aside from considerations of the suffering sustained by the individuals in these areas, they are a drag, first of all, because they fail to produce at the same rate as the rest of the nation. . . . They are a drag, too, because the unemployed and the underemployed are transformed from taxpayers into tax users. They not only are unable to contribute to the support of their communities, their States and their Federal Government, they simultaneously turn to tax-supported programs—unemployment compensation and public assistance, chiefly—to sustain themselves.[2]

As of mid-1962 there were 873 designated areas plus 50 Indian Reservations in 47 contiguous states (only Vermont was free of one), Puerto Rico, the Virgin Islands, Guam, and Samoa. These areas had an aggregate population of 35,000,000 and a labor force exceeding 13,000,000, of whom over 1,000,000 were unemployed— a rate of 8 per cent (national average was 5.5 per cent). In some areas the jobless rate had reached 30 per cent.

The most prominent regions of designations were (a) the coal problem areas (the Appalachian, Eastern Interior, and eastern Oklahoma-Texas fields), (b) the cut-over region from northern Minnesota to northern New York, (c) the lumbering areas of the Pacific Northwest (from Montana to Washington to northern California), (d) the textile centers of New England, and (e) labor surplus areas in the Southeast—a broad belt from North Carolina to eastern Texas.

Provisions of the Act for these areas were as follows:

[2]Victor Roterus, Remarks at Annual Conference of the Association of American Geographers, Miami Beach, Florida, April 24, 1962.

1. Loans to help new businesses to get started and old ones to expand—but not to relocate.
2. Loans to help finance new public facilities (such as sewers and roads) which a community must provide in order to aid businesses creating new jobs—but not relocation of jobs.
3. Programs to train jobless workers.
4. Technical assistance to help an area plan and execute its own program of economic development. This program, known as the Over-all Economic Development Program (OEDP), is the area's own blueprint for progress.

> After an area was officially designated, it had to formulate its OEDP before ARA assistance was given, in accordance with the principle that "economic development must percolate up from the community, not trickle down from a central source." Accordingly, each area had to provide its own initiative, do its own planning, and generate risk capital. "Self-help" was the underlying philosophy, as the ARA offered only training, council, and "seed money" to help the local economies grow.
>
> Within a year of the Act's passage, 515 areas and 20 reservations had submitted their OEDP's, well over half of the designated units.

Economic Development Administration

The Area Redevelopment Act expired in 1965 and the Area Redevelopment Administration which had been created to carry out the work of this act ceased to exist. Two new acts designed to replace the ARA were passed in 1965. Most closely related to the spirit of the old ARA Act was the Public Works and Economic Development Act. The second of these landmark acts, the Appalachian Redevelopment Commission Act, is significant because it introduced the concept of large multistate regional planning units. The notion of multistate regionalism has, since 1965, been carried forward under Title V of the PWED Act so that today the Appalachian Regional Commission is only one of several regional commissions administered by the U.S. Department of Commerce's Economic Development Administration.

Some of the factors leading to the birth of the Economic Development Administration and its impact on the regional planning process as we know it in the United States are described as follows:

> The Area Development Administration program was criticized on various counts, but the principal objection was directed to its orientation to small areas. Such areas, critics charged, were often too small; first, to have the variety and volume of resources to be viable or development-worthy; and second, too small to contain a growth center, central place or trade center in or around which economic development could be reasonably expected to take place.

Consequently, when the Area Redevelopment Act expired in 1965, the new legislation to take its place (the Public Works and Economic Development Act of 1965) emphasized two additional types of areal units for economic development purposes. One of these additional units is the "economic development district", which was defined as a group of adjacent counties or areas which: (1) together are large enough to have the resources to permit effective economic planning and development (generally considered to range from 5 to 15 counties in extent); (2) contain at least two redevelopment areas (generally one-county in dimension); (3) include at least one "economic development center"; and (4) have been officially designated by the U.S. Department of Commerce on the recommendation of the state in which the district is located. The other new areal unit which the Economic Development Act provided for (in Title V) was the "economic development region." These regions, to be designated by the Secretary of Commerce with the concurrence of the affected states, were: (1) to be bound by geographic, cultural, historic and economic ties; (2) to be within contiguous states (except for Alaska and Hawaii); and (3) to be lagging behind the Nation in economic development as indicated by various criteria. These criteria included unemployment, family income, outmigration, slow growth, industrial readjustment and the level of public facilities. The definition of the new multi-state regional unit was largely patterned after Appalachia which already had been designated by previous specific legislation. Generally, the Economic Development Act extended the Appalachia idea to other large areas of the nation whose economies were lagging.

Thus, within one program of the Federal government, it has been found advisable to approach economic development problems from three levels of the areal hierarchy—local areas (generally about a single county in extent), multi-county districts (generally about 5 to 15 counties in extent), and multi-state regions (consisting of all or parts of contiguous states). In reality, since the programs of the Economic Development Act involve state cooperation and participation, a fourth level of the areal hierarchy, represented by the states, is also involved.[3]

Some planners feel that in the not-too-distant future we will have "wall-to-wall regional planning." Judging from the areas covered by economic development districts (Figure 31-3) and regional commissions (Figure 31-4), this assertion does not seem to be unreasonable.

Interregional Connections

As Figure 31-5 shows, the pattern of economic areas can be broken down first into two great families, subsistence and exchange; the latter can be further classified into two subtypes, nodal and uniform. The message of the map is twofold: (a) The *subsistence* world is confined largely to the tropics and to the very high latitudes, and (b) the *exchange* world is basically a single far-flung area functioning around one great *node*, or *core*, that straddles the North Atlantic ocean. This focal zone in the world's economy extends from east-central Anglo-America through west central Europe. Most of this nodal

[3]Victor Roterus, "The Area Hierarchy and Economic Development Planning Problems," *American Industrial Development Council Journal*, Vol. II, No. 4, October, 1967. Also see "Multistate Regionalism," a report by the Advisory Commission on Intergovernment Relations which was published by the U.S. Government Printing Office in April, 1972.

Figure 31-3

ECONOMIC DEVELOPMENT DISTRICTS

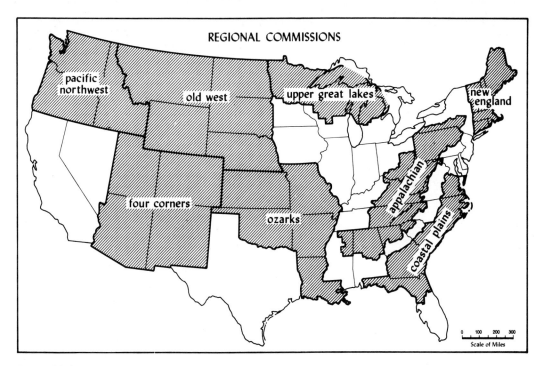

pacific northwest

old west

upper great lakes

new england

appalachian

four corners

ozarks

coastal plains

0   100   200   300
Scale of Miles

Figure 31-4

area is situated in the Northern Hemisphere, but outliers have sprung up (in Latin America, Africa, and Australia) whose economies mesh closely with that of the core. Sometimes the term "integrated commercial world" is applied to this vast exchange area. This nested-hierarchy theory receives good supportive evidence on this map in that diverse uniform regions, each of which is homogeneous (for instance, major cropland regions, major ranch land regions, major forest regions, and major mining areas), are all functionally integrated with the economic life of the great industrial core flanking the North Atlantic. Consequently, the world's major sea lanes converge on this supernode, linking it with distant places.

(We might make a case for transferring the category "plantation agriculture" from the subsistence world to the exchange world. At least the concepts of plantation farming as we presented them in Chapter 12 would make such a change defensible.)

REGIONAL PLANNING

Having inspected the world pattern of production, exchange, and consumption of economic wealth, we cannot help but anticipate the future and ask normative questions. What kind of a pattern is most desirable? How does the ideal pattern differ, if at all, from the present pattern? Is it possible to change the pattern, so as to conform with the ideal? If so, how can this be done?

On an enormous scale, the process of answering these questions is similar to the planning a family does in determining the best possible use of the house and the property it occupies. Many scientists now believe that large groups of people occupying large areas can also cooperate in following orderly plans for increasing the

returns from their lands and properties without sacrificing the values of freedom. As a result of this conviction, more and more areal planning is being done in the United States and elsewhere on at least three distinct levels: *city planning*, *state planning*, and *regional planning*.

City Planning

City planning, in which the regional method of analysis is applied to individual cities, is rooted in the conviction that the problems of cities—traffic congestion, parking congestion, residential blight, dead subdivisions, need for conveniently located parks, and so on—can be solved by research and foresight.

Improving a city clearly calls for organized schemes and efforts. Cities do not grow spontaneously into efficient areas of human habitation. In fact, a city is like a house. One can build a house by the hit-and-miss method, a room here, a room there, and continue to tack on rooms and additions from time to time as needs arise. But no part of such a house is related, by forethought, to any other part: They just "happen" to be built against one another. The result is a monstrosity that is badly designed, awkward, inefficient, and costly to maintain. The tragic fact is that most cities have grown just this way—without forethought of plan or pattern. The settled areas have continually expanded and spilled over haphazardly into the hinterland. From time to time new sections are tacked on to the community, and the result is often a monstrosity with fantastic street patterns, awkward traffic snarls, areas of blight—all of which makes for a less efficient community, one that is increasingly expensive to service and maintain.

In contrast, a house may be carefully designed by an architect, so that its parts fit together. In such a house

PATTERN OF WORLD OCCUPANCE TYPES

Subsistence World

Extensive subsistence agricultural regions

Intensive subsistence agricultural regions

Nodal Regions

Urban-industrial world core
Major cropland
Major ranch land
Major forest land
Major sealanes

Transition Areas

Plantation agriculture

⊙ Major mineral producing areas

Figure 31-5 (*Courtesy Allen K. Philbrick and* Economic Geography.)

there is an orderly arrangement of rooms and passages. It is efficient. It is pleasing to look at and live in and economical to maintain. Likewise, a community may grow according to an orderly arrangement. This is where city planning has a role to play. City planners are the architects who design the city. Two main jobs confront them: designing new areas and redesigning older areas.

Design of New Areas. Expansion of a city into the countryside calls for a blueprint for the transformation of farmland and other rural land into efficient accretions to the urban totality. As the planner gazes out over the rural-urban fringe he must face such questions as: Where should schools be located? How much land should be set aside for each school? Where should major thoroughfares be located? How should interstitial areas between thoroughfares be laid out—with winding street patterns, or grids, or some other design? What areas should be zoned for apartments, for large-lot single-family dwellings, for small-lot single-family structures? Should land be set aside for shopping centers? If so, how much and where should it be located? Will there be a need for land for industrial uses? (If so, it should be demarcated in large parcels—at least a few hundred acres—zoned to keep other users out and situated near

railways, main highways, and on land which is not too valuable.) The general thinking by planners now is that at least 5 per cent of a city's land should be set aside for recreational purposes. Hence, the need for deciding what parts of the farm land to be annexed should be devoted to parks, golf courses, wildlife refuges, or other types of recreational uses. Additional questions deal with matters like positioning storm sewers in such a manner that heavy rains and melting snow can run off with no flooding. Rural land adjoining a city usually is not faced with a serious problem at this point (unless it is in a valley bottom) since most of the earth's surface is covered with soil into which much of the water seeps. Water which isn't absorbed by the soil often is retarded in its run off by pasture grasses or other ground cover. But when such land is transformed into city, it is almost entirely resurfaced—and water-proofed! Roofs, streets, driveways, and sidewalks absorb no water—neither do they impede its run-off. Heavy rains and melting snow produce volumes of water which must be quickly conducted away to prevent flooding.

But the city planner's design for the urban fringe cannot be executed if the land is outside the city's jurisdiction. Hence, the urgency by many cities to annex the fringe while it is still in a rural state—before urban types of buildings are constructed beyond the city limits.

462

Annexation. The question of annexation is a complex one with several pros and cons. From the standpoint of the city, the main advantage to annexing rural land is that the city can be sure that the land is laid out in a manner which fits in with the over-all city plan. Furthermore, as the fringe is built up, property taxes paid by its occupants will flow into the city coffers—thereby expanding the municipal tax base. The main disadvantage is that, for the first few years after annexation, the city is likely to spend more to service the fringe (with fire protection, police protection, schools, street maintenance, snow-removal, and so forth) than it receives in tax revenues from the fringe. This is the main reason why some citizens of the city resist vigorous annexation policies, preferring to wait until the fringe is occupied sufficiently so that its property taxes at least come close to equalling the cost of services the city will render it. A factory or commercial establishment in the fringe is often looked upon as a juicy plum, and is coveted for annexation, since the principle is almost universal that such properties are taxed at a higher rate than the services they receive are worth.

The other side of the annexation coin is the attitude of the fringe dwellers. From their viewpoint there are also both advantages and disadvantages. By annexing to the city they generally stand to benefit by receiving better fire protection (therefore lower fire insurance premiums), storm sewers, better schools, and other services. On the other hand, the cost of such services is likely to raise their taxes above the level formerly paid to their rural governing unit. Moreover, there may be a loss of certain freedoms, often things which on the surface seem trivial but which mean a great deal to some fringe dwellers. For example, some cities have ordinances governing parking in residential areas and prohibit a resident from leaving a car anywhere except on his own property.

Regulations by which cities can annex land are carefully proscribed by state governments in the United States and by national governments in most other countries. These laws differ somewhat but one such set of

controls stipulates that for any parcel of fringe land to be annexed the following conditions must be met. (1) A petition must be circulated describing accurately the boundaries of the fringe parcel which is proposed for annexation. (2) The parcel must be contiguous to the city. (3) At least 50 per cent of the land owners in the fringe must sign the petition favoring annexation. (4) Such signers must own at least 50 per cent of the acreage in the land to be annexed. (5) The city council must vote to annex the parcel.

Under such rules, confused gerrymandering of city limits can result, since petitions can be drawn up to annex highly irregular shapes of land areas—in order to include favorable voters and exclude those resisting annexation.

Redesign of Old Areas. City planners also face the problems of built-up areas within the city. In some instances these areas are chaotic in design and obsolete in construction, necessitating a complete overhaul. In others the problems are less severe and require less stringent measures. The treatment of these older problem areas can be divided into three categories: urban conservation, urban renewal, and urban redevelopment.

Urban conservation involves no change in land use. Rather, by neighborhood clean-up campaigns, by enforcing building codes and sanitation ordinances, it aims to encourage the upkeep and maintenance of houses, stores, and other buildings, thereby resisting the incidence of blight.

Urban renewal, which is more involved is applied to areas already blighted. Generally it entails no major change in land use but may call for the demolition of obsolete structures and the replacement by new structures performing the same function—for example, replacing slums with new apartments.

When the Phelps Dodge Corporation built a new smelter in a remote valley in southwestern New Mexico, they also had to build the planned community of Playas to house their employees. In what ways are the planning problems faced here different from those faced by the builders of Sweden's new suburbs? (*Courtesy Phelps Dodge Corporation.*)

Urban redevelopment is the most ambitious form of redesign and calls for the bulldozing of large areas of land and building up an entirely different layout with new street designs and functions. The construction of Cobo Hall along downtown Detroit's riverfront, Stuyvesant Town in New York, Lake Meadows in Chicago, and the Civic Center in Los Angeles are examples of such remedial surgery.

Today the concepts of city planning can be used to weave present and future developments into a logical pattern. In many cities, planners have actually revamped portions of the old pattern—by widening old streets, providing open spaces with parks and boulevards—but at high cost. Yet the cost may be even higher if cities are allowed to deteriorate at the present rate. It would seem evident that every citizen should be familiar with city planning and should be encouraged to do what he can in the years ahead to encourage wise planning by the city in which he settles.

The Planned Town. Some cities were well planned in advance and laid out in great detail prior to settlement. Around 3000 B.C. the city of Kahun, Egypt, was laid out in rectangular form, housing slaves and artisans working on the nearby Illahun pyramid. In approximately the same period the cities of Mohenjo-Daro and Harrapa (in the Indus Valley) were laid out in a regular grid pattern. Beginning around 400 B.C. several Greek towns (such as Olynthus, Priene, and Miletus) were designed and laid out on a grid pattern with an extra large "block" in the center devoted to the *agora*—the market place which served as the center of business and political life. There appears to have been comparatively little planning of cities during Roman times although occasional military towns apparently were laid out on a grid basis.

In the eighteenth century a new type of city plan, *the Baroque*, was adopted in designing several European cities which functioned as political or religious centers. This plan featured radials—major thoroughfares which focused on the royal palace or a great cathedral like spokes on the hub of a wheel. Lateral streets were sometimes circular, conforming to the shape of the city wall. Karlsruhe and Mannheim in Germany and Versailles, France, are examples of Baroque cities.[4]

In the Western Hemisphere, Philadelphia (planned in 1682 by William Penn) and Savannah, Georgia, are early examples of planned cities. In 1791 George Washington hired a French planner, Charles L'Enfant, to design this nation's new capital city. Early in the 1800's planners laid out a radial street pattern around Detroit's business center and a grid pattern for most of Manhattan.

But throughout most of the history of urbanism, city

[4]For an interesting discussion of the types of cities which developed in past ages see Arthur Gallion's *The Urban Pattern* (New York), 1950.

In 1959–60 the City of Kalamazoo, Michigan created the nation's first open-air mall. Three blocks in the heart of the central business district were ripped up and replaced with a landscaped mall for use by pedestrians only. By 1970 the mall had deteriorated to the point that a second major renovation was needed. The second renovation was completed in 1972. (*Courtesy City Parks Department, Kalamazoo, Michigan.*)

planning has lain dormant, and most cities grew on a hit-or-miss basis, becoming increasingly crowded and congested and, in the opinion of some people, ugly environs in which to live.

A renaissance in city planning has developed within the past 50 years. Nearly every American city of 10,000 has a city planning department, which, in large cities such as New York, Los Angeles, and Chicago, is staffed by scores of employees. And in Europe increasing attention to planning is being paid by both local organizations and branches of the national government. In some countries, principally Britain and Sweden such planning has given birth to several "New Towns."

The "New Towns". In the last several years there has been a rebirth of the "New Town Concept"— the building of a new city according to a predetermined plan. These have become increasingly numerous since

World War II and appear in diverse parts of the world. Examples are Brasilia and Volta Redonda, Brazil, and Pyskowice, Nowe Tychy, and Nowa Huta in Poland. Examples in the United States are Levittown, New York, and Levittown, Pennsylvania, which were ventures by private planners, and Oak Ridge, Tennessee, and Richland, Washington, which were planned by the Federal Government around atomic energy research plants. But the most spectacular examples of New Town planning in recent years have occurred in Sweden and Great Britain.

In Sweden, most of the new towns have been built in the countryside encircling major cities, for example, Kortedala outside Göteborg. There are over 20 new towns around Stockholm of which Vällingby, Farsta, Högdalen, and Bjorkhagen are examples. In the postwar period most of Stockholm's expansion has been channelled into a series of new suburbs west and south of the central city and located along a subway system. Each of these suburbs (usually built on forest land owned by the city) has a shopping center adjacent to a subway station. Around the center are apartment houses of varying sizes and forms and on the periphery one-family dwellings, or row-houses. New Towns generally have from 5000 to 25,000 inhabitants, three-quarters of whom live in apartments within walking distance of the center with its supermarkets, banks, and other business facilities. Some shopping centers are larger than the rest, and their department stores serve several suburbs for less frequent shopping. Vällingby, located 8 miles west of downtown Stockholm, is one of the largest centers. Its shops were opened in 1954. The woods between the suburbs are as a rule left intact for recreation. All new town suburbs have been planned by the city planning agency, but they have been built by private contractors, and most property is owned by cooperatives and private firms.

Britain likewise has a considerable number of new towns, constructed, for the most part, after passage by Parliament of the New Towns Act of 1946 and the Town and Country Planning Act of 1947. Objectives of this legislation were partly to decentralize population from overcrowded and poorly housed areas within the great cities, partly to disperse industry, and partly to rehabilitate depressed areas. Authority to carry out this legislation was given the Ministry of Town and Country Planning. The designated powers were threefold: (a) designation of the site of a new town after consultation with local authorities, (b) establishment of a Development Corporation responsible for planning and building the new town, and (c) provision of loan funds to the Development Corporation, repayable to the Treasury. After a town is occupied and has established its own local government, the Development Corporation is dissolved.

There are over 25 new towns in Britain, 11 of them located in a ring around London at a distance ranging from 20 to 80 miles from the center of the metropolis. The others are scattered in different parts of the country but usually near a metropolitan area. As for functions of the new towns, three types are discernible.

The new towns in the London Ring (Table 31-1) were originally designed to absorb people from the British capital. Most of them were built on sites where a small settlement already existed with established water supply, electricity, and communications.

A second type of new town is that positioned in depressed areas, usually old mining zones, where unemployment is high, housing poor, and the need for economic and social rehabilitation great. Examples are Cwmbran (near the eastern margin of the South Wales coalfield), and Newton, Aycliffe, and Peterlee in the Durham coal area. This trio of settlements is not concerned with metropolitan spillover but with the regrouping of existing population for better living conditions.

The third type of new town is designed around a major industry that is new to the site. A new mine on the Fifeshire coalfield (about 50 miles northeast of Glasgow, Scotland) led to the founding of the town of Glenrothes to accommodate mine employees and their families and employees in services. Somewhat similar is the town of Corby, about 60 miles north of London, which actually began in 1934 as a new town built around a new steel mill. The steel company itself designed a town and built 2300 houses. But with postwar development, the need for expansion convinced the Town and Country Planning Board that growth should be provided for under the New Town Act.

Thus, new British towns came into existence to perform quite different roles.[4]

State and Regional Planning

State planning applies to a whole state the concepts just discussed. As yet, very few states in the United States have true planning departments. This does not mean that planning is absent. States do plan for the building of roads and purchase of land for state parks or forests, but generally such planning is done by the state highway department or the state forestry department rather than by a state planning department. State planning is much less developed than city planning. Where state planning departments do exist, they have frequently been created to dispense federal funds rather than to actually *plan* per se.

Regional planning is the name given to the design for large areas, such as groups of counties or river basins— areas that often cross over political boundaries. Soil conservation districts, drainage districts, watershed areas, and more recently, the Economic Development Administration's economic development districts and regional commissions are all specialized applications of the regional planning principle.

The agency for such regional planning may be a private organization, such as the Wisconsin Valley Improvement Association, an organization of businessmen, public officials, and other citizens concerned about solving problems facing the economy of the upper

---

[4]For further information on both British and American new towns see the excellent book by Marion Clawson and Peter Hall, *Planning and Urban Growth, An Anglo-American Comparison,* the Johns Hopkins University Press (Baltimore and London), 1973.

Table 31-1

New Towns in Britain, January 1971*

	Date of Designation	Original Population	Target Population (All Populations in Thousands)		Distance from Conurbation or City Center (Miles)
			Original	Revised	
CONURBATION OVERSPILL TOWNS					
Greater London					
Stevenage	1946	7	60	105	32
Crawley	1947	9	50	80	31
Hemel Hempstead	1947	21	80	—	25
Harlow	1947	4	60	90	25
Hatfield	1948	8	29	—	21
Welwyn Garden City	1948	18	36	50	23
Basildon	1949	25	50	133	29
Bracknell	1949	5	25	61	30
Milton Keynes	1967	40	250	—	49
Peterborough	1967	84	190	—	81
Northampton	1968	131	300	—	66
Birmingham (West Midlands)					
Telford (Dawley)	1963	70	90	220	34
Redditch	1964	32	90	—	14
Liverpool (Merseyside)					
Skelmersdale†	1961	8	80	—	12
Runcorn†	1964	28	100	—	14
Manchester (South East Lancashire/North East Cheshire)					
Warrington	1968	122	200	—	18
Central Lancashire	1970	240	430	—	30
Newcastle Upon Tyne (Tyneside)					
Washington†	1964	20	80	—	8
Glasgow (Central Clydeside)					
East Kilbride†	1947	2	45	100	9
Glenrothes†,‡	1948	1	32	95	58
Cumbernauld†	1955	3	70	—	14
Livingston†	1962	2	100	—	26
Irvine†	1966	36	116	—	26
Development Area Towns					
Newton Aycliffe	1947	0	10	45	—
Peterlee	1948	200	30	—	—
Cwmbran	1949	12	55	—	—
Newtown	1967	6	11	—	—
Other Towns					
Corby	1950	16	40	80	—
TOTAL		1,210	2,709	3,270§	

Sources: F. J. Osborn and Arnold Whittick, *The New Towns: The Answer to Megalopolis*, 2nd ed. (London: Leonard Hill, 1969); Frank Schaffer, *The New Town Story* (London: Macgibbon & Kee, 1970), *Town and Country Planning*, January 1971; and gazeteers.

*From Marion Clawson and Peter Hall, *Planning and Urban Growth: An Anglo-American Comparison*, The Johns Hopkins University Press, Baltimore, 1973.

†Also served development area purposes, and receives development area aid.

‡Not originally designated for Glasgow overspill purposes but received this function after failure of original purpose (development of new coal mine in Fife coalfield).

§Including original targets for towns where these were not revised.

Wisconsin River Valley. Their best-known slogan, "One Less River To Boss," epitomized the spirit of the project.

But most regional planning is carried on by governmental agencies. In the United States the Tennessee Valley Authority was the first large-scale effort. The TVA and the Appalachian Regional Commission are probably the most familiar examples. In Britain, the Town and Country Planning Ministry has performed exhaustive research in analyzing land use and many other phenomena as a basis for planning decisions. The Netherlands, Sweden, and numerous other countries are actively engaged in regional planning.

Inevitably this topic leads to political debate, since regional planning is a type of activity which on the one extreme may be carried out entirely by groups of citizens apart from the central government or, on the other extreme, may be carried out entirely by the state—as in the Soviet Union. In between is a broad transition zone from which men must choose the degree of authority for planning they desire to vest in government.

In conclusion, it must be admitted that it is impossible in a text of this type to deal at length with the concept of regional planning.[5] But the field has become an

[5]Interested students will be stimulated by reading Robert Dickinson's *City, Region and Regionalism* (London), 1947, in which he traces the historical background of regional planning and the regional method of analysis.

area of study in itself. And as interest in this problem has grown, many colleges have begun to offer degrees in City and Regional Planning and the number of professional planners is growing.

RETROSPECT AND PROSPECT

This book was written in the conviction that a person can better understand the world, knowing something about the spatial variation and areal relationships of economic activities. Accordingly the authors had two goals in mind as they wrote: (a) to give readers information about spatial variation in economic endeavor (knowledge of areas of economic activity), and (b) to encourage them to develop their ability to apply the geographic method of analysis.

Throughout the book, ideas and facts have been organized directly or indirectly around three basic questions that, the authors believe, constitute the distinctive geographic method of analysis. Since it is the method that is the hallmark of geography as a science, the authors hope that readers will remember the basic questions long after they have forgotten the facts that constitute the content of these chapters.

Figure 31-6 (*Courtesy Tennessee Valley Authority.*)

Two of the major problems confronting the science of economic geography involve the third basic question of the geographic method as employed in this textbook. The chances are that the next few years will find economic geographers giving considerable attention to the identification of those relationships which are the most significant. Theoretically, the spatial arrangement of economic endeavor might be found to be related to a host of other variables. Which of these relationships are the most significant ones? Investigation of this problem inevitably leads to the problem of the measurement of relationships. What are the most meaningful methods for measuring the relationship between economic endeavor and other variables?

As it sheds increasing light on the spatial arrangement of economic production, exchange, and consumption, the science of economic geography will help us all better understand the world in which we live. It will contribute to our understanding of newspaper, television, and other reports of the problems and actions of nations.

It will be of help to businessmen facing questions of where to locate factories, wholesale distribution facilities, retail outlets, or other service establishments. It can be of assistance to city planners and national government authorities facing decisions of how to make the best use of the available resources—both physical and cultural.

This swings our attention around to what many people feel to be the single most important function of college education: to develop skill in handling questions —both formulating and answering them—skill, in fact, in making decisions. But this immediately raises another question: How does one know when he is making the *right* decision? Economic geography—or any science— can answer the question "What is?" But science alone cannot answer the question "What ought?" It can only provide information and insight that the individual and society can manipulate in accordance with those value systems which they have chosen on the basis of their life philosophy. May college education be a healthy stimulus to student and teacher alike in choosing those value systems (and the means to those ends) that will help realize the best in life for the world's population.

SUGGESTED READINGS

BLAIR, JOHN P., "Industrial Decline, Vertical Integration, and Geographic Concentration," *Growth and Change*, July 1975, pp. 34–37.

BOAL, FREDERICK W., "Urban Growth and Land Value Patterns: Government Influences," *The Professional Geographer*, 1970, pp. 79–82.

CHAPIN, F., STUART, JR., *Urban Land Use Planning*, Urbana, 1965, 498 pp.

CHURCH, R. J. HARRISON, "Some Problems of Regional Economic Development in West Africa," *Economic Geography*, 1969, pp. 53–62.

DELAPLAINE, JOHN W., and HOLLANDER, EDWARD D., "Federal Spending for Human Resources Helps the Growth Rate in Depressed Areas," *Growth and Change*, January 1970, pp. 28–33.

DIEM, AUBREY, "An Alternative to Unplanned Urban Growth: The Case of Stockholm," *The Canadian Geographer*, 1965, pp. 193–204.

FOWLER, GARY L., and DAVIES, CHRISTOPHER SHANE, "The Urban Settlement Patterns of Disadvantaged Migrants," *The Journal of Geography*, 1972, pp. 275–284.

GIBSON, LAY JAMES; BARR, JAMES L.; and O'KEEFE, TERRENCE B. "Measuring the Community Economic Base: A Comparative Analysis," *American Industrial Development Council Journal*, July 1975, pp. 7–35.

———, et al., *An Economic Development Strategy for Bisbee, Arizona*, U.S. Department of Commerce, Economic Development Administration, 1975, 151 pp.

HANSEN, NILES M., "How Regional Policy Can Benefit from Economic Theory," *Growth and Change*, January 1970, pp. 20–27.

HELBOCK, RICHARD W., "New Towns in the United States," *The Professional Geographer*, 1968, pp. 242–246.

HOFFMAN, GEORGE W., "The Problem of the Underdeveloped Regions in Southeast Europe: A Comparative Analysis of Romania, Yugoslavia, and Greece," *Annals of the Association of American Geographers*, 1967, pp. 637–666.

HUNKER, HENRY L., *Industrial Development*, Lexington, 1974, 323 pp.

ISARD, WALTER, *Introduction to Regional Science*, Englewood Cliffs, N. J., 1975, 506 pp.

KING, PAUL E., "Mobility of Manufacturing and the Intrastate Redistribution of Employment," *The Professional Geographer*, 1975, pp. 441–448.

KUEHN, JOHN A., and BENDER, LLOYD D., "A Dissent: Migration, Growth Centers, and the Ozarks," *Growth and Change*, April 1975, pp. 43–48.

———, and WEST, JERRY G., "The Ozarks: Highways and Regional Development," *Growth and Change*, July 1971, pp. 23–28.

LEWIS, W. CHRIS, and ALBRECHT, STAN L., "Attitudes Toward Accelerated Urban Development in Low-Population Areas," *Growth and Change*, January 1977, pp. 22–28.

LINGE, G. J. R., "Governments and the Location of Secondary Industry in Australia," *Economic Geography*, 1967, pp. 43–63.

MCKAY, JOHN, and WHITELAW, JAMES S., "The Role of Large Private and Government Organizations in Generating Flows of Inter-Regional Migrants: The Case of Australia," *Economic Geography*, 1977, pp. 28–44.

MABOGUNJE, AKIN L., "Manufacturing and the Geography of Development in Tropical Africa," *Economic Geography*, 1973, pp. 1–20.

MELEZIN, ABRAHAM, "Soviet Regionalization: An Attempt at the Delineation of Socioeconomic Integrated Regions," *Geographical Review*, 1968, pp. 593–621.

MORRILL, RICHARD L., "On the Size and Spacing of Growth Centers," *Growth and Change*, April 1973, pp. 21–24.

MULKEY, DAVID, and DILLMAN, B. L., "Location Effects of States and Local Industrial Development Subsidies," *Growth and Change*, April 1976, pp. 37–43.

MURPHEY, RHOADS, "Aspects of Urbanization in Contemporary China: A Revolutionary Model," *Proceedings of the Association of American Geographers*, 1975, pp. 165–168.

RICHARDSON, HARRY W., and RICHARDSON, MARGARET, "The Relevance of Growth Center Strategies to Latin America," *Economic Geography*, 1975, pp. 163–178.

SCHWIND, P. J., *Migration and Regional Development in the United States, 1950–1960*, Univ. of Chicago, Dept. of Geography, Research Paper No. 133, Chicago, 1971.

SEMPLE, R. KEITH, GAUTHIER, HOWARD L., and YOUNGMANN, CARL E., "Growth Poles is São Paulo, Brazil," *Annals of the Association of American Geographers*, 1972, pp. 591–598.

———, and RICHETTO, JEFFREY P., "Locational Trends of an Experimental Public Facility: The Case of Nuclear Power Plants," *The Professional Geographer*, 1976, pp. 248–253.

SMITH, BRUCE W., and HILTNER, JOHN, "The Fiscal Impact of Urban Expansion," *The Professional Geographer*, 1975, pp. 449–453.

SVART, LARRY M., "Environmental Preference Migration: A Review," *Geographical Review*, 1976, pp. 314–330.

TILL, THOMAS E., "Industrialization and Poverty in Southern Nonmetropolitan Labor Markets," *Growth and Change*, January 1974, pp. 18–24.

TOLOSA, HAMILTON, and REINER, THOMAS A., "The Economic Programming of a System of Planned Poles," *Economic Geography*, 1970, pp. 449–458.

WHITE, GILBERT F., "Geography and Public Policy," *The Professional Geographer*, 1972, pp. 101–104.

WOHLENBERG, ERNEST H., "Interstate Variations in AFDC Programs," *Economic Geography*, 1976, pp. 254–266.

index

471

makes, *table*, 281; and raw materials, 282-283; world pattern, 285-286

Automotive triangle, 279

a value of regression line, 431-432

Awad, Mohamed, 30

b

Backhauls, 272

Baking, 221-222 (*photo*, 220): correlation with population, *table*, 221

Balance of movements (*cities*), 396

Balance of payments, 354-356

Balance of trade, 351, 353-354

Bananas, 138: international trade, *table* 138

Barley: international trade, *table*, 132; world production, *tables*, 38, 124

Baroque city plan, 464

Barr, James, 395

Bartholomew, Harland, 387-388

Basic employment, 394-395, 402

Bauxite, 177, 253: production by nations, *table*, 255

Bedford, Indiana, 180

Beef cattle (*See* Livestock raising)

Beet-sugar, refining in U.S., 228-229

Beimfohr, Oliver, 398

Belt, defined, 7

Benelux Customs Union, 358

Berry, Brian J.L., 343, 392

Bessemer, Henry, 207

Bindibu tribe, 25

Bioculture (*See also individual types*): defined, 79; location of, 153-154, 160-161; and man, 160-162; relationship to total employment, 159; and soil, 162; types, *diagram*, 154; in U.S., 155-157

Biotic pyramid, 57-58

Bituminous coal, 166-171 (*See also* Coal *and* Mining)

Bjornevatn (or Kirkenes) field, 175

Blast furnace, 263-264 (*diagram*, 264, *photo*, 261)

Boal, F.W., 414

Boswell, Indiana, nodal area, 453-454 (*maps*, 451, 452, 453)

Boundary line of region, 456

Bourne, Larry, 413

Breaking-point theory, 449-450

Breese, Gerald, 404, (*table*, 406)

Brewing, commercial, 229-230 (U.S. *map*, 229)

Bridge industries, defined, 225

Buffalo, New York, flour mills, 226

Building-material minerals, 180

Bulk-break point transportation centers, 227

Burges, E.W., 416

Burton, Ian, 398

Bushmen of Australia, 25

Butte, Montana, copper district, 177

Butter, 97

b value of regression line, 432-433

C

Cacao, 67, 137: international trade, *table*, 138

Calcium, 178-179

Caliche, 179

Calves (*See* Livestock raising)

Camayura tribe, 25

Campos, grass varieties, 84

Canada: dairying, 96; iron, 173, 175-176; manufacturing, 317-319 (*map*, 318); oil, 195

Canals, 332-334: and mining, 208

Cane-sugar refineries, 228-229

Canning and freezing, 220-221 (U.S. *map*, 220)

Capital, risk (*See* Risk capital)

Carp, 39, 151

Carrying capacity of habitat, 82-83

Cash-grain: corn, 125; correlation with flat land, 434-435; in mixed farming, 101-102

Catalan forge, 207

Catfish farm, *photo*, 148

Cattle ranching, 82-90 (*for dairy cattle, see* Dairying): carrying capacity, 82-83; contrast with nomadic herding, 83; drive, *photo*, 84; and farming, 87; feedyard, *photo* 86; history in U.S., 87-90 (*map*, 89); natural requirements, 83-85; and population, 85-87; ranch, *photo*, 90; trade, 86-87; U.S. sales, *map*, 106; world pattern, 82-87 (*map*, 105)

Caucasus oil field, 187, 189, 192, 197

Cause and effect, 7, 10

CBD (central business district) 410-417 (*photos*, 364, 411): changes, 412-413; delimiting, 411-412; and industry, 414-415; patterns, 416-417; problems, 413-414; and residence, 416; subsidiary centers, 414

Census, U.S. (*See also* Population): of Business, 378-380; classification of urban settlements, 370-375; districts, *map*, 316; of Manufacturers, 214; of Mineral industries, 203; tracts (small areal units), 403

Central city, 372, 374-375

Central place, 362: theory of, 396-398, 440

Central twin city, 372

Centrifugal forces, in Colby hypothesis, 417

Centripetal forces, in Colby hypothesis, 416

Cerro Bolivar mining district, 173

Characteristics of economic activity, as basic question, 7

Charante tribe, 25

Cheese, 97-98

Chernozem soils, 108-109, 128

Chicago: industrial structure, 311-312; population pattern, 405-406; *Tribune* circulation area, *map*, 391

Chickens (*see* Poultry)

Chile, nitrates, 179

China (*See also* Intensive subsistence farming): coal, 166, 170

Christaller, Walter, 396-398, 440

Chromium, 176

Cinchona tree, 68

Circulation system of world, 324 (*See also* Transportation and transportation machinery)

Cities (*See* Service centers)

Citrus fruit, 120-121 (*map*, 121; *photo*, 120)

City planning, 461-462: annexation, 463; of new areas, 462; of old areas, 463-464; planned towns, 464

Class rates, railways, 329

Clawson, Marion, 465

Cleveland: manufacturing area, 311; population pattern, 405-406 (*table*, 406)

Cleveland (England) iron ore field, 172

Clustered pattern of cities, 398

Coal, 166-171: anthracite, 166; bituminous, 166; drift mining, 205; Europe, 166-168 (*map*, 168); international trade, *table*, 171; lignite, 166; and manufacturing, 171; open-pit and underground mining, 204-205 (*photo*, 168); production regions, 166-170 (*table*, 167); reserves, 170-171 (*tables*, 169, 170); seams, *diagram*, 205-206; trade, 171; unit train, *photo*, 439; U.S. 169-170 (*table*, *map* 169-170); U.S.S.R., 168-169 (*map*, 169)

Coastal shipping, 334

Cobalt, 176

Cod War, 62

Coefficient of correlation, 433-434: for copper industry, *table*, 251; for machinery industry, *table*, 436; for manufacturing, 214-215 (*table*, 215); of geographic association, 426 (*table*, 427)

Coefficient of linkage, 426

Coefficient of similarity, 426

Coffee, 138; international trade, *table*, 138

Coir, 67

Coke, 263-267

Coker, J. A., 211

Colby, Charles, 416

Collecting, forest, 67-68

Commercial areas, 409-414: CBD, 410-414; commercial strips, 414; dispersed businesses, 414; shopping centers, 414

Commercial bioculture (*See breakdowns under individual types*): animal farming, 149-153; dairy farming, 92-99; fishing, 54-65; food manufacturing, 220-230; forest gathering, 67-78; grain farming, 124-133; Mediterranean agriculture, 114-122; mid-latitude crop farming, 139-147; tropical crop farming, 135-139

Commercial core, 409, (*photo* 412)

Commercial economy, defined, 22, 49-50

Commercial farm types, 155-157

Commercial manufacturing (*See also individual idustries*): four periods, 295-296

Relationships: as basic geographic question, 7-9; causal, 7-8; consequential, 7-8; and correlations, 7, 9-10; cultural, 8; internal and external, 8-9; physical, 8; probabilistic, 10
Renewable resource, 75
Renewal, urban, 461-465
Residuals from regression, 436-438
Resources: conservation, 211; non-renewable, 211; preservation, 211; pyramid, 204
Retail trade in cities, 378-379; gravitation, law of, 450; per capita, by metropolitan areas, *table*, 378
Rice (*See also* Intensive subsistence farming): dry and wet, 37; harvesting, *photo*, 42; international trade, 45-46, (*table*, 132); lowland 37; paddy, 37; production, world, 124; yields per acre, *table*, 38
Risk capital, 279-284
Roads and highways, 330-332 (U.S. *maps*, 331-332, *photo*, 401)
Roadside as tertiary settlement, 367-368
Rock River Valley, labor and transportation costs, 313
Rodgers, Allan, 305-306
Romania, oil, 186-187, 194
Roterus, Victor, 459, 460
Rubber, 137-138: international trade, 138
Ruhr valley, 168
Rural settlement, 369
Russia (*See* U.S.S.R.)
Rye, 38, 124

S

Saar valley, 168
Saguenay River, aluminum manufacturing, 255
Salisbury, Neil, 424
Salmon, 63
Salzgitter, 173
Sand, 180
Satellite city, 393
Savanna, 84: defined, 25
Savannah, Georgia, 464
Scale of economic activity, coarse and fine, 293
Scandinavia: iron, 174-175
Scatter diagram, 223, 387, 430-431, 433, 437: defined, 223-224
Scavengers, 39
Schefferville, 175-176
Schumann Plan, 211, 358
Seals, fur, 62
Seasonal precipitation, 41
Secondary manufacturing, 241, 251
Secondary production, defined, 4
Sector pattern of city, 416
Sedentary primitive cultivation, 32, 34
Selected service, 379-380
Semi-shifting cultivation, 32
Service and refrigeration machinery, 296

Service centers, 361-376, (*photos*, 368, 369, 377): areas and shapes, 386-392 (*map*, 389); CBD, 410-414; central city, 370, 372-373, 375; city, 369; classification by employment, 382-383; conurbation, 369; economic differences, 378-384; employment in 380-382, 394-395, 402; hamlet, 368 (*map*, 367); locational patterns, 364-367, 396-399; megalopolis, *map*, 370; metropolis, 369; millionaire city, 369; and mining, 208-210; and money, 391, 393, 396; Nelson's classification system, *tables*, 384, 387, and people, 385-386, 391, 392-393, 402-409; percentage of population in, by nations, *table*, 364; and personal income, 384-385; population of, 402-409; rank-size hypothesis, 375; road side, 367-368; size categories, 367-376; Standard Metropolitan Statistical Areas, 373-375 (*map*, 374); town, 369; trade, external, 390-392; trade, internal, 392-396; transportation and trade, 378-379, 389-394; types of services, 379-380; urban, defined, 369-372; urbanized area, 371-372; urban patterns, 416-417; urban place 370-371; U.S. Census categories, 370-373, 375; use of land, 409-417; U.S. pattern, 365-367; village, 369; world's largest, *table*, 370
Settlement patterns, 396-399: clustered, 398; dispersed, 396; linear, 398; random, 399
Shallow waters, 57-58
Shapes of urban settlements, 388-389 (*map*, 389)
Sheep (*See also* Livestock raising): in U.S., *map*, 89; in world, *map*, 83; Shenhsi-Shanhsi, coal field, 170
Shipbuilding, 286-287; (*map*, 288, *photo*, 286, *table*, 287)
Shifting cultivation, 32-33
Shoemaking, world *map*, 240
Shoppers' mall, *photo*, 464
Shopping centers, 414 (*See also* CBD)
Siddall, William, 379
Sidewalk farmers, 130
Siegerland, 173
Siemens, Sir William, 207
Sigatoka, plant disease, 136
Silesia, 172
Single-family housing, 416
Slash-and-burn farming, 32 (*photos*, 30, 33)
Slums, 416
Slurry, 337
Smith, David, 448
Smith, J. Russell, 39
Smolski, Chester, 387
Soft-drink bottling, 222-224
Soft wheat, 127
Softwoods, 69
Soil (*See also* Chernozem soils and Podzol): in dairying, 98; erosion, 162 (U.S. *map*,

162); forest, 71; in grain farming, 128; impact of bioculture, 162; in intensive subsistence farming, 42; leaching, 32; in mixed farming, 108-109; organic matter, 32; in primitive cultivation, 32
Sorghum, 37
South, the, as industrial region, 313-314
Soviet Union (*See* U.S.S.R.)
Soybeans in U.S., *map*, 103, *photo*, 103
Sparrows Point, 269
Spatial variation, 6
Special-industry machinery, 299
Specialization (of labor), 49
Spindletop oil well, 190
Spring wheat, 128
Stafford, Howard, 398
Standard consolidated areas, 375
Standard deviation, 383-384
Standard metropolitan statistical areas, 373, 375, (U.S. *map*, 374)
State planning, 465
Steel, 262-270: characteristics, 263-264; consumption, U.S. *table*, 269; and markets, 267-269; mill, *photos*, 268, 269; production, world, *map*, 271; *table*, 270; raw material, 264-267; regions of the world, 270; transportation, 269; triangle, 262; in U.S., 262-269
Steppe, 84
Stevens, George P., 403
Stockyard, 224
Stone, 180
Store machinery, 298-299
Stouffer, Samuel, 450-451
Stranded areas, 458-459
Strassendorf, 388
Straw, 41
Strip mines, 204-205
Subcontracting, 277
Subsistence, economies (*See also* India: farm problems): cropping methods, 37-38; defined, 22; fishing, 39-40; intensive subsistence farming, 36-48; primitive cultivation, 31-34; primitive gathering, 24-26; primitive herding, 26-31; settlement, 44-45; transportation, 45
Subsistence world, 460-461
Suburb, 393, (*photo*, 455)
Sugar cane, 137: centrales, 208; harvest, *photo*, 139; manufacturing, 228-229; international trade, 137-138
Sugar refinery, *photo*, 228
Suitcase farmers, 130
Sulfur, 180
Survival location factors, in steel industry, 262
Sustained-yield forestry, 76-77
Sweden, iron, 174-175
Sweet potatoes, world production, *table*, 124
Swine, world *map*, 104
Symbiosis, 221, 269
Syracuse, New York, *map*, 372

POPULATION DENSITY

Tropic of Cancer

Equator

Persons per square kilometer

- 250 or more
- 150–249
- 50–149
- 25–49
- 10–24
- Less than 10

Scale at Latitude 35°

0   500   1500   2500 Miles

0   2000   4000 Kms.